169

THE OUTLINE OF
MAN'S WORK AND WEALTH

WILLIAM RITTASE, FROM "FORTUNE."

THE CONQUEST OF TOIL

This single colossal unit machines all the castings for an automobile frame. Its solitary attendant is no Robot: he is its watchful, intelligent controller. But with it he does work that would formerly have demanded the toil and attention of a great multitude of skilled men.

H. G. WELLS

THE OUTLINE OF MAN'S WORK AND WEALTH

TWO VOLUMES IN ONE

ILLUSTRATED

GARDEN CITY PUBLISHING CO., INC.

Garden City   New York

CONTENTS

v

PAGE

CONTENTS

HALFTONE ILLUSTRATIONS

xiii

LIST OF CHARTS

A NOTE ON THE ILLUSTRATIONS. Pictorial diagrams have been added at certain places in this book where the presence of some sort of visualized statistics seemed desirable. For the most part they have been based on data supplied by United States government bureaus; in certain cases they have come from other sources.

To the Bibliographische Institut of Leipzig thanks are due for permission to borrow a number of symbols used in their published charts.

THE OUTLINE OF
MAN'S WORK AND WEALTH

INTRODUCTION

The Object of This Work and the Way in Which It Has Been Written

§ 1. *An Account of Human Activities throughout the World and of the Reasons for These Activities*

THIS book is intended to be a picture of all mankind to-day, a picture of living mankind active, working, spending, making and destroying. There are, we are told, one thousand nine hundred million human beings more or less. They all breathe, eat and sleep, and they are otherwise engaged in the most various activities. They coöperate with one another, and they are in conflict with one another. They die, but continually more are born to take up and extend the activities the dead have relinquished. We seek here to give all the activities in one crowded picture. And further, as our show goes on, we shall put and seek an answer to certain questions that arise naturally out of this spectacle. What sustains all this world-wide activity? Why do these millions live as they do? What are the various manners of living, and what are the motives that lie beneath these various manners of living? That is what we have to display and attempt to elucidate. The "How" is first to be shown and then the "Why?" has to be answered.

Such a general picture of all mankind about its business has not been attempted before. It would have been impossible before the present time, and had it been possible it would have been of doubtful utility. Now it has become possible, and it has been attempted because it is needed. Never before has there been this need and desire to "get the hang" of the world as one whole. Quite suddenly it has come upon us.

There have been some very great changes in the circumstances of human life during the past hundred years or so. If in the past anyone had made a survey of all human activities, he would certainly have treated his subject as a huge work upon Geography. He would have described human life country by country, and illustrated and explained their differences and the differences of race and custom. But to-day that is not at all the best method. It is not the best method because of the increased and increasing ease with which communications can now be made between man and man, so that, while in the past men lived in a mosaic of little communities, each almost completely independent of the others, each with its own little but sufficient histories and its general ideas and its moralities, now we are in more and more effective relationship with all the other people in the world, and such mosaic pictures of thought and knowledge suffice no more.

Geography has become something different from what it was. Now we get news of those once inaccessible peoples hourly, and we trade with them, we cannot now dispense with that trade, we can serve and injure them to an extent that would have seemed fantastic in the days of King George the Third. Goldsmith once wrote of the remoteness of China and said that if a Chinaman was killed every time a gun was fired in France or England no one would hear of it nor care in the least if he did. Nowadays we should hear quite a lot about it. And as a consequence of this "abolition of distance" almost all our political and administrative boundaries, the "layout" of the human population, have become, we begin to realize, misfits. Our ways of doing business, dealing with property, employing other people, and working ourselves have undergone all sorts of deformation because of this "change of scale" in human affairs. They are being altered under our eyes, and it behoves us to the very best of our ability to understand the alterations in progress.

Suppose, to borrow an idea from Mr. Bernard Shaw, some young man or young woman, instead of being born in the usual fashion, were to be hatched out of an egg at the age of twenty, alertly intelligent but unformed and uninformed. He or she would blink at our busy world and demand, "What are they all up to? Why are some so active and some so inactive? Why are some toiling so industriously to produce things and some, it seems, doing nothing but consume? Why is this? What is going on?"

This book would be our answer.

§ 2. *The New Education*

The new revolution in human affairs, this modern "Change of Scale" has happened very swiftly, and it has crept upon us one day after another so insensibly that it is only now we are beginning to realize the nature of the thing that has happened to us. The World War of

1914–18 was for great numbers of people the first revelation of how closely states and empires were being pressed together, and how impossible it was now to prevent the concussions of a conflict from affecting every state and person in the world. Indians starved in Labrador because the Paris fur trade was disorganized; they could sell nothing, so that they could not buy sufficient ammunition to kill their food.

It is only now after the World War that people have begun any serious and sustained attempts to grasp the new state of affairs and to break away from the old traditions that had, under modern conditions, brought them so close to disaster and which still keep them in manifest danger of perhaps even greater catastrophe. It has taken a dozen years for the full necessity for such a break-away to be realized by any considerable number of people. But under the continuance of international stresses and social discomfort that number is growing. There is an increasing desire to part from the old limited interpretations that once were serviceable and that now guide us more and more unsatisfactorily, and to look at life plainly in the new, more formidable aspects it now presents.

First here and then there the idea was repeated that for a new time there was needed a new education. You could not run a world reborn, it was suggested, with the senescent ideas of a world that had passed away. This new education was to be not so much a resort to new methods as the continuation of the old methods with a new content. The educational progress of the pre-war period, so far as ways of teaching went, had been very considerable, and it might well be trusted to continue. But there was a growing·dissatisfaction with what was taught, with the "educand,"* with the system of ideas about life in general, the *ideology* (to use the word as it is now used by thinkers of the Left) built up in our schools. That no longer corresponded with realities. Reform was attempted in the schools, but schools, it was soon realized, can be reformed only very slowly and only with the assent and stimulus of outside opinion. So that it was inevitable that at first this world-wide movement towards a new ideology, a new way, that is, of looking at ourselves and the world about us, should be most evident and vigorous among those who had left school, among intelligent adolescents and adults, consciously anxious to adjust themselves to the alterations in the world about them.

The first distinctive movement for a new education took the form of the New History movement. History was the subject most obviously

*Maxwell Garnett: *Education and Citizenship*.

in need of revision. The New History was a revolt against local, national, and "period" history. It was an assertion that the history of mankind is a single whole and can only be comprehended as a whole, that we must have a just conception of human origins and the general development of human life before we can form any proper picture of the place of our own nation or city or village in the world, or make any proper plans for our political conduct.

It is for the specialist student to say how this New History movement originated and who were its pioneer exponents. Long ago Lord Acton was saying such things to historians as, for example: "It is our function to keep in view and to command the movement of ideas, which are not the effect but the cause of public events." That is precisely where we stand. The advocates of the New History tell the story of man as a whole, because they want to see political institutions advancing towards world unity, and because that advance is only possible upon a ground of minds prepared for it, expectant of it, and understanding its necessity.

But the conception of a new education has proved to be an expanding one. It involves, we discover, something more than the understanding of history as one process. History reaches back to pre-history, and that passes insensibly into palæontology. The new education also involves, therefore, the assimilation of certain broad biological ideas that have been making their way slowly but surely from the laboratory and specialized biological course, towards the general instruction of the young and the guidance of mankind. And biology also illuminates the nature and working of mind, out of which spring the guiding ideas of History. We live in a world very badly informed of the many pregnant things biology has made manifest. A second factor in the new education is Modern Biology.

The content of a third portion of the new education is still in a far less developed state than either its history or its biology. It is far less developed and far more urgently necessary amidst the perplexities, pressures and conflicts of our time. That is a general conception of economic life, of industrial processes, trade and finance. It is to assist in bringing out this most undeveloped side of a modern ideology, that this present work is produced. It is intended to sketch out the missing third side, the economic side, of the ideological triangle.

We have remarked that this attempt to build up a modern ideology is going on at present chiefly in the minds of adolescents and adults outside the ordinary educational organizations. No doubt there are many teachers and schools already astir with the new ideas, but they are exceptional teachers and schools. The present state of affairs is a queer and paradoxical one. People leave school and then for the first time hear properly of the new history and of the leading ideas of modern biology which are essential to a modern ideology. They learn for the first time of socialism and of communism, of monetary and financial questions, of tariff issues, and of all the vast tangle of property and business. All this has been kept from them. They have had hardly an inkling of these things at school. And yet such things are the very substance of the lives these people must live. They do what they can to supply the deficiencies they discover in their school teaching and to correct its manifestly antiquated and reactionary influence upon them. Meanwhile the schools are taking the children of these people as they come along and very actively *putting them back among the old ideas*.

For example, while the adult world is learning painfully but steadily that aggressive nationalism is a disastrous obsession, a vast majority of our children are still being made into just as ardent little patriots as we were made before the war. They are even drilled, put under military discipline, made to wave flags and sing militant songs, and are given history teaching of a combative, romantic and narrowing type. This is no doubt a temporary state of affairs. As the modern ideology of the intelligent adult becomes more lucid, assured and complete, he will discriminate with increasing confidence and effect against the traditional teacher in favour of the enlightened one who certainly exists beside his reactionary confrère. One may easily become unjustly impatient with the school teacher. The school teacher cannot outrun public opinion. If he does so, he loses his job, and there is an end to the matter. The first battles for the New Education of our new world must be fought in the adult mind.

§ 3. *Apropos of Roger Bacon*

This present revolt against established teaching and traditional ways of living and managing human affairs is not unprecedented. Again and again individuals or clear-minded groups have set themselves to change the *ideology* of the world about them. The first and perhaps the supremely important effort for a new view of life and a new way of thinking came in the great days of the Academy of Athens, and there was another struggle for a new method at the end of the scholastic controversies in the period of the Renascence and the New Learning, when experimental science dawned upon the world. A third phase was the organization of modern ideas by the French Encyclopédistes. Upon these major movements of the human mind, these real new phases of human thought, we shall have more to say in our second and fifteenth chapters. But there is one isolated figure in history which must always be very sympathetic to those who are working on the reconstruction of contemporary ideology, the figure of Roger Bacon in the thirteenth century. He, however, does not mark a turning point in human ideas. He failed. The turning was to come later. But he was a pioneer who foretold the modern world, and he gave very clear indications of how mankind could achieve most of the things that have since been achieved. He was the first of the moderns, seven centuries ahead of his time.

He met with great opposition. He spent his declining years in prison, deprived of writing material. To the end, in spite of his suppression, he remained an obedient son of the Church. His dominant idea was to liberalize the teaching of the Church, and he imagined a Pope leading Christendom to exploration and research, power and abundance. He foresaw the modern world in substance even if he saw it still papal in form, but he did not see the centuries of waste and bickering, the endless petty wars, the schisms in the Church and the intricate mischief of princes, the great pestilences, the social disorder, that intervened. He had not taken the measure of mankind.

He was by no means a serene and superior person. He scribbled, he scolded, he was tiresome and almost entirely futile. Everybody about him was too brisk, active, able, and preoccupied with immediate things even to attend properly to a vision that to him was as plain as day. They found no sense in it. Two centuries of the liveliest history followed his death; it was the age of codpiece and crucifix, torture chambers and oubliettes, Plantagenet ambitions and the Wars of the Roses, peasant revolts and frequent famines, a romantic rather than a happy age, until at last successive epidemics of filth disease swept away half the population of Europe, and skulls became a leading theme in decorative art. When at the close of the sixteenth century Francis Bacon revived the vision of science, the Catholic Church was already entering upon its present defensive phase, and crabbed and scattered manuscripts that nearly everyone had forgotten were all that remained of the hopes of Roger Bacon.

His name remained indeed, but it remained as the name of a legendary magician.

Industrious biographers, loyal to their subject, have sought to trace a certain continuity between his ideas and those of Gilbert, the friend and instructor of Francis Bacon, and it has been shown that Columbus, unaware of his existence, quotes him at second hand as one of his inspirations. But if Roger Bacon started anything at all, he started very little. It is doubtful if Clement IV, who asked him to write, ever found time to read him. He had interested Clement before the latter became Pope. Then came his one gleam of opportunity. Would he set out his ideas for his friend to consider? In great haste Bacon poured them out in an *Opus Majus* and sent that with an *Opus Minus,* already done, and some other works. Perhaps Clement never saw these manuscripts. Probably nobody ever read more than scraps of them until the tenacious modern student came hardened to the job. There is no hint in Bacon's story of ally, colleague, or disciple. No band gathered about him. He passed, and the stream of events closed over him.

Yet what he had to say seems to us now the plainest common sense in the world. He wanted the frowsty, pretentious Latin teachers of his time to burn their atrocious translations, abandon their narrow and tedious methods, learn Greek and try to understand what Aristotle really had to say, explore the scientific treasures available in Arabic, turn from books to observation, and make experiments to check their dogmas. Vision and power would reward them. Steamship, aëroplane, and automobile: he saw them all, and many other things.

He could not say it plainly and loudly enough. He had none of that quality which lays hold of wilful men and marshals them to coöperation. He saw opportunity passing, within arm's length, as it seemed, and he lacked the power or the subtlety,—or was it the luck?—to rouse any living contemporary to the quality of that opportunity. Not for two more centuries was mankind even to finger the magic skirts of scientific knowledge—that most indifferent of benefactors, that most bountiful of givers.

It is perhaps because of his bickering uphill struggle, his desperate impatience, and his endearing weaknesses that Roger Bacon appeals now so strongly to those who are battling and toiling to-day in the same old struggle against the conservatism of educational institutions and the lag in progressive development that ensues. At first all educational reform is uphill. That is unavoidable. And all reformers are disposed to self-pity and moods of despair. They know no better. We still fight the enemies that he fought, but with a better hope. We still fight as he put it, "Undue Regard for Authority, Routine, Popular Prejudice and a False Conceit of our own Wisdom." A False Conceit, that is, when we should still be learning. The old tradition necessarily has all the prestige in such conflicts; it has the advantages of the defensive; it sits fortified in the high places and in the habitual assent of men. The reformers are often men no better than, or even of inferior quality to, the established men they attack. To be inspired by an intensive realization of a need does not make one the all-round superior of one's uninspired antagonist. And by the standards of the old education, anyhow, by the accepted standards, that is, it is inevitable that the reformers should appear to be defective, uneducated, minor and presumptuous men. Roger Bacon had the appearance and many of the defects of a presumptuous man. And no doubt to-day many of us who work for the new education have an air of presumptuous arrogance that is far from our real measure of ourselves. David and Jack the Giant Killer must have been in a sense presumptuous men. Even Adam displayed a certain arrogance when he accepted the task of replenishing the earth and inaugurating a world new-made.

The analogy between Roger Bacon and those who are working to-day for a new education must not be carried too far. For Roger Bacon there was no supporter in the world except one short-lived Pope. For the new educationist now an immense support is possible, for he can appeal over the heads of established authority to the Sane Man throughout the wide world. Roger Bacon was living in an age of authority, and we are living in a democratic age.

We who are concerned with the development of the new education have had to learn many things, and particularly we have had to realize that we possess this power of appeal from the scholastic authority to the general public. At first we were too much disposed to follow Roger Bacon and make a direct attack upon the school and university curricula. We were disposed to harass overworked and hampered teachers because they did not instantly turn their faces towards the new dawn. We waited upon education ministers and education departments and were officially rebuffed. When we could see a thing so plainly, it was difficult for us to realize that it might not be at all apparent yet to these other busier and more closely occupied people. And because of the resistances we encountered some of us were inclined to find ourselves new Roger Bacons, crying prematurely and ineffectively of the possibilities of a better world against an obdurate obscurantism, and so lapse into a self-righteous indolence. We did not realize that now it is through adult education by means of the book that the final definitive revolution of the educational organization must be brought about.

§ 4. *The Outline of History and the Science of Life*

The writer's *Outline of History* affords an excellent instance of the way in which the intelligent adult reader can be brought in now to correct the bias of scholastic usage. Although it has had an immense popular sale, that book was not planned nor written for a popular sale. It was conceived as a school book.

It was the outcome of the writer's experiences in his war propaganda work and in the foundation of the British League of Nations Union. These experiences convinced him that the idea of the League of Nations might be anything or nothing, according to the historical prepossessions of the particular person concerned, and that there could be no effective reorganization of human political affairs until the conception of human solidarity was far more firmly established in men's minds than it is at the present time. He came to apprehend the entire dependence of the political reactions of men upon the picture of history that existed in their minds. He realized that these pictures varied extraordinarily from class to class and still more so from country to country. Nearly all history teaching hitherto had been partial and partisan, and consequently men came to the peace discussions of the time with the best natural intentions and (all unawares of their state) with the most perverted ideas. For the new time there was needed a new teaching of history, the history of man's rise and achievement as one story; history could be treated no longer as a national rather than a universal subject, and it was necessary, if the efforts to reorganize the world at the end of the war were to have any permanent effect, that they should be erected on a common foundation of universal history.

In this belief the writer was not alone. Nor was he in any sense a pioneer. He takes his own experience because it is the handiest experience, because he knows it best, because indolence and egotism dispose him to do so. But in America, even before the war, under the influence of such writers as Breasted and Robinson the teaching of history as one whole was already under way. There has been now for some years an increasingly important New History movement in America. There was no particular originality therefore in the writer's insistence upon the urgent need of this important educational adjustment, and it was only after he had made various appeals to other historians and teachers that he set about writing the *Outline of History* as a proof that the subject could be brought within the compass of a college course, and as a demonstration of the method of treatment which would make it most valuable as an ideological basis for the new time.

No one could have been more astonished than he was at the great popular success of the *Outline*. He went to bed, so to speak, educational reformer and he woke up best seller. He discovered—and it was as great a discovery for his publishers as for himself—that there existed an immense reading public in the world which was profoundly dissatisfied with the history it had learnt at school, and which was eager for just what the *Outline* promised to be, a readable, explicit summary of the human adventure. The book sold and continues to sell enormously— on that promise. Not only does it sell, but several other excellent popular general histories, Van Loon's, for example, have appeared beside it. It has been translated into most civilized languages. Altogether, in all its editions and translations it has found more than two million purchasers, and its sale is still going on. In 1930, for instance, a dollar reprint of an old edition ran to a sale of 450,000 copies in the United States. The writer has at least an average share of egotism and vanity, but nothing will convince him that this immense success is due to any extraordinary merit in the writing of the book. It is a book done in a humdrum fashion, which derives any largeness and splendour it has entirely from its subjects. But it was for a while the only thing that even promised to satisfy the urgent need of intelligent people everywhere for a new and wider view of the human adventure, for a new and wider view made sufficiently clear and accessible for the time and attention they could afford to give it.

Now the discovery of the vast new public by the *Outline of History* was a very astonishing and important thing for all of us who were feeling our way towards a new education and the establishment of a new ideology. Throughout the world there existed this immense multitude of alert and hungry minds, ready for and seeking a wider and more serviceable vision of the past that has made the present, than the schools had given them. Instead of boring away in an uphill struggle for the schools, we could appeal directly to this great adolescent and adult stratum of ordinary intelligent people, and afterwards, with that immense support, turn to the reformation of the schools.

A vision of history as one whole is, as we have already remarked, only one part of a modern system of ideas, and it was natural, therefore, after the encouragement of this first success, to think of supplying the two other main factors for a complete modern ideology. These two other factors, as we have already put it, are biology and economics. The *Outline of History* gives the story of man's origin, his races, his tribes, communities, cities, states and empires, his wars and migrations, the development of his arts and implements, and the series of events that have brought him to his present situation. But on the one hand some account of what is known of the nature and possibilities of life,—what this thing Life is and how it works,—and on the other, some explanation of the toil and motives that bind mankind together in an uneasy unity, are needed to round off the view of existence to which a modern man must adjust himself.

The success of the *Outline of History* had given the writer a peculiar advantage for the launching of these two other needed Outlines, and so he set himself to the problem of their production. Circumstances had given him the opportunity to get this work done in a fashion, and once it has been done in any fashion, it is made easier for abler men with ampler organization and resources to do it over again more lucidly and thoroughly. The reader must not suppose that the producers of the pioneer modern ideology of which this is the third part, have any illusions about the quality and permanence of their work. The *Outline of History* must serve until a better outline replaces it, and so must the outline of Biology and the outline of Economics we are now introducing. As soon as they can be replaced by fuller and more lucid versions of what they have to tell, their usefulness will cease.

The first of these two to be made was the outline of Biology. For reasons we need not dwell upon here it was thought better to call this second work the *Science of Life*. The writer's early training had been biological, and he has always retained a lively interest in biological thought, but the mass of knowledge that has been accumulated since his student days rendered it necessary to call in competent assistance. He found it close at hand in the persons of his friend Professor Julian Huxley, grandson of his own biological teacher, and his own son, G. P. Wells. They produced a résumé of contemporary knowledge in this field, which gives the general reader the sum of what is known about his body and his mind, discusses the origin and evolution of life, surveys all the multifarious spectacle of living things on land and in the sea, brings together all the main trends of psychological thought and culminates in a special study of the very peculiar and exceptional biology of mankind. The publication of the *Science of Life* crowned the labours of two years and more of hard collaboration, and then it was possible to take up the last and most difficult enterprise of all, this outline of Economics, this popular account of the business and toil, the give and take of our strange and unprecedented species.

It has been so perplexing and heavy a task that it is necessary to make clear to the reader the broad facts about the difficulties encountered and give the reason for the form in which, after several false starts, abandonments, and renewed attacks, the work has now been cast. The reader has to be taken into the writer's confidence to that extent. Two convenient conventions, namely an imaginary encyclopædia and a museum of reference, have been adopted, and without them it is difficult to say how this outline of human activities could be exhibited at all. Behind the *Science of Life* there existed actual museums, textbooks, encyclopædias and the like, for the collaborators to summarize. Behind the present outline of economic science there exist indeed certain museums of which we shall tell more fully later, dealing very interestingly with one or other aspect of our many-sided subject, and a vast undigested mass of fact and material, not yet gathered into any ordered arrangement available for summarization. These things are coming into existence, but they are not yet fully here, and so we have had, as it were, to anticipate them and manage as well as possible as if they were already in being.

§ 5. *The Urgent Need for Sound Common Ideas about Work and Wealth*

Of these three systems of knowledge and realization which must make up a modern ideology, the third, in order as we have taken them, is not only the most elusive and difficult to assemble, but the most urgently necessary at the present time. Since the Great War the economic stresses of the world have become more and more painful and distressing. By comparison preceding ages are beginning to assume an air of the most idyllic tranquillity. We are coming to believe that before our time the ordinary human life passed in a peaceful, unchanging security from the cradle to the grave. It might be limited, it might be oppressed, but it was sure. The peasant child learnt to scare crows and plough and so forth, and grew up and ploughed and ploughed his patch to the end of his days. The townsman had his trade or his little shop, and it kept him, and he left it in due course to his son. The lawyer, the doctor went about his business; the woman of the gentler sort was loved and married and lived happily ever afterwards in a round of household duties. The seasons brought the harvest and the hunting, Yuletide, May Day, and the happy summer weather.

In truth things were never like that, but multitudes of people thought they were. The wheel of life seemed to them to be turning in orderly fashion from age to age, they did as their fathers had done before them, life was an even flow of small but sufficient events. Over the hills and far away was adventure, perhaps, but it did not threaten them. Young men went off and returned no longer young, with parrots and lacquer boxes and suchlike objects to witness to other worlds of taste and work, unlike but as stable, it seemed, as our own.

And that life was understandable. The way in which its few and simple parts joined together was plain. It was at hand. One saw every stage from the sowing of the seed to the baking of the bread, from the gathering of the wool to the making of the garment. One saw master and man, and if there arose any doubts about the explanation of the world, the priest at the altar had a wonderful way of dispelling them.

But now we all begin to realize we are living in the break-up of whatever system existed before our time, and that in a great disorder a new system may be coming into being. All sorts of forces are at work disorganizing us now but with a tantalizing air of producing some larger strange organization to which we must adapt our lives. We work, and the things we make are taken away and we see no more of them. Our streets are full of strangers who pass and give way to other strangers. Great factories arise in our familiar landscape, and we do not understand why they have arisen or what they produce. We buy and consume exotic foods. We are employed, we are thrown out of employment, things become dear, or cheap, or inaccessible and we cannot trace the causes of these fluctuations.

It seems all beyond our control. We cannot find out who controls it. Is anyone controlling it? The newspapers tell us this or that about it. They are disturbing and alarming. Vast multitudes, we learn, millions are being thrust out of employment. There is plenty, locked up. There are dire want and misery. Then we find ourselves called upon to decide between politicians who demand that this shall be done and politicians who demand that that shall be done. It appears that we in our muddled multitudinousness are being called upon to make decisions. This immense tangled affair, we gather, is our affair. In various rather obscure ways we have been made responsible for it. We have to vote.

But how can we vote when we do not get the hang of it? Has anyone got the hang of it? Are there any people anywhere in our world to-day who have a really comprehensive vision of the economic world process as one whole? Apparently not. And yet we ordinary people have it thrust upon us, that whatever control can be exercised over this immense complex tumult of world change, must be exercised through our voting and our assent.

When the present author wrote his *Outline of History* he was writing down and doing as exactly as he could for other people what in any case he had to do for himself, to get all the phases of history into one story and in their proper relation to one another, so that he could understand the international problems that unfolded after the war. And now again in this work he is making a practically parallel effort. He is doing it not only for the sake of the reader, but for his own sake. He is trying to assemble and select out of the infinitude of facts in the world about him the cardinal and significant facts that will make the whole mass of working, producing and consuming, one understandable spectacle. He is attempting a book, a survey of the world, a scheme and map of *doing,* which will enable him to say to anyone whatever: "This is the whole world of work and wealth, of making and getting and spending, and here at this point is your place, and this is where you come in. The map is not a very large-scale map, and consequently you and your sphere of activity may not loom very large, but here and not elsewhere is where you are. And so far as can be ascertained the reason why you are at this point and why you do this or that and want to do so and so is as follows. . . . And further there are reasons here given why you should act in a certain fashion and what certain things are justifiable for you and what certain others are not. This world of making and fetching and carrying and buying and selling to which you give the greater part of your waking life is ruled by certain laws, obsessed by certain defects (which perhaps you may help to cure) and threatened by certain dangers you may help to avert. In fact, I am attempting to make for myself and you a complete chart of economic life, not simply to help you to steer yourself through the confusion, but also to supply a common ground upon which we two can coöperate in this great experiment of life; this adventure of mankind.

"Just so far as this attempt is successful, then so far, instead of our present feeling of helplessness against the waves of want and loss and of elation and prosperity that sweep over our lives and the lives of those about us, we may presently find ourselves with ideas in common, with convictions in common, and with a workable plan of campaign for the stabilization and betterment of this strange eventful world."

§ 6. *Some Difficulties and Problems in the Writing of This Book.*
Museums of Industrial Progress. The Device of an Imaginary En-
cyclopædia

And now let us give the reader some account of the very great difficulties that have been discovered and circumvented in getting this work
into shape.

The *Outline of History* was written by a single author who took his
work to specialists for verification or correction; it was largely a summary of predigested material. But the *Science of Life* was done in a
different fashion; there was an immense body of very technical science
in existence, and the work was best done in collaboration with two
able experts. The writer's first conception of this third book was as a
collaboration also. He thought he would call it the *Conquest of Power*.
It seemed to him that it would be possible to treat all the spectacle of
today as being, in its essence, mankind escaping from toil through the
development of power machinery. The work was to tell of the development of invention and science, and then it was to trace the transformation of everyday life, the spreading change in the forms and fashions
and methods of everyday life, through this change in the economic
basis. Two well informed collaborators were to gather the bulk of the
material and assist in the synthesis.

It seemed laborious but possible in these terms. It was only after the
project was launched and the first instalment of "material" came to
hand that the profound difference in conditions of this enterprise from
its predecessor became apparent. It was only then that the author
realized how purely customary our productive, manufacturing, credit,
monetary and trading systems are. The mass of fact to be dealt with
was not only far larger, but it had undergone nothing like the same
sifting, scrutiny and classification as the biological material. It had
hardly been approached scientifically. We know far more exactly about
foraminifera and tadpoles than we do about many business operations,
and we are far more in agreement how that sub-human life is to be
thought about and told about. The author found himself urging his collaborators towards a dark jungle of fact in which there were no textbooks and only very incidental and limited museums. That sort of
clearing, exploratory, synthetic effort was demanded, in which collaborators, advancing in triumvirate formation, might easily become an intolerable drag on the work. It would be all too easy to collect enough
material to overwhelm us while leaving the larger part of the jungle

unexplored. And nothing annoys a collaborator who aspires to be a colleague more than to tell him to scrap his material and either begin again or resign. Yet there was no way to avoid such masterful repression. Experiments in statement would have to be made, chapters written and torn up, methods of treatment tried out and abandoned, before the right way of doing it was discovered.

As it was surveyed in this collaboration stage the *Conquest of Power* presented itself as a continually swelling mass of fact. The job was to digest it. Because of the ease of aggregation compared with the difficulties of synthesis, any group of collaborators would be committed slowly but surely to the writing of an encyclopædia. That would take years of toil and might never reach completion.

Presently, as it became more and more plain to me that the development of the world's current economic life has much more in it than merely the introduction and consequences of power machinery, the projected title of the enterprise was altered to the *Science of Work and Wealth*. An ever growing series of industrial developments was sketched out. We should have, we thought, to tell the history of steam from Hero's engine to the latest turbine. We should have to trace the development of the metallurgy of every sort of metal. We should have to tell the full story of electrical development. There would have to be lengthy explicit accounts of the utilization of coal, plans, diagrams, photographs of old-fashioned and modern gas works, a pursuit of coal-tar products to their ultimate ramifications, a history of wild and of cultivated rubber, and—in the fullest sense of the phrase—so on and so on. Interminably. When that much was done we should have got at least a technical encyclopædia. We should have accomplished in a book what the Science Museum at South Kensington and—more explicitly and fully—its daughter the Deutsches Museum at Munich—set out to do. And it is a journey of nine miles to walk once round the galleries of the Deutsches Museum! Our enterprise was already becoming colossal and interminable.

But all that would only be the first portion of the design of the *Science of Work and Wealth* as it was opening out. For this account of materials, mines, foundries, factories, engines, machines, was only the framework of what we had to do. So far as that part went we might have sat down in the Deutsches Museum with notebooks and cameras to turn it into a book. But there would still remain great fields of activity untouched, for which we should have to go elsewhere. The technical museum could, for example, take us as far as the "textile fabric," but to trace the textile fabric to the stylish dress via the costume designer, the milliner and the shop, opened a new and practically unexplored field. The immense activities of distribution, selling, advertisement, the fluctuations of fashion, all fell within the boundaries of our project, but for these as yet no Deutsches Museum exists. That department of anthropology has still to assemble such partial collections as have been made so far. And when it came to catering, to modern food distribution, to the new ideas that are being embodied in contemporary housing, to the hotel industry, to tourism, the material was still more hopelessly scattered, and, in any completeness, unobtainable. And still other vast areas of interest stretched beyond, the pay envelope and the counting house, the farmer's loan and the bank, the financier and the douane. At the douane were national flags and soldiers in uniform. . . . And after all that came the enquiry why all this vast multitude did what they did.

In the face of this unordered multitudinousness the projected collaboration had definitely to be broken up. Some other way had to be found to synthesize this complex spectacle. It was by no means easy to find that other way. I will not weary the reader with the details of this search, the hesitations, the ponderings and goings to and fro. The problem was to reduce this colossal project to manageable dimensions. It had grown until it had become the scheme for an encyclopædia, a whole technical literature, and there still remained vast hinterlands to explore. It had outgrown itself beyond realization. Yet nevertheless, I perceived, it retained a shape. It had not become a mere chaos of material.

Might it not be possible therefore to give merely the gist of it, the idea of it? For example, a scheme for it might be prepared, a rather detailed synopsis. This could be printed and circulated—more or less restrictedly. It would at least give the framework of essential ideas soundly and clearly. Then perhaps it would be possible to reorganize the task on the lines of a multiple collaboration. My mind still harped for a time on comprehensiveness, organization, a concentrated encyclopædism. I would not indeed produce the *Science of Work and Wealth* itself, but an infant, prepared, if the gods willed it, to grow up into the *Science of Work and Wealth*. It could be issued as, let us say, "*Work and Wealth*—A Project for a Review of the World's Economic Life."

That I may call the first phase of the reorientation of the project. Perhaps such a synopsis, I thought, would be as much as I could actually do towards the enterprise. It would be a sort of interim report upon a work in hand done in such a way that presently other hands might take it over. It would be the pencil outline for a fresco which would have all the colour, substance and detail the sketch could merely indicate. It would be possible to broach all the leading ideas and anticipate the main discussions of that contemplated work—that was the main point. It was to be a forecast—but a substantial forecast, much more than a mere agenda—of the whole thing. . . .

On that I went to work, but as the work got done, I saw more and more clearly that I was not writing a synopsis but a book. I was doing what I had been wanting to do, in a fresh, compacter and altogether more convenient fashion. What I was writing was not indeed that encyclopædic, all too vast and detailed *Science of Work and Wealth* that I had found at first so alluring and then so oppressive. But it was its essential form and ideas made all the clearer because they were not embedded in hundreds of illustrations and collaborators' detail. I changed the title. I gave it another title, the title of *The How and the Why of Work and Wealth,* to make it plain to myself that I was doing something starker and less massive than the original project. We were to deal with industry but not technology, with finance but not accounts and statistics. Motives and direction were to be the primary substance; detail was to be secondary and by way of illustration. That title was good in so far as it kept the bare aim in view, but gradually, as the work approached completion, as it broadened and opened out and its spectacular quality became plainer, this title also was felt insufficient, and it was rechristened finally, *The Work, Wealth and Happiness of Mankind,* under which title is has appeared prior to this revised edition.

The discovery of that final title was extremely difficult. It had to be descriptive, expressive, and attractive. It had to tell the reader what he was getting. It had not to promise too much or to terrify unduly. It had to present a candid attractive brow to the world, broad rather than high. Various suggestions were tried over. The footnote below is a sort of vault in which some of the condemned lie in state.* They all help to show the objective of this work. It is now neither a synopsis nor the complete encyclopædia once contemplated, but a real summary, and I hope a serviceable summary, a world display, of the present mental and material poise of our species. It can be read right through. But that projected encyclopædia would never have been read through, because

---

*A Survey of Civilization, What Mankind Is Doing, The Human Complex, The Fabric of Society, The Fabric of Human Society, The Panorama of Mankind, The World of Work and Wealth, The World at Work, The Work and Play of Mankind, Work, Wealth and Play, The Activities of Mankind, The Human Ant-Hill, Homo Sapiens, Man in His World, Homo Contra Mundum, How Man Exists, Man Conquering and to Conquer.

it is only the broad issues that interest us all in these questions, and the technical details of engines, researches, industrial processes, mining, agriculture and so forth, except in so far as they illustrate general principles, are speedily tiresome to those not immediately concerned with them. We all find a certain pleasure in watching work in process but nearly all of us are bored if it is explained to us too fully.

That need for the limitation of detail was brought home to me very vividly by a shrewd friend I had taken to the South Kensington Science Museum. We spent an hour or so over the development of the steam engine; we went on to the story of the ship. Then we went up to the evolution of optical science. My friend began to show signs of brain fag. We went to that central place on the top floor which gives a glimpse of all the floors and galleries. "This is fascinating," said my friend, "but it isn't like reading a history or a novel. It doesn't take you on from a beginning to an end. It's a multitude of strands woven together. Each one is different, but they all go the same way. I would like you to tell me now what it is all about; to take me to this exhibit or that to illustrate this point or that, but I have no use for it all. I like to know it is here. I like to know what the main divisions are. But nobody sane would want to explore all these galleries, just as nobody sane would dream of reading through an encyclopædia from beginning to end. This stuff is for reference. You tell me what it is all about—if you can."

I felt the wisdom of these remarks still more profoundly at Munich as I made my nine-mile pilgrimage through the Deutsches Museum. I would spend a profitable hour or so upon a hundred feet of exhibit and then walk on, taking the bright objects about me for granted and blessing the wisdom and industry that have assembled them. These things have to be done and made accessible, but it is no part of the new education to inflict them in mass upon everyone. What the new education has to give to everyone is a conception of the broad stream of mental growth and purpose upon which all these things are carried along. Then let everyone specialize in the section that attracts him most.

This remains an experimental book. It has all and more than the faults of the *Outline of History* because it is less of a compilation. It is slighter and even more provisional. It has little of the scientific assurances of the *Science of Life*. But its claims are enormous; let there be no mistake about that. It represents all current human activities and motives—all and nothing less. It is a first comprehensive summary of the whole of mankind working or playing or unemployed; it seeks to show the jockey on the race course in relation to the miner in the pit, the baby in the cradle, the savage in the jungle, the city clerk, the fish-wife, the lord-in-waiting, the lord chancellor on the Woolsack, the Soviet envoy, the professional cricketer, the shopwalker, the street-walker, the dealer in second-hand microscopes, the policeman, the news-vendor, the motor-car "bandit," the political gangster and the university professor. It will have failed of its object so far as any particular reader goes if that reader does not find his own niche clearly indicated in this descriptive fabric. He must be able to say, "Here I am, and this is how I stand to the rest." Or at the worst he must be able to say, "Here in this lot I should find myself, if the scale were bigger." It has to establish the reader's economic citizenship, *place* his economic rights and duties. It has, among other things, to supersede the vague generalizations on which Marxism rests and concentrate and synthesize all those confused socialist and individualist theorizings of the nineteenth century which still remain as the unstable basis of our economic experiments. It has to be that much sound and thorough, or it would not have been worth doing.

In other words, this is a sincere and strenuous attempt to make eco-nomic and social science come alive and be personal. It is a book within the compass of my writing and your reading, but behind it still looms the original, the vaster conception of a huge modern encyclopædia of human skill, knowledge and relationship, the whole *Science of Work and Wealth*. That phrase I use repeatedly in what follows—to suggest a conspectus of modernized economics, the entire literature of the subject and all such studies now in progress. And radiating from our work stretch out the galleries of the South Kensington Museum and the Deutsches Museum, and beyond these, other museums and the anticipatory phantoms of galleries that do not yet exist, a museum that Henry Ford is trying to assemble under von Miller's inspiration, and other museums that as yet no one is trying to assemble; museums of advertisement, of selling and the like, museums of educational methods and apparatus. At one point I raid towards art museums, music libraries and libraries of gramophone records. For all human achievement falls into our prospectus. . . . The reader, after this explanation, will not, I hope, resent my frequent allusions to these collections assembled or still to be assembled. It it a device of very great convenience. It makes a picture that could be made in no other way.

The abandonment of the idea of a triumvirate of collaborators for this work has left the writer wholly responsible for its tone, content and general arrangement, but it has not meant an abandonment of assistance. In fact, it has rather released him to get special help from a great number of people, instead of restricting his channels of supply to two helpers. The first start had already produced a sketchy framework of the undertaking and a certain amount of more or less useful material had been assembled. Moreover, one of the original triumvirate, Mr. Edward Cressy, the well-known writer and popularizer of industrial technology, although he had felt unequal to the labour of collaboration throughout, retained a keen interest in the enterprise; his experienced hand is evident in the earlier chapters, and his advice has been helpful at a number of points. Mrs. G. R. Blanco White, who was originally consulted about certain passages connected with money and banking, upon which subjects she had written various articles and memoranda, took up the matter with so lively and understanding a response, that finally the whole plan was put in her hands and discussed with her, and she became a real collaborator upon the entire work. The special chapter on Women, though it does not by any means present her particular views, was inserted at her suggestion and has been closely argued with her; a considerable part of the material on actual labour conditions comes from her; she assembled the Congo and Putumayo histories; she collected the substance of the summaries of wealth-getting careers, the diagnosis of the current world slump is mainly hers and she has read and prepared proofs for press. Another friend who has contributed material to this book, subject of course to the freest editorial handling, is Mr. J. F. Horrabin, M. P., my collaborator-illustrator in the *Outline of History*, to whom I am indebted for particulars of legislative work as it is done in the House of Commons. It is very pleasant to have his hand in the third as well as the first part of this trilogy. To Madame Odette Keun, the novelist and descriptive writer, I am also greatly indebted. She has assembled material for me, contributed to the discussion of colonial conditions, read and re-read the entire typescript and all the proofs, and throughout she has insisted on the utmost clearness and explicitness in everything she read. Where so much matter has to be condensed there are great possibilities of fogging, and her sharp, critical mind has been of the utmost value. I do not know whether thanks are most due to her from the reader or from myself.

Outside this inner circle of people who have had, so to speak, a finger —or several fingers—in making the original manuscript, I have to thank a number of others who have, in the measure of the demands made upon them, helped me or my collaborators very generously and freely. I went to Munich to see what the Deutsches Museum could do for me, and I had some very stimulating talk with Dr. Oskar von Miller, the virtual creator of that wonderful display, and afterwards I visited Sir Henry Lyons at the South Kensington Museum and followed out the broad lines of his scheme of development. The important share these great collections have had in suggesting my method of dealing with otherwise unmanageable masses of detail, has already been explained in this Introduction, and it will be obvious throughout the entire work.

I have to thank Dr. C. S. Myers, who allowed me to see the working and intentions of his National Institute of Industrial Psychology and who put me on to the admirable Home Office Museum in Horseferry Road. I am also very grateful to Mr. E. W. Murray, who showed me over that museum and made its meaning plain to me.

Some years ago Professor Carr-Saunders visited me and discussed this project at its very beginning, and subsequently I had a very profitable talk about the general scheme with Professor Henry Clay. His *Economics for the General Reader* has been a steadying handbook in the writing of several chapters. Professor Carr-Saunders has since read the proofs of the entire work for me. His care, criticism and knowledge have been of great value. But he is not to be held responsible for the opinions expressed or the tendencies displayed. I am the only whipping-boy for this work.

Another adviser has been Mr. Graham Wallas. Years ago among the Swiss mountains we discussed Ostrogorski's fruitful studies of modern democracy, then newly published, and it has been very pleasant to link up this present work with those earlier trains of interest. Outside an all too limited circle of special workers on both sides of the Atlantic, few people realize how much contemporary thought about political and administrative matters owes to the obstinately critical and enterprising mind of Graham Wallas. To Dr. Finer of the London School of Economics my thanks are also due for helpful counsel. Dr. Finer has taken the civil services of the world as his particular field of study, and I am very fortunate to have had his aid. Mr. Eric Simons of Edgar Allen & Co. has "vetted" Mr. Cressy and myself so far as the account of the steels goes in Chapter II, and Sir Frederick Keeble and Mr. A. P. Allan have played the same generous rôle for Chapter III. Mr. R. A. Duncan has read Chapter V to its great benefit, and so has Mr. Clough Williams Ellis. My son Frank Wells has also made some useful suggestions upon this architectural section. Lord d'Abernon, Mr. Maynard Keynes and Mr. Thomas Lamont have read the typescript of Chapter IX and discussed it with me. Mr. Lamont does not in any way endorse that chapter, which he regards as Utopian, but he has made some very friendly and helpful comments on its statements. My friend Mr. Leif Jones, an "old parliamentary hand," read and discussed the account of Parliament with me. Lord Olivier read over the population and race chapter (XIII) and advised upon it, giving me in particular a very useful note on the state of affairs in Jamaica, and Lady Rhondda has read the chapter on Women and commented thereon. My daughter-in-law Mrs. G. P. Wells has looked up and checked much indispensable material and helped ably with the proofreading. And my friends Professor Harold Laski and Mr. Kingsley Martin have read the entire proofs from beginning to end, to my marked profit.

Mrs. Blanco White has received very useful help from Mr. Robert R. Hyde (of the Industrial Welfare Society), Mr. R. G. Hawtrey of the Treasury, Mr. John Hilton of the Ministry of Labour and Mr. J. F. Darling, Mr. W. Crick and Mr. Parfett of the Midland Bank. Mr. R. G. Hawtrey has read through and discussed the typescript of Chapter IX and saved me from several errors of fact and presentation. Mrs. Blanco White consulted Mr. H. W. Nevinson and Mr. J. H. Harris of the Aborigines' Protection Society for material about Putumayo. Among others to whom I am indebted for ideas, material, answers to questions and permission to quote, are Sir Robert Hadfield, Sir Josiah Stamp, Professor T. E. Gregory, Sir R. A. Gregory, Mr. Percy Redfern, Professor Miles Walker, Mr. Cloudesley Brereton, Mr. W. Clarke Hall, Professor Soddy, Mr. E. M. H. Lloyd, M. André Gide, Mr. Raymond Fosdyck, Professor Malinowsky, Sir Basil Thompson and Mrs. W. H. Thompson (Joan Beauchamp). My debt to the new Encyclopædia Britannica is manifest and is acknowledged at a score of points. But it is almost impossible to recall and name all the friendly and interested people on whom I have upon occasion inflicted lengthy descriptions of this project during the various stages of its growth, and who have given me hints, criticism, counsel and ideas. M. Henri Barbusse, Mr. Maurice Hindus and Mr. Michael Farbman, for example, have brought me their personal impressions of Russia. I have found the excellent talk and published views of Mr. Edward A. Filene particularly illuminating upon modern distribution and the relations of the manufacturer to the retailer, and I cannot say how much I owe in the correction and steadying of my ideas, to the conversation of my friend Sir Arthur Salter.

The publication of this book produced a voluminous correspondence by which I have profited in revising it for a new printing. I have particularly to thank my friends Dr. Delisle Burns and Mr. Eden Paul for reading it through and sending me their very helpful notes. And among other correspondents who have made valuable general criticisms of the book as a whole are Mr. R. A. Duncan, Mr. Ernest Slater, Mr. P. E. Percival, Mr. B. C. Allen, Mr. Jonathan Griffin and Mr. Robert Donington. And the book on its first publication had a good and helpful press.

In a number of footnotes the reader will find the names of numerous books that have served me. For a couple of years I have read very little that had not some bearing upon this task and I have met no one with something to tell, whom I did not try to turn to account for this work. But in view of the breadth of the field to be covered, it is impossible not to realize that there must be many good books I have missed and many authorities I might have consulted with advantage and did not do so. These authors and writers must forgive my ignorance and not suppose themselves wilfully ignored. This outline was altogether too vast to do exhaustively at the first onset. The alternative to doing it as it has been done was not to do it at all. And it had to be done.

It remains a sketch, an adventure. It is, I recognize, the least finished work of a trilogy, because it is the most novel. In the long run a better work of the same substance must replace it. Or it may share one destiny with its two companions and be fused with them for a common purpose. A further fusion, concentration, stripping down and simplification may be ultimately attempted. At present the *Science of Life* overlaps the opening chapters of the *Outline of History;* our first chapter of this present work does the same, and the concluding sections of the *Outline of History* merge insensibly into the economic and political problems we deal with here. They are all contributory sketches to that complete but clear and concentrated Account of Life, which it behoves us to give to our children, that summary of fundamentals on which the collective energies of a new generation must be based.

Mankind is living too ignorantly and casually, and such education as exists is limited, incoherent and confused in its statement of reality. That is the chief cause of unhappiness in the world to-day, and that is the evil against which the triple effort of these books is directed.

CHAPTER THE FIRST

How Man Became an Economic Animal

§ 1. *Economics Is a Branch of Biology*

THE first thing to ask of this vast intricacy of human activities in which we live is, What as a whole is it? What is its nature? How did it arise? What do we know of its history? When and how did this world of work and wealth begin?

We must go back first to historical biology, the prelude to history. In the *Science of Life* there is a careful account of the beginnings and ascent of living things, of the dawn and primary nature of human psychological processes, of the development of man as a social animal and as a reasoning creature,—an account which culminates in a special book devoted to Human Biology. At that point this present work takes up its task. Economics, which is neither more nor less than the academic name for the science of work and wealth, is spoken of in the *Science of Life* as a branch of ecology; it is the ecology of the human species. Ecology deals with the welfare of species generally: how they hold their own in their environment, and how they depend upon and serve other species of plants and animals; how they prosper and increase or suffer and decline. It is the science of the balance of life. Economics is the science of the balance of human life and how it prospers or decays. We have to deal here, in this survey of work and wealth and happiness, with the position and prospects in space and time of practically the only economic mammal, *Homo sapiens*. That is the wide framework of our undertaking.

By economic animal we mean an animal that prepares and stores food socially. Ants and bees are economic animals. Almost immediately we will explain how it is that man differs from all other vertebrates in being economic.

Until recently economic science and discussion have ignored biology and outraged psychology; they have dealt with a sort of standard and inalterable man; it is only now that it becomes possible to bring economic realities into line with these more fundamental sciences and treat them as evolved and evolving facts. But in no field of knowledge has there been such vigorous advance during the last quarter of a century as in the study of social origins. A vast, rapidly organizing mass of fact becomes available for educational use and for application to the economic life of mankind.

The way in which the knowledge of social origins has grown upon the minds of the intelligently curious during these past five and twenty years is a process as fascinating as the development of some long desired picture upon the plate in a photographer's dark room. There was a steady and at first almost unconscious convergence of originally very remote researches. Psychoanalysis, coming from the mental clinic by way of the study of mental stresses, dreams and childish thought, has illuminated mythology and primitive mentality very vividly; archæological discovery, the science of comparative religions, anthropological speculation and mental physiology have all been approaching the interpretation of the rapid and marvellous conversion during the brief space, astronomically speaking, of less than a million years, of a rare and rather solitary and self-centred species of primate into an economic animal with a continually developing social range and a continually increasing biological interdependence. For that is what has happened in and since the Pleistocene period. Man ceased almost suddenly to be an ordinary animal, eating its food where it found it, and he became very rapidly indeed an unprecedented species, leading an economic life resembling only quite superficially the social economic life of the ants, bees and termites. He achieved this social economic life, not as the insects did, by the development of organizing instincts, but by the interplay of motives in his cerebrum. The nature of this transition lies at the root of any sound economic study. A review of human work and wealth and happiness cannot be either sound or helpful unless it rests firmly on this fundamental biological fact.

The *Science of Life* tells the story of the evolution of the cerebral cortex in the mammals, and the way in which hand, eye and brain have educated one another, shows how a new power of abstraction and planning crept into existence with the appearance of the primates and, with a resort to vocal and visual symbols, imposed itself upon the wasteful trial-and-error methods employed by mentalities of a lower grade. And further, biology demonstrates how these symbols of sound and gesture, which appeared at first as a mere means of communication, rendered possible the immense and rapid mental organization of *Homo sapiens:* immense in relation to the intelligence of any other living creatures. Man's rapid yet insensible transition from the casual feeding of all other sorts of vertebrates, to economic foresight, was the direct outcome of this mental organization. All this is explained quite clearly in the *Science of Life* or any equivalent biological summary that may exist. And thereby the way is cleared for a sound psychological approach to human economics.

Up to the beginning of the present century such an approach was impossible. Historical and economic speculation was profoundly vitiated by the tacit assumption that man in the opening phases of his social life saw things as definitely, apprehended consequences as clearly, and generally thought as we do now. Historians had still to realize that either geography, climate, or human nature could change. And among other fundamental failures of imagination in their thought, the economics of the last century carried back into the remote past the distinctions we make to-day between the religious and material interests of man. Primitive man was supposed to be mentally already a business man, driving bargains and reaping the "rewards of abstinence." Abstract thought was ascribed to him. Popular writers upon pre-history, anxious to make their subject sympathetic, have always been disposed to exaggerate the resemblances between the life of a man or woman in the late palæolithic age and the life of to-day. They made out the early savage to be a sort of city clerk camping out; they presented the men of Ur and early Egypt as if they had been the population of Pittsburgh or Paris in fancy dress. They minimized or ignored the fact that these people were not only living under widely different stimuli, but reacting to them in ways almost as much beyond our immediate understanding as the mental reactions of a cat or a bird. "Human nature," they said, "never changes." In truth, it never ceases to change.

Anyone who will spend a little time in looking over the carvings on a Maya stele or the representations of Indian gods, and who will reflect that these strange and intricate forms were made with intense effort and regarded with the utmost gravity, that evidently they conveyed meanings that were felt to be otherwise inexpressible, may get some intimations of the width and depth of the mental gulf across which we moderns, with our abstract terms, our logical processes and our prompt rejection of irrelevances and unorthodox associations, must strain to conceive the earlier thoughts of man. Dreamlike and childish is what we call these images now, and dreamlike and childish they are, but such was the quality of the mental atmosphere in which the enlarging social life of humanity began. Man began his social life dreamingly, amidst fear and fantasies, before he could talk very much. Speech and social organization grew complicated together. His fantasies still haunt our social institutions.

The exponent of the science of work and wealth has to bring out all this. The task before the workers in the field of modern economics is to use all this new work to fertilize their barren abstractions. The ideas of Frazer, of Jung, of Atkinson play upon and enrich each other. The last haunting suggestions of a "social contract," of the idea that human society was a deliberate arrangement between intelligent people like ourselves, is being cleared out of our minds by this play of thought between the mythologist and the psychologist, and the way is being opened to a proper understanding of the social mechanism.

§ 2. Primitive Man Haphazard as an Animal

Let us recapitulate the broad facts about human origins that have been assembled during the last half century. They are the necessary foundation for all our subsequent generalizations about social interaction.

Man was already a tool-using and fire-making creature before he became man as we know him to-day. Several species of *Homo* have existed on the earth, of which *Homo sapiens,* all mankind now living, is the sole surviving kind. And not only do we know now of other species of man, but we now know also of other genera of primates, Hominidæ also, nearer to us than any ape, and yet not men in any sense of the word: such types as *Pithecanthropus,* the man-ape of Java, and *Sinanthropus,* the ape-man of Pekin, manlike creatures below the tool-using level. There is a rapidly growing body of knowledge now about these sub-men and early men whose lives preceded humanity. One year gives us Rhodesian man; a little later comes this *Sinanthropus*—the sort of Missing Link our grandfathers demanded before they would believe in the animal origins of man. While I write someone may be actually excavating another important fragment to fit into the jig-saw picture of man's origin. Some two or three million years ago or so, there was, it is manifest, a considerable number of species of these quasi-human creatures, "ground apes," perhaps, rather than arboreal creatures, similar in many respects to their cousins, the clambering or climbing great apes, of which the gibbon, orang-outang, chimpanzee and gorilla still linger in the dwindling tropical forests of our planet. Before very long we shall be able to picture their manner of life.

Apes, these early sub-men, and man, constituting together the class of Primates, had and have certain distinctive advantages over most other great mammals. One of these advantages is the possession of exceptionally good eyes. The primates see far more clearly and exactly than the run of mammals. If they do not see so swiftly as a cat or dog, nor are so quick to detect movement, they have a far better apprehension of the form and relations of things. There is a distinctive area of precise vision on their retinas. No other mammals except the monkeys possess this area of distinct vision. And the fore limbs of all the primates had been developed by a phase of arboreal life into more and more competently prehensile organs. Hand and eye therefore worked together with the brain in a rapid mental development. All the early primates were exceptionally wary and ingenious animals, and all very ready and able to use sticks and stones for their immediate ends. A chimpanzee, as the *Science of Life* describes very clearly, will display contrivance quite beyond the range of any other mammalian type. Several of the early species of *Homo,* perhaps all the genus, seem not merely to have caught up sticks and stones for use, but to have shaped and adapted them to particular ends. The sticks have perished; the stones endure.

Many of the more recent geological deposits abound in stone, and particularly in flints, which have certainly been chipped deliberately to point and shape them. It was once supposed that these eoliths, as they are called, were the work of real human beings like ourselves, but it is more probable that they were made by one or more kindred species now extinct. The ancestry of modern man is still difficult to trace precisely. Finds will have to multiply very greatly before we can fill in our genealogy with complete assurance.

The most near and interesting of these extinct human kindred is the species of *Homo* known as the Neanderthal Man (*Homo neanderthalensis*). He differed from our own species (*Homo sapiens*) in his teeth (which were flatter and more complex, without our rather larger, and so more beastlike, canines), in his want of a chin, in his inability to turn his head back and up to the sky, in the fact that his thumb was not so exactly opposable to his forefinger, and in minor differences in his limb bones. Features of his jaw bone make it doubtful if he could use articulate speech of the human kind. The movements of his tongue may have been restricted, but then he may have resorted to gesture or other methods of symbolism. *Homo neanderthalensis* had a fairly big brain, but it was bigger behind and narrower in front than that of *Homo sapiens.* We do not know if he met and interbred with *Homo sapiens* (as dog, jackal and wolf will interbreed with each other), but we do know that he made quite well-shaped implements, buried some of his dead with their tools and ornaments beside them in caves, and used fire. His later implements show more skill than the earlier ones and come nearer to the *Homo sapiens* type of manufacture. So we conclude that the capacity for these things was common to the ancestor of both this species and *Homo sapiens,* and that man was already a fire-using, tool-using animal before he was completely man. And his tool-using must have involved primitive feelings about personal property. Even our ancestral sub-man, the common ancestor of these two species or races, must have trailed an increasing amount of gear about with him. His economic pilgrimage had begun.

Early man of our own line, *Homo sapiens,* was too intelligent to be easily drowned and fossilized, and were it not for this habit of interment he shared with the Neanderthaler, we should know very little indeed about him. We should know as little of him as we do of the other quasi-men who did not bury their dead. But so far as our present records go, the indisputable *Homo sapiens* came upon the scene some forty thousand years ago or more, a distinct race if not a distinct species, and he was then a hunter, wandering in small family groups from pitch to pitch, living like all the rest of the great mammals on the food he found from day to day, fruits and roots, small game, and sometimes a larger kill, using fire for cooking and to keep off hostile beasts, and extending his natural powers by means of stakes, clubs and shaped and sharpened stones. He was certainly not a very numerous race at that time. He had still to develop extensive social habits. He probably wandered in small family groups as the great apes do to-day, and he may have been as rare as they are.

§ 3. *The Dawn of Social and Economic Life*

From this wandering and hunting condition man, true man, that is to say, the species of *Homo* to which we belong, presently made a very extraordinary stride forward. He seems to have made this stride very rapidly from the biological point of view in something between five thousand and ten thousand generations. To geologists and astronomers that will seem a mere instant of time. We have as yet few material traces of this transition. It is possible that this stride forward was taken in regions now submerged and so far inaccessible to scientific exploration. But the most subtle and ingenious probings into human habits, traditions and mental reactions have pieced together the probable outline of the processes by which this stride was achieved. They constitute a complex and fascinating speculative literature, rather too ample and fascinating for intense treatment here. The drift of it, and especially its mental aspect, is given in the *Science of Life*.

The gist of the change was that while hitherto man had subsisted upon the natural food supply of the country in which he lived, he now began to cultivate and store food, keep other animals to be a source of supply to him, live in larger communities than heretofore and establish definite permanent settlements. He had become an economic animal. From the point of view of biology this was a quite extraordinary new departure. Except for a few rodents of which the beaver is the most remarkable, no other mammal, no other vertebrate, has even begun to develop in this direction. Rabbits and gophers associate but do not store; squirrels store but do not form coöperative communities. Dogs and wolves hunt in packs but take no thought for the morrow. Even with the beaver, it is questionable if there is a deliberate storage of food. No mammals cultivate. We have to go to the insect world, to the ants, termites and bees, to find any parallel to human societies. They too are economic animals which are settled in communities and do not live from hand to mouth.

Yet, though the change meant a transition from one sort of life to a sort of life so fundamentally different that scarcely any other vertebrated species displays it, and though it was fraught with the most astounding possibilities for this planet and it may be for the whole universe of matter, it yet went on in all probability generation after generation, age after age, without any very sudden and violent revolutions in human usage. The herdsman, the builder, the cultivator, were already latent in the watchful, ingenious early human wanderer. Already, before his economic life developed, he was talking, he was imitating, he was in his manner experimenting. One thing led to another, and the unforeseen of yesterday became the familiar of to-day. *Tradition* appeared and grew and changed, unaware that it ever changed. Man's increasing ingenuity and curiosity increased the number of his implements and possessions. He had to keep these impedimenta somewhere, and perhaps a store place was the first thing to tie the developing varieties of *Homo* to a definite settling place. Moreover, it was convenient to have a hearth where a fire could be kept alight, for early fire-making had its difficulties. So agriculture found man already disposed to root himself to place. He must have passed through this great transition from animal wandering to economic settlement almost unawares. The story of human work and wealth does not begin, therefore, like something suddenly begotten or hatched out; it does not open as a play does with a curtain suddenly rising on Act One: it dawns.

§ 4. *The Domestication of Animals*

The interest of *Homo sapiens* in other animals was the lively interest of a hungry hunter who was sometimes hunted. He lay in watch and puzzled his brains about what these other animals might do and what might influence their comings and goings. Spears, arrows, traps, fish-hooks are among his earliest productions.

He imitated these beasts, and in his quickening brain, which must have been very like the brain of a bright child of to-day, he suspected his imitations affected the behaviour of his enemies and his quarries. Dances to influence game seem to have begun quite early in his history; they may have been among his first rituals. He shaped the form and move-ment of his fellow animals in gestures. His opposable thumb and finger made it easy for him to record these gestures and scratch and smear likenesses of beasts on rocks and wood: feats, it would seem, beyond the abilities of *Homo neanderthalensis*. He drew and painted beasts on rocks and in caves, and we discover them now with vast appreciation. He recorded his hunting for us to see, and even made pictures of his camp and dances.

It is a pretty question whether man picked up the dog as an associate, or whether the dog picked up man. The relationship may have begun like the relationship of the lion and jackal, when the latter merely fol-lows the former about to pick up the remains of its kills. Early dog may have hovered about early man, and the superior sociability of the dog may have begun the first rapprochement.

Nature is a great friend of coöperation; it is a gross libel upon her to say she is always "red in tooth and claw." On the contrary, she has something like a passion for making living things interdependent. She elaborates and confirms every disposition to associate. One of the com-monest utilizations of the hovering cadger is as a watcher and warner. The rhinoceros and crocodile, for example, have their attendant birds which are vermin pickers and scouts. And for the dog which hunts naturally with other dogs it would be easy to help round up deer, or cattle, or horses, in association with man. At any rate, the dog opens the list of domesticated animals. He was sleeping and barking about the human group while it was still a group of wandering, tool-making beasts.

And man with his dog, though he consumed the herds of reindeer, wild horse, wild ass, wild cattle and sheep that drifted in search of grazing grounds as the age of forests gave way to the age of open plains in Europe and Central Asia, did not pursue them with an inveterate hatred. He protected them as far as he could from the competition of other beasts, wolves and so forth, which wasted them; he sought to restrain their wandering beyond his reach and protection. The possible gradations between hunter and herdsman and between truly wild beasts and beasts that have come to tolerate the approach of men are insensible.

At the end of his great stride from the palæolithic wandering life to the neolithic territorial life, we find man has domesticated dogs, oxen, sheep, pigs, probably goats, the ass, and possibly also in Central Asia the horse. The distinction between domestication and farming is not clearly marked, and we cannot say when or where man attained the latter stage. Breeding in captivity is the characteristic of this phase of control. Oxen came to be used as draught animals, and with them man probably took over the major agricultural operations from woman. For the management of flocks and herds the dog was essential and was well qualified for this both by natural intelligence and by his hunting instinct.

Now, all these creatures brought with them various very convenient by-products—teeth, horns, bones, hides, and hoofs—for the use of man. We find the list of man's material and impedimenta growing longer. He could not change his dwelling place so frequently. Property limited his movements, tied him down to one spot, at any rate, for considerable periods of the year; and as his surroundings grew more familiar, as danger passed from an unknown to a known and calculable element in his environment, as the necessity for constant alertness diminished, came the opportunity for reflection and experiment.

And now commences another development. Man was struck by strange imaginations about these beasts who were becoming his intimates. He began Experimental Zoölogy; he tried to breed the unlike together and to interfere in normal breeding. Mythology is full of fantastic hybrids, from the cockatrice to the minotaur. These legends are the fossils of experimental dispositions that once filled his mind. They show what he was after. At some stage man added the sturdier mule to the tale of his servants and helpers. And also he discovered the changes produced in the temper and texture of animals by castration. There was a curious phase of mutilation in human development which still appears transitorily in boyhood and girlhood. Man chopped himself about, he circumcized, he lopped off limbs, he tattooed, he trepanned, he knocked his teeth out. Evolution had given him the flint knife, and he used it—as a boy will still use a knife—on himself and others.

Moreover, he made certain experiments that must have seemed at first very queer things to do. He tried the milk of these domesticated beasts. We are so accustomed to rely on milk and milk products that it is hard for us to imagine a time when a resort to such nourishment must have seemed unnatural and even monstrous, yet there may have been such a time. There must have been mental phases in these early experiments like the fantastic dreams and imaginings of a little child. Before Freud few people dared to confess what things had passed through their heads during their years of innocence. The ideal child was supposed to have a mind of the genteelest whiteness; it was held that we were born in a state of perfect self-suppression instead of having to learn it for long, painful years. . . . All these opening phases of human life still remain to be worked out. The earliest of the agricultural communities we can trace, had milk, butter and cheese, as well as meat.

§ 5. The Beginnings of Settlement and Sustained Work

And while man was thus becoming an experimental zoölogist, he was at the same time acquiring a very considerable practical knowledge of plants. As a wandering hunter he must already have had an extensive acquaintance with edible fruits and herbs, nuts, roots and the like, and it is hardly to be imagined that his concern for the movements of the beasts he tracked and the herds he followed left him regardless of woodland and grass.

But he probably knew of grass and grain without much regard to their phases and processes. One may doubt if in his primordial hunting stage he recognized the relation of seed to tree or of season to fruit and flower. We cannot say with any precision yet at what stage in his development man realized that there was an annual cycle, a year.

We contemporary human beings are taught so much from our earliest years, we are told that this is so and that is so with such reiterated conviction, that a multitude of ideas seem to us to be in the very nature of things, whereas it is merely that at a very early stage they have been built into the fabric of our minds. Children of three or four will say

quite confidently that the world is round and that the year goes from
summer to winter and from winter to summer; and it is hard to purge
these ideas from one's consciousness and imagine an adult mind without these particular assumptions. But the world of the early men was
flat and went on forever, and the weather changed, grew hotter and
colder, snowy or rainy, sere or green, and it was only the very oldest
and most observant who could have had a chance of noting any established rhythm in these phases. When the year had been discovered, it
had still to be measured and mapped out. An accurate calendar is a
thing of the last two thousand years. Before then man was still struggling to catch the sun and stars and failing to get them. They slipped
away through his reckoning of years and centuries, and put him wrong
with his sowing.

Just as it is hard to conceive a mind to which extracting and drinking
the milk of cows must have seemed a marvel, so also it is hard to conceive a mind with no idea of sowing a seed. But such must have been
the intellectual state of the early wandering *Homo sapiens*. He no more
looked forward from seedtime to harvest than a cat or a gorilla. It helps
us to realize a little that age of primitive ignorance when we learn that
several savage peoples remained ignorant of the connection between
sexual love and offspring right up to the nineteenth century A. D.

The men of twenty thousand years ago (or thereabouts), who have
left us the rock paintings, the carvings and implements of the late
Palæolithic Age, had already got to a much higher level of intelligence
than that. They probably had an annual migration following the reindeer and horses they ate, and a clear idea of the annual round. It is possible they had even found out the directional value of the stars, and in
what seems like the representation of a bridle on one palæolithic carving of a horse head, there is reason to suppose that they employed the
horse for draught purposes in their migrations. But to pass from that
life to the life of the settled agriculturist must have involved certain
steps of which we have at present only very perplexing and incomplete
intimations. They were difficult steps to make, and there is plain evidence that they were made in a roundabout way and with much confusion of thought.

To the modern mind, ploughing, manuring, sowing, weeding,
harrowing, reaping, seem all such plain, common-sense proceedings that
it is difficult to realize that none of them was in the least an obvious
thing to do to our remote ancestors. They had to feel their way, generation by generation and age by age, to clear ideas about these proceed-

ings. They did all sorts of things, and the harvest resulted; they had no method of determining what was essential or what was inessential among the things they did.

One of their misconceptions lies at the root of a vast complex of religious and ceremonial practices which still survive. Somehow the first crops were associated in the human mind with the killing of a human being. That is a very strange association from our current point of view, but it is an indisputable fact. For some reason that is now extraordinarily incomprehensible to us that killing seemed to our forefathers to be as necessary as the seed scattering.

Moreover, with no calendar in existence, and no proper measure of the year, it was extremely hard for primitive man to hit on quite the right time for this conjoint sowing of blood and grain. The stars, man had come to know, went through an annual change of position in the sky; the altitude of the sun at midday increased and diminished as the year passed. His clumsy and bloody sowing had to be mixed up therefore with a clumsy, toilsome, and superstitious astronomy. As he emerges to our vision from the archæological obscurity of his first essays on agriculture, we find his settled communities everywhere dominated by a temple and by a priesthood associated with the observation of the sun and stars and devoted to periodic human sacrifice. He did not dream it was possible to sow or reap without them. He did not dream it was possible to live without them.

The temple and the sacrificial priest were of primary importance therefore to the economic scheme of the first settled communities. They embodied a primitive science, however loaded it may have been with guesswork and error, and a primitive religion, full, perhaps, of needless terrors and cruelty, without which mankind might never have passed over from the earlier phase of lonely savagery and casual subsistence to its present condition of economic interdependence. The first religions were as practical in their purpose and as closely interwoven into the texture of life as a hoe or a cooking pot. They were as necessary and inseparable a part of early social life. There was no nonsense about religion being too "spiritual" for business use in that stage of human development.

Biologically this change from a wandering to an economic life was a great success. Very rapidly *Homo sapiens* became a numerous animal instead of a rare one, first perhaps in some region now beneath or round about the Mediterranean, and then spreading slowly and multitudinously over more and more of the available land surface of the globe.

He became more numerous than any other species of the primates had ever been. His habitat grew wider and wider. He varied his agriculture considerably to adapt it to a variety of favourable conditions.

With the beginnings of settlement, regular work came into the life of mankind. Work we may define here as exertion when there is no immediate bodily urgency. It is exertion for a remote end. It is undertaken when one is neither hungry nor thirsty, lustful nor frightened nor sportive, in order that later on one may not suffer want. Man, the wandering savage, was probably very much on a level with his fellow beasts; he led his life in obedience to continual urgencies and made his first inventions in a kind of play. His first work was implement-making and fire-feeding. He worked like a gipsy tinker. Hunger and fear and other bodily cravings kept him on the move.

The primitive human communities were certainly very small family groups. The things *Homo sapiens* ate were few and far between and hard to find; quite a wide area, therefore, was needed to sustain a single family. The same is the case with the great apes to-day. They cannot live thickly. A tribe of hundreds in the Early Stone Age would have meant starvation.

Primitive organization was probably not very rigid; there were no records to *fix* things; there could have been little pedantry or exactitude about relationship in truly primitive man. There are sound reasons for believing that the typical primitive social group of man, as of the present-day gorilla, consisted of an old male, a female or so and one or two young. The old man generally drove off the young males as they grew up and became obnoxious to him. But though that was the typical it was not the only sort of group. Young males might keep together for a time after they were driven off; the old man might be killed and his group coalesce with some other group. But the patriarchal family was the dominant type. The only division of labour was the natural difference of masculine and feminine function. The male did more of the fighting, and the female bore, fed and slapped the young. Most of the minor chores were probably put upon the women. They wanted them done more than the men wanted them done.

That was the scale and type of the first human communities. But with growing intelligence and the development of the huntsman-herdsman life, as the forests of a moister age gave place to grass plains, there was a great biological advantage in a larger community with numerous men in it who could hunt in agreement and fight if necessary to retain their hunting ground.

The human community grew social exactly as other animals have grown social, as the African lions seem to be growing social to-day, by an increasing toleration of the young by the old, especially on the part of the males, and by a retardation of full maturity. The basis of all human society is the taboo, restraint, the prohibition of certain impulses. A system of taboos grew up to bar the women of the tribe from the young men and mitigate the disruptive violence of sexual jealousy. There is a world-wide taboo among savages between a man and his sisters and his step-mothers and his half-sisters. There are at least traces of such a taboo in all human societies. A young man who wanted a woman of his own had to steal her from some other group (exogamy). All over the world linger the vestiges of exogamy and marriage by capture. The idea of incest as a sin is an almost universal tradition among human beings, and it finds no equivalent among apes or other animals. There is no instinctive bar to incest in any animal. This taboo of incest may have been the foundation of real human society. It made it possible for father and sons and sons-in-law to endure each other. It made it possible for the group to grow larger and safer.

The psychoanalysts trace the moral conflict in our minds back to its roots in these primordial prohibitions and suppressions, without which social life could not have existed. They do it very convincingly. Through the taboo system humanity underwent an immense training in self-restraint. Diffidence and a respect for taboos were woven into the normal human soul. The sexual side of the moral conflict developed.

Imperceptibly a gradation of duties arose. The old man's headship and prestige were enhanced. The men specialized as hunters and fighters, and the women kept camp. There was probably much individuality about these early communities; there is no reason to suppose they were all of one pattern. Anthropologists are exact-minded men; they forget at times that primitive men are not so. Usually the headman was the depository of wisdom, but often the rôle of medicine man, who drew pictures and did incantations, may have fallen to someone else. And the older women must have done a lot of talking and telling. There must have been endless conflicts and alliances of mind and brain. The prestige of some old men outlived them; they haunted the dreams of the tribe; their strength and their influence were invoked; medicine men saw them in visions, undertook to speak for them, and the first tribal gods were evolved.

From the gradual development of the mysteries of agriculture and the adoption of a mainly vegetarian dietary by such taboo-respecting tribes,

the first settled and numerous human communities arose. As these developed, security increased, and with it the need for work. But man
has no passion for work; he has to be broken in to work, and social
history is largely the record of the attempt to break men in. Or, to be
more exact, of men to break other men in. The dawn of economic history shows us humanity already busy upon the job of putting the work
on to someone else.

The social conflict is already in full progress at the very beginning of
a numerous society, and it goes on through all the rest of history. No
such temperamental adaptation as seems to have occurred in the case
of the ant and the worker bee has ever been achieved by man. That is
the point where he differs most widely from the economic insects. These
creatures have produced a real worker type, a multitude of individuals
who seem to have no other desire in life than to toil in certain definite
ways and live and die for the collective good. The insect worker works
by instinct. Humanity has never produced a real worker type. None of
us toils by instinct. Mankind can produce with ease classes prepared to
give orders, disdain work and enjoy privileges, but the workers remain
not a class but a residual mass, subordinated without enthusiasm, betraying no essential willingness for a subordinate rôle. That is why it is
so unjust to tell the sluggard to go to the ant for moral instruction. The
ant *likes* work for its own sake. It is morally incapable of inaction.

One thing that has stood in the way of such a separation of our
species as we find among ants and bees is the varying economic processes of the human community, which have called sometimes for one
type of toil and sometimes for another. And we shall show as this work
proceeds, that the resistance in the human soul to a life of mechanical
toil has lasted long enough and proved stout enough and is operating
now under such new conditions as to make it improbable that a human
"worker" type will ever be evolved at all. We are not travelling the same
road therefore as the economic insects. The resemblance of our society
to their societies is more apparent than real. Man is travelling a road
of his own that no form of life has ever trodden before, towards unprecedented destinies.

§ 6. *The Rest of the Historical Overture*

This dawn of human economic association has been treated with a
certain fulness here because of its great structural importance to the rest
of this work, but the further history of the expansion and complication

of mutual help and service must be dealt with more compactly. It must be not merely descriptive but psychological. The whole science of work and wealth indeed, that is to say all economics, is ultimately psychological. Human beings are associated through their brains, and, except in the very early stages of family life, in no other way. They are associated, not by instinctive mechanism and innate class differences as the social insects are, but by different idea systems in what are otherwise closely similar animals. The science of work and wealth is the history and analysis of these operative systems of ideas.

In his temples, laws, customs, man has left us, fossilized, as it were, the data to reconstruct these idea systems that have served to bind him to his fellow men. The history of human communities—political history, that is to say—is, as the *Outline of History* shows, fundamentally a history of developing means of communication and the possibility and realization of larger and larger communities. It is the story of a secular change of scale in the dealings of man with man. The economic history of mankind must be *pari passu* a history of the growth, changes, and replacements of the inducements, beliefs, symbols, and methods that have made social coöperation possible and determined the character of its development. The common worker in the early communities before the dawn of written history, like the common worker now, must have gone about his work because somehow he found himself *there* and his work was what it seemed he had to do. If he had no instinct for work, he had acquired a habit of work, he acquiesced in its necessity. And backing up that sense of necessity in his mind, and arresting any primitive impulse to revolt, there were tradition, religion, awe, there was a belief in ruling Powers, in gods or a god, justifying the scheme of things, a "synthetic personified sense of the Tribe" as the god of the Tribe, as lord, director, and protector. Behind the taskmaster loomed the temple and the possible anger of these gods. To rebel against work was to go out of life into nothingness.

This religious tradition took on the individual's developing ideas and emotions as he emerged from his infantile subjection to mother and father. His childhood was prolonged by it. He grew up out of sonship to his father only to become one of the "sons" of the tribal founder or the tribal god. He never emerged completely from the mental habits of sonship. He never became a free, self-centred adult beast like the primordial *Homo*.

This was not a trick played upon him. It was the way everything grew up about him; it was the way things had come about. It caricatures and modernizes those early social phases to suppose that priests, secular rulers, and leading people were not equally subject in their minds to their lord and god, or that they could release their minds to the extent of being cynical about the personal advantages given them by the general faith in a tribal symbol. They played their part in perfect good faith, not questioning the fairness of their advantages. They were the elder brethren among the sons, and they recognized obligations commensurate with their privileges. They felt that the god was on their side, but also that the god was standing observant over them.

But at some quite early stage the developing human community was invaded by another and harsher conception of relationship. Side by side with the sons of the god and their sisters and womenkind appeared another sort of human being, more definitely cast for the rôle of toil—the slave.

The domestication of animals and the domestication of strangers must have involved very similar mental processes. You took the pups of the wild dog and the children of your enemy and subdued them to your purposes. Mutually destructive tribal warfare passed by a series of variations into tribute-levying and actual conquest and class enslavement. The *Outline of History* tells of the going and coming of conquering rulers over the early civilizations. That had begun when the curtain of history proper rises. It was already established. The nomadic tradition, becoming militant, would impose itself upon the agricultural tradition, and the armed monarch would rule beside the priest. The change in the social structure was not great. Successful wars would bring captives and gang labour in their train. A harsher type of toil would spread and prevail in the larger communities, a type of toil more consciously under human compulsion and mentally less acquiescent.

But we can deal only in the broadest outline with the development and interplay of ideas in what we now call the ancient civilizations. The relation of the everyday working life to the temple and the symbols of authority can be traced in Sumeria and early Egypt and in those strange survivals of the tradition of a remote past, the Maya, Aztec and Peruvian societies. It was one social pattern—with variations. The cultivator was the base and main substance of the community. Proprietorship, like sovereignty, still undefined but apprehended, vested essentially in the god or god-king or chief of the community, and balanced against or overruled the customary property of the worker in the thing he worked upon, land, ship, utensil or what not. There was community ownership vested in god or chief and there was user ownership, the ownership of implements. A third type of ownership manifests itself in relation to personal adornments and precious objects. But man in the early societies was not very clear in these matters; he was not very clear about anything; he knew nothing of exact definitions and logical thought; he probably did not distinguish types of ownership or detect the various roots of the "thine and mine" idea. For thousands of years ideas of possession, deference, authority and subordination grew definite or fluctuated and were modified in relation to this or that new occasion.

Through a long procession of favourable centuries inter-related systems of tradition established themselves in the minds of men, and the social man whom we can still understand without any great difficulty was gradually and surely established in the Old World, in Egypt, in Mesopotamia and in Central Asia. Dynasties came and went, and conquests stimulated or deflected the process of civilization. Language extended its range and became more precise. The word won its way slowly against the visual image as the chief implement in human thinking and feeling. Pictorial representation opened the way to writing and an increasing definition and fixation of words. Slowly, through scores of centuries, the symbols and metaphors which still frame our thoughts were hardened and set by time. The mental and emotional dispositions of *Homo sapiens* in the great warm river valleys, became more and more akin to our present "humanity."

Age by age, man sharpened and fined his words and idioms, as age by age before he had sharpened and fined his flints. As thought grew fine and exact, the more primordial thinking of the earlier mythologies took on a monstrous and incredible quality. The ancient gods and legends began indeed to puzzle their inheritors. Men, feeling their way to the methods of reason, to generalization and abstraction, looked for more "reasonable" explanations. Twenty-five centuries ago in Greece the modern mind was already pecking its way out from the shell and membranes of tradition and mythology in which it had been incubated —profoundly unconscious of its origins. A fresh phase was beginning in human life. The age of exact reasoning was dawning.

And about twenty-five centuries ago that extension of economic contacts and the development of trade and trading classes and trading cities which had been going on with a comparative gradualness from the days of the first localized civilizations, quickened very considerably. Money and the money idea became increasingly operative. It brought profound and subtle changes into economic life. Money relaxed and released property and made credit processes of a quite unprecedented rapidity possible. Men could now undertake impossible payments and pile up debts as they had never done before. Usury grew. Some day the science of work and wealth, the new realistic political economy, will gather all that is available about the methods of early trade before currency and accounting and find what there is to be found about the trading, for example, of Cnossus and Tyre and Sidon. It seems to have been plain barter. Then the appearance of new, more abstract methods will need to be traced. The onset of money and reckoning was a very cardinal event in man's development. The money community which came into existence in the first millennium before Christ, was an altogether more mobile form of association than the barter and service civilizations that had preceded it.

In the *Outline of History* the Roman republican and imperial system is treated as the first instance of a "money" community. Its economic operations were far more extensive and fluent than those of any preceding great community, and it arose out of a sea conflict between two commercial republics, and not upon the basis of a great alluvial area inhabited by cultivating peasants and conquered by nomads, as the "ancient" despotisms had done. It carried the Western world forward into larger and less stable social methods. China, India were far less affected by money and continued to revolve in the traditional alternatives of conquest and dynastic change for another thousand years.

Religion in the Roman Empire was less integral to its social and economic life—more aloof and less intimate. Human society had no longer the same need of its binding power. Money was providing a new nexus. Religion, as people say nowadays, became "spiritualized."

The extending Roman system made a greater use of the slave gang than any previous system and staggered so soon as its wars were no longer a source of captive toilers. The expansion of the city of Rome and its citizenship was by the scale of world history a rapid and unstable expansion. It never really worked out the conflict of methods between serf, slave, and wage labour. Its wealth was hectic, and it consumed its population. Its crash was a stupendous event for mankind. Disorganization came from within, and the barbarians tumbled into the ruins—with an air of conquest. The common people, sunken from the normal free farmer level, had no spirit to resist the Hun, the Northman, or the Arab. For them it was only a change of masters.

Our modern world arose out of the wreckage of that crash, and so it is that the history of Rome must play a larger part in this overture than any Eastern history. The professors of the science of work and wealth, who will presently be teaching our youth, will some day examine the expansion and collapse of Rome as essentially an economic process. Here we have to go with less than scientific assurance. The thesis of the *Outline of History* is that the facilities for insolvency provided by ill regulated money, the inherent impermanence of a slave system, the failure to develop a representative governing system as the Empire grew—or even to realize that such a thing was needed—the failure to produce sympathetic coöperating "educated" classes in sufficient abundance, difficulties in communication, the nomadic wedge in the Danube plain, and possibly climatic changes and epidemic diseases, all contributed to that series of disruptions and reunions and disruptions which makes the history of Europe and western Asia, the history of the Empire in the West and East, throughout the Middle Ages. The monetary system was too loose and elastic, and the administrative system not responsive, elastic and sympathetic enough for the Empire to work. Gibbon's analysis of the Decline and Fall is all too deeply coloured by his anti-Christian bias, for Christianity, that amazing mélange of ancient rituals with new spiritual ferment, was a symptom rather than a cause in the vast, unsound expansion and collapse of the first great money-credit system. The *Outline of History* tells for how brief a period the Roman Imperial System really worked, and to the *Outline* the reader will have to go for the divergent fates of the Latin and Greek Empires, for an account of the barbaric driftage of the Dark Ages, and the slow resumption of order as the feudal system crystallized out of the confusion.

The Social and Economic History of the Roman Empire, by M. Rostovtzeff, 1926, is a work of great learning and acute analysis. It is a very important first step in the analysis of the Roman downfall. His conclusions (p. 486) are that: "None of the existing theories fully explains the problem of the decay of ancient civilization, if we can apply the word 'decay' to the complex phenomenon which I have endeavoured to describe. Each of them, however, has contributed much to the clearing of the ground and has helped us to perceive that the main phenomenon which underlies the process of decline is the gradual absorption of the educated classes by the masses and that consequent simplification of all the functions of political, social, economic and intellectual life which we call the barbarization of the ancient world. The evolution of the ancient world has a lesson and a warning for us. Our civilization will not last unless it be a civilization not of one class but of the masses. The Oriental civilizations were more stable and lasting than the Greco-Roman because being based chiefly on religion they were nearer to the masses." To which we may add that these civilizations were also simpler in structure and less permeated by those social solvents, money and credit operations.

With the Church and the Holy Roman Empire, with the development of states and kingdoms and the rise and fall of powers and empires in Europe and Asia we need not concern ourselves now. For that too the reader must go to the *Outline*. Our concern is rather with the fate of the productive and business ideas and methods of the Roman and Byzantine world, throughout the long scrimmage of the Decline and Fall. What was holding out in Constantinople, in Venice, in such perennial places as Marseilles, and in Egypt and Persia, in the way of buying and selling and hoarding and credit, while Goth, Hun, Northman and Moslim swept to and fro? Here we can put the question, but we can offer no complete answer. No one can tell us yet, even in the roundest and most speculative figures, how the volume of trade in the Mediterranean varied between 300 B. C. and A. D. 800. We do not even know how populations expanded and contracted during those times; and indeed we knew nothing exact about populations until the dawn of the present era.

And again, what the routine of daily life was like, how people kept house in castle or shrunken town during the worst of these centuries, is only vaguely known. The peasant dug and harvested and hid—as ever—as he is doing now in China. And he was made to work and yield to his brigand master. But where did the leaders, the brigand nobles and brigand princes get their clothes and ornaments made? Who did the dressmaking for the ladies of the Merovingian court, and how was it paid for? Had it all shrunken back to the worker who was kept in the household—who worked for keep, protection and small rewards? A little band of workmen gathered about every castle and manor and increased as order and prosperity returned. Manifestly some sewing and painting and carving and hammering and building were going on right through those ages of confusion.

Here we do but summarize the facts of that survival. And then came the slow economic recovery that becomes traceable after the eleventh century, the steady recovery of overland trading in mediæval times, the rise of mercantile shipping and overseas trade, the outburst of exploration, and the reappearance of wealth. A multitude of towns emerged to prosperity and importance; the Rhineland, Provence, and northern Italy led in the revival of an agreeable productive life in the West. The artizans multiplied, and the peasant went to market more abundantly. Would that we could refer here to some thorough and penetrating comparison of the developing monetary and banking systems of the rapidly healing world with those of the past! But such a comparison has still to be made. Two new devices in human affairs presently began to play an increasing part in the world's restoration; representative government and joint stock enterprise, at first unlimited and then with limited liability; and here again, to take us beyond mere general remarks, there is a call for some synthesizing mind.

The economic spectacle changes in its character more and more as our historical review approaches our own time. History was not repeating itself; history never repeats itself; but men have a curious disposition towards historical repetition. Statesmen and churchmen, as the *Outline* tells, wasted the energies of the Western world in a hundred fantastic attempts to recall the vanished Roman Empire. As persistently that Empire refused to return. Only after 1918 did the world escape finally from that retrospective obsession. Amidst the political and traditional confusion of a thousand years new forces and new orientations grew continually more evident. A greater world, indifferent to tradition, was coming into being. Before the close of the eighteenth century, man had already come to a knowledge of the whole round globe on which he lives, and was rapidly developing his means of access to every part of it. Unprecedented "empires" extended into regions Cæsar never knew. Organized science appeared and invention quickened. It was prosperity coming back to mankind, but with a new face and new methods. A new world-wide productive, trading, financial and monetary system was growing up.

Trade expanded continually from the sixteenth century onward, population increased, and the industrial revolution arrived. There was a vigorous search for productive energy. And at first for "hands." The idea of tapping natural sources of mechanical power was scarcely stirring as yet. Problems of business and social organization exercised imaginative minds. One could quote Fielding benevolently finding work for poor children and laying the foundations of factory sweating, and Defoe with great enthusiasm depicting a purgatorial land of hope for Moll Flanders in the West Indies. Many quite good men, in their zeal to get people working, were advocating every variety of compulsory toil. Las Casas, the champion of the oppressed American Indian, introduced the Negro to America and the questionable benefits of Christian teaching.

But slavery was hard to revive, because no sweeping conquests were in progress, and so wages labour became widespread and at length almost universal. There had been a long struggle in the fifteenth century after the pestilences had depleted the labour supply, and particularly the urban labour supply, to retain the serf at his task and hinder his wandering off in search for wages, but wages servitude had won. Gang slavery reappeared indeed in the plantations of America—to fight a losing battle. There were a conscience and a criticism abroad that the Roman world had never known; and forces beyond its utmost imagination, new slaves without souls or resentments, were coming to take over the toil of the subjugated. The first of these new slaves which came to the rescue of the old was Steam. With the first hum and clanking of power machinery, with the bitter servitude of the machine minders to the inventions that will at last abolish such poor creatures altogether, our historical overture to the contemporary human panorama must culminate and end.

CHAPTER THE SECOND

How Man Has Learnt to Think Systematically and Gain a Mastery over Force and Matter

§ 1. *Directed Thinking*

BUT before we go on to the actual panorama of present things, we must, if the whole spectacle is to be made understandable, go a little more fully into one particular aspect of history, the history of human thought. Human thinking has passed through several stages in its evolution, and most of us repeat those stages in our individual lives. The way we do business with each other and set about the affair of life is conditioned altogether by the way in which we think. Most of us do not think enough about thinking.

We have explained how round about five and twenty centuries ago the appearance and wide use of money and monetary credit in the world produced a new epoch in human affairs. It was an epoch of enlargement and extension. Mainly through the action of this new flux, money, the huge, unstable Roman system and the associated Byzantine system were able to develop—and collapse. But much more than the expansion of a novel political and economic system occurred at that time. These political expansions and instabilities were reflected in men's thoughts about life and divinity. These were intellectual consequences of far greater and more permanent importance than the material changes. In the *Outline of History* the appearance of syncretic and universal religions, for example, is traced to the expansion of these empires; they destroyed the prestige of the local and national gods. The idea of widespread brotherhoods and world unity dawned.

And simultaneously came a slower and ultimately still more important change in human affairs, though for a time it did not have anything like the same conspicuousness amidst the general appearance of life. This was an intellectual movement, a change in the way in which man did his thinking and came to his conclusions. He began to be more careful of the mental processes through which he took hold upon things. He began to think about thinking, to take care about his thinking and to learn to think.

That was destined to have gigantic effects later on. We are indeed living amidst its gigantic effects, but at the time, for twenty centuries indeed, this intellectual revolution and reconstruction was an affair of the study and classroom, and the mass of mankind knew nothing about it. Even those who were concerned in it may not have realized its full importance.

Let us be perfectly clear about this "learning to think." Children, like primitive man, have still to learn to think; they do a large part of their thinking by imagination. That is, so to speak, the natural way with the untrained mind. Their thinking is a flow of images with which impulses to act are connected. Images and scenes are suggested and give rise by various forms of association to others. The whole flow is pervaded by a sense of wilful activities. It is spontaneous and uncontrolled. Many people in adult life are able to recall a time in their lives when they did all their thinking in that fashion. Many adults never think in any better way.

In the mental flow of child or savage, moreover, things are not distinguished very clearly from persons; they are thought of as quasi-persons. That is another great difference between the untrained and the trained mind. All things are liked or disliked; they can be friendly or inimical. The world of primitive thought is a drama in which the thinker conceives a rôle for himself. The flow of fantasy proceeds and gives an agreeable or disagreeable quality to this or that imagined line of action, which is followed or rejected accordingly.

The thought of the young child, the thought of the primitive mind, is a type of mental activity differing from dreaming only in its closer touch with reality, in its more frequent checking through the waking senses. Otherwise it is a quite undisciplined and undirected flow. There is hardly any use in it of generalizations and abstract ideas. There is no critical element asking, "But is this sound? Is this true?" Everything presented in the flow that is not itself physically real is apprehended in a symbolical and often a personified form. The idea of the winds, of the seasons, of the tribal organization, of the obligation to do right, for instance, appears under the guise of personalities or personal relationships. Everything is supposed to *do* something. Everything that happens is supposed to be *done*. The wind blows. It seems natural to ask: Who blew it? The river flows. Who poured it out? The sun rises. Someone has driven it up the sky. So we get Boreas or Auster, Father Tiber, Apollo, the charioteer of the sun. Every tree must have a spirit, just as man has a spirit, and how can there be thunder without a Thunderer? Father and Mother, at this mental stage, furnish patterns for the imagining of gods. Jove-pater stalks across the universe terrible and incalculable—with an immense beard and a voice of thunder. We cower to the bosom of the Earth Mother, mother of all the gods. She is the nourishing Mother, the Cow-goddess Athor, Mother Nature. The unsophisticated savage remains a child throughout life. To the end of life the primitive mind thinks in this way. Throughout the opening cycles of human history there was no other method of thought. All mankind thought then as our children think now.

This corresponds to what Comte called the mythological phase of human development. It has recorded itself in a vast mass of imagery in language and of images and pictures in the world. The gods and monsters who sprawl across an Indian or Maya sculpture frieze are thoughts embodied. Osiris, Horus, Anubis, and Isis express ideas of command and obligation and of good and evil for which man could devise no simpler, less encumbered expression. The eyes that a savage paints on the prow of his canoe betray this same entanglement of his mind with personality.

Only very gradually, as minds ripened and as mankind ripened, does an exacter discrimination and disentanglement of essentials appear, and logical thinking begin. The mythological passes insensibly into the metaphorical. With an increasing vocabulary, abstraction becomes possible to the growing mind. We *disentangle*. Goodness and benevolent power in the world can be thought of without evoking the figure of an armed and crowned chieftain bearing all the symbols of majesty; a boat can be considered as a floating contrivance which does not need an eye. The mind begins to arrest and examine its flow of association; to classify things in this way and then in that; and to pick out what is necessary from what is accidental and incidental.

On that follows "logical" thinking. Man, as he "grows up," begins to reason things out instead of dreaming them out. He begins to control his predispositions and observe a logical coherence. He restrains and criticizes his impulsive judgments and responses. He struggles to control and direct their sequences. He begins to squeeze the inessential associations out of his metaphors and symbols. The Athenian philosophical literature, culminating in Plato and Aristotle, records man's definitive adoption of what psychologists call *directed thought* as distinguished from *undisciplined thought*. The paraphernalia of personification which was once necessary had become an inconvenience and a burden. Gods, demi-gods, demons and fates faded into figures of speech and receded from the arena of judgment, while concepts of a more abstract order, forces and matter, atoms and reactions, were adopted to replace them. Much that was inessential still lurked in the new terms and abstractions, but the effort to get rid of that inessential element continued.

So, in that phase of human development which opened about six centuries B. C., man definitely ceased to take the results of his mental processes for granted. A scrutiny of those processes began. He had found them clumsy and inexact and he had set himself to sharpen them as once his ancestors had set themselves to sharpen flints. He had set himself to chip off the unnecessary.

And also he had ceased to take the world of appearance about him for granted. He had begun to scrutinize and question his world.

In the *Outline of History* Plato is taken as the typical exponent of a novel and inspiring idea, that man is able, if he will, to change his way of living. Aristotle stands beside him in that account, as the first organizer of the collection and classification of knowledge. They questioned custom, and they questioned appearance. Each of these men was in reality greater and less than this, but it is convenient here to use their names and their outstanding qualities as landmarks. We pick them out to simplify our story. In these two men we find the human mind turning upon its primitive methods and seeking a clearer and more serviceable form of interpretation, that will give, they realize, a hitherto unimagined mastery over fact and one's practical reaction to fact. Man, as they embody him, man in the Athenian phase, wrestles with his impressions, classifies them, seeks to clear and order them by exactly defined words, because he is realizing that ignorance is danger, and knowledge, power. He is changing from responsive imaginations to logical thinking, directed towards the attainment of practical working truth.

The psychological chapters of the *Science of Life* deal rather more fully than is possible here with his substitution of orderly and directed thinking for the symbolism and imaginative play that was once the only human method, and which is still perhaps the most ordinary way of thinking. And in the *Science of Life* how this arose out of the still more primitive blind try and thrust of the animal life is explained very simply and clearly. Animal behaviour, it is shown, has three main stages of complexity. ("Main stages," we write; not distinct and separate stages.)

First, instinctive and conditioned responses; then, imaginative thought before action; then, logical thought before action. It is unnecessary to repeat that fuller exposition here.

This change-over from a mental life that was merely experience-checked imagining to an analytical mental life aiming at new and better knowledge and leading on to planned and directed effort, is still in progress. It is the greatest change in the methods and nature of conscious life that has ever occurred. It is still only partly achieved. Over a large range of his interests man has still to acquire the habit of thinking with self-control and precision.

§ 2. *The Criticism of the Instrument of Thought from the Beginnings of Directed Thinking Onward. Nominalism and Realism. Experiment. The Renascence of Science*

The philosophers of the Athenian and Hellenic communities of the sixth, fifth, fourth and third centuries B. C. inaugurated the logic-restrained and question-guided thinking of the modern world. But, as we have said, it was a beginning only. It was not the whole stride that had to be made, and we must not exaggerate even while we recognize its essential significance. Man did not, at that time, fall suddenly into a perfected way of thinking. He sought precision. By no means did he attain it. Day cannot come without a dawn, but the dawn is not the day.

That age of intellectual vigour in Greece marks the breakaway from mythological imaginative interpretations, and it marks also the first repudiation of tradition. The Utopianism of Plato is the first announcement of man's ability to depart from tradition in his acts and institutions. The Science of Aristotle displays a realization of the need for, and the possibility of, attaining a growing orderly body of tested knowledge and directive ideas, for the use of our race. It was to be new and increasing knowledge. That widening departure from tradition is the fundamental subject matter of this book. We are only carrying out to-day the intellectual release that Athens began.

Let us state clearly the full importance of that release. The *Science of Life* deals fully with the appearance of *tradition* in human evolution, shows how it was at first a progressive innovation and how greatly it accelerated social development, how it dispensed with the slow attainment of hereditable characters through mutation and selection, and also how it is now giving place to a still swifter process of social adaptation, due to the systematic interrogation of fact, organized research, and *planned development* that was latent in the new way of thinking. This transition from tradition to deliberate planning which is now in progress, is at least as great an event in evolution as the transition from unassisted heredity to heredity-plus-tradition which carried man above the level of the brute. The man who orders his knowledge and thinks things out is as far above the natural man of impulse and traditional usage as the latter is above an ape which has not even tradition but only instinct. They represent three successive stages of vital adjustment.

The Hellenic world conceived and shaped the instrument for modern thought and prepared the human mind for that widening breach from tradition, that forward-looking attitude, to which it is now committed. But, outside certain fields where the need for observation and experiment was limited, Greek scientific achievements were, by our modern standards, small. Greece made only the first step towards effective knowledge. There were many more further steps to be made before even such mental efficiency as we can boast to-day was attained. The instrument of modern thought was invented and shaped in the Hellenic age, but it had still to be sharpened and relieved of many clumsy associations. A long succession of active brains had still to work upon that task—a task that is still far from completion.

Moreover, that bright beginning in the eastern Mediterranean was hampered, checked and arrested by unfavourable political and social conditions. The *Outline of History* tells how the small and scattered band of original thinkers, which constituted the whole intellectual life of the Hellenic world, was slowly swamped and stifled by the conservative traditions of Egypt and overwhelmed by the vast expansion, disturbances and collapse that constituted the history of Roman Imperialism. That first intelligentsia, the Hellenic intelligentsia, never arrived at any sufficient facilities for conducting experiments or exchanging and discussing observations and results. Indeed, it had a very insufficient sense of the need for multitudinous experiments. It was overconfident of this new process of logical thinking it had developed, and unsuspicious that the new method had its own peculiar dangers and pitfalls.

What were the imperfections of the new method of directed thinking? What was still unsatisfactory about logical reasoning as the classical world understood it?

That there was an unsatisfactoriness appears plainly in certain of the dialogues of Plato, but in a manner and with an application that does not fit in very conveniently to contemporary needs. The essence of the unsatisfactoriness that appeared was this: that there was a question how far words were *accurate*. Were words as true as material facts, or truer, or less true? If they were truer, then a logical conclusion was truer than an experience, and that, on the whole, was the classical assumption.

I write "on the whole" because this assumption was then already being questioned. It may be difficult for many minds to realize that any people have ever been disposed to think that words were truer than experienced things. But the fact is that not only have men in the past continually tended to treat words as more real than material facts, but that now, at the present time, men, you and I included, are tending to do exactly the same thing. We suspect and resist that tendency now, but many people have so far given way to it as to believe that in words they had a means of penetrating beneath experience and appearances down to profounder truths. The tangle between the One and the Many, between the Ideal expressed by the word and the Individuals assembled under the word, arises out of this disposition. It was only through the toilsome discussion and bickering of many generations of men in the later Middle Ages that the processes of this directed thought, which was and is still replacing the more primitive uncriticized flow of associa-tions, were cured, to some extent, of its early disposition towards an independent arrogance, a false profundity and overconfidence, and re-called to a closer relationship to the verities of life. As briefly as possible we will put the bare elements of that great debate before the reader. He may then be willing to admit that those "Schoolmen" who wrangled through the centuries were doing a very indispensable work, too little appreciated by this contemporary world of ours—which indeed could never have existed without their wrangling.

Everybody has heard of this wrangling, of the great mediæval con-troversy between Nominalism and Realism, but the ordinary educated man, because of his insufficient and misleading education about such matters, is still all too ready to suppose that it was some extraordinary, remote, dry-as-dust conflict of pedants, that can have no possible interest for him. He thinks it was a dispute about some dead issue which has no possible bearing upon his life. He has not been told the truth of the business. That conflict has never really ceased because it has not yet been fought to a definite conclusion; it is still going on all about us under an endless diversity of masks and forms, and there is not a thing in our social, political and economic life that would not have been profoundly different if these controversies had never arisen.

The essence of this vast dispute between Nominalism and Realism which was already beginning in the Greek discussion between the One and the Many, and which is still far from a final conclusion, may be stated in a few paragraphs. Indeed, one may get very near the heart of the matter in a sentence. We have already said that there are three ways of thinking about words; one may think they are truer or less true than fact, or that they are *accurate* and fit fact exactly. For the Realist the word was truer than the experience; for the Nominalist the experience was truer than the word.

The human mind is a very imperfect instrument, just as the human eye is a very imperfect instrument. And just as the eye is prone to "optical illusions," so the human mind has its innate disposition to certain intellectual illusions. Chief among these is this disposition to trust to words, to names; the disposition, for example, to regard any unreal conception to which a name has been given, or any group of things to which a name can be given, as being thereby made actual and different from all other things. The mind trusts too much to the symbol or word it has adopted. The *name,* the *word,* which is man's implement, can easily become his master. He is disposed to believe that things that are called by the same name are necessarily all alike and altogether alike. He falls into that sort of acceptance very readily. He is always slipping into the error of confusing similarity with identity, and supposing that things that have one common quality or a few common qualities have all their qualities alike.

So he is apt to believe that all atoms or all herrings or all sheep or all Englishmen or all sovereign states, are exactly and in every detail alike because they are spoken of by the same word. By that word they are made one. He takes refuge from the infinite variety of existence in the *word,* which he can then reason and dogmatize about. He will say "all sheep" do this or "all Englishmen" do that—meaning that mostly they do. His untutored disposition is to treat the name of a group of things as though it expressed something fundamental and essential, and to ignore the endless variations that shelter under every common noun. This assumption that a name has something real and quintessential in itself, that there is an ideal and perfect sheep, for example, over and above all individual sheep, is the essence of philosophical Realism. The denial that a name is anything more than a label put upon an assembly of more or less similar but never identically similar things in the essence of Nominalism.

There is, we must note here, an unfortunate conflict between the common use of the word "realist" and its proper original meaning. The contemporary reader has to be warned of that difference in usage if he is not to misconceive all this section. In the great controversies of the Middle Ages, the Realists were those who followed this more natural but deceptive human tendency to treat names as expressing something more real than actual existences; while those who held that names were not in themselves real, that they were *only* names, labels just stuck upon things for our mental convenience and susceptible of infinite shifting and alteration, were called Nominalists. The Realist believed only in the reality of words and the general ideas they embodied; the Nominalist believed only in the reality of things and individual instances. The Realist believed that all individuals are imperfect specimens of the perfect "type"; the Nominalist ignored the perfect type. The mediæval Realist was what we should nowadays call an idealist, a Platonic idealist; the Nominalist was the facty man.

This is evidently almost the exact opposite of our modern use of "realist" and "realism," and in order to keep this distinction before the reader's mind, we spell "Realism" here, when it means the philosophical teaching and not insistence upon "actuality," with a capital R. That vast necessary controversy that went on in the Middle Ages was essentially a struggle of the human mind to escape from the innate vice of Realism, from the phantoms, the delusions created in the mind by primitive uncorrected Realist thought, and to look directly and discriminatingly at things themselves.

"Very nice," says the modern Nominalist, after the most clenching deductions, "and now let us try if it is so."

Both sides in that huge wrangle went far and stated excessive cases. Roscellin, an extreme Nominalist of the eleventh century, for example, held that a name, a word, was no more than a *flatus vocis,* vocal wind. But from the time of William of Ockham onward (fourteenth century), and indeed from the time of Abélard (twelfth century) the recognition grew that names and classifications might carry more or less weight and convey more or less truth. Words had to be scrutinized. There might be false as well as true conceptions in the mind. Some words were truer than others, they implied a higher degree of similarity than others, but none were as true as fact. When every name, every word, was marked with a note of interrogation, the way of escape from Realism lay open.

To escape from Realism is to escape from hard classifications, from the harsh judgments, assurance, uncompromising attitudes and dogmas that arise from hard classifications, and to move towards qualified statements, the examination of individual qualified statements, the examination of individual instances, enquiry, experiment and careful verification.

Here we will not attempt to follow the fluctuations of that immense dispute. The practical defeat of Realism over large areas of human interest was obviously a necessary preliminary to the release of experimental science. You could not get men to look at reality until verbal Realism was abandoned. It was so much easier to deduce your beliefs from first principles than to go out to make observations, and according to Realist ideas it was a sounder process. The protest of Roger Bacon was the outcry of a Nominalist in a Realist age. The Realist still ruled completely in the universities and over the teachers for a century after his death.

It was Roger Bacon who was first to ascribe to experiment its proper importance in the pursuit and discipline of knowledge. It was he who first insisted clearly that logical processes must be constantly checked by facts. On that account we take him as we took Plato and Aristotle—as a landmark in human development. He serves to mark a further step in the escape of the human mind and will from their original limitations. It was not so much what he did as what he said that gives him importance. His own actual experimental achievements amounted to barely anything at all. But he was almost the first human being to stress the supreme importance of verificatory experiment in the search for knowledge. He stands out as, in effect, insisting that no words could be trusted without the test of experiment.

His writings led straight to the scientific method of extending and using knowledge. One hears a great deal about the "scientific method," and it is often spoken of as though it were a distinctive method of thinking. But it is not a distinctive method of thinking, but only a distinctive method of using the logical method of thought already in existence, but of using it in a new spirit, a spirit of distrust. Your logic might prove that a thing should be so; your experiment then had to prove that it was so. "Observe, try, record, speculate logically, try out your speculation, confirm or correct, *communicate to other investigators, hear their communications, compare, discuss logically,* establish and so onward"; this, for all practical purposes, is the method of science. Apply as occasion arises. Eschew all *a priori* methods, for you do not know enough about your brain to trust it to work without this constant experimental checking. Check it by other brains, but above all check it by facts. Distrust every term, every name, you use. Logic is very serviceable as an aid to judgment but not as a final judge. All the terms you use *fit loosely on fact*. That is the key persuasion behind the experimental method. Keep trying back to fact. Such was the working scientific method of the nineteenth century, that age of material progress, and it is still the working scientific method at the present time. It is a repudiation of all philosophy that is not perpetually verifying its propositions.

Upon that working philosophy, upon that insistence that every assertion must be checked by fact and by the scrutiny and corroboration of other eyes and ears and minds, all the material triumphs of the scientific worker during the last century have been made. He sets himself to master the things at hand as thoroughly as possible. That is his essential and personal job. If there are limitless implications in these immediate things, he believes that they will unfold themselves and become plainer as his work proceeds. But he will not anticipate such progressive revelations. He will not trust his mind except when it remains in the closest touch with fact and with the concepts of his fellows. He will not tolerate the philosophies that merely project the peculiarities and obsessions of the human mind upon the universe, and declare that this is Truth. The rôle of philosophy from the point of view of the scientific man is not the attainment of wisdom but the perpetual accompaniment and criticism of man's thinking—to avoid follies and remove obstacles.

The detachment of the human mind from its Realistic predispositions remains incomplete. Mankind still believed in the fixity of animal and vegetable species—which were supposed to vary about a perfect type—until less than a century ago, and in the identical similarity of atoms until a quarter of a century ago; and in the world of international politics the Realist way of thinking holds almost undisputed sway at the present time. That intellectual error lies at the root of the greatest dangers that threaten our race. Men's hearts may be in the right place, but their poor heads are still befogged by the magic of names. Plainly a man who takes the Nominalist way and regards such a word as "France" as merely a name covering a great area of country, climatic and social associations, and about forty million human beings of very diverse kinds (numbers of them not even speaking French), will regard international politics from an entirely different angle from a Realist who finds in the word France something more real and vital than any single individual or thing that contributes to the ensemble of that idea. "Russia" is another magic term of this sort for the Realists; "Mother India" again, or the "Old Country," whichever it is. Since we do not teach the significance of these words "Nominalist" and "Realist" in our schools, nor give any sort of training in analytical thinking, we are Nominalists or Realists as our mental temperament or luck may determine, and the Nominalist and Realist of contemporary life, all unaware of this difference in the very elements of their thought, find each the other stupefyingly obtuse. Each cannot see what is the matter with the other's mind. The Realist "patriot" calls his brother Nominalist "traitor" or "cosmopolitan scoundrel," and the like, and is amazed that he does not wince; the Nominalist humanitarian calls the Realist obdurate dogmatist or romanticist and accuses him of a perverse taste for contention and blood.

At a considerably higher level we find the contemporary mathematician who has still to learn the real meaning of "experimental verification," and who is habituated to treating the schemes of concepts in his brain as truer than fact, at odds with the modern biologist. Still constrained in the logical net, he shakes his head at the "unphilosophical" ease of the latter's mental movements. He objects to conclusions that are not final and exactly proved. He has not learnt to rest in a provisional conclusion, and clings to the delusion that purely symbolic processes can win truth from the unknown. His symbolic processes never do win truth from the unknown, but he fancies that they justify an attitude of disapproval towards the pragmatical acceptances of practical science. But in the long run perhaps even the mathematicians will become scientific.

The Nominalist emancipation of the human mind proceeds slowly, but it proceeds; the boundaries of once hard classifications become transparent and manifestly provisional. The discovery of Evolution, the realization, that is to say, that there are no strict limits set to animal and vegetable species, opened the whole world of life and its destiny to Nominalist thinking. The realization by the world of mathematical physics that the universe can be represented as a four-dimensional universe of unique events has abolished the conception of a quantitative equivalence of cause and effect and made every atom unique. Only the indifference of school and college to current thought has prevented every thinking person from becoming a Nominalist by the present time.

§ 3. *The Practical Nature of Renascent Science*

Two fundamental ideas came with the experimental method in the renascent world of the later Middle Ages, to qualify, extend and empower the first great releases of the Hellenic period. One of them is the *changeableness of substances* leading on to the possibility of changing them, and the other is the possibility of *deliberately releasing power*. Neither of these ideas is in evidence in Hellenic science. They were latent in it, perhaps, but they were not in evidence. Their appearance in effective action marks a profound difference between the Old World and the New. The deliberate "Conquest of Substances" and the deliberate "Conquest of Power" are entirely characteristic of our modern world.

There were deep enquiries into the nature and constitution of matter in the ancient world, such as the wonderful guesses of Lucretius, but these were speculative exercises of the mind, prompted by the desire to explain, rather than the passion for effective knowledge. The science of Aristotle is largely descriptive. The herbalist sought practical knowledge, but to the Old-World mind substances were what they were, just as plants and animals were what they were. You knew about them, but you did not probe into them. And neither was there research for power. Curious mechanical toys were made—and there at the curious stage they remained. There was little experimental work, and the philosopher did not deign to share in and scrutinize the practical secrets of the metal worker and suchlike artizans. Archimedes would not have the construction of his practical contrivances recorded. They were beneath his dignity as a philosopher—mere artizan tricks. The highest aim and the only honoured aim of that earlier science was to know.

It is only as the obscure, secretive science of the late Middle Ages emerges to publicity and discussion that we find these new conceptions of *interference with substance* and the *release of force* in action. The alchemist we discover looking for the elixir of life and the transmutation of baser metals into gold. From alchemy chemistry developed into "iatro chemistry," the chemistry of medically useful substances. All the ancient aloofness of the philosopher gentleman had disappeared by the dawn of the new time. Roger Bacon is full of practical promises, they made the substance of his message, and Francis Bacon died through a chill contracted when making a crude experiment upon the preservative use of cold. He got out of his coach to stuff snow into a fowl.

The science of this new phase was concerned not with the essential nature of things as the old had been, but with the properties of things and what you could do to them and with them. It was more modest because it did not set itself to explain, and yet it was bolder because instead of merely accepting and describing, it set itself to use and alter.

It did not pontificate about fact; it grappled with fact. It was philosophically more modest and practically more courageous. It sought practical ends and presently, and almost inadvertently, it found itself penetrating far more profoundly into the nature of things than the exalted philosophers of the Hellenic world had ever been able to do. But that profounder knowledge came by the way; it was found by the wayside to actuality. Science did not even stoop to conquer. It stooped to practical things and conquest ensued.

This modesty of approach and this bias towards practical issues may have been forced upon renascent science by the religious intolerance of Christendom. If so, there is something to be said for intolerance. The Hellenic philosophers had nothing to forbid their seeking fundamental knowledge, but in the late Middle Ages scientific enquiry could only be released by that compromise of the later schoolmen which distinguished sharply between "spiritual" truth which was the *higher truth,* and rational truth, the everyday truth of normal experience and the secular mind. In that way the reconstruction of astronomical ideas which has gradually released the human imagination from an earth-centred universe to the immensity of space, and the realization of organic evolution that has opened to man the limitless vistas of time, have been possible without a conflict to the death between science and religion. There have been disputes and discussions of a very far-reaching kind, there have been forced recantations like Galileo's and martyrs like Bruno, there have been skirmishes in the Garden of Eden and quarrels about the Gadarene swine, but the combatants have never finally clinched. At the close of the nineteenth century science worked upon lines that implied a conception of the universe which was rigidly fatalistic, side by side with the picture of free-will, unqualified initiative and moral responsibility, presented by the religious teacher. It was an intellectual incompatibility which did not interfere very greatly in the steady extension of the multitude of substances that were being made available for human purposes or in the continually increased utilization of extraneous power. Science worked and religion attended to the immaterial needs of mankind.

§ 4. *Ultimate Truths Are Outside the Diagrams of Experimental Science*

In recent years very extensive readjustments have been made in the general formulæ which the man of science has used to simplify and systematize his facts. These readjustments have occurred mainly in the world of physical science; they have affected the steady advance of biological and social science very little. It is the professor of physics who is most concerned. The philosophical concepts that have served to guide and sustain his enquiries hitherto have been, so to speak, under repair. He has had to alter his general diagrams.

The reader will have heard endless echoes and repercussions from these enquiries into philosophico-scientific technique, even if he has not deliberately studied them, and so it is well to explain how far they concern us and how far they do not concern us in this work.

Some recent experiments and observations have jarred heavily with the general philosophical ideas that have hitherto satisfied and served the scientific worker. His diagrams have had to undergo a considerable revision. They were much too naïve and "obvious." In certain fields he has had to question the essential reality of that framework of space and time in which he—in common with the man in the street—has been wont to arrange his facts. He has had to scrutinize the ideas of time and eternity afresh. He has been brought to consider Euclidean space as only one of a great number of theoretical spaces, and to replace it by other and subtler concepts of space that seem more compatible with these recently observed facts. The old issue between predestination and free-will has in effect been revived in terms of mathematical physics. Is the universe a fixed, rigid time-space system, or has it movement in still other dimensions? Is it a continuous or an intermittent universe? The mere asking of such strange questions is very exciting to the speculative mind. But they do not affect the practical everyday life, either of the individual or of mankind, and we note these interesting developments of modern thought here as fascinating exercises for the intelligence outside our subject altogether.

It may be that we exist and cease to exist in alternations, like the minute dots in some forms of toned printing or the succession of pictures on a cinema film. It may be that consciousness is an illusion of movement in an eternal, static, multi-dimensional universe. We may be only a story written on a ground of inconceivable realities, the pattern of a carpet beneath the feet of the incomprehensible. We may be, as Sir James Jeans seems to suggest, part of a vast idea in the meditation of a divine circumambient mathematician. It is wonderful exercise for the mind to peer at such possibilities. It brings us to the realization of the entirely limited nature of our intelligence, such as it is, and of existence as we know it. It leads plainly towards the belief that with minds such as ours the ultimate truth of things is forever inconceivable and unknowable. It brings us to the realization that these theories, the working diagrams of modern science are in the end less provisional only in the measure of their effective working than the mythologies and symbols of barbaric religions.

But it does not give us any present escape from this world of work and wealth and war. For us, while we live, there must always be a to-morrow and choice, and no play of logic and formulæ can ever take us out of these necessities. To be taken out of these necessities would be to be taken out of existence as we know it altogether.

It is impossible to dismiss mystery from life. Being is altogether mysterious. Mystery is all about us and in us, the Inconceivable permeates us, it is "closer than breathing and nearer than hands and feet." For all we know, that which we are may rise at death from living, as an intent player wakes up from his absorption when a game comes to an end, or as a spectator turns his eyes from the stage as the curtain falls, to look at the auditorium he has for a time forgotten. These are pretty metaphors, that have nothing to do with the game or the drama of space and time. Ultimately the mystery may be the only thing that matters, but *within the rules and limits of the game of life,* when you are catching trains or paying bills or earning a living, the mystery does not matter at all.

It is this sense of an unfathomable reality to which not only life but all present being is but a surface, it is this realization "of the gulf beneath all seeming and of the silence above all sounds," which makes a modern mind impatient with the tricks and subterfuges of those ghost-haunted metaphysicians and creed-entangled apologists who are continually asserting and clamouring that science is dogmatic—with would-be permanent dogmas that are forever being overthrown. They try to degrade science to their own level. But she has never pretended to that finality which is the quality of religious dogmas. Science pits no dogmas against the dogmas of the ghost worshippers. Only sometimes, when perforce science touches their dogmas, do these latter dissolve away. Science is of set intention superficial. It touches religious dogma only in so far as religious dogma is materialistic, only in so far as religious dogma is a jumble of impossible stories about origins and destinies in space and time, a story pretending to a "spirituality" that is merely a dreamy, crazy attenuation of things material. And even then does it touch these dogmas only because they involve magic irrational distractions, interferences and limitations of the everyday life of man.

I wish that there was a plain and popular book in existence upon the history of scientific ideas.* It would be fascinating to reconstruct the intellectual atmosphere that surrounded Galileo and show the pre-existing foundations on which his ideas were based. Or ask what did Gilbert, the first student of magnetism, know, and what was the ideology with which the natural philosophers of the Stuart period had to struggle? It would be very interesting and illuminating to trace the rapid modification of these elementary concepts as the scientific process became vigorous and spread into general thought.

Few people realize how recent that invasion is, how new the current diagram of the universe is, and how recently the ideas of modern science have reached the commoner sort of people. The present writer is sixty-five. When he was a little boy his mother taught him out of a book she valued very highly, *Magnell's Questions*. It had been her own school book. It was already old-fashioned, but it was still in use and on sale. It was a book on the eighteenth-century plan of question and answer, and it taught that there were four elements, earth, air, fire and water.

These four elements are as old at least as Aristotle. It never occurred to me in my white-sock and plaid-petticoat days to ask in what proportion these fundamental ingredients were mixed in myself or the table-cloth or my bread and milk. I just swallowed them as I swallowed the bread and milk.

From Aristotle I made a stride to the eighteenth century. The two elements of the Arabian alchemists, sulphur and mercury, I never heard of then, nor of Paracelsus and his universe of salt, sulphur, mercury, water, and the vital elixir. None of that ever got through to me. I went to a boys' school, and there I learnt, straightaway, that I was made up of hard, definite molecules, built up of hard definite indestructible atoms of carbon, oxygen, hydrogen, nitrogen, phosphorus, calcium, sodium, chlorine, and a few others. These were the real elements. They were shown plainly in my textbook like peas or common balls suitably grouped. That also I accepted for a time without making any fuss about it. I do not remember parting with the Four Elements: they got lost and I went on with the new lot.

At another school, and then at the Royal College of Science I learnt

*But *Man and His Universe*, by J. Langdon Davies, is good, readable and suggestive, and Ginzburg's *The Adventure of Science* also comes very close to my wish. I may add Holmyard's *Chemistry for Beginners* and Alexander Findlay's *Spirit of Chemistry* as agreeable books for the general reader who would like to expand the matter of this necessarily very brief section. Finally as the proofs of this book pass through my hands, my attention is called to a still closer approximation to my desire in E. A. Burtt's *Metaphysical Foundations of Modern Science* (1925).

of a simple eternity of atoms and force. But the atoms now began to be less solid and simple. We talked very much of ether and protyle at the Royal College, but protons and electrons were still to come, and atoms, though taking on strange shapes and movements, were intact. Atoms could neither be transformed nor destroyed, but forces, though they could not be destroyed, could be transformed. This indestructibility of the chameleon of force, was the celebrated Conservation of Energy, which has since lost prestige, though it remains as a sound working generalization for the everyday engineer.

But in those days, when I debated and philosophized with my fellow students, I was speedily made aware that these atoms and molecules were not realities at all; they were, it was explained to me, essentially mnemonics; they satisfied, in the simplest possible arrangement of material models and images, what was needed to assemble and reconcile the known phenomena of matter. That was all they were. That I grasped without much difficulty. There was no shock to me, therefore, when presently new observations necessitated fresh elaborations of the model. My schoolmaster had been a little too crude in his instructions. He had not been a scientific man, but only a teacher of science. He had been an unredeemed Realist, teaching science in a dogmatic Realist way. Science, I now understood, never contradicts herself absolutely, but she is always busy in revising her classifications and touching up and rephrasing her earlier cruder statements. Science never professes to present more than a working diagram of fact. She does not *explain,* she *states the relations and associations of facts as simply as possible.*

Her justification for her diagrams lies in her increasing power to change matter. The test of all her theories is that they work. She has always been true, and continually she becomes truer. But she never expects to reach Ultimate Truth. At their truest her theories are not, and never pretend to be, more than diagrams to fit, not even all possible facts, but simply the known facts.

In my student days, forty-five years ago now, we were already quite aware* that the *exact* equivalence of cause and effect was no more than a convenient convention, and that it was possible to represent the universe as a system of unique events in a spacetime framework. These are not new ideas. They were then common student talk. When excited journalists announce that such intellectualists as Professor Eddington

---

*See, for example, my own undergraduate essay in the *Fortnightly Review,* July 1, 1891, "The Rediscovery of the Unique"; and see also L. Silberstein upon "The Time Machine," 1894, in his *Theory of Relativity* (1914), p. 134.

and Professor Whitehead have made astounding discoveries to overthrow the "dogmas of science," they are writing in sublime ignorance of the fact that there are no dogmas of science, and that these ideas that seem such marvellous "discoveries" to them have been in circulation for more than half a century.

No engineer bothers about these considerations of marginal error and the relativity of things, when he plans out the making of a number of machines "in series" with replaceable parts. Every part is unique indeed and a little out of the straight, but it is near enough and straight enough to serve. The machines work. And no appreciable effect has been produced upon the teaching of machine drawing by the possibility that space is curved and expanding. In this book, let the reader bear in mind, we are always down at the level of the engineer and the machine drawing. From cover to cover we are dealing with practical things on the surface of the earth, where gravitation is best represented as a centripetal pull, and where a pound of feathers weighs equal to a pound of lead, and things are what they seem. We deal with the daily life of human beings now and in the ages immediately ahead. We remain in the space and time of ordinary experience throughout this book, at an infinite distance from ultimate truth.*

§ 5. *The Organization of Research*

Let us consider how this collection of working diagrams up to date, this practical thing, Science, is perpetually being added to and perpetually being clarified and made more serviceable.

There was a time not so very long ago when an isolated man of independent means might still conduct investigations of primary importance and make great additions to knowledge or profound changes in ideology single-handed. A man like Cavendish, the great chemist, or the Abbé Mendel, could work on his own resources and could leave notes and observations behind him to lie undeveloped and disregarded for a long time. But now we think a great deal more in each other's minds than we did. It is often difficult and sometimes impossible to trace the authorship of modern key phrases and words and terms. Who, outside a small specialized world, knows, for example, who first used "genes" or "auto-suggestion" or "metapsychics" or "values"? No doubt

*Our discussion of the relations of science to human life, philosophy and belief in the four preceding sections has been necessarily very bare and swift. The reader who would like a longer and fuller treatment of these questions will find it in W. C. D. Dampier-Whetham's *History of Science and Its Relations with Philosophy and Religion*.

the answer is to be given in each case, but few of us trouble about the answer. The new term is thrown out, and suddenly we are all using it. We do not want to be bothered about questions of copyright. Patent rights in a new terminology are no longer recognized. A score of men turn a corner at about the same time and at once indicate their sense of a new direction by the same inevitable phrase that no one had ever dreamt of using before.

To-day, in an increasing number of subjects, teamwork research prevails, and in many it is the only possible method. In the *Science of Life* the rapid production of valuable results by the teamwork in genetics under Morgan in New York is described.

A history and discussion of the social and economic basis of scientific work from the very beginnings of scientific thought would be profoundly useful. Where did scientific questioning really begin? The priesthoods of the early civilizations had a considerable accumulation of knowledge. How had it been accumulated and reported? It seems to have undergone a slow but steady progressive development. Gradually the archæologists, and especially the Egyptologists, are disentangling the material to answer that question. For the last century or more workers, in Egypt especially, have been getting together and cataloguing and classifying the material for the understanding of these remote mental processes, but now, and with the inspiration of a psychology suddenly become boldly speculative and analytical, we are more and more able to realize the current assumptions and reconstruct the thought of past periods.

I doubt if the Egyptians had any idea of research. I suspect that even a very intelligent Egyptian or Sumerian priest supposed that everything was known that could be known, even if he and those about him did not know it all. He had no suspicion of limitless seas of knowledge accessible but unexplored. For him there existed already—Wisdom. All one had to do was to learn and learn, to seek out mighty Sages and learn more. And if he observed something that he had never heard of before, then I suppose he put it on record not as anything new but as a mere provisional replacement of some part of the mosaic of Wisdom that had got mislaid. I doubt if any Egyptian priest, however original, ever thought in the form of fresh discovery. Even when they were most original the ancients were always, they thought, restoring Wisdom. They were, they imagined, in conflict not with virgin ignorance but with corruptions.

Knowledge and skill, conditioned by such views, advanced slowly, backing forward and bowing to the past. Maybe that here or there a man had a momentary glimpse of the limitless seas of things still unknown that lay outside of and encompassed Wisdom,—that Wisdom knew nothing about. But not for long did that glimpse last. Such a thought, if it occurred at all, must have traversed the mind of an Egyptian priest, very much as a terrified mouse dashes across a room. It was there. It was gone. Even to-day the intelligent visitor to Egypt, walking through her long colonnades, recalls something of the fixed recurrence, the finality, to which the world of the great dynasties had attained. Everything was known, they supposed, and across the dark river waited Anubis the Accuser, Horus the Saviour, and—if the scales did not condemn the pleading soul—eternal bliss with Osiris, stereotyped also forever. That was life. That was all.

It seems plausible to suppose that the first scientific questionings began where traditions came into conflict. My own coarse guess is that the southward swirl of the Aryan-speakers across the Asiatic and Mediterranean civilizations did much to loosen the roots of old ideas, that the clash of strange languages led to a new curiosity about meaning and so to logical analysis, and that the development of a class of independent, prosperous, but not too opulent people with leisure made the play of doubt effective. They sat about and talked and reasoned a little; they wrote, and copies were made of what they wrote. They began to ask such questions as, "How do we know what we know?" Much of that discussion was forgotten or lost again. When at last the story of enquiry and record is fully traced out it will seem marvellous how narrow and precarious were the first springs and rivulets that have swelled to the science of to-day.

What was the first dawn of associated scientific work? The Museum at Alexandria, perhaps. All associations in the ancient world had to be religious associations, or they were regarded as dangerous conspiracies. The Alexandrian savants therefore dedicated themselves to the Muses. They were patronized by the Hellenic Pharaohs. What well-nigh imperceptible drops in the general flood of contemporary human acceptance were these Hellenic sages who set out upon such enterprises as the measurement of the globe! How flimsy was the thread of occasional and precarious letters that linked minds in Alexandria with kindred minds in Athens and Syracuse!

The renewal of the scientific process in mediæval Europe is often ascribed rather absurdly to the dissemination of the Greek literature, after the fall of Constantinople to the Turk. But science died in Imperial Rome with all that Greek literature at hand. Some necessary freedom or protection had disappeared. Nobody was, in fact, left free to care for it. The revival was due much more to the reappearance of certain social types, and particularly of *secure, freely thinking, independent people,* people of "means," stimulated by, but not absorbed in public responsibilities. They could give curiosity play and amuse themselves with dreams of magic discovery. Half seriously and a little furtively these fortunate amateurs took up the search for the secret of transmuting metals and the mysteries of longevity. We have noted the new streak of practicality in the science of the Renascence. The "curio" came before the museum; the pottering odd experiment before the definite enquiry.

Embryonic modern science was closely mixed up with art. Philosophy wrangled. Art observed. Dürer and Leonardo were scientific pioneers. The universities droned along blindly with the oral teaching of traditional wisdom; they were on the side of tradition. Modern science owes few of its initiatives to them.

Mercantile motives and the vast raids of the Mongols set the process of geographical exploration at work again. It had been suspended from the days of the Roman ascendency. Its effect in effacing the delusion that everything was known extended far beyond the geographical field. The unrest and doubt that spread out from this Mongol thrust was probably much more important than the Greek stimulus. The revival of Greek studies at the Renascence did not so much start new ideas in men's minds as confirm and stimulate what was already stirring.

The difference between the mentality of a sixteenth-century gentleman of intellectual tastes and a mentally vigorous Egyptian priest must have rested primarily in the relative realization by the former that there was a limitless, accessible circumambient unknown. There the sixteenth-century gentleman was in advance of the priest. But also he was intensely individualistic, and there he seems to us nowadays to have been less "modern." The priest had a sense of belonging to an organized system; albeit it was a tradition-preserving system. The founders of modern science worked for a time almost independently. They met first in the early academies: the Academia Secretorum Naturæ of Naples, 1590, suspected of the black arts and closed by the Pope; the Academia dei Lincei, of which Galileo was a member, 1603; the Academia Naturæ Curiosorum of Madrid, 1657; the Académie des Sciences, incorporated in 1666 after thirty years of informal meetings (including Descartes, Gassendi, Pascal); the London Royal Society

(1662, after informal meetings dating from 1645), and presently a variety of specialized scientific societies.* But they assembled under no sense of obligation, just out of fellow feeling, for the social gratification of their curiosity, and perhaps also for the sense of a possible need for mutual protection against the hostility of the traditional. The greatness of Bacon's *New Atlantis* lies in the clear recognition by its author of the need for coöperation in research.

The first modern coöperation in research seems to have been made under the auspices of royal and wealthy persons, to form collections and horticultural and zoölogical gardens too expensive for a private purse. There the royal and wealthy of the seventeenth century recall the memory of Asoka and the Ptolemies. To begin with, laboratories were individual and private. The first men to earn a living by experimental science were, I suppose, the assistants of scientifically inclined gentlemen. They emerged to distinction like the groundsmen and professionals in the games of cricket and golf. Until they could teach their employers. . . . Then gifted young men began to be "discovered" and assisted in their own investigations, and research institutions appeared. The accumulation of facts and generalizations presently led to public lectures and movements for the diffusion of scientific knowledge.

The material for this story is still scattered in hundreds of biographies and collections of letters. It is all very recent, an affair of three centuries at most. But when it has been collected and arranged the compilers will have done their task ineffectively if they do not display a steady change of attitude on the part of those who were engaged upon that accumulation, towards the knowledge they had procured and tested.

Only in moments of insight and exaltation did the curio-collecting nobles and gentlemen of the sixteenth and seventeenth centuries realize this mighty new directive system they were evoking. This amusing and surprising little pet creature, this Natural Philosophy of theirs, was to grow into a dragon that would sustain the world, but of this they had no idea. For the most part science was a toy or an ingenious way of discovering new money-making activities, and presently it became a useful weapon for teasing the parsons. Or it aroused wonder. By imperceptible degrees we shall find the idea of scientific research as an important public function entitled to systematic support, and the associated idea of science as a devotion and a primary end in life, creeping into the record. Science ceased to be a recreation and became a pursuit.

---

*M. Ornstein's *The Rôle of the Scientific Societies of the Seventeenth Century* (1928) may interest the reader who would like more detail here.

These new views about the importance of science have arrived very recently; within the lifetime of many who are still living.

Such stories as that of the Smithsonian Institution in Washington, of the Institute Pasteur, of the London Royal Institution, and of the Rockefeller group of endowments, would repay a careful scrutiny. They would reveal progressive stages in which men say more and more distinctly, "This Science is a great and mighty business." From such beginnings followed the progressive public organization of research.

The activities of the gentlemen who launched Natural Philosophy upon the world, needed to be supplemented by work of a coarser type before it could realize its vast potentialities. There were practical men, mostly millwrights and often of no education (Brindley could scarcely read and could write only with difficulty) who understood the pressing needs of the day and the practical difficulties in the way of overcoming them far better than the learned. They experimented in a crude practical way. To their help came some Natural Philosophers (Rennie and Smeaton were F. R. S.) and also some military engineers bringing traditional skill of a certain kind. Out of this contact and collaboration arose the civil engineers. The civil engineers bridged the gap between pure science and practical application; they linked the toy with the needs.

Scientific research is still in its prentice stage. It is still undergoing rapid change and development, and still greatly encumbered with military, naval, and other patriotic entanglements. Its organization for intercommunication is complex and imperfect. The Institute for Intellectual Coöperation at Paris, with Madame Curie as instigator, has directed its attention to this latter group of problems—I know not with what energy, resources, or effect. Organized world-wide research is still a promise rather than an achieved reality, and yet every year the astounding harvest of science and invention increases in mass and length and breadth.

It is interesting to glance at the relations between the scientific process and the older and newer universities of the world. Belatedly those venerable seats of learning which preserve the university tradition in its greatest purity gave their recognition to the new knowledge and, as far as they could, made it amenable to the established routines of syllabus and oral lecture, notebook and examination. They did not receive it humbly; they tried to annex it and assimilate it to their ancient concepts of learning. They did all they could to give it a quality of "scholarship." Enquiry was taught as far as possible as if it were traditional Wisdom. Chairs were set up for this and that, the boundaries of "subjects" were marked out, subjects that could, in fact, coalesce or split into a score of fragments in a year or so, and "degrees" were instituted in science just as they had been for centuries in the "fixed" subjects of erudition. The universities conferred "degrees" of Bachelor, Master and Doctor of Science; that is to say, bachelors who knew some, masters who knew most, and doctors who knew all. They arranged for the young to pass from the innocence of the first year undergraduate to the complete and final knowledge of the robed and hooded Doctor. He was then to be considered a finished scientific *scholar*. Scientific men were appointed to professorial chairs, and the universities, by an insistence upon oral teaching and administrative duties, sought to wean them from too sedulous a pursuit of research.

Only very reluctantly would these venerable institutions recognize the primary importance of research and the essential insignificance of scholarship to the man of science. Abraham Flexner, in *Universities, American, English and German,** shows how much leeway modernization has still to make up. The constant fluctuations and extensions of the scheduled sciences, the perpetual eruption of crude *new* matter, worried the learned mind extremely and are still a cause for reproach on the part of scholars. They complain that science never really knows its own mind. It is perpetually correcting itself, perpetually superannuating its generalizations, never achieving a classical finish in its statements, never becoming Tradition. . . .

Slowly they are learning better now. University science becomes more and more scientific. The grants, the endowments and workers multiply. The science side grows ever greater and overshadows "scholarship" more and more. Knowledge is no longer despised because it is new, nor revered because it is mellow.

Scientific research in a review of human activities must be regarded not only from the point of view of a collective function, but also from the individual's point of view. Research work in itself becomes a career nowadays. It is clear that if the progressive development of human society is to continue, there must be a steady increase in the proportion of scientific workers to the total population. Very little attention has been paid to the social types and classes from which these workers are now drawn and the spirit in which they approach their unending coöperative task.

Scientific research is the modern form of the religious life. It gives

*Quoted in *Nature*, April 18, 1931, p. 543.

courage and a fundamental serenity. It is the securest refuge from the distresses of the human soul. The laboratory becomes the pathway to great adventures and limitless service. Its interrogations may send off men and women to every part of the world and direct them to the strangest experiences. Its pay and endowment are the least of its rewards.

But we are anticipating issues that will be better developed at a later stage. Let us turn now to the practical consequences of the scientific scrutiny of human conditions. The main practical sciences of the eighteenth and nineteenth century were chemistry and physics; the study of *substances,* that is, and the study of *force and movement.** The one has led to a vast increase in the materials used in social life; the other to a systematic conquest of natural power.

§ 6. *The Conquest of Substances.*

It would be a fine large task in itself to compile a great book, a Book of Substances, giving a really full and orderly record of the subjugation of matter to human needs, a review of all the stuffs out of which Man shapes the tools, implements, machinery, clothing, furnishing, housing, bridges, all the impedimenta indeed of our civilization. It would tell how man has passed from the flint to stainless steel and the sterilized scalpel, and from the walls of the rocky cavern, or a shelter of tree branches and leaves, to towering steel-framed buildings of reinforced concrete. Man was once an animal which picked up things by luck and took them and used them for what they were; he has become a planning creature, making and shaping objects more and more after his heart's desire. That in brief would be the theme of that unwritten book.

Such a Book on Substances would open with a résumé of the materials used by the earliest men we know. The list would be a brief one. Some of the Hominidæ below the human level may have made a free use of sticks and unshaped stones, and may have already begun the shaping of flints. Animal substances, tusks, teeth and bones particularly, and skins, with some rude anticipations of leather-dressing, were added to these primary elements of the human equipment, and also clay, as a pigment to smear and as a substance to mould and dry. Vege-

*Under chemistry we here put botany, which was at first not so much a biological study, a study that is of *living* things, as a systematic development of the lore of the herbalist, with a view to the recognition of plants and the use of plant materials.

table fibre began to be twisted and woven. The first traces we have of *Homo sapiens* show him at this stage. The early Neolithic people had already a pretty taste in stones and were finding gold and setting a high value on it. Mining began before the Neolithic period. Palæolithic peoples mined for flints. Their workings are to be found in many places.

At first metals were only known through chance finds of gold and copper and meteoric iron, and then came the discovery of how to reduce certain metals from their ores. The first metallurgists worked in copper and bronze, and then came iron. The furnace improved. The furnace opened the way to glasses and enamels. A large field of knowledge, still rapidly growing, would have to be explored and summarized for this history of human materials. The Deutsches Museum at Munich gives models of primitive mines and the hearths and furnaces of savage people. It shows in a charming model, negroes smelting iron ore. It gives a series leading up to the blast furnace. It unfolds in an illuminating series of exhibits a complex stream of stories about metal winning—for every metal has its own history. The furnaces tower up, their interiors blaze more and more blindingly, the conquered and chastened metals pour more and more obediently to the casting.

All these advances, if one traces them carefully and intelligently, were prettily interdependent. One step here depends on the completion of a quite different step there. Ancient biology, for example, was greatly retarded in its development by its unawareness of the possibilities of magnification by properly shaped glasses or globular water flasks. It never suspected animalculæ therefore. Steel was known, iron was known, but neither was handled in large masses, and so the ancient world knew of steam only as the moving force of curious toys. The simple and obvious idea of railways which must have occurred to road makers again and again could find no material for its effective realization in the ancient world. A sort of rails—stone wheel tracks—are found in such excavated Roman cities as Pompeii and Pæstum. At that point the railway idea sat down, baffled. It had to wait a couple of thousand years before the rolling mill could turn out iron rails.

This History of Substances we have imagined, would go, comparatively speaking, at an ambling pace even up to the opening decades of the nineteenth century. Man's building operations at that time were still determined by the properties of a few building stones and a few types of mortar and cement, his clothing was either natural wool or silk or cotton, his dyes were "natural" dyes, his list of metals and alloys had hardly grown since the Roman Empire, and his steel was a kind of hard iron. And then came novelties. He began to work iron and steel upon a larger scale. The use of coal in metallurgical operations assisted that. That again led to a control of steam power. At the great museums of South Kensington and Munich the relationship of the development of the steam engine to a large handling of iron and steel is manifest. *Puffing Billy,* that early locomotive, is built up of a patchwork of plates of iron bolted together. It has become almost comic in its clumsiness to modern eyes. The relatively large modern engines are built up of castings, many of which would outweigh the entire *Rocket* or *Puffing Billy*. The first *Puffing Billy*—there were several engines of that name— weighed three tons without fuel or water, and with four wheels it broke the cast-iron rails provided for it and had to have the load redistributed over eight wheels. (The vanadium high-test cast-steel frames of the electric locomotives recently built for the Norfolk & Western Railway, U. S. A., weigh nearly 9.8 tons.) Side by side with the name of Watt, the name of Wilkinson the iron founder should be remembered. The one could not have developed his ideas without the other.

Tinplate and coal gas were other cardinal events in the reawakening phase of human affairs. Rubber, wild rubber, crept into trade and industry, an unimportant stuff at first, destined to become a gigantic interest. In my childhood you rubbed out pencil marks with it. It had little more importance than that. Petroleum was a considerable find that also falls within the last seventy years.

Towards the middle nineteenth century the tempo of the narrative in our Story of Substances would quicken perceptibly. New metallic elements were being investigated; new alloys tried. Rubber began to be put to new uses and mixed with this and that. Such artificial substances as vulcanite and ebonite, combinations of raw rubber and sulphur, were being made and tried out for all sorts of purposes. The idea of artificial substances inspired a growing multitude of patentees. The deliberate conquest of substances was being undertaken. Every day new substances were being discovered and led into the factory.

The headlong substitution of "made" materials for "natural" materials during the last sixty or seventy years is an extraordinarily important fact in this present summary. At the opening of the scientific period, man was still going humbly and submissively to the rock or the plant or the sheep or the silkworm and taking what was given him as the directive and limiting conditions of the building or weaving. Now he makes his pastes and pulps into whatever texture or fibre he needs.

Once steel was steel, a rather uncertain but powerful substance. Now, as we will tell later, there are hundreds of kinds of steel, and each knows precisely what is expected of it, and in understanding hands behaves accordingly. An array of once undreamt-of new metals has come in to enrich the resources of metallurgy.

In order to exhibit this array with anything resembling completeness, a sedulous canvass of great groups of industry would have to be made. So much novelty is continually being poured into industrial life that if we were to be up to date we should have to go to the fountain-heads. And also we should have to take stock of all the new raw materials, formerly unused, which are the basis of this ever increasing array of made and prepared substances.

But it is possible to sketch out one or two striking developments that have occurred in the list of industrial substances during the last century, and this shall be done in the next section. That Book of Substances I have just projected for an actual encyclopædic *Science of Work and Wealth* would be a filling up of the gaps and an amplification of the particulars of this and the following section.

But it would go further. It would take up the question of quantities, a thing we cannot even begin to do here. To make the story complete there would have to be an estimate of the visible and probable supplies of ores and of animal and vegetable substances, of oil and coal. That would be—in other words—an outline of Economic Geography and the distribution of present and potential supplies of raw material about the earth. This would broaden out at last so as to amount to a résumé of the chemical composition of the entire globe, considered as a ball of raw material for economic exploitation.

§ 7. *Some Typical Modern Materials*

We will not attempt any complete inventory of useful materials here, but let us at least stroll about the human warehouse and see what is lying about in it and what invention and discovery have recently brought in and made available.

If it were possible to summon the whole *Science of Work and Wealth* into existence here, if we could thrust out our hands and eyes into the year 1940 and turn over the two or three hundred thousand pages that may then exist, we should find long, fascinating chapters devoted to the story of coal and oil, the story of iron and steel and of the metals and non-metallic minerals. There would be long descrip-

THE CONQUEST OF SUBSTANCES

A TYPICAL industrial plant such as is found on the outskirts of any great
city. This particular picture shows part of a coke by-product system. The
stack in the foreground is coal.

THE CONQUEST OF POWER

BUILDING part of a giant hydro-electric system. This is one of the
pipes which will lead water to the turbines.

tions, stage by stage, of mines and foundries, of the processes by which lead, tin, and other familiar metals are brought at last, tamed and submissive, to our hands. Modern discussions of the better utilization of coal would have produced their inevitable fruits. The already rich and eventful history of the distillation of coal, the story of gas and of the by-products of coal gas, would have had new chapters added to it. The oil chapter would tell of the refinery and of another great multitude of secondary materials arising out of oil. Here we can but intimate and sketch. We should read of copper refining—for the electrification of the world depends on copper; we should be told of the conquest of aluminium and of all that its lightness and strength make possible. On tin, they say, the food supplies of our urbanized world depend. But there the aluminium container and the "paper" carton may save the situation.

Had we limitless space the account of the distillation of coal would lead on to a description of aniline dyes, one only of the endless outcomes of that distillation and that would carry us on to an account of the dyes of former days, how rare and limited they were, and we should realize the great outbreak of colour in dress and furnishing and of scents and medical substances—as well as of frightful explosives—that the modern chemist has made possible. How did the colour of a ballet or a pantomime scene in the early nineteenth century compare with that of one to-day? I believe we should find it was extraordinarily flat and unsubtle.

Under the heading of nonmetallic minerals we should read in that great collection of details we have imagined, an account, for instance, of the finding and trade in various precious and semi-precious stones and a little about diamond cutting and why it fixed its headquarters for so long at Amsterdam. No such discursiveness is possible here. And then there would come a survey of the materials of the potter and the glass-maker and the comparative study of the ancient and modern cements. A brilliant array of modern pastes and enamels would follow. The vast architectural possibilities of reinforced concrete would be touched upon. But its fuller treatment would be better left for our chapter on the housing of mankind.

I seem to see before me a vast display of exhibits to comprehend long-cloth, paper, celluloid and a multitude of other such substances, brought together under the heading of "The Utilization of Cellulose," the substance of the ordinary vegetable cell wall. One branch of that utilization is the production of artificial silk. Hundreds of ingenious minds, crystallizing their results in thousands of patents, have led step by step to this one new item in the world's clothing.

The world's production of artificial silk in 1927 was more than 125,000 tons. A quarter of a century before, artificial silk was unknown. The story of artificial silk is a story of steadily accelerated invention. Réaumur, in 1734, suggested that artificial silk might be made from the solution of a gum. But the chemical knowledge of the time was insufficient to develop the suggestion. A hundred and twenty years later Andromars made cellulose nitrate by treating cellulose with nitric and sulphuric acids. This could be dissolved in a mixture of alcohol and ether, and when it was forced through a fine orifice, the alcohol and ether evaporated, leaving a filament of nitro-cellulose which could be converted into cellulose again without appreciable loss of form. That thread was the clue to the practical achievement of an artificial silk fibre.

For a time the technical difficulties of manufacture remained insuperable; Andromars' artificial silk fibre was a scientific curiosity and nothing more, and then a Frenchman, Chardonnet, worked out a commercial process. His attention was drawn to the matter while a student under Pasteur, when the latter was pursuing his famous investigations into silkworm disease. For thirty years Chardonnet struggled with his problem and at last worried through to success. He took out his first patent in 1884. His process is still in use, though the cost of the alcohol and ether was at first a serious disadvantage. Effective methods of recovering these had to be discovered.

A parallel process in which cellulose was dissolved in an ammoniacal solution of cupric hydro-oxide was worked out in France in 1900.

In 1902 Cross and Bevan discovered viscose, or zanthate of cellulose, a new and better material for the fibre, and from that time things went swiftly. By 1927 viscose formed 84 per cent of the world's artificial silk output. Three years later the same chemists invented the acetate process by which celanese is produced. All varieties of artificial silk are now known as *rayon*.

The raw materials used are cotton linters—the short fibres produced when cotton is "ginned" to remove the seeds; or wood pulp, obtained from spruce—usually *Picea excelsa;* and an abundant supply of pure soft water. From these materials not only rayon but also artificial horsehair, wool, narrow ribbon exquisitely delicate and fragile, films, sheets, and plastic masses of cellulose or cellulose acetate are now obtained.

When treated with camphor, cellulose forms celluloid, the material of camera and cinema films, of trinkets, toilet requisites, and toys, of collars, of cutlery, brush, umbrella and walking-stick handles, and of a thousand and one things, formerly made in bone, ivory, glass, china, leather, cotton, linen, wood, or metal. A sheet enclosed between two sheets of glass forms the unbreakable material used for the wind screens of motor cars.

Compounds of cellulose and acetic acid (the acid of vinegar) are used as "dope" for aëroplanes. They form a durable, glossy, and extremely tenacious film over wood, metal or fabric, and are replacing other forms of paint and varnish on account of the more attractive finish. Thin sheets of this material are used for wrapping food, and a film deposited on wire gauze forms a substitute for glass. All this variety of substances have been won from wood pulp and cotton refuse in the last fifty years.

It would be an interesting special study to trace the progressive introduction of animal and vegetable substances to industrial use. Leaving the ore heaps and chemical works behind us we should carry out our survey to the open, to the plantations and forests and wildernesses, where the "first state" of our substances is to be found. Some day we shall have precise estimates of the wild wastage of fine timbers that has gone on, and industrious students will have put in order the records of the modern search for fibres and paper, pulps and vegetable and animal oils. A history of materials if it is to be complete must also pursue the fur trapper and tell of fur farms and of the tragedy of sealing. How far is man killing off the whale and the ivory animals? There have been very hideous massacres of penguins for oil; it is a particularly moving story of waste and cruelty.

There is an interesting story behind this vehement search for animal and vegetable oils. Fifty years ago the chief demand for such oils came from the soap industry. Nobody thought of eating them or could have eaten them.

Soap is essentially a sodium or potassium salt of a fatty acid. The fatty acids are present in animals and plants in combination with glycerine. When these glycerides are treated with caustic soda or caustic potash the soda or potash displaces the glycerine, and soap is the product.

Tallow, obtained by boiling animal fat, was used for centuries for soap-making as well as for candles. Palm oil from Africa and olive oil from the Mediterranean region were employed for the choicer toilet soaps. And of these oils there was enough and to spare, until margarine became an article of manufacture. Margarine, however, is also made from animal oil, vegetable oil, or mixed oils. The principal raw materials are the oils of the cocoanut palm kernel, cotton seed, soya bean, or other plant products, and the fatty tissues of the caul and kidneys of cattle. These ingredients are mixed with skim milk which has been pasteurized and inoculated with lactic acid forming bacilli to make margarine. Most people over fifty can remember the introduction of this new synthetic and cheaper rival to butter and recall the prejudice it aroused.

Now the manufacturer of margarine soon outbid the soapboiler for the better qualities of oils and fats. A scarcity arose, more particularly of the harder oils or fats. The difference between soft (fluent) oils and hard oils or fats is as a rule a difference in the amount of hydrogen they contain. The former have less hydrogen than the latter. It was the hard fats the margarine makers and the soap makers wanted and struggled to obtain.

The chemist in his laboratory, at that time, could produce a hard fat from an oil by the addition of hydrogen. But his processes were difficult to carry out on a commercial scale. The problem was solved finally by employing a general reaction discovered by Sebatier and Senderens. They passed hydrogen through the fat heated to a temperature of 140°C. to 200°C. in the presence of a finely divided metal such as nickel. Not only did this harden the oil, but it deodorized it. So suddenly not only were soft oils turned to hard, but whale and fish oils, which formerly had had a limited utility owing to their objectionable smell, were brought to the aid of the soap-boiler and butterman. The balance of supply was restored, and the quantity available was enormously extended. To-day whale oil can not only be used for soap, but also for margarine, salad oil, and other articles of food. So black olives lie wasting now in the olive orchards of Provence while native labour gathers the material for the world's salad oil in the East Indies and the African forests, and the whalers of the Southern seas supplement their efforts.

While the invention of margarine captured a great supply of hitherto unassimilable oils and fats for food purposes, the story of milk products shows us the reverse process of utilizing a periodically excessive supply of nutritive material for industrial processes. Milk has a constituent called casein. It is an albuminous substance similar to the white of egg. It is the curd which is precipitated when rennet or a dilute acid is added to milk, or when milk sours naturally. When dried it forms a white powder, and of this powder about ten thousand tons are now produced annually in the United States alone.

The buttermilk or skim milk from which it is obtained has a limited value as a food for domestic animals. But the white powder is used in confectionery and certain manufactured foods, in cosmetics and ointments, as an adhesive material for glass, china, paper, wood, and other substances, in printing and sizing cotton fabrics, for waterproofing paper, and for making distempers.

When the dried powder is compressed and then hardened by soaking in a solution of formaldehyde, it can be machined and polished. Alone or mixed with various filling materials or colouring matter, this moulded and indurated material imitates ivory, horn, bone, tortoise-shell, amber, ebony, and ornamental minerals like malachite. It is fashioned into toilet trinkets, inkstands, cigarette holders, the handles of cutlery, brushes, and umbrellas, and scores of other articles. The colouring and translucency of many of these things are exquisite. How many people realize that the manicure set and the morning milk have a common origin?

Another series of artificial substances of great modern importance are the synthetic resins. Natural resins are gummy liquids which are exuded by trees, especially conifers. Amber is a fossil resin that has been valued since prehistoric times. But that is not the amber you will buy nowadays in the Rue de Rivoli. Resins differ from gums in being insoluble in water, and they are extensively used in varnishes. It has been found possible to make substances similar to natural resins by acting with formaldehyde on phenol and other products of coal tar or by subjecting these products to the action of heat, light, alkalis, or strong acids. Other synthetic mixtures are also made, to which coal tar does not contribute. Some of these false resins become harder and insoluble under the action of heat. The natural ones exhibit a contrary behaviour. These artificial products are used in varnishes and as insulating material for electrical apparatus. Since they will withstand a high temperature they have an advantage over rubber, ebonite, and celluloid. Bakelite, for example, which has become popular in a hundred varieties of bright-coloured ware, retains its form and properties when most other materials would soften or decompose. It is one of the most important insulating materials used in the electrical industry. Another variety of resin is made from urea, or from thiourea, a by-product of the gas works, treated with formaldehyde. This can be tinted and is used for table and decorative ware of extraordinary delicacy and colour.

The American petroleum industry dates from 1859, when Colonel Drake drilled the first well at Oil Creek in Pennsylvania. Before that enterprise the American output (used as fuel) was only 2,000 barrels a year. To-day it is more than 900,000,000 barrels, or nearly 500,000 times greater, and more than 70 per cent of the output of the world.

Petroleum is a complex mixture. By distillation at successive temperatures, the oil refiner obtains gases, naphtha, illuminating oils, lubricating heavy oils, and a residue of coke, pitch, or asphalt. Naphtha, on redistillation, is separated into petrol or gasoline, commercial naphtha, and benzine, used in dry cleaning. Similarly illuminating oils and lubricating oils yield different grades, each suitable by quality or price for a particular purpose. The heavier oils yield vaseline, petroleum jelly, and other now familiar substances. Paraffin wax, so largely used in the electrical industry—and for chewing gum!—is separated by cooling.

But the constituents do not exist in the proportions required by the modern world. The light oils have become more valuable than the heavy oils. So the heavy oils are subjected to the process of "cracking." A quick rise in the temperature of the still causes them to decompose, with the formation of lighter oils. In this way the production of illuminating oils, and particularly of petrol or gasoline, has been greatly increased during the last twenty years. A natural balance has been adjusted to meet changing human needs.

And so building up that spectacle of the world's activities which is the object of this work, we must add to the scientific experimentalists and research institutions we have already evoked as the nucleus of the modern economic world, a multitudinous array of toil and enterprise. We must fling across our canvas an impression of mines and foundries scattered about and digging into the skin of the world, innumerable quarries of every sort of stone, oil fields with their gaunt cement works, brick fields, the production of clay and feldspar for potteries, coal mines, peat cutting, forestry, and lumbering, saw mills and paper mills and a spreading increasing variety of plantations for rubber, sericulture, cotton, flax, hemp, sisal, factories for cellulose products and all the widespread extraction and preparation of the stuffs out of which the appliances of civilized life, its tools, machines, houses, clothing, and so forth are made. Here, except for our glance at margarine, we will say nothing of food. With food production we will deal later. That is the task of hundreds of millions of cultivators, the fundamental task of mankind, but here already we have millions at work of every race and colour, in every climate, winning and assembling the crude materials of modern industry in ever increasing variety and abundance.

A special chapter of outstanding liveliness in that great Book of Modern Substances would give the history of plantation rubber—with the Congo, Putumayo, and the Stock Exchange in the picture. They are not in our picture as yet, for we have still a long way to go before we come either to the tragedy of defenseless peoples invaded and forced to labour by alien enterprise, or to the problems of overproduction and planless cultivation in our still essentially haphazard world. But here we may at least glance at the happier aspect of a new substance woven into our economic life. A hundred years ago rubber was as unimportant as electricity. The very name reminds us of its chief use, the rubbing out of pencil marks. (Have we not all of us in our infantile artistry suffered from the sulphur streak of the cheaper kinds?) Or the stuff served as the material of a bouncing ball. The Spaniards found the natives playing with solid rubber balls when first they reached South America.

The extensive utilization of rubber dates from 1839. Then it was found that heating rubber with sulphur (vulcanization) made it stronger and more elastic. With more sulphur still it became harder and even brittle. In my boyhood ebonite was used for trinkets, and the incorporation of paraffin wax and other petroleum products with rubber had begun. Ebonite toys were irritatingly brittle. Very fine rubber, containing oil, was in use for such things as the tubes and teats of feeding bottles. And it was in silk-elastic also and particularly in those dreadful and now happily vanished objects, spring-sided boots.

That was about all I can remember of rubber sixty years ago. It was still a mere accessory substance. It would hardly have been missed had it vanished altogether. Consider what has happened since then. Consider its use for electrical insulation alone. If by some miracle rubber suddenly ceased to exist, what would happen to our streets and homes? Silence and darkness. The telephone would cease to ring. Seven eighths of the wheeled traffic would stand immobilized in the streets. Within a lifetime rubber has passed from the status of a supplementary elastic substance to a position of fundamental importance.

At first it was a wild product, it was made from the latex of various forest trees and plants of which *Hevea brasiliensis* was the chief. It was collected, often under dreadful conditions, in Brazil and the Congo Free State. (We shall have a grim story to tell later about that.) In my childhood a few thousand tons of this ball rubber was all the rubber output in the world. Under the pressure of new demands, of which the bicycle tire was the chief, the price rose, the hunt for wild rubber became more urgent and cruel, and the total product rose towards fifty thousand tons by the end of the century. Meanwhile the economic botanists of Kew were working out the problems of its cultivation. It was first successfully grown in Ceylon, and there followed a boom in rubber plantations; they multiplied in Malaya, the Dutch East Indies, Ceylon, Indo-China, India, Siam, and tropical Africa. The output of the cleaner and better plantation product has risen to over six hundred thousand tons, and prices have fallen until further production has become unprofitable. The quantity becomes the more impressive, and its bearing upon human work becomes plainer, when we remember that rubber is derived from a milky fluid which trickles at the rate of four or five pounds a year from cuts in the bark of trees, into small vessels hung beneath the cut. From that sticky treacle its drawn-out threads pass now to weave intimately and indispensably into the entire fabric of contemporary civilization.

All this, which we treat in a few brief crowded pages of evocation here, would unfold in a full and complete *Science of Work and Wealth* into a great mass of clear and well illustrated descriptions. This section is the intimation of a great volume. It would have to be a volume if once it began to expand. This material is the sort of thing that must be done either very fully or very compactly. There is no middle distance for a landscape of staple industries. Either you must see them from a remote distance, a reek of tall chimneys, clusters of strange sheds and retorts, tangles of conduits, gigantic dumps, a distant rumble of trains and machinery, or you must go right up to the blinding heat of the electric furnace and the intimate roar and beating of the machines. You must count the chimneys, weigh the fuel and assemble the records of output. At present we are doing no more than an aërial reconnaissance of all this side of human life.

As Crawford's admirable antiquarian work has shown, a man in an aëroplane cannot only see more deeply into the sea than a man in a boat, but he can observe a multitude of land secrets, old ridges, ancient roads and enclosures, and differences in soil and texture that are altogether hidden from the man in the field. But the airman can see nothing of the daisies and knows nothing of the lurking life in the hedges and by-ways. Here we are, so to speak, aëroplane economists, more concerned with the past and the general hang of things than with particular instances.

§ 8. *The Story of Iron and Steel*

But though we have every desire to avoid overwhelming the reader (and the writer) by masses of detailed technicality, there is one chapter in the vast catalogue of modern substances which is so integral to our account of the modern world, that we cannot avoid treating it with some particularity. This is the development of the iron and steel industry which was vitally necessary to the conquest of mechanical power.

In 1700, iron was made in Britain with charcoal in small blast furnaces. Steel was got by heating pure wrought Swedish iron in contact with charcoal. This *blister steel,* so called because the process of manufacture resulted in the formation of blisters on the surface of the metal, was broken up, bound into faggots, reheated and beaten to *shear steel*. That was the only iron and the only steel in England, and there was not very much of either. How much, we do not know. In other countries matters were at as low or a lower level. Bars, fetters, railways, small cannon were the largest workings of iron; a sword blade or a breast plate was the maximum piece of steel.

In the early eighteenth century coke began to replace charcoal in the blast furnaces. Coke permitted heavier charges, heavier charges involved longer contact with the fuel, and a more fluid iron was produced. Coal-fired reverberatory furnaces appeared after the middle of the century, and puddling and rolling followed. Foundry and forge tended to concentrate on the coal fields, and industrial units grew larger. Shear steel gave way to cast steel for many purposes, on account of the relative cheapness of the latter, so soon as crucibles could be found capable of standing the high temperature necessary to melt steel. But shear steel (double shear steel) is still used—for high grade carving knives, for example, and suchlike purposes. With this new abundance of steel, cutlery, fine-edge tools, steel springs became abundant in the world, facilitating scores of new processes and making hundreds of new conveniences possible.

By 1800 the world's output of iron and steel was perhaps over six hundred thousand tons.

By 1820, the production of pig iron in the world passed the million mark. Crawshay of Cyfarthfa could not turn out five hundred tons of bar iron in 1787; in 1812 he produced ten thousand tons. That was how things were going.

This flow of iron and steel into human resources made itself apparent in a number of useful things that had hitherto been impossible. In the latter half of the eighteenth century, not only was wrought iron being largely used, but cast iron was being extended to a number of purposes. The first iron bridge (cast iron) was constructed across the Severn in 1777–79 by Abraham Darby. An iron canal boat was built and launched by Wilkinson in 1787. Cast iron was used for tramway rails from 1767, and wrought iron on the Stockton and Darlington railway in 1825. Iron in quantity had solved that problem of the railway, which had entirely baffled Roman civilization.

In 1788 about half the pig iron produced in England was puddled. The steel was made almost wholly from imported iron, and employed only for cutlery, tools, and springs. The amount must have been relatively small. Nowhere in the world was steel used for anything but cutlery, tools, weapons and springs.

Cast iron, wrought iron, shear steel and cast steel were all available for human use in 1800. There were several grades in each. The quality depended upon the purity of the ore, whether the fuel was coke or charcoal, and upon the judgment of the workman. The purest ore was Swedish magnetite, but there were also inferior varieties of iron from Sweden. Some ores contain phosphorus, and iron containing this element is "cold-short," or brittle when cold. It was used for little but nail-making. Iron melted by coke was liable to contain sulphur. This caused "red-shortness," that is to say brittleness when red hot.

A sample of steel in those days was found to be suitable or unsuitable on trial. Even rough chemical analysis was hardly available as yet and quantitative chemistry had still to come. A sample was examined by breaking and noting the fracture. That is still used as a rough test to-day. But there were neither testing machines, nor quantitative methods of analysis, nor metallographical methods. No organized knowledge, in fact, but merely empiricism and experience.

Neilson's invention of the hot blast in 1829 introduced an economy in fuel and enabled the Scottish blackband ironstone to be smelted. The temperature of the blast was raised to 600°F. That was a great achievement for the time. To-day temperatures of about 1800°F. in the blast furnaces are not unusual. Wrought iron continued to be made by the laborious process of hand puddling for many years. In 1856–60 the Bessemer process of blowing air through molten pig iron to burn out impurities and then adding carbon and other ingredients to make steel came in, and for the first time steel became cheap and available in bulk. Castings of steel up to 25 tons became possible. The open hearth appeared in 1864, a gas-fired furnace in which pig iron and scrap iron are melted in an oxidizing atmosphere. Steel castings of over one hundred tons became possible, and the quantity of metal produced increased and increased. From one American open hearth two hundred tons of metal have been pouring every three or four hours since 1927. We have several hundreds of tons of steel to-day for every ton of iron or steel the world could produce in 1800.

Each advance in the size of iron and steel castings opened up new possibilities of handling and utilization. Lifting appliances for heavy weights, for example, could only exist when metal was available in huge castings. Otherwise you could not make a sufficiently big crane. In 1800 not more than a ton or so could be lifted. To-day 5-, 10-, and 20-ton cranes are common and castings of 50 or even 100 tons may have to be moved. Generally any casting of more than 100 tons is made in two or more parts to be bolted together. But a 50-ton mass can be handled with more ease to-day than a single ton lump in 1800.

In America 11 per cent of the steel produced is used in the form of pipes. The production of pipes was a very difficult process in 1800, and little if any iron pipe was made. There are two methods of pipe-making to-day: either a flat sheet is rolled and the edges are welded in a longitudinal joint, or the metal is rolled over a pier to form a cavity and a seamless tube is produced. Seamless iron pipes are also made by means of centrifugal casting. The high pressures now being tested in power stations (600 pounds to 1,200 pounds per square inch) would be impossible without seamless tube. So one thing leads to another, and impossibility after impossibility crumbles away before the advance in substance control.

The electric furnace came into use in 1890. It is largely employed in the manufacture of the alloy steels used in motor-car construction, and for the stainless steels. Since it asks for water power rather than coal, it has been extensively developed for tonnage steels in Italy, where there are 200 furnaces in operation. The high frequency electric crucible furnace has been introduced since 1927. With this, the highest classes of tool steel can be produced. It contrasts very vividly with the crucible furnaces it is replacing. Formerly you had men standing astride white-hot coke furnaces, enduring the most terrific temperatures as they lifted out the pots of steel by their sheer unaided strength. Now, at the pressing of a button, eight times the quantity of metal is poured out, in a fourth of the time.

The world output of pig iron in 1927 was 85,270,000 tons, and there had been an increase in every decade since 1800. The production of steel in the same year 1927 was 100,180,000 tons. This disproportion is due to the fact that large amounts of steel scrap and iron ore are used in steel making and that a considerable amount of steel contains elements other than iron and carbon. The figures are not comparable. Steel has largely replaced wrought iron for all constructional work and for parts of machinery where strength, resistance to shock, and durability are required. We may compare the 85,270,000 tons of pig iron with the annual output of 650,000 tons in 1800. It is 131 times as great. But the increase in the quantity of steel would be even more striking if the figures were available. To-day we have hundreds of tons of steel for every ton of either wrought iron or steel available in 1800.

And meanwhile steel, which was a distinctly mysterious iron product in 1800, has had its composition studied, analyzed and controlled.

In 1800 steel was just the substance of a knife blade or a sword. It was one substance, so far as was known. But now we have on our economic bill of fare not one steel but dozens. There are first the carbon steels. These contain iron and carbon with only traces of other elements: phosphorus, sulphur, silicon, manganese. All tonnage steel (steels made in large quantities) contain 0.3 per cent and upward of manganese. There are seven grades of carbon steel known as: extra soft, structural or mild, medium, medium hard, hard, spring, and carbon turning-tool quality. It is the first two grades which have so largely replaced wrought iron. The softest cannot be hardened. It can be case-hardened. (Case-hardening consists of heating the metal in contact with carbonaceous material whereby carbon is absorbed, giving a surface of harder steel.) It is workable either hot or cold, and is used for thin sheets, which are cold-rolled, rivets, which have to be beaten out, pipes which have to be bent, and smith's bar.

Structural steel is used for bridges, boilers, and railway rolling stock. Medium steel is used for shipbuilding and machinery. Medium hard for large forgings, parts of locomotives, car axles, rails. Hard steel for wheels, tires, wood-cutting tools, etc.

All these carbon steels can be forged and machined, but with increasing difficulty as the carbon content rises. From medium steel onwards the quality depends largely on the heat treatment to which they have been subjected. Hardness is increased at the expense of ductility, and is often accompanied by brittleness.

The following table from the Encyclopædia Britannica indicates the kind of variation:

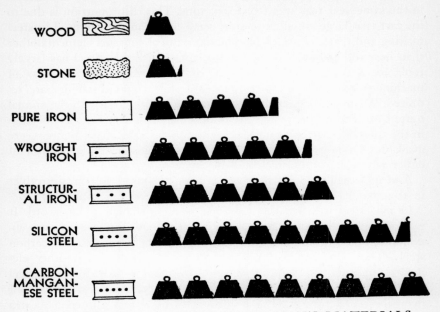

THE GROWING STRENGTH OF MAN'S MATERIALS

THE size of his structures, and the scope of his activities, have depended to a great extent on the materials which man has had at his command. Each weight in this chart represents a load of ten thousand pounds to the square inch. To develop from wood or stone, the earliest building material, with a useful strength of about ten thousand pounds per square inch, to the latest steels, which will carry ninety thousand pounds and more, has taken many hundreds of years. There are harder and stronger steels known than the carbon-manganese alloy shown above, but they have as a rule other qualities which make them undesirable for general structural uses. The figures for strength are from the United States Bureau of Standards.

Material	Ultimate strength
Rivet steel	50,000 lbs. per sq. in.
Medium hard	75,000 " " " "
Spring after quenching	200,000 " " " "
Spring steel	150,000 " " " "

These seven grades have a total extreme difference of carbon content of only 1.2 per cent (from 0.08 per cent to 1.2 per cent). They illustrate the extraordinary effect of minute quantities of this element on iron, and they show the remarkable accuracy with which metallurgical operations are now conducted. A hundred tons or more of metal may be poured into a mould and not differ from the required proportion of carbon by more than 0.1 per cent. Other elements, particularly manganese, nickel, chronium, tungsten, molybdenum, cobalt, and vanadium, when present in certain proportions, have a powerful influence on the qualities of steel. Manganese in quantities below 1.0 per cent strengthens and toughens iron. Very strong castings are made with 1 per cent to 2 per cent manganese.

Silicon steel, or to be more precise silico-tungsten steel, is used for long-span bridges, boilers and in shipbuilding. It has a strength greater by 10,000 pounds per square inch than other kinds used for boilers. Its ultimate strength is 120,000 pounds per square inch, and a test piece stretches 23 per cent before breaking. A 0.9 per cent carbon steel with 1.65 per cent manganese, undergoes very small distortion during heat treatment (hardening and tempering) and is used for dies and gauges. Hadfield's manganese steel has 11 per cent to 12 per cent manganese, and 1.0 per cent to 1.2 per cent carbon and was for long the toughest material known, though it has now given pride of place to the austenitic nickel chrome steels. It resists shock and wear, and is used for tramway points, dredger buckets, crusher jaws, and the like purposes.

A carbon steel tool has a relatively low limit of cutting speed. If the speed is too high it becomes hot, loses its temper and its edge. Higher speeds were found to be possible with the tungsten-manganese alloy invented by R. Mushet between 1860 and 1870. This was self-hardening by heating to a high temperature and cooling slowly. Similar steels containing tungsten and chromium were used in America. It was supposed that the temperature of hardening should not exceed 815°C. to 845°C. But Taylor and White (Bethlehem Steel Co., Pa., U. S. A.) after twenty-six years' research discovered in 1900 that if heated to 1040°C. to 1100°C. its hardness was greatly increased, and the tool would cut at a red heat without loss of edge. This was the first of a number of high-speed tool steels. No need to cool off; no need to slow down: they drive on. In some cases cobalt is added to these steels, and it will be news to many readers that there are now several high-speed tool "steels" which do not contain iron. Stellite, for example, has cobalt 55 per cent, tungsten 15 to 25 per cent, chromium 15 to 25 per cent, and molybdenum 5 per cent. More recent and more important now than stellite is tungsten carbide.

The practical consequence of man's conquest of these new materials may be gauged by the fact that, with a particular quality of steel in the lathe and the same depth of cut, a plain carbon steel cuts at 16 feet per minute, an air-hardening steel cuts at 26 feet per minute, or, after quenching, 60 feet per minute, and a modern high-speed steel 100 feet per minute or more. With softer material and lighter cuts a speed of 150 to 175 feet per minute is attained. Under favourable conditions tungsten carbide will remove the metal at over 300 feet a minute. The writer has seen it cutting cast iron at as high a rate as 400 feet a minute.

I will not dilate here upon nickel, chromium, and nickel-chromium steels. The effect of each element is to toughen steel and to enable hardness to be secured without brittleness. They are more effective in this when used together. Stainless steel has more than 10 per cent (often 13 per cent) of chromium. Nickel steels are used in bridge and structural work generally and for boilers. They are heat-treated for guns, engine forgings, and shafts. Chromium steels are used for projectiles, grinding rolls, and roller bearings, and with nickel or vanadium for armour plate, or, heat-treated, for axles, machine parts, and gearing.

At one time aëroplane and automobile were entirely dependent on tungsten steel, because it was the only steel possible for the permanent magnets in the magneto until chrome steel (for cheaper types) or cobalt steel became available. Tungsten can be produced in a ductile form and is then used for the filaments of electric lamps. It has entirely superseded the earlier carbon filament, and it made wireless telephony and broadcasting possible. The earlier forms of thermionic valve essential to a receiving set could not have existed without tungsten. . . .

But enough of such facts have been given for our present purpose. We must draw back before the serried facts overwhelm us. The little steel sword blade of our great-grandfathers has become the framework of bridge, railroad, ocean liner, skyscraper, and ten thousand other things. In a locomotive or motor car to-day you will find a score of different steels, all beautifully adapted to the work. I will not attempt to estimate the hundreds of thousands of patents, the scores of thousands of inventive minds, that have gone to the making of this one chapter in the multitudinous history of substances. I have left the tale abbreviated, cut down, and only half told, and side by side with it could be set a score of parallel tales.

An adequate Book of Substances alone would make a stupendous volume. You would never read it; you would only read in it. You would insist upon a comprehensive index and go to it ever and again for a fact. Here you have been given all and more than you need. One adviser has already remarked that some of the pages immediately preceding this read like "extracts from an article in the 'annual review' of a technical journal"—and how else could they read? And such a Book of Substances would give only the material basis of the spectacle of human activities, the material basis only of the life of work, wealth, and enjoyment we are setting ourselves to survey. It would be only an introduction to the more crowded books that would follow it. Happily our main argument is possible without the actual production of that interminable catalogue.

§ 9. *The Conquest of Power. Sources of Power*

And now we come to a group of facts so important to the modern world that, as I have told in the Introduction, I thought of calling this entire work by its name, the *Conquest of Power*. There is also a reverse title to that: the *Abolition of Toil*. Yet it is not merely that mechanical power has replaced toil over a vast proportion of the field of human effort. That is only a part of what has happened. There has been an enormous *addition,* an altogether disproportionate extension of the energy available for human ends.

We have distinguished in man's history a prehistoric, casual-living, sub-human stage; a stage in which social life and tradition appear and human life is retrospective and ruled by precedent and historical legend; and this present third stage in which we are living, with science and design rapidly ousting tradition from its domination over human life.

The age of tradition was also the age of toil. The traditional social life is and always has been pyramidal, with a mass of toiling workers as its base. This modern life that opens before us seems likely to have an entirely different structural scheme.

Toil, like tradition, is a distinctively human thing, made possible by the intricate reactions of the human cerebral cortex. Toil is sustained work done against the grain and giving no essential satisfaction in itself, done because the individual indisposition for it is overcome by some more powerful system of motives. A few of the more intelligent gregarious animals have also been made to toil by human compulsion, horses, oxen, and the like, but outside the list of these exceptions there seems to be no real toil in animal life. Most living creatures will not stand toil. They will resist to the death. The "workers" of the ants and bees are not toilers: they work by instinct; it is what their structure dictates and what they want to do. The scarabæus, rolling its dung balls, is no more toiling than the nightingale singing in a tree.

But human *"toil"* is not instinctive, not as people say a *"natural"* thing. Work may be a natural thing. Much human work, the work of a sincere artist, writer or inventor, for example—expressive work, as we call it—is not toil in the sense in which we are now using the word. It does not go against the grain. But the spectacle of human history shows us a long succession of generations in which a great majority of the community was *subdued to labour.* The muscular force of this labour class, doggedly applied, was the main source of power, the driving force of the social mechanism. The community could not have gone on without that subjugation.

In a brief century or so science and invention have rendered the bulk of this muscular exertion superfluous. It is no longer necessary that man should virtually enslave his fellow man; he has found new slaves, gigantic slaves, out of all proportion mightier than the human hands and muscles that hitherto have thrust and moulded obdurate matter to human ends.

A complete history of the Conquest of Power* would open with a brief review of the sources of power in the early civilizations. It is a meagre list of accessories. Except for the department of transport, wherein wind and stream and pack animal played important parts, for a certain limited use of wind wheels and water power as well as beast power for grinding and irrigation it was human muscle that kept things going. Even on the sea the galley was preferred to the sailing ship.

From this review of the ancestral equipment the record would pass on to the pryings and guessings of more ingenious spirits of the Middle Ages. At the time such enquiries must have seemed the oddest, obscurest, least important of activities.

The Quest of Power, by H. P. and M. W. Vowles (1931), gives the story from windmill and water wheel onward, very interestingly and in ampler detail than was desirable here.

Each machine was a curiosity because it was unique. It was designed for a particular purpose. This purpose loomed so large that it obscured the general principle. Whatever the motive power—wind, water, horses, or bullocks might be used—it was part of the machine. The first idea of a Prime Mover, capable of driving a variety of machines, appears in the work of Leonardo da Vinci.

The sixteenth and seventeenth centuries produced a number of pioneers whose work, like so much pioneer work, was more notable for its failures than for its successes. But as children say in the game of "hide and seek," they were getting hotter and hotter. Then, suddenly, like a new and splendid theme taking possession of a musical composition, deliberate invention and discovery break into human history.

That fuller story of the Conquest of Power we are imagining would note the early attempts to use steam, and it would "feature" James Watt very prominently at the opening of the new phase. It would trace the increasing efficiency of steam generating. It would give pictures and descriptions of the older and most modern types of steam engine. The steam turbine has opened a new modern chapter in the history of steam. From the turbine the Power Book in the *Science of Work and Wealth* would pass to a second type of power production, the internal combustion engine, in which the intervention of steam is dispensed with and the explosive combustion of a jet of gas or a spray of finely divided liquid is applied directly to give the thrust of the engine.

How rapid this development has been may be illustrated by a few facts. The "Otto" gas engine of 1876 was the result of 100 years of effort, largely fruitless, except for the temporary success of the Lenoir engine six years earlier. The fuel was town gas—far too expensive for large scale use. Dowson in 1878 exhibited a gas producer in which cheap coal slack was employed, and Sir Frederick Bramwell prophesied that within fifty years the gas engine would replace the steam engine as a source of power. He was wrong. He underestimated the world's capacity for power. He did not foresee the variety of purposes to which power would be applied. It was not clear at the time that steam engines of ten, twenty, and to-day of over fifty-thousand horsepower would be built.

At that time the oil engine had not appeared. Daimler invented his petrol engine in 1884, the year that saw the first steam turbine. Parsons' first patent for a reaction turbine was followed a year later by De Laval's patent for an impulse turbine. Priestman invented the first medium oil engine in 1885, and in 1892 Diesel patented the heavy oil engine with which his name is now inseparably connected. The first Diesel was built in 1895, but it took twenty years to work out the subsidiary problems of this type. These three stages in the evolution of the oil engine used successively cheaper forms of fuel, while the actual consumption of fuel in medium and heavy oil engines per brake horsepower has been reduced since 1890 by more than one half. In the last few years the oil engine has been ousting the steam engine in a hundred different fields. The heavy oil engine competes now with the steam engine in driving factories, in pumping, the production of electricity, in the propulsion of ships, and is even threatening the steam locomotive. How great the success has been for ship propulsion is indicated by the fact that in 1931 of the total world tonnage only 56 per cent consisted of ships fitted for burning coal, while 28.5 per cent consisted of ships fitted for burning oil and 13.5 per cent of motor-ships. Sailing ships accounted for only 2 per cent. In 1914 ships burning coal accounted for 88.8 per cent of the total tonnage, sailing ships for 8.1 per cent, ships burning oil for the very small proportion of 2.6 per cent and motor-boats for 0.5 per cent. The Italian motorship Augustus, built in 1927, is 32,650 tons burden.

The light oil engine made the motor car and the aëroplane possible. Since 1915 the weight per horsepower of an air-cooled engine has been reduced from 3 lbs. to 1½ lbs. The accuracy of workmanship and delicacy of adjustment of these high-speed engines are among the great mechanical triumphs of the age. They run at from 1,000 to 4,000 revolutions a minute. For the sake of simplicity suppose the speed is 1,200. Then there is a revolution every twentieth of a second. In half that time, in one-fortieth of a second, the engine makes a stroke. At each stroke the valves open and air and fuel are admitted, or the mixture is compressed, or it is exploded, or the valves open and the spent gases are swept out. The spark which fires the mixture must take place at exactly the right moment. It must be adjusted to an almost infinitesimal fraction of a second. The inlet valves open and close with marvellous precision. The exhaust valves act in turn, though they are at a bright red heat. High temperatures, high pressure and high speed are here brought into coöperation in a way which would have amazed the engineers of an earlier generation.

Let us explain here a few of the more important developments in the utilization of fuel.

The special advantage of a *gas* is that it can be intimately mixed with the proper amount of air for complete combustion. Only a slight excess is required. A *liquid* fuel possesses a similar advantage. The lighter oils are vaporized before burning, and the heavier varieties are broken up into a spray by a jet of compressed air. Liquid fuels have the special merit that they are easily stored and so can be transported economically over longer distances. The burning of a *solid* fuel is by comparison slow and irregular and from 120 to 150 per cent more air than is required for combustion has to pass through the furnace and flues. The use of mechanical stokers and continuous agitation of the fuel may facilitate the removal of ash and increase the rapidity and regularity, but they hardly affect the excess of air which lowers the furnace temperature.

The distillation of coal in retorts yields gas, ammoniacal liquor, tar, and coke. This process has been in use for the public supply of gas for over a century. A modification of the process in which the yield of gas and liquid products is of secondary importance is employed in the preparation of the hard, dense coke for metallurgical furnaces. Coke-oven gas is now used to supplement the gas-works product for public supply. But coal (usually breeze or slack) and coke can be converted wholly into gas (producer gas or water gas) by blowing air, or air and steam, through the hot material. Gas obtained by the distillation of raw coal contains mainly hydrogen (about 40 per cent), methane (21 to 28 per cent), and carbon monoxide (8 to 15 per cent). The new low temperature carbonization process gives percentages of 29, 49, and 8 respectively. From 5 to 8 per cent of nitrogen is present also. Producer gas is carbon monoxide, and water gas is carbon monoxide and hydrogen. Both these gases contain a large percentage of nitrogen, which serves merely to dilute the mixture.

Coal contains excess of carbon which can only be converted into combustible gas by burning in a regulated supply of air. It is this air which brings in the diluent nitrogen. Attempts have been made to convert coal, with the exception of the small percentage of ash, wholly or almost wholly into combustible liquids and gases, mainly in order to increase the supply of liquid fuel, but this work is still in the experimental stage. The competition of gas and petroleum has, however, led to another way of using coal—particularly the breeze or slack, which is too small for many industrial purposes. The material is ground into a fine powder, dried and fed into the furnace through a nozzle by the aid of compressed air. Combustion then takes place, as in the case of a gaseous or liquid fuel, and only 20 to 30 per cent excess of air is required. There were tentative experiments on this method forty years ago, but the main progress has been made in the last ten years. The annual consumption of pulverized fuels is now about 150 million tons. It is used for firing cement kilns, in metallurgical furnaces, and for steam-raising.

All these ways of using fuel aim at economy but do not necessarily involve a reduction in consumption. The tendency is for power spread ever more widely over the world to exploit new or old sources of raw material and to provide increased facilities for transportation and other public services. The capacity to employ power seems to be illimitable. And yet fuel, solid, liquid or gaseous, is not inexhaustible. Oil can never satisfy more than a fifth of the world's present dependence upon coal. And the coal "in sight" will last, at the present rate of consumption, for twenty generations or so. Twenty generations back in our own history takes us to the Hundred Years' War, the Black Death, the First Statute of Labourers, the Peasants' Revolt, and the First Navigation Act. The changes since then have been many and, in a sense, revolutionary. But the changes in the next period, especially as they affect human life and work, will appear more numerous and still more revolutionary to those who will look backwards as we do to-day, but over twice the length of time.

As it nears exhaustion, coal may become more valuable as a source of raw material for the chemical industry than as a means of obtaining mechanical power.

Here, were we aiming at encyclopædic completeness, would be the place for a survey of the automobile and aircraft engines of to-day. In that encyclopædic expansion there would have to be a great mass of information about modern engines and a vast multitude of figures and diagrams. Such details would be interesting to those with a special aptitude for these things; for most readers they would stand unread as reassuring and confirmatory matter, and they would add nothing to our general exposition.

But a point we have to note here is the extreme transitoriness of this phase in mechanical evolution, in which power is derived from the combustion of natural substances like coal and oil. The employment of steam was the means by which man broke through to the idea of power machinery; and it was only with great advances in metallurgical science that the explosive engine became possible. But these advances have now been made, and man turns again to the wind wheel and to water power, to the force of gravitating water, of which indeed since the very beginnings of his economic life he had made a dribbling little use, for water-lifting and the like, but which he could never use properly before our present phase of metallurgical attainment because of the inadequacy of his water wheels and his lack of transmission contrivances. Dr. Herbert Levenstein* speaks of the coal-power and oil-power age, "the age of fossil power," as a mere incident in the economic evolution of mankind. "It will have lasted, when it is over, for a shorter period than the Moorish occupation of Spain."

Now, with the electric current discovered and at his disposal, man has no difficulty in transferring the force of the windmill or water wheel to the most distant points of application, and the advance of metallurgy has converted the flapping wooden wheel of the old-world miller into a mighty interceptor of the rush and weight of stream and waterfall. The economic world turns back from fuel to this ancient and hitherto scarcely exploited resource of water power. So long as the world spins and the sun shines and the rain falls, there will be no end to the perpetual renewal of water power. It is the widow's cruse of economic life. So long as the wind blows, the wind wheel also will gather momentum. It is possible that in the near future the use of fuel will be confined to such freely moving mechanisms as ships, cars, and aëroplanes, or to the generation of power *in situ*. From the factory or from the fixed transport line, fuel-driven engines may disappear altogether.

The revival of water power is extraordinarily recent. It waited on the electric lamp, which came about 1880, and on the combination of engineering and electrical knowledge in electric generator design which was only achieved completely within the next decade. It was about 1890 that big hydro-electric power plants began to appear, and they were stimulated in some cases by the discovery of electrical processes of manufacture. Aluminium, carborundum, calcium carbide, graphite, and a host of other things were more economically produced, or could only be produced, by electrical energy. In Ontario and Quebec, where there is no coal, the hydro-electric plants are producing power that would require 30,000,000 tons of coal a year. What would the extent of the manufacture and the facilities for transport in that million square miles of country be like if they were dependent upon coal?

In India, also, where the coal supply is concentrated in one great series of deposits, hydro-electricity has probably a great future, although the difficulties caused by the seasonal nature of the rainfall will have to be overcome. Already at least 50 per cent of the cotton mills and other large industrial concerns of Bombay use electric power, which is pro-

*Address entitled "But an Apprentice in Nature's Workshop," Soc. of Chem. Indus., July 15, 1930.

vided by utilizing the heavy monsoon rainfall of the Western Ghats. A scheme is in operation in Kashmir, and another is projected in the Punjab by which forty-seven towns will be provided with light and power. In addition there is likely to be a considerable electrification of agriculture, as electricity can be used to work pumps that will either prevent the water-logging of irrigated land or raise water to the level required for irrigation purposes.

In Canada, water provides 600 horsepower per thousand of the population; in Switzerland, 500; in Norway, more than 700; in Sweden, more than 200; in the United States, more than 100. In Great Britain, the source of power remains the coal supply, and water power accounts for only a very small fraction of a horsepower per thousand people.

Here perhaps we may make a remark in anticipation of the chapter we shall devote to the housing of mankind. People have seen in the easy distribution of power a possibility of scattering population more evenly over the countryside. But in spite of the ease with which electricity can now be distributed over long distances, there is little sign at present that this is going on. Electrical power distribution is tending rather to form concentrations at new centres either near the source of power or where it is convenient for interrelated industries to use one another's products or by-products. The population map changes, of course, as the methods of utilizing power change, but so far no dissolution of the great town is occurring.

Are there still any undeveloped possibilities of extracting power from the movements of air or water? An exhaustive Power Book would summarize the present phase of the still unsolved problem of using tidal force. And further it would have to note and describe one or two odd and as yet impracticable contrivances for the direct capture of radiant solar energy. In the Kaiser Wilhelm Institute at Dalhem, Dr. Lange has run a small electric motor by sunlight, passing the light through a photo-electric cell. This little motor of Dr. Lange's may figure in the economic histories of the future as Hero's steam engine figures in those of to-day.

Many suggestions have been made for utilizing the internal heat of the earth by means of deep bore holes in the crust. In an indirect way this source is already being tapped. From steam which issues from the earth at Ladarello, in Tuscany, Prince Conti obtains over four thousand horsepower, and there is a similar scheme under development in California.

A high temperature is not necessary to produce power. A vapour engine, like the steam engine, requires water at a temperature which will produce vapour, and water at a lower temperature which will condense it. The difference between the energy of the vapour at higher temperature and its energy at the lower temperature, is the energy available for external work. Such a difference of temperature exists in nature between the warm surface waters of the ocean, especially in the tropics, and the cold water which flows along the ocean floor from the poles. After preliminary experiments in Belgium, Dr. Georges Claude is constructing a large-scale engine based upon this principle on the coast of Cuba. At Malanzas Bay bottom water can be pumped from the depth of a mile and a half through a 13-foot pipe and used to condense the steam given off in a low-pressure chamber by the hot surface water. There is a difference of 14°C. between the cold and hot water, and this, it is alleged, will suffice to run a practicable and paying plant. Here we may have another way of utilizing the heat of the sun on a larger scale than those devices of mirrors, lenses, and so forth, which attempt to employ the concentrated rays to produce a high temperature.

We mention these various notions here for the theoretical interest rather than for any immediate practical value they possess. They help one to grasp the idea of man's return from combustion as his source of power to the spin of the earth, the tides and currents of the seas, differences of velocity, pressure and temperature in the incessant stir of the world machine. All combustion sources are vanishing sources. In the end the rotating planet must become man's sole dynamo, the Prime Mover for all his mechanisms.

§ 10. *Transmission of Power*

Having got his power, man's next problem is the application of it to the task to be done. The power has to work this or that apparatus or drive an implement in contact with material undergoing manufacture; it has to be transmitted to the point where that is done. First our encyclopædia would discuss rope, chain and belt drives in the factory, with the problems of friction that arise, and then come to the use of compressed air and impelled water as power transmitters.

The transmission of power by toothed gearing is very ancient. The "teeth" were wooden pegs driven into the rim of a wheel. From the fifteenth century to the nineteenth actual cogwheels were made of cast iron, brass, or bronze. In the latter half of the nineteenth century they began to be made of steel. But in spite of the teeth being cut as nearly as machinery would allow to the exact geometrical shape, so that they would "roll" upon each other, there were still inequalities which produced noise.

One of the difficulties of applying the steam turbine to ship propulsion was the high speed of the turbine and the relatively low speed at which the screw propeller is efficient. The toothed gearing then available was far too noisy. The noise arose from errors in the machine in which the teeth were cut, and which were unavoidable. Sir Charles Parsons showed how to distribute these errors all round the wheel and succeeded in producing gearing which is very nearly silent, and in which less than 2 per cent of the power is wasted in friction.

Again belts and ropes passing over pulleys have been used for many centuries. They extend the range of transmission from a few feet to a few yards. The range is further extended to a mile or more by the use of high-pressure water. Though electric lifts are becoming more common, there are still many hydraulic lifts in docks, harbours, factories, warehouses and hotels and blocks of offices in large towns. How many people realize that the latter depend upon a public supply of water at high pressure laid under the streets like the ordinary water mains?

During the last twenty years some beautiful hydraulic transmission devices, using water or oil, have been invented. They are used to transmit power to machinery and to control the power transmitted according to requirements.

Compressed air has long been used, though it is not very economical since heat is evolved on compression. Nevertheless, air is found to be convenient for many purposes. The South African mines use nothing but compressed air.

During the war a Roumanian—M. Constantinesco—devised a method of transmitting power through water by waves. The water was contained in a long, closed, flexible pipe, and the waves produced by a series of taps on one end. These are reproduced with little loss of energy at the other. It was used first to "time" the discharge of a machine gun on an aëroplane so that the bullets would pass *between* the blades of the propeller. It has since been applied to rock drills.

The hydraulic and wave transmission devices, together with many forms of flexible coupling of the last twenty years, are ingenious additions to methods which sufficed for many centuries. They are novel in principle or design, and they indicate that neither mechanical ingenuity nor the application of scientific principles is exhausted in this field.

The next subject in order would be the electric generating station and electrical distribution. Our encyclopædia of reference would have to explain how the powerful rotation we have won from steam or water is made a source of electric current. It would expatiate upon the working of a dynamo and give pictures of dynamos and power stations. Then the description would proceed to spread out for us our living wires and cables, marching across country, burrowing underground, carrying power to farm and factory, home and road.

Electric energy was not produced on a very large scale until the late eighties of last century, nor was it transmitted very long distances. To-day, two or three hundred thousand horsepower is utilized more than two hundred miles from the source. The voltage, or pressure, at which the electricity is conveyed has risen in forty years from 10,000 to 220,-000 volts. For testing the equipment of such a line, apparatus yielding electricity at 1,000,000 volts is employed, and a flash of artificial lightning 17 feet long is produced by its discharge.

Wonderful it is to reflect that a hundred years ago the very idea of a power station distributing driving force to road, car and factory, lighting and heating cities, and so forth, would have been incredible, and that even the "power house" with its rackety steam engine, driving the machinery in a factory by band transmission, is not a hundred and fifty years old.

§ 11. *Points of Application*

Consider now the various points of application of this power we can distribute so widely. The domestic and agricultural ends it serves are very diverse. But for most industrial purposes the point of application is the tool. In our second chapter, § 7, we have described how the development of steel alloys has permitted a more and more rapid use of tools. We have noted already in our historical introduction, how improvement in one field waits on improvement in another. Here in the correlation of metallurgical exactitude and tool precision we have a modern instance. Our story of the machine tool is a history of ever increasing speed and precision.

In the eighteenth century the art of working in metals was in a very primitive state. The cylinders of some of the early engines were of wooden staves, held together with iron bands, like a barrel. Before Watt entered into partnership with Boulton, he complained bitterly of the lack of skill displayed by mechanics. Some of his cylinders differed from circular section by a quarter of an inch! The machines used for boring them were that much clumsy and inaccurate.

Maudslay, towards the end of the eighteenth century, improved the lathe. But the most important step towards precision was taken by Whitworth. He introduced standard screw threads and made a machine that would measure to a millionth of an inch. The test piece could not be touched with the finger if an accurate measurement was required. The warmth of the hand caused it to expand by an amount which was measurable by the machine. Sellers rendered similar service by standardizing screw threads in America.

The next stage towards accuracy was the introduction of gauges. Rule and callipers were not sufficiently delicate, so the work was tested by standard rings, plugs or notched pieces of metal. Then limit gauges came into use. It is easier to machine a piece of metal *between* two dimensions than to an exact dimension. So gauges were made in pairs, and the work was made larger than one and smaller than the other. Work is now accurate to within a thousandth or a two-thousandth of an inch.

Parts of machines made in this way are interchangeable. It was no longer necessary to make a single machine. Parts could be made in dozens, hundreds or thousands, and stored. Any set of parts, selected at random, could then be assembled, and they would fit as perfectly as if they had been made individually for the purpose. Mass production became possible. Sewing-machines, typewriters, cash registers, bicycles, and a host of things became plentiful and, with the advent of automatic and semi-automatic machinery, relatively cheap. The process was extended upwards to heavier machinery. To-day a motor car and a 250 horsepower Diesel engine are assembled in the same way as a cash register.

Before passing to the stores, the parts are inspected to ensure that they are within the prescribed limits. In some cases an optical test is used. The part is projected in profile upon an enlarged drawing on a screen, and any slight departure from accuracy is revealed. The drawing is usually made with double lines representing the limits allowed, and if the image falls between these lines it satisfies the conditions. This method was introduced recently in a works where gauges had been used for years and had acquired errors. Machines failed to work properly, the cause was discovered, and the projection method convinced men who were loth to believe that the fault lay in overconfidence in a traditional practice.

Automatic and semi-automatic machinery has been evolved by making it self-acting, first in respect of one motion, and then in respect of another. It has been built up slowly, one step at a time. For a human being to repeat these motions in exactly the same way required an almost superhuman capacity for taking pains. Few craftsmen possess the delicacy of touch, the patience, and the conscientiousness to produce the parts by the methods in use seventy or eighty years ago. But with artificial aid, accuracy is largely independent of individual human qualities. The machine makes the machine. Operation requires little effort, muscular or mental. It has become machine-minding, and women, girls, and boys have largely replaced men.

How wonderful it is to watch some of these machines at work! Some of them, fed with bar or strip steel at one end, turn out nuts, bolts, screws or washers by the thousand. A big machine is fed with little rods of wood at one end. These are next seen stuck in holes in a travelling belt which winds over pulleys. This belt moves so that the ends of the wooden rods are dipped in hot paraffin wax; then, after an interval for the wax to set, in a composition; and finally delivered as matches neatly packed in boxes. Another machine takes in tobacco and paper and delivers cigarettes, filled, rolled, wetted and sealed almost faster than the eye can follow. The Barber Knotter, used to join up a new set of warp threads to an old warp, will pick up the two threads and tie them together with astonishing accuracy and speed. If it fails once, it does not pass to another pair of threads, but makes a second attempt with the original pair, and with a second failure, a third attempt. After the fourth failure the machine stops, and the operative is called upon to adjust it.

Or take another exhibit. The world now consumes more than six hundred million electric lamps every year. The tube from which the bulbs are blown is drawn out continuously from a furnace which operates twenty-four hours a day. A single works may turn out ten thousand miles of tube a year. The machines not only draw the tube but cut it into lengths. Another machine receives the tube and converts it into a bulb ready for receiving the filament.

Automatic machines are not exactly an innovation, but their use received a great impetus during the war. Before those feverish years, the employment of such machines increased only slowly. They were employed for a few articles for which there was a large demand. Men are naturally conservative, and many manufacturers would have continued to follow traditional methods if they had not been forced by military necessity to adopt new ones. One result was relative cheapness of production. Another was the creation of a productive capacity far exceeding the demands of a world at peace and financially crippled.

Millions are unemployed now because a proportion can supply the present needs of mankind. To this issue we shall return later.* Here we will throw out a question or so that will reappear for adequate treatment in the later parts of this work. Is this gradual shrinkage of employment to continue, or can the work be spread over a larger number of hands by reducing the hours (or years) of labour, and providing work for all? How will that square with our present business methods? For some chapters these questions must remain floating questions, until we have opened up several new series of considerations that are essential before we can even suggest an answer.

*See Chapter VII, § 5, Chapter X, § 7 and Chapter XIV, § 1.

CHAPTER THE THIRD

The Conquest of Distance

§ 1. *The Increasing Range of Modern Life*

THE preceding chapters have been, as it were, preparatory to the essential material facts we have to consider. We are now in a position to set about our summary of man's activities, our actual world in its present phase of evolution from local and transitional to world-wide and measured and planned economics.

In the next three or four chapters it will be convenient to use that non-existent *Science of Work and Wealth* to which we have already made reference, as though it were a work actually at hand, even more frequently than we have done already. And also these museums yet to come must be invoked again and again. We go through these chapters in great danger of technological avalanches. Whenever the detail becomes too abundant and threatens to encumber the development of the general argument, or where material has been altogether unattainable, we will wave a hand towards phantom galleries or carry over by a reference to the encyclopædic contents of that imaginary work.

When some years ago I made the first rough notes for this work, I planned to begin with food. I thought we could open our survey with the present food supply of mankind and tell how man eats—and how he gets his food. That had an attractively fundamental air about it. One must eat to live. And the rest follows. But so soon as I came to the detailed planning of this part it became evident that we must first deal with the transport systems of the world. The world a century or so ago was living upon food that grew at its door. The modern eater in the great modernized communities stretches his hand halfway round the world for every other mouthful. This increase of range is a prior consideration to any treatment even of the eating, much more of the clothing or housing of mankind.

Extended range of action is indeed the key idea to almost all the great problems with which mankind is at present confronted. In the

Outline of History it is shown how this has acted as an expansive force politically and how the salvation of man from the ever more destructive and disorganizing activities of war is now only possible through the establishment of a World Pax. The revolution in transport has made all existing governments provisional. It has "abolished distance" and jumbled them up together. In this work we must extend these political conclusions to the whole of the economic life. It has become infinitely easier to-day for a New Yorker to trade with a man in Pekin than it was for him to trade with a man in Maryland a hundred years ago. It is necessary to say something of the processes by which things have come to this pass before we can study the developing consequences.

§ 2. *Railway and Steamship*

A full and exhaustive account of world transport would have to begin with a brief review of transport in the past and the progressive escape of mankind from geographical limitation. Here we can but glance back for a moment to our historical opening and say something about the more or less concurrent invention of wheel and road. The Hittites had roads. The great Persian roads that figure so importantly in classical history were but an extension of that more ancient system.

What seem to have been the primary civilizations had, however, little need of road or road transport, and in Mesopotamia and Egypt road systems remained undeveloped. These first states grew up upon the courses of great rivers, and the river was the connecting link that bound the village to the city and the cities into a state. Man learnt to navigate on these rivers before he put out to sea.

For a long time sea communications were too precarious for essential economic interchanges. There was overseas trade in ornaments and luxuries generally, in rare metals and substances and the like. Probably kidnapping and slave-trading played a large part in the early stages of overseas merchandising. The seaman could lapse very easily into piracy; the shore trader become a wrecker. And early navigation was a very marginal and subsidiary thing to the general economic processes of that time. The general life would have lost only a gleam of colour and a touch of variety if there had been no sea trade at all. There was one exception in the case of Rome during its period of maximum expansion, but otherwise overseas shipping was not a vital organ in economic processes.

Coming on from the older phases of human prosperity to the modern

THE CONQUEST OF SUBSTANCES
COAL unloader at the Berwind Coal Docks, Superior, Wisconsin.

THE CONQUEST OF SUBSTANCES

POLISHING sheet glass. Under this grinding and polishing machine the glass, in two trips under the wheels, one for each side, is given a smooth finish. In grinding, more than thirty different sorts of abrasives are used, from coarse sand to the most delicate rouge. The abrasives are arranged in a precise order and so proportioned that they give the highest polish obtainable.

renewal of progress it is interesting to note the development of the canal system in the opening phase of the new industrial age. It will serve to remind us of an important fact already noted in the *Outline of History*, that the industrial revolution preceded the mechanical and scientific one. They were two separate processes which became confluent. One had a precedent and the other was new. There had been an industrial revolution and a factory system (book-copying, e. g.) in Rome. And these eighteenth-century canals also were the revival of a very old idea which had been worked out in China ages before.

But a new intellectual activity was afoot. A certain William Smith, a surveyor engaged in canal-making in England, noticed the relations of strata and fossils in the earth in which he worked, and evoked stratigraphic geology as a by-product. He gave body and reality to the speculations of the scholars and philosophers. The traditional cosmogony, the literal authority of the Bible and much else, was drowned by accident in the waterways of the English Midlands. Research and innovation were thereby disencumbered from a very heavy obstruction.

The Marquis of Worcester's *Century of Inventions* (1663) was an early indication of the essentially practical stir that distinguished the intellectual revival of post-mediæval Europe from the phase of Hellenic vigour. That book described a vague, unrealized steam engine, the intimation of what was at hand.

The steam engine arose as a pumping engine, a clumsy mechanical Dinotherium. The first one in use was Savery's, in 1698. For a whole century the steam engine did little more than pump. It came out of the mines at last (1803) to meet with the old obvious idea of rails and give us the railway. A road steam carriage had already been made in France in 1769 by Cugnot. The steam railway had become possible because iron rails had become possible. But it was still extraordinarily clumsy by present-day standards, because the conquest of the necessary substances was only beginning. Stephenson's *Rocket* was made of "cast and wrought iron and a small amount of brass, while, as Sir Henry Fowler has pointed out, specifications for fifty-five separate metals are now required for a modern locomotive."* An encyclopædic *Science of Work and Wealth* with unlimited illustrations would have space to tell the subsequent history of the railway in full and "feature" its more vivid episodes. It would show by period maps how the railways, once they were begun, spread through the world like nerves in a developing embryo. Let us give, at any rate, a few salient facts from this mechanical

*Sir Richard Gregory in a lecture on "Science and Labour."

drama and leave such filling in as the reader who is specially interested in this field needs, to his further reading.

September, 1930, witnessed the centenary of the opening of the first railway, in the modern sense of a public steam railway, between Liverpool and Manchester. There had been tentative railways or tramways with steam locomotives in colliery districts and on the northeast coast nearly twenty years before this event. But though George Stephenson was an ardent advocate of steam traction, the use of that method on the first railway was decided only at the last moment, after competitive trials. The result was so convincing that a number of lines were constructed during the next few years. At first it seems to have been the capacity, and the speed over short distances, rather than the increased range that attracted attention. The new lines were short. They had a strictly local value, and some of the large systems—the Midland more especially—were created by the amalgamation of small and relatively local concerns.

Passenger traffic, also, was underestimated. The advantage of carrying heavy stuff in big loads loomed so large in men's minds that no one seems to have realized the importance the new methods of transport would assume for travel and journeying. And so, too, no one visualized the social and political influence of the new means of communication. These unforeseen consequences as they were revealed stimulated the expansion of railways enormously, and railway development became a mania in the thirties. In 1825 Great Britain had only 26 miles of line; in 1850 there were more than 6,600 miles; in 1870, more than 15,000 miles; in 1890, more than 20,000, and to-day, 24,000. France and the United States began to experiment with steam locomotives in the year that the Liverpool and Manchester railway was opened. Germany and Belgium were five years later.

From these beginnings the railway spread rapidly over the world. Content at first to join up neighbouring centres, engineers soon began to visualize lines which would cross continents and bring distant peoples into direct and easy communication. The first transcontinental line spanned the United States in 1869, rising 7,000 feet above sea level in the Sierras, crossing 700 miles of desert and hundreds of miles of country inhabited by tribes of hostile red men. The last spike of the Canadian Pacific was driven in November 7, 1885. By the end of the century the Trans-Siberian Railway was in operation, and the duration of a journey round the world had been reduced to thirty-three days. The Australian can now travel by train from Perth to Adelaide, and

Africa is the only continent still incompletely spanned by the iron road.

By 1924 there were nearly 238,000 miles of line in Europe, 316,000 miles in North America, 55,000 miles in South America, 81,000 miles in Asia, 37,000 miles in Africa and 30,000 in Australasia. North America and Australasia now have more than 22 miles for every 10,000 of the population, Europe 528 miles and Asia only 0.8 miles. The ratio of mileage to population is naturally highest in a large country with a thinly scattered population. In Africa it is low because there are so few lines. Gold, diamonds and wild forest products make small demands upon transport. Cultivation of the soil and manufactures are necessary for abundant railway expansion.

The story of these engineering achievements, of the knowledge and skill which have been employed, of the hardships and dangers from rigours of climate and pestilence which have been incurred, would fill many volumes. The way has been blasted along the face of vertical cliffs and through the hearts of mountains. Stephenson had to pump water out of the Kilsby tunnel on the London Birmingham line for eight months. The first of the great Alpine tunnels, under Mont Cenis, seven and a half miles long, occupied fifteen years in construction. The St. Gothard Tunnel, twelve and a half miles long, took ten years. The temperature at the working face arose to 100° F., and water entered at the rate of 3,000 gallons an hour. The Simplon, of the same length, but begun a quarter of a century later, required only eight years—the result of improved appliances. The Gravehals tunnel on the Bergen-Oslo Railway is only three miles long, but involved thirteen years of labour. Steep gradients on the Jungfrau Railway and on the Canadian Pacific between Hector and Field have been overcome by spiral tunnels inside the mountain.

Rivers have been crossed by tunnels and bridges. The boring of the Severn Tunnel occupied thirteen years. Four times water flooded the workings and brought progress to a standstill. In some subaqueous tunnels the excavation has been only a few feet below the bed of the river. The men have a "shield" behind them and the water is kept back by compressed air. In 1880, when the Hudson River Tunnel was under construction, the air blew out through the river bed, water rushed in, and twenty men lost their lives. A "shield" is used in driving through soft ground whether water is present or not. And so accurately are the surveys made that the deviation from the true direction is trivial. In the 12½ miles of the Simplon Tunnel the error in direction was 8½ inches, and in level only 3½ inches. The Hampstead tube had an error in direction of ¼ inch and in level of ⅛ inch. The amazing "truth" of the base of the Great Pyramid, the sides of which, over 750 feet in length, have only a mean error of 3/5 of an inch from those of a perfect square, has long been a marvel to posterity. But this is better.

The railway evoked the great bridge. Before 1850 the longest iron span was that over the Wear at Sunderland—234 feet. The Britannia Tubular Bridge over the Menai Strait (1846–50) has two spans of 460 feet. The Brooklyn Suspension Bridge (1870–83) has a span of 1,596 feet, and the Williamsburg Bridge (1895), a mile away from the Brooklyn, a span of 1,600 feet. That towering mass of steel, the Forth Bridge, was opened in 1890. It has two spans of 1,710 feet, and for twenty-seven years this was the greatest distance which engineers had attempted to cross in one leap. But in 1917 the Quebec Bridge, which crosses the St. Lawrence in one span of 1,800 feet, was opened for traffic, after a disastrous failure ten years earlier. The present stage in bridge-building is illustrated by the magnificent arch across Sydney Harbour, and the still more magnificent structure spanning the Hudson River.

Throughout the growth of this network—more than three quarters of a million miles in a century—steam traction retained its supremacy and is only now being seriously challenged by electricity and the Diesel engine. In the little *Rocket* were embodied all the principles of the modern locomotive, though not its size and form. It had coupled driving wheels, a tubular boiler, and the exhaust steam was discharged up the chimney to increase the draught.

As the volume of traffic increased, locomotives have become larger and more powerful. Size in Great Britain is limited by the distance apart of the rails and the height of tunnels and bridges. The pioneers who determined these conditions did not imagine the future boldly enough. Brunel alone, whose mind ran to big things (he was the designer of the *Great Eastern*), adopted a 7-foot gauge for the Great Western Railway, but Stephenson's curious choice of 4 feet 8½ inches had secured too strong a hold for this to become general.

Though the locomotive, on this account, could not be made much larger, it could be made more efficient. Various improvements were made in the valve gear which controls the admission of steam to the cylinders. Then the boiler, and especially the firebox, was improved. Compounding, by which the steam was expanded successively through the cylinders, was introduced, chiefly in countries where the cost of coal justified the additional expense of construction and maintenance. With the higher pressures rendered possible by boiler plate of higher quality, compounding became more common. Then the steam was superheated on its passage from the boiler and more power obtained from the same quantity of fuel. The increased pressures now being used for stationary engines (there is a power plant in America using steam at 1,200 pounds the square inch) are spreading to the locomotive. Until 1895 the pressure did not exceed 160 pounds on the square inch. Then 200 pounds was tried. While a common pressure to-day is 250 pounds per square inch, there are several using steam at 350 to 400 pounds. Experimental engines using steam at 850 to 900 pounds are under trial, and at the time of writing one is under construction which will use steam at 1,700 pounds—more than three quarters of a ton on every square inch of internal surface.

These improvements have been made possible by metallurgical advance, and they have been stimulated during the last twenty years by the increasing cost of fuel, the competition of electricity and the influence of the Diesel engine. Steam-turbine locomotives and Diesel locomotives are already the subject of experiment. Apart from main principles, the modern steam locomotive is an amazing contrast, not only in size but also in performance and complexity, to the simple little engine that satisfied the Manchester to Liverpool trials, 100 years ago.

The development of railways depended upon their capacity and speed as compared with other forms of transport, and speed with safety depended not merely on power, but also on effective control of train movements. Traffic was at first regulated by "policemen" with flags and lamps, and later by the familiar semaphore. When these signals were worked mechanically they were "interlocked" so that a wrong signal could not be given.

The invention of telegraphy by Wheatstone and Morse permitted the movement of trains to be flashed almost instantaneously along the line, and enabled the approach of a train to be anticipated with a far greater margin of time. This stage was reached in 1850.

The range of signalling was again increased when signals were operated by compressed air or by electricity or the two in combination, and to-day the elimination of human error is being achieved by the use of automatic methods by which the train gives its own signal of approach, or picks up the signal and stops of its own accord. Eleven thousand miles of road and 8,500 locomotives in the United States were provided with automatic train control apparatus by 1928.

Meanwhile the amenities of railway travelling have been enormously improved. The open trucks for third-class passengers had a very brief existence. Seats have been upholstered, carriages warmed, and facilities for eating and sleeping provided. In spite of isolated instances to the contrary, the punctuality of trains is extraordinary. The cheapness and range of railway travel have enormously enriched life for millions who, in an earlier age, would have been doomed to a narrow and monotonous existence.

On the other hand, railway transport is inelastic in many respects. The units are large, the demand cannot always be foreseen, and the fixed track limits the area from which passengers can be drawn. For this reason road transport has become a serious competitor, and it is perhaps unfortunate that the motor bus developed so much later than the steam locomotive. Instead of coöperating in the provision of a close network of economical and efficient transportation, the railways may buy up the bus services as they did the canals, solely for the sake of maintaining the returns upon lines which are, or threaten to become, unremunerative.

But it is in goods traffic that railways stand in greatest need of improvement. There is, perhaps, no more uneconomical appliance than a railway truck. It has been estimated that one per cent of a truck's life is spent in running full, three per cent in running empty, and ninety-six per cent in standing in sidings. Before the war British railways were laying down sidings at a far greater rate than running tracks. They were becoming warehousemen—of empty trucks. On the Continent and in America nearly all wagons belong to the railways. In Great Britain about half of the 1,280,000 belong to private owners. Railway company trucks stand empty, heavy capital expenditure is involved in sidings, and time is lost in sorting out trucks when required. In common with many other aspects of industrial activity, transportation has grown upon altogether too narrow lines. It has neither been planned with vision nor administered with enterprise. It is burdened and cramped by tradition and routine, and each form of enterprise tends to treat an alternative form, not as a collaborator to be encouraged, but as a competitor to be crushed.

Why, people are asking, should the railways be cluttered up with coal trucks for the home trade in districts where canals are lying idle? Why invest capital twice for the same purpose? The annual fuel requirements of any particular area can be forecast with tolerable accuracy. Coal could be stored. A steady stream of barges would convey the requisite quantity to many districts, and enable a seasonal demand to be met by uniform production at the coal face.

Transport by canal, railway and road has developed independently, and it needs now to be organized as a whole, as coördinated and co-operating rather than as competing units. And road or cross-country motor transport needs to be used to provide existing networks with a finer mesh, and to extend the systems into areas, rich in natural resources, which have not yet been able to bear the capital cost of a permanent way.

The first electric railway was exhibited by Siemens at Berlin in 1879. But electric generators and motors were then in their infancy. Ten years were to elapse before big machines were available, and another ten before many of the details of transmission were worked out. The Liverpool Overhead Railway and the City and South London Railway were opened about 1890. Then several short lines were converted from steam to electricity. Meanwhile the New York, New Haven & Hartford and other American electric lines were opened, and electrical working adopted for the tunnel sections of the Swiss railways.

The advantages of electricity were more obvious, and the difficulties of introduction and operation less in the case of short suburban and interurban lines with a heavy passenger traffic. By distributing motors along the train, the grip on the rails was increased. Electricity secures quicker acceleration than steam, and less time is lost in increasing or decreasing speed when leaving or approaching a station. It had obvious advantages, too, on underground lines and in long tunnels which are difficult to ventilate. As the power from a large central station is more flexible than that of a steam locomotive, there were also advantages in the use of electricity on main lines with steep gradients. And so the new method of traction has gradually invaded the domain of the steam engine.

That, however, could not be done in a day. It required cheap power such as can be obtained most economically from falling water. Hydro-electric development was a powerful stimulus. Then there was an enormous field to be explored. The most economical pressure for the transmission of electrical energy; whether it should be direct or alternating current, and, in the latter case, whether it should be single-phase or three-phase; the most satisfactory method of communicating energy to the train; the best type of motor: these were only a few of the questions which had to be investigated. Each one of them carried a mass of detail in the design of auxiliary devices. Throughout the nineties and beyond, the patent offices were busy in registering new ideas.

The most wonderful achievement during the last ten years is the equipment of automatic sub-stations. The line is divided into sections of a dozen miles or more in length, and each section is supplied independently with energy from the central power station through a sub-station. The sub-station contains machinery or apparatus for transforming the high-tension current into one of low enough tension to be communicated to, and used with safety on, the train. The overhead lines are liable to have produced in them surges of electrical energy from lightning flashes; the sub-station machinery may be overloaded by too many trains on the section, and a number of irregularities may occur which formerly required an operator to observe them and make the necessary adjustments. This is now unnecessary. The sub-station can be, and often is, entirely automatic. When an irregularity occurs the machines correct themselves or stop. And the man in charge of the control station can see, by glancing at coloured lamps on a board, whether each control device is doing the work for which it was designed.

As yet we are only on the threshold of this phase of transportation. Omitting urban and interurban lines, there are only 6,500 miles of electrified track out of 563,000 miles. The United States has less than 1,500 miles out of more than 236,000 miles of line. Great Britain has 400 miles out of 20,000. Italy has made use of her immense hydro-electric resources in the streams which flow down the southern slopes of the Alps. She has 670 miles of electric railway out of 12,500 miles. But the greatest development has been in Switzerland. The figures—595 miles out of 1,852—hardly reveal the truth. No less than 67 per cent of the track is electrified and 85 per cent of the trailing-ton miles is accomplished by electrical power. Man has been observing, experimenting, discovering, for scores of generations. Within the last three he has achieved the railway, and within the last one the electric train.

We turn now to the modernization of shipping and the struggle of the sailing ship against extinction. The story of shipping is a continuing story of growth in size, power, and speed. We will not dwell here upon the safety and comfort of modern ocean travel, and we can speak only in general terms of the main economic and political effects of ocean transport. As the *Outline of History* insists, the second British Empire, that is to say, the present British Empire which arose after the separation of the United States, is essentially a steamship empire. It came with the steamship, and with the appearance of air transport and the diminishing importance of the steamship in world communication it is bound to undergo great changes either of adaptation or dissolution.

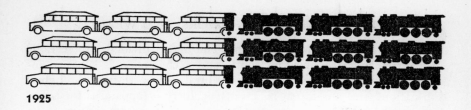

1925

1929

THE ROAD DEFEATS THE RAIL

THE changes in transportation habits that new modes of locomotion have produced.

Each bus represents one hundred million passengers carried in the United States by busses during the year.

Each locomotive represents one hundred million passengers carried in the United States by railways during the same period.

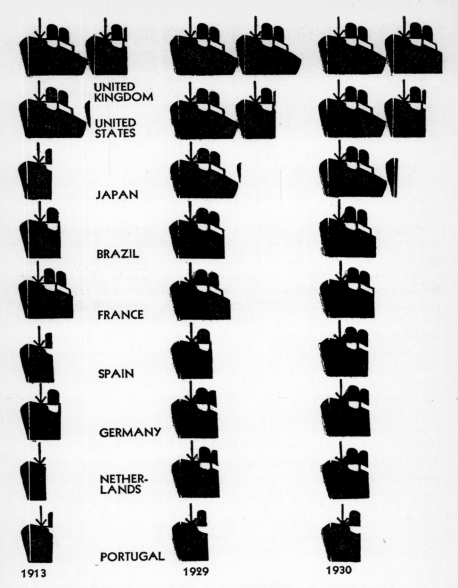

UNITED
KINGDOM

UNITED
STATES

JAPAN

BRAZIL

FRANCE

SPAIN

GERMANY

NETHER-
LANDS

PORTUGAL

1913   1929   1930

THE WORLD'S WATER-BORNE COMMERCE

Here, for the year before the war, and for the two most recent years for which figures are available, is a graphic delineation of the world's water-borne commerce as indicated by shipping entries for the principal maritime countries. Each ship represents fifty million registered tons entered. Domestic shipping is not included.

The steamship phase has so far lasted little more than a century. In 1777 a Frenchman bought one of Watt's engines and used it to propel a boat along the river at Lyons. Symington exhibited a steamboat on Dalswinton Loch in 1788. The *Charlotte Dundas* clove the waters of the Clyde in 1802. Fulton's *Clermont* navigated the Hudson in 1807. By 1823 more than 300 steamboats had been built in America for use on rivers and lakes, while in Great Britain steamers came into use in a tentative way for coasting and cross-channel trade. The first vessel using steam crossed the Atlantic from America in 1818. But in this and later ships steam was used only as an auxiliary to sails. Steam, as the chief agent of propulsion, dates from 1838.

While all steamships have increased from these beginnings in size, power and speed, those built for the Atlantic passenger service have undergone the most uniform and extensive development. The Cunarders of 1840 were 207 feet long, with engines of 740 horsepower. From this length and power they increased slowly to 500 feet, and 5,300 horsepower in 1880. In the same interval the average speed increased from 8.5 to 15.5 knots. The greater length and speed were facilitated by the use of steel in construction. Composite ships, with wooden frames and iron plating, were built from 1840, but it was the invention of Bessemer steel (1856–60) which led to the great increase in size. Brunel anticipated events by building the *Great Eastern* of iron, 680 feet long, in 1859; but she never fulfilled expectations, and it was forty years before another ship of her size was attempted.

In the opening of the twentieth century, came a vigorous competition between the German, British and American ship builders for the trans-Atlantic trade, and great floating palaces of 700, 800 and 900 feet appeared. Ships are now on the stocks which will be 1,000 feet—333 yards —in length. The *Leviathan* (U. S. A.) weighs just upon 60,000 tons and is 907 feet long; the *Majestic* (British) is equally huge and is eight feet longer. The *Bremen* (German) is just under 900 feet, but she is narrower and about 8,000 tons lighter.

The earlier vessels were driven by paddles, which take up a great deal of space amidships and are in the way when entering and leaving dock. The screw propeller was patented in 1836 and first used in 1839. The first large vessel to be provided with this means of propulsion was the *Great Britain,* designed by Brunel. She was 320 feet long and was launched in 1844. But the paddle was not displaced for large steamers until the sixties, and it is still used for boats which ply on rivers and lakes. Paddle vessels of nearly 8,000 tons are used on the Great Lakes to-day. Twin screws were tried from 1862, but only obtained popularity on the fastest boats. The maximum growth, however, in size and speed, could only be attained by the use of three and four screws.

Meanwhile, an ever increasing economy was sought in the engine room. The compound engine was introduced in 1854, the triple-expansion engine in 1873, and the quadruple-expansion engine in the last decade of the century. Further economy was secured by the steam turbine first tried for ship propulsion in 1894. The first merchant ship was provided with turbines in 1901. There were, at first, many difficulties and disappointments. There were difficulties arising from construction which were overcome by improved materials and design. The high speed of the turbine and the low speed at which a screw propeller, working in water, is efficient, were conciliated by improved gearing. Alternatives to toothed wheels which have been tried are the Foettinger hydraulic and the electric systems. In the former the turbine drives a centrifugal pump, which forces water through a water turbine on the propeller shaft. In the latter the turbine drives electric generators, and the propeller shaft is driven by an electric motor.

Again, in contrast to the steam turbine, operating with or without a reciprocating engine, and acting through gearing, water power or electricity, is the Diesel engine. Until after the war the Diesel engine had only been tried on cargo boats of relatively low tonnage. But it has been applied far more widely than steam for cargo vessels, and has invaded the field of the turbine on passenger ships. The *Britannic* has Diesel engines of 20,000 horsepower, and an Italian vessel, similar engines of 27,000 horsepower. During 1930 the net increase in the world's steam tonnage was 148,176, and of motor tonnage 1,468,235—an amazing development in less than fifteen years. The advantages are simplicity, compared with the turbine and its auxiliaries; smaller storage space for oil than for coal, and fewer men required to run the machinery. So far as shipping is concerned, an oil age has already begun.

About 70,000,000 tons of shipping are available for the world's needs. They have enabled human beings of different races and tongues to meet and mingle. Raw materials have been carried nearly round the world and exchanged for other raw materials and goods. But until fifty years ago most articles of food were perishable. Apart from a somewhat limited trade in live cattle, meat, fish, fruit and vegetables had to be consumed within a few hundred miles of their source. Only salted food could be kept for any length of time. The preservation of food by cooling it below the temperature at which the bacteria of putrefaction were active began in the middle of last century. The first cargo of beef was sent from America to England in 1877; the first cargo of mutton came from Australia in 1880. Scientific investigation has fixed the most suitable temperature for preserving every article of food for which there is a distant market. Many foods have ceased within the last thirty years to be "seasonable." The world dines at one table, and the fare is vastly richer and more varied than it ever was before. Could anything illustrate more simply or more forcibly the difference created by the railway and the steamship? Mining and manufacture lead to great concentrations of population which far exceed the food-producing capacity of the immediate neighbourhood. Yet they labour for the rest of the world, and the rest of the world supplies them in greater abundance and variety than they could produce directly for themselves. But this is anticipating our next chapter.

We may glance here at the question of freight charges, and particularly at the ideas of David Lubin and the more experienced work of Sir Arthur Salter. Lubin dealt with the question of freights before the war; he wanted to fix them instead of leaving them to a complex process of haggling; he wanted an international transport at fixed rates on the model of international postage. His suggestions are full of mental invigoration.

Salter's work, *Allied Shipping Control,* arose out of his experiences with transport problems during the war. Enormous economies were effected by putting all the allied shipping under a common direction. At one time American wheat was going to Italy, while Indian wheat was passing it *en route* for England. The wartime pooling of shipping put a stop to such absurdities—"for the duration." The American wheat was turned aside to London, and the Indian to Italy, and thousands of miles of transport were economized. "For the duration." Thereafter everything was allowed to lapse back into the hands of the private profit-seekers.

A complete survey of transport by rail and sea would give typical pictures and descriptions of modern docks and trans-shipment methods. It would involve a great history and description of harbours. At first these were the natural mouths of rivers or sheltered bays, with staging of timber or stone to facilitate loading and unloading; then, in the order of elaboration, a bay sheltered from the waves by an artificial embankment or sea wall. The sides of the river or the shores of the bay would next be excavated to provide a number of huge tanks, separated or confined by massive concrete walls. On these walls appear cart tracks and then railway sidings, and at length miles of railway, bigger and bigger open sheds, tall warehouses, machinery for pumping and for loading vessels with astonishing speed and economy of human effort, great chutes for loading a ship with ore or corn carried in bulk. (On the Great Lakes 12,508 tons of ore have been loaded in 16½ minutes, and unloaded in 3 hours and 5 minutes.) Corn is poured into a ship down a chute and sucked out of it through great tubes from which the air is continuously withdrawn by a fan—waterfalls of grain, and reversed waterfalls with the grain pouring upward.

Provision has to be made not merely for cargo but for the repair of ships. Where it is not considered desirable on the ground of expense or urgency to construct a permanent dry dock, a floating dock is used. There is one at Southampton, and another at Singapore, either of which will accommodate the largest ships. A floating dock is like an immense box, open at the top and ends. Or it may be likened to a steel trough. The sides and bottom are hollow and are divided into compartments into which water may be admitted or from which it may be pumped. The dock is sunk by admitting water, the vessel is moored over it, the water pumped out, and as the dock rises the vessel is lifted out of the water. The Southampton dock is 860 feet long and will lift 60,000 tons; that at Singapore has a lifting capacity of 50,000 tons. They are floating factories, portable shipyards, equipped with workshops and machinery to enable any kind of repairs to be carried out. That at Singapore was towed all the way from the Tyne. There or elsewhere you could, if necessary, build a ship.

Another great item in the spectacle of modern transport is the development of ship canals and particularly the development of Suez, Panama, the Manchester Ship Canal, the St. Lawrence chain and the Kiel Canal. To the present generation all these great waterways are accepted with little emotion or understanding; to our parents and grandparents they were objects of awe and admiration. Conceived in earlier times merely as substitutes for roads or rivers, canals in the latter half of the nineteenth century became also links in oceanic communication and terminal extensions which enabled oceanic transport to penetrate deeply into land areas. A few canals by-pass tempestuous or dangerously crowded seas. To the first class belong Suez and Panama; to the second the Manchester Ship Canal and the St. Lawrence chain, the Amsterdam Canal, and the New Orleans Industrial Canal; instances of the third type are the Corinth and Cape Cod canals. In a number of cases the canal route is not only safer but shorter.

The Suez Canal, opened in 1869, occupied ten years in its construction. It was merely the last of many efforts, none completely successful or permanent, to connect the Red Sea with the Mediterranean. The history and legend of these efforts cover more than three thousand years. Before work upon the existing canal was commenced the proposal was debated for more than half a century. It was accomplished by the labour of a quarter of a million men and the expenditure of twenty million pounds. Half as much again has been expended in widening, deepening and otherwise improving it. In 1870 only 451 ships made the passage. By 1927 the number of ships had increased to 5,545, and the tonnage was 28,962,048. How would trade have developed in the Mediterranean and the Far East, and what would have been the political history of Europe had it never been undertaken?

The history of the Panama Canal would afford material for a modern epic. The earlier years were grim with tragedy. De Lesseps, elated with his conquest of the sands of Suez, utterly underestimated the magnitude and difficulty of the task in Central America. In spite of heroic efforts, he failed. Between 1879 and 1887, no less than £66,000,000 was sunk in the enterprise, and 16,000 men died from disease. The United States government took over responsibility in 1904. By 1914 the work was completed at a total cost of £75,000,000. Two factors contributed to the American success. One was modern medical and sanitary service—particularly the steps taken to prevent mosquito-borne disease; the other, military discipline. There was a tendency among the civilian engineers at first employed to quarrel with one another or to leave for more remunerative posts. To secure loyalty and continuity President Roosevelt replaced them by military officers. Military officers could neither disobey orders nor seek other employment. In 1927, 5,475 ships with a tonnage of more than 27,000,000 used the passage. There is thus a peculiar symmetry in the flow of traffic through the Suez and Panama canals, the easterly and westerly exits from the North Atlantic system.

The Manchester Ship Canal has enabled that city, situated 45 miles from the sea, to become the third port in Great Britain. A similar but far deeper penetration is affected by the chain of canals along the St. Lawrence, and the Welland Canal between Lake Erie and Lake Ontario, still under construction. A small ship can now be loaded at Manchester and discharge its cargo at Chicago. A limit to the size of vessel is imposed at present by the St. Lawrence canals which permit only a 14-foot draught. It is proposed to deepen the channels throughout the whole length, and the next generation may see the largest cargo vessels moving athwart the south Lancashire landscape and so out to sea, and ending their journey by passing through cultivated fields for hundreds of miles to a port a thousand miles from the ocean.

The traffic on these inland waterways is amazing. The Sault Sainte Marie, between Lake Superior and Lake Huron, carries more than 85,000,000 tons a year—more than Suez and Panama together.

On these narrow ribbons of water traffic is concentrated. Dispersed on the wide oceans is a mass, stupendous by comparison, whose total bulk defies the imagination. Millions of horsepower and hundreds of thousands of men are moving thousands of millions of tons from those who have to those who need, with ever increasing speed and no regard for distance. No central mind directs this world circulation; and yet a routine is perceptible which suggests conscious coöperation and a purpose clearly seen, an order, as it were, crystallizing out of chaos. Can the inorganic world with its atoms and molecules, its crystalloids and colloids, show anything more wonderful or inexplicable than human transport at its present stage of development?

There is another aspect of the development of great ships and controlled shipping and water transport at which we can glance here only for a moment. That is the elimination of human suffering that has gone on at the same time. We do not mean simply the heroic sufferings of shipwreck and famine and natural disaster; those we can in a sense tolerate. But it is certain that in the past the small sailing ship far from land, remote from the influence of women and children and all social restraints, was all too often a pit not simply of deprivation but of cruelty. The galley slave was a slave, but throughout the eighteenth and early nineteenth centuries the sailors, often beguiled aboard, were among the poorest and most evilly entreated of labourers. Almost inadvertently science and invention have lit and cleansed those miserable caskets of oppression beneath the tall masts and the bellying sails of the old order of things at sea.

§ 3. The New Road and the Airway

A new chapter of the history of communications is opened when we consider the modern revival of the road. The macadamized road was the high-water mark of roadmaking in the pre-railway era. With the coming of the automobile a new phase in the history of roads opened, roads of a harder, firmer type appeared, more or less freed from the filth of horses and the disintegrative beating of their hoofs. The internal combustion engine, rubber tires and new road surfaces have interacted in the evolution of our modern road traffic, a multitude of illuminating problems of traffic control and of road- and town-planning have arisen and are arising out of this evolution. But of town-planning we will write later. A full encyclopædia of *Work and Wealth* would have to expand copiously upon such problems as the possibility of a closer coöperation of road and railway through the transfer of large package units from chassis to truck.

And then we turn our attention to the air. The very recent but very complex story of the achievement of mechanical flight has still to be written. At present the organization of air services in a practicable form is enormously hampered by the jealousies and frontier impediments of the seventy-odd petty sovereign divisions with which our developing world is still entangled. *The Science of Work and Wealth* would have, of course, a full and fully illustrated review of the latest development of aircraft and it could weigh the merits of the airship against the aëroplane. Here, we must say to the reader, is a way of going wherever you like about the world, very swiftly and agreeably, so soon as you are sufficiently tired of the traditions of nationalist and imperial conflict, to turn to these new powers and conveniences.

The internal combusion engine lies at the root of both these developments, the automobile and aviation. They came in a necessary sequence. The automobile was the inevitable predecessor of the airship and aëroplane. Until a fairly reliable light engine had been worked out upon the ground, where sudden stoppages did not involve disaster, sustained flying was no more than a dream. The early "gliders" in the gliding machines, Lilienthal, Pilcher and Chanute, were plainly and consciously preparing for the advent of an efficient engine. So soon as sure and sufficient power was available, both flying and the navigable balloon became inevitable.

The automobile story is still a confusion of claims and disputations. Gottlieb Daimler (1885–86) was early in the field, but it is alleged that Siegfried Narkus in Austria had made and driven a four-wheeled car with an internal combustion engine as early as 1875 (Encyclopædia Britannica). By 1897 a lot of people were busy making experimental cars of various types, in France, Germany, England and America. To show the manner of the growth and do justice to these experimenters would require furlongs of museum gallery. It took a dozen years and the toil of many thousands of inventors before a really trustworthy car, that would not only take its driver out but bring him home again, had become a marketable commodity. In 1897 there were ninety cars upon the roads of the United States; in 1906 the hundred thousand mark was passed, in 1913 the million and in 1928, twenty-one million. There is now (1931) a car to every seven people in the United States and to every sixty people in Great Britain and France.

The aëroplane followed fast on the car. The world of inventors was in labour, so to speak, with the automobile in 1896–97. That was the great time of road trials and freaks. The corresponding years for the aëroplane were 1909–11. By 1903 Wilbur and Orville Wright had already added a petrol motor to the gliders with which they had been experimenting since 1900 at Dayton in Ohio. They were certainly flying in 1905. Santos Dumont flew in 1906, and Farman, at the Voisin works at Issy near Paris in 1908. In July, 1909, Blériot flew across the English Channel, and from that date onward the record is crowded with flights of increasing length and height. The Atlantic was first crossed in 1919 by Alcock and Brown.

The very earliest speculations on the possibility of mechanical flight were based upon flapping wings. The significance of soaring, with wings placidly outspread, was not at first apparent. And though Sir George Cayley in 1809 stated the principles upon which a heavier-than-air machine could be employed, a hundred years elapsed before this became an accomplished fact. The balloon, invented by the Montgolfier brothers at the end of the eighteenth century (1783)—lifted by hot air, hydrogen or, after 1821, coal gas—had buoyancy, it was capable of lifting a load up into the air, but its direction was that of the wind. In 1852 Gifford fitted a steam engine to a balloon and propelled it at five or six miles an hour. But a larger machine, built three years later, came to grief. During the Franco-German War a balloon which had a propeller worked by eight men was used. In 1885 Renard and Krebs constructed an airship, *La France,* propelled by a nine horsepower electric motor. This machine flew over Paris and attained a speed of fourteen miles an hour. But that was about as far as the lighter-than-air machine could go until the internal combustion engine came to its assistance. This association became possible at the dawn of the twentieth century. In 1901 Santos Dumont flew a navigable balloon, like a fat flabby fish, for seven miles out and home, round the Eiffel Tower.

The earlier French airships were "non-rigid." They consisted of a lozenge or fish-shaped envelope containing the gas, and the car for pilot, passengers and machinery was suspended from a net, embracing the fragile gas container. The "rigid" type, in which the fabric is stretched

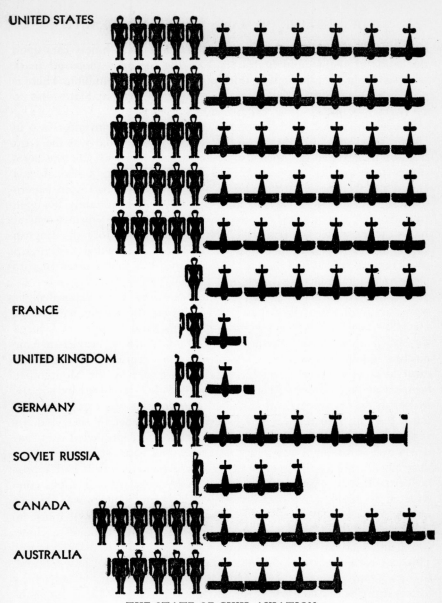

UNITED STATES

FRANCE

UNITED KINGDOM

GERMANY

SOVIET RUSSIA

CANADA

AUSTRALIA

THE STATE OF CIVIL AVIATION

EACH plane indicates one million miles flown, and each figure indicates twenty thousand passengers carried. Only the principal flying countries are shown. It is interesting to note that during the period shown, more than seven hundred million passengers were carried by railroads in the United States, compared to less than half a million carried by plane. The statistics on which this chart is based were compiled from United States government sources, and are for the latest year available, 1930.

over a sausage-shaped metal framework, and the gas is contained in "ballonnets" in separate compartments of the larger vessel, was developed in Germany by that great experimentalist, Count Zeppelin. He was at work before the end of the nineteenth century. He was the first to make a rigid airship (of aluminium covered with silk and linen and containing hydrogen). It made successful flights before the end of 1900. But his Zeppelins remained very tender and fragile for ten years. It was only with the invention of duralumin (an alloy of aluminium) in 1909 that a really adequate, strong and light frame for a rigid airship became possible. Duralumin has five times the strength of aluminium and is nearly as light. During the war France and Great Britain developed non-rigid types of airship, and by 1918 the latter country had several hundred of them for scouting and coastal patrol. Italy showed a preference for semi-rigid ships—non-rigid envelopes stiffened by a metal keel. Germany, keeping the lead Count Zeppelin had given her, went on building rigid airships of the largest size and using them very effectively, and until 1916, when the L 33 was brought down near London, there was no information available outside Germany as to their design and construction.

Experimental work with large airships is less easy than with aëroplanes; airships are infinitely more costly to build. They are relatively fragile, and when a disaster occurs they are more expensive in human life. Until hydrogen can be replaced by the non-inflammable gas helium, the menace of fire will always be associated with them. Helium is the next lightest element to hydrogen, and although abundant in the sun's atmosphere, it is on earth a gas of rare occurrence. It is found in various natural gases and in the water of some mineral springs. It is widely distributed, but only in very small amounts; it is obtainable in considerable quantities in America alone. The supplies are manifestly limited, and this puts yet another obstacle in the way of general airship development.

The armament competitions of the opening decade of the twentieth century, and then the war, were tremendously stimulating to both airship and aëroplane construction. At the outset of the conflict aëroplanes were used only for reconnaissance and to mark for gunfire. By the end of the war an elaborate system of air fighting existed, and night after night great air raids—in which the big aëroplane of the Handley Page, Gotha type presently ousted the more vulnerable Zeppelin—bombed the belligerent populations behind the fighting lines.

The Peace of Versailles released the accumulated possibilities of the civil transport aëroplane. The first regular air services had already been established before the war in Germany in 1912, when rigid airships were used. By 1920 there were three British and two French companies providing cross-channel services by means of aëroplanes. The British interests were subsequently (in 1926) concentrated in Imperial Air Services, Ltd., which operates between England and France, Switzerland, Germany, and Belgium. British Empire routes were also established in Africa, the Near East, India and Australia. But the British Empire is not very happily planned for air transport. Britain has a very central maritime position, but the main air services of the future are more likely to radiate from the centres of the great land masses of our planet. By 1926 the route mileage of the world's air transport had reached 50,000, and the number of miles flown in that year along these routes was nearly 17,000,000. This progress testifies not only to great improvements in the design and construction of the machines, but also to the increase in efficiency of the internal combustion engine. In 1915 the lightest water-cooled motor weighed 4 pounds per horsepower, and the lightest air cooled engine 3 pounds. To-day the weights of these engines are more than halved.

Apart from transport, the aëroplane is being used for many economic and administrative purposes. Vast areas where the population is sparse and means of communication poor are being surveyed from the air. In 1925 and 1926, 120,000 square miles were mapped by aërial photography in Canada. Rivers and coast lines and routes for new roads and railways have been surveyed in the United States, and in Australia the extent and form of the Great Barrier Reef have been recorded. The forest areas of Germany, Canada and other countries are being determined in this way. Mineral resources in Africa and the United States are being investigated. Town surveys have been made in the United States and Germany. The Canadian Salmon Fisheries are being policed by aëroplanes, and cotton and other crops are being sprayed or dusted with insecticides or fungicides by low-flying machines.

Few people before 1918 could have believed that archæological work would ever be undertaken in an aëroplane. But thanks mainly to the energy of one man, Mr. O. G. S. Crawford—who learnt the business as an aërial photographer at Arras during the war—the aëroplane has become now a most important instrument in reconstructing the life of the past. An aërial photograph reveals details in the texture and quality of the ground which are totally invisible to a man on the surface, and the long unsuspected vestiges of ancient settlements and the prehistoric layout of the land have been elucidated to a very remarkable extent in this way.

From its very beginnings, civil air transport has found itself entangled amidst the narrow political boundaries of the past. An International Convention for the Regulation of Aërial Navigation was ratified by many countries in 1922. This was followed by an International Commission for Air Navigation on which twenty-five states were represented. The Commission acts as an advisory body to the governments which send representatives on such questions as customs, licenses and certificates of airworthiness, and the establishment of lighting systems and the provision and dissemination of meteorological information—a strange complex of fiscal, legal and scientific services.

It is plain that we are still only in the beginnings of this new age of road and air transport which the internal combustion engine has made possible. The new highroad and the airway are at about the stage the railway had reached a century ago. The actual mechanism, the automobile or the aëroplane, that is to say is in existence in a working state. It is the development of the network that has now to be undertaken. Over great parts of the world the normal automobile cannot yet be used because of the want of modern roads. Either it must be replaced by automobiles of a special type and toughness—like the Citroën cars used in the North African desert and the crossing of Central Asia—or it cannot be used at all.

Still more is regular and trustworthy air travel restricted by ground conditions. Night flying and long distance cannot be considered safe until invention and organization have collaborated to anticipate and deal with the at present very heavy risks of fog. But, as we shall see in the next section, conquest of fog by the development of beam wireless and particularly of the new micro-rays, to which fog and rain are transparent, is close at hand. There is also needed a great effort in the development and application of meteorological science, so that the aviator may plan his route with assurance, free from the dread of adverse surprises by rain, snow, fog and tempest. Only by evolving a cosmopolitan organization can meteorology achieve that manifest task before it.

Week by week, year by year, at this point, at that, the road map and air route map of the world are being elaborated and redrawn, and every change in these maps involves political, social, and economic consequences of the most fundamental order. The transport framework of a new world system is being pieced together in spite of a thousand traditional antagonisms and impediments.

§ 4. *The Transmission of Fact. The Present Moment Becomes World-Wide*

But this chapter is concerned not simply with Transport, but with all methods of communication. We are considering not only how men and things can be moved about the modern world, but also the movement of information and ideas. Mankind seems to be approaching a phase when we shall realize and think almost as if we had one mind in common. Political disorder and various sorts of uproar delay the attainment of that phase, but there is an element of inevitableness in its advance. We move towards a time when any event of importance will be known of almost simultaneously throughout the planet. Everywhere it will presently be the same *"now."*

The story of communications, written regardless of any limitations of space or time would deal with signalling, with semaphores, smoke signals, practised by every savage people from the Picts to the Polynesians, and the like, and then go on to the story of electrical communication, with the electric needle, the telephone, the dawn of radio communication and the possibilities of the wireless transmission of visual impressions, as its chief episodes.

We may perhaps glance at a few facts in this latter story. It all falls within the compass of a century and a half. Until the end of the eighteenth century few of the phenomena of electricity were recognized; its nature was a subject of speculation rather than organized experiment Volta had shown how to produce a continuous current of electrical energy in 1793. In 1819–20 Oersted discovered that a wire conveying a current would deflect a magnetic needle; in 1825 Ampère studied the forces exerted between a current and a magnet and between two currents of electricity; and in 1832 Faraday showed that when a current was started or stopped in one wire, another current in the opposite direction was "induced" in a neighbouring wire. At the time these things, the germs of all the telegraphic and telephonic developments of to-day, seemed curious minor facts.

Soon after Oersted's discovery, attempts were made to transmit messages by the deflection of a magnetic needle. In 1820 Ampère constructed a telegraph which had twenty-six wires and twenty-six needles —a wire and a needle for each letter of the alphabet. It was not until 1836 that a measure of success was achieved by Gauss and Weber in Germany, and Cooke and Wheatstone in England. Wheatstone's first instrument had five needles, but these were reduced to two, and in

1845 to one. The letters were arranged on a dial, and the needle pointed to a particular letter, according to the signal received. The instrument had the merit that no special knowledge or skill was required to operate it.

Meanwhile Morse, in America, adopted a different plan. He devised a code of "dots and dashes" by sending a current along the line for a shorter or longer period and recording them by a pointer, or "pencil," which pressed against a moving strip of paper while the current flowed. His first patent was taken out in 1835. By 1851 there were fifty companies using the Morse code in America. In Europe the needle instrument prevailed, and the Morse code and system did not come into use until 1861. In 1853 duplex telegraphy was invented. By this method two messages could be sent simultaneously over the same line. Edison invented quadruplex telegraphy, by which two messages can be sent in each direction simultaneously, in 1874. These are two out of scores of refinements which increased the speed and range of electric communication. The needle instrument and the dot and dash apparatus were supplemented, and to some extent superseded, by printing telegraphs, in which each letter is produced in type on a moving strip of paper. During the last twenty years it has become possible to transmit facsimiles of letters and photographs.

Transmission under water demanded elaborately constructed and insulated cables, and created many unexpected problems. England and the Continent were joined in 1851. A cable was laid between Ireland and Newfoundland in 1858, but it broke three years later. The first permanent Atlantic cable was laid in 1866. More sensitive recording instruments than those which sufficed for land lines were required. These were found, first, in the mirror galvanometer, and secondly, in the siphon recorder, both invented by William Thomson, afterwards Lord Kelvin. The siphon recorder has a siphon dipping into a vessel of ink. The long limb of the siphon, drawn out to a fine point, rests upon a moving strip of paper. The signals are received by a sensitive galvanometer with a suspended coil of wire instead of a needle, and the deflections for dots and dashes are in opposite directions. These deflections are communicated to the siphon, which traces a straight line so long as no message is coming through, and a wavy one when signals are being received. The dots were indicated by waves on one side, and the dashes by waves on the other side of the line.

By the aid of a number of subsidiary devices, the speed of cable transmission has been increased from 15 letters a minute in 1858 to

2,500 letters a minute at the present day. There are now more than 3,000 submarine cables in the world, with a total length of about 300,000 miles, and 21 of these lie between Europe and North America. The whole of that network of intercommunication has been established within eighty years—the lifetime of a single individual. It has effected a revolution in method of government and in the conduct of business. It tends to make the world one unit to a greater extent even than the railway or the steamship. It permits of instantaneous decisions in places remote from one another. It annihilates time—in some cases it antedates events. An incident in the Far East may be known in England before the hour by Greenwich time at which it occurred.

The transmission of human speech, with its vowels and their consonantal modifications, was a more delicate matter than the transmission of dots and dashes. From 1854 onward inventors were busy on this problem. Some means had to be devised to cause an electric current to vary with the vibrations of the human voice, and then to reproduce these vibrations at the receiving end. The problem was solved in 1876 by Graham Bell. Briefly, his apparatus consisted of a transmitter and a receiver with a connecting wire. The transmitter was composed of a flexible ferrotype disc, a disc that is of very thin sheet iron, gripped by its edges and fixed opposite the end of a magnet. Round the magnet was a coil of wire through which a weak current of electricity flowed. When a person spoke to the ferrotype plate it was set in vibration. Its approach to and recession from the magnet altered the magnetic field and caused corresponding alterations in the strength of the current which set up similar vibrations in a disc in a similar instrument at the receiving end. The chief modification since then is in the transmitter. This consists of a box with a flexible disc on one side. It is filled with granules of carbon, through which passes an electric current. A person speaking to the disc causes it to vibrate, and the vibrations are communicated to the carbon granules. This causes variations in resistance and consequent variations in the strength of the current.

So it became possible for one person to speak to another at a distance, and the next step was obviously to devise methods of getting into communication with the person with whom speech was desired. Here again was a new field for invention and enterprise. Switchboards through which a number of subscribers could be put into intercommunication were devised. The first was set up at New Haven, Connecticut, in 1878, with several thousand subscribers. In London in the same year the subscribers were less than a dozen. To-day there are about 20,000,000 telephones in the United States, roughly one to every six people, and there are more than 30,000,000 telephones in the world.

The distance over which messages could be sent increased. Many improvements had to be made in auxiliary apparatus before long-distance telephony was possible. For long-distance lines, the feeble currents which represent speech have to be reinforced by valves such as are used in wireless telephony. But with no unreasonable delay the chief towns of Europe and America were brought into communication, and the human voice was carried across the wide seas. In the towns the telephone operator is gradually being displaced for local calls by the automatic exchange, a wonderfully ingenious arrangement by which any subscriber can call up any other in the area by "spelling" the number on a dial.

But now a new phase in communication was to appear—the transmission of signals and speech without connecting wires. This development began in the mind of a mathematician and in the laboratory of a professor of physics. Like the preceding developments, it was a triumph of pure science. In 1865 Clerk Maxwell published his electro-magnetic theory of light in which he suggested that electricity was propagated through space by a wave motion similar to that of light. About 1887 Hertz detected these waves. It was known that when electricity jumped across the gap, a spark was produced. It was known, too, that when the discharge took place between large metal plates or coils of wire the spark was not a single flash, but a series of flashes caused by the electricity surging backwards and forwards millions of times a second. This surge in the circuit which contains the spark sends out waves. Fitzgerald had suggested in 1883 this method of producing electric waves, but there was no way of detecting them. Hertz formed a circuit composed of two conductors "connected" by a straight piece of wire with a gap in it. The conductors were charged with electricity by an induction coil—a coil similar to, but larger than, that which thousands of people have used for administering "shocks" to their friends. When the spark jumped across the gap, sparks also passed between pieces of metal placed very close together in other parts of the laboratory. The electric waves had reached them, a similar surge was set up, and with each oscillation a spark passed.

These pieces of metal served their purpose for confirming the existence of the electric waves and enables their properties to be studied. But a more suitable form of detector was invented by Branly, and in 1896 Marconi took the step which rendered possible the wireless transmission of signals. He connected one of the terminals between which the spark passed to a long wire slung in the air, and the other terminal to a metal plate buried in the earth. The "earthed" aërial radiated waves far better than any other device, and has remained an essential element in wireless transmission ever since.

Marconi brought his apparatus to England and demonstrated its practicability over a distance of $1\frac{1}{4}$ miles on Salisbury Plain. Before the end of 1897 he sent signals 14 miles. In 1899, messages were sent 85 miles. In 1901, received by an improved detector, messages passed between Poldhu in Cornwall and St. John's, Newfoundland, a distance of 2,000 miles. In their course the waves kept to the curvature of the earth, surmounting a "hump" of the Atlantic 125 miles above the direct line joining the two stations. This result could not have been predicted by the scientific knowledge then available. The practical test revealed a new fact of enormous importance to future development. Electric waves would spread over the surface of the earth and be within range of millions who had the means of detecting them.

Further advances were rendered possible by new devices, more especially by the thermionic value which could be used not only to detect signals but to amplify them. We have no space here to describe these devices, nor the hundreds of others which played their part in the development of wireless telegraphy.

We pass on to the next stage in this amazing story of achievement—the transmission of speech. For this purpose the original Marconi system of producing waves was unsuitable. The sparks were violent intermittent disturbances which produced short trains of waves, each of which rapidly died away. If you throw a stone into a pond it sets up a train of ripples on the surface. If you then throw another stone in the same place, another train of ripples is set up. If, instead of throwing a stone, you dip your hand into the water and move it rapidly and regularly up and down, you will send a continuous stream of waves over the water as long as you keep up the motion. If the movement upwards and downwards of the hand is slow, the distance from crest to crest of the waves—the wave length—is longer than if the movement of the hand is quick. It was the persistent hand and not the occasional stone, that voice transmission, as distinguished from signal transmission, required.

An alternating electric current flowing with extraordinary rapidity and regularity up and down the aërial was necessary to produce the continuous waves required for wireless telephony. Several rival systems of wireless transmission produced waves of this kind, and a new method was available after 1913, when it was discovered that the valve, hitherto used for detecting and amplifying the signals, was itself capable of acting as an oscillator and of radiating electric waves. The transmission of speech was then achieved by imposing on the continuous waves much coarser variations corresponding to the vibration of the human voice. The speaker's words are received by a microphone, which is really a sensitive telephone transmitter. The electric current flowing through the microphone is modified by his voice and conveys these modifications to the outgoing wave. This wave conveys the modifications to a distance, where they are rendered audible in a telephone receiver or a loud speaker. Such, in brief, is the general procedure by which wireless telephony has been accomplished.

By 1920 our world by land and sea was everywhere throbbing with dots and dashes and living words. For half a dozen years Europe and America had been in wireless telephonic communication. The British government had projected a chain of wireless stations. The most remote parts of the Empire were to be brought into communication. All over Europe and in North America there was intense activity, when suddenly the whole practice of long-distance transmission was changed by a most curious circumstance.

No branch of applied science has ever exercised such a fascination for the man in the street as radio transmission. Advance had been so rapid, the field was so new, that the physicist and the engineer had not swept it clean. They had left things to be discovered—mostly new arrangements of the parts, of which there is a bewildering variety. That was a great opportunity and stimulus for the gleaning amateur experimentalist. But while opportunities for private experiment in reception were unlimited, those for experiment in transmission were limited to wave lengths which did not interfere with public service. For public use, the relatively long waves were monopolized, for the earlier investigators had found these to be the most effective for their immediate purposes.

Consequently the amateur was forced to use short waves. But he was not necessarily limited to short distances. In 1921–22, American, British, French, and German amateurs were communicating with one another across the Atlantic with far less power than that required by the big stations. Through their efforts it was realized that for the longest distances the short wave is the more effective, and the cost of equipment less. This was especially the case when it was further discovered that with a special form of aërial the short waves could be radiated even more effectively in the form of a beam with very little spreading. This beam aërial consists of a number of parallel wires hanging vertically and in a straight line. If the row of wires is north and south the waves are radiated east and west. If the row is east and west the waves proceed north and south. They form a beam with a very slight divergence, whereas long waves spread fanwise over a wide area. If similar, but more numerous, wires are hung behind the others, they form a screen, and the waves are radiated only from the front. This beam wireless has the same relation to the long wave wireless, that a focussed searchlight has to an unshaded arc light. By beam wireless England is now in regular communication with South Africa, India, Australia, Canada, the United States and other countries. Long-distance lines in America also employ this method.

In April, 1931 (says *Discovery,* May, 1931), a new "ultra short wave" radio equipment was demonstrated. Conversations were exchanged between Dover and Calais on a wave length of only eighteen centimetres, using aërials of less than an inch in length, with a power of half a watt —which is just sufficient to light an ordinary flash-lamp bulb. In this new apparatus, the sound of the speaker's voice at the transmitting station is carried to a "micro-radion" tube where waves called "micro-rays" are generated; the waves oscillate at a rate of sixteen hundred million times a second. After concentration by an ingenious combination of two reflectors into a fine pencil of rays, somewhat similar to the rays sent out by a searchlight, the waves are transmitted into space. An important feature of the micro-rays is that they are not subject to the "fading" effects encountered in ordinary wireless transmission, and they are not absorbed by rain or fog, as is the case with light rays. The demonstration has shown that wave lengths of between ten and a hundred centimetres can be used for commercial transmission. This gives a great range of difference in transmission and nearly a quarter of a million micro-ray instruments will be workable without any one of them interfering with another.

Wireless communication was rapidly adopted for use at sea. All ships making long voyages are equipped for it, and by the direction finder they are able to ascertain the point of the compass from which signals come. It is also destined to facilitate aërial navigation very greatly. An airman can already find his way to the aërodrome through darkness or fog by noting the direction and strength of signals which are continually emitted for his guidance. And these new micro-rays will manifestly play a large part in the complete development of such vitally necessary facilities. The aëroplane of the future will have micro-ray eyes, and it is within the limits of scientific possibility that that which these radio eyes will see may be translated again into direct vision for the pilot.

The broadcasting of entertainments began in Canada in 1920. In 1922 the British Broadcasting Company was formed. In America, many broadcasting services were established by private enterprise. The isolated farmer, the aged and infirm, the sick are brought into touch with the world. The colonial settler, a hundred miles from a railway, can hear during his dinner hour the weather forecast, the crop reports, market prices, as well as many things remote from "the daily round, the common task." In Europe a man may, by merely turning a knob, hear music in variety, or speech in one of half a dozen tongues. What is distance? Where are political boundaries when man can speak to many men across a thousand miles of space?

The possibilities are boundless. And yet as we go to press official announcement has just been made of a difficulty which may, for a time, block progress and largely frustrate the efforts of all these scientists and inventors. The ether is becoming overcrowded. Powerful stations, broadcasting variety entertainment, are so increasing their range as to interfere with reception thousands of miles away. Even signals of distress from ships at sea are said to have been drowned. There is a destructive competition going on in the ether which in the end will benefit nobody and lead to nothing but a deadlock unless it can be solved by international agreement.

Yet manifestly more is still to come. Television is already possible on a small scale. The unsurmounted difficulties here are still immense. To appreciate these, consider the simpler case of transmitting a photograph by electricity. The original picture is divided into a number of minute squares. Each of these squares is illuminated in turn by a spot of light until the whole photograph has been explored. The light reflected from the surface will vary in intensity according to the light or shadow of the part illuminated. This reflected light falls upon a cell sensitive to light—a vacuum tube having the inner surface coated with a metal that changes in resistance as light falls upon it. So, as the spot of light runs over the picture and explores it, the current through the cell varies with the light and shade and conveys these differences to the outgoing waves. At the receiving end these waves act on a mirror galvanometer which regulates a minute beam of light in an otherwise darkened chamber, falling successively on a series of small areas of a piece of sensitized paper. This paper, on development, yields a copy of the original photograph. This process of transmission may take ten or fifteen minutes.

In television a distant person or object has to be explored in the same way by a spot of light. That is not difficult. No photography is involved. At the receiving end corresponding spots of light, of greater or less intensity, according to the light and shade of the original, have to be thrown on a screen with such rapidity that the last has appeared before the first has faded from view. When anyone looks at an object, an image is formed on a sort of screen—the retina, at the back of the eye. This image persists, after the object has been removed from sight, for one tenth of a second! On this elementary fact of the persistence of vision the cinema rests. But see the limiting time conditions imposed on television! The distant person or object must be explored ten times a second, and the transmitted image formed on the screen with the same rapidity. The apparatus must be capable therefore of working at least three thousand times faster than that used for transmitting a photograph. The difficulties in achieving this rapidity are partly mechanical, and partly they lie in securing a sufficient intensity of light to illuminate a large area. At present the transmitted picture could be contained on a postcard.

But who dares say that these difficulties will not be overcome? The time may yet be when a man will talk to another a thousand miles or more away, and each may be able to see, life size, every movement of the lips and every changing expression that indicates the other's mood. Everyone in that concentrated and intensified world will be living, so to speak, in the next room from everybody else and able with little effort to step into that next room to speak to a friend or make an explanation to remove a misunderstanding. The whole world will be a meeting place.

§ 5. *Print and Film*

This recent and dazzling development of electrical communications which has made the present moment world wide must not blind us to the major importance of that larger organization of human communications which is concerned with the establishment of ideas, the supply of ordered knowledge, the maintenance and development of common understanding—namely, the printed word. Electrical communication is a matter of the past century; the book has been developing for more

A MODERN DESCENDANT OF THE *ROCKET*

THE oil-electric engine of the Canadian National being lowered into place. This locomotive, the 9000, will take a heavy train across the continent in sixty hours, an unprecedented speed, at infinitely less cost than heretofore.

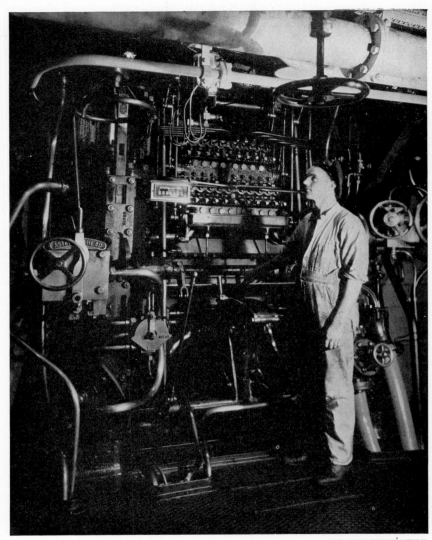

OIL OUSTS COAL

ONE of the battery of Diesel Engines on the new motorship *Britannic*.

than two thousand years; the newspaper, in its modern form, as an addition to the world's mental power, is a thing scarcely two centuries old.

We live in the light of a hard, crude alertness to events. It is a glaring and unshaded light, which casts strange shadows, but it is light. Few of us realize the darkness and the remoteness from current reality which characterized the minds of our great-grandparents. They had a few well printed books, bound in leather and handsomely out of date, a small news sheet, and a monthly magazine as their chief sources of information. That was all.

The *Outline of History* tells in brief the main factors in the story of the book, because an outline of human history is necessarily a record of continually growing communities, and necessarily it deals with communications as matters of primary importance. Such figures as Alexander, Cæsar and Napoleon are mere passengers carried about by the real moving forces of life; the use of cavalry on the Persian roads, a new system of monetary trading, the sailing ship and the highroad. The entire contents of the *Outline of History* might easily be rearranged under five successive headings: (1) Before Speech (2) Speech (3) Writing (4) the Printed Book (5) Mechanical Transport and Electric Communication, each indicating a revolution in communication and involving a new, larger, and more complex social organization. The printed book and map revolutionized the world at the Renaissance; the newspaper followed hard upon manageable paper and printing.

And here again our museums come to our aid. This time we can refer to actual museums. There are already many miles of galleries treating of the making and use of books. There are also vast collections of filed newspapers, and now such of the primitive machines as survive are being taken care of and found floor room. In these museum galleries it is possible to trace the first origins of the press in the classical white notice board, the "album," in the news letter and news sheet, and go on from that, step by step, until the throbbing great printing machinery and the stir and rush of a well equipped newspaper office are brought before our reader.

We dare not embark upon the story of newspaper work and the adventures of newspaper men. Interesting it would be to trace the thrill of excitement from the moment of a crime to the arrival of the reporter and the headline proclamation to the world. How is reporting done? That would be a queer chapter in the detailed story of human activities. Our picture, in its fullness, would include the government representative making his communication to the gentlemen of the press and the interesting, tactful and precarious work of a foreign correspondent. The editing and make-up of a paper would be shown.

The rôle of the newspaper in modern life is profoundly important. On the one hand it touches the book, on the other the pulpit, the lecture-theatre and now the radio talk. It is the modern man's daily reminder of things greater than himself, of a life of the race exceeding and comprehending his own. Every day that reminder comes to him. Few of us realize how the intensity of the individual life is diminished and the individual life *generalized* by the newspaper. To that we must return later when we come to review the education, formal and informal, of the modern citizen.

The newspaper is so much with us now that it is already difficult to imagine a world without it. Still more difficult is it to realize what an extraordinary and possibly transitory thing it is in social life—in the form in which we know it now. It does work now vitally necessary to a modern community, and it does it very crudely. It began simply and frankly enough as a purely informative news sheet. It was produced as that and bought and paid for as that. But from the very earliest stages it became evident that it had other uses. It was extraordinarily convenient for all sorts of announcements, which had previously been made chiefly by criers, by notices on church doors and suchlike frequented places, and its use for advertisement became rapidly profitable. It could, in addition to the news it supplied, supplement its interest by the discussion of public affairs.

Its rapid expansion in the nineteenth century was associated not merely with the spread of elementary education but with a revolution in paper making. The rag-made paper of the past could never have been produced in sufficient quantity for the modern press. Wood pulp, wrote Lord Northcliffe in the eleventh Encyclopædia Britannica, is at the roots of the expansion of the modern newspaper. The machinery to produce it in great quantities became available in the last quarter of the nineteenth century, and with that came huge printing machines, folding machines and the like, making the printing and distribution of a couple of millions of copies in a few hours easily possible.

The vast demands of the daily press are being met by a ruthless destruction of forests and have encouraged the planting of quick-growing soft timber at the expense of hard constructional varieties, which are also being exhausted to serve other human needs. It has been estimated that the present European demand for soft woods exceeds the annual growth of existing forests by three thousand million cubic feet.

From the first the newspaper was developed on commercial lines. It betrayed little ambition beyond profits, and little consciousness of the rôle it was playing in the expansion of our new and larger world with which it was being evolved. Its successful proprietors, with a few distinguished and redeeming exceptions, have sought to give such news only as appealed to the commoner sorts of mind, to provide excitement and entertainment even at the cost of veracity, and to gather "publics" which would present an attractive field for well paid advertisements. Their temptations have been immense. They have been naturally and necessarily on the side of private adventure against comprehensive control. They have a bias against an orderly commonweal. Our press is an adventurer's press. Few newspapers have any interest in supporting or defending a soundly organized public service, nagging attacks on public services are a world-wide newspaper feature, but every newspaper has an interest in a shabbily conducted, privately owned transport system which is advertising to keep its passengers in a good temper, or in a purveyor of quack medicines or trashy foodstuffs sustaining a legend of merit by a lavish expenditure in display. No newspaper again has any interest in the exposure of fraudulent or adulterated commodities, unless such an exposure will frighten or flatter the owners of competing articles, to its profit. It has no organic links with political issues. Serious discussion may easily bore its readers; ridicule and caricature of men in difficult positions are not only easier to do but more acceptable to the ordinary man. It can offer or refuse, it can in fact sell, "publicity," that most precious commodity, exactly as it is disposed. The marvel is not that the ordinary modern newspaper succumbs too often to these manifest temptations, but that it has not been altogether overwhelmed and degraded by them, that it still in its way, performs something of its necessary function in the new community. It does, as we have said, generalize its habitual reader and open his mind, however crudely, to a wider, more various life beyond his own.

But what needs to be made clear and is by no means clear to a generation born amidst newspapers and brought up on them is the extremely recent and the extremely provisional nature of the press as a social and political organ. Nobody seems to have foreseen how the community would be generalized by letterpress and by a universal habit of reading, and still less did anyone scheme or contemplate such a task of sustained information and direction as a better form of newspaper might undertake. The newspaper, a mere petty excrescence upon life in the early seventeenth century, is discovered to be a necessary part of our modern social organization. Now that we have it and observe it we realize that it is not only a vitally important organ, but also one still in the process of development and social adjustment.

One important aspect of this development is the rapid disappearance of free competition due to the increasing primary costs of producing and distributing a modern newspaper. There was a time when anyone with a small capital and hope and energy could start a newspaper with a reasonable prospect of survival, but that time has gone. Though there are far more *copies* of newspapers sold nowadays, there are fewer newspapers. F. L. Allen (in *Only Yesterday*) gives the aggregate newspaper circulation for daily issue in the United States as 28 million in 1914 and 36 million in 1926, but during that time the number of daily papers sank from 2580 to 2001 and of Sunday papers from 571 to 541. And of these more and more are falling into groups under the control of a single proprietor. The newspaper Forum ceased to be open to all comers. Publicity is being cornered. And under the free play of economic forces nothing can be done to prevent this.

The cinema, with its recent development, the talking cinema, destined it would seem at a not very distant date to be modified and mitigated into the artistic "sound film" in which talk will play a minor rôle, is a more modern and even more startling case of a new, important method of intercommunication gone very seriously astray. So far it has been developed chiefly on its "amusements" side. The story of the cinema is a worse record than that of the newspaper so far as the waste of serviceable opportunity through triviality of conception goes. Its obvious uses for educational purposes have still to be developed. The universities and schools of the existing régime lack the vigour and enterprise to control this new and powerful instrument for the distribution of mental impressions.

To that we must return later. A broad treatment of modern education will be the culmination of our enterprise, and in this chapter it will suffice to mention only the development, manufacture and distribution of the "movies."

Our imaginary economic museum, in its immense and spacious fashion, will have room to give an account of the making and display of a typical talkie-movie from the moment of its invention to its final disuse as a superannuated film. (I grow more and more pleased with the storage accommodation of these museums of ours.) And here again we shall be forced to note the inconvenience of outworn political traditions that now hamper, and may continue to hamper indefinitely, the worldwide spread of ideas by the cinema, in the interest of national antagonisms and national profiteers, the quotas, the customs dues and all the "blackmail of frontiers."

Another system of world communications, the international post, shows a better spirit at work. The creation of the Postal Union, marks a phase of sanity breaking through the chronic spites of nationalism. The growing facilities of letter transport over great distances were first realized in America, and in 1862 the United States suggested a conference which was held in Paris in 1863. Wars interrupted the movement for some years, but in 1875 the first International Postal Convention was signed at Berne and the Postal Union brought into being. It has survived all the stresses of conflict that have since torn the world, and to-day, so far as letters go, our planet is practically one. Forty million million letters pass through the organized postal services of the world every year, besides newspapers, books and parcels in great quantities. One scribbles a letter in a room in Manchester or Chicago and with a minimum of delay it starts on its journey, to a solitary Pacific island, to a factory in Soviet Siberia, to a boy on a battleship, to a prisoner in a jail. More than a hundred million letters a day are rustling about the world.

This Book on Communication again, like the Book of Substances and the Conquest of Power, is given here in the briefest outline. But the *Science of Work and Wealth,* rest assured, if and when it comes into existence, will give by its unrestrained pictures and descriptions an illimitable store of interesting and curious detail, helpful but inessential and quite impossible to summarize. And when the *Science of Work and Wealth* has laid down the world's roads and railways, launched its fleets and traced its multiplying airways through the blue, it will turn round and tell the reader just how he can travel to the ends of the earth, how he may talk to and see his friend wherever he is upon the planet, and what are the facilities and conditions for sending a ton of goods from anywhere to anywhere.

And so the scale and tempo of the modern process will be set for the survey of feeding, clothing, housing, protecting and keeping in health and order, that will follow.

CHAPTER THE FOURTH

THE CONQUEST OF HUNGER: HOW MANKIND IS FED

§ 1. *The World Eats*

EVERY day upon this planet about 1,900,000,000 people eat, and eat at least enough to keep themselves alive. In no part of the civilized world now does death from starvation figure as a dominant item in the mortality list. There may be many deaths to which wrong or insufficient nutrition is a chief contributory cause, in India and China, particularly—some million or so a year. Arnold Lupton calculates for instance, in his book *Happy India,* that in 1919–1920 the total food available per head per day for the whole of the Indian population was only 1.2 lbs of grain, rice, fruit, vegetables and sugar. This is below sufficiency. But by the scale of 1,900,000,000, the deaths from actual starvation do not bulk large. We come now to the fashion in which this primary need of the species *Homo sapiens* is met.

It is doubtful if ever before the world has carried and fed so immense a human population as it does to-day. Even in the most prosperous and fertile phases of the early civilizations it may be questioned whether the total came to much more than a few hundred million, and the boldest estimate of the numbers of our race in late Paleolithic and early Neolithic times would probably fall within the compass of a million or so; who were far more closely occupied by the food hunt and for the most part much nearer famine than any human community to-day. As for still earlier stages of our evolution, have we not already called attention to the fact that the great apes must needs be rare and unsocial creatures because each small group of them requires square miles of rich tropical forest for its food supply? Throughout all history until the present age famine has been a periodic experience. To-day, in spite of the world's immense unprecedented population, it is restricted local accident.

The Neolithic Age was an age of more food—and of proliferation up to the limits of the food supply.

§ 2. Fertilizers

In Chapter I we have stated the broad facts, as they are known to-day, of man's agricultural beginnings. If we were to expand the subsequent history of food production until we came to present conditions we should next have to compile a history of the growth of agricultural knowledge and method.

So soon as agriculture passed beyond the flood lands of the great rivers, where the soil is annually renewed and refreshed, the fact of soil exhaustion pressed for attention. The soil demanded intervals of rest and refreshment. The history of agriculture tells of the passage from natural husbandry with resting fallow lands, to the realization of the value of legumes, beans, vetches, etc., in restoring fertility to the soil, to the modern rotation of crops, and so on to the systematic restoration of soil by natural and artificial fertilizers. From that it goes on to modern intensive cultivation with every possible artificial assistance and acceleration of nature's generosity, and to the scientific breeding and feeding of animals.

In the past century there has been a great revival of irrigation in many parts of the world, often with an astonishing increase in productivity. For example, in India the estimated annual value of the crops raised on areas receiving State irrigation is more than the total capital outlay on the works themselves. The Lloyd barrage, completed in 1932, irrigates fifteen million acres of land once absolutely desert. In the future perhaps irrigation in India will be linked with a widespread use of hydro-electricity, since there is no objection whatever to the use of the same water first for obtaining electric power and then for irrigation.

The story of artificial fertilization falls broadly into three well marked stages. By 1840 the labour of botanists like De Saussure and chemists like Liebig had shown that in addition to air and water, four materials were essential to plant life—nitrogen, phosphorus, potassium and lime. The replacement of these elements after cropping began to be studied systematically. An empirical use of fertilizers already prevailed. Manuring with natural products, with humus (mould), dung and lime, had been practised for centuries. Now it was realized that the necessary nitrogen, phosphorus and potassium could also be introduced from other sources. The developing science of chemistry set itself to discover and prepare the most suitable forms of these additional plant foods. The first factory to make a successful chemical manure was opened by Lawes in 1843. Liebig had made an earlier attempt, but his enterprise was a failure because he fused his materials together and rendered them insoluble. The fertilizer prepared by Lawes was superphosphate of lime, obtained by treating bones or mineral phosphates with sulphuric acid. Bones also began to be used directly, ground up more or less finely; mineral phosphates were employed; and the Basic Bessemer and Siemens processes for steel-making provided basic slag, supplying phosphoric acid, particularly useful for pasture on heavy soils.

Potash was obtainable only by burning wood (pot-ashes) and sea-weed, until the discovery of immense deposits at Stassfurt about the middle of the century. It is now obtainable from flue dust in certain industrial operations, and other natural deposits are being worked. An attempt is also being made to recover it from the bed of the Dead Sea.

The first phase of the nitrogen industry (1839–68) was the use of guano, the accumulated droppings of sea birds, mostly from Peru. Then—as the guano deposits approached exhaustion, nitrogen, com-bined in a suitable form and in large quantity, was discovered near the surface of certain arid areas in Chile. The ordinary saltpetre is nitrate of potash; Chile saltpetre is nitrate of soda. With the development of gas manufacture this source was supplemented by ammonium sulphate. The ammoniacal liquor obtained during the distillation of coal is neutralized by sulphuric acid. These were the only sources of agri-cultural nitrogen until 1906, when synthetic nitrogen appeared.

Artificial fertilizers, and the restoration of fertility by a rotation of crops, are at present used mainly in the intensive farming adopted in thickly populated areas. They are not employed in the vast wheat-growing regions of the world. The ultimate effect of growing the same crop year after year without making up the loss is exhaustion of the soil,* and nitrogen compounds are so soluble that if they are not used up quickly they are washed out. At the British Association Meeting in 1898 Sir William Crookes emphasized this tendency to soil exhaustion. He pointed to the growing demand of the world for wheat, and the limited supply of mineral nitrates. And it was he who first suggested the abstraction of nitrogen from the inexhaustible store in the atmos-phere.

Lord Rayleigh had shown a few years previously that when an electric discharge passed through air, oxides of nitrogen were formed

---

*It might be inferred that continuous cropping led to a continuously declining yield. This is not so. The field at Rothamsted, cropped with wheat year after year to which no fertilizer or manure has been given, has yielded about 12 bushels an acre since 1875 with-out showing any tendency to diminish further. The experiment began in 1852 and a decline occurred in the first twenty years, after which the field stabilized. *Carr-Saunders.*

and could be isolated under proper conditions. By 1907 a process based on this reaction was in commercial operation. The fertilizer produced by this process is calcium nitrate. Another method was found in which nitrogen was passed over lime and charcoal, when calcium cyanamide was formed. Put into moist soil this yields ammonia. These original processes are gradually being superseded by one invented by Haber in Germany just before the war. In this a mixture of hydrogen and nitrogen (from liquid air) is passed at a high temperature and pressure over finely divided platinum. The resulting ammonia is then converted into the sulphate or other compounds. One of these, of great utility, both as a fertilizer and in the manufacture of the synthetic resins we have described in Chapter II, is urea.

In 1903 the total output of agricultural nitrogen expressed in metric tons of pure nitrogen was 352,000, and it was all in the form of naturally occurring nitrogen compounds. In 1928 the amount used was just close upon 2,000,000 metric tons, of which 1,019,200 owed their nitrogen to the air.

So much for the scientific and practical development based on a chemical theory of fertility.

But Berthelot, the great French chemist, early expressed a suspicion that fertility was not entirely due to normal chemical reactions, and by 1880 research was actively at work upon this doubt. While nitrates were found to be immediately effective, ammonium compounds were apparently inactive for twenty days.

In 1887 Warrington in England and Winogradsky in Russia detected and isolated special types of bacteria which changed ammonium compounds into nitrates. There are, in fact, two stages in the change, and each is due to a specific organism. One changes the ammonium compound into a nitrite, and the other converts a nitrite into a nitrate. Both of the types of bacteria concerned are called nitrifying bacteria. Ten years later it was discovered that the nodules on the roots of leguminous plants (peas, beans, clover etc.) contain colonies of a third type of bacteria which enable the plant to absorb nitrogen direct from the air in the soil. The last are called nitrogen-fixing bacteria. With their discovery a biological theory of fertility was super-imposed on the older chemical theory.

But even these two parallel explanations are insufficient for the complete account of soil fertility. Since 1900 it has become recognized that both the chemical and the biological changes are dependent upon physical conditions. Temperature and moisture are to some extent functions of the physical condition of the soil—the fineness as well as the character of the particles, the closeness of packing and so on. And there is in many cases an optimum state of division and distribution of the fertilizer. The water-holding capacity of the soil, which is no less important than the food supply, is in large measure determined by the physical conditions of the soil particles, for the roots of plants require, on the one hand, water wherewith to supply the leaves, and air wherewith themselves to live. So that if all the soil space is occupied by water the plant dies of suffocation, and if it is all occupied by air the plant perishes by drought.

The farmer of former times discovered by experience the advantages of thorough cultivation, of liming and marling, of natural manures and of rotation of crops. But he did all this by rule of thumb and tradition. He knew nothing of the vast complexity of mineral substances and of living organisms, nor of the marvellous changes that go on in the chambers and corridors of the soil. And it will perhaps be another century before he can interpret these with the same certainty with which an experiment in a chemical laboratory can be understood.

§ 3. *The Mechanized and Electrified Farm*

Machinery is rapidly coming to the help of the farmer, and a steady "electrification" of agriculture is in progress. Cultivation for endless centuries was carried out entirely by hand labour and the use of animals. It was always a conservative industry, modifying its methods only in response to some urgent stimulus. The application of machinery to agriculture came later than in mining or manufacture. It marked the change-over from agriculture for immediate consumption to agriculture for marketing. In England the outburst of mechanical invention of the eighteenth century was coincident, in the latter half, with the enclosure of land and the associated revolution of agricultural practice. There appeared the drill (sowing machine), harrow, reaper, winnowing machine and haymaker. A primitive type of threshing machine was introduced in 1798. These machines came into wider and wider use continuously thoughout the nineteenth century.

The use of machinery in America dates from about 1850, and in the wide, unbroken stretches of the newer countries there was greater scope for it than in the small enclosed fields of older civilizations. Here the sheaf-binder first saw the light. It not only cut the corn, but tied it into bundles ready for stooking. To-day in the drier areas of California and

Australia, where the wheat ripens on the stalk, a machine is used which cuts off the head and threshes and bags the corn. The stubble is then burnt and its mineral constituents restored to the soil.

In the latter quarter of the nineteenth century the steam engine began to replace horses. The first step was obviously to secure speed and economy of human effort in the heavier and more laborious operations. Ploughing, harrowing, and threshing were accomplished by steam. Because the heavy steam engine pressed heavily upon and consolidated the soil, it was sometimes, and still is, used in a fixed position, and the plough hauled backwards and forwards by chain tackle.

The greatest service was rendered to all agricultural operations by the development of the oil engine. This rapidly came into use for barn machinery, such as hay, chaff, and root cutters, cake and seed crushers. The earlier oil tractors for ploughing and cultivation were heavy machines with the same disadvantages of weight as the steam tractor and suitable only for large farms. But small machines drawing a two-furrow plough soon became available and are now widely used. With a tractor it is possible to plough five acres or more a day as compared with one by a man and a horse. It has been calculated that ploughing absorbs from 15,000 to 20,000 horsepower hours per square mile, and other mechanical cultivators from 7,000 to 10,000 horsepower hours. You must multiply the horsepower by eight to get the equivalent in superseded man power. So while the agricultural population decreases annually in comparison with the town population, the world production of food increases. Machinery, scientific cultivation and the improvement in the strains of agricultural plants necessitate rural depopulation.

Steam and oil power are now being supplemented, and to some extent displaced, by electricity. This form of power is less suitable for many agricultural operations because of the need of a supplying cable. On light land the oil tractor and on heavy clay the steam-tackle plough are preferable. Electrical ploughs or cultivators are, however, used on the Continent and in America under favourable conditions. Current is conveyed by a cable wound on a drum on the tractor. But it is in the farmhouse, yard, and outbuildings that electricity is of the greatest service. Much work, especially with animals, has to be carried out before daylight and after dark. The byres and stables are lighted first. Then the housewife demands a washing machine. Then comes electric dairying. Milk is drawn from the cow by an electric milking machine which absorbs only one sixth of a horsepower. With a herd of fifteen cows the saving in time is one and a quarter hours a day. The milk is now cooled in an electrically operated refrigerator, the cream is separated in an electrically driven separator, and churned in an electrically driven churn. The utensils are sterilized in an electrically heated chamber. If the cow's drinking water is warmed, she yields more milk.

In the barn, electricity is more convenient for driving the various choppers, cutters, crushers and mixers, machines for corn shelling, husking and shredding, grain cleaning and grading, hoisting and elevating, than an oil engine. The tendency is to use separate electric motors for each machine, so that overhead shafting with pulleys and belts is avoided. Out of doors electrical energy is used for pumping, including domestic water supply and irrigation. Add to these such household utensils as cookers, kettles, irons, vacuum cleaners, toasters, and the manifold uses of electricity on the modern farm become even more impressive.

In Sweden experiments are in progress in warming the soil by an underground cable in order to promote early growth. Seeds for garden crops are being irradiated by ultra-violet light, which is also used to supplement sunlight in greenhouses. Poultry houses are lighted morning and evening in winter. The hens thus have a longer daily period for exercise and food. They are found then to lay a larger proportion of eggs in winter when hitherto there have been a shortage and high prices. The total output per hen does not seem to increase; she simply becomes a less seasonal bird. When all the poultry houses in the world are lighted we may expect eggs to be a uniform price all the year round. But the consumer will have to pay the electric-light bill.

Progress in the use of electric energy has been hampered by the scattered population of agricultural areas and the high capital cost of transmission. In the United States this is five times as great per head as for the average town consumer. In England there are electrically operated farms in Sussex, in the neighbourhood of Chester and elsewhere. An extensive experiment is proposed in the eastern counties. On the Continent there has been a more vigorous development of electrified cultivation because of the prevalence of cheap electricity derived from water power. Between 1924 and 1927 the number of farms in the United States supplied with electricity increased by 86 per cent. In the latter year there were 227,442 farms supplied from public sources, and probably a larger number with private plants. It has been estimated that 600,000 or nearly 10 per cent of the farms in America are using electricity in these various fashions we have noted.

PRODUCTION

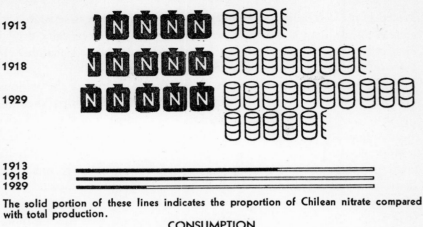

1913

1918

1929

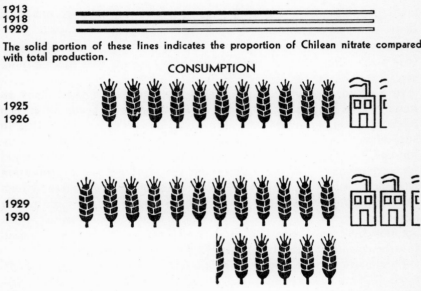

1913
1918
1929

The solid portion of these lines indicates the proportion of Chilean nitrate compared with total production.

CONSUMPTION

1925
1926

1929
1930

N 100,000 metric tons of Chilean nitrate	100,000 metric tons synthetic nitrogen
100,000 metric tons utilized as fertilizer	100,000 metric tons used for explosives and other commercial uses

THE WORLD'S NITROGEN SUPPLY

NITROGEN is a vital element in both war and peace. This chart shows its production and consumption before the war and in 1931. Until the development of various processes for securing nitrogen from the air, the world's nitrogen supply was largely in the hands of Chile.

§ 4. The Spectacle of Cultivation: The Vineyard and the Bee Keeper

To make a complete picture of contemporary food-getting we should next have to review various special aspects of the business, contrasting new ways with old, in market gardening, in the working of orchards, vineyards, and plantations generally, in dairying, pig-keeping, cattle-ranching, and fisheries. A year or so ago the British Empire Marketing Board produced a wonderful film of the herring fishery showing the journey of the herring from the shoal to the market, but I am afraid it is too Utopian an anticipation to suggest that our encyclopædia should be supplemented by films for use in the study. Whether our science museum will be able presently to provide permanent sideshows of this sort is another matter. Films and moving-picture peepshows are used in the Kensington Science Museum and at Munich. From the cattle ranch, the sheep run and the levelled fields and the quay, from the terraced hillside and the marshalled orchard and orange grove, we should follow the beasts and fish and the grain and the fruits and the roots and so forth on their journey—often now a journey halfway round the world—to become food for the table. We should give a stirring picture of the slaughter houses of Chicago (one of the earliest instances of mass production). We should assist at fish-drying, at the preparation of haddock and kipper, and we should feel the chill of the modern refrigerator car and the storehouse for frozen meat. Jam should have its meed: the fruit-picking, the boiling, and the canning.

The bee keeper, ancient and modern, demands at least a section. We should tell of the passing of the beehive and the end of the annual slaughter of the bees. With the beehive the grindstones of the old windmill have passed away. The world was full of windmills and beehives when we sexagenarians were children. We should have to treat of modern flour-handling and of modern bread-making and biscuit factories. And after food production would follow a review of food transport and methods of modifying and preserving food, chiefly with a view to its use during unproductive seasons or its removal to remote markets. Butter, cheese and such new milk products as condensed and powdered milk must be dealt with, and the preparation of those "cereals" which play so large a part now in the nursery and on the breakfast table. We should need a long chapter on the canning and food-packing industries. Close to that comes the manufacture of meat extracts. Nowadays, not only meat extracts but vegetable juices stand ready prepared for the cook's hand.

I find myself with an assortment of items about the history of feeding that have still to be arranged. Each by itself has its special interest, but the assembled mass of information would be overwhelming. Our complete encyclopædia would have an account of margarine—a long and interesting chapter that would be now—in the history of edible substances. Margarine is edible substance won from the comparatively inedible. It is made from various animal and vegetable oils, so treated as to resemble butter in every respect except its vitamin content. We have told already (Chapter II, § 6) how it stole the fats from the soap-boiler, and a full history of salesmanship should relate how the popular mind was won over, by changes of name and novelties in marketing, to the new comestible.

And there would have to be the story of wine. The trivialities of creed and controversy have, alas! estranged Mr. Hilaire Belloc from me, to my infinite regret, though they leave my admiration for his vigorous writing undiminished, or how gladly would I get a special chapter from him on wine, with supplements from colonial agents-general, anxious to recommend their particular brands of Cape hock and Australian Burgundy—Mr. Belloc objecting or not, as the case may be—in vivid footnotes. Nowadays the grapes are often crushed by mechanism, but still in the Province of Champagne red feet dance to music in the wine press. They may go on doing so. I am told that the twigs and seeds get crushed nowadays in the cement presses and yield unhelpful additions.

Beer and cane sugar, syrups and treacle, would give another sunlit chapter to that unwritten encyclopædia of ours. Cocoa and chocolate would have also to be told about. The entire grocer's stock indeed would be traced to its origins and explained. Or rather it must be dealt with at its origins and traced step by step to the grocer's counter. It would be a book of bright little marvels. And the reader, the nine-out-of-ten reader, would never read all that mass of detailed information. He would dip into it and find it amusing until he began to tire. He would skip and turn it over and stop here at this picture and there at a headline. And then he would stop reading. Most of it he would take as read, which is precisely what we are doing here. We are merely taking two steps instead of one. We are taking it as written, and then we are taking it as read. The result is exactly the same.

Now, passing very briefly over the marketing of this food stuff, for marketing is to be dealt with later, we wave a hand to the modern kitchen, with its gas cooking and its electric refrigerators, make the customary contrast with past conditions, and pause at the breakfast table and the dining-room door.

§ 5. *Substitutes and Adulteration*

We freeze food, we store it, we move it over immense distances and modify it in hitherto unheard of ways—and we have increased our gross supply enormously. But certain less agreeable aspects of modern food production must not be ignored in this survey. Science casts a shadow wherever she distributes her benefits. New substances are not always unmitigated blessings. It is impossible to deal completely with the feeding of mankind unless we bring into the picture the ingenuity and industry that are lavished in—how can I put it?—supplementing the supply of recognized foodstuffs by calling in, as unobtrusively as possible, substances less obviously nutritious and appetizing. The harsh word for this is "adulteration."

When I write "harsh word," I have in mind a gentleman charged with supplying a lubricating grease into which he had put 40 per cent of chalk, which, unhappily for the machinery and him, happened to be mixed with iron filings. "Oh," he protested to his barrister, "we don't call *that* adulteration. That is a most objectionable word. We call it 'loading'." In matters of food and drink, the gentler, more acceptable term is "substitution." Originally adulteration was understood to be plain cheating, and the adulterator had little to say for himself when he was found out; his adulterated stuff was destroyed, and he went into the pillory or was branded, nailed by the ear to any convenient woodwork, or otherwise roughly handled.

But the increase of knowledge and human subtlety have complicated this question. The idea of artificial and synthetic foods has a peculiar charm for the practical substitutionist, and the conception of suggestion comes in as a very real help when one is detected in misdescription. There may be substitution in series giving the most remarkable results. In one delightful instance a firm was prosecuted for selling something called lemonade crystals which was labelled "Pure Fruit Juice and Sugar Only." It was shown that neither fruit nor sugar was used in their manufacture. The "accepted substitutes"—ingenious phrase—for lemon juice and sugar in the trade are citric acid and glucose. But this particular firm had procured its citric acid from a purveyor whose idea of an "accepted substitute" for citric acid was tartaric acid. And tartaric acid also by the charitable customs of commerce can have an understudy, and so what this firm of caterers was finally handing out to thirsty little boys and girls was a "tartaric acid substitute"—of which they did not know the composition. Analysis showed it to be dirty phosphoric acid. The label had not only the lying words quoted above but a picture of a large yellow lemon in vivid contrast with a lovely green leaf. The defendants alleged that this was to help people to "realize that it tasted like lemons"—which my informant declares stoutly it did not do. All the more need for the helpful label, the defendants might argue. It is distressing to think of the virtuous teetotaller, who has avoided alcohol as a deadly poison throughout his life, betrayed into the consumption of this sinister brew of glucose and old bones.

This is but an outstanding instance of an all too prevalent disposition to put a brave face upon dishonesty. S. L. Bensusan, the well known writer on British Agriculture, has recently come upon and made a happy use of a private and confidential memorandum issued by the British Food Manufacturers' Association upon Jam.* Jam, Mr. Bensusan protests, should be made of sound fruit and sugar alone. Swedes and vegetable marrow, dyes and so forth, are inadmissible to the housewife's preserving pan. But this federation sets up certain standards for "First Quality" and "Second Quality" jams, and its guiding instructions to the patriotic jam-maker leave Mr. Bensusan and ourselves astounded. "First Quality" jam for the British market need not have more than 50 per cent of fruit, and second quality more than 20 per cent. The "fruit" may be brought from abroad in tubs with preservatives; it may be eked out with any old vegetable pulp as an "acceptable substitute," the want of seeds in this pulp may be supplemented by the stale stock of the seedsman, it may be livened up with citric, tartaric and malic acids and brightened with any "permitted" colouring matter, and there it is, First Quality British Jam. What Third Quality Jam for the millions can be like is known only in the deepest recesses of the British Food Manufacturers' Association.

In a systematic treatment of this question we should find ourselves confronted by certain main types of justifications and excuses. There are "preservatives." Some, it is alleged, are quite harmless, but that is no reason why the consumer should not know clearly that they have been employed, just as he has a right to know that food has been kept in a refrigerator. Most preservatives employed seem to be injurious in vari-

*New Statesman, Dec. 20, 1930.

ous degrees, and some are a plain danger to health. Yet they may be arranged in an unbroken ascending order of virtue until you come to the time-honoured practices of salting beef and pork, smoking hams, hanging game and putting sugar or lemon in your tea. Is there any really "natural" food except unmixed fresh raw fruit?

Next to preservatives come various colouring matters employed to restore our confidence in faded and jaded substances. It is a fine line that separates decorative and encouraging from deceitful coloration. It needs a still finer discrimination to distinguish between the modern "flavouring substance" and the herbs in the soup or the mint English cooks put with peas and potatoes. Finally there is the bulk substitution of one cheaper and less reputed foodstuff for another. It is called by the more reputable name, to help the imagination and stimulate the receptive juices of the consumer. Why should they not be stimulated?

You see that this is not a simple case of wickedness and adulteration on the one hand and goodness and no adulteration on the other. We can pass by imperceptible degrees from the poisonous scoundrelism of those lemonade sellers to the makers of the most desirable foodstuffs and condiments and to every sort of innovator in dietary. What of the breakfast cereal? What of the sausage? When Raleigh came to Europe with the potato, did he realize that he was bringing over an "acceptable substitute" for wheat flour?

A constant warfare goes on between two types of alert intelligences in this field of food supply, a conflict which indeed extends far beyond catering into almost every field of human activity. People are being shabbily active and intelligently cunning in the feeding of mankind, and they are spending their lives and finding their profits in degrading human food, but at the same time another active class is making the most strenuous efforts to increase the quantity and quality of human nutrition and to restrain and defeat the sordid interests that would poison and enfeeble us. The campaign for more and better food is a world-wide and on the whole a not unhopeful one. We have already glanced at the conflict of the same factors in the problem of journalism, where we found sordid considerations and unimaginative self-seeking cheapening and corrupting that general supply of information and discussion which is now so necessary to civilized life, and we have found the countervailing forces as yet undefinable and ineffective; but as regards the more urgent matter of food, what we may call antiseptic organization is better developed. There is a great body of legislation for the protection of the people's food in every civilized country; there is an organization of analysts and inspectors.

Our projected *Science of Work and Wealth* would tell in full of the development and organization of this new preventive service—for its beginnings date only from the middle of the nineteenth century. Before that time the only check on adulteration, except for outbursts of popular indignation and municipal action (taking the form of market control), was through the Revenue service, which naturally confined its attention only to the sophistication of dutiable articles. An interesting part of that history would be the passing and working of the Federal Food and Drugs Act of the United States of America (1906). That marks a very important phase in the history of the American stomach, and also in the history of private enterprise. From being a country where private enterprise had carried the adulteration and misbranding of food to extremes, the United States now ranks among the most wholesomely nourished lands in the world.

There is also the American Consumers' Service, Inc., to be noted, which reports to its subscribers on the real value of commodities offered for sale—with especial reference to adulteration.

But manifestly a completely satisfactory food supply for mankind is only possible when we know what is to be scheduled as completely satisfactory food. Scientific food control awaits the advance of physiological science. Until such schedules are produced, legislation must aim mainly at the suppression of misdescription and leave the individual, with such guidance as his doctor can give him, to choose among his poisons. We must still have our substitute lemonade, perhaps—but with a plain intimation of the bones or other refuse from which it derives its refreshing acidity. In the place of that green and yellow picture of a lemon, if a decorative label is still felt to be necessary, a slaughter house or a knacker's yard must be pictured as attractively as the artist can contrive.

§ 6. *Dining and Drugging*

A new chapter opens, and the reader's appetite is revived when we turn from the caterers' stores and the substitutionists' problems to the dinner table.

And here we have to consider not merely what people eat but how they eat it. One interesting change challenges our attention, the gradual replacement of the private dining-room by the restaurant that is now in progress. I do not know if anyone has yet attempted to trace and measure this steady replacement of private by collective feeding.

Feeding used generally to be a very unobtrusive and intimate affair. Even cats and dogs like to turn away from us a little to finish up a bone. The peasant, the small householder of only fifty years ago, either never fed abroad, or on such rare occasions as he did, took his little packet of food with him. The employee brought food with him to his work or went home to eat. Large classes of inferior people were too shy and awkward to eat in strange company, and the banquets of the rich were private. People ate together in the refectories of monasteries and nunneries, in military messes, in university college halls, at public banquets and city feasts. They ate at the dreadful tables of boarding houses. There were almost always associative links to bring the eaters together, except when one was travelling—and travel was rare. But now everywhere the little tables of the restaurants increase, and so does the proportion of meals taken by the average man in promiscuous company.

A pleasant subsection of our encyclopædia or museum would deal with table furniture and decoration. We should see tablecloths and mats and serviettes, china and glass, forks and fish knives and flowers, replacing bit by bit the dipping in the bowl, the loving cup, the troughlike habits of the past.

Equally interesting and laborious would it be to get together a comprehensive account of the large-scale catering connected with this change of habit from secret to open eating. Our encyclopædist would have to go behind the scenes of a great restaurant and display the cooks at work and the organization of the service. For the present the interested reader will find much quite trustworthy information in Arnold Bennett's novel, *Imperial Palace*. Is there a limit to this increase in collective feeding? That we shall be better able to discuss after we have dealt with the development of collective housing, as we shall presently do.

Another specialized section would be necessary for our tobacco and cigars. Carmen no doubt will demand a place on the scene. We should have to tell how far machinery and the machine-made cigarette have superseded Carmen's nimble fingers. In the days of Dickens most cigarette smokers rolled their own cigarettes; it was a very foreign and rather sinister thing to do. Now few have the skill, and there are hardly any private cigarette machines. I doubt if you could buy one. Who put the pocket "cigarette machine" on the market, and who or what has hustled it out of existence again?

And after all that spectacle of feasting it would be necessary, I feel, to call for doctors and drugs—and here more particularly drugs. Diet from the point of view of health and medical treatment has been dealt with in the *Science of Life,* but if our detailed survey is to cover the whole complex of human activities, the work of the medical man must have proper attention. I have found very great difficulty in weaving the doctor and surgeon into this scheme of human living so far as their normal professional activities go. And the dentist. But I think here is a place for them so far as they are to be considered vis-à-vis with the eating individual.

Much of the physician's work can, of course, be considered and dealt with when the organization of the modern city and the public control of public health is again considered. Surgery again may be made a sort of side chapter to a treatment of scientific research. And there must be a little world of admirable human beings making the beautiful apparatus and instruments that subserve such work. I do not know where we should place it in our encyclopædia, and I find it ungracious and impossible to ignore it. Here, at any rate, with a sort of logic we can note the preparation, manufacture and distribution of drugs. It is, I believe, a very neat and interesting industry indeed. The unobtrusive tabloid and the urbane ingratiating capsule have banished most of the horrors of the dose. The comic writer can no longer wring any laughter from the black draught. We live in a time when the black draught is forgotten. But in the eighteenth and nineteenth centuries it was almost as cardinal in domestic life as "washing day." We still talk of a man "taking his medicine" when he has to face the consequences of some rash act, but in this age that phrase has none of the suggestion of nose held and bold gulping, that it once possessed.

How far the drug industry interlocks with the manufacture of meat and vegetable extracts and with condiments and perfumes, I do not know. To find out and tell the public would be a task as fascinating as it would be laborious. And since no one would read a complete description of this matter all through unless in preparation for an examination, we need not set ourselves to the task. We need do no more than think of the various groups of factories and laboratories, the clean and skilled workers, the bottling machinery and canning machinery busy with ever increasing efficiency upon these myriads of supplementary products.

§ 7. *The Peasant, the Basis of the Old Order*

Having eaten, drunken, and rectified ourselves we can face certain fundamental issues that underlie our description of food production. These issues are indeed fundamental to the whole process of social and economic evolution.

We can no longer dispense with detail by waving the reader to imaginary encyclopædias. We must sit down here to direct and exact discussion.

We will imagine that we have really looked over various voluminous and well pictured descriptions of scientifically planned plantations and that the picture of the organized production over large countrysides, of this or that item upon the daily menu of mankind, is before us. But when the reader goes about the world, particularly when he is in an aëroplane over Europe, southwestern Asia, India or China, he sees no such widely conceived and widely handled areas of production. For the most part he sees the best soil and the most convenient regions parcelled out into extraordinarily small patches and being cultivated by methods that any full rendering of the possibilities of modern production will assure him are antiquated and obsolete. He will find if he enquires into the matter that these little patches are held individually and managed independently. He is in the presence of the most obdurate obstacle to the effective modernization of the world, the peasant. The peasant is the type, symbol and substance of localized traditionalism. He is the basis of the old order and a misfit and anachronism in the new. He, with his whole family, work upon and live upon his holding of land. He and his family constitute an almost autonomous social unit.

A couple of centuries ago, practically all mankind was living on local produce. Foreign trade was a trade in luxuries, superfluities, and accessories. Fosdick, in his *Old Savage in the New Civilization,* cites an account written by a Massachusetts farmer of the year 1786 of his economic life, which has happily been preserved for us. All his meat, bread, vegetables, fruit and (maple) sugar, he grew himself. His clothing came from his own wool and flax and leather of his own tanning. His house was built from his own trees, and he had his own forge. All he needed from the outside world were a few such things as salt, pepper, lead bullets, gunpowder, tools and weapons, and few of these things came from overseas. These needs he satisfied easily by selling a fraction of his wheat or cattle. The human world, save in the regions given over to nomadism, was a world of such small localized cultivators, and its towns, industries, churches and monasteries, courts and armies, such as they were, were all resting in the last resort on the indefatigable toil of the man with the plough and spade, *working in the vicinity*.

There was one important breakaway from this generalization before the modern era, the case of Rome during the mightier phase of the City-Empire. Then the subjugated provinces, and especially Sicily and Egypt, sent a great tribute of foodstuffs in exceptionally large ships to the capital. The economic life of all Italy indeed during the days of imperial expansion, shows a movement of essential produce unequalled in quantity and distance elsewhere in the ancient world. Where there are very large rivers there had also been, since the very earliest days, an important concentration of produce to aliment city aggregations at crucial vantage points. Since the beginnings of history there have been such pre-railway great cities, for example on the Nile, on the Euphrates and Tigris, on the Ganges and the great Chinese rivers.

But these were exceptions to the general state of human affairs. The immense majority of the race was dispersed in a village plus small-town pattern, and each repetition of the pattern was economically autonomous and capable of carrying on by itself, if necessary, for an indefinite time. Indeed, it had to be so autonomous, because there were no means of either taking away or bringing produce in bulk. If production failed, the district starved. In the past men could die of famine in Cheshire while Kent had a glut. And the fundamental dots in this stippled pattern of human society, the individual dots that made the circles of relationship, made the rosette of villages and township, were the hand cultivator, the peasant. Alterations in the status of the peasant there have been again and again. In the story of Pharaoh's dream of the lean kine and the fat kine we have the memory of a deal in which the burthen on the peasant is increased. And the château-burning of the first French Revolution finds its parallel in most of the social cataclysms of the past. The superincumbent pressure is thrown off, and the peasant recovers his surplus produce. But whether the peasant was getting a greater or lesser share out of his total yield, whether he was serf or debtor or free and prosperous small farmer with no master above him, did not in the least alter the fact that the economy of the community was entirely based on him. He conditioned the lives of his tyrants and masters and parasites. They might come or go, they might vary widely, but he remained. He was the essential thing. Nothing in the nature of industrial England or industrial Belgium was possible before the nineteenth century, no countryside carrying millions of industrial workers and having a food production out of all proportion smaller than the needs of the population it carried.

§ 8. *The Passing of the Peasant*

Essentially the modernization of food production means the supersession of this small localized self-directing cultivator, peasant or peasant-like. Here we will speak only of the mechanical organization, the material pressures, concerned in the process. It will be more convenient to leave until later the mental and social stresses this supersession involves.

We have mentioned already the expropriation of peasants in favour of an estate system with slave labour, as a phase in the Roman development. This probably diminished the total output per head and thinned out the population of the countryside, but concentrated a large share of the produce as profit in the hands of the slave owner. The decline and fall of the Empire, the cessation of the slave supply, meant the restoration of the soil to the peasant.

It was a thousand years later, in the British Isles and under entirely new conditions, that the supersession of peasant holders appeared again. In the south and east of England the dispossession of the peasant was associated with sheep-farming for wool export, but it was also directly related to the appearance of new agricultural methods that superseded the strip husbandry and common grazing of the ancient traditional system. It was not merely that the peasant was dispossessed in England; the more important fact is that his methods were set aside. His labour was economized by production on a new scale. Specialization ended his autonomy. Cultivation was less and less for immediate use and more and more for the market. And his home industries were overwhelmed by town products. In this new process of estate aggregation the countryside population was actually reduced while the surplus of production was greatly increased.

It is unnecessary to trace in detail here the phases of the process that replaced the English peasant almost altogether by the agricultural labourer. It is one typical local instance of a world-wide struggle that is still going on, with many fluctuations and setbacks. It is a fight between the individualist "family farmer" on the one hand and organization and (later) machinery on the other. In Denmark the small cultivator has persisted by a surrender of much of his individual freedom to coöperative organization. He has survived by combination. The English peasant was extinguished before he and his world had reached a level of knowledge and education that made such a voluntary association for collective purposes possible. The English small-holder to-day is a new social type still upon its trial and still learning the lessons of coöperation that the Danish peasant mastered two generations ago. He is not in the old tradition. He is a return to the land.

Since the end of the World War there has been a great extension of large mechanized farms in America. The end of the free land policy coincided with the immediate post-war boom, and many farmers sold their land at top prices about 1920, with the result that when prices fell many farmers and tenants were burdened with high rents and debts. Agriculture was stimulated to a new technique and much agricultural machinery was sold, often on the hire purchase system. Many small farmers had to sell out. There was a "thinning of the comparatively densely sown farming democracy of the middle west." Already in 1926 over 9000 corporate farms were in existence, with a gross income of over 709 million dollars (almost 6 per cent of the total agricultural gross income of the United States.) These corporate farms are very varied, including fruit farms, cattle breeding farms, dairy farms, sugar plantations, mixed farms, cotton growing enterprises and wheat farms. One large sugar refinery in Louisiana owns an estate of 10,000 to 12,000 acres of sugar canes. In some cases, for instance in California, the small farmer continues management subject to the instructions of business headquarters, which sell the produce and finance production. Factory farms proper are however run by the aid of movable labour and machines, and are unburdened by any superfluous expenses for housing workers and settling villages. They reflect the mechanical character of modern America (says Professor M. J. Bonn, from whose book *Prosperity,* published in 1931, these facts are taken) far more clearly than do industrial undertakings.

They resemble somewhat the Russian Sovkhozy, the modernized collective farm as it is being worked out in Russia. The Soviet government is trying to pass at one stride from conditions that prevailed in fifteenth-century England to an organization of agriculture comprehensive beyond anything hitherto known in the world. A strenuously modern conception of social organization is seeking to impose itself upon a mediæval peasantry, and there is a conscious and acute struggle between peasant and estate—which in this case is a government estate. Upon its issue depends the whole future of Russia. A successful resistance by the peasant spells regression and defeat to that vast experiment. A triumph of large, coördinated cultivation means, on the other hand, an educated countryside, dominated by schools and research stations, and playing a large part in the establishment of a new social order throughout the world.

This primary problem of the Russian revolution, the problem of the peasant, was the main topic in a conversation between the present writer and Lenin in 1920. Lenin was then very hopeful of a progressive organization of publicly owned estates, district by district and province by province. The peasant method of life was to be fought and beaten in detail, first here and then there. The peasant, said Lenin, has great resisting power in his own place, but he has not the nation-wide solidarity nor the alertness to bestir himself to combat an attack on his dearest habits and prejudices when it is going on in another part of the country. So that by concentrating all the resources of the Soviet government first in one province and then in another, all Russia would at last be won to modern agriculture and reconstructed from the ground up. Special, specially favoured, regions were to be chosen for the establishment of great communal estates, which were to produce upon modern lines, and the peasants of unregenerate districts were to be won over to submit in their turn to communal organization by the spectacle of the super-productivity, comfort and vitality upon these estates.

That was the project of Lenin in 1920. It seemed to me a quite reasonable and hopeful method. But it was never pursued. The famine year of 1920–21, the economic blockade of Russia by Western Europe, and the crippled state of Russia's industrial plant, delayed its realization. The necessary machinery was not at hand. The peasants underproduced because they got no satisfaction out of their extra production. The Western world, with its conservative traditions, held aloof, and no machinery or commodities of any sort could be got to stimulate the peasant to toil. The N. E. P. of 1921, the new economic policy, was a desperate attempt to save the immediate situation, a reversion to many of the liberties of private accumulation and ownership that had been abolished. Trading and production for profit reappeared in the towns, adventurers with foreign capital came bargaining into Russia, and the abler peasants grew richer than their fellows again. In a few years Russia began to resemble the United States of a century ago. Profits and social inequality developed on a scale that threatened every ideal and hope of constructive communism.

This temporary arrest of socialization began in 1921. Lenin fell ill and a struggle for the succession began. That development of a socialized estate system in chosen localities did not go on, as it could and should have gone on. There was a delay of eight years. There was a distinct drag in the modernization of Russia for those eight years. The temperamental Slav was, it seems to me, in a phase of lassitude. He dislikes measured steady work; he likes to take things by storm—and many things cannot be done in that way. So, I say, it seems to me; but reputable observers see in that interlude of eight years a period of recovery, necessary for the accumulation of energy for a fresh push forward. Trotsky and Zinovieff protested in 1927 against the gradual recession from socialist ideals, but the protests were set aside. Their protests, said Stalin, Lenin's successor, were premature. The time was not ripe.

Then, in 1928, Stalin awoke to an extravagance of energy. Not by parts, but as a whole, should Russian agriculture be made over. The N. E. P. was disavowed and set aside. The richer peasants, who had been evoked by the N. E. P., were suddenly denounced as the enemies of Russia. They were persecuted, and their children were persecuted and denied ordinary educational facilities. The time was ripe at last. Russia was to be made over by the Five Year Plan, which was to abolish the peasant for ever in favour of the collectivist estate, scientifically controlled. Russia was, in fact, to do in five years what the capitalist system has been painfully feeling its way towards for centuries. Was it, is it, an impossible undertaking? We must remember Russia has the experience of those centuries to help her, American machinery, American agricultural experts in prairie cultivation, and a very real but rather incalculable fund of enthusiasm to draw upon.

We are still watching that effort. It is the most interesting thing in contemporary history. Such pioneer reporters as Henri Barbusse, Maurice Hindus and Frazier Hunt tell of great changes and enthusiasm, infectious enthusiasm; they seem to have felt success in the air. And we get excellent propaganda films full of sunshine, hope and promise to tell us of the Five Year Plan sweeping ahead of schedule time. The screen displayed the building of the railway from Turkestan to Siberia very vividly and told me in continually increasing type:

TURK-SIB WILL BE READY IN 1930

TURK-SIB WILL BE READY IN 1930

TURK-SIB WILL BE READY IN 1930

TURK-SIB WILL BE READY IN 1930

Possibly it is something old or cold or bourgeois in my blood, that mingled a broad streak of scepticism with my appreciation. A question of temperament comes in here, and the reader should know of it. I do not like Dostoevsky or Tolstoi; I dislike the epileptic temperament; I am the antithesis of a Slav, and I bore away at things. I like things done without haste and without delay. I do not like things in front of schedule time any more than I like them behind time. So I doubted. But in May I learnt that my scepticism in this instance was unjustified. Turk-Sib was ready—and seven months of 1930 had still to run. Turk-Sib is running. Good for Russia! Good for Stalin! So far.

So far, because witnesses also return to testify to a terrible misuse of the new machinery, of harvesters taken to pieces out of mere childish curiosity and rusting in the fields, of the new wine bursting the old bottles and then running to waste.

In March, 1930, the Western world became aware of a check in this big thrust that was to carry rural life in Russia with one stupendous rush from mediæval to ultra-modern conditions. The young communists in charge of the transformation were rebuked for excess of zeal; they had driven too hard, and they must relax. All over Russia the Kulaks, the richer peasants, were slaughtering the stock they had accumulated rather than surrender it; their persecution had been not merely unjust but intolerable, and they were in revolt.* The attempt to foment a "class war" between the peasant with a dozen head of stock and his neighbour or his brother or his cousin with less or none, had failed, and the peasants were holding together. Perhaps this was only a first assault and a first repulse. Perhaps these Russian revolutionaries who have been in so extreme a hurry and so convulsive in their methods have learnt deliberation from this check and thrust forward all the more effectively for the lesson.

The Russian experiment will be an enormous stride in the modernization of the world, if it succeeds; but even if it is heavily checked and delayed, or even if it fails altogether, it is only one part of a world-wide thrust towards the single organized human community. Russia is a very forward country because it is also a very backward country. Its issues lie bare and plain. There is none of the complex closeness, the elaboration and masking of conflict between the scientific and instinctive forces, that one finds in the Atlantic communities.

*Between March, 1929, and March, 1930, sheep decreased by one third, and pigs by two fifths, and horned cattle by one fifth. There was a famine of meat and dairy produce. Farbman in *Piatiletka. Russia's Five-Year Plan.*

Soviet Russia is double faced. She is communist and instinctive on the one hand, and she is state-socialist, scientific-planning and organizing on the other. She is mediæval and modern, revivalist and cold-blooded. There are, for example, two entirely different types of experiments going on there in agricultural reconstruction, experiments with a curious parallelism and a curious indifference to each other; these are (1) the "Kolkhozy" and (2) the "Sovkhozy." They serve to illustrate a curious two-sidedness that runs through all this Russian revolution. The Kolkhoz (1) displays the old sentimental unwashed sweating "democratic" side, all natural virtue, brotherhood and kisses. The rich peasant is dispossessed, the poor are exalted above him, and the whole village attempts collectivist democratic management—with, however, as Hindus and the propaganda film make clear, a bright young man from Moscow as persuader, adviser and redeemer. On the other hand (2) the Sovkhoz is a state plantation, a really scientifically planned and directed modern large-scale organization of production with disciplined and trained workers—the big cultivations in Turkestan, for example, or the "Gigant" in the Caucasus, the vastest wheat-growing estate in the world, measuring fifty miles from north to south and forty from east to west. One thing cripples the Sovkhozy greatly. The best lands are already thickly settled by peasants, and so they have fallen to the Kolkhozy. The Sovkhozy have to take up lands hitherto uncultivated, either because they are poor lands or at a grave distance from consuming areas. They carry no village population; they are run to produce wheat (or some other single crop) for the towns or for export. The two thousand square miles of the Gigant have a total population, including engineers, families and subsidiary staff, of 17,000—of which, by the by, over 16,000 were under thirty years of age in 1930.

These Sovkhozy make straight for a new world order, but it is very doubtful if the Kolkhozy do anything of the sort. The Kolkhoz seems to be the old Tzarist Mir in a state of emotion. It is Rousseauism pretending to love machinery and taking it to pieces out of sheer childishness, misusing and destroying it. Recently Russia has been sending out admirably made, good-humoured, and attractive films about the new departure, in which peasant beggar women or social outcasts of a highly idealized sort, are represented as suddenly taking control of affairs, adopting all the latest devices of scientific agriculture, and founding and organizing elaborately mechanical coöperative estates. It is quite charming nonsense, but it seems to be sent out in perfect good faith.

Socialism did not originally include and does not necessarily include now any insurrectionary or "primitive" element. Its essence is scientifically planned construction as opposed to individualistic *"laissez faire* and all will come well."* It was Marx whose mind was dominated by the prevalent political democracy of his time, who twisted up progress with crudity, and determined this curious Russian "squint," so that we are never quite sure to what Russia is looking and what her next step will be. Russia is, in fact, a vast area of moody and fluctuating economic experiments distracted by two points of view, and for that reason alone even her warm well-wishers—and I am one—are left doubting whether her constructive effort will succeed or will relapse finally into a mere barbaric chaos of insecure petty cultivation at the present Chinese level.

The change in the Russian landscape is at any rate remarkable. Joan Beauchamp, who visited Russia in 1927 and again in 1930, describes it very vividly in a pamphlet, "Agriculture in Soviet Russia," as she noted it from the train. In 1927 the age-long tradition of strip cultivation still held sway, "implements of the most primitive kind" prevailed, "a third of each family's land lay fallow each year," and "each peasant wasted much of his working time walking from one to another of the many strips into which his holding was divided." In 1930 a great proportion of the strips had vanished; they survived mostly close to the towns and villages (no doubt for vegetable growing and townsman odd-time cultivation). Elsewhere the small peasant holdings have been replaced either by vast state farms using the most up-to-date machinery, or by "peasants' collective associations which have gathered together all the horses and machinery they could beg, borrow, hire or confiscate."

"I travelled from Moscow down to the Northern Caucasus during the recent harvest, and it was fascinating to sit at the carriage window and observe all the different methods of agriculture in use as the train sped on. Sometimes we passed through districts where all the land was divided into tiny strips on which men, women and children were working by hand, aided only by the simplest implements. Here a peasant was cutting a strip of perhaps a tenth of an acre of wheat with a sickle, handful by handful, while his wife followed after, gathering the handfuls into sheaves. Next a lad ploughing half an acre or so with one horse. Then we would run into a district where already the strip system had been abolished and fields of wheat, barley, or oats of a reasonable size began to appear. There we passed long lines of reapers, with scythes sweeping rhythmically, followed by women in bright headscarves, bending down to tie the sheaves. At times we travelled for kilometre after kilometre through uncut wheat, waving far away into the distance. On the edges of some of the larger stretches of corn horse-drawn reapers, such as those still used on many English farms, were at work, often following one another in squads of three or four. Sometimes we came upon large pieces of land which the peasants were bringing into cultivation for the first time. In one such field, at seven in the morning, I counted no less than eighteen horse machines about to start work. Wherever the strip system had been abolished a good deal of machinery of the most assorted types was in use, and the method of traction varied almost as much as the type of machine—here and there a tractor, more often a pair of bullocks, occasionally a camel, but most often, horses.

"Most of the villages seemed to consist of one-storeyed mud houses with barns or cowsheds attached, though a number of the newer houses were made of wood with red zinc roofs. In many districts new houses were being built of bricks with zinc roofs, but all appeared small, and very few had more than one storey. Not far from the villages, running along beside the railway for a kilometre or so, there was often a strip of rough grazing land where herds of cows or bullocks grazed, watched by children. Harrowing also seemed mostly to be entrusted to the children, who hailed us joyfully as they sat perched on the harness of whatever animal happened to be dragging the harrow. . . ."

The expropriation of the peasant as it occurred in Britain through enclosures and a change of scale in farming, and as it is being attempted in Russia through governmental socialization, are extreme instances of the release of production from petty individualism. Changes in cultivation over the rest of the world have for the most part been of a less drastic type. In the older countries, still under the sway of the traditions of a long past of peasant culture, we find a great variety of peasantdoms still prevailing, more or less mitigated to fit modern exigencies; here the peasant enslaved by the usurer, here grown larger into an acquisite free farmer, here in barbaric regions the slave cultivator of a local chief, here sharing profits and here paying rent in kind or money to a landowner inheriting from some sort of expropriating brigand. One widespread result of the war in eastern Europe, in Esthonia, for example, has been the breaking up of great estates and a relapse towards—if not actually to—peasantdoms.

In vivid contrast to the ancient deep-rooted peasantdoms of Europe and Asia are the conditions of cultivation in the new lands that have been opened up to cultivating occupation in recent years: the modern ranch and farm in America, Australia and New Zealand, and the exploitation of new irrigation lands. There the cultivator, starting *de novo* with modern appliances, works directly for the market and not for his

HUMANITY IN MOVEMENT

THE Grand Central Station, New York. It is estimated that more than sixty-eight million people used the terminal in 1929, of whom forty-seven million were passengers. The remaining twenty-one million used it as a thoroughfare to the surrounding office buildings, hotels, and streets, or to meet and bid good-bye to passengers.

THE PRINTED WORD

FED by a giant roll of paper, huge presses like the one in this picture print, cut, fold and pour out a continuous stream of newspapers ready for distribution. The white arrows show the direction of the moving papers.

own consumption, just as the new Russian Sovkhozy do, whereas the primitive peasant worked entirely for consumption and at most traded only, or yielded reluctantly, the small surplus of his output.

The story of New Zealand is particularly illuminating. As that very modern community rushed into being there was extensive land grabbing. It seemed probable that a big private estate system would be established, with tenant cultivators. Vigorous legislative opposition, and particularly graduated taxation, has checked this tendency. The great estates have to a considerable extent been broken up. But the proportion of small cultivating holders, that is to say, holders of less than half a square mile, has not increased. The increase is in holdings of from half a square mile to eight square miles. With modern coöperative methods of machinery and selling, an active Agricultural Department and state electric power, New Zealand seems to be working out a satisfactory and prosperous modern agriculture with owning cultivators farming upon that scale. Neither peasant nor landlord appears in the scheme, and the stratum of modern-spirited farmers exercises very considerable political power. For many types of cultivation the large farmer, who will be in effect neither complete owner nor debtor nor rent-payer, but a fairly free occupier, financed through phases of difficulty by a state cultivators' corporation, selling mainly to its marketing board, assisted by its laboratories, sustained by its common services and in the ultimate resort under its control, may prove to be the final best through long ages in the future before us.

Different climates, differences in contour and soil may vary the optimum area for unified farming, from the hundreds or even thousands of square miles possible over prairie regions to the few acres of an orange farm or a vineyard. New Zealand, it must be remembered, is a sheep-farming country where the farms rule large. The unit of enterprise may prove to be much smaller in urbanized regions, where fruit, vegetables, flowers, poultry, and highly manured, intensely cultivated dairy farms will be at a convenient distance from a market. But these are differences in scale rather than differences in spirit. The smaller holdings contemplated will be something very different from the strips of the past, and the worker altogether different in quality and outlook from his peasant predecessor. He will be growing for the market as an item in a comprehensive scheme. The general principle of a limited, controlled and directed individualism with an overriding state landlord runs through all the most hopeful schemes for agricultural reorganization.

§ 9. The World's Catering Is Still Unorganized

There are two other questions, both very speculative, that we have to consider before we leave this subject of the world's eating. The first is how far our present reorganization of our food services upon world lines is still incomplete. It is vast and elaborate, but it is still haphazard. Immense economies and readjustments will have to be made before the constructive intelligence can be satisfied by the state of affairs. Let me quote again from Raymond D. Fosdick who in his *Old Savage in the New Civilization* has said already exactly what has to be said here.

On the surface of the earth there are to-day living 1,900,000,000 people.

"We know precisely the quantity of food necessary for this vast population. That is one of the additions to our knowledge which the new science of statistics has given us. We know, moreover, where this food is grown and raised. We know the quantity of exports and imports for each of the sixty-five nations of the world. We know the primary and secondary sources of supply for particular countries. We know, for example, the amount of wheat that Germany would ordinarily import from Russia, and Russia failing as a granary, the amount that has to come from the United States or the Argentine. We know the dependency of the United States upon other nations for coffee, tea, cocoa, sugar and many other products, and the dependency of other nations upon us for wheat and beef. In other words, through modern statistics we are able, in our generation, to get a complete picture of supply and demand in relation to the world's food.

"And yet is it an orderly process that we see? Is it a process that has been worked out to obtain a maximum of benefit for the human race and a minimum of suffering and waste? Has organizing intelligence been applied on a world-wide basis to the production and distribution of food? The question answers itself. In spite of all our knowledge, this essential phase of the world's work is a chaos, a haphazard, drifting arrangement in which sheer chance plays far too prominent a part. As if natural hazards like crop failures or animal diseases were not enough, the human race adds to its own confusion by tariff wars and discriminatory regulations and cut-throat competition and a hundred other exhibitions of international folly. Consequently, part of the world is hungry while the rest of the world has food in quantity. Eastern Europe starves while the farmers of our Middle West burn their corn for fuel. Asia is underfed while North America hunts a market.

"Here is a vast problem that is calling for the organizing intelligence of mankind. The field has been surveyed and the factors are known. What we need now is synthetic thinking, constructive brains, a plan, laid down in world terms, that will disentangle and weave together in a common system the complex details of our present arrangement."

There is one powerful argument for a revision of the legal, political and educational traditions that at present rule mankind. That such a revision is pressing upon us is the conclusion to which all this review of human work and wealth is taking us. The next section will reinforce that argument very strongly and underline it with a note of urgency.

§ 10. *The Limits of Plenty*

The second wide question we cannot ignore is the possibility of a progressive exhaustion of essential supplies. As we have shown in the *Science of Life,* every species has hitherto eaten (or starved) according to the current year's resources. A limiting factor in the expansion of life, lies in the restricted and diminishing supply of available phosphorus. And we are now beginning to take nitrogen from the air in the manufacture of artificial fertilizers, a process that may easily attain such a scale as to produce within a few score centuries a perceptible change in the composition of the atmosphere. "The solution of the nitrogen problem by Crookes," says Professor Armstrong, "has brought us nearer to destruction rather than saved us, by hastening the depletion of irreplaceable phosphatic stores. We can clearly foresee in phosphorus the limiting factor to the world's progress." Professor Armstrong is not a miracle of judgment or knowledge, but these words of his command respect.* Man is able to do what no other animal species has done: he is able to draw upon the accumulations of energy in the past and to anticipate his normal periodic supplies. He is doing so now, and it is a task awaiting the early attention of research students in economics to assemble and summarize everything that may illuminate the problem of how far man's consumption of food is exceeding his proper income and invading the capital upon which his future depends. In the *Science of Life,* in the Book on Ecology and in the Book upon Human Biology, attention is drawn to this fact that for the last two centuries *Homo sapiens* has been increasing at a rate that almost justifies the phrase "a breeding storm," and it is suggested that even now the human popula-

---

*My suspicions are confirmed as I go to press. Mr. C. J. Williams, a director of a well known firm of fertilizer manufacturers, writes: "I would like to point out that there is enough in one phosphate mine, namely the Gafsa Company's mine, to supply the whole world for sixty years, and the North African coast from Gibraltar to Egypt is practically all phosphate, and is being shipped regularly from Morocco to Egypt all over the world."

tion may have passed the security point and be greater than it should be for a prosperous sustained biological equilibrium.

We have already raised this question in our outline of a Book of Substances. But now we are able to put the matter in a more concrete form, as a picture of all this feeding and feasting we have displayed, the smoking and wining and drugging, going on without apprehension, prevision or guidance upon dwindling supports over an abyss. It is a primary issue of unknown urgency, calling aloud for earnest and sustained study and for collective controls, conceived not upon national or imperial, but upon absolutely comprehensive world-wide lines.

CHAPTER THE FIFTH

THE CONQUEST OF CLIMATE: HOW MANKIND IS CLOTHED AND HOUSED

§ 1. *The Wardrobes of Mankind*

SO SOON as our 1,900,000,000 people are assured of food, the questions of clothing, shelter and ornament arise. The search for comfort begins. Man—and still more woman—arrays himself against the elements and to encounter his fellow creatures. He dresses, he arranges his personal background.

When first I planned that voluminous undertaking, the *Science of Work and Wealth*—that project which turned out at last to be only the necessary vast eggshell, the phantasmal embryonic wrappings from which this present work was born—I put down the title of two great books. One was to be How Mankind is Clothed, and the other How Mankind is Housed. As soon, however, as the attempts to assemble the material began, it became evident that these two systems of human activity were in fact inseparable. They are both in essence now, man's conflict with climate and the weather. And so far as the treatment of industry goes furniture is one indivisible link. Such substances as textiles and leather would have to come in twice over if the two subjects were separated, though little more than the lie of the seams separates a shirt from a pillow case or a pair of boots from the cushion of a smoking-room armchair. The productive processes are the same. And hat, parasol, umbrella, tent, shelter, shed, hut, hovel, and house have, as the biologists say, a plain morphological as well as functional connection. They are all represented by the shell of the snail.

First we should have dealt with the general materials for clothing and furniture. There would have been an account, an immense account, like endless galleries in a museum, of natural and artificial fibres, and of modern spinning, weaving, knitting and netting. After that would have come the colouring and printing of these fabrics. Leather and skins generally, demand a chapter by themselves. Then would have

169

come the shoemaker, hosier, hatter, tailor and dressmaker. A discursion of fashions follows naturally on that. I think our encyclopædia would have omitted the soul of clothing unless it included an account of dress designers and their methods and profits and a survey of modern dressmaking and millinery as they have developed in such typical centres as Paris, London and New York. That could be made intensely interesting—for everyone with enough money to "dress." How are fashions launched and sustained? And one could tell of the subtleties of "exclusive" fabrics, made only for this or that dressmaker, and of the perpetual stealing of models and infringements of copyright. We could show the rich lady from the Argentine or the United States coming to Paris, and all the decorative traps and lures that are set for her money. We should have a wonderful and amusing chapter here—and I should like to have it written by some student with misogynic tendencies and a meticulous industry.

Such a discussion of dressmakers and decoration, even the suggestion of such a discussion, may seem frivolous to some readers and altogether beneath the dignity of "economic science"; but indeed it is not at all frivolous. The fashions are not merely a sort of decorative crest to the business of clothing mankind. All the world nowadays follows the fashions. There is no stable, staple costume left anywhere any longer. We may glance back at the past when for large sections of the community costume was as prescribed almost as military uniform. That fixity occurs now only in very out-of-the-way places, and every year it is more difficult to find any out-of-the-way places. There have been local reactions towards traditional costume in Spain and Italy, and in Brittany the priest and public opinion are effectively conservative of local modes. Apart from such exceptional cases the treatment of fashionable clothing is an essential part of the treatment of clothing in general. The mannequin parade in the Paris club or hotel links inseparably now with the shopping of the lodging-house "slavey" on her afternoon off, or the gala costume of the Kentish fruit-picker with money to spend. It is all one process of a continually varying demand and a continually stimulated production.

It might be interesting and profitable here to go into the question of what should be included in the modern man's wardrobe. I am not thinking here of the wardrobe of a smart man-about-town. But what should a sailor, or an agricultural labourer, or an engine driver, or a clerk in a modern civilized community possess in the way of hats, shirts, boots, shoes, suits, and ties and collars? And what in fact does an exceptionally prosperous individual of these classes buy for himself nowadays? That ought to be ascertainable, but I know of no one who has attempted to ascertain it. I think we should find a considerable gap between the equipment that is reasonably desirable and the equipment actually possessed in most cases. I think we should find the world is shockingly underclothed to-day by the criteria of either efficiency or desire.

In the first place every worker in a soundly organized community should have proper working clothes, and by that I mean not simply overalls, but such underclothes as are best for him to toil and sweat in. I doubt if the expense and trouble of procuring this working costume should be left to him. They are the concern of the efficiency-seeking director as much as the space and lighting of his work-place. The *Daily Worker* (March 12, 1932) gives an account of an electric battery factory in Moscow in which this provision is made as a matter of course. The modern agricultural worker, quite as much as the miner or factory hand, should have his working costume. And men and women are mere industrial slaves if there is not a considerable part of their waking life spent out of working clothes. That means suits and dresses and fresh underclothing into which they can change. The old-time peasant almost everywhere had his or her traditional "best," the go-to-meeting array, the provincial "costume." This was handed from one generation to another. It might be amusing to give a series of illustrations to show how alike those "old-world" costumes were and how distinctive they were felt to be. The modern worker has little need for such parade costumes for feasts and rare occasions, but more for varied personal clothing during his ever increasing leisure. He wants first his sound and adequate "producer" costume as this or that sort of worker, and next his sufficient and satisfying individual "consumer" wardrobe as a free and independent citizen. The Lancashire operative usually has a "berryin 'at," for funerals and state occasions, a last trace perhaps of the peasant's "best" regalia.

I believe myself that the present underclothing of the world is disgustingly dirty, ragged and defective. A contract to put that right and keep it right would set every woollen and cotton and rayon factory in the world enlarging itself and working overtime. And would keep it working overtime until fresh factories arose.

It is not simply for the oily mechanic, the miner and the farm hand, that we have to consider this two-sided wardrobe. There is an old-established but increasing disposition in most of the organized work of the world to put the worker on duty into a uniform. In the past he was usually expected to share or bear all the expense of that. When I was a draper's apprentice the clothing expenditure of the shop assistant's wages was controlled by the fact that the men had to appear behind the counter in a white shirt and collar, black tie, black tail coat and dark gray trousers, or some such similar rig—it varied with the establishment—while the shop woman was under similar obligations. For shop assistants living in, this meant that from a quarter to a third of their wages was earmarked for uniform. In off time there was nothing for it but to go on wearing the same things. As a natural reaction against this obligation, it was the supreme ambition of every assistant to possess a coloured lounge suit. That was the symbol of one's (temporary) freedom, one's citizenship, one's manhood. One felt, when one wore it, no longer a shop hand but a man. One might be anyone in mufti. A select few treasured the equivalent of the peasant's gala costume in a cherished dress shirt or so, a white waistcoat, and a carefully folded evening-dress coat and trousers. They wore this gear at chapel dances and genteel occasions of that sort. Heads of departments got to tweeds and deerstalker caps. Nowadays there are thousands of young men in plus-fours who have never handled a golf club in their lives but who wear them as the outward and visible escape from some quasi-uniform imposing occupation.

I do not know how it is with the clothing of shop assistants to-day. Nor do I know on what terms the hall porters, hotel waiters, busdrivers, railway conductors, postmen, delivery boys, lift attendants, and the like, that increasing band of uniformed men and women, are clothed. The social effect of the uniform, however, is very plain. The uniform limits both control and obligation. It is no longer an affair of lord and inferior; your personalities disappear in the formalized relationship. The first obligation of the man in uniform is to respect his uniform—as the scientific worker must respect his research or the doctor the public health.

Cheap, smart, stylish clothing, I am told, has revolutionized the factory life of women. The conditions under which girls are asked to work must have a certain compatibility with their clothing. Girls looking as they think like ladies, expect to be treated as they think ladies (working in a factory) should be treated, and the result is an extraordinary rise in the standard of cleanliness, language and manners.

Uniform expresses rôle, and as community-planning develops and the laying out of towns and architectural scheming become more extensive and influential in people's imaginations, the idea of a personal as well as a functional rôle may influence men and women in the direction of "dressing the part" even out of the employment hours. Their costumes will become indications of how they wish to be treated. They will express their conceptions of their own characters. We may be moving towards an age of much more varied costumes than the world has ever known before.

With all this an encyclopædic volume on clothing would deal copiously—in relation, no doubt, to museum displays—and then it would come to the making of the clothes in question. It would deal with the typical varieties of clothing factory, the mysteries of standard shapes and sizes, the processes of distribution and the eternal struggle between the economies of standardization and the incurable craving of every living individual for something distinctive. And so we should come back at last to those "exclusive" fabrics and designs to which we have already alluded. "Exclusive" designs—if we may be paradoxical—may become more general. As workers are released by improved productive methods from staple production, the proportion engaged in the design and making of distinctive clothing may increase.

§ 2. Cosmetics

Before we leave this matter of clothing, it may help to make our picture of social life complete if we say a little more about adornment. No human activities witness so directly to the almost universal resolve, at once heroic and pathetic, to make life gay and lovely as those which constitute the cosmetic industry.

In the last thirty years and especially since the war this has become an immense industrial interest. In 1929 manufacturers' sales of perfumes, cosmetics and other toilet preparations in the United States of America amounted to $193,440,550, as compared with about one fifteenth of that amount in 1899. There were 815 factories in operation with over 13,000 employees and using 12,150 horsepower. These figures do not include small establishments reporting production of a smaller annual value than $5000. This figure of annual manufacturers' sales would probably have to be trebled for an estimate of the prices actually paid by the ultimate consumers, for profits in this trade run high, and to this would have to be added the upkeep of numberless beauty establishments, the wages of probably thousands of more or less skilled employees, masseurs, rubbers and the like, electric current used in treatment and other expenditures. Professor Nystrom estimates that in 1930 three quarters of a billion dollars were spent on beauty culture and cosmetics. In all ages, far back into pre-history, we find human beings have painted and adorned themselves. The Cro-Magnon people painted themselves like Red Indians; all India seems to paint, if only caste marks upon its forehead; nearly all savages smear themselves abundantly. Museums are littered with the rouge cups, trays, manicure sets, mirrors and pots for greases and messes, of the pretty ladies of Sumeria, Egypt, Babylonia, and thence right down to our own times; but never can the organization of human adornment have reached the immensity and subtlety shown by these American figures.

To our fourth chapter we have given the title of the "Conquest of Hunger," and this present chapter goes on under the caption of the "Conquest of Climate." But, as we have noted already in our remarks about dressmaking, mankind is not for a moment content with mere nourishment and covering and shelter. In a world in which, as we have shown, there is a frightful deficiency of underclothing, as many people as can are already striving for beauty, dignity and general effectiveness in their costume, and we have noted how clothing and conditions of employment can react upon each other. Here, under this heading of cosmetics, we face a still franker manifestation that man does not live by bread alone nor build his houses simply to keep warm and dry. This section goes beyond those necessities into another sphere of conquest altogether, the attempt to conquer happiness and beauty. And to keep something of youth still—something more desirable and far more evasive than bread or board. In 1928 to 1932 there was a great slump in American life, as we shall see in a later chapter, but while all other industries suffered the beauty trades went bravely on to a record of £200,000,000 in 1931.

Let us consider the effort to be pleasing that a modern woman in comfortable circumstances will make to-day. If our present hope that comfort and abundance are spreading down now steadily from class to class is to be justified, this is what most women will be doing in no very distant future.

It is an average well-to-do woman we are describing, intent, she says, upon her duty of pleasing mankind. She goes now to the beauty shop for massage at least once a week, and there, according to her physical condition, she has electric treatment or rubbing with creams, the application of hot and cold lotions; she has her face put under a "mask," an affair of beaten-up eggs and other ingredients which tightens on the face, she has it covered and rubbed with ice. Then her eyebrows must be plucked to a fashionable form, and there must, especially if she is of a dark complexion, be treatment for any casual hair, for an incipient moustache or the like. Her neck must remain round and youthful; it must be treated for sagging, and her hair, even if it does not need to be dyed, must be washed, marcelled, or water-waved and rubbed with a tonic. Good hair tonics are specially expensive. Once a week at least the hands must be manicured, and generally the nails are coloured as well as polished. A little pedicure may come in here. Few people can be trusted to cut and arrange their own toe nails well.

After this weekly or bi-weekly cleansing and refreshment our lady goes home. But she does not go empty-handed. She will need a selection of scents; and she will carry off bath salts, lotions, eau de cologne (costly when well alcoholized), and perfumed soaps. We will say nothing of her dental care, because that is a part of normal hygiene. During the day she will want to clean her face, and this is done, not dairymaid fashion, with soap and water, but with cleansing cream which takes off powder, rouge and dust and prepares the facial ground for reconstruction. Then comes skin tonic or liquid astringent to tighten up the skin, reduce any puffiness under the eyes and remove what remains of the cleansing cream. Then all over face and neck is put a "foundation" or "vanishing cream," and on this goes the powder (there are various powders according to the part of the body), rouge (red, orange, or dark red, according to the type and fashion), lip salve, and "kohl," black powder or liquid, for the eyebrows, the upper eyelids, or just under the eye, or at the hair roots on the temples.

If her face feels tired and there is no time to go for massage, our lady puts on some very expensive "day cream" and lies down for one or two hours. It has quite a wonderful effect, and when it is taken off again with cleansing cream and astringent, the face feels back in its teens. A "muscle oil" also is very helpful in tightening up the muscles of the face, neck and shoulders and diminishing the wrinkles at the nostrils.

After the triumphs of the evening the lady cleans her face before retiring with cleasing cream and liquid tonic. Then, if her face is thin, she puts on a thick, oily, very *nourishing* cream, or if it is fat, a *reducing* oil, and if she can bear it she goes to sleep thus anointed. But if she finds it unendurable she gets up again and wipes it off.

Also she must put cream on her hands to keep them white, and special cream on her nails. And also, perhaps, if she has been advised to that effect, she will put on a "wrinkle eradicator"—a band of rubber tied tightly round her forehead—and a "chin reducer," made by experts, of elastic and herbs, to brace up and keep her chin muscles within bounds.

But, you will say, this is a very exceptional woman, and indeed this is a very superfluous section to insert in a survey of world economics! By way of answer you are referred back to the figures from the United States Census of Production given in the opening paragraph of this section. There are a million women in the United States alone with an average annual expenditure of something like £100 on these things.

§ 3. The Dissolution of the Home

A comprehensive survey of housing would begin with the housing of the past. That was highly localized both as to design and material. We recur here to the motif of "delocalization" which runs through all this work. Housing is now more and more independent of local resources, though it is still dominated and will always be dominated by climatic conditions. You can bring any material now to a place, but you cannot take its weather away. The partial release from locality produces a certain discordance in many populated landscapes, because of the incoherent variety of forms and material now possible, but the weather is a steadying and harmonizing influence.

Here some very pretty pictures will come to mind. Compare the slant and structure of roofs in snow country with those in hot countries and windy lands, the characteristics of marsh, riverside and seaside building, the variations of window space, of the height and size of rooms, of the construction of verandas, loggias, sun traps and sleeping porches with variation in sunshine, windiness and rainfall. There is little need to tell here of the rapidly increasing comfort of the modern house, because we are all living through that improvement; consider, for example, the appearance of the bathroom and the enormous brightening of the evenings that has come with the electric light.

But the electric wires and the water tap take us on to another phase of the development of modern housing, the enormous development of collective services in the modern community. Water was laid on to the home in London in the seventeenth century, and domestic gas lighting came early in the nineteenth. The cholera epidemic of the middle nineteenth century stimulated the development of drainage and sanitary organization in Great Britain and made the English for a time the propagandists of domestic and public sanitation—until the Americans took the good work out of their hands. Our museum should show the rapid development of domestic interdependence in the modern town and give sections on water supply, drainage, sanitation, the destruction of refuse and the distribution of hot steam (as in New York), gas and electricity. And it will point us also to the household end of the telephone, with its new access to shop, doctor and mechanic. Here too a thoroughly exhaustive account of the decreasing autonomy of the modern home would have a few pictures from the London *Punch* of the eighteen sixties to remind the happy present of the vanished horrors of "washing day." A description of the working of a modern laundry seems indicated here. All these collective services tend to replace the structurally separated house by collective buildings, mansions of flats and the like, and the high and rising value of land in urban agglomerations stimulates this tendency.

And there is another side to this increasing collectivism of modern life, and that is the increasing disposition towards collective housekeeping on the part of women. The modern household is not only invaded at every point by collective services, but it is also assailed and superseded by them. For all its improved facilities, the separate home irks people nowadays more than it did. Women, especially the abler ones, rebel against domestic preoccupations. Men object to a life with preoccupied women. Domestic service, especially in the small household, is more difficult to obtain than it was. It would be interesting to give an account of some country house or château of the eighteenth century for the purposes of comparison. The owner, like Trimalchio in that immortal banquet Petronius has preserved for us, could boast that everything he consumed was grown on his own land and prepared by his own dependents. Even his town house was served by his own mules and wagons from his own estates. Against this former autonomy of the rich we have to set the history of the modern hotel industry. Formerly "hotel" was the name of a great private town house; the seventeenth century knew nothing of what we call hotels. There were inns. You brought your lackey with you, if you had one, to secure proper service. The real dreadfulness of these inns glares through the fun of such a novel as *Humphrey Clinker*. In Russia, towards the end of the nineteenth century, you still brought your bedding, your tea, and even your provisions to the inn. You do that now over the greater part of India.

Over all Asia, indeed, the caravanserai still rules. And these accommodations existed only for travellers. For those making a longer stay there were "lodgings." Fielding's account of his *Journey to Lisbon* describes an actual lodging in the Isle of Wight for the edification of posterity.

Athwart these memories we evoke the advance of the Hotel Industry, as the provision of a care-free comfort and abundance, at first for the very rich, now for the well-off, and presently for most people. We note the hotel branching out into the service flat and mark the progress of the residential club and country club.

With these advances there comes a considerable change in the status and quality of domestic service. From being a personal dependence with indefinite duties and a general obligation to obedience and obsequiousness, domestic service in a flat system becomes definite in its functions and with a certain personal detachment that marches better with modern conceptions of human dignity. In a London service flat or in a London club a modern bachelor is assisted in his domestic affairs by human beings he may neither rail against nor threaten nor burden with unexpected and uncovenanted tasks. But yet their assistance can make him extraordinarily comfortable. He can telephone that his rooms are to be ready before he comes to London, and he will find them in spick-and-span order. A maid will call him in the morning and bring him his morning tea, a valet carries off his disordered clothes to brush and puts out a fresh suit; a newspaper drops into his letter box. He finds his bath prepared. He telephones down to a central kitchen or restaurant for any meal he needs, and it is served him. Tea is served, and clothes are put out for him during the day. If an electric light or a lock goes wrong, a skilled mechanic comes up to set it right. The tenant's utmost trouble in the matter is to ring up the housekeeper or head steward.

He has never "engaged" any of these helpers. He never gives them "notice." Often he does not know their names. He goes away for a month and may find one replaced. He may ask a friendly question about that, but it is not his business. He knows nothing of the religion, politics, private life of these competent professionals. Such a system of relationship would have been inconceivable in A. D. 1850. Then these people would have been part of our bachelor's private household; he would have been their patriarchal tyrant, and they (and he) would have suffered all the limitations and inconveniences of their being fixed upon his back.

§ 4. *The Landscape of Homes and Cultivations*

This secular disappearance of the autonomous household through these double and alternative processes, the collectivization of its services on one hand and collective substitutions on the other, open up the prospect of an entirely new series of patterns in the layout of town and country. The life of the well to do citizen tends to divide itself between a town apartment with a stereotyped fashion in its fundamentals and either a country club or an individualized cottage or bungalow, and the large-scale map of our populated regions alters in accordance with these tendencies. The regrouping of urban centres and dispersed out-of-town homes and resorts is going on now with extraordinary rapidity and demands a new planning of roads, open woods and other common lands. The idea of "Town-Planning" is a new one in the Anglo-Saxon world. Before that idea became prevalent, towns grew unchecked. They grew higgledy-piggledy, but their growth never came to any crisis that challenged control until the present era of continually advancing and varying transport facilities. And "Town-Planning" still remains very uncertain because of the endless devices and methods of transport that have still to be tried out and judged.

But though Town-Planning came as an afterthought to the great urban aggregations of modern Europe and America, the idea itself is an obvious and ancient one. The cities of the old civilizations were planned, as often as not, as wholes. The idea came as a novelty to Renaissance Europe and has never since been lost sight of in Germany. Such eighteenth-century cities as Karlsruhe were carefully planned. Sir Christopher Wren tried to plan a new London after the great fire, but he was defeated by haste, greed and vested interests.

Before the modern housing map can be made out in detail it will be necessary to work out the proportion of urban and diffused urban population to the country worker and to the delocalized elements—free to live anywhere—in the grand total of people whose needs have to be provided for. There will necessarily be great local variations in these proportions and in the nature of the local activities. They will presently become calculable, but thus far estimate and guesswork have had to be used. It will become more and more possible, as surveys become more exact and statistical methods are perfected, to determine the proper sites for factories and industrial fields and to scheme out systems of intercommunication between them and the residential districts, to plot out the great schools, colleges, directive and research stations, the clinics, the hospitals, rest houses and playgrounds, the theatres, dancing-places and museums, of an advancing social order. Such a planned distribution of populations is called "zoning." There are already planning schemes which regulate the number of individuals in a locality; the Welwyn Garden City plan, for example. Such regulation is necessary, if adequate breathing and recreation space is to be maintained. The Ministry of Health fixes an upward limit to the number of persons per acre in urban regions in Great Britain.

But all this planning has to be given substance and reality in a world already covered with fields, hovels, farms, châteaux, villages, towns, and cities, whose forms and distribution have been determined by an interplay of forces and feelings that have now passed away or changed beyond recognition. We can look about us and see the old towns of yesterday with their citadels and fortifications, their casernes and iron-barred palaces, their cathedrals and town halls and market houses, giving place incoherently to the thrusts and pressures of our new occasions. All this dissolving and changing human landscape must be brought at last to the measure of a quantitative survey. And that survey must comprehend the rapid advance in building and engineering methods that is going on, and the attempts of power supply and water supply and every extending collective service to keep pace with the changing, experimenting and developing contours of façades of the rehousing of mankind.

Happily, in this field, it is only when we come to political frontiers that we impinge upon the traditions of patriotism and war. The local struggles of expanding municipality with urban and rural district councils, the conflicts of new avenues with ancient slums, may be severe and intricate, but, at any rate, we do not teach in our schools the inviolable sovereignty of Paradise Alley and Muck Lane, we do not stir up in them a more than religious fervour to remain for ever what they are, nor invoke all the forces of romance and sentiment towards bloodshed in the cause of old insanitary suburbs inconveniently situated upon our outlets, but "rightly struggling to be free." The most formidable obstacle is the individualistic landowner whose obstinacy, greed and defensive energy have necessitated and probably will in many cases still necessitate a long political and legislative struggle.

§ 5. *Modern Architecture and the Possible Rebuilding of the World*

At a later stage in the development of this survey we shall point out the probability of community-buying taking the place of individual-buying in respect to many commodities and services. In no field is this more practicable and probable than in the plan and rearrangement of town and countryside. It will be convenient to anticipate the conclusions of that discussion here and to review the tendencies of contemporary rebuilding. A steady enlargement of the enterprises, an increasing boldness and comprehensiveness are to be noted. The time may not be very remote when whole districts and townships and cities may be systematically reconstructed upon one single plan.

Most people have still to realize the vast extensions of available material, the changes in method and outlook that have come to the modern architect. The most fundamental change is the replacement of natural materials by reconstituted and artificial ones, and particularly steel framework and ferro-concrete building. In our story of the steels we have noted the development of structural steel. Most steels will corrode unless specially protected, but the metallurgist may be trusted to deal with that difficulty. So far, steel frameworks have been made in large forgings and riveted together, but now welding is coming into use, particularly in America. New alloys, lighter to handle and fix, may be counted upon with confidence. Even now buildings can be made upon a scale and of a complexity beyond the utmost imagination of the builders of a hundred years ago. Before our age the technical problems of architecture were concerned chiefly with the piling up of weights. Great buildings were really "stately piles." Now they can have a new openness, grace and variety, and they can soar up to heights unthought of before. They can also be built with what a hundred years ago would have been an incredible speediness.

Up to the present the original mud hut has been clearly traceable in modern building. Cement, mortar, the dried brick are all mud at one remove. All building has hitherto been a wet process. Now it becomes the "dry" putting together of fully fabricated parts. And as R. A. Duncan has pointed out in his essay in *Science and the Art of Architecture*,* building is ceasing to be a skilled handicraft and is becoming an affair of mass production, far more rapid and capable of rearing much more massive edifices.

In the place of massive walls of brick and stone, hollow walls of metal-sustained composition are not merely possible but most practicable and economical, so that a room can be like a vacuum flask and maintained at a steady temperature impervious to heat or cold; it can be lined with soundproof materials; or it can be built of tinted or clear

*Journal of the Royal Institute of British Architects, June 7, 1930.

toughened glass and saturated with sunlight. And while the house of earlier times was a mere accumulation of masonry boxes with clumsy fireplaces for ventilation and staircases from floor to floor, the modern building becomes more and more like an engine, with tubes for air, hot and iced water, sanitary apparatus of all sorts, wires for heating and lighting, telephones, speaking tubes and the like. The house of a hundred years ago compared with the modern house is halfway back to the cave.

Reinforced concrete is already a great stimulus to rebuilding, especially the rebuilding of big blocks of offices, warehouses and retail stores. Because its speed of construction is quicker than any other method, the capital invested becomes remunerative in a shorter time, or a business is not interrupted for so long a period. It is also cheaper than any other form, and that also encourages rebuilding and expansion. The rigid framework permits of lighter walls, less weight, a taller building with a greater capacity on a given area. A steel-frame or ferro-concrete building has a greater range of upward extension than one of stone or brick. These new structural resources not only make the entire fabric light but permit a much larger area of window space and therefore larger rooms. This window space means better day lighting, especially in the murky atmosphere of northern manufacturing towns. The side and back elevation of the newer warehouses in Manchester, for example, appears to be "all window."

Many steel-frame buildings have masonry fronts; but the masonry is only a veneer. The "bricks" or "blocks" used to fill the spaces between the steelwork have often no structural qualities—they are merely "fillers."

For dwellings man still builds with little bricks, like the men of old. It seems difficult to replace the small rectangular "block" by the "slab" which is suggested by the vertical walls. But "wooden" bungalows are frequently covered wholly or partially and lined and ceiled with asbestos cement sheets, or covered with roughcast sheets which consist of a thin cement sheet mounted on expanded metal, like a coarse wire net. For interiors three-ply board is being used, and cheap panelling employing this material is now available. Slates are rapidly disappearing as roofing material, and the slate quarries languish. But tiles are more varied in pattern and colour, and may do much to produce beauty even in a small dwelling.

When there are museums to do justice to the march of structural knowledge, the ordinary man will realize what a large amount of vigorous experiment and innovation is in progress. I spoke the other day to an architect of the problem of noise in flats, and he rattled off a list of devices and compositions to meet that one trouble; Cabot's quilt, acousticon plaster and a score of others. But so far, where there is glass, it is difficult to bar out noise from the exterior.

It is small wonder that not only young men and women with an artistic and constructive drive in them, but also business men, financiers and publicists concerned with the problems of human employment, turn their minds more and more definitely to the immense possibilities in comfort, creative work and beauty and happiness of this ever renascent art. Before them a by no means insurmountable barrier of social and business usage and political stupidity stands in the way of a complete reconstruction of human habitations, in which only a few lovely, memorable or typical buildings now in existence will be spared. At this stage in our work this may seem a very bold prophecy, but when the reader has got through our twelfth chapter he will probably be quite ready to accept our very confident prophecy that, *if our present civilization does not crash,* it can hardly avoid this stupendous rebuilding. It is not only that man *can* do it. It is not only that it stirs the imagination as if with trumpets to think of its being done, but, as we shall show, it will *have* to be done to sustain the economic working of our world. We shall have to rebuild to keep the economic machine running.

As it is, England is being rebuilt at the rate of a complete new world in a hundred years, and the economic life of a New York skyscraper is estimated at thirty years. A friend reading this passage foretells a licensing of buildings which will require the clearing of the site when the license expires.

The layout of that rebuilt world is also amenable to imaginative reconstruction. In the first place considerations of economy point to a continuation of the present processes of agglomeration. Plumbing, sanitary convenience, power distribution, and so on, all necessitate close grouping. Transport facilities release even the horticulturist, the flower and vegetable grower from the necessity of sleeping and living in his spare time close to his work. To resort in fine weather to the sea, the forest and wild, the open country, is a very powerful desire in most human beings, but that can be gratified by the use of tents and light pavilions and need not prevent the concentration of permanent habitations in handsome soundproof, sweet and clean compound buildings. A village, a town, a great city need no longer be an accumulation of huts, hovels and discordant, inconvenient old houses. Now it can be planned and made as one complete architectural undertaking.

This is not any sort of Utopian dreaming. It is going on now. Everywhere in the world building schemes are becoming bolder and more comprehensive. The ever more deliberate organization of industry, the scientific reconstruction of factories, with which we shall deal in Chapter VII, advance step by step with the progress of habitation. We can foretell with as much assurance—subject to the one proviso we have already made—that the twentieth century will be the Era of Rebuilding as we can call the nineteenth century the Era of Railways and Steamships. Let the thoughtful reader of English to whom a great public library is accessible compare the article upon Architecture in the Eighth Edition of the Encyclopædia Britannica with the current edition. It is a different subject; it is an account of a different world.*

§ 6. The Lighting of Town and Countryside

One of the least obtrusive and yet one of the greatest, biologically speaking, of all the great changes in human life that have occurred since 1800 A. D., has been the immense development of artificial lighting. Quietly, steadily, a little more every year, the evening lights have been turned up. To anyone from Stuart or Georgian times who might return to contemporary life, nothing would seem more remarkable than the night-time brightness not only of interiors but of streets and roads. And it is a change still in progress. What we have is only an earnest of the lighting still to come.

Man is a daylight animal. So were his ancestors, and so are all the primates. We are creatures that see with an unparalleled and exquisite precision in a good light. But we are in darkness and groping at a stage of illumination when most other mammals can still see effectively. So while the carnivores prowl and the herbivores creep to their drinking places, the gorilla squats with his back to the tree in which his family nests, and man goes into his cave or camp or clearing with a fire to keep off inimical beasts. From twilight to dawn, except when the full moon comes with its magic and excitement, or when he talks and wrangles or indulges in some mystical singsong or dance, savage man is out of action. Dawn rouses him, and sunset dismisses him.

This daylight phase of human life lasted almost to our own times.

*The reader who finds this section attractive will probably like to read Le Corbusier's *Urbanism* (translated into English by F. Etchell as *The City of Tomorrow*).

Man was busy from dawn to sunset—"for the night cometh when no man can work." The torch, the fire, and the dim oil lamp remained the chief illuminants until the coming of the candle. When one thinks of the crabbed, uncertain lettering of the manuscripts, and the chill small flame of the lamp, one begins to realize the heroism of the student burning "the midnight oil." (How many men like Pepys laid down their pens and put their books aside in early middle age because of blindness?) "Wax candles," says the Encyclopædia Britannica, "are probably of Phœnician origin," and candles massed on a candelabrum were the typical illuminant of temples and palaces (the golden candlesticks of Solomon's Temple, e. g.). The eighteenth century saw the candle at the zenith of its career. Massed candles could give churches, palaces, and public gatherings a soft brilliance that seemed at times dazzling against the background of the circumambient night. But even the roads and lanes about the palace itself were black or had their blackness made visible by swinging oil lamps or transitory linkmen.

A new phase arrived at the very beginning of the nineteenth century with the use of coal gas. The lighting of streets and houses became brighter. There was a simultaneous advance in gas and lamp lighting. Lamp wicks were improved, and better burners devised. At first the gaslight was a naked flame owing all its illuminating power to the incandescence of its own constituents, but later the burning of the gas was used to heat lime to incandescence. The "limelight" has survived as a proverb for the conspicuous, long after its theatrical use has disappeared. Presently petroleum, paraffin, and the mineral oils and fats came to the help of the lamp and candle in their struggle against gas. The gas was enriched by various admixtures. All through the nineteenth century the standard of nocturnal brightness was rising. Lighthouses also were spreading and multiplying about the world and calling continually for brighter lamps. Nineteenth-century London and Paris had already developed a night glare beyond the utmost dreams of Babylon or Rome.

Then came the electric light. Its first form was the spitting arc light fluctuating with its violent flushings, and then the incandescent filament lamp. Jablokoff's arc light (1876) was the first practical arc light. The inventiveness of Edison and Swan made incandescent lamps a possibility four or five years later than this, and thirty thousand of them were alight in 1882. At first the filaments were of carbon, and then came the far more efficient tungsten filament. Steadily electric light rivalled and then surpassed all the combustion lights.

Gas made a gallant struggle as an illuminant against its newer rival. Auer von Welsbach, while trying to improve the electric lamp filament, hit upon the modern "gas mantle." This is a mantle of cotton or pumice dipped in nitrate of thorium and cerium and burnt. The thorium and cerium salts are reduced to their oxides, thoria and ceria, which become brightly incandescent in the gas flame.

Man has now at his disposal a great and increasing variety of electric-light sources, which continually become cheaper, more powerful and more manageable. He has gaseous vapour lamps in which the current passes through a glass tube of attenuated gas; this tube can be bent to form designs and letterings, it can be as long as twenty feet; its decorative possibilities are immense; such are the Neon tubes whose ruddy orange brightness is a familiar note now at night in every city in the world. This Neon light has great penetrating power in a fog. And there are little incandescent lamps, scarcely larger than pin heads, with which man can explore a hollow tooth, and powerful ones for searchlights that sweep the sky. He can tint and temper these lights in the most various ways. He can make them stimulating, or he can make them restful and tranquillizing. And he has now the utmost freedom in grouping them. Before the electric light came, every light on earth was burning upward; it had to stand on a base; it had to be fed regularly and jealously guarded from other inflammable material. From all these limitations the designer is now released. Now man can put lights under the bedclothes or in his mouth, upside down and where he will.

At the present time, *white* light of the Neon type, "at a low price is the goal of a very considerable amount of research. Its development in the future will involve a very extensive reorganization of both lamp manufacture and power distribution. More light and cheaper light seem to be inseparable from any reasonable forecast of the future."

Upon all this "conquest of darkness" there follows a vast revolution and extension of the possibilities of architecture, housing, and living generally. A room at night can be lit more delightfully than was possible even with sunshine in the days before electricity. Colour can be thrown upon walls and buildings and changed and varied. There need be no permanent patternings on walls or scenery; everything can become a screen for projected lights, form, and colour. Great advances have been made in the science and use of reflectors, and light can be concentrated upon this or that special point or poured out (in flood lighting) over wide surfaces. Already a number of fine buildings have come into existence, built as much for flood lighting from beneath at night as for the slow creeping of the downward daylight across their façades. The time is upon us when city life at least will have all the assured freedom of vision and movement that daylight alone permitted in the past.

And nocturnal light spreads out upon the highroads—and upon the air routes—from the city to the once black and silent countryside. We have now upon the highroad a sort of symbolization of the conflict between individualism and collectivism. When the automobile first came, it was rare, it had to travel at night upon roads whereon it never encountered another light except a distant house window, the lantern of a carter, or the glare from the eyes of a startled sheep or cat. All the driver wanted to do was to see ahead of him. There was a steady competition to produce continually more brilliant and far-reaching lamps, until head lamps became veritable searchlights. That was all very well until the automobiles multiplied. Then headlight dazzled headlight, and automobiles had to feel their way past each other, dipping their lights, turning them down, going slow. The night highroads became confusing and distressing and dangerous to drivers. The local authorities and automobile associations accepted and still largely accept the powerful individual headlight to-day and put up reflector signals and warnings on the country road. But in the towns the headlights must be turned down, and now the disposition is to spread out the lighting and light the highroad. Great lamps can be hung high above it, but the more convenient form of road illumination now (involving a more exact levelling of the roads) is cheap white flood lighting at a level below the car body. It seems highly probable that the time is near when the automobilist will save his headlights for the lane and by-way, and that the great roads of the future will run lit and silent, luminous white bands across the night landscape. Instead of the continual conflict of individual glares there will be a steadfast light along the track. There will be collective lighting instead of personal lighting. Amidst the dark landscape flood-lit houses will shine like glow worms, and indolently wandering searchlights pick out trees and shining waters. One will have to go far from the artificial brightness of the roadways to recall the clear softness of moonlight or the bright stir and glitter of the stars.

Among other consequences of the present revolution in lighting will be the probable disappearance of those lonely workers, the lightship men and the lighthouse keepers. For now anything that can be moored or fixed off a coast can have its lighting controlled from the shore; there is no need for the imprisonment of men to tend those lights.

§ 7. *Protective and Regulative Services of the Modern Town and Countryside*

A survey of the layout of population in town and country would be incomplete unless something was said of the marshalling and protective services of the modern community. The older civilizations fought fire, imposed sanitary controls over epidemic disease and filthiness generally, and kept order in the streets only in the most rudimentary fashion.

One might write a history of civilization in terms of police and public order, in which attention would be concentrated throughout upon the growth of organized controls and protections in the developing body politic. I cannot decide in my own mind which is most symbolical of social organization, a lighthouse, a cadastral map, a ship's wireless apparatus or a traffic policeman. But I incline to think it is the traffic policeman. The stage is not so very remote—indeed, it is still theoretically in existence in most countries—in which every man was expected to do his share in keeping order, suppressing fires and performing similar public duties whenever he was called upon. Sheriffs, constables and so forth, came into existence primarily as directors and marshals of the common effort and became the nuclei of special forces only by degrees. In the small, highly localized, toilsome but uneventful countryside community of the past, there were few real strangers, crimes were almost family events, and the necessity for an organized control of such things as traffic, public cleanliness, and personal safety did not appear. The great towns of mediævalism in Europe, India and China were dark, insanitary, dangerous tangles, and it did not seem they could ever be anything else. But the change in human methods of communication which has made all the world neighbours has conversely made the man in the street a stranger, and the organization of his protection and direction struggles to overtake the sweeping reconstruction of our homes and ways and roads that is now in progress.

The city, to begin with, we may note, was a planned and unified affair. It centred on the *arx,* it was walled and well organized, the brain and heart of a small countryside. The typical Greek city was this; even Rome was this in its beginnings. The sanitary planning of kingly Rome or Cnossos was sound and adequate. But so soon as political organizations enlarged to the scale of kingdoms and empires, cities began to lose their figures and spread. It is only now that the modern architect and the modern policeman are setting out to get these vast, loose, flabby monsters into shape again.

The story of the modern police, after the historical retrospects usual in such studies, would begin in good earnest in the seventeenth and eighteenth centuries. Crime and the mob were getting out of hand during that period with the growth of a larger economic framework that admitted of quicker escapes, ampler hiding places and less controllable gatherings. A large part of police duty was, to begin with, repressive. Mobs out of hand, rioting, was a marked and distinctive feature of eighteenth- and early nineteenth-century history. The first French Revolution became a riot on a large scale until a whiff of grapeshot cleared the streets. The nineteenth century saw the steady development of a police not simply of repression but of order. As my friend Eden Paul remarks here; "Crime is getting out of hand again. Motor bandits, gangsters, bootleggers, using modern means of transport and modern weapons, appear. The 'repressive' brutality of the police, third degree, etc. is the brutality of people exasperated by their own inadequacy." They too have to be modernized.

Any history of police would have to note continually the steady increase of directive duties and the relative diminution of the more primitive repressive functions. Less and less does a modern police constrain us to do this or that, and more and more does it become a service of specialists associated with the layout of roads and habitations, dissolving congestions, arresting annoyances, averting dangers, assisting people to do what their education has presumably disposed them to do.

I think in an encyclopædic expansion of this present survey there might be a long and interesting chapter on fire-fighting, tracing its organization from primitive neighbourly helpfulness to the splendid disciplines and equipments of to-day. In the uneventful life of the newspaper-less past a fire was not without its consolation of excitement. It must have stirred up everybody and been a nine-days' wonder. People must have talked of all they did and thought and felt. And who set the place alight? The cloth hall of the town of Thaxted in Essex still preserves the iron hooks on long poles that were once used to drag the thatch from burning houses, and some of the water buckets that were passed from hand to hand along the street. From that sort of thing we have ascended stage by stage to the watchtowers and ever-ready engines and fire escapes of a modern great city.

And the ordinary man in the street is no longer a helper but a nuisance at a fire. Precautions against fire were admitted very reluctantly to the list of public functions. The earlier fire brigades were paid or kept up to the mark by insurance companies. Great fires sweeping away

whole quarters of the congested cities of the time, are normal incidents
in the history of the Middle Ages. They are much less important relatively under contemporary conditions. It is lamentable to note how
much of the records of the art, literature and science of the past has
been destroyed by fire. The Great Fire of London swept out of existence
all the apparatus of Gilbert, that most interesting of all our scientific
pioneers. Fires at Dantzig, Copenhagen and Petersburg did much to
diminish the tale of early telescopes, and all Volta's original apparatus
was destroyed by a fire at Como. Priestley's library and apparatus were
destroyed by mobs in 1791, another aspect of inadequate protection.

The agglomeration of the modern community in cities, residential
districts and organized areas of production, not only created a new
need for systematic regulation and protection but raised also another
set of problems through the wearing out of its fabric and its accumulation of waste material. In addition to the activities of constructors,
engineers, builders, furnishers, and the like, in addition to the activities
of police and firemen, there are the perpetual repairing and replacement of material that go on, the wrecking and removal of outworn
buildings and other structures, the removal of débris, the dustbin and
the dust destructor. There is a vast industry of salvage in the modern
social organism. I am told by a competent adviser that the Waste
Trade, considered altogether, is the fifth greatest industry in England.
It salvages everything from old iron, rusted girders, scrapped machinery
and brick rubble, to bottles, bones, rags, worn-out tyres. It is a filthy
and at present ill-organized service in which much sweating, insanitari-
ness and dishonesty prevail.

The defilement of scenery is one of the minor evils that arise from
the ill regulated extrusion of waste materials. I would like to give a
picture of that once beautiful corner, the Pont de Nice at Grasse, to
illustrate that point. The picture would not reek and smell, however,
and so it would give only a very imperfect idea of how a backward
municipality may still defile the world. This dump engenders a plague
of flies and forms a sort of club and prowling place for a miscellany of
mongrel dogs. In the Middle Ages excrement, waste, and débris lay
where they fell; filth and rubbish were everywhere, but they were
diffused. The effort to banish these offenses precedes the effort to
destroy them and leads to hideous concentrations. While I cry aloud at
the Pont de Nice, my friend Bernard Shaw bewails with equal bitterness the dumping of London rubbish at Welwyn. But in this field too
the type that prefers service to profit is at work, the community is not

content, and steadily things improve. An encyclopædic *Science of Work and Wealth* would have a huge illustrated section on scrapping, house-breaking, salvage and the manner in which the struggle against foul offensive accumulations is being waged to-day.

So we add to our growing catalogue of human activities the increased multitude of people engaged in building and building regulation, in planning layout and in rebuilding and rearranging habitations, in keeping roads and drains open and working, in maintaining every sort of security and order, in preventive hygiene and in the suppression of fire. Here too we must glance at the hospitals, with the ambulance organization and at the medical profession. These are the scavengers of damaged and scrapped humanity.

We have surveyed now—superficially enough but sufficiently for our present ends—all production, all transport and all the services of order; we must next note, as compactly as possible, a third main mass of occupations, *distribution*.

CHAPTER THE SIXTH

How Goods Are Bought and Sold

§ 1. *Old and New Shopping*

HERE we make our first step from the appraisal of the mechanism and material of civilization towards social psychology. Hitherto we have studied the forces and materials of production and considered how things are got and made and consumed. We have come now to a point where the question of their distribution has to be considered. We have to take up the relations of the consumer to the producing organization.

Had we the limitless pages of an encyclopædia to fill we would give here a picture of an Egyptian market, tell something of the desert trade in the early empires, and glance at the export industry of Cnossos in jars, beads and so on, making such guesses as are customary of the spirit and motives of the buyers and sellers. Trade in luxury articles went to the very boundaries, went beyond the boundaries of the known world. Imperial Rome had trading stations in India, and thence probably commodities drifted off into the unknown. With a brace or so of historical students to help us we might go on to an account of the Venetian and Levantine trade of the Middle Ages and the commerce that kept the mule passes over the Alps open and in repair. How much of that remains to be deduced and inferred? What sort of caravans and companionships followed the ancient "green roads" of England that are still traceable over her hills? What occasions brought them? The refrain of the slow breaking-down of barriers, the slow transition of economists from local to cosmopolitan would run through all that history.

The markets of 1750 were emerging gradually from a still very local and limited condition of things. Trade beyond the local bounds remained very largely an affair of luxuries, delicacies, accessories, and smallish manufactured articles. Spices for pickling winter provisions were important. But cotton, tobacco and sugar were beginning to travel in considerable bulk across the ocean. Guns and pistols, cutlery and fine textiles, went back in exchange. Wine and oranges moved north from France and Spain. Voltaire distributed the watches he was teaching the Swiss· to make, by letters of recommendation throughout the courts of Europe. Enough business existed to sustain a system of wholesale markets and exchanges.

It was by insensible degrees that this system accommodated itself to the ever increasing bulk of material handled and to the increasing importance of the masses, the peasant, and the labouring "proletariat" as purchasers. It is quite recently that the masses have been thought worth while catering for. Before the middle nineteenth century, shops hardly existed for anyone below the prosperous middle class. For instance, there was no such thing as a furniture shop to cater for poorish people. Such poorish people went to sales and got second-hand stuff. The home in which I was born was furnished about 1855. I do not believe there was ever a new thing in it. It was a second-hand outfit, half-worn carpets, slightly damaged chairs; even our library was replenished at auction sales. Everything was "good" but in decay. And all the food and domestic material came from little individual shops, each with methods and characteristics of its own. Mrs. Bean's butter we thought better than Mr. Martin's, and there was nothing to touch Mrs. Bean's tea. She got it out of a great canister and weighed it and packed it up in a paper parcel. Soap was weighed and cut off; mustard one got from the chemist, also weighed for every purchaser. It would be very interesting—and in places rather pathetic—to trace the appearance and development of the great "popular" department store and the ousting of the small, independent shopkeeper.

Three main types of modern distributive organization exist. First of all comes *the department store,* the concentrated giant store with an immense radius of delivery, to which people go for clothing, furnishing, provisions, *et cetera*. Then the *chain stores,* the syndicated shops for more immediate necessities, the multiple shops everywhere at hand, that now supply tobacco, everyday groceries, milk, meat and so forth. And, as a special and important type of department store, in Europe, and particularly in Great Britain, we have the machinery of *coöperative buying,* by coöperative societies, the surviving tangible fruits of Robert Owen's socialist beginnings. In management and organization, this third class tends to resemble the department stores, the difference being that the object of the coöperative administration is ostensibly for service and not for profit. Gains in the coöperative shop are understood to reduce prices or they are returned to the members of the society as a "dividend."

An interesting type of store is the Woolworth type, in which a miscellany of articles is offered at a uniform price. These stores cut prices by eliminating travellers and advertisement and buying lines of goods by the million direct from the manufacturer.

The activities of the man behind the counter do not end with his handing out the goods demanded by the consumer. If he does less weighing and packing and measuring nowadays, he does more selling. Every capable shop assistant is alert, not only to remind you of any need you may have forgotten or suppressed, but also to "introduce" new goods to you that you have never thought of getting before. He is a propagandist of consumption. Through all distributing organizations— least so, perhaps, in coöperative stores—runs this idea of salesmanship. Salesmanship tries not only to make things attractive to you, but also it seeks to make buying easy for you. And in the last few years, in pursuit of the latter end, it has evolved the Instalment System. This marks a new phase in distribution. Great multitudes of people are now in possession of goods that they partially own. They have paid an "advance"; they pay for two or three years to complete their purchase, and meanwhile, in case of default, the seller has the power of recovering the goods.

There was considerable criticism of instalment selling in its early stages. Young people, it was thought, might sink into debt at the outset of life, sacrifice economic freedom for immediate advantages of comfort and equipment. They would lose the power of discontinuing or changing their employment, lose, in fact, the right to strike. But this line of thought disregarded the fact that at the worst they would have to surrender a partially used and paid-for commodity that otherwise they might never have possessed. It was also held that in a time of depression the supplying companies would cease to receive the bulk of their instalments, and that they in their turn would be unable to observe their obligations to the banks that had financed their enterprise.

Tested in America by the very grave slump of 1930, these fears seem to have been exaggerated. Buyers have kept on paying; resumption of the goods involved has not increased. In the United States three quarters of the automobiles sold are sold now on the instalment system, and furniture, refrigerators, radio apparatus, pianos, washing machines, important books at a high price, jewelry and suchlike goods, are largely marketed upon the new lines. When it comes to perishable articles such as boots and fashionable clothing the security is manifestly not so good; the instalments must be spread over a shorter period, and, by taking up references and exacting collateral guarantees, the methods of the seller approximate to those of the ordinary private loan monger. About 13 per cent of the retail trade in the United States is instalment selling, and its annual total is estimated at £1,200,000,000.

The social consequences of this new method of distribution are still a matter for speculation. Instalment buying seems likely to diminish savings, hoarding and popular investment. Instead of putting money by to get something, people will get something and then pay for it with the money they would otherwise have put by. They buy first instead of buying last or not at all. There is a quickening of the production, distribution and consumption of goods.

§ 2. *Teaching People to Want Things*

And now we have to bring into our picture one of the most highly illuminated aspects of modern economic life, advertisement. There is great need of a history of its wide extension, new methods of appeal and increased penetration during the past half century. That history would deal with media, the newspaper, the circular, the shop window and the bookstall, the wayside house and the railway carriage, the roadside board and the hoarding. It would glance up at the aëroplane writing advertisements in smoke across the sky with letters one mile or so long. It would consider the advertisement side of the cinema and radio. There is deliberate and open and there is also masked and incidental advertisement. There is a point when advertisement ceases to attract and begins to irritate or bore. People can be habituated to disregard an advertisement. I have already written a rather amateurish essay on the psychology of advertisement in *The World of William Clissold*. But there are serious books on the subject: Professor Dell Scott's *Psychology of Advertising;* T. Russell's *Commercial Advertising;* H. L. Hollingsworth's *Advertising and Selling;* Sir C. F. Higham's *Advertising, Its Use and Abuse,* and works by H. Gale, S. R. Hall, A. T. Poffenberger, E. K. Strong, and others.

Turning now from the methods to the social function of advertisement, we may point out how necessarily advertisement is a part of the replacement of individual by widely organized marketing. The old trader and his shop were known in the neighbourhood. The talk of the countryside was their sufficient publicity. But the new trader may be at the other side of the mountains or the other side of the world. As he cannot show his face, he must show a placard. He has to create a giant, a nation-size or world-size personality, for himself and his commodity. The common man to-day buys his screw of tobacco or his packet of cigarettes from a Briareus as big as a continent. Picturesque and amusing as the methods of advertisement often are, this side of the question is far less important and interesting than its aspect as a new system of intercommunication and its bearing upon social psychology. The advertisement organization of to-day can spread the knowledge and use of a new commodity and all the changes in habit and custom a new commodity may bring with it, with the utmost rapidity throughout the world. It can break down social habits and usages in the most extraordinary way. It can suggest new conveniences and economies of time and labour, indulgences such as cigarette smoking and gum chewing, taking a daily bath or resorting to winter sports. It can make us feel uncomfortable after our coffee or doubtful whether our throats are not suffering from a previously unsuspected irritation.

The story of cigarette advertisement should be amusing and edifying. Half a century ago Europe knew nothing of the machine-made packet cigarette. Then it spread with incredible rapidity about the world. It was found that there could be such a thing as de-advertising a commodity. One day a certain firm was so ill-advised as to proclaim that its particular brand did not "irritate the throat." Hundreds of thousands of people thought that over, coughed in an investigatory and suspicious manner, and gave up smoking cigarettes.

At present it seems arguable that there is great waste and overlapping in this field of activity. And it is only slowly and recently that a genuine system of ethics for marketing generally and salesmanship in particular has developed. Is it necessary to protect the public more strongly than it is protected at present against misstatement and furtive falsehood in advertisement? In Great Britain there is a considerable general legal control and much effective local legislation against sky signs, tiresome processions, flashing lights and other irritating media. In the United States much has been done through the federal government's control of interstate trade to check lying and unwholesome suggestion in advertisements, more particularly in the advertisements of medicines and drugs. America moreover is the centre of the Associated Advertising Clubs of the World, whose motto is "truth in advertisement," and furthermore, this association has established a National Vigilance Committee to keep the profession above reproach. In the future it is quite

A MODERN ORCHARD

A THOUSAND-ACRE orange grove in Southern California, typical of the wholesale food production of to-day.

THE MODERN PORK BUTCHER

THE General Foods Company packs pork chops in a cellophane-like sub-stance, boxes them and passes them through a freezing chamber, 50° below zero (lower picture). The side of the freezing chamber is removed in the picture at the top to show the boxed chops (light band in the middle of the picture) between the upper and lower rollers that carry them along.

possible that the check upon the statements of Briareus, as he hands out our goods, will be much more stringent. The main body of the advertising profession will certainly be on the side of such a censorship. Competition in falsehood ultimately discredits all advertisement. It may be possible to bring side by side sample advertisements for the last century and the present time, to show the advance in dignity and integrity that has already occurred.

The extension of professional advertising from marketing to politics and the public service will open up another issue of very great interest. For the modern man the daily newspaper already fills to a certain extent the place of a daily religious service. It takes him out of himself and reminds him of all the world. It makes a miscellaneous appeal. Formerly, in the days of fixed traditional attitudes the newspaper took the side of some definite party in politics; it discussed morals and public affairs in its "contents," and its advertisements were mainly marketing —and invitations to entertainment. But now it is much more "newsy" and much less educational in its contents, and on the other hand the advertisement columns become a forum for appeals and proclamations of collective importance.

But here we are passing away from marketing and looking again towards the question of public education. We will go no further in that direction now. All our later chapters will point towards education, and finally the chapter on Education will crown and complete our work. But to our growing enumeration of human activities we now add the placard and the handbill, the aëroplane writing across the heavens, the sky sign flaring and blotting out the stars, the displayed advertisements of the newspapers, the monstrous letters on the cliff face, the hoarding making its discordant proclamation athwart the rural scene, the rain of samples, the pestering cigarette tray, the perpetual nagging of our wearied attention in railway carriage and street car and restaurant and hotel room, the bawling loudspeaker, the interlude advertisements on the cinema screen (in France more particularly) and the association of the radio (in America) with advertisement. And every one of these things means a swarm of people busy in making and diffusing the glad tidings of goods to be bought; a whole world of clamant activities.

§ 3. *Fluctuations and Vagueness in Distribution*

The present distributing methods of mankind are in a state of violent fluctuation. Fifty years ago most commodities reached the consumer

through three well defined stages. First the producer, whether manufacturer or grower, sold his produce to the wholesaler. Then the wholesaler sold to a retailer, who either sold in a shop or hawked the goods
about the country. The retailer unpacked and repacked the goods; he
cut up the cloth and calico, he chipped up the sugar loaf, weighed out
the tea and butter. This seems, under modern conditions, of which increased efficiency in advertisement, packing and postal enterprise are
the chief, to be at least one stage too many for stability, and the history
of distribution for the past half century is largely the history of a
struggle to squeeze out some one of the three stages. The manufacturer
brands his goods and advertises them to the consumer; he may even, in
the British boot trade, e. g., distribute through his own shops; retail
shops unite to buy directly from the manufacturer; or as a third way to
the desired end, the wholesaler cuts out the retailer and breaks out as a
system of chain stores. Chain stores may thus arise either as whole-
salers' shops, manufacturers' shops, or by an enterprising retailer adding
shop to shop and cutting out his wholesaler.

In America there has been a great development of mail-order houses
selling their goods, not by displaying them in shops, but by describing
them in catalogues and circulars which are distributed by the million.
Mail-order houses appeal to a scattered population; they do for the
country people what the great department store does for the concentrated urban population. The illustrated and explicit price list takes the
place of the department displays.

Every modification in methods of communication and carriage is felt
at once in the distributing world. Each involves changes, novelties and
abandonments, in warehousing and storage. The architecture of warehouses varies with improvements in handling. The old-fashioned retailer
kept his goods on his premises and showed samples in his shop window.
Now a dealer will keep a brightly lit showcase in a railway station, a
hotel, an arcade or an exhibition of goods; he will receive your order by
post in an office miles away, and pack and deliver your goods from some
quite remote centre.

The breaking-up of the old retail-shop tradition has also broken up
the ancient traditions of the shopman. Formerly, in England and
America, he was indentured as an apprentice, for four or five years
learnt the "art and mystery" of selling, lived on the premises and
worked upon time-honoured precedents. As businesses grew in size
and the personal contact between the employer and the apprentice
diminished, the instruction of the latter in merchandising became more

and more a pretense, and as the standard of living in the community rose, the long hours, the bad food and crowded housing of the living-in system became less and less tolerable. Now apprenticeship and living-in die out, and a vast variety of salesmen (often specially trained by their employing firm) take the place of the old "shop assistant."

The present existence side by side of old types of shop and new marketing experiments leads to a vast amount of overlapping in the distributing trades. In England there is a shop of some sort for every forty-five inhabitants, and one person in every twenty-five is a non-productive distributor. This seems a very heavy burthen of not very skilled activities upon the general population. Our world is in fact full of goods (with sellers behind them) looking or wandering about rather vaguely in pursuit of the consumer. A typical instance of the planless-ness of our distributing machinery is the wild multiplication of petrol pumps along the roads, twice as many as are needed, since the coming of the automobile. For half these adventurers struggle, failure and frustration lie in wait.

No figures are available of waste through the deterioration of unsold goods, especially in the provision trade. Indeed, the science of distribu-tion is still in a very backward, merely descriptive state. The general impression among financiers and business men, is that distribution in the modern community is loose, unstable, adventurous and very waste-ful. But that is not the fault of the distributor. It is not only that shopping and selling change with the progress of transport and mechanism generally and with facilities for advertisement, but, as we shall see later, that customers are also in a state of flux. Purchasing power drifts from class to class. The rich and the middle class change not only in taste and in intelligence but in character. The process of monetary deflation (which we shall explain later) shifts purchasing power from the customers of one type of shop to those of quite an-other sort. Inflation will provoke a feverish buying of "valuables" to hold against a rise. Deflation tempts the possible customer to restraint, to save his or her money.

E. A. Filene tells us that "the average article sold by department or other retail stores to-day costs the consumer two, three, four, often six or eight times its production cost." This does not seem to be a very exact average, but the statement is very illustrative of the huge unprecise interception of money due to the uncertainty and experimental dis-organization of the distributing machinery of the modern state. This high cost to the consumer is not, Mr. Filene says, due to profiteering, it is due to waste. He quotes research work by C. N. Schmalz (Harvard Bureau of Business Research) to show that the net earnings of a series of department stores studied, varied between 1.1 per cent loss and 1.6 per cent gain. His own ideal seems to be a combination of department stores with chain stores. He would have great department stores at all the centres of distribution, and each department, for boots and shoes, automobiles, watches or what not, would be in a chain with the same departments in the other great store buildings throughout the country. This vast organization would deal directly with the producers; the middleman would be cut out entirely. This is "mass distribution" to balance mass production. As a third factor in the modern distribution of goods Mr. Filene advocates the credit union system, by which groups of employees and neighbours guarantee one another for the repayment of emergency loans. All these are expedients for bringing the individual buyer into a less wasteful relation to Briareus and eliminating secondary middlemen, credit retailers, loan-mongers and the like parasites upon popular distribution. At a later stage (Chapter X, §7) we shall have something to say about collective buying.

§ 4. Coöperative Retailing

A note is necessary here on that very distinctively British method of distribution, the coöperative store. This is an attempt to replace the retailer by a combination of consumers, and it is practicable and efficient just as far as its members represent a stable and homogeneous community, with similar needs and similar habits and ideas. Then in the case of such commodities as coals, boots, groceries, ironmongery, it can effect great economies. The members are the owners of the organization, and the profits made on the trading—or as coöperators prefer to say, their surplus payments—are returned to them as a "dividend" in the proportion of their purchases.

In Britain there are 1,364 of these societies, varying in the number of their members from a score or so (in a small village society) to a quarter of a million. They vary as greatly in their range and enterprise. Many are little more than profit-sharing grocery stores; others are complete profit-sharing department stores and carry on bakeries, laundries, dairy farming, and a multitude of services and productive activities. They run libraries, travel guilds, schools, dance halls, entertainments, periodicals and building societies. About £3,000,000 of house property is owned by coöperative societies in Britain and they carry £7,000,000 of advances made to members for the purchase of their own houses. This various multitude of voluntary associations is federated to the Coöperative Wholesale Society (there is a separate C. W. S. for Scotland), and there is a Coöperative Union of Great Britain and Ireland for legal, educational and propagandist purposes. The retail coöperative societies of Britain employ upward of 170,000 workers, and their gross sales in 1929 were £217,000,000 of which nearly one-tenth was returned to the purchasing members as "dividend." About one in eight of the British population is a member of a coöperative society, which means that over one third of the family households of Britain buy more or less of the goods they consume through coöperative retail stores.

In Finland, Denmark, Belgium and Switzerland coöperative retailing is equally well developed, and the rest of Europe north and west of the Danube is not far behind. The coöperative movement in France was originally and is still mainly a coöperation of producers with which we are not at present concerned. Consumers' coöperative societies in France number over two million members which works out at below one family out of five or six in comparison with the British one in three.

Nothing to compare with this great network of distributive machinery is to be found in the United States. The life of the common man there is far more individualistic and adventurous and less stable, defensive and protected than in Europe. He buys on his own. For the year 1928 the retail buying in the United States has been estimated at forty-one thousand million dollars. Of this only one hundred million is ascribed to coöperative retailing. More than half of the grand total was effected through small private adventure shops which are perpetually opening, going bankrupt or closing down. Not one in ten of such small businesses struggles through to a success in America. The rest of this distribution was done by great profit-seeking systems, department stores, chain stores and mail-order organizations.

So much for coöperative retailing. But it is only one aspect of the coöperative movement. The broader implications of that movement will be dealt with more conveniently after we have considered the general conditions of productive employment in the next chapter.

CHAPTER THE SEVENTH

How Work Is Organized

§ 1. *Putting the Personnel into the Picture*

ONLY in the preceding chapter have we begun to take what is called the "human element" into our account of the world processes of production, distribution and ordered life. We have been looking hitherto not so much at peasants and farmers as at fields and estates; we have reviewed factories and warehouses rather than workers and traders. Even in the agricultural sections where we have displayed the strips, the peasant type of cultivation passing away and giving place to estates and large farming, we have said hardly anything of the peasant giving way to the agricultural labourer. We shall have quite a lot to say about that before we have done. And were all the science of work and wealth that we have summarized thus far, actually assembled and written and illustrated in all its confirmatory but oppressive vastness, we should still have no more than a display of factories running like automatic toys rather than as complexes of human coöperation; we should see the automobile in mass production being built up bit by bit upon its endless band, the biscuit passing magically from dough to box, and so on through a thousand industrial process series without a hand to help it. Now we have to enter a fresh field of description. It is time we brought working human figures into this world spectacle of cultivation and production we have evoked.

What we have to consider now, the marshalling of workmen, foremen, managers, directors, experts and experimentalists in due order, might be treated in reference to any one of ten thousand different series of productive operations. Each would have its own characteristics, but each would exemplify the same broad facts of industrial organization. We might, for instance, survey the working of a modern engineering plant, a shipyard, a factory for making typewriters or cash registers or clocks and watches. Or we might give a distillery or cement works or a shredded wheat factory. Essentially we should deal with it now as a "manned" factory, a factory considered as a human going concern. For

202

each or any of these concerns an account could be rendered of employees, their types, their numbers; how they are directed by foremen, how all the various groups are coördinated by the manager and his staff. An adequate survey of a modern factory would include a discussion of the housing, feeding and sanitation of the staff; its recreations and rest places, its welfare organization and casualty stations. We will not ask yet what inner forces hold the wills of all this personnel together; that is for a next stage in our surveying. *Why* they do it all, comes later. First we must ask *what* each one does.

In doing this we leave our museums behind us. They have been most useful so far as a system of reference, but now they fail us, and we push into a region where as yet no comprehensive museums exist. The Science Collections at South Kensington and the Deutsches Museum display the material organization of modern production with great completeness. You may, for example, see the layout of a whole machine shop in either, presented as a working model. You can make the wheels go round. Everywhere there are working models of machinery. Compressed air and electricity are used, and the visitor can put the wheels and so forth in motion either by pressing a button or in some cases by putting a penny in a slot. For certain types of boy, and even for some modern girls, such museums are a preferable substitute for Paradise.

But no figures of workers animate these factories and machines in motion. Imagine, however, that this idea of working models has been carried on to a further stage and extended to the provision of model plants, in which minute workers are seen carrying out their operations, and the business and labour handling of the raw material are traced to the finished product in terms of living individuals. In such a model we should see not only "the wheels going round," but also the little figures which pull over the levers to set them going. Little coloured threads could run from the captains to the noncommissioned officers and men of this personnel. At the side of each model plant would be diagrams of the numbers, pay and hierarchy of the workers. Such models may or may not be practicable. Imagine models of local industries conceived on this plan, animated "personnel models" to adorn the local schools of every industrial region. The intelligent youngster could say not merely as he does now, "This is what happens to the stuff and that is how the wheels go round," but "This is father," and "That is the person I intend to be," and later on such a youngster would go to work with a sense of participation in a complex team job that few of the myriads which industry annually swallows now possess.

Whether such industrial models can really be made or not, I do not know; but the idea of them is also the idea of our present approach to Organization. We begin to put in the human figures in our panorama of human work. We have to pass in imagination through the field or the machine or the selling service, note the gang leaders and foremen, and so come to the manager's office, the board of directors and the departments of research and suggestion.

Illustrated descriptions of typical industrial plants at work bulk large in that encyclopædic dream, *The Science of Work and Wealth*. But we need not wait for them now to discuss the broad questions these organizations raise and illuminate. The pictures, the descriptions, the models remain to be made, but for the present they can be taken as given. Even before this substantial preparation is realized, it is still possible to open up the main issues of staffing and management in general terms.

§ 2. *Guild and Trade Union*

Let us begin our survey of the personnel of production and distribution at the base, with the individual who actually ploughs, sows, reaps, tends beasts, hews coal, stokes furnaces, lays bricks, saws timber, spreads cement, weaves, hammers, casts, blows glass, tends machines, handles goods for sale, fetches and carries, packs parcels, enters items into books, typewrites, transmits telephonic or telegraphic messages, steers ships, guides vehicles: the fundamental *worker*. How is the worker put to his job, paid, ordered and kept going?

The modern world grows to-day, day by day, in unbroken succession out of the old world of toil, and the tradition of the worker is still one of subjugation and compulsion. He or she behaves and is treated as inferior. During the ages of toil the fundamental worker was either the cultivating peasant, a pressed man, a serf or a slave outright. We have considered already the new forces that tend to wrench the practical ownership and control in agricultural production from the peasant and to make him an agricultural labourer and so industrialize agriculture. We have stated the essential facts of this process as it is displayed by Great Britain and Soviet Russia. We have noted too—though as yet only in the most general terms—the liberating effect of money in the past, and how in our present organization the wages worker plays a rôle in mine and factory and plantation which replaces and renders unnecessary the individual and gang slavery of the past.

Yet to this day the crack of the whip and the rattle of the chain haunt the thoughts of many people when labour is discussed. To many it seems impossible that anyone would work unless want and hunger stalked the unemployed. The worker they think has to be kept down and compelled. They cannot imagine contented and participating labour. But there are others who can, and their faith and their efforts to realize their conviction play an important part in the making over of the world that is now in progress. The conditions of the modern worker are still undergoing rapid development as the scale and mechanism of production and exchange expand and evolve, and any account of the labour organization of mankind, however full and detailed, which fails to recognize that every method and institution of to-day is provisional and entirely transitory, will necessarily be losing value from the very moment it is made.

The full *Science of Work and Wealth* would have to include some elaborate masses of fact about the mutations of the labour institutions of the world as machinery and power have developed. There are three main strands of evolution interweaving in this reorganization of work. First, there is that industrialization of the peasant with which we have already dealt. Next, there is that numerical expansion of the craftsman class of mediæval life, and that change in the scale and nature of its activities which has given us the mass of skilled, and the greater mass of semi-skilled, manufacturing workers of to-day. And thirdly, there is the struggle of the unskilled worker, the economic successor of the gang worker, the mine slave, the galley slave, the plantation worker, the excavator, the pyramid builder of the old order, towards a tolerable life: a struggle in which he is helped by the steady substitution of mechanical power for the muscular ingredient of his task. The broad drift is towards a fusion of all three types of worker into one huge body of semi-skilled workers working at their various jobs under skilled direction, and having a common type of mentality and an unprecedented sense of solidarity. The incessant changes in the method and apparatus of production are abolishing many types of the highly skilled craftsman, and the universal spread of education is bringing the black-coated, white-collared clerk down—or to put it more truly, is bringing the semi-skilled worker up—to a common level of respect.

Neither the peasant nor the gang worker of the past developed any autonomous organization worth consideration; the one was ruled and directed, so far as he was ruled and directed, by his owner, his lord, his creditor and the market demand, and the other was herded to his task by his overseer. But the more intelligent and more valuable craftsman has always organized locally throughout the ages in the local interests of his craft. The societies he formed in the days of the Roman Empire do not seem to have survived the general débâcle of Western economic life in the Dark Ages, but with the gradual return of social order and prosperity, associations of craftsmen appeared side by side with merchant guilds. Manufacture was handwork; the productive group was a small one, a master, a journeyman or so, and a prentice or so, all hoping to become masters in their turn, and the craftsman guild concerned itself chiefly with the restraint of competition and the material and spiritual welfare of its members.

There was no essential and permanent antagonism then between employer and worker.

We know very little of the internal organization of such larger enterprises as cathedral building, the greatest collective effort of mediæval times, but there is little record of labour troubles in these undertakings. The lore of the masons was elaborately secret, and the literature of freemasonry throws little light on the actual working of the job. The cathedrals, however, grew very slowly by modern standards. Evidently they were not so much the work of crowds as of not very considerable bands of men levying their pay as the pious provided it, and doing their work year after year. The cathedrals were early instances of what we shall refer to at a later stage as "collective buying." The original "secrets of the Freemasons" were probably geometrical drawing, quarrying and chisel work combined with the political and religious activities necessary to keep that collective buying alive.

Many productive arts remained purely domestic throughout the Middle Ages. It was only in the fourteenth century, with the general broadening out of life and a steadily increasing volume of trade, that the increasing size of the unit of production released the possibility of antagonism between employer and worker. The number of journeymen relative to the number of masters was increasing to an extent that opened up the possibility of remaining journeymen for life to most of them, and with that they began to organize to maintain wages and keep down the tale of hours for the working day. The fifteenth century saw a considerable amount of trouble upon such issues.

The devastation of Germany by wars and the enlargement of trading and productive operations in less troubled regions of Europe ultimately submerged most of the industrial organizations of mediæval times. They were elaborate in their methods and inadaptable. Machinery crept into use, and already in the seventeenth century, before the advent of

power, the process by which capital accumulated and some small producers prospered and grew while others declined and fell into employment by the former, was well under way. The gap between master and
man widened: it became a class distinction. The industrial revolution
—with its "division of labour"—preceded the mechanical revolution with
its economy of force and attention, by some decades, and at first the
mechanical revolution did no more than emphasize and exaggerate this
process of class differentiation. In one branch of industry after another,
work began to be done no longer by the hands of individuals but in
squads, in companies, in battalions.

The first organization of the new scale industry was directive; it
came from the entrepreneur. He planned his merciless factories and
arranged the duties of overseer and time-keeper. The character of the
new industrialism departed more and more widely from the traditions
of mediæval craftsmanship in the direction of gang work. The first
organization of industrial labour, suffering under these conditions of
degeneration, sprang from no preceding organization. It was entirely
defensive. It was the outcome of intolerable distresses. It was a fight
against long hours and sweated work, a fight against the mutual competition of hungry workers and against the advantage this gave to the
bargaining employer. At first such organization was illegal, and the
long story by which the collective bargaining of the workers won its
way to recognition is to be read in the Webbs' *Industrial Democracy*
and the Hammonds' *Town Labourer, Skilled Labourer* and the *Rise of
Modern Industry*. The trade union began its career, regardless of craftsmanship or the need and quality of the product. It was an urgently
necessary protective fighting organization to protest against long hours,
insufficient wages and the individual degradation of the industrial
worker. It spread easily and naturally to many fields of unskilled labour,
where the workers could be easily assembled, and less easily to such
workers as the scattered seamen, and still less easily to the agricultural
labourer.

By the nineteenth century there was already a wide gulf in interest
and feeling between the directive and exploiting elements in industrial
production on the one hand and the worker on the other. The nature
of that gulf is of vital importance in our present study. For many years
it has been an antagonism—on both sides. A great majority of employers
have been attempting more or less consciously to get the most out of
their workers and to pay them as little as possible; the reciprocal effort
has been to lighten toil, shorten working hours and raise pay. Through-

out most of the nineteenth century this warfare has smouldered or raged over the whole field of employment. The employer has fought for the right to discharge at will, to lock out as he chose, to play off the urgencies of the unemployed at his gates against the resistances of the worker within. The chief weapon of the employed has been the strike. Here again an expanded treatment of the law and practise of industrial conflict, the organization of militant unions, the conflict around the open shop, the history of great strikes would make a vast, tragic section of our encyclopædia in which many acutely interesting passages would be embedded in a dry tangle of highly technical detail. To-day all the lower ranks of workers in our industrial plants are potential strikers; and the special organizers and officials of the trade union and of its more militant dissentient subsections must be shown in those working models of ours, flitting obscurely but effectively round and about the industrial plant. They maintain a certain standard of life against the exigencies of work. Our picture will not be complete without them.

At any time almost any of these concerns, these coöperations, these great services, of which we have imagined a series of working models under our eyes, may begin to run slowly or stiffly or stop, stop short for an hour or a day as a warning strike, or stop at the onset of some conflict that will be fought to a finish. The average annual loss in working time actually caused by strikes is often grossly exaggerated. Professor Carr-Saunders puts it—for the thirty-two years between 1893 and 1924—as about the equivalent of one day's holiday each year. Their more serious effect is the dislocation they may cause in completing or obtaining contracts.

This relationship of antagonism between employer and employed is the most important fact of our present phase of economic development. It has been manifest in the past, but never to the same extent. Is it an inevitable relationship in a modern economic system? In the middle nineteenth century there were many who thought it was. They believed that the economic process could not go on without a margin of want and the resentful resistance of the worker. They displayed a stern fatalism for others and were happy to feel themselves luckier and more deserving than the common run. But there are various schools of opinion which deny that necessity. The Communist would obliterate the employer and so solve the problem. He carries out the idealism of democracy to its economic conclusion. He believes that in some way the masses can exercise a directive will over economic life that eliminates all need for compulsion and changes the spirit of direction. Work, when the mystical dictatorship of the proletariat has given place to its still more mystical goal of the classless, the homogeneous, community, will be spontaneous and joyful. It is not a very explicit doctrine, and so far Communist rule in Russia has not so much as manifested a stormy disposition towards it.

But quite outside the adherents to the Communist creed there is a growing multitude which is convinced that this great antagonism in our economic life is not essential, that it marks a mere phase in evolution, that it can be reduced almost or altogether to a vanishing point, that without any violent revolution or breaking up of society, while carrying on with the world as a going concern, there may be a steady reconstruction of the economic life of our species that will produce a willing and effective coöperation of everyone engaged upon it. These more hopeful spirits can point now to a great number of instances where better pay has been proved to mean happier and better work, where shorter hours have been more productive than long hours, and where the spirit of coöperation has been evoked to mitigate or replace the crude compulsion and resistance of the first harsh phase of modern industrialism.

§ 3. Industrial Democracy: Workers' Control

In studying the progressive organization of the semi-skilled labour which is becoming the main labour mass in town and in the countryside alike, a very great number of more or less parallel efforts have to be considered, all aiming at the restoration of a sense of participation on the part of the worker.

The nineteenth century was the age of democratic ideas. It was pervaded by the assumption that the maximum of justice and directive wisdom was to be attained by a universal uniform distribution of votes, and so we find such a book as the Webbs' *Industrial Democracy* (1897) filled largely with an account of the quasi-parliamentary administration of labour organizations. The problem of the control of the secretary was a grave one from the beginning, and all sorts of constitutions have been devised to prevent executive councils and officials getting out of hand. The secretary can bully and dominate because of his close and continuous knowledge of the society and the difficulty of tracing his acts and assembling a meeting competent to judge them. He has also great opportunities of selling his society. But the secretaries of all societies are necessary evils, and a great book could be written upon their inconvenience and disloyalties.

Industrial Democracy, for all its thirty years and more of life, is still the best general introduction to the development of labour organizations and to their main type of defensive activity; the insurance of their members against discriminatory treatment, their collective bargaining, their experiments in regulating hours and processes, restraining the competition of boys and non-members, insisting upon sanitation, securing protective legislation, and so forth. In the past third of a century great advances have been made in the state enforcement of sound labour conditions, and much that was once a matter for trade-union regulation is now the subject of legal enactment. Here again the mass of fact is vast and tangled, and an encyclopædic *Science of Work and Wealth* would give an ordered array of statistics as useful for reference and confirmation as it would be unattractive to any but the highly specialized reader. Every great industrial country presents its own distinctive method of approach to these problems and has its own types of solution.

The industrial democracy of the nineteenth century was defensive and restrictive; it meddled little with business direction except to object when the interests of the worker seemed to be threatened, but since the beginning of the twentieth century there has been a strong disposition to incite the organized worker to usurp or assume (whichever word you prefer) some or all of the functions of the directorate. This re-unification of industry by the upward extension of the workers' will, was formulated in England in the opening decades of the twentieth century as Guild Socialism, but the idea, in many variations, of the autonomous organizations of masterless coöperating workers has spread all over the world. What is practically the same conception of workers' control has played a considerable and not very happy part in the industrial experiments of Soviet Russia, and there were various very substantial attempts to realize it in Italy after the war and before the onset of Fascism. We have no space to tell in detail of the formation, struggle and failure of the National Guilds in Great Britain after the war, nor of kindred experiments in other countries. The British National Building Guild of building-trade workers executed a number of contracts between 1920 and 1922 and did good work before it got into financial difficulties. For a time the "shop steward," a representative of the workers in the discussion of various details of method and discipline with the employer, assumed an importance he has not retained. He was a war-time product who acted for the workers during the emergency disablement of trade-union organization.

A sore point in the existing relations of employer and employed is the general absence of any judicial process in the dismissal of workmen. If the employer comes down to the works in a temper he can still sack the first man he sees. In Germany an attempt has been made to remedy this. Statutory works councils have been set up in all establishments above a certain size. These councils consist of workmen only, and whenever a man is dismissed they can examine into the circumstances and if they think fit they can bring the matter before a special court. If the employer cannot show that the dismissal was dictated by the economic position of the concern or cannot prove that it was "just," he must either reinstate him or pay compensation. See Guillebaud, *The Works Council—A German Experiment,* 1928.

In America the restriction of immigration since the war has cut off a bountiful supply of cheap and helpless labour and produced very great changes in labour conditions. From a state of harsh conflict and forcible suppression there has been a powerful thrust towards constructive experiments. For example, employers have organized their workers in "company unions," comprehending all the workers in a plant, electing employee representative councils or work councils. These company unions develop what are called "welfare features," such as the sale of the company's securities to its workers at rates below those to be got in the open market and the purchase of insurance to cover all the workers employed by the concern against sickness, old age and death. This type of organization tends to break up the old nation-wide trade unions and runs (says the Encyclopædia Britannica, Article, *Trade Unions*) to a membership of several millions.

Another type of experiment lies in the direction of a trade union undertaking the responsibility for production. The business in return gives the union a share in the gain from increased output. This method worked so well between the Machinists' Union and the Baltimore & Ohio Railway Co. that it has spread to a number of other railway systems in the United States and Canada. Similarly the Amalgamated Clothing Workers' Union has taken over many of the duties of management and supervision from the manufacturers, has studied and effected considerable economies in production, and done much to educate and increase the efficiency of its members. This tailors' union has been outstandingly successful; it has accumulated funds, made loans to employers and carried through a big coöperative housing scheme in New York City.

§ 4. Profit-Sharing

Another line of attempted reconciliation between the "two nations" of employers and employees, a line of reconciliation proceeding from the initiative of the employer, lies in profit-sharing, a peculiarly French invention. A French profit-sharing system was in operation as early as 1820 and there are a number of such businesses still active. The Paris Bon Marché has a scheme at work dating from 1880 by which all its share capital is now in the hands of past or present employees. Similar schemes have been operated in Great Britain and America following upon French precedents. The employees of the British Gas Light and Coke Company, the largest gas company in the world, have acquired £750,000 of its ordinary stock as their share in its profits. The Zeiss works in Jena, manufacturing glass lenses, are run on a profit-sharing scheme that has proved a great success.

But such successes are exceptional in the history of profit-sharing. The method has many drawbacks; its outstanding success are few and generally due to the enthusiasm and integrity of the managing employer; it does not increase and spread through the general body of industry. It fails to excite much enthusiasm in the ordinary worker, who is apt to consider it as a mere complication of his pay, and the trade unions regard it as a method of shelving the proper adjustment of wages. It raises many delicate and debatable questions about what are profits and what are receipts from the consumption of capital, and what proportion of the annual surplus may legitimately go back into the business for depreciation and expansion. It is in fact an encumbering quasi-benevolent device; it leaves the primary functional opposition of employer and employed untouched, and we note it here mainly to distinguish it clearly from the essentially structural innovations, the real resumptions of responsibility and participation by the organized workers, that have sprung from the Guild Socialist conception.

§ 5. Continuous Employment and Waiting About: the Possibility of Lifetime Jobs for All

One chief hardship of the worker in the modern industrial world is the uncertainty of his employment from day to day and in many cases from hour to hour.

Comfortable prosperous people know little of the tedium, wretchedness and disappointment that have characterized and still characterize, great fields of employment through the "waiting about" forced upon the workers by the chancy, *undercalculated* and inconsiderate nature of a large proportion of industrial operations. Men have to stand at dock gates, waiters queue up outside restaurants, men and women sit inactive in clothing shops waiting for work to be given out, they assemble in silk-weaving establishments, in steel works, glass works and so on, *earning nothing* until they are beckoned to their task. Until recently it was not even the custom to pay actors and actresses for rehearsals. Few prosperous people realize that to be an out-of-work is often as binding and far more tedious than to be in employment. They think of being out-of-work as a leisurely, free state, disagreeable only through its concomitant of want.

One might imagine from this that one great objective of trade-union effort would be to secure continuity of employment. But that has not been the case. There are alternative evils to be considered. Labour under contract is hampered in the strategy of collective bargaining. And a contract for continuous employment without definite conditions for treatment may become very easily a practical slavery. The ancient English contract with farm servants for a year, the yearly bond of the Northumbrian coal miner, the annual hiring of the Staffordshire potters, have now, for that reason, become matters of history. It is only when the contract is amplified by a very rigorous definition of the rights and remedies of either party, when there is a well defined schedule of the customs of the trade and the precise duties of the worker, that the latter can feel secure against aggressions and deprivations. We find therefore that the worker is forced to choose between two uncertainties: uncertainty of continuous earning on the one hand, and uncertainty of treatment on the other. His adjustment between these two sets of considerations is a complex task which is still going on.

Contemporary industrialism has been evolved in relation to a labour class numerically always in excess of the demand for its services. Industry has been wont to take in workers as it needed them, by the hour, day or week, and to drop them again directly they were unwanted. The community had to carry these workers for the primitive type of employer during his intervals of relative inactivity, and he was never called to account for their upkeep. Such education as these workers got was provided either by charitable bodies or the general community, and when they were disabled or superannuated they again went on to public resources. There was little or no recognition of the indebtedness of the employer to this floating population of impoverished people which served to cheapen his labour supply. That did not come into his figuring. The drain they made on the general resources was not charged to him.

Education in the early stages of the industrial revolution was trivial, poor relief was a minimum, and it was only as the standard of efficiency and economy rose, as education became public and expensive and assistance for the out-of-work increased, that people began to think of any bookkeeping as between the social cost of the worker's birth, life, and death and the finance of industry. The common man of to-day has become a much more manufactured and costly product than the common man of a century ago. Then he was, one may say, a wild product, like a chance mushroom in a meadow; the employer picked him and consumed him; now he is a cultivated product, and the organized community which has made him asserts its right to control the exploitation of his abilities.

Professor Carr-Saunders calculates that the cost of producing a boy for the labour market in Britain (1930) is well over £350. The government returns show an educational expenditure of £100; food and clothing amount to at least £200, and rent and social services certainly add another £50 to the total.

The industrialist of the early nineteenth century lived like an animal that ranges in the woodland; he reaped his profit with no thought of whence it came and with an unshaken confidence in his own right to live. But all that has changed and continues to change. The industrial concern is becoming more and more dependent on public resources for the quality and intermittent support of its labour supply, and the world at large grows impatient with the factory's habit of absorbing and then excreting workers into the general community without the slightest regard for social decency. Sustained unemployment means degeneration; and the right of industry working for private profit to take the young people society has provided, has civilized and to some extent educated, use them intermittently for a term of years, and throw them out in a state of diminished usefulness in order to avail itself of younger, fresher and cheaper material, is being questioned more and more acutely.

The possibility of greatly reducing casual and short-term employment can be approached not only from the point of view of the public services, but also from the point of view of the employer. Casual labour is rarely loyal or zealous labour, and a considerable effort is being made by many employers to diminish or eliminate it altogether from their works. As I was planning this section a significant document dropped into my letter box, an American publication, the *Survey Graphic,* giving an account of the labour organization of Messrs. Procter & Gamble, a firm of soap-makers (about whose products and standing I know nothing). This firm claims to guarantee a minimum of forty-eight weeks' employment in the year to ten thousand employees. It is not quite clear if they have other employees outside the privileged ten thousand, but if so, they are apparently probationers and few in number. This is a very interesting and plausible claim, and probably it is the anticipation of something likely to become much more general. There is no reason why that much foresight should be practicable only in soap-making. Messrs. Procter & Gamble are satisfied that they reap a full reward in the increased good-will of their people. Any business organization capable of figuring out its production as exactly, they say, may reap a similar reward. That seems acceptable. It depends entirely on the figuring out.

It appears reasonable to argue that this "waiting about," this immense amount of slack in the economic machine, this running waste of unemployed hours and energies, is neither a necessary nor a permanent state of affairs. Its continuance is due to the statistical insufficiency in our body politic. But the trend of things is all towards sounder statistics and better forecasting.

Let me throw out here a broad thesis for the reader's consideration. The total life product of a worker, the money earned during the working years, should be equivalent to all that worker's expenditure and all the expenditure upon that worker, including the overhead charges for directorate and government, from the cradle to the grave. If it is less, he is a parasite; if it is more, he is being robbed and is carrying nonproductive social elements upon his shoulders that he ought not to carry. These seem to me to be sound propositions, giving a definite intimation of the way in which economic life may and should be measured and organized.

In the more calculable days that lie before mankind the economist should be able to state with ever increasing precision the amount of productive work required from every citizen to earn his life subsistence and his freedom for the residue of his time and energy. As these estimates become more precise it will become possible for the State or for some world-wide labour organization to make a deal with the ordinary worker, to undertake to find him or her employment for as many years as it may be necessary to work off that contribution, and to guarantee a life income in return. Such an organization would be responsible to the worker for his maintenance, and it would make its arrangements with the public or private service or production concerned, for his employment.

§ 6. The Amelioration of the Factory

Turning now from the current methods of employment for the mass of workers in our human ant-hill and the way in which these methods may develop, let us consider a very interesting field of enquiry and experiment which falls under the term "Scientific Management." This term we owe to Frederick Winslow Taylor, and as exemplified by him it was essentially a reconstruction of industrial processes after a close study and analysis of every step in the process under treatment. For example, he dealt with shovelling in a large steel plant, watched and timed workers, tried out movements and showed that they were using ill-chosen shovels, lifting excessive weights here and insufficient weights there, and missing the easiest way of performing their tasks. By altering the types of shovel used and carefully teaching the shovellers, such an improvement in the process was made that the average wages of these men was raised 63 per cent while the cost of handling was reduced 54 per cent.

Another research of Taylor's led to great improvements in the transmission of power by leather belting and to the redesigning of lathes. The same methods applied to the general planning-out of work to be undertaken, led to conspicuous economies in the moving about of material, the elimination of delays when stuff had been used up and more was required, the arrangement of work spaces in the order of maximum convenience and so forth.

Particular attention was given to prevent machinery standing idle. Inactive machines, vacant floor space, swell the overhead charges without adding to the product. Work thus closely watched can no longer be left to the old type of foreman. Its direction becomes educational; the foreman must be, to a large extent, a teacher and demonstrator and a specially trained and skilled man.

So in our review of contemporary human activities we must add now to the worker, foreman, shop steward, overseer and suchlike traditional officials in all really organized businesses, a new small group of very important people who are planning, watching and charting the processes of production. From the point of view of the worker, his task is made less laborious and troublesome but more effective. He is to work in the best air and the best light; his temperature and comfort and mental tranquillity are studied to enable him to give his best; he is relieved before the fatigue stage sets in. Such are the concepts and methods that are spreading now throughout the industrial world.

By way of contrast to efficient modern going concerns, a study or so of early nineteenth and Victorian enterprises might be very useful and entertaining. The material for such studies, I should imagine, must still exist in abundance—accounts, balance sheets, plans of layout, estimates —but how far it has actually been digested and made available I do not know.* I may be wrong here. Perhaps more than I think of the directive intelligence of the smaller, more limited and more controllable business of from fifty to a hundred years ago was carried about in people's heads; perhaps the great part of Victorian management went undocumented, its once living records long since decayed in the cemetery.

In our modern plants we shall certainly find not merely a more adequate documentation, but a distinctness and definition of parts in the organism which were either unorganized or absent in the more primitive economic structure of the nineteenth century. There are, for example, the beginners who replace the old apprentice fags, those who are indeed working in part but who are also in part learning. For them the factory is half a school, a specializing school. For them there must be a special teaching and controlling staff. The modern factory has to deal with the general educational organization of the community in a spirit of give and take. The educational authority has to come into the business as the protector of the 'prentices to see that they are really taught and not used merely as cheap junior hands, and the industry seeks to extend its influence into the schools to secure a better type of worker in its shops.

Another modern section in a business organization outside the everyday round is the research staff, concerned with the systematic investigation of problems arising out of the work and in the search for novelties, improvements and economies. Both these sections are correlated nowadays with great educational and investigatory organizations outside the works, with the school, the technical college and the scientific side of the university. The days when it was possible to distinguish sharply

*Such men as T. G. Ashton, G. W. Daniels and others have made studies on Victorian cotton, wool, brass and iron production. *H. J. L.*

between business organizations and public educational and social institutions have passed away.

In America such great industrial organizations as General Motors, the Ford Motor Company and the Westinghouse Electric Manufacturers have established training institutions to meet their own particular needs, and these interlock closely with exterior schools. For instance, we find the University of Cincinnati, Antioch College in Ohio, the Institute of Technology at Flint (Mich.), and the Technical High School at the city of Dayton (Ohio) all in close coöperation with the General Motors organization at Dayton. The engineer students pass to and fro between the shop, the classroom and the laboratory.

The increasing correlation of the organizing forces in the factory with public research and education to-day is well displayed in that pioneer institution, the National Institute of Industrial Psychology in London.* Here, under the direction of Mr. C. S. Myers, there is a continual coming and going between school, employer and public official. "Planning" is studied, that is to say, the layout of plant, the routine of processes, the storage and transport of material. Fatigue is exhaustively scrutinized: its relation to hours of work, to lighting, to temperature, to the movements of air in a workroom. Winslow Taylor's ideas are adapted now to this new industrial process and now to that. In addition, work is going on continually with the object of making a trustworthy classification and tests for nervous and mental types, so as to fit the job to the worker and avoid the distress and wastage of setting the wrong sort of individual to an uncongenial job. Employers send applicants for posts under them, to the Institute for tests and examination, instead of trusting to their own casual impression of the aspirant; parents may bring youngsters for advice as to the choice of a *métier*.

At first the work of Winslow Taylor and the larger enterprise of the London Institute were regarded with considerable suspicion by the workers themselves as being no more than an attempt to put them under increased pressure and reduce employment. Winslow Taylor, in his classical instances, seems always to have insisted that the workers concerned should have a substantial share in the economies effected in the form of increased wages. The question of the reduction of employment is one best deferred to a later stage, but the dread of any increased stress through "Scientific Management" is already dispelled. The Institute has got a number of expressions of approval from workers with

---

*The ruling ideas of the Institute are set out in *Industrial Psychology,* by C. S. Myers and others (1929). See also *Business Rationalisation* (1932) by C. S. Myers.

whom it has dealt. Says Factory A: "Could we not have more like this? It has made it a lot easier for us." "It feels much safer now; we can get on with the work much quicker." Factory B echoes: "It is much better now; we can stick to the job without being fussed about." "It's fair now; it divides the work up—share and share alike." And a worker from Factory C says: "When we heard of the changes you were giving us, we were that glad we all felt six foot high. . . . I wish you had been here when I was a girl; I wouldn't look the old hag I do now."

It is interesting to contrast the conditions of the actual worker at work, now and in the past. The toil of the Lancashire cotton-mill hands or the sweated Sheffield cutlers of the early industrial period was immeasurably inferior in ease, dignity, comfort and leisure to that of their current successors. Already it is difficult for us to realize how enormously and needlessly cruel were the relative ignorance and inexperience of the pioneer age of power production. With no profit to the employer worth talking about.

In 1830 England was leading the world in the development of the new industrialism; she was the supreme industrial country. Let us see the price in humanity that she was paying, recklessly and needlessly, for that ascendency. In those days a cotton hand would be getting from four shillings to five shillings and sixpence a week, his wife three shillings and his children from one shilling each, upwards. The budget of a family of weavers who were paid at the current highest rates showed that after rent and working expenses had been deducted from their earnings of eighteen shillings, ten shillings and tenpence a week was left for the food, clothing and other needs of seven people. This is rather more than the amount available for the same objects in the families of the lowest paid unskilled London labourers in 1912. But four people had to work sixteen hours a day to earn it, as against one man working a ten-hour day. Moreover, bread cost then sixpence halfpenny for a four-and-a-half-pound loaf of household or brown bread. Many families, although in full work, were obliged to obtain relief from the parish.

This sample cotton operative at the age of thirty could probably already look back upon over twenty years of toil in the mill. Six or seven was the age at which most children started to earn, although some began younger. Our man might at that date have been one of the pauper children sent from all over England by their parishes to a life indistinguishable from slavery in order to relieve the local ratepayer, for that practice was not stopped until 1816. Or he might have been a child whose father had been told that if he would not bring his children to the mill he could not be allowed parish relief. Once brought there, the child would have been obliged to work thirteen, fourteen, or fifteen hours a day for six or even seven days in the week and all the weeks in the year. Factories were known where girls of eighteen worked eighteen hours a day for five consecutive days a week; others where workers were often kept on all night. Even seven days' work was exacted. The engines, it is true, were stopped on Sundays in order that a Christian population might go to church, but the children were required in many cases to turn up as usual and clean machinery. Such were the wages, such the hours, under the leading industrial state of the world only a hundred years ago.

From time to time the Commons, urged by the better employers, passed Acts limiting the working hours of apprentices to twelve, but no method of enforcing them was provided, they were not carried out, and outside the very best mills, real relief did not come except in the matter of night work, until the passing of the Acts of 1847 and 1850. For all those interminable working hours the children stood, or walked, or crawled under the machines, collecting cotton waste. One employer, known as humane, calculated that his children during their work walked upwards of twenty miles. They also walked from their beds to the factory and back again. There were meal-times—an hour and a half in all—for adult workers, but not for children. They had to clean the machines and to eat their food as they worked among the oil and dust and flue. If they grew too tired, the overseers beat them to keep them at work; their fathers beat them to keep them awake so that they should not fall into the machines. Everyone spat to get rid of the flue that settled in their lungs—it was stated in evidence before Sir Robert Peel's committee (1816) that when spitting failed to achieve this purpose emetics were freely given.*

We are told to-day that there has been exaggeration in the attacks made on the early factory system, that many mills were clean and airy, so that the operatives who worked in them were better off than those who ate and slept and worked in the damp cellars necessary for the home weaving of cotton, that brutal masters were an exception, and that the children of the home-workers toiled as long and were often more cruelly treated than those who were at the mercy of employers and overseers. That may be true. The English are a kindly race, and the presence of onlookers is always a check on cruelty. It is certainly

*Hammond: *The Town Labourer*, p. 158.

true also that the housing conditions of the time were sufficient to account for any amount of typhus, typhoid and tuberculosis.

Here is a description of a district in Spitalfields inhabited by weavers in the year 1840; Manchester is described as "even worse." "Ruinous buildings, streets without sewers, overflowing privies and cesspools, and open ditches filled with a black putrefying mass of corruption infecting the air for miles round, render the district the abode of disease and death. There are streets and alleys from which typhus fever is never absent the year round."* And the new machines brought their own occupational diseases—consumption from the cotton flue, stomach diseases for the weavers who sat pressed forward against the beam of the loom, cancer for the mule-spinners, consumption again for the girls on worsted spinning who, "exposed to a constant spray of water from the frames, were compelled to spend the greater part of the day in wet clothing; and the introduction of hot-water spinning merely increased the heat and dampness of the air."†

Flax mills were described as even more unhealthy, the Sheffield grinders were killed by sandstone dust, the metal-workers were blinded by sparks. Every trade seems to have produced its own scourge. And the new machines were run so fast that it was painful to keep up with them; accidents were continual; when workers were killed in the course of their employment they were not thought worth the trouble of an inquest. Many factories were dirty, dark and airless; in many the workers were locked in, at a temperature of 80°, without water—forbidden, in fact, to drink—without lavatories, and under what they certainly regarded as a prison-like and brutal discipline.

As for brutality, it has to be remembered that the wage-earners were helpless. In the huge new towns there was no public opinion, and no custom to protect the men in any established rights. They might not combine to negotiate with their masters or even to secure that these latter observed the law. Each individual must make his own bargain for employment, those who complained were prevented from obtaining fresh jobs and had nothing to keep them from starvation but the workhouse. In such an atmosphere blows and brutal punishments seem normal. Nor had the worker any help from public opinion. Respectable people, with their minds still obsessed by the thought of the French Revolution, regarded him as potential Jacobin.

Even the physical consequences of these inhuman conditions roused

*"Report on Handloom Weavers," 1840, p. 681.
†Pinchbeck: *Women Workers and the Industrial Revolution*, p. 137.

in the comfortable classes not pity but repulsion and fear—their very diseases and deformities set the industrial classes apart as alien, sinister and dangerous. The only possible method of dealing with them seemed to be violence, and it was an age of evictions, transportation, whippings, treadmills and pillories; capital punishment was inflicted for any felony. To go out on strike was commonly treated as an offense.

The only possible answer for the victims was to return savagery for savagery. Magistrates were terrorized so that they were afraid to convict rebellious operatives, and employers and their agents were intimidated so that they dared not give evidence. The first standards of fair treatment set up, the unions, were maintained so far as they could be maintained by a reign of terror.

Turning to the vital statistics of the industrial operative of a hundred years ago we find that whereas miners seldom lived beyond fifty, the weavers were said to die soon after forty. At thirty-five their earning power began to decline. Slaves must have been very cheap indeed before any slave-owner would have thought it good management to kill his men so young. But then the slave-owner had to buy his slaves, while the community in the opening phase of industrialism gave its young without fine or fee into the hands of the industrial employer.

A hundred years ago things were at this stage in England. But in this still disunited world things do not move forward at a uniform pace, and one land after another blunders through the same experiences as its fellows—knowing little or nothing of the lessons they have learnt. China industrially is a hundred years behind western Europe, and there to-day one can see a population entering upon an entirely similar phase to that from which the men, women, and children of industrial England are emerging.

The silk factories of Shanghai to-day can show conditions which vary only in detail from those of the British industrial revolution. The children who crawl in them do not choke their lungs with cotton, but they scald their fingers picking cocoons out of pans of boiling water and die of blood poisoning in consequence. The smell must be worse than that of the dirtiest cotton mill that ever defiled Lancashire, for it is added to by unwashed babies slung under the frames and the putrefying insects in the cocoons.

Egypt, again, tells a parallel story. There came to hand by the same post (January, 1931) the news of a weavers' strike in Lancashire against a proposed lowering of their wages and labour conditions "to meet foreign competition," and an account of the sort of competition they have to meet in a report upon the Egyptian cotton mills of to-day. There we have now, just as we had in Lancashire a hundred years ago, the ill-organized factory, the ill-arranged machinery, because Egyptian flesh and blood is so cheap. "Half the workers are under fifteen and many under nine." . . . "I saw with sorrow in several factories the almost automatic hitting of the children with canes and whips by the overseers as they moved up and down, to spur them on to their work." . . . "There was some hitting of the children on the head, a really dangerous practice." . . . "The mills run from 5 A. M. to 8 or 9 P. M., but no one in authority seems to find it necessary to see that individual young workers, or groups of them, have any regular pause for a meal." . . .

A report upon conditions in the Cairo silk-winding and hand rug-making shops is equally bad. "Tiny children of five and a half years and upwards working like rapid machines in the hand-work shops, with all expression of childhood gone from their faces." . . . In a rug-making shop a child suffering from the painful, dangerous and infectious disease of trachoma was at work, crowded close to other children. In the cigarette and tobacco factories children work among dangerous processes and imperfectly guarded machinery.

If there is one redeeming feature in this account which differentiates it from the contemporary descriptions of Lancashire a hundred years ago, it is that it is not, as it were, a voice crying to empty heaven, but the evidence of Dame Adelaide Anderson, a distinguished British Inspector of Factories (a type of official which did not exist a century ago), published in the *Review* of the International Labour Office at Geneva, a publication effective enough, at any rate, to produce at once assurances from the Egyptian government that steps are now being taken to remedy the worst of these conditions.

It may not need as long as a hundred years, perhaps, to bring Egypt into line with the state of affairs already established in Lancashire. The pace of progress may be quicker for China and India as the world moves towards unification.

In India indeed actual factory conditions have been rapidly improved in the past thirty years. A fairly high standard of safety, ventilation and sanitation has been introduced. The minimum age at which children might work in factories has been advanced from seven years in 1881 to nine years in 1891 and twelve years in 1922, and children between the ages of twelve and fifteen are now limited to six hours' work a day. The majority of Indian cotton workers are men, although many women and children are still employed in jute factories, and also on the Assam tea plantations. The housing conditions in Bombay however are still extremely bad, the infantile death rate is monstrous and the workers are habitually in debt. In Japan 80% of the cotton workers are women, and numbers of peasant girls work in the cotton mills on two or three yearly contracts, part of their wages being paid in advance to their parents. Until recently these girls were sold for fixed periods to the mills for lump sums paid in advance to the parents. These conditions we say are transitory, they are passing away as you read. Here, by way of reassurance, is a description of the newer phase in the cotton industry. The mill described is still not Utopian, but it is sufficiently developed from primitive conditions to show the nature of the new order to which we still seem to be moving.

If a cotton operative of 1831 could be taken over one of the Lancashire mills to-day what would catch his attention first? Probably, the new machines, stately, complex, precise and beautiful compared with the crude mechanisms which enslaved him. Then, surely, the scarcity of human beings. In a room where a dozen great carding machines are delicately gathering up their film of cotton he might see no one at all. The seething, wretched, mill-ground humanity of his experiences has vanished altogether. If he spoke of it he would be told, "There should be a girl about." Minding an avenue of shimmering spindles which would stretch from one side of a broad road to the other he would see two men and a boy. Two healthy men and a well grown boy. The weaving sheds where women work might seem more familiar to him, for women, invincibly possessive, bring little bundles with them into the spaces between four looms where each rules over her tenter, stamp them with their personality, and so to speak domesticate them. But now new looms are coming which will need but an eighth of a man's attention —the old factory swarm is gone forever.

Next our returned cotton slave would remark the light, the extraordinary amount of light, the clear atmosphere, the absence of little children and the air of alertness, intelligence and self-respect that reigns among the workers in a good mill. Noisy it would still be—we are not yet able to control our noises—but he would be shown lavatories, cloakrooms, water to drink and to wash in—the place so arranged generally that our now expensive workers may combine and harmonize to the best effect with the costly machinery they control. If he talked to this generation of his great-grandchildren he would find independence in the place of hopelessness, social humour for his bitter class hatred, and technical interest in improvements for his blind, agonized obstruction to every economy of toil.

But the most fundamental change, productive of these others, is that the worker is no longer an isolated individual or even a member of a helot class. He is a voter, a citizen with acknowledged rights and an acknowledged value, whose state concerns itself perforce with his safety and the decency and cleanliness of his surroundings, sees that he is compensated for accidents, and makes provision for sickness, unemployment and old age. He is also, if he is wise, a member of a respected and powerful union which guards his hours and wages and champions him in any case of ill-treatment or injustice.

This much can be found in any ordinary mill. But our present system can be run to yield far more than this. Cotton has been chosen for description in this work, instead of the mines or the metal industries, to illustrate the worst possibilities of industrialism in a phase of eager, profit-seeking enterprise. In England, moreover, cotton is a hard-hit export trade which handles a low-priced article. It must compete now with the output of India, China and Egypt. Yet such a firm as Tootall, Broadhurst, Lee & Company of Manchester, working with modern conceptions of scientific management and sympathetic intelligence superadded, is able not only to train but to educate the young people in its Bolton mills, teaching, besides English subjects and gymnastics, physics, mathematics and drawing to the boys, and cooking, sewing and housework to the girls. These last domestic arts are taught not only in a modern kitchen, but also in a typical Bolton cottage, so that the pupils may see what can be made of the sort of home they may one day possess. For all the employees of this firm there are a library, games clubs, musical and dramatic societies, a dental clinic and a welfare department.

The firm we have named is merely an outstanding instance of the civilization of industrialism. It is a leader in a general movement. The process is being universalized slowly, alas! but surely. Probably very few of our readers have visited the Home Office Industrial Museum in London. It is not a popular place of resort, but everyday business men of the better type who are building or reconstructing factories go there for warning, advice, information, and inspiration; problems of industrial diseases and discipline are brought there by factory inspectors or employers, and studies are pursued by students of social and economic problems. It is fascinating to see how the orderly trained mind is extending security throughout our crowded, busy ant-hill. Here in one place is a grim collection of broken apparatus, hooks of cranes, chains, bearings, and torn, scorched and blackened electric fittings that have gone wrong; every one of these has caused the death of one or more workers; it is, indeed, a sort of "Chamber of Horrors" in that respect; but every one of these exhibits has been the basis of an enquiry and vigorous preventive measures. There are series of studies of, for example, the causes of explosions in industrial plants, of eye accidents and their prevention, of lighting in relation to fatigue and eye strain, of protective clothing, of the particular dangers and necessary precautions in the pottery, the bakehouse, the laundry, the printing hours, shipbuilding, housebuilding and so on. Veiled by dark covers that must be drawn aside, there is a terrible series of wax models; arms and hands, faces and bodies discoloured and distorted by anthrax, lead poisoning, silicosis, dermatitis and a number of other industrial diseases.

Almost every new industrial process, particularly when it involves new materials, needs to be watched in the interests of the worker. Working in pitch and paraffin has brought to light unsuspected dangers of skin cancer; the increasing use of chromium has made chrome ulceration a special problem. There are X-ray photographs of choked and diseased lungs, and there is an exposition of the precautions, regulations and prohibitions that have resulted from these studies.

We have just mentioned the disappearance of flue from the cotton factory. At the Home Office Industrial Museum one may see how dust, chips, filings and flue are sucked away from the worker and out of the factory atmosphere. Another considerable section of the museum is devoted to the prevention of fatigue, to comfort, rest rooms, sanitary accommodation and kindred problems. The London Home Office Industrial Museum is only one of several. There are similar collections in Milan, Berlin, Amsterdam, Paris, Lausanne and elsewhere. They are not merely in evidence and protest against the headlong, ignorant exploiter. Associated with them is a very definite and increasing element of control and punitive power.

Such is the contrast of a modernized scientific industrialism with the hideous lawless exploitation of the opening phase—in Egypt, India, and China to-day; in Lancashire a century ago—when the promise of the new order is yet masked by the greedy incompetence of the profit-seeking employer and the ancient black tradition that servitude, to be productive, must be ruthlessly imposed. In these industrial museums the spirit of the trained, educated man is made visible, steadily overcoming the dull brutality and rapacity of the primitive entrepreneur.

They are among the most significant and hopeful of the signs and portents of that world of organized foresight towards which human affairs are moving.

They will move in that direction more and more rapidly as increasing masses of people grasp the significance of what is going on and throw their influence into the scale on the side of scientific control as against "free" individual profit-making. Steadily, as world unity is organized, the whole of man's industrial life throughout our planet will be raised to the level and beyond the level indicated by that museum in Horseferry Road to-day.

§ 7. *Vestiges of Slavery and Tropical Forced Labour*

The backwardness, the heedless cruelty, revealed by contemporary reports upon the factories of Egypt, India and China is not only dreadful in itself, but it pulls dead against all the progressive forces of the more highly organized European and American communities. On the one hand we have the civilized factory we have just described, and on the other we have the soul-destroying factories of the backward countries, undercutting all but the very highest grade of Lancashire product and obstructing further advance. We have this discord of easy modern productiveness with ancient traditional greed. The responsibilities of the International Labour Bureau at Geneva in this respect alone are colossal. The establishment of a common standard of employment throughout the world remains a distant objective to which we move forward only very slowly.

But there are still graver aspects of contemporary production, due to the present irregular distribution of civilization and order—aspects that cannot be ignored in any survey of contemporary human activities. It is unhappily true, as Bombay and Cairo testify, that civilization does not necessarily follow the flags of civilized states. Modern machinery and commercial greed can outrun the modern administrator very easily. In the darker, the less illuminated regions of the world, the worst impulses of barbarism and modern business enterprise can meet and mingle to produce far more frightful consequences. There is, then, not even the pretense of paid employment; there are outright slavery and a form of enforced production under threats and duress more horrible than any slavery can be.

The extent to which slavery itself still exists is not always realized. Lady Simon, in her book, *Slavery* (1930), puts the number of "owned persons"—that is, persons who may be sold as chattels—at considerably over four million. But these actual slaves do not as a matter of fact constitute a formidable economic threat. They are confined for the most part to Arabia, the northern two thirds of Africa, China, and the wild territories between India and China; they are not employed on industrial work nor even in handling valuable crops for international commerce. Slave labour is extremely inefficient—it is estimated that it takes two slaves to do the work of one free man. It is unintelligent and unambitious, devoid of any incentive to improve. It is not really cheap, for slaves cost money to catch, to breed, to buy, to train and also to maintain. They receive no wages, but they must be fed and clothed, housed, tended in sickness and incessantly supervised. As against efficient modern labour the slave does not pay. Slavery as an economic method is moribund; if it survives as an institution it will be in the form of domestic servitude.

In this form it is still a social problem. The faster it can be stamped out, the better. But it is another aspect of human helplessness which challenges our attention when we are considering threats to the Atlantic standard of life. This is the system of peonage or forced labour. It is in effect, as we shall see, the economic *consumption* of backward and ill-organized races. It is far more profitable than slavery, and in some cases it is even more cruel. There are, at any rate, reasons for keeping slaves strong and well. They possess a money value, and a man must be drunk or negligent, stupid, a miser, mentally diseased, or out of temper before he will damage his own property. Slaves may, of course, fall into the hands of callous or morbid persons. Where they have been captured and marched long distances to the slave markets they must have passed through extremes of suffering. Where women are used deliberately to breed children for sale or sold as prostitutes they must often be among the unhappiest creatures on earth. But each slave, until worn out, is of value to someone. If human beings must be ill-treated or damaged in order to make them work, or killed in order to terrify their companions, it is cheaper not to buy them in the beginning.

PUTUMAYO

The natives who were tortured in tens of thousands and killed or starved wholesale by the rubber companies of the Putumayo and the Congo were not slaves. Technically they were "free" and under the legal protection of governments which rank as civilized. Their freedom

THE MECHANIZED FARMER

"DISKING" an orchard in the Pacific Northwest with a gasoline tractor. Tractors of this type are used on hilly farms in many parts of the United States for ploughing and other agricultural operations, where a steam tractor would have difficulty in negotiating the slopes.

THE LATEST STAGE OF HUSBANDRY
A CATERPILLAR tractor and drag at work.

only added to their misery. At this moment the Africans who are being flogged and robbed on the cocoa plantations of St. Thomé and St. Principé are supposed to be indentured labourers who have entered into contracts of service of their own free will.* Sir Roger Casement's reports on the Putumayo were written only twenty years ago, and some of the men against whom his most serious charges were made are believed to be still alive, free and in possession of their fortunes and probably still engaged in their appalling activities.

The forest-rubber region of Central South America is mainly the watershed of the Putumayo River and its confluents. These waters go on into the Amazon, and they flow through a land of tropical forests. The district of Putumayo belongs to Peru, but it is almost surrounded by Ecuador, Colombia and Brazil, and at the time of Casement's report, in 1910, it was not in fact subjected to any real form of legal government. It is separated from the lower reaches of the Amazon by thousands of miles of swamp and jungle, and from the coast to the west by the Cordillera Mountains.

In 1907 it was inhabited, according to the official estimate of the Peruvian government, by about fifty thousand Indians. They were not warlike people—in fact, that they were gentle, docile, and almost defenseless, is clear not only from the testimony of travellers and missionaries, but from the fact that only once or twice did a few of them venture to revolt against the oppression the economic utilization of rubber brought upon them. Until the last quarter of the nineteenth century they were visited by very few white men. Most of them could call their lives their own. Then adventurers from Colombia began to come down the rivers in search of wild rubber trees, bringing Indians to collect the milk for them. At first these newcomers traded with the natives, selling them rubbish in order to get them into debt, or inducing chiefs to pledge the labour of their clans. When such trading failed to produce as much rubber as they wanted, they resorted to terrorism. Each of these men considered the particular river on whose banks he had settled and the Indians who lived by it as his property: he kept all competition out of the district, maltreated the natives as he chose, and carried off and kept or sold the women and children.† The agents under his authority were half-tamed Indians, usually from some tribe belonging to another river, who were trained as guards and allowed to

*Lady Simon: *Slavery*, p. 144.

†Annual Report of the Minister of Justice to the Peruvian Congress, 1907, p. 782. Official Peruvian Government Press.

carry rifles. They themselves were compelled to force the forest Indians to bring in the quantity of rubber which had been fixed by the master and to follow them and hunt them down if they tried to leave the district. In return for this the guards were allowed to bully the natives as they pleased. The women and children were theirs to play with.

By 1910, however, when Casement's report was made, these early Colombian pioneers had almost disappeared, bought out by the Peruvian Amazon Company, which was amalgamated with the firm of Arana Brothers. But the joint firm, largely controlled by Julio Arana, carried on the old methods, though its agents now replaced the independent adventurers. It, too, relied on control by armed Indian guards, of whom Casement stated that though many he met were demoralized ruffians, capable of any crime, others, he thought, ill-treated the natives because they knew that if they did not do so they would themselves be murdered.

It was by mere mischance, from the company's point of view, that his visit was paid at all. In 1904-05 Arana Brothers had recruited about two hundred Barbados natives who were British subjects, and some of these men complained to the British Consul at Iquitos, the local headquarters of the company, that they were not only being refused the right to return, and used as slave drivers rather than workers, but that they were themselves subject to the grossest ill-treatment. These complaints bore out accusations which had been made in a book, *The Andes and the Amazon,** written by W. F. Hardenburg, a surveyor who had travelled through the district making a survey for a railway on behalf of the Peruvian government, and the British Foreign Office sent Consul General Casement to inquire into the question. He was of course afforded facilities by the Peruvian government and was accompanied everywhere by the Peruvian Amazon Company's principal representative.

His report† confirmed the very worst of the rumors which had been current. The Barbados Negroes—men of a semi-civilized class, some of whom could read and write—had not only been forced to commit crimes against the Indians, but had themselves been the victims of gross ill-treatment. But their own cases fade into insignificance beside what the report reveals of the victimization of the natives. These unfortunate beings, men, women and children, were systematically tor-

*Fisher Unwin, 1907.

†British Parliamentary Papers, Miscellaneous Nos., 1912. References unless otherwise stated are to this report.

tured and flogged. They were flogged regularly, with twisted whips of rawhide, if the loads of rubber they brought in did not reach the weight required, and arbitrarily if anyone chose to flog them. Of the natives Casement saw, he reports that quite 90 per cent bore scars as the result of their floggings—some of the worst scars he found on children of ten or twelve (pp. 33–35). In one house containing the fifteen Indians who served as servants to a settlement he found only one small boy unscarred. Deaths from flogging were frequent (p. 37), due as a rule to putrefaction of the wounds.

After the whip the most common instrument of torture was the stocks—two heavy wooden beams with leg holes cut in them, which were closed down one over the other when the legs had been inserted. Victims were confined in these for long periods, often with their legs forced so widely apart that they suffered extreme pain, and in some stocks the holes were so small that the beams could not be closed without cutting and crushing the flesh (pp. 41–42). Not infrequently natives were flogged when confined in these machines and then left to die of hunger—an eyewitness spoke of having seen them "scraping up the dirt with their fingers and eating it" and "eating the maggots from their wounds" (p. 39). Another method of punishment was to hold them under water until they were nearly drowned (p. 38), or to hang them by the neck with their toes just touching the ground until they were almost strangled (p. 39); one witness spoke of men being flogged while in this position. When the rubber had to be transported to the coast, which happened three times a year, the Indians were forced to carry it for about sixty miles, over a path "fatiguing to a good walker quite unburdened," and without any food but what they could bring with them. The principal representative of the rubber company himself told Casement that "hundreds" of them perished during the forced marches. One load of rubber weighed by Casement was just 50 kilos (100 pounds).

Large numbers, too, of the natives were shot, either as reprisals, after the one or two occasions when a revolt was attempted, or from mere wanton savagery. One witness speaks of Indians killed for sport—tied up to trees and used as targets (p. 66). Other individual crimes described by more than one independent witness are too revolting to have been the work of sane men. These dreadful accounts are for the alienist and criminologist rather than for the economic student.

It is obvious that under such a régime the Indian women and children were at the mercy of any white man or native guard who liked to amuse himself with them (p. 46). The Barbados men stated that they themselves were offered native "wives" at every station, but not as a rule allowed to take these women on with them if they themselves were shifted.

The general outcome of this combination of greed and ferocity may be stated briefly: Between 1900 and 1911 the amount of Indian-gathered rubber shipped to England through the Iquitos customs house was almost 4,000,000 kilograms—an amount which must have fetched between £1,000,000 and £1,500,000. The number of Indians deliberately murdered during this time or killed by starvation "often purposely brought about by the destruction of crops over whole districts" (p. 158) was at least 30,000, which is at the rate of under £50 per life tormented and destroyed. In 1906 the population had been estimated at 50,000. In 1911 it had fallen to 8,000. The difference between 30,000 and 40,000 is attributed to deaths from disease. That the coercion was so greatly intensified during these six years as to bring about this average yearly diminution in the population of 7,000 was due to the flotation by the Aranas in 1907 of a British company. In order that capital might be attracted from British investors it was necessary to show a high output, and during 1906 nearly 3,000,000 extra kilograms were extorted from the natives. It is to be regretted that the Aranas' search for British support was sufficiently successful to secure not only money but interest in very influential quarters, and that in consequence the pursuit of the Putumayo facts is not so easy as it might otherwise be.

Since Casement's reputation suffered later from the part that he played in the Irish rebellion, it may be as well to state that the most damning evidence was not taken by Casement alone, but in the presence of other members of the Commission, and often of officers of the company or of the British consul at Iquitos, and that all the allegations made were confirmed by the report of Dr. Paredes, the head of a judicial commission dispatched to the Putumayo by the Peruvian government in 1911. Other reports by Peruvian officials dating back to 1905 are quoted by Hardenburg in his later book *The Putumayo, the Devil's Paradise*.* The facts were beyond dispute.

Yet nothing effective was done, and so far as one can learn, nothing effective has been done. Before even drawing up his main report Casement had provided the British government with the names of the principal criminals, and these had been telegraphed to the Peruvian government at a time when most of these men were still openly in the

*Fisher Unwin.

district. They were, however, allowed to escape, some of them dragging with them large numbers of captive Indians either for sale or for continued forced labour in other parts of the forests. Two were known to have crossed the border into Brazil and to be continuing the collection of rubber there. The Brazilian government seems to have made genuine efforts to arrest them but, owing to the wildness of the region, failed in its purpose. Dr. Paredes issued warrants for the arrest of no less than 237 persons, but after he returned to the capital he "ceased to fill any judicial function," and only nine of the warrants were made effective. Even of the nine men arrested, none were brought to trial. Casement, revisiting the country at the end of 1911, found that the half-hearted attempts to plant rubber trees which had followed his former visit had come to an end again. A month later his first report was published by the British government; it had been kept private in order to give the Peruvians some inducement to undertake reforms, but when it became clear that there would not be any reforms the facts were made public. For a time the press of the world rang with the scandal. The British courts ordered a compulsory winding-up of the British company. Sir Edward Grey instructed British consuls throughout the world to report in future on the treatment of native races within their districts. Then came the war and a multitude of distractions. Facts to-day are hard to gather. What happened to Arana and his agents, and what is happening now in the rubber forests, nobody knows.

CONGO RUBBER

The havoc wrought in the Putumayo district, bad as it was, may be considered as almost trifling and accidental beside the devastation caused by the French and Belgian rubber companies in the Congo. Their individual crimes were no worse—you cannot do more to people than torture them to death—but in every other respect the Peruvians and Colombians are distanced by their European competitors. In the first place, the area of country and the number of victims concerned were very much greater, and the period of misrule longer. The two Congos, French and Belgian, cover an area of 1,600,000 square miles, rather larger than Europe without Russia. In the Belgian Congo the native population was reduced from over 20,000,000 in 1890—some observers, among them the English explorer Stanley, placed it at 40,000,000 —to 8,500,000 when an official census was taken in 1911. There seem to be no figures available for the French Congo. They are probably smaller, partly because the area concerned is only two thirds of the other, partly because the French part of the country was never so densely populated. But it seems likely from what evidence we do possess that the proportion of survivors was much the same. In a debate which took place in the French Chamber on February 19 to February 21, 1906, it was stated that according to official documents in one region alone 20,000 natives out of the 40,000 who had lived there were destroyed in two years.

Secondly, the outrages of the Putumayo were perpetrated by a few hundreds of persons working for a private company in a region where no governmental control existed. It was an escape from control. The wholesale massacres of the Congo, on the contrary, were carried out either by the actual forces of the State, or by mercenaries hired by wealthy companies who enjoyed the full support of their governments and were defended by them with ardour in their respective parliaments. The one scandal happened in a remote frontier district; the other was systematically planned in Europe by persons holding exalted positions and was deliberately carried on with the aid of many well known European newspapers, a skilful propaganda, and a widespread system of bribery. The originator, the mainstay and the chief beneficiary of a system which has killed more human beings than the European War, was King Leopold II of Belgium, and every influence which can be wielded by an astute and wealthy king was wielded by him in order to ensure its continuance.

The Congo Free State was formed in 1884, under the name of "The International African Association" "for the purpose of promoting the civilization and commerce of Africa and for other humane and benevolent purposes." King Leopold, who was the head of this association, represented that his agents had drawn up treaties of amity and friendship with the independent native rulers of the Congo, and he persuaded the other European powers to recognize him as absolute and personal sovereign of the greater part of the Congo basin in return for various assurances embodied in the "Congo Act." These included a promise that he would put down the slave trade then being carried on by Arab raiders; a guarantee of "complete freedom" to the trade of all nations, another guarantee against the granting of any trade monopolies or favours, and a general pledge that he would "watch over the preservation of the native tribes." He was enabled to obtain this position of trust partly because he bore the reputation of a wise ruler and a philanthropic man, partly because of the English support which was forthcoming for the son and namesake of Queen Victoria's favourite uncle.

This accomplished, he set about to do four things: assume possession of the land and its products; stop private trading; especially in rubber and ivory; raise an army among the savage tribes of the Upper Congo, and organize propaganda in Europe. By 1890 he had recruited some thousands of soldiers—in many cases by downright slave-raiding. His circulars* promise bonuses of 90 francs for every man over 1 metre 35 centimetres in height, 65 francs for youths over 1 metre 35 centimetres, and 15 francs for male children over 1 metre 20 centimetres. The next step was to get permission from the European powers to impose duties on merchandise in order, ostensibly, to fight the Arab slave-raiders. There were at that time both English and Dutch firms established on the Lower Congo, and protests were made by them as early as 1890 that the policy of the Congo Free State was ruining private trade and stirring up strife among the natives. The King, however, replied to these protests by a widespread newspaper propaganda, and obtained permission from Europe to exterminate the Arabs, and £1,000,000 from Belgium to carry on the war in return for his leaving her the Congo in his will. He succeeded in driving the Arabs from the Congo and in getting possession of the enormous stores of ivory which had been in their possession. Then he turned to his other objectives.

In order that the reader may form a picture of what his actions effected, he must be told something of the state of the river country and the natives who lived in it as Stanley found them on his voyages in 1879 and 1882. The river banks were at that time the home of a flourishing population which he estimated at forty millions. He saw large numbers of centres of population, each containing from 5,000 to 40,000 people—settlements extended for hundreds of miles along the waterside. The tribes had reached a certain level of civilization—they made beautiful cloths and ironwork, carried on a number of other skilled crafts, cultivated a large variety of vegetables as well as maize and sugar cane, kept their gardens as well as Europeans could do, and were above all enthusiastic merchants who made long voyages up and down the river and maintained trade relations with the distant tribes of the interior. These people were savages—there were even among them a certain number of cannibals—but the foremost Belgian historian of the Congo said of them at that time, "They are warriors only for defense; they are

*Quoted in debates in Belgian Parliament, March, 1905; March, 1906. Official shorthand reports.

one and all traders."* It is as well to stress the fact that their rulers held the land in trust for the tribesmen and "early explorers of the Congo; Catholic and Protestant missionaries with long years of experience in different parts of the territory; British consuls, indeed a whole host of witnesses" testify to the jealous regard of the native population for their rights in land.† This land King Leopold proceeded to appropriate. By an official decree of July 1, 1885, he declared that "vacant land must be considered as belonging to the State."

By vacant land, it subsequently appeared he meant all land not actually built upon, the forests in which the various tribes hunted and collected the raw materials for their trading and their crafts. In 1891, his armies being prepared, he forbade the natives to collect or sell rubber or ivory to merchants, or merchants to buy them from the natives. This practically destroyed the whole private trade of the area, for it was for rubber and ivory that the goods of the European firms were interchanged. Henceforth, any native who collected rubber for anyone but the State was a poacher, and the merchant who bought it of him a receiver of stolen goods. The merchants protested, but with no result, and they were finally forced to abandon their business.‡

Next, by secret instructions dated Brussels, June 20, 1892, the King informed the Governor General of the Congo State that the officials of the State were to "exploit the produce of the forests." To induce them to do this he would pay a bonus on rubber and ivory "proportionate to the cost of exploitation"—that is, the *less* the native received for what he brought the greater was to be the payment to the official.§ When news of these instructions reached Europe, the German government protested that it was a violation of the Congo Act to which Germany had been a signatory. Leopold, in a reply dated December 11, 1895, signed Edmund Van Eetvelde, denied that any bonus was either in existence or in contemplation. It was, in fact, the pivot of his organization.

Next a system of "taxes" was imposed on the natives—they were ordered to bring in certain amounts of ivory, rubber, or whatever produce of value the district produced. When the forests were ex-

---

*Wauters: *L'Etat Indépendent du Congo.*

†E. D. Morel: *The Black Man's Burden*, p. 115.

‡The full story of these events may be found in E. D. Morel's three books: *King Leopold's Rule in Africa* (Heinemann); *Red Rubber,* and *The Black Man's Burden* (Parsons).

§Official shorthand report, Belgian Parliamentary Debates.

hausted the natives were compelled to labour themselves or to bring in food for those engaged in forced labour.* Officials were informed of the amounts they were required to collect and given a certain time in which to collect them. Refusal to furnish the required amount was to be considered as a revolt and punished by force of arms, and by taking hostages.

Under this system, between 1899 and 1906 alone over £13,700,000 worth of rubber was collected by the natives of the Congo.† Within a year of its inauguration the Lower Congo looked "as though a tornado had torn across it and destroyed everything in its passage."‡ The amounts fixed as "taxes" were so great that it was impossible for the tribes to produce them. They refused, or failed, their villages were raided and burned, their women carried off as hostages to be redeemed, if they were still alive, by payments in rubber.

The report of one of the remaining Belgian merchants says, "There is not an inhabited village left in four days' steaming through a country formerly so rich; to-day utterly ruined. . . . The soldiers sent out to get rubber and ivory are depopulating the country. They find the quickest and cheapest method is to raid villages, seize prisoners, and have them redeemed afterwards for ivory." If we add that one or two black soldiers armed with rifles were left as sentries in every helpless village with no one to call them to account, and that as a check on their wasting cartridges they were told in many cases to cut off the right hand or sexual organs of their victims, dry them, and bring them in baskets to their superiors, one for each cartridge used, we have the essential features of the system.§ As for these superiors, whether King Leopold's own officers, or the officials of the great companies to whom he had farmed out part of his territory, it may be as well to add that they were not allowed to resign. If they left their stations they were prosecuted for desertion or died or were killed on their way to the coast. ||

For twenty years this procedure was pushed methodically further and further inland under the name of "pacification." In 1903 a traveller named Murdoch, in 1907 another called Scrivener, travelled up the Congo for weeks together without meeting a single human being, past "long miles of ruined mouldering villages thickly strewn with skele-

---

*Official shorthand report, Belgian Parliamentary Debates, July, 1903.
†*Red Rubber*, p. 36.
‡*The Black Man's Burden*, p. 120.
§British Government White Book, Africa, No. 1, 1904.
|| *Red Rubber*, p. 88.

tons"* where once there had been a dense population. In groups of villages estimated in 1898 to have contained about 140,000 inhabitants, in 1903 under 18,000 were left.† The country of which these statements were made was part of King Leopold's "private domain."

Matters were even worse in the concessions. The Abir Company—an organization managed by a council consisting among others of a Belgian senator, the Grand Master of King Leopold's court in Belgium, a prominent banker and member of parliament, an ex-governor general of the Congo, and a Belgian nobleman—"enrolled thousands of natives, armed with rifles and cap-guns, to force the rubber output upon the general population. It kept some 10,000 natives continually at work all the year round collecting rubber, and some 10,000 men, women, and children passed every year through its 'hostage houses.' . . . When certain areas became denuded of rubber, the remaining male population was carried off wholesale under escort and flung into another area not yet exhausted, their women handed over to the soldiers."

It can hardly be necessary to add to this picture by the enumeration of atrocities. Of course, there were atrocities, tens of thousands of them, there were intended to be—they saved cartridges. And they were filthy and bestial beyond description. One official seems to have punished men who did not collect enough rubber by forcing them to drink the white man's excretion.‡ Another made the natives eat the rubber if it was badly prepared. The Court of Justice at Boma—there was a court, and great play was made with its existence in Europe—decided that the subsequent illness and death of the Negroes concerned could not be attributed to this as the "introduction into the stomach by the mouth of an elastic substance was not productive of after ill-effects."§

The reports of these atrocities were, of course, challenged. From the first complaints of the European merchants settled on the river to the last debates in the Belgian Parliament, every criticism of Leopold's administration was met by official denials, by a widespread counter propaganda, and by allegations that the criticisms came from corrupt or interested persons or formed part of political plots. Occasionally new "humane" regulations would be published in Europe in order to impress public opinion. In 1903 an edict appeared in Brussels to the effect that the natives were only to work forty hours a month at rubber-

*The Black Man's Burden, p. 124.
†King Leopold's Rule in Africa, pp. 238–41.
‡Memorial to Congress from the American Missionary Societies, January 16, 1905.
§Red Rubber, p. 106.

gathering. In 1906 three inspectors were appointed. But slowly information leaked out—always disputed, always contradicted by King Leopold's ministers and the heads of the Catholic party in Belgium, in spite
of the courageous protests of the Catholic missionaries on the spot.

There is no need to go into the nature of the evidence here—it may
be consulted by anybody on the shelves of the Anti-Slavery Society in
London. Or the names and numbers of the parliamentary papers, and
British and American consular reports which confirm the statements of
travellers and missionaries and of officers and officials themselves entangled in the system may be found in Mr. Morel's books. In case any
reader has been made sceptical by war-time stories of atrocities, let him
consider that Leopold II was defending himself and his closest friends
against these charges for over twenty years. In this task he spared
neither time nor influence nor money. And year after year, in speeches
and books, openly published, Morel and the other principal members
of the Congo Reform Association accused him of deliberately inciting,
bribing, and even commanding his officers and soldiers to wholesale
murder, rape, arson, the feeding of troops on human flesh, mutilation,
and torture of every description. They accused the King of doing this
deliberately and systematically, to an accompaniment of lying and corruption, for the sole end of amassing a personal fortune. They published
the names of many of the responsible heads of the concession companies; they made their charges specific and personal in the highest
degree. They were well known men living as a rule in England, whose
courts would not have hesitated for a moment to condemn them if
what they said overstepped the limits of legal proof. And no one of
them was ever prosecuted for libel.

That the Leopoldian régime endured in the Belgian Congo for
twenty years was due to the fact that the man responsible for it was a
king, and a king who had enjoyed until middle age a reputation for
virtue and benevolence. The Congo Free State had been brought into
being amid such torrents of eloquence about helping the natives that
it took ordinary people a long time to make the necessary complete
reversal of their opinions. From the beginning Leopold had realized the
need of a complicated defensive organization at home. Side by side
with his system of terrorism in Africa he built up a system of propaganda and corruption in Europe. To begin with, he farmed out large
areas of the Congo territory—in all perhaps two fifths of the whole—
to companies of persons whom he thought it advisable to influence. He
kept half the shares in each of these companies for himself; the rest

were held by court officials, journalists, bankers, judges, etc. These enterprises soon became enormously profitable. Paid-up shares of the A. B. I. R. Company of a par value of £4.6.6 were freely dealt in at prices between £700 and £1,000. This in itself constituted a barrier against reform, for every step taken to expose the system brought down the value of the shares—which finally, when reform was complete, fell to a few shillings. In addition, the existence of a market in these shares gave the King an opportunity of placing his inside knowledge at the disposal of journalists, financiers, or politicians whom he wished to bribe. He enlisted the general support of the Clerical party in the Belgian Parliament and the unwavering loyalty of their leader, M. Woeste, by various political concessions, though individual Catholics supported the Socialists in their demand first for reform and then for annexation. In Belgium itself the King had the further advantage that he ruled the Congo Free State not as a constitutional monarch, and not in his capacity of King of the Belgians, but as an absolute monarch and purely in his personal capacity.

Even so he felt unsafe; he needed accomplices against a possible day of reckoning. He lay open to the attack of hostile philanthropists in France, Germany, and England. He therefore set about inducing the French to introduce his system into the French Congo. He employed journalists to contrast the enormous profits made by the great Belgian concessions with the small trade done in the "undeveloped" French territory. A wave of speculation in Belgian rubber shares coincided with this effort and attracted the attention of French financiers. Finally, in 1899, after what a well known French writer described as "scandalous financial and political intrigues, bribery and corruption," Leopold succeeded. Within a year the French Congo had been parcelled out among forty financial corporations each with a thirty-year charter. Many of them were partly financed by Belgian capital, and their directorates interlocked with those of the great Belgian concessionaire companies. An attempt was made to extend the system to French West Africa and the German Kamerun. There were powerful trading firms in the first of these colonies, and they combined with the officials to defeat the proposal. In particular the Governor General of French West Africa, M. Ballay, opposed a system which required "a soldier behind every producer." The German government did grant two concessions to Belgo-German companies, but after a year the privileges of these groups were cut down and further applications for concessions refused.

The French Congo lies to the north of the Belgian—it is a country covering 600,000 square miles and carrying just before the war a population of 5,000,000. At the time when the Leopoldian system was introduced, such trade as existed was largely in the hands of trading firms who had established themselves along the sea coast and on the lower reaches of the river Ogowe. Under the new system the concessionaire companies considered themselves entitled, by their charters, to sole possession of all the rubber and ivory in their respective countries, and it followed that trade in these commodities between the natives and any third party became illegal. The natives were forbidden to approach the trading stations. The local administration—which was to receive a royalty of 15 per cent on the company's output—imposed a tax payable in rubber itself, and to be paid to the companies. When, failing legal redress, a revolt occurred against this new state of affairs, the concessionaires sent out their raiding bands, the government its columns of soldiers, to burn and slay from one end of the country to the other.

In 1905 somebody got hold of a batch of suppressed reports made by officials appointed under the De Brazza régime which had preceded this modern exploitation of the Congo. They were published, and they revealed to the French public a state of affairs the exact parallel to what, by that time, was known to be going on in the Belgian Free State. Here all over again were the murders, the mutilations, the women carried off wholesale for the use of troops, the hostage houses, and the atrocities. Tens of thousands of natives were stated to have perished during these first five years. French feeling ran high at these disclosures. The government of the day was alarmed into sending out De Brazza, the former governor, to report on the new régime. His instructions (since published by his widow) contain passages urging him to make it clear that the French system was not similar to the "proceedings of methodical tyranny" which were being carried on in the Congo Free State.

It is true that the French government had not reserved large areas for systematic exploitation on its own account which could be compared to Domaine Privé or the Domaine de la Couronne on the other side of the frontier, but its administration and its armed forces were supporting the concessionaire companies in a system which was identical to that carried on by the corresponding Belgian companies. De Brazza confirmed this. In a way, this was unfortunate. The English Foreign Secretary—Lord Lansdowne—had suggested that an international conference should be held to discuss the affairs of the Congo, and had the French been able to enter such a meeting with a favourable report in their hands the Government of France might have agreed to it. As it was, France joined with Belgium in resisting the calling of a conference, and the proposal was dropped.

De Brazza died on his way home from the colony; his staff were forbidden to draw up a report from the material they had collected, and all that happened was a three days' debate in the French Chamber (February 19–21, 1906). The demand for the publication of De Brazza's material was defeated by 345 to 167, and although charges naming most serious crimes were made against particular companies, and it was proved that the government inspectors were recommending their dissolution, no steps whatever, either then or subsequently, were taken against them. On the contrary, the travelling inspectors, who had at least reported, though their reports had been suppressed, were removed in 1911.

By that time matters were improving in the Belgian Congo. There is no space in this book for a history of the Congo reform movement, and it is enough to say that in 1908 the Congo Free State was formally annexed by the Belgian government under the name of the "Belgian Congo," and that reforms were set on foot so that the worst features at least of the Leopoldian system disappeared. In 1913 the Congo Reform Association was able to meet in London and to dissolve itself in the belief that its work in the Belgian Congo was done. But in the French Congo it is feared that matters are still far from satisfactory. The latest account which we have in English is *Travels in the Congo* (*Voyage au Congo* and *Le Retour du Tchad*), by M. André Gide, the well known French writer. These two books were published in 1927 and 1928, immediately after his return. M. Gide seems to have gone out on a semi-official mission with no idea at all in his mind that he would be interested in the treatment of the natives. He says that when he had been there for a few weeks he could think of nothing else. Where the natives were under the direct control of the French government he found them poverty-stricken—sometimes starving—but free, once their rubber tax had been paid. This tax was estimated to take them one month's work in the year. But in the interior, where concessions have been granted, he found the old evils still going on. He arrived at one spot six days after a black sergeant had shot twelve men, massacred fifteen women with an axe, and shut five young children up in a hut and set fire to it.* The native who first brought the news to M. Gide's party was thrown into prison for having done so, but

*Travels in the Congo, pp. 65–66.

M. Gide was able to get him released and the agent of the company prosecuted—with what result the book does not say.

He also found women, some with babies at the breast, forced to make a great embankment of earth which more than once gave way and buried the women and children at the bottom. This "murderous road" was to enable the representative of the Compagnie Forestière to drive along it once a month in his car. He was told that a month before a native had been flogged to death, in the presence of M. Pacha and M. Mandivier, the company's agents, for not bringing in enough rubber.* A chief told him that he had seen ten men die in a single day as a result of ill-treatment. He found children of both sexes taken away from home with halters round their necks and made to work for six days without pay or anything to eat. Again his informant was imprisoned.† He was told by a government medical officer that the Compagnie Forestière breaks all the sanitary regulations and propagates sleeping-sickness in districts free from it by its system of recruitment; that it is "ruining and devastating the country."

Nevertheless, one gathers from what M. Gide does not say that matters are better than they used to be. From systematic massacre things have toned down to such unsystematic murder as we have here described. But it is difficult to get exact information—or even to find out how many concessions are still held by the companies or what they are doing with them.

This account of the massacre of primitive and barbaric societies by the uncontrolled forces of modern industrialism, enterprise, and finance, threatens to grow out of proportion to the rest of our review of human life. It has run away with the pen. And yet only one side of this monstrous rubber story has been told. There is another, later, rubber history almost as depressing if not as horrible as the story of forest rubber. This is the story of plantation rubber. From blood and torture we pass to dismal servitude. In *Asia* for February, 1931, M. Luc Durtain gave an account of work upon the rubber plantations of Indo-China. It is a description of brutal compulsion and unhappiness, inflicted in this case upon Annamese victims.

From this history of rubber-getting a complete description of this aspect of barbaric servitude to modern economic demands would go on to the long, intricate black record of forced labour in South and Central and West Africa, less atrocious, perhaps, but equally un-

*Ibid., p. 70.
†Ibid., pp. 148–49.

righteous and unhappy. From rubber it would pass to gold, to diamonds, to cotton and copper. Everywhere there is the same story of greed, of haste. The same crying need for controls is manifest. It is a history of things unforeseen. It is a crowning demonstration of the diabolical possibilities of uncontrolled and uncriticized profit seeking. Supremely it is a story of the new powers and forces that have come to man, running wild and crazy in a last frenzy for private and personal gain.

King Leopold, that *reductio ad horribile* of the obsolete advantages of monarchy in the modern world, is only a crowned and glorified symbol of a world-wide undisciplined spirit of acquisitiveness. The new economic life has come upon mankind unheralded and unpremeditated, and first it caught and enslaved the poor and the children of Great Britain and western Europe, and now it has spread throughout the earth. The old traditions of trade and gain and government are insufficient to control it, and we are still struggling to discover new forms and methods of control. It feeds and expands the life of hundreds of millions which could never have come into existence without it, but also there are those other millions it crushes and torments.

But there for the present we must leave this part of our spectacle. At this stage of our survey we are not ready to discuss any solution of the problems that are raised in these two sections. We must go on for a time with our examination of the developing new world economy that plays such havoc with the unprepared; then we must go into the question of the motives that keep people toiling, seeking gain, helping, oppressing, and destroying one another. After that we shall be able to bring the operations of finance and the wealth scramble that are so largely responsible for these stresses into a rational relationship with the present governments and the present education of mankind.

Then and only then shall we be able to return with sound comprehensive ideas to the problem of these sufferings, ideas which will enable us to measure our hope and plan our activities for ending such distresses for evermore. In these matters indignation is not enough. Indignation without restraint is little more than a vindictive impulse to extend the area of a wrong. It is the clear head and the thought-out plan that will lead us to a happier world. Let us therefore resume our general description of the organization of modern production.

§ 8. *Rationalization*

Any talk of the organization of businesses nowadays will evoke the word *rationalization* at a very early stage. And just as *democracy, dictatorship, ideology* and *realism* are all used nowadays to mean something the reverse or almost the reverse of their original significance, so *rationalization* also is an inverted term. To rationalize has one meaning in psychology, another meaning in the sociological writings of Max Weber, and quite another in the loose discussions of modern politicians and business men. We are using it here in its current popular sense.

It is one of those words which are really easier to understand than to define. Mr. Urwick, in his very illuminating book, *The Meaning of Rationalization,* gives a pleasing variety of "definitions" by a number of people who for the most part do not define it at all. They talk of the "spirit of rationalization" and what it is intended to do. The gist is a repudiation of haphazard—of uncontrolled—"evolution" in a number of fields where it has hitherto ruled; a recognition that planned and calculated design and adjustment are needed throughout the whole world of economic life. Such are the root conceptions of this work, and they are conceptions that have been growing more and more plainly acceptable for some years. Their practical application has been, so far, more effective in the United States and Germany than in Britain, but their discussion has been, as are all such discussions nowadays, world-wide.*

An outstanding, indeed a heroic, exponent of rationalization in Germany was Walther Rathenau. It was the late Lord Melchett who popularized the word in England. At times he used it—evidently with "anti-Socialist" controversy in his mind—almost as if it were the antithesis of nationalization; his reasonable point being that business can be better reformed and reconstructed from within by business men, than from without by politicians. But the word has a much wider sweep than that would give it.

It took some time for the leaders of British financial and industrial thought to arrive at this idea of a planned remodelling of business organization. Their ideas, because they have an older tradition, remain much more "individualist" and "evolutionary" than those of their American and German equivalents. At the end of the war their first apparent impulse, unhappily too effective, was to escape from all coordinating controls and stampede back to the happy days of detached profit-seeking before the war. It took quite a long time for them to discover that the days before the war were no longer available as an objective, and meanwhile other countries moved forward intellectually and practically.

---

*A clear and interesting sample of the spirit of Rationalization up to date is Donham's *Business Adrift,* with an Introduction by Professor Whitehead (1931).

Rationalization is often confused with headlong amalgamation. It is nothing of the sort. It may be easily possible to carry the coalescence of business organization too far. Points may be reached, varying with the particular industry concerned and with regional conditions, at which the advantages of economies are balanced by the difficulties of management and direction, and beyond these points there may be an increasing loss of vigour and effectiveness with increasing scale. With regard to certain overriding broad services such as transport, the rational distribution of various staple products, and the like, there may be no real essential obstacle between existing conditions and a rationalized world control; but with regard to much of the business of the world the most favourable dimensions for autonomous businesses may be reached at a far less universalized level.

In some, and possibly in many, directions attempts at unified organization may have already been carried beyond a favourable extreme. And they may have been carried in the wrong direction. Combination should aim at material industrial advantages. So far as "rationalization" means that, it is little more than what was known before the war as "coöperation"—in restraint of injurious competition. There should be physical economies; less fetching and carrying, less waiting and delay, a steadier employment of power, a better division of labour, a shortening of time, less "splash," the elimination of intermediate profits. Such are the legitimate ends of the rationalization process. We do, however, find a type of merger which is merely financial, a merger to monopolize a market rather than serve a public better. We can but glance here, anticipating various issues we shall have to raise later, at the way in which national tariff arrangements may facilitate such merely financial profiteering combinations. World-wide free trade and a world-wide common commercial law might result not in an increase but in a break-up of many large industrial constellations, at present operating rather in restraint of trade than for economy of service.

How far the size of an industrial concern may be increased depends also very largely upon the level of intelligence and honesty and the facilities of intercommunication in the community in which the concern is operating. These set temporary and removable limits to super-organization, but there are also very definite maximum limits to every type of control and association, limits due to irremediable mechanical difficulties, just as there are definite material limits to the size of every type of animal and vegetable organism. There is a relation between the intricacy and largeness of a job to be done and the amount of gray matter to be devoted to it. The most powerful mind conceivable cannot give more than four and twenty hours of attention to the details of a task. As the breadth of a control increases, its complexity of intervention must diminish.

In addition to these essential limitations to the concentration of control there is an immense variety of forms of human production and transmission, where the need for a very high degree of detailed freedom is imperative. A very precise limit is set, for example, to the activity of multiple retail shops. They can distribute standardized things, but they are useless or vulgarizing and mischievous when they attempt to deal in objects in which a certain individuality is essential. You cannot have chain shops to sell pictures. You cannot, as another example, have satisfactory mass-produced costumes for women. People weary even of cigarettes, cakes and tea in uniform packets, and where a chain-shop organization has bought up all the groceries of a countryside, it is not uncommon to find little enterprises springing up, "Ye Olde Tea Shoppe," or "Lavender's Parlour," or suchlike quaintness, in which a couple of maiden ladies will sell recommended teas of obscure purveyance and home-made cakes, at Bond Street prices, and do very well by it. Their human inefficiency seems more welcome than the hard, limited certainty of the packet. Similarly, there is always room for the small manufacturer of "special" individual cigarettes in the smarter quarter of any city.

When we come to the selling of any kind of work into which a strong element of artistry enters, the objection to wholesale dealing is fundamental. It would be interesting to find out how far the big general stores of America and Europe, which attempt to deal in everything under the sun, have been obliged to make such departments as bookselling, tailoring, furniture and so forth, autonomous and self-subsisting. It would be equally interesting to find out how far such an industry as that of the dress fabrics of Lyons has had to follow the same process. Distinctive designs are produced exclusively for special buyers who make costumes for a select clientèle, and this must necessitate independent or quasi-independent small manufacturing concerns. I believe that it would be possible to trace a very widespread process of internal decentralization and rehabilitated freedom, in modern production and trade. Many great concerns may prove on examination to be like the present British Empire, an association of practically independent organizations with nothing to link them except the "golden link" of ownership by an overriding company—a sort of parallel to the golden-link function of the imperial crown.

Rationalization, we repeat, is not amalgamation. Economy, research in common, exchange of information, exchange of services, elimination of competition in buying and selling alike, mutual financial accommodation, agreements to share out work so that one concern may concentrate upon this type or model of production and another upon that, these are among the essentials of rationalization. For a conception of economic life that is all adventure and speculation, jostling cut-throat competition for profits, conflict and waste, rationalization substitutes the idea of a planned, statistic-ruled system, adequately and efficiently productive and distributive. For conflicting completely separated businesses, it substitutes the idea of interrelated and confluent businesses. It is in fact Nominalism instead of Realism applied to the titles of firms and the names of undertakings. Because a mass of activities are assembled for a time under one name, that does not mean we are dealing with a permanently distinct organization in conflict with similar organizations. Rationalization sets its face against that delusion; it is indeed essentially a revolt against that delusion.

Naturally rationalization comprehends the idea of scientific management and stimulates its application. Expressing as it does the feeling that for every process there is a best way which is the right way, *it involves the repudiation of the idea that individual profits are the test and end of business success.* The discussion of motive in social life is a very important one; we shall devote to it the whole chapter following this one, but here we must note that rationalization is in effect a renunciation on the part of its advocates of any priority of the owners' profits over the health, vigour and future development of the service or industry rationalized. That is a profoundly significant change of front in the world's business life. And advances upon that new front must bring us at last logically to the realization of the whole world as one organized business system.

§ 9. *The Coöperative Movement**

We have already noted the characteristics of coöperative retailing in our account of the buying and selling of goods. But coöperative retail-

*See *Self and Society:* a collection of essays published by the C. W. S.; B. and S. Webb: *The Consumers' Coöperative Movement;* P. Redfern: *The Consumers' Place in Society;* E. Poisson: *The Coöperative Republic,* and Professor Bernard Lavergne: *L'Ordre Coopératif.*

ing is only one aspect of a constructive movement of very great significance in our present welter of economic experiment and reconstruction. It is mainly confined to the more highly industrialized countries of Europe. Differences in phase of economic development have checked its appearance in America. In our account we shall have to glance at various considerations that will be dealt with more directly in our subsequent chapters (VIII) on social motive, (IX) finance, and (X) wealth. It is impossible to consider the coöperative movement as concerned solely with economic method and mechanism.

In its wider sense the term "coöperation" covers all that rationalization implies and more also. As Professor Henry Clay points out, "every sort of voluntary association to restrain reckless individual self-seeking, cut-throat competition,"* and the like, is essentially a coöperative association. Price agreements, cartels, trusts, trade unions, employers' associations, all fall within the term.

But when we speak not of coöperation generally, but of the coöperative movement as it is manifested through such organizations as the English and Scottish Coöperative Wholesale Societies, the French Consumers' Coöperative Societies, and their associated propaganda, then we are dealing with something at once more specific and more far-reaching than any mere combination to control competition. The movement looks beyond immediate relief and economies to a new world, to the Coöperative Republic, the Coöperative Commonweal. It carries its projects of rationalization right up to the social and political reconstruction of the human community. It is a theory of society based on the idea of man as a consumer. The customer has looked at the world, and this movement is the outcome.

Since Britain and France were the first countries to experience the industrial and mechanical revolutions, it was natural that in these countries also the first attempts should be made to stem the destructive effects of the chaotic individualism these changes released. There are records of the coöperative buying of food by workers to protect themselves from the rapacity of retailers before the end of the eighteenth century, but it was only after the end of the Napoleonic Wars that systematic attempts to arrest the storm of reckless competition, of underselling and underpaying, of sweating and social degradation, began in real earnest. Robert Owen in England, and Fourier and Saint Simon in France, are the outstanding figures of that new effort. We

*Economics for the General Reader, Chapter VI, § 3.

owe both the word "socialism" and the phrase "coöperative movement" to Robert Owen, and in their early stages the ideas conveyed
by these words were closely akin. They spring from the same root.
We have no space here for a history of the development and variation
of socialist ideas. The basal concept of the coöperative movement as
distinguished from other branches of the Owenite stem was the voluntary combination of individuals into associations for producing, buying
and selling, for mutual aid and for the education of their children.
These associations were to form, so to speak, the nuclei of a new social
life amidst the stresses of the old. They were to succeed and multiply
and coalesce at last into a new human society. Socialist thought moved
away from this idea in the direction of the "social revolution" of the
Communists or of socialization through the development of public
services (Fabianism). The coöperative movement, on the other hand,
seeking to "crystallize" a new world out of the current disorderly lique-
faction of the old social order, narrowed down to small voluntary
associations.

For some decades the history of coöperation was one of experiments,
for the most part unsuccessful. The idea produced, however, devoted
workers and thinkers like George Jacob Holyoake in England and
Charles Gide in France; it found willing and untiring, unsalaried
officials and organizers; it tried and tried again to achieve realization.
All men are not self-seekers, or there could be no coöperative movement to-day. Only gradually was it realized that the systematic development of a growing and spreading coöperative organization must begin
at the consumers' end. It was in 1844 that the Rochdale society hit
upon the idea of a "dividend," which we have already described in
Chapter VI, § 4, and found in that idea the way to solvent and efficient
coöperative marketing, and about eighteen years later there were
enough successful coöperative retail societies in operation to found the
still vigorous and expanding British and Scottish Coöperative Wholesale Societies. Concurrently propagandist and educational organizations
were formed. From that time onward the history of British coöperation
has been one of discreet but steady expansion, until there are now
6,000,000 members of the British consumers' coöperatives representing
certainly over 18,000,000 of the population. For a time the coöperative
idea in France was applied chiefly to production groups, but in 1885
a nuclear consumers' coöperative appeared at Nîmes, and the movement has now attained to a membership of over 2,000,000. It is strictly

a workers' movement. Even in Great Britain it has never spread upward to the middle classes.

The coöperative movement has always been quietly but persistently propagandist and enterprising. And it has always displayed a strongly cosmopolitan disposition. Its tentacles spread throughout Europe and reach to India and Japan. Gradually the difficulties in the way of producer coöperation have been studied and solved. In Ireland, in Russia, Italy and other mainly agricultural countries the unit coöperative society has been a society for the joint purchase and use of agricultural machinery, for mutual credit and for marketing. The Coöperative Wholesale Society trades as a unit with the Russian coöperatives, and British coöperatives farm, manufacture, finance, publish and educate, as well as trade.

And yet one may doubt whether this movement, as it exists at present, will ever crystallize out into that promised new world. That new world, it would seem, needs something more, much more, than is to be found in this sane and discreet extension of membership and activities. It may be overtaken by other forces, more powerfully and rapidly constructive. It is significant that the coöperative movement has failed to take root in America. It has been nipped in its initial consumers' retail phase, as we have noted in Chapter VI, § 4, by the competition of the more vigorous and varied department and chain stores. Trade-union enterprise has anticipated some of its productive possibilities and the greater mobility of the population has been against it. The modernization of economic life has reached such a point in America that the possibility of slow progressive crystallizations has passed.

In Russia all the coöperatives were abolished in 1920, and restored, with a difference, in 1924. How far they can now be regarded as voluntary associations it is impossible to say. In Russia, excluding the Ukraine, they include 15,000,000 members, and they conduct nearly half of the country's retail trade. Their federal organization, the Centrosoyus, conducts great trading operations with the English Coöperative Wholesale Society. In Italy again the National Union of Coöperative Societies was suppressed in November, 1925, and replaced by state control. The organization ceased, in fact, to be a voluntary coöperation; it became a state machine. While in America economic development had apparently rendered the coöperative movement unnecessary, in the Bolshevik and Fascist State Socialisms its organizations have been seized upon and incorporated with the governmental machinery.

In the perspective of a western European point of view the coöperative movement is seen to grow, but, to be slightly paradoxical, it grows without animation. Professor Lavergne, in his sound and ample book *L'Ordre Coopératif* (Volume I, 1926), is confident of the merits and future of coöperation. By a series of metamorphoses, he says, "the coöperative, formerly a petty district shop distributing small necessities, has become big industry and big business, destined heir of those great public services whose direction overstrains the political State. It is profoundly important to the social sciences to demonstrate that the coöperative principle—which leads towards a happy democratization of incomes—can supplant both the old ideal of State socialism and the more recent idea of municipalization. From the facts, too long neglected, of coöperative progress, the lesson emerges luminously, that both private capitalism and socialist régimes can pass on to a new order which combines their merits and has none of their defects." P. Redfern, in the Encyclopædia Britannica article, cites facts which seem to justify Professor Lavergne. He tells of the International Coöperative Alliance, "a minor league of nations" with 85,000 societies in 36 countries, the International Coöperative Wholesale Society representing 28,000,000 members, of a Special Coöperative party (of five members) in the British Parliament, to which 423 societies with a membership roll of 3,281,971 persons are affiliated. He tells of great educational and propagandist activities. To these we may add Lavergne's account of the coöperatives of communes and municipalities in Belgium to run light railways, electric distribution, and other public services. But in contrast with Lavergne, Redfern ends his article—doubtfully.

There are 6,000,000 coöperators in Britain. What proportion of them see anything more in coöperation than the source of that useful "dividend"? Twenty-eight million adults would be a mighty force to bring about a coöperative world state or at least a coöperative Europe, but how many of that 28,000,000 would even trouble to attend a public demonstration in its favour? The movement has prospered through the passionate devotion of a few hundred or a few thousand men. How far have they imparted their passion to the masses of the movement? For my own part I can testify that, though one English adult in eight is a coöperator, and though I talk freely with all sorts of people, I have never heard any single person boast that he was a member of this great movement. I know several people whose eyes brighten at the words "social revolution," but none who become exalted at "coöperative republic." And never have I overheard anyone anywhere pointing to an exceptionally beautiful car, or a fine bicycle, or tasting tea or coffee or butter, or noting a lovely dress stuff or a wonderful costume, or admiring the decoration of a fine public building, say: "That is *our* stuff, coöperative stuff. Those others cannot produce stuff like ours." But then I belong to the south of England, and the north, I am told, feels very differently. There such popular music-hall stars as Gracie Fields sing songs in favour of the Coöps which are received with enthusiasm, and the Glasgow housewife would never "go past the Coöp." But even in Glasgow, would a man feel proud to be told that he looked as if he had been rigged out at a Coöp?

In Sweden too, a correspondent assures me, there is much loyalty and pride among coöperators.

Enthusiasm and distinction may increase. The European coöperatives supply good honest goods at honest prices but they do not lead in the production of better and novel goods. They do not supply *interesting* goods. The privately owned shop can beat them at that. They may evoke partisan excitement, but they do not evoke pride. They have grown to great things in a hundred years, but they have to grow still more rapidly in this age of new bigness if they dream of leading the world. Or as Mr. Redfern puts it: "Whether the movement can lead a stubborn world decisively along this coöperative road, probably will depend more and more, not only on its numbers but also on its power to enlist intelligence, and develop in all ranks a leadership capable both of creating enthusiasm and producing everyday conviction amongst the masses of mankind."

Which is not to say that the coöperative movement will be so much defeated and disappear as be overtaken—as it has already been overtaken in Russia and Italy—and incorporated in bolder and wider enterprises with a more explicit plan and a deeper emotional drive.

§ 10. *The Public or Private Direction of Big Industries and General Services*

What do we find playing the rôle of a head to the greater number of businesses and services, of economic coöperations, that is to say, in the modern community? It is sometimes a proprietor, but not so frequently as it was a century ago. It is more often a partnership. Most businesses and services confess to a founder, to a single man who, either alone or in congenial partnership, made the concern in the first place. But most typically, nowadays, the business or service has become a company, and the headship vests in a board of directors on which the original organizer or his heirs sit dwindling in relative importance. The company has created a body of shareholders who in their annual meeting exercise certain limited powers of criticism and of changing the directors. And the directors in council deal with the managers and so forth who run the operations of the concern.

But side by side with businesses and services directed in this way we now find others run by managers and officials appointed by the elected representatives of city, county, country or other governmental constituencies. Except for the final bookkeeping of the concern, these publicly owned services and industrial plants bear the closest resemblance to their privately owned and organized parallels. The criticism of the shareholders' meeting is replaced by the criticism of the voters. There is no distribution of profits: that is the essential difference. The profits, if any, go to reduce charges or relieve taxation. The tendency is to keep profits down and give better and cheaper services or products to the general public. Sometimes, where there are no profits but losses, the loss is justified on the grounds of the common convenience. These public enterprises have increased in proportion to the private profit-making concerns during the last half century, and their development and substitution for the latter is one practical outcome of socialist thought and propaganda.

A vast, voluminous literature has been devoted to the rights and wrongs and the relative efficiency and vigour of initiative of these two forms of economic process. The two classes of enterprise are connected in practice by many intervening forms. There is no hard-and-fast boundary. At one end of the series you have concerns run on privately owned premises and working entirely with privately acquired material. But few businesses attain to considerable proportions without trenching on roads and waterways and the like, requiring concessions from public bodies and access to material in the public domain. They then—like the railways—expose themselves to public responsibility and a measure of public control. If a public body will not take over such businesses, it must still inspect and restrain them to the best of its ability. If it does not provide directors, it provides controllers and inspectors. And if the publicly owned service has no shareholders, it has had to begin more or less with a capital outlay, and that has had to be provided by an issue of bonds secured on the rates and taxes of the community. Few people can tell a privately owned from a publicly owned omnibus, or a company glass of water from a municipal glass of water. Comparatively few Londoners, for example, know whether the water they drink has yielded a profit to anyone or not.

It is alleged in the controversies between Individualism and Socialism, controversies still garrulous in their decay, that the search for profit has an enormously stimulating effect upon the energy, enterprise and responsiveness of a concern. The profit motive plus competition is regarded as the perfect method of adjusting supply to need; the consumer is supposed to have unlimited leisure to pick and choose and go from one firm to another. In practice various forms of rationalization are destroying competition, and few of us have the leisure to hover over and judge most of our purchases. The critics of Socialism assert, moreover, that a profound moral difference exists between those who work under the direction of proprietors seeking profit and those who work under the direction of elected persons. The former are understood to be kept up to the mark by the balance sheet; they are alert, enterprising, energetic, economical; they have been chosen for their profit-making fitness, and they must continue to display that fitness, for upon it they depend for their positions. But transfer these men to a publicly owned concern, and at once they change in character; they become slack, extravagant, careless, they feel themselves above criticism and irremovable. The same manager who will work with disinterested zeal for a company and choose his subordinates with an acute regard for their suitability and loyalty will, so soon as he becomes a manager under a public body, evoke a vast crowd of relations and dependents to whom he will distribute places with an utter disregard for their suitability. Moreover, the public business is amenable to the politician, and the politician, they say, will be swayed by the votes of the workers more than by the votes of the public he serves, and he will sacrifice the interests of the business to his private ends and the exigencies of his party—while no private owner would ever dream of sacrificing the quality of a product or service to the exigencies of finance.

Most of this we would dismiss at once as preposterous nonsense if if were not for the fact that it is a quite fair summary of much that is said and written as anti-socialist argument.

We are dealing here with a limitless chaos of accusations and excuses through which we might blunder interminably, sinking now into morasses of twaddle and now entangling ourselves in libel actions. The plain facts of the case seem to be that as businesses grow beyond the scale of one-man concerns, they become impersonal in character, and that by the time they have reached the dimensions of a railway system, a modern catering organization, an urban water or milk supply, the differences between public and private ownership cease to be matters of structure, organization, or working efficiency, and remain only differ- ences in the spirit of the direction.

Publicly conducted business may be in many cases unenterprising be- cause of the ordinary politician's habit of following, rather than leading, public opinion and his dread of popular hostility to changes, but privately owned business may more easily develop conspiracies to monopolize markets or raw material, and so restrain innovation. Private- profit, coöperative, municipal, and State directorates all tend to develop characteristic faults; none are perfect. All work better in the light of intelligent criticism, for the responsible official is by the nature of his training more responsive to good repute than to gain. But criticism must be intelligent and fair and open. Adequate criticism is the pre- servative of all human affairs, and while public concerns may suppress criticism by governmental action, private businesses have shown them- selves extremely able and energetic in controlling the press—which is their medium for advertisement—for the anticipation and strangulation of adverse comment. (Newspapers are very chary of publishing the names of advertising firms convicted for adulteration, for example.) The public authorities of a region at a low level of social organization and general education are incapable of conducting even quite limited businesses; but public authorities and government departments admin- istering large areas, scientifically organized and sustained by an intelli- gent community, may be able to direct production and service with an efficiency far exceeding that possible under a profit-seeking group. It is a question of scale and of quality.

It would be easy to cite local authorities, state governments, small sovereign powers, which have fallen more or less completely under the sway of great business organizations altogether too powerful and efficient for them. The great trading companies of the seventeenth and eighteenth centuries, the East India Company, for example, exceeded and subdued governments and became themselves quasi-states. The armament industry, as we shall tell later (Chapter XII, § 9), played the rôle of a super-state in Europe. Gangs of politicians can seize control of the State and sell the State's authority to private entrepreneurs. That flat opposition in thought, of private control versus public control, is therefore a misleading one. It throws a false simplicity over the vast and intricate variety of ways in which human coördination can be arranged and worked.

Later on (in Chapter X), in certain studies we shall make of particular instances of wealth aggregation, we shall note the way in which the private ownership of great economic utilities lends itself to the purposes of the financial adventurer. Publicly owned utilities are not subject to such mischief because the rapid and violent changes in control due to the forced or panic selling of their stocks and shares, cannot occur.

§ 11. Grades of Social Organization

What has gone before makes it very plain that for every sort of collective enterprise there must be grades of organization whose practicability and applicability depend on the interplay of a number of mutually interacting variables.

For example, there is the state of the general intelligence and of the public understanding of, and acquiescence in, the enterprise. The telegraph has been hampered in its extension through some parts of tropical Africa by the artistic preference of the natives for bracelets and anklets of copper wire and their lack of sympathy for unguarded property. The early development of letter boxes in several European countries was delayed by the temptations offered to the facetious young. Large-scale agriculture in Russia has had to struggle against the love of the peasant for taking machinery to pieces and his lassitude in the phase of reassembly. The willing coöperation of the public is essential to the spread of every new invention and the working of almost every public service. At every level of intelligence and public spirit there is a type of organization which will prove most successful with the public— and there will also be types above and types below its requirements.

Similarly, for every factory there is a relationship between the work and the available personnel. Women and men cannot work together unless a certain minimum of restraint and decency has been attained. You must drop all sorts of methods if your workers cannot read. There must be certain standards of honour in effective operation. A sanitary service in French North Africa attempted to restrain the eye disease so prevalent there by distributing lotions for the eyes of the children affected. It was necessary to entrust the distribution to native agents, who, forthwith, put a price on the stuff, set up as quack practitioners and largely defeated the end for which they were employed. The honesty of the staff in any retailing concern is not simply a matter of discipline and supervision; it is also a matter of the general social tone of the employees. All sorts of modern trading operations become impossible with a filching staff or a filching clientèle. The old Phœnician traders bought and sold with arms in their hands. The abolition of haggling in retail trade released vast possibilities of distributive organization that did not exist before prices became fixed. In the West End of London anyone with a banker's reference can have goods sent to his home on approval, and one may confidently buy goods without even asking the price until the bill comes home.

The extension of the idea of function to the trader and manufacturer and the increasing confidence of the buyer open wider and wider possibilities to trade and manufacture. Every step towards general honesty in regard to metal, coins, notes and cheques diminishes friction and enlarges the vigour and scope of economic operations. In ordinary life every one of us knows the difference in speed and precision of dealing, between the fair dealer with a conception of a legitimate due and the fellow who watches for a chance of a smart turn on us, and who seems unhappy in his trading unless he leaves resentment in his wake.

We may ascend the scale to the financial and economic advantages of government enterprises. What can be done in comprehensive production by public ownership where there is a conception of public duty and an intelligent public alert to enforce it, is altogether beyond what can be attempted in a society where political success is regarded as a legitimate opportunity for unrestricted gain.

But we will not multiply instances to show how dependent our economic development is upon these matters of atmosphere, on the grade and quality of popular education and the existence of an effective public opinion. All we wish to establish here is that for every level of education and public morale there is a limit to the size and complexity of businesses possible. What would be unwieldly at one stage becomes practicable and easy in another. The obvious course for the great city would be fantastic absurdity in a kraal. These considerations lead us on to what is the very quintessence of this work, to the truth that with every grade and type of human social, economic and political association, there should go a certain definite philosophical foundation of a certain sort and a certain quality of educational training. The educational and practical factors should interlock, each sustaining the other. Educational revolutions must accompany economic and political revolutions. All economic enlargements, all economic progress, demand an adequate corresponding modification of teaching in the schools. They are ideas in action. They fail or they prevail by the ideas they encounter.

To the relationship between the ideas in a man's head and the part he will play in social and economic life we will therefore direct our attention in the next chapter.

CHAPTER THE EIGHTH

WHY PEOPLE WORK

§ 1. *The Persona and Conduct*

AND now we open up the fourth, the final and most important, section of our examination of human activities, the portion devoted to Will and the organization of Will. We have to enquire what forces within mankind keep all this great economic system going.

We have thrown a picture on the screen, so to speak, showing our contemporary world ant-hill at work and being fed, clothed, housed and induced to buy this, that and the other necessity or luxury, and in this picture, thus far, the men and women who work and buy and sell have been represented for the most part as moving about like neat little toy men and women in a working model. For all we have said hitherto, the participants in most of the operations might be wooden dolls wired to move and play their parts in the general scheme. Well-disposed dolls. No word have we said yet of those deep discontents that lie at the root of strikes and labour troubles generally, nor of disloyalty to the general task of production.

But now we have to get inside these puppets and make them come alive. We have to ask why they work and buy and sell. Why do they carry on at all? Why do they do it? Why do they stand it? How do they feel about it? We have to redeem the promise of our opening and explore the psychology of work and wealth.

At the outset we made it clear how large a part suppression played in the socialization of man. We have reiterated the essential difference of man's social life from that of any other social creature's. While the social life of the insect world is essentially instinctive, and the various workers, soldiers, queens and what not, are moved by simple inherent impulses to play their part in the biological and economic whole, *Homo sapiens* has undergone no such adaptation and specialization. He plays his individual part through a balance of motives. He is *educated* to his rôle. It is rare that he is completely fitted to his job. Generally he does what he has to do with a very considerable amount of internal conflict

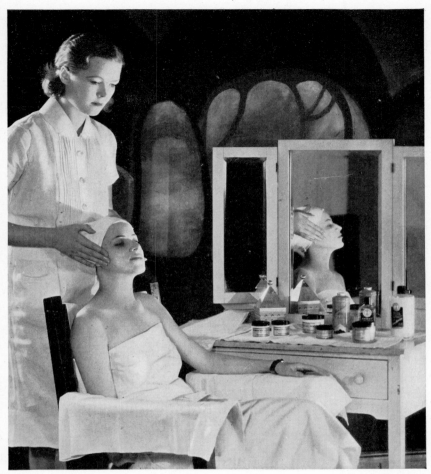

THE MODERN WOMAN CONQUERS AGE AND FATIGUE

A BEAUTY parlour.

NEW YORK: THE UNIQUE CITY

LOWER NEW YORK, seen from the air. Most of the larger buildings showing in light colour have been built within the last five years. New York illustrates many of the soaring possibilities of modern architecture; but it may be doubted if the cities of the future will follow its pattern. Its narrow, restricted area, its foundation upon firm rock, and the peculiar social economic conditions that have promoted building upon small lots without a general plan, have given it a bristling verticality that may remain its own special distinction.

and external friction. At bottom he is still a highly individualized animal, resentful of subordination, competitive and exclusive, demanding freedom and the world for himself.

But he is also amenable to fear and affection and capable of self-restraint and reservation. In the *Science of Life* we have traced the growth of the human community through the establishment of the primary taboos, and we have shown how ideas of superiority and inferiority, of leadership and obedience, were established in youth and sustained, imposed, upon the unwilling mind of adult man. From his very dawn into the world *Homo sapiens* is a creature at war within himself; he has a moral conflict; he controls his impulses, he does things that he dislikes, and in particular he toils to escape other possibilities that he fears will be even less agreeable. This internal conflict is essential to the nature of man. He can never escape from it; never return to the simple internal unanimity, the "state of innocence," the direct unencumbered reactions, of lower animal types. But he will not be content with a bare recognition of the restraints upon him. He will shrink from the unpleasant fact of his own unwillingness. He will always be seeking consciously and subconsciously a personal adjustment of this conflict; he will always be trying to group his motives about as agreeable a conception of himself, within the range of his possibilities, as he can contrive.

A man's guiding and satisfying idea of himself is what Jung calls his *"persona."* It is a very well chosen term. The original meaning of *persona* was the mask worn by an actor in the Greek and Roman drama. It gave his "character," it was what he thought he was. In his hand he carried his *rotulus,* his little roll on which was written the part he had to play in the story, his *rôle*. It was what he had to do. From the very beginnings of the human adventure and throughout the whole world to-day every human being is steering a cherished persona through the allurements, buffetings and frustrations of life. That is "conduct." Every one of these busy puppets we have seen making and buying and selling in the great economic spectacle we have displayed has a persona, an idea of himself, either more or less harmonized to and accepting the rôle he has to play, or more or less in rebellion against that rôle. The continued, progressive working of this continually more complicated and continually more centralized economic society of mankind is dependent upon the sustained harmony between its operations and the hundreds of millions of personas involved in them. Beneath the material processes of economics lies the social idea; its driving force is will. The clearer the idea, the better organized the will in the personas of our species, the more hopeful and successful the working of the human ant-hill.*

§ 2. *The First Class of Persona: The Peasant Persona and Types Mainly Derived from It*

The earlier subjugations of man to toil were comparatively crude. Fear of the stronger individuals, the chief and leading men within the tribe, was sublimated as a sense of obligation, and the disposition to accept their rule was sustained by the greater fear of wandering from the tribe into the wilderness. The retention of immature characters has been a frequently recurring event in animal evolution. The common man, as he grew up, escaped less and less from the natural subordination of childhood. As life grew more secure and · productive and laborious, toil came to him as part of that subjugation.

In those obscure ages during which human society developed, in that phase of the taming of the human animal to subordinated associations into which the archæologist, the psychoanalyst and the student of primitive expression now probe, there were built up traditional systems of personas, or, if you prefer the phrase, "ideals of rôles," to which we find men adapted, as writing and record develop and their mental lives become accessible to us. We find them subdued to the conception of the classes to which they belong. We find them all saying to themselves, "This is what I am. This is what is becoming for me to do. This is what I will not endure." It is manifestly necessary, if we are to carry this survey into the field of mental reactions, that we should attempt here some sort of classification of the primitive types of persona. Man, as history in the narrower sense, history in human record, dawns, has ceased to be a spontaneous wild man, he has brought himself into a community through this self-reference to an ideal of a rôle.

*The reader will find much that is said here in terms derived from Jung put in quite another terminology in, for example, Chapter XVII (Wages) of Henry Clay's excellent *Economics for the General Reader*. His is the more orthodox phrasing. There the willingness to work is studied in relation to what is called the "standard of life" of the worker. A man's standard of life, his conception, that is, of what is due to him and his proper scale and quality of living, is not, of course, his whole persona as we have here defined it, but it is, from the economic point of view, a very important factor in his persona. But the persona brings in a vast motivating complex over and above the standard of life; it brings in his sense of obligation, of what it is graceful and becoming to do, his pride, what is honourable or insulting for him; and we believe that for the purposes of social and political as well as economic analysis, the wider mode of approach adopted here is altogether more comprehensive and effective.

What, then, are the chief forms of these operative rôles?

Here we shall have to break at times into what is almost untouched ground. Into it we must go with humility, apologies and the firmest resolution to explore it as thoroughly as we can. Social psychology has hardly begun. It is extraordinary that it was not begun long ago. Economic science, in all its schools, has been accustomed and content to work upon the crudest assumptions about motive, that it is possible to make. The Marxist indeed makes some pretensions to psychology with his phrases about a "class-conscious proletariat" and a "bourgeois mentality" and the like. He shows at least an awareness of differences of persona. But under the stresses of political and social combat such phrases have long since degenerated into mere weapons, aspirations and terms of abuse. So discredited and warped are they that they will be of no use to us here.

The basal mentality of that traditional social order from which we are now emerging seems to be that of the types for which we have used the general name of peasant. The distinctive character of the peasant type of persona is its complete acceptance of the idea that toil is virtue, and its close, intense adhesion to property and the acquisition of property. All over the world and continually peasants murder for property. Wherever there is a peasant countryside the newspapers rarely go for many weeks without an account of such a murder. Murders of passion characterize towns and the middle and upper classes. The peasant lusts and breeds, but without any pride or romantic play. He trains his young to toil at an early age, to getting and to avarice.

His suppressions make him prone to envy. His soul is equalitarian. His hostility to exceptional display imposes a standard costume and decorum upon any countryside where his is the dominant ideology. Housing and furniture too are standardized there, and the slightest departures from the rigidities of usage provoke a bitter resentment and moral condemnation. Everywhere in Europe and Asia where the peasant persona rules, sentimentalists delight to prate of its lovely local costumes and customs, its music and art. Everywhere, except for differences due to conditions of climate and natural resources, these costumes and art are practically the same, the industriously made lace, the bright buttons, the white linen, the red and black colourings, the tedious repetitive carving, the traditional music, the staid dancing, the plaintive and tragic song. It is essentially and visibly the same from Biscay and Brittany to China.

The peasant's persona is subdued to a life of hard monotonies and stereotyped pleasures. He is always under the observation of his neighbours. He is much worried about his character and personal prestige; he exists because of his reputation—for this or that—for his good thatching or his skilful pruning of the vines. When he is sober he is afraid. He is afraid of his lord, afraid of the opinion of those about him, afraid of lawyers with "bits of writing," and of priests with mysterious powers over the gates of heaven and hell. Drink releases a fund of suppressed brutality and self-assertion. With pestilence or bad seasons the subjugated imagination escapes very readily into superstitious observances. The puzzled and distressed peasant is never very remote from the ancient blood sacrifice. His religion is primordial, it is unsophisticated superstition, entirely unspiritual.

All these realities must, by a psychological necessity, be made to appear in the peasant's consciousness of himself in the most pleasing light possible—interwoven with a palatable presentation of any individual idiosyncrasy he may possess. He asks no why nor wherefore to explain his work and his property. There they are. What else could you have? But about himself, against any lurking doubts he must be sturdily reassured. He sees himself therefore as a good honest fellow, the friend of that friend of his, the local god or the Good God, as the case may be. That god also is as possessive and jealous and as hostile to strange ways and displays as his Maker. The peasant's God and the peaant stand upon their "rights" and do what they like with their own. The peasant is free from affectations and fal-lals, and none can better him at a bargain. Let anyone who would do him an injury beware. But nothing "stuck-up" or arrogant enters into his composition. He can be shrewd as well as worthy. He "knows his way about" and is far too wise to make enemies of the rich and great. A certain humour helps him to swallow and ignore any humiliation that may come to him. He will laugh and, later on, get the better of them. The mills of the peasant, he flatters himself, grind slowly, but they grind exceeding small. On such terms with himself he finds his rôle in life endurable. It is a great consolation to reflect that many are (deservedly) worse off than himself.

Derived very directly from this fundamental type of human persona is that of the mediocre town dweller who has drifted in from the countryside. The normal townsman is indeed a transplanted peasant. This peasant-minded townsman is under the same necessity to reconcile his egoism to a laborious and inferior rôle, and he displays the same consequent exaltation of toil as a virtue, the same self-congratulation upon simplicity, sardonic humour and sagacity, and the same disposition to avarice and a tenacious adherence to a residuum of "rights." He is brought into closer contact with a greater number of people, and that gives him a greater mental quickness. He needs a livelier sense of the instability and ultimate humiliation of those of better estate than himself, because their better fortune presses upon him more closely.

In most forms of popular religion throughout the world, the theory of compensations hereafter has been a useful help to equanimity. The priest, amidst the closer population of the town, has always been less of a medicine man and more of a consoler than upon the more superstitious countryside. He has played a helpful part in the reconciliation of man to his destiny during the ages of toil. In the end he still assures us, Lazarus will corner the water supply of Dives. And the affections and relationships of family life have afforded the peasant type throughout the world, the consolations of authority and self-esteem which it has had to relinquish so largely in its outward social rôle. He clings to his family, therefore, as he clings to his scrap of property, and resists any infringement of his absolute ownership of either. They constitute his inner freedom, his private assurance, his self-respect. To lose them is to become a lost soul, a wanderer or a slave. He may have to submit, as peasants in Russia and central Europe submitted until quite recently, to such little infringements as the *"droit du seigneur."* But after all that was soon over and he was left master in his own hovel, free to beat and compel. It was just another tax in kind which you evaded if you could and yielded if you had to.

Arising out of this great and world-wide system of tradition and interpretation, which gives us the peasant type of persona—the prevalent type of human persona still—are others, essentially of the same nature, but liberated or disturbed by certain broad modifications of condition. In the town and in the countryside individuals may prosper exceptionally. They may get enough property to give employment to their less successful fellows or to lend them money and entangle them in debt. The acquisitive and competitive sides of the peasant mentality may lead them to a position in which they may even come to defy their original traditions so far as to indulge in display and open arrogance. The rich townsman, the moneylender and middleman, the big peasant and farmer of mediævalism, all arise out of the main mass of peasant-minded society in a logical development of its ideas.

Nearly all the early pioneers of the modern large-scale industries arose in this way, and brought with them into the developing new conditions the grasping conceptions and domestic severities of their origins. The social history of Lancashire cotton or Birmingham metal goods would illuminate this very plainly. Even to-day, the persona of the big business man remains fundamentally a peasant persona. What the Communists call the "petty" and "big" bourgeoisie are in reality only the primordial peasant writ urban or writ large. They are "kulaks" one stage further on. One peculiar value of the "Five Towns" novels of Mr. Arnold Bennett lies in the clear, convincing, intimate, and yet almost unpremeditated way in which he shows the industrialized peasant mentality of the employing class in a typical industrialized region, the Black Country, waking up to art and refinement, to ampler personality and new ideas.

But while on its upper face the main peasant-souled mass of the human community throws up this prosperous minority, this crop of "well-off" families, on the lower side it produces, through excessive breeding, through selective competition—once in small quantities, and now, through changes in the scale of production, in abundance—a number of "expropriated" individuals to whom the Communist, with his infallible inexactitude of nomenclature and his ineradicable passion for sham erudition, has applied the term "proletariat." The typical modern proletarian is generally without children, that is to say without "proles"; he has lost his grip upon any property and is unable to sustain and control a family. He is a quite landless and homeless man denied the normal consolations of his kind. He may fall into this condition from the peasant and town tradesman level, or, as happens nowadays with increasing abundance, he may be born to these conditions. In the former case the persona to which he squares his conduct and consolations may be a very rough adaptation of the fundamental peasant persona; in the latter, it may be something much more distinctive.

Now the psychological make-up and disposition of these expropriated people, these proletarians—for we have to accept that word now—is of very great importance to our present study. As small ways of trading, cultivation and manufacture give place to larger ways of doing these things, great numbers from the old peasant-townsman stratum will be forced down towards the proletarian level, while a small proportion will clamber upward to ownership and direction in the new giant concerns. Those forced down will be obliged, in sheer defense of their self-esteem, to deprecate family and property. An element of adventure, defiance, and sentimental brotherhood will be required for a satisfactory persona. All are either unemployed or threatened by intermittence of unemployment, and that too gives a chronic uneasiness. The proletarian wants change of general conditions, therefore, and is not afraid of change. In that he differs absolutely from the peasant who is still holding on to property.

Our Western business community has neglected altogether to study the new type of persona—our Western business community seems indeed to neglect the study of everything that does not make obviously for immediate profit—but the Communist has made some plausible generalizations about it. One considerable error seems to me to be his exaggeration of the power and sincerity of the proletarian sentiment of brotherhood. He has developed this alleged disposition to fraternity into an inspiring but misleading cant. And also he mistakes a craving for change due to uneasiness, a desire to upset the uncomfortable arrangement of things for a creative desire.

Here we are under no compulsion to idealize the proletarian. Generally speaking, he is a poor creature, and in the mass he may disgorge great accumulations of envy and be dangerous, destructive and cruel.

It is also a grave error in the communist ideology to confuse the true proletarian persona with that of organized labour in Britain, France, Germany and elsewhere. A large part of such labour is not and never has been truly propertyless and proletarian; it has never parted company with the simple domestic industrious saving ideals of the peasant types. It has generally savings to its credit. In America it has almost always savings to its credit. And its trade-union and political leaders are essentially like any other members of the peasant-townsman class who have "got on." They have personas closely akin to those of rising business men.

A much more fundamental error on the part of the Communist is his assumption that the types and classes we have dealt with thus far, the acquisitive people growing rich and the working people growing poor, constitute the whole of contemporary society. They do indeed constitute its greater mass and impose their characteristic types of persona upon the great majority of human beings, but they are no more the whole of the human community than flesh and bones, viscera and blood vessels are the whole of a human body. The nerves and brain and the endocrinal glands may seem out of all proportion less, but until the activity of these controlling systems is reckoned with, our account of human physiology is very incomplete and altogether misleading.

It is only fair to admit that Communism began its career with a realization of the need of a psychological analysis of human society, but for various obscure reasons that movement has been continually the victim of its own phrases, and it early fell into slavery to "the materialistic conception of history." This phrase, however carefully it may have been qualified originally, has had the effect of insisting upon the *entire* supremacy of economic considerations in human life. Naturally, therefore, every type and class of human being that did not fall into simple economic categories was ignored. But man was man long before he became an economic animal.

For strategic purposes Communism has now become entirely dogmatic. That has given it enormous revolutionary effectiveness at the price of any scientific development of its ideas. Perhaps we of the Atlantic world are too disposed to be ungrateful to the vast experiments Communism has made and to underrate its achievement. But there can be no doubt that its dogmatism sets a very definite term to its usefulness in the world, and that ultimately it may become like every other rigid motivating system that has preceded it, a mass of mental encumbrance to human thought.

THE FISHERMAN, THE PEASANT OF THE WATERS

We may note here the variations of the peasant type that appear where fertile rivers flow and where land meets sea. There appears fishing. The fisherman is a water cultivator. Fishing has produced its own distinctive types of habitation in pile dwellings which still survive in the Celebes to-day, and which, because of the facile preservation of their remains, figure so largely in the archæology of the Neolithic period. The Swiss lake dwellings, the Glastonbury finds, mark important points in the history of our knowledge of this science. Fishing probably crept down the rivers to the sea and mingled with the casual life of the longshore prowler looking for shell fish and edible seaweed and leaving his "kitchen middens" of shells for posterity. Probably fishing clung to the shore and rarely went out of sight of land until the Middle Ages. Inland people ate river fish or none at all, and oysters brought from Britain were, as everyone knows, a Roman luxury, but sea fishing as an industry and a regular food supply is of recent origin.

The fisherman in our study of personas has to be distinguished quite sharply from the seagoing man. Maybe the latter learnt the first tricks of navigation from the river and longshore folk, but from the very beginnings of history we find him trader, slaver and pirate, and he falls under the second broad class of personas we shall next consider. The first real sailors linked the seaways with the desert routes, but the villages of the fishermen spread along the rivers, dotted lagoons and sheltered in coves and inlets away from any ports or cities.

The expansion and industrialization of fishing came only with the general expansion and industrialization of enterprise in the fifteenth and sixteenth centuries. Its most picturesque and romantic extension was whaling. Since the beginnings of human association men have no doubt attacked stranded whales or whales in shallow water. Since palæolithic man did not hesitate to attack an embarrassed mammoth in a swampy place and even trap the monster in a pit, he would certainly have set about a whale had he got the slightest chance to do so. The Esquimaux have killed whales among the ice from time immemorial, and wherever there were fishing boats we may be sure that men would find the presence of whales offshore provocative and exciting. But the arts of shipbuilding and navigation had to precede any attempt to push the assault further. It was only after the sixteenth century that the systematic extermination of whales became a business enterprise, and the same period saw the invasion of fishing by larger ships and apparatus and the methods of capitalism. In the broad issues that concern us here, the psychology of the industrialization of the seas and ocean does not differ materially from the industrialization of the land.

§ 3. *The Second Class of Persona: The Typical Nomad's Persona and Its Variations*

Let us now bring in certain other strains of tradition to this account of human motivation. Our general problem of why people carry on in, and submit to, social and industrial life, and how the progressive organization of human life is to be sustained, will then take on quite a new and different appearance.

And first there is a very considerable range of ideas that come into modern life from the mentality of the aggressive nomad. We write "aggressive nomad" and not simply "nomad." Our introductory history has followed the Bible in its recognition of the early schism between Cain and Abel, between the cultivator and the herdsman. This was a regional climatic difference between arable and periodic pasture lands. In the one, cattle were accessory; in the other, cultivation was incidental. Normally the nomad led a life almost as inaggressive as the cultivator, but his mobility made him more easily a thief, a robber, a raider, a merchant, and at times a cultivator. Cattle was naturally his money of account. Outside the arable levels of recently deposited soil, "the great alluvial valleys" in particular, he wandered into ore-bearing districts and became the first metallurgist. The gipsy tinker, with his distinctive morals and traditions and pots and pans, is the last decaying survival of the nomadic life in western Europe.

But at times, as we have told in the *Outline of History,* the herdsman gathered in strength and raided "for keeps." Then he founded kingdoms and autocracies and ruled the men with the peasant personas. He had, and has to this day where he still maintains his freedom in the Asiatic midlands, an entirely more robust and swaggering tradition than the peasant. Fundamentally he despises work. His spirit towards property is "easy come and easy go." Not to get easily and give freely reflects upon his force and vigour. His love is fierce, romantic, personal and not nearly so prolific as that of the cultivator in constant need of "hands" for the soil. He gambles, and he does it with pride and elegance. Waste is a glory to him. He is, and in his persona he knows himself to be, a fine, reckless, desperate fellow.

Such have been the quality and disposition of kings, aristocrats, soldiers and ruling classes since the social world began. From them by snobbery and imitation, through romantic poetry, literature, art and example, this tradition has soaked into the general imagination of mankind. It introduces an element of conflict and fluctuation now into most personas in the world. Even the young peasant sits in the village cinema theatre to-day watching the familiar situations of romance unfold, and imbibes new notions altogether of what it is to be a man.

And upon the ideology of the nomad and the sword the incessant search and fight for territory and ascendency, the essential forms of our political life are framed. It seems perfectly natural to us to see a king with spurs and sword; we should never dream of seeing him with a hammer or a spade. These are the implements of the robbed and subjugated. It was only in the nineteenth century and under the menace of the peasant-minded moralist that kings began to flaunt their virtues and imitate the bourgeoisie. As indeed it was only in the same period that the acquisitive classes won their way to spur and coronet. The onset of great-scale production was altering all the values of the old dispensation.

The Communist confuses this predatory tradition of the robber nomad with the tradition of the acquisitive peasant type, growing rich.

In modern life the two mingle extraordinarily, but that does not make them the same. They are and remain different threads. They make indeed the personas and conduct of people in dominant positions muddled and confused, but mixture and confusion do not mean assimilation. The strands are fundamentally different and essentially separable. The present solidarity of the rich with the royal and "noble," based on mutual accommodations and common fears, is an apparent solidarity that will probably fail to stand any great social or economic strain. The aristocratic woman sells herself and her pride of caste in marriage for money, and her family finds a compensation in the snobbish imitativeness of the newly rich. She feels herself that she has not so much sold herself as captured money. But recent revolutions have greatly cheapened "nobility," and its prestige declines as the social confidence of the plutocracy increases.

I do not know how far we may be able to establish and demonstrate the ideological confusion and indecisiveness of collective initiative, this mélange of the rich boor and the proud baron has produced in the directive classes of the modern European community. Presently some shrewd student of social psychology will gather and focus the light of letters, memoirs, well informed novels and plays and reports of divorce proceedings upon this clash of cultures.*

§ 4. *The Third Class of Persona: the Priestly or Educated Persona and Its Derivatives*

But now we must consider a third great system of tradition, a third great system of personas and self-esteems. This in the early stages of society was represented by the priest. From the beginning the priest represents a type of persona more or less detached on the one hand from the family idea and the obsession with property of the peasant, and on the other from the personal assertion and lordship of the aristocrat. It would be extraordinarily interesting to work out the evolution and ramifications of the priestly type of persona. In that we should find a mass of indications of the utmost value in our final estimate of the need and destinies of our planetary ant-hill.

It is a biologically important fact that generally speaking the priest has been as often as not unreproductive. The characteristics of the priestly persona are not therefore inherited; they are the outcome of a particular training, a particular system of suggestions, and not of any

*Sombart's *Moderne Kapitalismus* is illuminating here.

selective process. It is not necessary to breed an educated intellectual class. The Brahmin caste in India, which we may regard as an experiment to that end, shows no distinctive mental superiority. Priests over a large part of the world are drawn from every section of the community. Throughout Christendom for example, noble, trader, peasant have all contributed their quota to the priestly stratum.

I write "priest" here. But I intend much more than the specialized religious officiator in the modern scheme of things. "Cleric" might have been a better word, but then there is risk of confusion with the modern "clerk." Originally the priests constituted the entire learned class; the priesthood was all the learned professions. The Egyptian priest was doctor, lawyer, teacher and financier. His order supplied the only writers and poets. He was architect and artist. He stood at the side of the ruler as secretary and minister. The temple was bank, treasury and museum. This original monopolization of education by the religious organization is written plain over the history of those mediæval and Renascence European communities from which the contemporary world derives the bulk of its tradition. If there was any collateral development of writing and reading in ancient times it was probably in relation to the account keeping of nomadic and seagoing traders. The estate clerk and the court scribe may also have been laymen from very early times —but they must have been educated by men in the priestly tradition.

Until the Protestant Reformation universities were monastic in spirit and organization; the great statesmen were church dignitaries, and there was scarcely any intellectual life at all outside the priestly organizations. From this identification of intellectual activity with the clerical tradition arises a fact that is too often overlooked in progressive discussion. Liberalism is too apt to denounce "priestcraft" as altogether evil. Yet the progressive and revolutionary initiatives of the past have been almost entirely of priestly origin. True that in theory the priest has been the inflexible guardian of tradition, but in fact it has been priests and learned clerks who have led almost every breakaway from tradition that has ever occurred. Roger Bacon, that morning star of modernity, was a Franciscan. Huss, Wycliffe, Luther, Calvin, Knox were all priests, dissentient priests. Mendel, the founder of genetics, was a priest. And it is interesting to note how many of the pioneers of that most revolutionary of all sciences, anthropology, were priests. Even Karl Marx was a university product, a doctor of distinction.

Through the scholastic clerical tradition nearly all the intellectual growth of humanity has come. The contribution to human initiatives of the vast peasant-souled majority is small by comparison. A few starry men of genius break through, a Shakespeare, a Burns, but even these are expressive rather than critics and innovators. The aristocrat gave more, but not so very much more, his principal gift that pride which tells the truth, and even his loyalty and chivalry have a quality of plagiarism from the priestly conceptions of devotion. It was the Church that saved learning throughout the Dark Ages. From priestly sources all learning had to come, and only in learned circles could the flame of criticism and discussion be kept alive. At times the protection afforded that flame may have impeded the access of air, but it was better for us on the whole that it should sometimes have been in need of blowing up than that it should ever have been altogether blown out.

And now let us look a little more closely into the type of persona produced by the priestly tradition. Under this heading we shall have to deal not only with priests and ministers of religion, but with a vast world of quasi-disinterested effort, with teachers of every class, with writers and creative artists, with scribes and journalists, with doctors, surgeons and the associated professions, with judges and lawyers generally, with administrators, and particularly that excellent type the permanent official, with technical experts, and finally, most hopeful, various and interesting of all, with the modern scientific worker. All these types of persona have characteristics in common that mark them off quite definitely from either the proliferation of the varieties of acquisitive peasant townsman soul, or from the royalties, aristocrats, robbers and genteel social parasites, who constitute the predatory classes. In the modern professional soldier we have perhaps a type intermediate between the predatory and priestly group and deriving more and more from the latter tradition, and in the modern barrister the pretensions of an aristocratic protector of a client subdued to the exigencies of a hireling bravo, and mingled too often with the un-redeemed greed of the peasant. (So that it is with dire public lamenta-tions that he "gives up" a practice "worth" so much for some honour-able promotion that is not so heavily feed.)

The first distinctive element in this third and most important class of persona, the educated persona, is the conception of self-abnegation, of devotion. The individual is not supposed to work directly either for his own enrichment or for his own honour and glory. He belongs, he has made himself over, to an order consecrated to ends transcending any such personal considerations.

That is the essence of priesthood, of professionalism, and of all artistic and literary pretensions. The robber type has its devotions to king and chieftain, intensely personal and sentimental, often to the sexual pitch, but the devotion of the learned-priestly type is to a God or to a divine overruling idea. This idea runs through almost all the endless developments and variations of the learned-priestly type we find in the world to-day. The doctor, the solicitor, the teacher, the artist all have their professional standards and repudiate "mere commercialism." Neither the barrister nor the physician works for definite fees. There is a tradition of gratuitous service both in law and medicine, and in Great Britain a quack can sue for his fee while a registered practitioner is restrained from doing so by his professional organization. Even the undisciplined writers have their unwritten code, and when three prominent authors, Mr. G. B. Shaw, Mr. Arnold Bennett, and another, were invited by a great London general store to write matter for its advertisements for some enormous fee—with full liberty to say what they liked, praising or blaming as they saw fit—they all declined the proposal as an infringement of their priestly function, as an imputation upon that complete disinterestedness and spontaneity which is to a self-respecting writer the most vital quality of his persona.

The element of devotion in this learned-priestly tradition is absolutely essential to the processes of civilization. One cannot imagine the economic social machine running at all, without the services of this now very various class, these definitive or constructive public servants, these judges, doctors, teachers, writers, officials, more or less honest and trustworthy. And they are practically trustworthy and efficient because they have all been brought up to and educated in this type of persona. That is a point to note. These types are more "made" than the peasant, townsman, money-earning types, who for the most part take up the tradition in which they find themselves without much scrutiny, or than the robber, aristocrat, military types;—though the military at least develop now an increasing distinctive moral training. This third great class of persona is moulded and its qualities are evoked out of germs of purpose which remain latent in all the less educated elements of the social mélange. That is the key-fact to the study of social psychology.

Again we approach the culminating topic of our survey, education. But from that we will diverge for the present to discuss the secular change in mental attitude which the priestly-learned factor in human development is undergoing. In the traditional past, education has been the preserver and transmitter of tradition. The mass of the priestly-learned class was essentially conservative. It learnt, it repeated, it handed on. So it remains in bulk. But there has been an increasing development of critical and reconstructive qualities in that mass. The priestly-learned class has never been blindly obedient and disciplined. Because, behind his teacher, the novice has always been aware of the overriding idea, the Truth, the Deity, or the spirit of the order or profession he was entering. The bolder ones have always found confidence and strength in that. They would derive courage from it to question the authority of their immediate teachers. In the past almost all the great changes in teaching have been proposed as returns to the original orthodoxy, as rebellions against recent corruptions. "Reformations" have been due not to a defect but to an exaggeration of loyalty. It was clerics, not Jew nor Moslim nor pagan, who broke the Catholic unity of Christendom.

And though such dissentients might seek support in other quarters for their novelties, it is in *the ineradicable idea of disinterested integrity* which this priestly-learned class alone has fostered that the future of humanity resides. The innovating spirits of the closing eighteenth century pitted the expansive urge of the new industrial and financial bourgeoisie against aristocracy, and so created Liberalism. It was not the newcomers who produced Liberalism. They took to it very readily, but that is another matter. The socialist thinkers of the following decades sought for driving power in the discontent and resentments of the multiplying proletariat. But in either instance the "idea" came from the class that alone breeds ideas. A great mind-dominating organization like the Roman Catholic Church is for ever searching its own body for the infection of original thought and revolt, because it knows that the deadliest antagonists to its current procedure are the men who most intimately possess its tradition. It fears the good it has engendered.

All complex reforms of method and spirit come from within. It is lawyers who must simplify law and harmonize it with social biology and psychology; it is medical men who can alone readjust medical practice properly to modern ideas. The schools are the ultimate citadel which must be won, if the general character of human thought is to be changed. It does not matter whether most doctors, most lawyers and most schoolmasters and spiritual teachers are formal and reactionary or not. It is within the training of these professions that the redeeming impulse is to be found. Liberalism and Marxism, whether they are right or wrong, are mere phases in that great conflict for orderly creation to which the gathering liberation and gathering courage of the priestly-learned mind have brought humanity. They are not really in-surrectionary impulses from below.

§ 5. *The Civilization of the Entrepreneur**

Out of the interplay of a vast multitude of variations and distortions of these three primary types of persona, the peasant, the aristocrat-soldier-robber, and the priestly-learned man, arose the mental life, the tolerances, acquiescences, concessions and usurpations of the old tradi-tional life from which we are now emerging. Out of the development of these, out of their steady modification by circumstance and their deliberate remoulding by a new directive education, must come the mental life of this new phase of scientific purposive organization towards which our species is at present moving.

And here perhaps is the place for a preliminary look upon certain types which we may lump together roughly under the name of entrepreneur. The mentality of the industrial and financial entrepreneur who has thus far been the immediate agent in carrying mankind over from localized and petty to large-scale and mondial production and trade, is best understood if we realize that he comes mainly from the urban variation of the peasant type, for whom property, money, and visible triumph over one's neighbour are the criteria of success. The first exploitation of the gifts of invention and science was very largely an instinctive, unintelligent exploitation. And to this day the typical face of the big industrialist and the big financier has a boorish quality.

But there is no innate necessity for this. As the organization of busi-ness increases in complexity, the importance and freedom of the in-dividual owner may be dwarfed more and more by the necessity for directive assistants who will be trained and specialized men, essentially of the new innovating variety of the priestly-learned intellectual type, and with its inseparable inspiration of disinterestedness.

Here is an interesting field for some student of the social aspects of economics. It is a piece of work that has to be done. It will be pro-foundly interesting to explore novels, memoirs, interviews and reported utterances of all sorts to trace the progressive civilization of the entrepreneur during the last hundred years. Our investigator may even collect opinions directly from some of the more original outstanding industrial leaders of our time. The big business man as a powerful and irresponsible savage is probably quite a transitory phenomenon in the

*See R. H. Gretton's *The English Middle Class.*

development of the new world-wide civilization. The rationalization movement is essentially the organized expression of his entry upon a new phase. The chaos of competition becomes the oligarchy of production and distribution; the erstwhile plunderer of profits becomes a ruling and responsible economic aristocrat.

With, of course, exceptions.

§ 6. The Idea of Property*

The three main types of human persona differ most widely in their attitude to property. The first type is acquisitive, tenacious and preservative; the second is rapacious and consumes; the third professes to be more or less aloof from possession and gain, and to carry on the service of the community for satisfaction of a quite different type. Let us now look a little into this idea of property which is manifestly a very primary idea in binding man to man in a common effort and a mutual servitude.

We live and breathe in a world of property, just as we live and breathe in air, and yet that idea is as little analyzed as air was three hundred years ago. We—the generality—have as little ordered and explicit knowledge of its elements and pressures.

It is, for example, interesting to turn to the index of the latest edition of the Encyclopædia Britannica, that compendium of general knowledge and the current mentality, and note how far we are as yet from any understanding of the need for such an analysis. One finds a reference to certain legal articles thus:

Property: see Compensation, Conveyancing, Personal Property, Real Property.
Property, Devolution of: see Intestacy, Legitim, Will.
Property, Law of: see Real Property and Conveyancing.

And finally one little article, a column and a third long, on Primitive Property, in which alone is any realization of the fundamental significance of property ideas apparent. This is in a work which gives seventy-four columns of letterpress and forty-one page plates to Pottery and Porcelain!

The article upon Primitive Property is compressed, but does recognize something of the subtlety and variety underlying the apparent

*See Professor Laski's *Grammar of Politics*, chapter on "Property," and Tawney's *Acquisitive Society*, for a good classification of types of property.

simplicity of this fundamental concept of social ideology. Rivers, Lave-leye, Malinowski and other explorers of this neglected territory are mentioned. Indeed, in spite of the silences of the Encyclopædia Britannica, there is already available a considerable amount of work which converges upon the problem we are suggesting. But it is dis-persed in all sorts of books and publications. For example, we have the work of such a writer as Lowie (*Primitive Society*), the material gathered for us by Malinowski, piquant suggestions from that psycho-logical genius Jung, and the Yerkes' focussing of simian behaviour, a mass of such work indeed, all ready to be assembled in a larger synthesis. That assembling waits to be done by some competent and industrious student, but we may, with a certain confidence, throw out some general anticipations of its conclusions.

The idea of "mine" seems to be of much earlier origin than the idea of "me." Some birds, many predatory animals and gorillas, for example, seem to have very definite territorial ideas. Possessive jealousy is mani-festly interwoven into the very substance of many mammals. Man, as he began to discover himself, discovered himself an owner. The linkage between himself and certain objects, places and persons must have appeared as something obvious and necessary to him. And not only was there a "mine" in his awakening and clarifying consciousness to keep him snarling warnings at his brothers and sisters, but also there was an "ours",—all sorts of other larger things that rallied the pack to a com-mon defensive.

These primitive appropriations were already becoming definite and recognized in the very earliest societies to which our knowledge or imagination extends. The establishment of taboos, on which, as we have shown, human social life rests, concerned not merely sexual owner-ship but many other forms of ownership, *varying with the nature and use of the thing owned*. The ownership of weapons and adornments must have always been very personal and thorough. The ownership of a strip of meat still on the body of the tribe's last kill was not nearly so well defined. Many sorts of ownership, and particularly the owner-ship of one's own body and life, were very precarious and may have been largely dependent on the will of the tribal chief.

People write and talk of "primitive communism" and "primitive in-dividualism." But both communism and individualism are highly abstract ideas, too abstract for my taste altogether, and with a little mental slovenliness either can be applied to savage conditions. Dr. Frith, in the Encyclopædia article I have cited, very properly dismisses both these "labels." The statement I have italicized above and to which I return as the cardinal proposition in the matter, is that originally the significance of ownership was dependent altogether upon the nature and use of the object under consideration. In the development of savage ideas, as in the development of language, the particular came before the general. "My" meant what I have now or what I mean to monopolize: woman, axe, bead, sunny corner or cave. Certain things I might covet but dared not touch because they were taboo to the headman or to someone else. And, as the common use of language testifies, "my" went beyond the idea of property altogether when one talked of my master or my enemy.

From such indefinite beginnings, which indeed signified hardly more than that a thing could focus on "me," the intensification of "mine" progressed. The idea of "mine" tended to generalize. But the generalization of property was never perfect. From the beginning there seem to have been these plain divisions between, first, the crude absolute property of a man in his nose-ring or beads; secondly, claims on services and particularly sexual property with certain customary reciprocities and limitations; and, thirdly, property in which there was manifestly a communal interest, such as hunting rights and collective cultivation.

Sexual property we will not discuss at this point. It does not concern this review of human activities very greatly, and the points where it does come in may be conveniently deferred for a special chapter on woman. The progressive emancipation of women and the social protection of children, seem likely, as we shall see, to relegate it, at no very distant date, to the world of private feeling altogether.

But with regard to the other two categories of property there have always been in the human make-up two conflicting dispositions: the first, the disposition of the primitive ego-centred human animal to make "mine" as absolute and extensive as possible, and the second, the more or less lucid realization of the frequent incompatibility of absolute property with the general welfare. The craving for absolute property is perhaps the most vigorous survival of primitive impulse in modern life. The normal man's lust, for example, is far more under control. He even wants to own his property when he is dead, and resents any interference with his freedom of bequest.

Confronting this excess of primordial egotism is the law. The lawyer is the property-tamer. It is time the lawyer came into our picture. He defines property. Let us consider at what point he comes in. He is a specialization from the clerical type. Lawyer and judge are essentially men of the literate and devoted tradition. With an element of authoritative aristocracy. No class has been so bitterly satirized and reviled, but the very bitterness of the abuse reveals a recognition that from this class it is natural and reasonable to demand a conscientiousness and self-suppression beyond the normal limits. The peasant who curses the lawyer for selling justice and making all he can by it sells his own produce without compunction and makes all he can by it though other people starve. When every iniquity of the lawyers of the past has been admitted, we still find that there were abundant gentlemen of the long robe, haunted, even if they were not inspired and pervaded, by the spirit of righteousness. The illumination they shed may not always have been a beacon, but at any rate the wick never ceased altogether to glow, and down the centuries we see a succession of these unloved men boring away in their tedious frowsty courts, really struggling in that dim mediæval light to import some semblance of justice, some thought for the commonweal, into the limitless greed of robber barons, the unqualified imperatives of feudal chiefs and the grasping cunning of the baser sort. And they are still working to-day towards the satisfaction of this permanent social need—the exact definition of proprietary rights.

There has been, as we have just remarked, an age-long recognition of at least two varieties of property; that economic property in which the family, tribe, or other community had an intervening interest, and particularly land, *real property;* and that other more intimate type of possession, absolute property, *personality,* the bead, the spear, the dog, that was part of a man and was often made to "die" and be buried with him. These two main divisions still rule. But it is manifest they are not comprehensive. Copyright and patent rights are instances of a third variety of property, an expiring property of a peculiarly intimate character. Nor is either division, real or personal, more than a miscellany. There are in practice a great number of kinds of property which develop species and subspecies as the complexity of society increases, and every species and variety has its particular limitations of hold, disposition and use.

The law does in theory recognize at least two sorts of personal property, though the distinction has disappeared from the thought of the average man. To a lawyer a chattel, which may be owned absolutely, differs from a "chose in action," such as a copyright, in respect of which one merely has rights. Even in regard to saleable property, an owner may have more or less power. Before property in human beings disappeared it was gradually modified until, from the right to kill and torture slaves, we arrived at the present position, when a man may not grossly injure even his own children, but controls them only for their benefit. Our property in animals has been limited quite recently by humanitarian legislation.

According to the law of England, all land is the property of the king, and its "owners" are his tenants. They have succeeded in establishing absolute rights against the spirit of the law, but the idea that land is held on trust is not deeply buried. During the privations of the last war public opinion supported public interference with owners who neglected to get all the food they could out of their land, and if similar action of this sort were proposed to-day it would be attacked not so much by lawyers as an infringement of elementary rights as by allegations that it would not work.

Indeed, against the whole range of individual rights, both in property and conduct, the law holds up the notion of public policy—a man may not act in a manner contrary to the public good. And the operation of this idea is not limited or governed by precedent, but varies freely with the moral and economic ideas of the age. On grounds of public policy judges have recently upset decisions relating to cruelty to wives, freedom of bequest and the doctrine that agreements to fix prices are illegal conspiracies. In the days of reverence for "economic laws" price-fixing was condemned because it checked their operation. With the passing of the school of economists who held this opinion the decision has been reversed. This attrition and modification of property is always going on. The lawyer knows it is going on, and his conception of property is of a very modified and graded ownership.

But in the thinking of the ordinary man—which is what concerns us most here—this is not clearly and habitually recognized. There is a discord between the existing legal realities of property and popular thought which still holds that "a man may do what he likes with his own."

Just as, long after Dalton and the discovery of the elements, my education began at the "fire-air-earth-and-water" stage of chemistry because of the lag of popular education, so in spite of current legal thought the ideology of the ordinary man begins with the idea of absolute property. And generally speaking it stays there. For the ordinary school teaches nothing about sorts of property. And the normal teacher knows very little of any property whatever. The ordinary man therefore is continually acting upon the idea that what he owns he owns absolutely, and he is continually being pulled up by restrictions and limitations which are discordant with this crude ideology.

Perhaps the nearest approach to absolute ownership—the complete power to do what one likes with one's own—lies in the change a man carries in his pockets and (provided it is not an heirloom) the ornamental ring he wears upon his finger. Next comes the money he has within reach or within call. The shadow of debt may lie on that, but otherwise his ownership is very complete. Beyond the range of such immediate property, his ownership could very well be treated as nonexistent, and his relationship to its object,—whatever it was,—home, land, stock or share,—treated as a personal claim or right to do merely this, that and the other definable thing with the object in question. It would work out to practically the same results. But it would work through a rather different mental process in the mind of the owner.

When we have grasped this fact, which is in the habitual thought of every lawyer, that property is a limited, definable, alterable claim, varying with the object concerned, a claim either upon a passive object or a debt or other claim for service upon a person or persons, we are in a position to measure the reality of such phrases as the "abolition of property" and the "abolition of private property" which played so large a part in the socialist and communist movements of the late nineteenth and early twentieth centuries. At what were these phrases really aimed, if it is true that we are always changing, abolishing and sometimes even extending property rights? Because, as we are showing, we might "abolish" property almost altogether and still leave things working very much as they do now.

We could quite easily call the owner of anything, "the person in charge," the official responsible for it. This would be a change of terminology, but it would not be a social revolution. It would be like the League of Nations device of calling tropical possessions "mandatory territories." We should by a verbal substitution turn owners into mandatories. We should "abolish property" in theory while retaining it as a working method of dealing with things and people until—if ever—a better way could be devised. By so doing we should open the mental door to a scientific revision of legal controls that would in the end reconcile all that is reasonable in socialist and communist theory with the utmost personal freedom that is socially permissible, and that is all we should do. The governments of the world might "abolish" all private property to-morrow by a series of declarations, and until they had devised that better way, those declarations would have about as much effect upon the everyday business of life, as the Kellogg Pacts have had upon the naval and military establishments of the world.

Let us make this clearer. The reality of property is this, that an individual called the owner, possesses rights of enjoyment, use and disposal over a thing owned, or he possesses certain claims for service or supply upon a debtor. Now the abolition, the destruction, of such rights and claims, as distinguished from their transfer to some other ownership, can mean only that the thing owned or the service claimed, if it is at all desirable, is flung out to be scrambled for, and that in the end someone else or something else will be found in possession, which, as Euclid says, "is absurd" because plainly you have not abolished anything if it reappears.

But if you cannot abolish property altogether, you can abolish the property of this man or that—on condition. The condition, the only way in which the property of any individual or class can be abolished, is that there exist a *competent receiver* for the property in question. This has always been the weak point in communist proposals, that they do not clearly indicate a competent receiver. And they do not indicate a competent receiver because in relation to most types and varieties of property there is no competent receiver. They are the first to denounce the national State as a competent receiver, or the parliamentary politician as a proper administrator of the confiscated spoils. A large part of the constructive task before mankind consists in the invention and creation of a competent receiver which will embody the commonweal. The Socialists' and the Communists' criticism of the working of private ownership in our economic life is often sound and very penetrating, but from that their transition to impossibly premature receivers is entirely too rapid. They mistake their statements of guiding principles for practicable working plans.

At the beginning of this section we asserted that we live and breathe in a world of property as we live and breathe in air, but, as we have shown throughout this chapter, the way in which the property motive works varies very widely. You may be induced to work in order to get and hold; you may get and spend without working, or you may work without wanting to get. Now this third alternative we have stressed, and to it we shall return again. We have shown that throughout the ages the proper conduct of human affairs has been very largely due to the continued existence of the educated devoted type of persona, in which the property motive is secondary or suppressed. To this type we must look for the organization and control of a competent receiver whenever we consider the removal of any sort of social activity from the spontaneous direction of private owners. And what the Socialist or the Communist is really after when he uses such phrases as the "abolition of property" is, in fact, the abolition of the property motive in economic life; that is to say, the abolition of the two most fundamental social types in favour of the third, the trained and educated type. The world has to become a world of men and women working to serve and not to own. To that possibility we shall return later. Here let it suffice to point out that the socialist idea is really the idea of a universal education for service, and that if it does not mean that, it means nothing at all of the slightest practical value.

At present an entirely educated world is no more than a speculative possibility. At present this world is a world of getting. The ordinary man works for himself primarily, and he works for others only in so far as he wants and needs to get from them.

§ 7. The Education of the Lawyer

The lawyer, we have said, is the property-tamer, and here, if we were being fully encyclopædic, we should give a lengthy description of the legal organization of the world. We should take the reader into law courts from China to Peru, discuss the legal procedure of the Moslim world, and the reason why the British barrister wears a wig, while his French confrère is adorned with a peculiarly shaped hat. We should glance back to the courts of Greece and Rome. But here again our convenient fiction of the *Science of Work and Wealth* must relieve us. It would be all there, and if it was there, the really interested reader would merely glance at it and then return to the main discussion. Here we will consider the legal organization only in the most general terms and think of it mainly in the forms it has assumed in the Atlantic civilizations.

What is the rôle of the legal organization in the social complex? In many respects the legal profession is one of the most antiquated types of activity in the world. It was one of the earliest to be detached from the primary priestly calling. It is still of very great importance indeed, though that importance is diminishing with the diminution of the traditional element in law and the establishment of codes. With the growth of civilization it will probably continue to diminish relatively to other fields of activity.

In his greater past, when law was a compromise between the will of rulers and the customs of a tribe or people, the lawyer was the sole repository of the law. At his best he upheld the rights of the common man against the encroachments of chiefs and kings. And his record is not a bad one. If his "bit of parchment" terrified the peasant, it often baffled the lord. He alone could state with authority what a man's rights were; it was his tradition to defend them; indeed, he had no *raison d'être* if he supported absolute power; and his skill subdued the hearts of rulers towards the current conceptions of mercy and justice. In those days, if the courts abandoned a man he was lost indeed.

Nobody is now in that position of dependence. We can read, we can write and argue to the point. Printing, popular education, representative assemblies and newspapers have made knowledge of the law accessible, and they have provided anyone who can attract attention with powerful if capricious defenders. The Public Trustee sets a standard for solicitors, judges may complain from time to time of the encroachments of, say, Civil Service regulations, but the battle thus started is no longer fought out in the courts of law but in Parliament. The lawyers have not so much to expound a common law known only to themselves as to administer word for word the statutes handed to them. Perhaps nine-tenths of the cases which come before the courts now are matters of statute law.

This is a limitation of the lawyer's function, and on the whole it is a change for the better. There is no such room in the administration of justice for individual beliefs and difference of culture as there used to be. An enlightened man, free to adjust the law to his own conceptions, would do more harm than good. For in most spheres of legal action what matters (within limits) to the members of a community is not so much how rights and obligations are parcelled out between them as that their rights shall be the same in this court as in that, next month as last month, and that they shall be enforced without fear, favour or distinction between persons. This is not so true of criminal law, but criminal law is only the sensational relief of the calling.

The lawyer, then, must know and follow precedent, and to this is doubtless due the wholly irrational scheme of his own professional arrangements. The modernization of the legal organization lags behind that of the medical services, lags behind the reform of the educational system. This is disastrously true of legal education. The barrister is a specialist. He influences the common life at few points; his general education, unless he becomes a judge, is of value chiefly to himself. Fortunately, for social reasons, it is the custom to give him what is considered the best education the country can offer. Solicitors, on the other hand, wield enormous influence. Now that clerical advice is less often sought than it was, we call on our solicitors to advise us at all those moments of crisis—death, marriage, disaster—when momentous personal decisions have to be made. The flow of inherited wealth, the employment of savings, our practical handling of all the vexed social questions, lie largely in the hands of our solicitors. No body of men stands so much in need of the widest and most generous equipment of ideas. And yet it is the custom to take them from school at the age when the mind should expand most rapidly and confine them to routine work in traditionally dusty offices, as though we were anxious to secure for our intimate counsellors men of stunted and dingy mental growth. Happily most of us are able to find men in the profession who have transcended these limitations. A day may come when the Incorporated Law Society will insist upon a modicum of social biology, psychology and modern economics for the professional qualification of a solicitor. It may even demand some elements of literary culture. Until that day arrives the adjustment of legal and social practice to modern knowledge will remain imperfect at many points.

§ 8. *"Scientific" Property*

We may recall here that brief history of human mental development we traced in the opening sections of Chapter II. We have shown how recent are abstractions, generalizations, and directed thinking in the development of society. We have reminded the reader how children and untrained minds are disposed to personify and to ascribe everything to agents and doers and deal with everything as a personal matter. They think not only of powers and inanimate objects as persons, but they think of tribes and communities as persons. They abstract with difficulty. We shall see presently (in Chapter X) into what difficulties human affairs have been brought by the inability of people to think of money except in terms of gold-bartering. Here we have to consider how recent and under-developed is the idea of common property, of any property, that is, not private and personal.

In the old civilizations two great personifications owned all the property that we should now consider collective, the God (administering through the temple priesthood) and the king. When tribal gods gave place to a universal God, he owned the earth and the fullness thereof. That conception of personal ownership came down to quite modern times. The road eighteenth-century Englishmen travelled on was the king's highway, the ships that defended them were the king's navy, anything otherwise ownerless, like treasure trove or an intestate's estate, was the king's. There was no difficulty then in proposing to expropriate an owner or a class of owners. God and the king were thought of as receivers of unlimited competence. And whatever restriction there was upon a man "doing what he liked with his own" was imposed in the name of the super-owner. "For everything a personal owner," has been almost a necessary principle of human thought, until the spread of socialist and communist views. Outside human interests, of course, were the things of the wild, wild beasts and birds and fish and the like, but they could only come into human affairs by being annexed and owned. They were owned so soon as they mattered. The feudal king owned the forests. Not even the seas were masterless; the Carthaginians warned the Romans off the western Mediterranean and, as Britons sang, Britannia ruled the waves.

But after a century of socialist discussion, after a century of thinking over such declarations as Proudhon's that property is robbery, we find ourselves released to take quite another view of property. We find it possible to start from a point absolutely opposite to that from which our grandfathers started. Instead of assuming the need for an owner for each individual thing, we can begin now with an absolute communist proposition, that everything belongs to all mankind, and try what result we can get by asking: To what persons or groups of people would it be best to assign the responsibility for protecting, controlling, exploiting or enjoying this, that, and the other division of everything? We can work downward from the conception of one human commonweal instead of upward from the basis of nineteen hundred million individual appropriations. We can do so now because the shock of that phrase "the abolition of property," reverberating for a hundred years, has released our minds. We can do now, with all the freedom of a scientific enquiry, what the lawyers through the centuries have been doing with an industrious elaboration, by instinct and rule of thumb, and attempt a really scientific treatment of the apportionment of duty, control and consumption over ownable things.

It was pointed out at the end of § 6 that it would be possible to "abolish property" to-morrow without any hindrance to our present occupations. But having done so we should then be in a position to ask each and every holder of property in the world to show reason why he should continue to administer that property, enquiring further whether his administration was the best possible for the human commonweal, and if not, by what means it could be transferred, with as little social disturbance as possible, to a better administration.

As a matter of fact, and with certain obscurities and indirectnesses, that is what is being asked in the world now, in a great variety of forms and phrases. What in any particular instance is the better administration? The first people indeed to imply this question by running into the arena with an answer to it were Herbert Spencer's Individualists, of whom Sir Ernest Benn is the most living British representative. They broke out in the middle of the nineteenth century replying, to an unspoken challenge, that the best social results, the greatest wealth, the greatest happiness, would result in leaving private property as it now exists, and as free, as untaxed, as uncontrolled as possible. Half of Herbert Spencer's writings were an indictment—a fairly sound one— of the contemporary State as a competent receiver. But by defending personal property as an institution they admitted that the institution of personal property could be called to account, and prepared the way for the world-wide discriminating and exhaustive enquiry that is now proceeding. They did good work in showing how incomplete, to the pitch of futility, was the socialist project until competent receivers could be indicated, but they satisfied no one by these instances of State stupidity that competent receivers were generally impossible.

Very much of this present work is, at its level, a contribution to the scientific conception of property. From first to last, indeed, it is a treatise on the management of the human estate, a balance sheet and report on current business, an account of the working of the world as a going concern. In this chapter upon motives we are concerned with property mainly because its acquisition is a social motive. The insistence of the Individualist upon the beneficent effect of a competitive struggle for acquisition, with private personal ownership as full, free and wild as possible, has to be taken into account. He tells us that men have a land hunger, a planning and management hunger, a passion for "founding a family." In a manner which he never fully explains, these base orientations of the egotistic drive, will, he assumes, work together for good, provided they are not thwarted and restrained.

But are any of these dispositions instinctive and ineradicable in the human animal? The social analysis we have made regards their domination over conduct as entirely the outcome of educational circumstances; they are great and powerful in the peasant and least so in the priest. The ideal "economic man" of the Individualist is simply the peasant,

bathed and in control of a business. The Individualist approaches this
complex question of human incentive too exclusively from the point of
view of the prosperous nineteenth-century protestant business man.
Mr. John Galsworthy has devoted a large part of his career as a novelist
to the meticulous study of the motives of a family of this type, the
Forsyte family, and more particularly to the life history of Soames
Forsyte, the *Man of Property,* and even nowadays, while practically a
contemporary, the reader is left wondering whether any real human
beings were ever so rigid and impenetrable as this constellation of
meanly discreet and discreetly respectable beings who figure in the
Forsyte Saga.

The thesis of this chapter is that both the peasant's craving for land
and tangible property generally, and the motive that made Soames
Forsyte want to own pictures, estate, wife, and everything else that was
seemly, is not a fundamental motive. The human animal wants a feeling of security, and it wants freedom and the feeling of power. Those
wants are truly fundamental. The ideology into which the peasant and
business man and other developments of the peasant have been born,
has moulded these natural, fundamental and ineradicable motives into
the form of tangible property, which carries with it to them the assurance of satisfaction for these essential desires. Their persona is that of
the struggling or successful owner, and they can see themselves comfortably in no other rôle. But the experience of the "educated" series of
types shows that the satisfaction of these desires (security, freedom and
the desire for power) can be guaranteed in quite other forms. And just
so far as it is guaranteed in other forms, so does the desire to possess
tangible property evaporate as a social motive.

This is well shown in the preference so many people display for irresponsible property, the preference for being creditors rather than
owners. We shall study the genesis of the "investing public" in Chapter X, and the characteristics of the modern rich in Chapter XI, and
then it will become manifest how profoundly and extensively the idea
of property is being changed from an array of material possessions to
entries in a bank account. The Individualist's picture of the modern rich
man as a property owner, owning, cherishing, increasing, extending his
estate and possessions, is already a dream of past conditions. Soames
Forsyte was behind his own times. Even the French peasant now, instead of hoarding, cleaning and counting his precious coins, sends his
money to the bank and buys *"bons."* The disposition to disencumber
oneself of property so soon as the human values it stands for, security,

freedom and the sense of power can be got in some other way, seems to be well-nigh universal. "Do it *for* me," says the modern successful man, working away at his own special task, and is only too careless of the competence of the receiver to whom he hands his gains.

The objective of any theory of Scientific Property must be just this release of successful people from their present obligation to own irrelevant property they do not want to administer or watch over, and conversely to release property from the absentee owner and the hands of those who do not want to administer it to the best advantage for the community.

We have said that the sub-man began the accumulation of wealth when he kept and carried a stone in his hand, and that our species tied itself to locality when it had accumulated more gear than it could conveniently carry all the time. There are many ways of viewing history, but from one angle it is to be seen as the piling up of more and more encumbering stuff. At last man is seen tied to the fields he has ploughed, the trees he has planted and the house he has built. We have written of his enslavement to toil and his present hopes of release. His personal release from his maximum encumbrance with property has also been going on—with intermissions—for a considerable time. He has gradually been freeing himself from tangible burthensome ownership by a process of monetary abstraction. To understand how that has come about we must begin with some elementary considerations about money.

§ 9. *The Complexities and Mutations of the Money Idea*

We will begin our exploration of this process of the "dematerialization," shall we call it? of property by a sketchy and generalized consideration of Money, of the money idea and suggestion, which becomes in abnormal cases the money passion. We are dealing here with a variable intricate complex. "Money" means in a thousand minds a thousand subtly different, roughly similar, systems of images, associations, suggestions and impulses. And this variety is disregarded in almost all our discussion of monetary questions. The general disposition is to treat it as something simple—if a little difficult to define.

Two convenient ways of discussing money present themselves. The first, the traditional, is to treat money as the development of a particular type of portable property and trace its progressive specialization as an intermediary in barter. The second is to consider money as the medium through which the general economic life of mankind is now being conducted and to criticize the laws and conventions determining its use from the point of view of the racial welfare. The convergence of the two methods brings tradition to the test of the creative idea.

A large amount of the literature of finance fails to distinguish clearly between these two different ways of approach or to realize that there are still imperfectly explored gaps between the current conclusions attained by one process and those reached by the other. In these still unmapped gaps lie the psychological processes by which money has achieved its present cardinal importance in economic life.

In our historical introduction we have glanced already at the onset of money. A sort of money of account seems to have preceded real money. A shield was worth so many head of cattle, and so on; the need for a numerical standard by which to envisage barter was early recognized. It is quite possible that debts were remembered in terms of such "proto-money," as soon as, or even sooner than, the time when metals —weighed at first and later stamped—began to be used as a convenient intermediary in trade. The tally conception of money, that is to say, may be older than the precious, portable, hoardable commodity conception. Gold and silver, copper and iron, became first the most convenient and habitual and then the standard materials for meeting the demand of the tally. With coinage they became the realized tally. But quite early in the story we hear of the Carthaginians using "leather" money, tokens or parchment bills; that is to say, the valuable metals were not handed about but set down somewhere in security, while the tally element of the money circulated by itself.

In a preceding section we pointed out that the idea of property is a *simplified* idea, that primitive man, with no general terms and no habits of generalization, thought of each thing and variety of thing according to its uses and conditions and had no general concept of material property at all. We noted that down to the present the law has always struggled with an apprehension that property is classifiable and should be classified. But the effect of money, even of money of account, was to help man very far towards an unsound simplification of the property notion. He was able to get out of sight of its variety by abstracting it as a monetary value. He began to think of everything as vendible, interchangeable and divisible. How far that extravagant extension of this idea of vendibility has been carried in human thought can be measured by the fact that such things as the crown (kingship) of Poland, wives, the command of regiments, the cure of souls, the caliphate, have on occasion been reduced to monetary values and sold and purchased.

And this simplification of property favoured also the extension of the idea of absolute ownership to all things. What you could buy and sell you could surely give, change or destroy. You could buy a slave—and break him. You could buy a picture by Holbein and burn it.

Further, crude conceptions of money undermined the feeling of joint and collective ownership and responsibility. It was easy to step from the idea that a collective property could be estimated in monetary terms to the authentic division of the total into the vendible shares. So that in both the ages of money, that is to say, under the Roman republic and empire and from the Middle Ages down to the present time, money ideology, by the facilities and enhancement it has afforded absolute individual ownership, has been potent in breaking up communal and collective systems and detaching customary owners from contact with and responsibility to the soil. In both the First (the Roman) and the Second (the Modern) Money Age there have been parallel changes that did not occur in any preceding phase of civilization. Debt was less restrained, it was incurred with great ease, usury assumed fantastic dimensions, and taxation developed to an unprecedented degree. The "poor" appear in the denunciations of the prophets; the proletarians take their place in the Roman constitution. For the first time "estates" arise from the selling up of dispossessed men. The accumulation of capital and the concentration of production in large enterprises become possible. The Roman process was already in its dégringolade before partnership developed into shareholding. Joint-stock enterprise and power-driven mechanism are two essential differences between the First and the Second Money Age.

We turn from the historical study of money, as the development of a system of conventions, simplifications and disregards, to its second aspect, to its study as a method of carrying on the work of the world. And that means beginning not with money as the measure of property, but with money as wages, conferring "purchasing power." At the outset of this second enquiry we must ask what is required of money. Just as man takes the horse and without much discussion of how that animal reduced its toes to one and what its life on the steppes and prairies of prehistoric times was like, castrates it and sets it to dragging carts, so those who approach the money idea from the second point of view seek to reduce this growth of conventions and acceptances, to the service of our economic life with as few concessions as possible. And just as the horse, because it is not a simple *ad hoc* machine but the product of a long organic evolution, has to be taken at times to the

THE CONTEMPORARY CITY

THE Chicago River, Chicago, showing the new Wabash Avenue draw-bridge in process of construction; the London Guarantee & Accident Co. Building at upper left; the clock tower of the Wrigley Building, right; Wacker Drive in the upper part of the picture, with the Michigan Avenue Link Bridge at left. A hundred years ago there was nothing but mud flats here.

FLOODLIGHTING THE MODERN CITY

THE Wrigley Tower in Chicago at night.

veterinary surgeon, driven with caution, fed with care, and sometimes put out to grass, so the money complex, which has never been a simple *ad hoc* contrivance, needs wariness and watchfulness in its economic use, or it may fail and fall or bolt with or overset the machine. Essentially both horse and money complex were evolved without human premeditation and are only partially subjugated to their functions.

Primarily money was a tally for property; it arose out of the needs of barter, but for the purposes of this second discussion money can be considered as primarily wages and salary; as the sure and reasonable reward of labour, the cheque for so much purchasing power. How far it can be, and how far it really is that, we must enquire. Here, at any rate, we can say that it is at present sufficiently that to keep the great world machine of production going. Because of their confidence in this cheque, the workers pour into the shops, mines, fields and factories we have surveyed in our earlier chapters. Destroy that confidence absolutely, and the machinery will stop dead.

Our generation has seen in two big human communities the practical loss of that confidence, and has some measure of the effect. I wish I could give statistics and photographs of scenes in Berlin during the final slump of the mark in 1922 and 1923. Berlin was a terrible city then; never had I been before in a city where nearly every human being was visibly dismayed and broken-hearted—except in Petrograd in 1920. The German collapse was due to very complex causes; the Russian state of affairs was mainly due to a frank and deliberate attempt to abolish money. It was to be made utterly worthless by the unlimited printing of paper money, and then it was to be replaced by cards with tear-off coupons like the rationing cards issued in Great Britain during the Great War. Every citizen was to receive a card periodically, with tear-off coupon for milk, meat, wine, clothing, transport, fuel, books, furniture, theatre, all his needs, and these coupons he was to exchange for these necessities at the communal stores. It was an entirely needless and clumsy experiment to make upon a population already sorely distressed. One insurmountable obstacle was that there were practically no goods worth talking about in the stores. There was a shortage even of flour. It had been quite impossible to improvise the organization of supply and distribution upon the new lines, and everyone was attempting evasions of the law against old-fashioned buying and selling. When I was in Russia at that time I found money still had value: ten thousand rubles was considered rather a better tip than a hard-boiled egg—I had provided myself with both forms of money—and there were still in-

dividuals who were not in urgent need of an egg, who did not want
it to decay on their hands, and preferred the reserve purchasing power
of money even though it might be difficult to exercise. Furtive trading
was going on in the north in spite of an iron régime of suppression, and
in Moscow and at wayside railway stations there was open selling. The
distinctive quality of money is the freedom of choice it gives its pos-
sessors, and this those tickets destroyed altogether. A certain peddling
of coupons presently arose between people anxious for more of one
thing and less of another, and after a time the complexity of supplying
goods to meet coupon demands became so great that the whole experiment was abandoned. What the worker needs, if you would keep him
working, is plainly a cheque for "anything money can buy" in return
for his services rendered.

Our modern economic organization, our whole modern human
society, has grown up on the assumption, the colourable pretense at
least, that the money distributed in wages does give that, and I cannot
conceive of it carrying on now in any other fashion without becoming
almost unrecognizably different. Our civilization can as little give up
the use of money now, as our bodies can the use of blood. The practical problem is to ensure the best blood possible—to keep out poisons
and contagions and avoid anæmia.

To these matters we will return in greater detail in Chapter X.
Within the limits of this present chapter we consider money only in so
far as it is a motivating idea.

§ 10. *A Résumé of the Coördinating Motives in a Modern Community*

Let us now recapitulate this chapter and state in general terms the
psychological essentials of modern economic and social coöperation. In
the first place, as we have pointed out, it is, at bottom, coöperation
against the grain. The human being, when fully adult, is still fundamentally a highly individualized and ego-centred animal, and his social
life is based on subjugation and education. In the past subjugation and
the retardation of the fiercer adult qualities, have been the prevailing
factors in the process.

Compared with the male gorilla, *Homo sapiens* never really grows
up. We have already pointed this out in § 5 of Chapter I. In every man
a war is continually going on between the gregarious instincts he has
retained from immaturity, his innate desire to conform to the opinion

about him, to be liked and respected by his fellows, on the one hand, and on the other his egoism, his desire to do the best for himself, to express himself fully and to dominate and prevail over others. This conflict is not so apparent in many of the savage communities, as it is in contemporary life. It reveals itself with the development of privacy and private property and with opportunities for individual enrichment. Civilized social life is based on the fact that the second, the egoistic system of ideas, can be mastered and modified by and subordinated to the first. Where the community accepts an ethic those individuals who disregard it can be forced to conform. The ethic itself can be changed by education. There has been an immense amount of mere subjugation in the past. In the future, we are going to suggest, education may largely replace subjugation. We may replace the broken and retarded individuality by a directed and self-disciplined individuality.

As we have seen, three main strands of tradition mingle in the process of breaking-in man to society. There is the peasant tradition with its exaltation of toil and its desperate clutch upon property, its fear, its political submissiveness, and its great power of passive resistance. There is the nomad tradition with its rapacity and handsome spending. There is the priestly tradition, the tradition of the trained and educated man with its repudiation of mercenariness, its conceptions of service and disinterestedness. How these strands interwove and interacted to constitute mediæval society is a matter of history. The civilized aristocrat touched thought and learning with a quality of enterprise, and the clash of cultures, of Latin Christendom with Arabic-Greek knowledge, released the scepticisms and enquiries that opened the way to the modern world. All these traditions still mingle in us and about us. Out of them we build our personas, our conceit of ourselves, our conception of our rôles and of what becomes us. But the proportionate influence of these three factors changes.

As we have seen, the new world-wide economic system that has been coming into existence in the last century and a half is rapidly superseding the independent small cultivator and the independent town trader and town artisan, by large enterprises employing wages—workers, foremen, managers and directors. With the diminution of that peasant-small-townsman stratum which was until recently the bulk of human society, goes the disappearance of the peasant-small-townsman type of persona. It is replaced by a complex of new ideals. Similarly the advance of social discipline has turned the aristocratic predatory type, partly in an instinctive effort for its self-preservation, to militarism and the maintenance of nationalist and monarchist institutions, and partly to a mercenary social mixture with the inflated entrepreneurs who have arisen from the peasant-townsman mass. The struggle for the new civilization with nationalist militarism is all about us—and is still indecisive. And meanwhile there has been an immense extension of education, *with all the strands of disinterestedness it brings with it*. The modern population is rapidly becoming a wholly literate one. The mentality of the learned clerk penetrates everywhere. Popular education has been recognized as necessary even by business entrepreneurs frankly anxious to keep the worker under. A machine civilization has no use for an illiterate citizen. The tradition-based mind is too inflexible for its varying and progressive needs.

The priestly-intellectual tradition has never set any value upon either the accumulation or the violent acquisition of property. Its disposition is to secure a position, through salary, savings or what not, in which it can operate freely, and then to take no more thought of money, but rather to get the work or service done. The satisfaction of good achievement is greater than the satisfaction of possessions. Our teachers arise out of this tradition and bring with them the same repudiation of accumulation and mercenary motives, which they instil into a larger and larger proportion of the population. The modern wages worker and that extending class, the salariat, do not even think of ever being wealthy; they are not in that competition; they want to be safe, comfortable and pleasant in their lives, free from anxiety, free from excessive labour, free to do their individual task well. For these ends they will be acquisitive of money. They do not want money for its own sake, and they do not want money for power. They want it to spend, they want it in the background for emergencies. They cannot do without it. When they come into the modern economic-social organization, this is the material end they have in view. This is the chief motive our developing modern economic organization has to reckon with. This search for security, comfort and liberty, is, as we bring consciousness into our review of human activities, the ruling motive which keeps the marionettes busy in our model industrial machine.

People say that modern life turns wholly on getting money. But the getting of money either by trading or other forms of "making money," or as wages, salary, rent and interest is now only in a small minority of cases an end in itself. The satisfaction of the demands of the persona constitutes, now as ever, the guiding principle of human conduct, and the value of the money system in the machinery is to be judged entirely by its ability to satisfy those demands. By that criterion we shall go in our subsequent examination of the currency system and its conceivable developments. Suffice it here to repeat that the modern persona is being steadily modified by education in the direction of substituting service of some type, and generally now coöperative service, for the pure acquisitiveness and desire for dominance of the traditional social scheme.

Compared with the localized economic systems of the past, the new order which is developing about us, which makes a larger and larger part of the human population, employees, workers, officials and specialists seems at the first glance to be abolishing freedom and making more and more people subordinated to a single world economic machine. But that is due to a common confusion between independence and freedom. Independence is no doubt being abolished by the synthetic forces at work, in the case of individuals just as in the case of sovereign states, but independence is not freedom. An "independent" peasant or small tradesman is tied, with scarcely a day's holiday, to his cultivation or his shop; he is the slave of local custom, and he must toil without surcease to the end of his days. An employee under generous modern conditions —dictated, be it noted, not by sentiment but by considerations of maximum efficiency—has daily leisure, holidays and an altogether greater meed of personal freedom.

Large-scale production and distribution release human beings to self-respect and initiative at every point in its organization. Domestic service in the past was practically personal slavery; the servant was at the beck and call of the employer from morning to night. Where mediævalism still prevails, as Lady Simon's admirable book on China has recently reminded us, domestic servants are still slaves. They are bought and sold. They are struck and beaten. In such backward countries as Italy servants are still beaten; I have seen a chambermaid beaten by the manageress of a hotel. But under collective housekeeping and in any large establishment servants become a "staff" with clear rights and definite limits to their duties. A great deal of nagging, bullying and oppression may still occur in any staff where the housekeeper, the head waiter or house steward is under-educated and evilly disposed; the new age is not the immediate coming of the kingdom of heaven; but in a well organized concern there are powers above the tyrant and modes of resistance against tyranny. It is possible to appeal against ill-treatment, and in the closely observed business of the ultra-modern type, friction will be perceptible in the lowered quantity and quality of the work and will be made the subject of enquiry.

PERSONAL SERVICE

At many points in the economic social machine there is still and probably there will always have to be direct personal service. There is the valet or courier to a busy man; there are the devils, amanuenses and secretaries, who eke out the powers of some person of exceptional initiative; there are the "companions" of the old and isolated. But a society which is replacing conceptions of advantage and dominance by the idea of disinterested effort will change such relationships very substantially even when it does not abolish them. The old way was for the principal person to behave towards his seconders as a lord towards inferiors. He was their substitute for motive; theirs not to reason why he commanded this or that. But in the atmosphere of an educated community he will be recognized not as a lord but as a specialist, and his claim for assistance will be based not on his highmightiness but upon his insufficiency. The valet or courier does things for him because, having regard for his preoccupations and limitations, he is totally unable to do them himself; the secretary supplements, extends, clarifies and checks his efforts. The secretary or valet is a protector of his principal from petty distresses and details generally. The relationship rises therefore from the level of subjugation towards the level of sympathetic aid and friendship. Exceptional ability can be recognized on either hand, and respect can be mutual and complementary. Occasionally to the end of time, the secondary person will have to show loyalty to the principal. Loyalty one may define as personal obedience to the initiatives of another even when those initiatives are not understood or seem to be wrong, obedience because, on the whole, the secondary person believes in the general rightness of the initiator, and in some distinctive unpredictable and inestimable quality that gives him or her the right to indisputable initiative.

CHAPTER THE NINTH

How Mankind Is Paid and Wealth Accumulated

§ 1. *The Counting House Comes into the Picture*

IN THE preceding chapter one or two fundamental things about money have been stated. It was at first a commodity like any other commodity. And there were various standards of value: cattle, land, for example, by which the relative values of things could be appraised. Metals were only one sort of standard by which things were valued. But in a slow, complex way money has become something more than a commodity. And now it is becoming something which is not a commodity at all. There is now, as we have pointed out, another way of looking at money, that is to say, as a guarantee of "purchasing power."

That was as far as Chapter VIII went with the discussion of money. It passed on to other aspects of human motive, for motive was its essential subject.

In this chapter this matter of money and monetary property is to be studied more closely. We are, as the heading of this section intimates, going to bring the Counting House into the picture.

But first let us step back for a moment and consider the whole plan of this work. The earlier chapters were designed to show the purely material development of the human community. We showed substances being subdued and handled; extraneous power brought into the service of man; food being made, treated and distributed, clothing, housing, roads, and ever increasing means of transport being provided, and at first there was hardly a human being, except for a few scientific workers and a customer here and there, in the spectacle. It was the mechanism of human life we dealt with and nothing more. Then, having prepared the scene and the stage, we brought in the workers and managers and set them to work.

But the way in which everyone was toiling remained unexplained. Why did they do it? We tried to get inside the heads of these workers, to make an analysis of their mental operations. We introduced the idea of the guiding "persona" in the mind. We showed how money came into human life to liquidate what would otherwise be an impossibly complex system of services and exchanges.

The design of those earlier chapters was to suggest a panorama of great productive and distributing plants, wide cultivations, housing, hotels, transport systems, research laboratories, and the like, but in all these presentations, certain oblong areas remained blank and no attention was given them. These blanks were the counting house and the board room. But now, after our study of motives, we are in a position to deal profitably with these necessary organs in the industrial body. We can now take into our purview the going to and from the bank, the question of prices and profits that underlie the more grossly material processes of the workshop and mine. Particulars about pay envelopes, tills, cash registers, estimating costs and determination of prices, are secondary and technical matters upon which we will not enlarge, but the going to and from the bank, the declaration of a dividend, are broad essential things to which we have to give our very best attention.

Why does the factory now increase its output and take on more hands? Why does it now slack off and slow down? Why does it raise or lower the wages it pays? What is happening? It is making profits or it is making a loss. The board room and counting house are getting or losing money. Through all the machinery of production and distribution runs money. Money is the blood of this monstrous economic organism we are studying, and finance is its circulatory system.

In the *Science of Life*, there is a chapter called The Living Body. There is an account first of the blood, then of the way in which it circulates about the body, then of the organs in which it is made, refreshed, cleansed, and finally of its working and control. This is not a bad plan to follow now with the blood of the great economic body of mankind. Only we have to bear in mind that while the blood and circulation of a human body have been perfected by millions of ancestral trials, successes and failures, the economic body of mankind is a new and unprecedented and untried organism that is struggling into being, a body experimental to the extremest degree and begotten not of like parents but by the flowing together of a number of smaller economic systems, themselves experimental and not tried out, but suddenly by the development of communications brought into our present larger synthesis of work and effort.

§ 2. *What Currency Has to Do and What It Is**

Now here our limitless museum of economic activities becomes extremely useful. Let us admit the enormous possibilities of curious and almost useless knowledge about money, and let us put it all in a great wing of that museum, and leave it there. (There is perhaps hardly a reader of this book who has not at some time stood on the threshold of a room devoted to numismatics—and turned away from that awful vista of yards and yards of idealized royal profiles and symbolized pretensions.) And further, in that remote wing we will imagine a most instructive exposition of old and new methods of gold-winning, and that there it is possible to trace every stage from the mine to the mint; learn about the finding of gold, the method of distributing the minted money and the immobilization of large quantities of it in reserves and hoards. That collection would also display the various types of paper and token money. Mints, assaying and the special nature and precautions of paper money printing would have their place. There would have to be a picturesque section devoted to the activities of the forger and the sweater of coin, a footnote section, so to speak, a museum exhibit of false money in the smasher's depot. All that history and detail we may take for granted here and pass on.

Moreover, if that display was to be at all comprehensive, it would have to include all the material for a précis of the varieties of monetary method, some of them still very primitive, operative or recently operative in the different sovereign states of the world. Laborious and tedious it would be, and yet discursively interesting, to trace how the widely dispersed right to mint money in the Middle Ages was gradually concentrated by the development of the modern national State, and how the steadily intensified obsession of the human mind by the idea of independent sovereignty since the Treaty of Westphalia has stood in the way of any international issues. The money of every country has been subjected to the advertisement of national symbols. Almost always, when a monarchy existed, one side of the current coin, at least, has been given over to the advertisement of the reigning prince. It is more than a little absurd that the gold sovereign which is now used by the British only for foreign trade should carry such advertisement matter, but the association dates from the remotest use of money, and few people seem to realize its present irrelevance. It is the visible re-

*A good and lively book not too long for the general reader is Professor Edwin Cannan's *Modern Currency and the Regulation of Its Value.* 1931.

minder that a matter of world-wide importance is still controlled by a patchwork of authorities all working for their own self-preservation, and none realizing fully or admitting frankly the functions money has to perform in a world-wide economic community. It is a picturesque survival from the quaint romantic past through which our ancestors worked their way darkly to our present use of money.

"It is surprising," said Sir Robert Hadfield in a recent address, "to realize how comparatively small in weight is the total quantity of this metal which holds such sway over our affairs. The production and stocks of gold are measured in ounces, whereas the metallurgist working in iron and steel reckons in tons.

"Recently I came across a most interesting and ably written pamphlet, 'Summarized Data of Gold Production,' by Mr. Robert H. Ridgway and the Staff of the Common Metals Division of the United States Department of Commerce, which throws much light on the part which gold has played in the history of the world during the past six hundred years. From a careful study of available records, it is concluded that the world's production of gold since the discovery of America, from the year 1493 to 1927 inclusive, amounted to 1,004 million fine ounces, including 1 per cent. for unrecorded or under-estimated output.

"Expressed in ounces, this sounds to be an immense quantity, yet in dead solid weight it amounts to about 30,720 tons, occupying a volume of slightly more than 56,000 cubic feet, or if we consider the whole of the gold produced in the world since the time of the discovery of America, this would go into a 38-foot cube. Not a very impressive block as regards size or weight to have ruled men's passions and destinies for more than half a thousand years! I wonder if its magic power is destined to continue. . . .

"The value of the actual and latest annual output, that is, for the year 1927, amounted to £83,000,000. From the weight point of view of a ferrous metallurgist this represents the miserable figure of only about 600 tons, or a 10-foot cube!" . . .

But we must turn away from that obscure and glittering miscellany of curious facts about gold. Our business with money is its functional value in the world organism; we are concerned not with what it has been (except in so far as this throws light upon its working now) but with what it is and what is now required of it.

We have dealt already (in Chapter VIII) with the psychological rôle of the money complex and shown how the bulk of the ordinary man's activities is based, however insecurely, on a belief in the practical trustworthiness of money. The money complex keeps the wheels of the modern economic world turning. That is the point of maximum importance about money, that *it works the worker*. Its relation to the worker is closely parallel to that of the blood in our bodies to the individual cell. It brings him alimentation and stimulus; it carries off his products.

Money guarantees, or to put it more truthfully, if the social machine is to work it should guarantee, to every worker who receives it as wages or salary, a certain definite purchasing power, and to every producer of a desired commodity, a reward in general purchasing power commensurate with the general need for his product. Then the worker or producer "knows what he is about." Work is done, services are rendered and goods produced under the most harmonious conditions. Money, then, from the point of view of the living, coöperating individual, has to be a trustworthy counter on which everyone can rely without further scrutiny. It must stand, steadily, for so much goods. On that basis everyone can deal. If a worker—in a world of steadfast money—is not content with what he gets he demands a rise in wages; similarly the producer raises or lowers the price of his commodity, and things adjust themselves by haggling and bargaining; the money throughout remaining a trustworthy and unchallenged counter of what is going on.

That is the ideal. That is money as it should be, seen from both the point of view of the general healthy activity of the community and from the point of view of the ordinary working individual. That is what almost everyone tries to believe money is—a sure thing—and something that will keep good. A worker who earns money wants to feel and should feel that to-morrow, or next month, or if he wants to save up for something, next year, the purchasing power of that money will be practically the same. Or, putting the phrase "purchasing power" into an equivalent expression, he wants to live in a world of stable prices. "Stabilized prices" is only another expression for trustworthy money.

But now, where are we to find the guarantees that the money we receive and pay is such a stable, trustworthy counter? Where and what is the guarantee that goods will be forthcoming and that prices are to "stay put"? The issuing authority, which is, under existing conditions, the State, the sovereign government (in the United States the federal government to which the states in that contract of federation, the Constitution, delegated the right of issue), or a controlled central bank working in more or less close coöperation with the State, makes or rather seems and tries to make, this guarantee. But it does so under rather difficult conditions. It is not itself in the position to supply the goods its money should guarantee and which the normal worker believes it will guarantee. Except in Soviet Russia the responsible State is not the prime producer of goods nor the distributor of goods. It is not in very close or effective control of the production and distribution of goods. It has no direct and exact means of preventing shortages or gluts. Its guarantee therefore is at most the expression of its faith and belief that, through channels outside its immediate jurisdiction, the necessary goods will be forthcoming. It implies that it will do its utmost to keep the money it issues in a stable relation to the supply of goods, and the confidence and security of the general working community rest in the prevalent belief in its ability and good faith.

This, let us repeat, is the ideal money seen from the point of view of the active individual and the point of view of the commonweal. We are not writing here of the actual money in our pockets, nor of the current state of affairs. We shall come to that later. We are discussing the money that ought to be in our pockets. And clearly this ideal money of which we are writing, can only serve its end of giving a fixed and definite purchasing power, if it is issued in strict relation to the volume of goods available. In other words, a satisfactory money must be a "regulated" money. The circulation must be, as Keynes terms it, a "managed" circulation. It must be barometric. If prices tend to rise, the issue of money should in some manner be restricted; if they tend to fall, the issue of money should be increased. For in no other way can the worker be sure of his due reward in satisfactions and consumable goods.

We are writing here of money from the point of view of its function of working the worker—of providing an incentive to toil. But that is a modern criterion. The idea of money represented *commodities in general* and controlled to that end is entirely modern. In the ruder past, money represented or actually consisted of one single commodity which experience had found convenient and reasonably stable for trading purposes, and the worker was much more frequently satisfied by payments in kind in lieu of or in addition to monetary wages. He did not live so entirely on his wages as the modern worker does—and he did not save to the same extent. His interest in commodity prices was less vital.

Nowadays statisticians give us "index numbers" to show the fluctuations in the prices of commodities. They will give an index number for any particular year to show the general state of prices for all the staple goods consumed by the community in that year. The determination of

TOTAL WEALTH	PER CAPITA WEALTH	PER CAPITA DEBT

INHERITANCE OF WEALTH AND DEBT

POST-WAR estimates of national wealth and debt, showing the inequalities of the debt burden under which children are born in various countries.

such an index number is a highly technical matter.* It is an approximation which can never become precise. But then every quantitative matter in life is approximate. The nature of the indications of the index number will vary with the importance attached to this, that and the other particular commodity. And manifestly our ideas of what is desirable in life, our ideas of what the normal citizen's life should be, will play an important part in the value given to this or that commodity. Social politics cannot be kept out of the index number. But under criticism and acute examination, index numbers can be worked out which will be more and more precisely indicative of the value of money in terms of material welfare—as it is judged by contemporary standards. A managed circulation of money would maintain such an index number at a constant level. The issuing authorities would watch the principal factors in general price movements, such as bank credit, money rates and the prices of raw materials; they would check their deductions by any increases or decreases in the production of goods and the figures of unemployment, and would then make up their minds whether the all important price index was likely to move. If they anticipated too great a rise in prices they would make money dear and restrict bank credit. If prices seemed about to fall they would counteract this by making money cheap and credit plentiful.

All this so far is fairly simple—until we come to working it out in practical detail. The principles are simple. They follow naturally upon our previous consideration of the rôle of money in human motivation. And if we were offering this explanation to one of Mr. Shaw's young men just hatched out of the egg, to whom we referred in § 1 of our Introduction, it would be quite natural for him to say: "Then what is all this bother about money? All this is quite straightforward. Your statistical department tells you—with ever increasing exactitude—how much money you need to have in circulation for the type and standard of life you desire, and you issue it and increase or restrict it accordingly." And if we told him that that was not at all what we were doing at the present time, he would be very much astonished.

When we told him that the issue of money in most of our communities was directly related to the amount of gold stored in certain national banks and treasuries, he would ask us why we chose to introduce this complication into a relatively simple matter. Why drag in the gold at all? What has gold to do with it? Why take this particular commodity of all commodities and pin your monetary issue to that? Why pin

*A good book for the general reader is Irving Fisher's *The Making of Index Numbers*.

money to any single commodity when it has to deal with all commodities?

We should have to answer this, and the first thing we should have to explain to him would be that this complication with gold has not been introduced into a simple business, but that the complication has always been there and that it is only now we are attempting to simplify it away. We should have to tell him that this institution of currency has grown age by age; that it has not been invented suddenly to serve its present ends; and that he must carry his mind back to a past when there was no such thing as currency at all. In fact, we should have to take him to those museum galleries we have already glanced down in the earlier part of this section and tell him the old, old story, how first all trade was barter, how the precious metals were found to be a most convenient intermediary in bartering—you bartered goods for them and afterwards bartered them for other goods—and so how it has come about that to this day the idea of barter, bartering gold, hampers our minds at every turn when we try to work the money invention. We want—to put the thing compactly—to give our ordinary working citizen a certain definite amount of purchasing power; that is the modern idea; but what we do in reality is to give him a bit of gold (or a bill or cheque representing—or purporting to represent—gold) which he then has to trade for what he wants. Our money is not yet actual functional money at all. It is a privileged commodity in disguise. We have built up our modern economic life on the wages system very rapidly and uncritically, and it is only now that we are beginning to see clearly and feel the consequences of the difference in nature between the functional money, the worker's cheque, we now require, and the metallic commodity that has hitherto met our requirements.

"But it would be perfectly easy now to cut the gold out of the story, would it not?", our young man out of the egg would ask.

We should have to embark upon further explanations to show why that is not so easy. To these explanations we shall now proceed. And first it may be advisable to show our egg-born enquirer some of the things that may happen to money when it is liberated from its dependence on gold, and not, as yet, securely tethered to a statistically satisfactory index number. Then he would realize why the world puts its trust not indeed in a golden calf but in a cube of gold measuring rather less than forty feet each way, and why it clings to that block in spite of the greatest strain and hardship, for fear lest worse betide if its grip relax.

§ 3. *The Inflation, Deflation and Devalorization of Currencies*

Let us tell that story as simply as we can and with as little use of technicalities as possible.

From the middle of the nineteenth century until the bills came in for that orgy of waste and slaughter, the World War of 1914–18, the progress of the world in wealth and prosperity had been unexampled and continuous. Indeed, for three hundred years after the break-up of Christendom that progress had gone on. Much of that advance was due no doubt to invention and geographical discovery, but the realization of the possibilities opened up by science and invention, was greatly facilitated by the stimulation brought about by an increasing supply of the precious metals, and—in particular since 1849—of gold. Before 1849 the stimulant was silver rather than gold—silver from the discovery of America onward with gold in the second place. And then gold.

Just how much that enhanced supply of metal for currency was necessary to the modernization of the world; whether the world could have been modernized without an abundance of money is a speculation into which we will not enter. The stimulation is undeniable. Upon successive floods first of silver and then of gold the world was carried from the toil civilization of the past to the power civilization of to-day.

In 1849, gold in great quantities was found in California; in 1851, Australian gold poured in abundantly, and then Canada joined the producers and, richest source of all, South Africa (from the eighties on). Eighty-five per cent of the gold raised in the world has been added to our monetary resources during the past eighty years, and well over half in the present century. This influx of gold provided the world for a time with a world currency, an informal world currency. No one foresaw, no one planned the sudden liquidation of world trade which resulted from this gold flood. It came. And reinforcing it was a steady development of banking and a use of cheques that were, in effect, an addition to currency. But of that reinforcement we will speak later. This increase in the amount and speed of currency, by a happy coincidence, did to all intents and purposes what an intelligent economic world control would have done deliberately. It met the increased productivity of the new railway, steamship, metallurgical era, with just the thing that was needed to prevent a great fall in prices, an arrest of production and unemployment; that is to say, it *increased the volume of available means of payment*. Money was more abundant, credit had increased, and it was easy to repay debts and launch out upon new enterprises. There were fluctuations and crises, but no break-downs; there were sixty years of advance and prosperity. For that period of maximum progress which ended in the war, all the chief countries of the world had currencies based on gold, currencies that underwent no very great fluctuations in regard to one another, and which increased in volume so as to keep pace generally with the ever increasing production and trade of the age. There were undulations in the process, and more particularly between 1873 and 1896, but no catastrophic fall. Mankind paid off the past and faced the future with confidence.

If our young enquirer, just out of the egg, had hatched out in 1910, let us say, we should have told him of the unparalleled merits of this great gift of Providence, the gold standard; we should have expressed no doubts of its permanence; we should have explained how it combined cosmopolitan economics with national integrity, and unless he had the shrewdness to ask certain penetrating questions we should have left it at that.

The war arrested and ultimately broke up this unpremeditated monetary cosmopolitanism. Following upon the outbreak of the war the belligerent governments withdrew gold from internal circulation and resorted to the printing press to replace it. Each in its own measure overprinted. At the close of the war the practical monetary solidarity of the world had disappeared, and the overprinting of paper money continued. Without any concerted action. The exchanges between the various national currencies were fluctuating in a manner that would have been incredible in the tranquil decades before 1914. Each sovereign power was struggling with its own monetary problems, and there was no world-wide realization of the need for an economic conference and board of control to deal with the world's economic situation as a whole. No one saw it as a whole. Providence had kept money working very well for sixty years—and people felt that the benevolent work would surely go on again as soon as things settled down. The Conference of Versailles, a gathering of politicians obsessed by the romantic nationalism of their school books, concentrated chiefly upon the elaboration of good rankling boundary disputes for posterity and upon punitive reparation arrangements that recalled the end of the second Punic War. And each power tried to get the better of the others. The sentimental generosities of the 1914 alliances were all forgotten. Every belligerent country was wounded, damaged, overstrained, irritated, greedy, afraid and in a state of inflamed patriotism. Each victor was resolved to get *something* for the victory. Each, therefore, presently set about the readjustment of its evidently very shaky money arrangements in its own fashion.

For the better part of a century finance had been cosmopolitan and had centred upon London. No one had planned that: it had happened. Finance now became national. A new spirit came into monetary affairs. As long as England had been the world's banker, the Germans, Jews, Italians and so forth, who had controlled the City naturally did not seek any undue advantages for Great Britain. They worked the gold standard by rule of thumb, taking only economic factors into account. Banking was an international service, centring in London. It had concentrated about the London nucleus, quite independently of English national quality. Financially London had never been a national centre, it had been a cosmopolitan focus. The City, throughout its gold-standard free-trading period, had existed not for Britain but for the world. All this was now changed. With the utmost ease the world forgot a monetary unification it had never fully realized.

Nearly every country in the world had been issuing more paper or token money for internal use than its resources justified. That is, there were more tickets for goods than could be honoured at the existing price level. So prices rose to restore the balance between tickets and goods. But in order to meet the interest on their debts, and to pay for war materials, swollen war salary lists, costs of demobilization, reparations, etc., etc., the separate sovereign powers (each in its own fashion) continued to increase the supply of these tickets. That is to say, independently and separately, they *inflated* the currency already in circulation. And with every increase of the volume of issued money, prices rose higher and higher.

Inflated money favours the worker and the active producers against the creditor, because one need not do so much or produce so much to earn a particular sum of money as one would have to do were the circulation not inflated. It is easier to pay off debts, to pay fixed rents, debentures, interest on loans, in a phase of inflation. Also the holders of the national securities, while receiving the monetary interest they had bargained for, get in effect nothing like the original purchasing power of their money. The community as a whole therefore is able to carry its debts more easily. It is true that higher money wages will be eaten into or even eaten up by higher prices, but these in their turn are made up for by increased employment. It is the family wage and not the individual wage which determines the level of working-class prosperity. Every belligerent government was heavily in debt for war expenditure to the creditor sorts of people, and inflation was a very convenient equivalent of bankruptcy. All the world was burthened with debt, and it would probably have eased the world situation immensely if there could have been a concerted simultaneous equivalent inflation of all currencies, if, for example—and disregarding various local adjustments and complications—an ounce of gold had been given three or four times its pre-war monetary value.

Gold at that time was actually cheap, but that was because it was not being used as a standard. It was cheap because it was in abeyance. So soon as there was an attempt to refer money back to gold, it appreciated, and the reality of the situation became apparent.

When an individual goes bankrupt he pays his creditors a fraction, a "dividend" of so much in the pound, to settle his debts. Money is, in effect, the acknowledgment of a debt from the community in general to the individual, and for a community the equivalent of bankruptcy is for it deliberately to pay only a fraction, a dividend, of the purchasing power its money originally represented. That is to say that monetary inflation is for a country what bankruptcy is for an individual. A concerted general inflation was indicated. Such a world bankruptcy would have relieved the situation altogether, and the general economic life, released and refreshed, could have been resumed at a new monetary level in much the same manner as before.

But nothing of the sort was possible in the feverish postwar atmosphere. Impossible reparation payments in gold had been imposed upon the protesting Germans, and the United States had been figuring out and building great hopes upon the debts (reckoned in gold) owing to her by her allies for munitions supplied them for the common effort. America returned to the gold standard in 1919. She returned to the pre-war weight of gold represented by the dollar. Any increase in the monetary value of gold would have enabled the defeated Germans and the debtor countries of Europe to pay with smaller amounts of it. But the more prices were brought down, the more onerous was the repayment of debt.

It is doubtful if this was done with any idea of increasing the burthen of the debt on the debtor countries. It is more probable that the American deflation was carried out in simple obedience to banking routine—because the Federal Reserve Bank of New York was losing gold—and without regard for the effect that it would have on millions of human lives. At all events, the value of gold was raised in terms of goods—the dollar rose 75 per cent in a year relative to commodity prices. Great Britain took the same course of supporting gold, partly because she did not like to allow the pound to fall too far below the dollar, and was already anxious to get back to the pre-war parity of 4.86. Partly, too, the great rise in prices which had taken place during the war—they had risen over three times from 1913 figures—had inflicted a sense of loss on the debt-owning classes, and British finance is in the hands of just those classes. To them any rise in prices savours of dishonesty, even though it may be accompanied by general prosperity, while falls in prices which create millions of unemployed and bring trade to a standstill nevertheless seem mysteriously "sound."

On the continent of Europe the reverse was going on. The French government, for instance, was seeing the franc fall and making no real effort to stop it because it was realized by the business world in France that this was building up French industry and clearing the country of debt. The other European currencies were fluctuating wildly, but the sum of their movements was always in the direction of inflation.

The monetary situation about May, 1920, was one of immense local inequalities. America was back at the gold standard. But there had been a great interruption of economic life and a great diversion of productive energy to supply munitions to the whole of the allies. There had been a lowered production of goods and an inflow of gold, and goods generally were relatively scarcer in comparison with gold than they had been before the war. Prices rose. There was a rise in prices, although there was no deterioration of the currency by the measure of gold. Prices in the U. S. A. in 1920 were, all over, $2\frac{1}{2}$ times as high as they had been in 1913; $\frac{247}{100}$ to be exact. In Britain the gold standard was still in suspense; Britain was using paper money; prices as compared with 1913 were $\frac{324}{100}$ and the pound note was at that level of inferiority, $\frac{247}{324}$ to the gold dollar. Instead of being at its gold parity, which is nearly five dollars to a pound (4.86), it was under four. Many other European countries were much further away from any gold equivalence. They had so increased their uses of paper and token money that prices were soaring to levels hardly measurable by index numbers. In France the rise in prices was slower. French prices took some time before they doubled the British figures. Denmark, Norway, Sweden, Holland fluctuated within still narrower limits.

Each country pursued its own course with a sublime indifference to the common weal of mankind. In America, there was a steady fall in prices. There was also a drastic restriction of credit. By the end of 1920 prices in America were 42½ per cent what they had been in May of that year, and at that level they remained fairly stable until 1929, when a new fall brought them down to the pre-war figure.

Meanwhile the British authorities set themselves to deflate their currency. The issue of money was restricted, credit was restricted; in two years prices were forced down to 50 per cent of the May, 1920, figure, and the process was continued until in a little over four years, parity with the dollar was attained. This involved a tremendous restraint upon business enterprise and a gigantic transfer of wealth from the producing to the creditor classes. People who had bought War Loan with pounds signifying so much purchasing power found themselves receiving interest in pounds of more than double that purchasing value. They were the lucky ones, and the general community paid for their luck.

The rest of the world did not sink so complacently under the yoke of the creditor. Many states did their utmost not merely to shake him off, but to destroy him. A number of governments inflated chaotically. Soviet Russia deliberately inflated the rouble currency to nothing and so pulverized every scrap of savings and abolished its entire creditor class completely. Germany, Austria, Poland and Hungary were all forced to follow the same path. They paid off their internal creditors with rubbish money. No other country went quite so far as these extreme inflationists. But everywhere prices reeled and leapt and staggered. Innumerable modest life schemes were wrecked, and every kind of business was disorganized. Everyone was forced to become something of a speculator; you lent your money, and you did not know whether it would be worth more or less when the time came for repayment; you fixed a price for a transaction, and when the paying time came you were ruined. The varying exchange values of these moneys as they rose or fell in regard to one another produced convulsive movements of goods from one country to another, and there was a vast amount of absolute prohibition of exports and imports, and later a great raising and elaboration of tariff walls, to keep home products at home or to save home industries from avalanches of imports.

The next stage after this phase of chaotic independent inflations was an attempt to return to the monetary cosmopolitanism of pre-war days by a *stabilization* of currencies, that is to say, by restoring the dependence of issues upon gold, either at the old equivalence or at a new equivalence. The American dollar had been put back to its former gold value, the pound sterling had been inflated but, as we have seen, a successful attempt had been made by restricting the issue to "deflate"

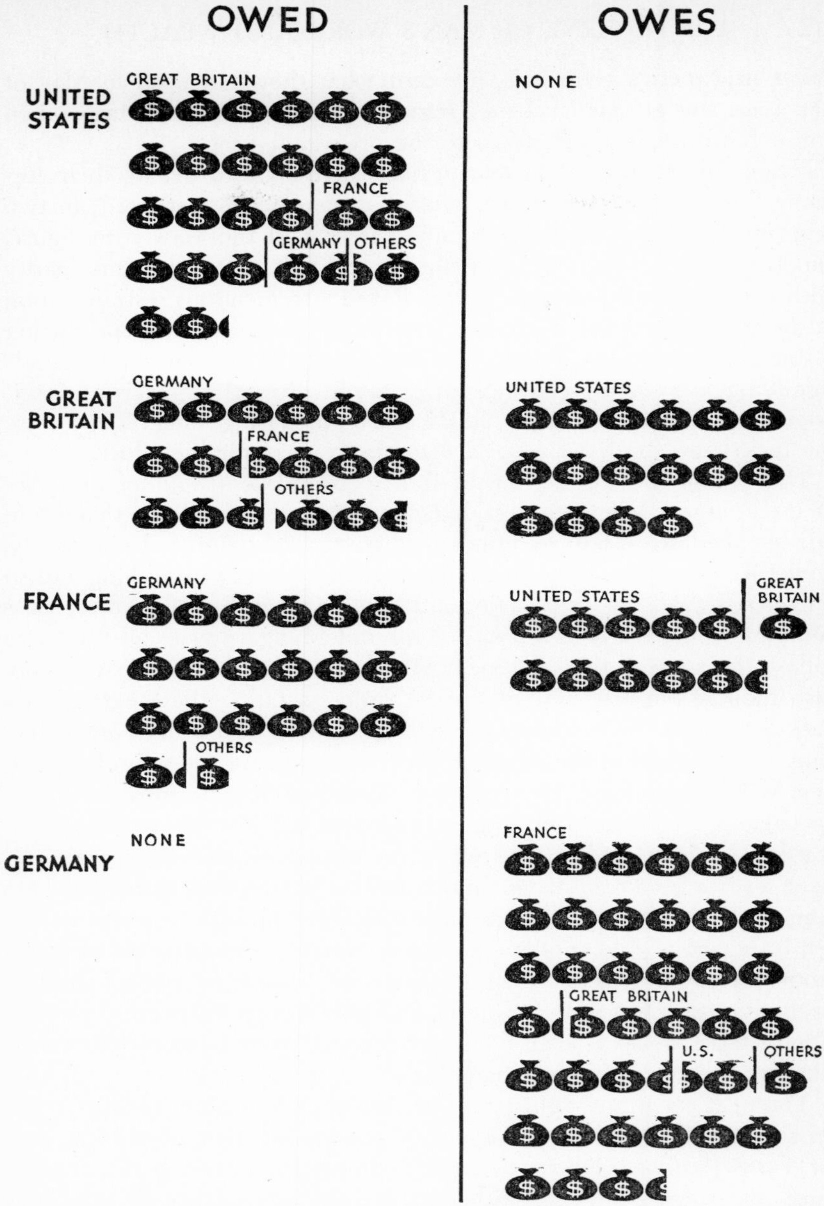

OWED

OWES

UNITED STATES

GREAT BRITAIN

FRANCE

GERMANY | OTHERS

NONE

GREAT BRITAIN

GERMANY

FRANCE

OTHERS

UNITED STATES

FRANCE

GERMANY

OTHERS

UNITED STATES | GREAT BRITAIN

GERMANY

NONE

FRANCE

GREAT BRITAIN

U.S. | OTHERS

THE STATE OF THE GAME OF INTERNATIONAL DEBTS

WITH units of $10,000,000 indicated by a single sack of gold, this chart shows the annual payments which should normally have passed between the principal debtor and creditor nations for the fiscal year ending June 30, 1932.

it up to parity with the dollar; while France, after an alarming plunge towards inflation, frankly accepted the new order of things by *devalorizing* the franc, which had been worth nominally about one fifth of a gold dollar, to a fixed equivalence of about one twenty-fifth. Italy also devalorized. Most of the other debtor countries devalorized.

So in the course of seven or eight years the world was brought back to something formally resembling its previous monetary conditions. Every country except the United States was still saddled with big external debts for war expenditure, payable in gold, and the United States was carrying a big internal gold debt on the same account. Soviet Russia had repudiated its external debts—at a grave injury to its foreign credit and trade—and abolished its internal debts, and most other European countries except Great Britain had had a more or less complete massacre and clearance of their internal obligations. But the workers and producers of Great Britain with its deflated currency, carried an undiminished weight of internal as well as of external debt. Indeed, as we have already pointed out, it was an increased weight so far as the internal debt was concerned, because Great Britain had borrowed enormously when the pound was at an inflation value, and was now paying back at a deflation value. Before, however, we can carry this question of reconstructing a world currency further, it will be necessary to take up certain other contributing issues that enter into the problem.

It will be convenient to return for a moment to our egg-born enquirer. He wanted to know why we did not cut out the gold altogether from our monetary methods, and by way of a partial answer we have informed him of these, the main facts, about the post-war inflations, deflations, and devalorizations. We had to break it to him that the world is not yet an economic unity. The world has not one monetary authority but many, and that is the sort of thing that happens when individually and separately states attempt to get away from gold. The countries of the world are economically interdependent and politically and financially they are independent. Thus far they have been totally unable to get together for any concerted monetary control. That is the gist of the trouble. Until they are able to get together effectively, any modernized world monetary system, released more or less completely from the gold tie and based on a steadily more accurate and trustworthy index figure, is impossible. It may be the plain common sense of the world situation, but it cannot be done. We cannot make money what it surely can be made, a due and trustworthy cheque for social services to the world commonweal. We shall remain at our present stage of comminuted barter. And everywhere money must continue to have uncertain purchasing power dependent upon the available gold supply, and be an unsatisfactory link in the economic machine.*

§ 4. The Gold Standard

After their various experiments in the inflation and deflation of their currencies most sovereign governments of the world had struggled back in a cowed state to the gold standard, that is to say, to barter, through the intermediate bartering of gold or gold notes, which worked so admirably in the great period of human expansion after 1850. But it was not working so admirably this time, for reasons that we will now very briefly examine.

One reason why the gold standard cannot work indefinitely is the inevitable drying up of the gold supply. The amount available from known sources is calculable, and its limits are in sight, and geologists are more than doubtful of the existence of any new gold-fields at present undeveloped. By 1950 competent authorities estimate that new gold production will have shrunken to a fifth of its present volume.† Consequently, while in the pre-war period reliance on the gold standard had the effect of a steady, stimulating inflation, gently dissolving away the relative purchasing power of the creditor, raising wages and encouraging the producer with rising prices, a new period of a restored gold standard is likely to have exactly the opposite effect. Adherence to the gold standard means a progressive deflation of the currency. It will never again have the effect it once had of a regularly and progressively inflated currency. It will tend now to make the patient inactive hoarders of gold the lords of the earth. Public debts under the new conditions will become more and more difficult to meet. Concerns with obligations towards debenture holders and the like will find their overhead charges becoming more and more onerous until bankruptcy supervenes. There will be, therefore, a strangulation of industrial activity and, from this cause alone, (there are several others) a secular progressive fall in em-

---

*A short but clear and stimulating little book which the beginner in these matters will find interesting to read side by side with this and the following sections is J. S. Wardlaw Milne's *The A. B. C. of £. S. D.*

†Lord Brabourne (January, 1931), at the annual meeting of the Consolidated Gold Fields of South Africa, said that in ten years' time the world's production of gold would fall from £85,000,000 to about £55,000,000, and that in a further five years South Africa, which is now responsible for half the world's output, would be giving no more than £10,000,000. From 1910 to 1919 the world produced £900,000,000 of gold; from 1920 to 1929 only £771,000,000.

ployment. All this follows necessarily if the gold standard is maintained indefinitely.

It is absurd that the general economic prosperity of the world should be at the mercy of an unknown probability, the probability whether fresh auriferous deposits will or will not be discovered, but that is how things are while we are ruled by gold.

On the other hand, let us note that the solution, which is quite possible and probable, of the problem of converting baser metal into gold upon paying lines, may also, at any time, if we are to hold to the logic of the gold standard, impoverish or altogether wipe out the *rentier* class and stimulate or overstimulate all the activities of the work and wealth of the world to an incalculable extent. To trust to gold is to put the economic life of the world at the mercy of the unforeseen. It is to rob the world of any pretence to economic justice.

But this approaching exhaustion of the gold supply is not the immediate factor in the unsatisfactoriness of gold as a monetary standard. In the pre-war period the most remarkable merits were ascribed to this metal. It was pointed out that it is almost incorruptible chemically; it could not be forged or fabricated, it has a magnificent stupid honesty. The quantity of gold in the world could be increased only by new production. It remained available even if it was used in the arts, as jewelry and the like. In a fluctuating world it was the symbol of stability. This was all very well in the pre-war period, when the monetary centre of the world was the cosmopolitan, unpatriotic City of London. Then, except for a regular and so not very disturbing amount of hoarding in Asia, all the gold in the world was forthcoming as coin or as a coinable or pawnable metal, and the instinctive unpremeditated cosmopolitan benevolence of the City was ascribed to it. But in this new post-war era of competitive nationalist finance this has ceased to be the case. The United States, which collects debts in gold and wants to sell without buying, has been taking gold out of circulation to an enormous extent. "America," said Lord d'Abernon in an interesting little book, *The Economic Crisis, Its Causes and Its Cure* (November, 1930), "has now the equivalent of 800 millions of pounds sterling in her Central Treasury; France has the equivalent of 414 millions compared with 160 millions five years ago; we" (Great Britain) "have only 150 millions, the same amount as in 1925. Therefore we are not responsible for the *maldistribution or corner in* gold."

This was published a year before the date of printing of this book. By September, 1931, the American accumulation had passed 1,000 mil- ·

lions and the French 500 millions and the British reserve was down to 130 millions.

This cornering of gold was a quite new thing in world economics. It was a breach with all the traditions of the City and all the usages of the expansion period. And it had been one of the chief factors in producing the present world-wide inability of everyone to pay debts or buy or go on producing.

"Since the time of Midas," says Lord d'Abernon, "there has not been a more paradoxical position than that in which America finds herself; for the central reserve vaults are bulging with gold, while in New York and other shipping points warehouses are overcrowded with wheat, with cotton, with copper; all unsaleable except below the cost of production."

In 1931 mankind was getting gold out of mines in South Africa and elsewhere in order to bury it again in treasuries—and to no other perceptible end. It seems a pity to spend all the labour of mining and transport on such an operation. "Ten countries," says the Interim Report of the Gold Delegation of the Financial Committee of the League of Nations, "acquired 1,055 millions of gold dollars during the three years ending December 31st, 1928, a sum equal to nearly 90 per cent of the total amount of new gold mined during this period." In 1929 France and the United States together took 538 millions of gold dollars or probably over two years' supply of new gold. To immobilize it.

National hoarding of gold had taken place before—notably when Germany went on to the gold standard—but it was on nothing like so large a scale. It was an artificial anticipation of the exhaustion of the gold supply, and it had the inevitable effects of discouragement and arrest of business (and human unhappiness) a fall in prices invariably entails. Gold which we had always supposed to be an honest incessant worker, incorruptible if stupid, had been led off unprotestingly from its appointed task to sleep in the national treasuries and work no more.

The Gold Standard had culminated in this Gold Scramble and it was plain that as a cosmopolitan currency it had failed altogether. The world staggered along with it for a time because of the impossibility of immediately imposing another. Exhortation like that of Lord d'Abernon, financial diplomacy, might induce the two great hoarders among the nations to release some or all of the stores of economic alimentation they had amassed, and there might be a helpful resort, as the League of Nations' Report suggested, to an extended use of cheques, credit transfers, and clearing-house, but these were obviously emergency reliefs, palliatives. Before the world, if economic progress was to go on, lay, it was evident, a vaster, more heroic task than any such temporary adjustments—namely, the establishment of a world money organized primarily to give the worker or entrepreneur his sure reward and divested of the last trace of barter. It was due to a conspiracy of favourable accidents that gold money, or money that consisted of tokens or tickets for gold, worked so well during the age of expansion. That age has taught the world what money can be, and sooner or later the human intelligence will see to it that what money can be, money shall be. Meanwhile an educational period of economic stresses and widespread discomfort and misery has come upon mankind. The dominant fact now in the world's affairs is the reconstruction of money.

§ 5. Currency Schemes

The experiences of the past century should have taught the whole world quite convincingly that it needs a currency, that is to say, money, purely as a counter, a cheque, between services and commodities. Such a money is, as we have shown, possible in the measure that trustworthy index numbers can be established. To keep the maximum of people at work, content and hopeful, the issue of currency needs to rather more than keep pace with the increase in the production of commodities. A continuous moderate inflation will be continually easing off the accumulation of debt. And this currency must be a world-wide currency; it can no longer remain under a divided control. All this seems to follow from the present facts of the world situation, when they are viewed broadly and dispassionately from the point of view of social interaction.

Circumstances have recently stirred up the general intelligence to the main factors of the currency situation. It has never hitherto been a very attractive subject. People have avoided it if they could, because it made them feel slightly uncomfortable and had an air of being highly technical and inconclusive—it was at once as intimate and as unconvincing as talk about one's liver—and general discussion has been further burked by dubbing anyone who raised the question, a "Currency Crank." Still, there may come a time when a man will be obliged to look his doctors in the face and consider the state of his liver, and the time has certainly come for mankind at large to consider the working of its monetary organization.

In the preceding sections we have done all we can to show that the elementary consideration of money need be neither obscure nor cranky. The broad lines of the matter become plain enough when we approach them for the study of social motive. It is only when the business is discussed in smart-looking, unsound technicalities and obscured by undefined terms and secondary implications that it becomes difficult. Here we have stuck to fundamental elementary considerations, and the conclusions to be drawn seem as plain as they are sound. It may appear to many that it would be a Herculean, an impossible, a "Utopian" task to bring about any world control of currency. But since plainly the alternative is disaster, that is no reason why the task should not be discussed and attempted.

For some years as the world's monetary situation has been unfolding and becoming demonstrative, there has been an increasing ferment of ideas and a great output of books on this subject. We cannot attempt any detailed examination of that literature, most of which is already out of date, but still it may be advisable here to summarize in the most general terms the nature of the proposals made.

This literature of monetary reform has some very distinctive characteristics. For the most part it has been extraordinarily superficial. Very few of those who have dealt with money have made any attempt at all to go down to its roots in psychology and material necessity. Currency reformers, as we have insisted already, have a way of beginning in the air, high in the air, even more detachedly and arbitrarily than did the old political economists. They assume international competition for prosperity and all sorts of secondary, questionable and transitory complications as though they are essentials in the matter. Few of them approach their subject from the point of view of world interests. And also, few of them are content simply to establish a working generalization. Usually they produce some Scheme or Plan for national, imperial, or (more rarely) universal adoption. They advance it with polemical vehemence. Few of them, except for a passing execration, take notice of the others, much less do they attempt any consideration, analysis or criticisms of previous and competing Plans, Remedies and New Models. Yet since many of them are active, bright-minded people, there is surely a wealth of half truths in this enormous accumulation of suggestions and proposals. Whether that wealth is in paying quantities is less certain. There ought to be an exhaustive classification and analysis of this chaos, and whoever attempts it may count with certainty upon a special circle of enemies of exceptional pamphleteering and epistolary power for the rest of his life. Here we can only note in the most general terms the leading types of project in order to illustrate our present attitude.

The first broad classification of monetary reformers is divided into two sections: (1) those who still cling to the barter core, who insist that some commodity be made the standard of value by the substitution of other commodities for all or some of the gold in use, and (2) those who have already turned the matter about from the point of view of the money manipulated to consider it from the point of view of the worker, and who have realized that money can be detached altogether from standard commodities. We might put together all that former class of projectors as the Old Money School and this latter the New Money School. An outstanding name among the exponents of the New Money ideas is Mr. J. M. Keynes,* whose common-sense suggestions are rapidly spreading into and saturating contemporary monetary thought. The conception of a barometric currency based on an index number is set forth very clearly in that work.

The difficulty that prevents the Old Money School from assimilating the newer views, is the difficulty of escaping from the desire for intrinsic worth in money itself. Whatever token or note is circulated, they seem

*A Tract on Monetary Reform, 1923: A Treatise on Money, 1931. But let us not forget that long before the war Arthur Kitson and Silvio Gesell were writing of managed currencies, though they did not use that term, or at any rate of elastic currencies entirely freed from commodity standards, and Major Douglas was active with his "scheme" before 1920. See Douglas's Economic Democracy and Credit Power and Democracy. Arthur Kitson's Scientific Solution of the Money Question was published as early as 1894, and his Money Problem, in 1903. Professor Irving Fisher of Yale was discussing money from the new point of view a quarter of a century ago and when the story of these ideas comes to be written, his influence will probably be found to bulk very large in their development. (The Nature of Capital and Income, 1906, The Purchasing Power of Money, 1911, e.g.) The history of the origin and interaction of ideas is the most obscure and difficult form of history and priority is rarely to be determined with any exactitude. In no field is this more true than in the one of currency discussion. Gesell will probably be a quite cardinal name in that story when it is unravelled. Most of his Natural Economic Order (Die Naturliche Wirtshaftsordnung) was published in Switzerland in 1906. The ideology of Silvio Gesell and his followers differs widely from that of this book. His doctrines are in agreement with the present work upon the necessity of increasing the amount of purchasing power in the world with increased production, but he would do so by giving the increased purchasing power to the individual producer. And while we would modify or thrust aside individual ownership of natural resources and productive organizations in favour of highly organized collective controls, he would modify or thrust aside the monopolistic and unproductive ownership of natural resources and productive organization in order to give individuals free access to them. From our point of view his projects are projects for chaotic production; from his, the conception of the organized world state we are unfolding here looks no doubt like a collectivist tyranny. Our whole enterprise involves a criticism and repudiation of the uncontrolled individualism of Gesell. We show that the socialization, education and civilization of Homo sapiens is essentially the restriction of individual impulse.

to think, somehow, somewhere it must be "presented" and something of value, a piece of metal or the like, handed over. That is the haunting idea that encumbers their minds. They will accept, as we shall see, the most remote and shadowy refinement of this presentation and payment, but they will not part with it altogether. They have a profound dislike, based on the horrid memories of the post-war currency convulsions, of any money that cannot be brought to the test in this fashion. "Sad experiences suffered by many countries," says Professor Cannan, for example, "have convinced the world that a currency . . . must be made to conform with some outside standard"—and he argues no more about it.

At bottom theirs is a mistrust of the probity and intelligence of their fellow creatures, of even their official and responsible fellow creatures. They believe that index numbers would surely be faked, falsified and manipulated. In the world of a managed currency they ask, they continue to ask, where are you to take your note and present it? The New Money School answers that it can be presented in any shop where you want to buy something. That, for the old school, is not enough. There is something, they feel, disingenuous in such a reply. Any commodity does not suffice them; they want a particular commodity.

Both classes of monetary reformers, the Old Money School and the New, can be divided into two main sub-classes; those who focus their attention upon national or imperial welfare, and those who take a wider view. The former subdivision of each class has hitherto been the more considerable, but the trend of events during the past few years is bringing more and more minds to the realization that nothing effective can be achieved in monetary and financial affairs, except upon a scale that transcends existing political boundaries altogether—upon, in fact, a planetary scale. As this realization becomes general, the projects of both the Old Money School and the New become cosmopolitan.

A considerable body of opinion in the Old Money School has turned towards silver, very naturally, for it is not so very long ago since silver stood in the place of gold as the chief precious metal. The history of silver as a standard of value is a long and very illuminating story, and it may help our exposition here to note one or two salient points. Before this present age of economic confluence began, people lived so "locally" (cp. Fosdick's New England farmer in our Chapter IV, § 4) that international payments were quite a minor interest in public affairs. International trade hardly affected the staple commodities of life. Countries could have quite different standards without serious inconvenience.

1493-1600	
1601-1700	
1701-1800	
1800-1850	
1851-1900	
1900-1925	
1926-1927	

FOUR HUNDRED YEARS
OF GOLD AND SILVER PRODUCTION

ONE of the problems of economists has been the vastly disproportionate increase in the production of silver over the production of gold. This chart, in which each solid black ingot represents the production of ten million fine ounces of gold a year, and each white ingot the production of ten million fine ounces of silver, shows the average annual production of these metals since 1493.

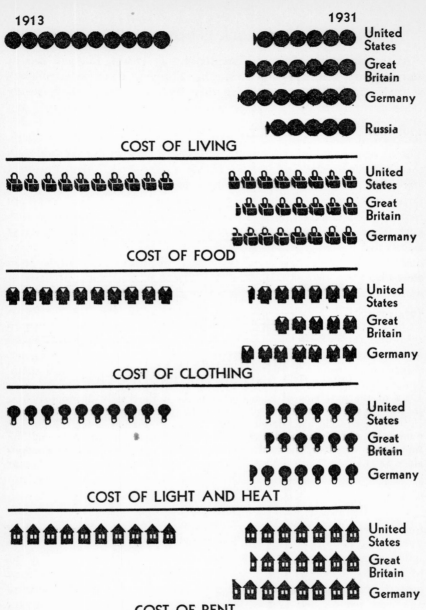

THE INCREASED MONETARY COST OF LIVING

THIS chart shows how the cost of living has increased since pre-war days. The 1913 unit of currency in each country is taken as standard; the symbols on the right represent the proportion of various commodities which the same unit purchased in 1931.

At the beginning of the nineteenth century (1819), England had its currency on a gold basis and most other European countries used silver as their standard. It was believed then that silver had a fairly steady value in regard to gold; 1 oz. of gold was supposed to equal 15½ ozs. of silver, and France (in 1803) on that supposition adopted a double standard of value, that is to say bimetallism; and for a time it worked. The ox of gold pulled the plough of industry amiably side by side with the ox of silver. The ratio in value between the metals in their uncoined state had not changed very strikingly for a long time. J. F. Darling (who makes proposals for the remonetization of silver through an Imperial bimetallic standard of value to be called "Rex"* combined with a restraint upon the export of gold beyond the Imperial frontiers) asserts that it held good for two and a half centuries. Bimetallic arrangements seem to be based on the belief that that ratio holds good eternally. Even that statement of Mr. Darling's is extremely "loose in its handle." There were considerable undulations in the ratio throughout this period. Under William III the ratio was close upon 1 to 16. In 1717, when Sir Isaac Newton was Master of the Mint, it was 1 to 15¼, and the value of the golden guinea was in consequence changed from 22 to 21 silver shillings. In 1760 the rate of exchange between uncoined gold and silver was 1 to 14.14 while the Mint was still maintaining gold and silver on the 1 to 15¼ ratio. How did it manage to do this? It was only coining gold. It had not coined any more silver, says Professor Cannan, after 1717, and it did not do so again until 1816. For a hundred years the English people made their old silver coins, for the most part very worn and reduced in weight, serve their needs. And after 1816 when new silver coins were issued, they were token coins of a less value intrinsically than monetarily, and the ratio did not matter.

Under the fourth dynasty in Egypt silver was more precious than gold. In the days of the Roman Empire the bullion ratio of silver to gold varied about 10 or 11 to 1. In recent years silver, demonetized, has fallen steadily in value; the bullion ratio has descended to 1 to 20, to 30, to 40, 50, 60, and still it tends to sink. On May 23, 1931, the price per oz. was $12\frac{5}{16}$ d., while fine gold remained at its fixed value of £4. 5. 0d. per oz. and standard gold about £3. 18. 0d. per oz. Greater ease of separation from gold, lead, copper, zinc and other metals, is one of the factors in this cheapening of silver. The production of any of those metals involves the production of silver also. No fall in the

*J. F. Darling, C.B.E.: *The "Rex": a New Money to Unify the Empire.*

price of silver can check this "by-product" supply. It has to be separated, anyhow. If the "gold mines" of the world were closed, there would be no more gold, but if all the "silver mines" in the world were shut down, there would still be millions of ounces of silver forthcoming.

In America at the beginning of the nineteenth century, the ratio adopted was 1 to 16, and this did not work, because then it overrated gold. It paid on those terms to change gold coins for silver ones in order to sell the silver abroad or for industrial use at home. The great gold discoveries, from 1848 onward, led for a time to a relative cheapening of gold. Silver began to be driven out of circulation even at the French rate. A fairly obvious fact then dawned upon the world, that there was no divinely fixed ratio of the two precious metals, and that whenever the relative production of one of them increased, the other went out of circulation (this principle is what is commonly called "Gresham's Law"). No system of bimetallism which is not based upon a comprehensive international agreement can overcome this difficulty. It is a difficulty which is bound to arise sooner or later whenever more than one substance is used as a standard.

Professor Henry Clay in his *Economics for the General Reader* points out that bimetallism, the joint use of gold and silver, would be a much more practicable method if all the mints in the world acted in concert to *fix* a price between gold and silver. They would then become a world combine, a world coöperative of precious metal buyers. The chief use of both gold and silver is for coinage; the mints are the chief buyers of both metals, and if they presented a united front to producers, instead of competing against each other for the gold output, production would have to adjust itself to the ratio they determined. The question of the ratio of bullion values would lose its importance. If either metal became more abundant, it would supply the bulk or all of new currency, and the output of its companion would be checked. This would not matter in the least to the general economic process if all the mints of the world were acting together. The rarer metal could not be driven abroad in accordance with Gresham's Law, because there would be no abroad to drive it to. And that nightmare of the exhaustion of the gold supply would be lifted from our minds at once. Such a combine of mints might prove a very helpful preliminary to a world currency control. But that we must consider later on when we take up the question of sovereignty. Let us return to our history of the gold-standard age which is now coming to an end.

In the 'sixties, with gold getting rapidly more abundant, the trend was all against the further use of silver, and in the 'seventies Germany and the United States adopted the gold standard. But (in the 'seventies) the gold output declined for a time, a fall in prices and commercial depression ensued, and the discovery of rich silver mines in America restored more than the former cheapness and abundance of silver. Wherever that metal was still acceptable for coinage it began to push out gold. There was an attempt to get along with a strictly limited amount of silver coin used as well as gold. Gold was to be coined without limit but silver only to a defined amount. This arrangement, the "limping standard," was adopted by France and a group of associated countries. Coined silver by this adjustment became more precious than uncoined silver; coined silver was silver that had been ennobled, so to speak; and forgery became almost an honest trade. All that the forger had to do was to buy silver and make coins exactly like the government ones.

Meanwhile the shrinking of the gold output, the shrinking that is of currency in the gold-standard countries, and particularly in America and Germany, was producing the inevitable consequence of deflation, that is to say, a fall in prices and a phase of world-wide depression (1885–86). These were the great days of the bimetallist agitation. Let silver be rehabilitated, and the required inflation would be achieved. In the United States the struggle for the free coinage of silver side by side with the free coinage of gold went on into the 'nineties; silver became the symbol of release for mortgagors and for every form of debtor, and in 1896 William Jennings Bryan made his great speech about "humanity," debtor humanity, and particularly the mortgaged Western farmer, being "crucified upon a cross of gold."

Then abruptly the Transvaal reefs came into play and the mines of South Africa began to pour so much gold into the world that, although the output of silver also increased in even greater proportion, the monetary tension was released without its intervention, and for a quarter of a century little more was heard of bimetallism. South Africa had pumped new life into the declining gold standard.

Now, in a fresh phase of falling prices, projects for the rehabilitation of silver are reappearing—still with no real solution whatever of the problem of fluctuating relative value that every attempt at a multiple standard must raise. The nearest approach to a reconciliation between the two metals, so that currency can be inflated by the addition of silver without Gresham's Law operating, is the proposal known as Symmetallism, in which a gold-silver alloy is suggested as the single monetary standard. That is really the most thinly disguised inflation imaginable. Exactly the same effect could be got by diminishing the gold value of a pound note and not bothering at all about the silver, because since silver is the cheaper metal it would merely be a diluent of the gold. . . .

Such are the primary facts which account for the present widespread disposition to replace the existing control of currency issues through the commodity gold, by more complicated controls bringing other metallic commodities to the aid of gold. The end sought is inflation. Or at least the end sought is a reversal of the process of destructive deflation that has been going on under the Gold Standard. Always the end sought is a local or general distribution of more purchasing power to producers and increased ease of debt payment.

We will not expand this section further by a more detailed examination of particular currency projects. They are all provisional projects. The broad issue is simple, and it is practically beyond dispute. The arguments that a managed currency, free of entanglement with any standard commodity, under a world board of control, is the best possible currency, are so overwhelming that any other scheme, plan, or project can only be regarded as a compromise, a political expedient, a way of getting round the supposedly invincible opposition of national policy, popular prejudice, and powerful interests, or of carrying on until that opposition can be overcome. In this work we do not admit that opposition is invincible. We believe that *Homo sapiens* is fundamentally sane—if sometimes disastrously slow and inattentive to his proper interests.

The question of carrying on is on an altogether different footing from the broad final necessities of the matter. One must distinguish sharply between the two sets of issues. The world's business must be carried on from day to day. That is a primary political principle. The release of the captive gold in the United States and France or a return to some form of bimetallism through the concerted action of the world's mints may do much for a time to relieve the strangulation of economic life that has been going on. A grave dislocation of the world's economic life, Professor J. W. Scott alleges, has been caused by the demonetization of silver, which has changed over India and China from purchasing communities to communities unable to buy and driven therefore to the worst forms of sweated production. Sir Arthur Salter cites figures which qualify this assertion very considerably. But the conviction is widespread that some manipulation of the standards in favour of silver may restore this lost balance. It is less questionable that the credit boycott of Russia has also driven that country to ferocious exportation at cut prices.

But we must not be lured into questions of current politics and current expediency. Our objects here are descriptive and scientific, not legislative or administrative. Our business has been to show as plainly as possible what money really is and the nature of the difficulties the world is encountering in its use, and there our part ends. It is for the reader to apply these facts to the problems of every day. The final settlement to be sought is the world organization of a New Money based on an index number, but a score of expedients may be necessary to avert disaster and gain time for the propaganda and establishment of the scientific method.

Let us in conclusion recapitulate the essential facts about the New Money idea. Barometric money, "managed currency" is paper money of which the issue and withdrawal are planned to secure stability of purchasing power in general. An index price of staple commodities has to be maintained. If it falls, issue is increased; if it rises, issue is restricted. So the primary end of a sure real value in wages is attained.

But a managed currency would have to be controlled by other factors as well as current prices. In certain circumstances, whenever, for instance, employment and production are increasing rapidly, an anticipatory increase of issue may be needed to keep pace with the general enlargement of economic operations. Where populations are increasing, more money will be needed to provide purchasing power for the additional human beings unless the general standard of living is to be forced down. As a special case of this we may note that as invention progresses an industrial plant becomes more elaborate and expensive, more capital is required to equip each worker in an efficient and modernized industry with the power, tools, machines, etc., which he will use in his task. The Federation of British Industries has estimated that this item has risen in England from under £1,000 before the war to over £3,000 in 1927. The new workers and the new machines are of course a potential source of greater wealth, but unless money is provided to balance this increased potentiality it will only tend to lower prices and dislocate trade. The whole literature of currency we have already noted is permeated by the feeling that the amount of purchasing power in the hands of the public should be subject to a continued slight increase. This is sometimes referred to as "inflation," but as long as it is only desired to *stabilize* prices there is no true inflation. Inflation occurs when prices are made to rise, and this too is often advocated as a method of devaluing money and thus gradually lessening the world burden of debt.

Were this policy adopted, in course of time each unit of currency would cheapen down out of common use and give place to a successor, as in France the double sou is giving place to the franc, and the franc to the five-franc note.

It is evident that the efficiency of barometric money depends very largely on the soundness of the index prices used. At present index prices are often very debatable. To make them quite trustworthy there is need for a trustworthy world-wide system of economic reports. That great and neglected pioneer, David Lubin, almost succeeded in creating a world bureau for the registration of production in Rome, but the war crippled that development for some time. We shall have more to say about his Institute of Agriculture later (Chapter XII, § 7). Slowly but surely it seems that the science of statistics will overtake and resume his fine ambitious effort. We shall become more and more able to anticipate shortages and abundances and the gross and relative values of commodities.

The science of statistics is still only in its infancy—a vigorous infancy. Every year the possibility of "figuring out" quantities in the human outlook increases and the problems of money and credit change. They change in the direction of managed currency and credit scientifically controlled. The rate of that change is dependent largely on the amount of knowledge and understanding available. To this idea we must return after we have directed the reader's attention to the speculative element in all contemporary business enterprises.

§ 6. The Bank

From an examination of these remarkable monetary counters by which our unconsolidated, fragmentary world civilization is still so painfully, so distressfully, endeavouring to compute its affairs, we must pass to the elementary phenomena of credit. We come back to the counting house and board room. We have to ask how the entrepreneur carries on, between the beginnings of his enterprise and the payment for the goods his enterprise has produced. We have seen him first paying out and later on receiving money again. Who hands him the money in the first instance, and why does he send his takings to the bank?

The history of banking is a comparatively simple one. It is easy to trace and understand its development from the time when it was a mere expedient for storing valuables and minimizing the dangerous transport of money by means of bills of exchange.

At first banking and usury had very little to do with each other. One was an affair of safe-keeping and the other was an affair of safe-lending. I suppose the earliest usury, the usury of the ancient world, was practised because cultivation had to carry on until harvest, or after a bad harvest, and the loan was material sustenance for which the cultivator pledged his future produce. Or else it was sustenance of the merchant until the ship or the caravan came home. Or it was supplied to the monarch embarking upon a raid or conquest that promised to be remunerative. In the ancient world, the temple was the primitive treasure-house, pawnshop and loan-office of the community, and some god the nominal lender. The priest was the first financial expert.

I do not know how far the financial expedients of the ancient world were carried over into the reviving economic life of mediæval Europe. What is desirable—I do not know if it is at present practicable—is a study of the evolution of ideas about credit loans and usury in the ancient world, an account of the financial methods prevalent under the Roman and Byzantine Empires and the way in which these ideas and methods emerged again, modified or not, after centuries of social and political collapse in western Europe, as social security was restored. There may have been a practical continuity. There may have been fresh initiatives. Ordinary history helps but little here. Scholars have always been disposed to condemn account books. What we want is a History of the Counting House. Few historians of the old school escaped sufficiently from the blinkers of language and national traditions to attempt anything of that kind. But a competent history of finance would have to flit from Constantinople to Venice, from South Germany to the Hansa Towns, and wherever credit was showing itself and new devices were working.

However wide and diverse that preliminary survey, the broad treatment of modern banking conditions would begin with the returning abundance of trade and money in the sixteenth century and the extension of arrangements for its deposit. The goldsmiths, who were developing into bankers, took care of money and issued signed receipts; the receipts were made payable to bearer and the bank note was evolved. It was an age of religious dissension, and the Christian temple never recovered the financial prestige and advantages of its Semitic and Egyptian predecessors. It kept the primary religious domination over marriage and burial and education, but the new economic developments remained outside its influence. It restrained the believer from usury, so that before the Protestant reformation produced a new Christian business persona, the Jews were given something like a monopoly of money-lending.

It was soon realized that the deposit and issuing bankers who were appearing could lend out part of their money in hand, so long as they had the confidence of the public and there was no danger of a run upon them. They were thus able to attract deposits by paying interest in the place of charging for their services, as they did at first. From these beginnings the banking organization grew rapidly. A long history of legislative control, the definition of banking activities, and the creation of national and central banks, would have to be given to display this growth with any completeness. But here again that capacious and inclusive *Science of Work and Wealth* of ours may very conveniently relieve these pages. The broad effects of the growth of banking were these. It utilized and vitalized savings. Under mediæval conditions, which held good almost up to the present time in India and China, savings were either hoarded as treasure or spent upon display, palaces, gold plate and jewels. Nowadays everyone has a paying use for savings, and they are all turned back, practically, for the animation of industry. Even the European peasant's stocking has unravelled and released its hoard. The bangles of the Indian women will follow the bank-ward movement. Business which in pre-banking days would have had to keep a treasure chest out of which to pay wages, buy material, finance particular operations, now goes to the bank for a short-term loan.

Unexpected consequences of banking convenience have appeared. The idea of the cheque was a very obvious and simple one, and yet its working out leads us towards results of a quite remarkable kind. The opening nineteenth century saw the rise of the cheque to an importance far exceeding that of the restrained and regulated bank note. Even allowing for the increasing production of gold, it is doubtful if the great economic expansion of that period could have occurred without the cheque. It let out the financial clothing of the growing economic giant who might otherwise have been strangled. If cheques were forbidden to-morrow, all the money in the country, even if no one held any for more than a day, would scarce suffice for half the needs of the very slackest working of our economic life. An enormous amount of the business of the English-speaking communities is now transacted by cheque without the shifting of a bank note or the movement of a coin.

The clearing-house has become an organ of primary importance in economic life.

The use of the cheque is by no means equally developed throughout the world, and its handling varies in different countries. French business, for example, is much more realistic than English, and for transactions of a few thousand or a few score thousand francs a larger proportion of at least paper money passes from hand to hand. But the experience of a century is making it clear that, except for the convenience of paper or coins for small immediate transactions, it would be possible now to dispense with actual concrete money altogether; it would be possible to sustain the general working of an entire economic system by clearing-house bookkeeping, by the continual transfer of money of account, of crude "purchasing power" that is, from one account to another.

This consideration alone opens out a very interesting prospect of the future of banking. If it is possible to get away from money to this extent, it may be possible to get away from it to a very much greater extent. There must be many imaginative and scientific minded bankers and statisticians who have already glimpsed something of a phase in economic development to which these facts may be pointing. If it has already become possible to carry on a voluminous tangle of productive and distributive activities with all the monetary side simplified down to cheque sorting and bookkeeping, may it not be possible, ultimately, to carry on the whole productive and distributory system of mankind on a basis of debit and credit entries of purchasing power to the account of this or that community or association or individual?

It is difficult to discover any inherent impossibility in such a suggestion. One can think, of course, of a jungle of manifest obstacles, at present trackless, but I should imagine that any banker who is not the mere creature and slave of routine, must apprehend to some extent this conception of a world system of current accounts and cheques, comprehensively embracing all his particular activities and providing a medium for the final adjustment of the main economic discords of our present world.

§ 7. *The Contemporary Evolution of Banking*

It is by the criterion of this possibility, the possibility of the banking system of the world becoming a complete guiding record of "purchasing power" from day to day, that we must appraise contemporary banking organization and usage. Banking falls far short of that possibility, but it is not at an immeasurable distance from it. The story of the *record of purchasing power,* the story of modern banking, that is, runs on lines closely parallel to the story of modern industrial development. We shall have to note the same rapid progress in a century or so from small completely independent personal enterprises enormously various in their character and trustworthiness, to vigorously competing companies, and so on to grouping, associated working and amalgamation.

But here the factor of State intervention, regulation and participation, is from the outset more important. In the United States, for example, there are legal restraints upon the opening of branch offices by banks. Consequently, small independent local banking concerns, of very unequal stability, take the place there of the local branches of the great amalgamations that one finds everywhere in Britain or France. The tradition of international malevolence also plays an even more important rôle in hampering the extension of banking systems beyond national boundaries than it does in restraining the production and distribution of commodities.

A full, illustrative and descriptive history of human credit methods would include an account of the earlier, more adventurous days of banking and of typical "runs," stoppages of payment and failures. Much material for this lies buried in the newspaper files of the nineteenth century. Those were the days of "romantic" banking. In America, for the reason just stated, local banks remain romantic. As the story approached contemporary conditions it would carry an increasing quantity of pictures of the typical buildings and other tangible property of banking concerns and give glimpses of strong-rooms, safe-deposits, and the like. Half the prominent street corners of London witness now architecturally to the great wealth of the modern banking corporations, and in Professor Soddy's *Money Versus Man* the reader will find a bitter protest against the extraordinary privileges that have favoured this accumulation.

The State gives banks the privilege of issuing money and then borrows money at interest from the banks. That, on the face of it, seems more than a trifle absurd. But we shall give a reason for that absurdity a few pages further on. The State, we shall find, is too afraid of its own temperamental fluctuations to issue money and reap the profit of the issue itself.

Our next exhibit, so to speak, in the banking section of our survey, will show the entrepreneur in conference with the bank manager. The rôle of the latter varies between that of the mere self-protective and

acquisitive money-lender and that of the sympathetic (and even encouraging and stimulating) associate. But there is always a risk that
sympathetic participation may pass into interference and control, and a
mind directed mainly to security and profit may see a business organization from a widely different angle than the point of view of the
creative entrepreneur. In all great industrial organizations there must
be a constant risk of conflict between material and financial considerations, and especially, when monopolies are created either by natural
conditions, patent rights or tariff protection, is there the danger of
holding back improvements in method while profits are still being made
upon obsolescent lines.

The whole trend of the mass of description and narrative our
imaginary encyclopædia would assemble, would be to show how far
we are as yet from that unified, simplified exchange of purchasing
power which is the ideal bank. Things have progressed far enough to
render that ideal conceivable and credible, but they are still at an incalculable distance from its effective realization. It is as yet only in his
moments of exaltation and lucidity that the banker is able to think of
himself as the guardian of the measure for human interaction; for
ordinary everyday purposes he is still under the sway of a long tradition
of profit-seeking. In the latter phase, if his practice is less satisfactory to
his higher nature, it is certainly more grossly sure and gratifying. Only
a change, not merely in his own ideology, but in the standards by
which people judge and esteem him, can alter that.

Such a change is certainly going on at the present time. A time may
come when profit-seeking banking will not be tolerated and all banking operations will be recognized as vital public services. That does not
mean that banks will be "nationalized." They tend through the natural
development of financial affairs to become quasi-public organizations
side by side with the politician's governments. Already "profit-seeking"
is a rather excessive phrase for most great banks. There is much legal
limitation upon their capital, and upon the dividends they may pay
their shareholders. They may have maximum and minimum dividends
fixed for them.

What are called central banks, about which we have more to say,
are in several countries partly or entirely the property of the State as
the chief or only shareholder. There is a great variety of such restraining arrangements, summarized very clearly in Kisch and Elkin's *Central
Banks*. There is more or less legal restraint upon all banking businesses.
The modern banker arose out of the townsman-trader tradition, but he

is rapidly assimilating the educated ideology. His manner nowadays mingles the reserve of the confessional with the alertness of a responsible controller. The vast amalgamations of Joint Stock Banks, banks of enterprise, that have occurred in recent years, tend to transfer the direction of banking more and more from bank "owners" to scientifically trained functionaries, who look not to profits but to promotion as the result of their work, and whose pride is rather in honour and prestige than in super-abundant riches.

The possible and probable development of the world's banking system towards a central exchange, a world clearing-house of purchasing power, becomes still more evident when we turn our attention to the way in which currency control is passing out of the hands of governments into the hands of a system of central banks. At first (in the eighteenth century, e. g.) bank notes were simply the promissory notes of banks to pay definite sums of cash at sight, and governments everywhere were the sole money-issuing authorities. Then in the interests of the public the banks were obliged legally to hold more or less adequate reserves of money to cover their notes. There was more and more restriction upon the right to issue notes, as the notes became more and more manifestly an accessory currency. Then from being accessory currency bank notes became the main currency. They are ousting metallic currency everywhere, except small-change metallic tokens. The period of monetary confusion that followed the Great War created a strong disposition to transfer currency issue from the direct control of politicians to expert management. Kisch and Elkin quote a declaration of the Irish Free State Banking Commission that is very significant:

"Mindful as it is of the disasters of past years in all countries where currency was issued by the Government, and recognizing the hazards which come from changes of Government, from the development of budget deficits and other evils from which no country has found itself immune, the Commission is definitely of the opinion that the management of the legal tender note issue should be placed in the hands of a non-political and independent body, which shall control the conditions of issue and shall have full control and custody of the securities it holds."

These are the ideas that have ruled the post-war development of Central Banks throughout the world. With comparative rapidity a network of these organizations has been created either by special modifications of the constitutions of preëxisting national banks, or by the creation of new ones, and from them it is, and not from the State directly, that the money now used by the ordinary citizen comes. This banking nexus, working with a considerable and increasing detachment from politicians, diplomatists and the press, is a comparatively new and most interesting organization in the economic life of the world. Its full possibilities are still largely unexplored.

We shall note in Chapter XI, § 10, and in Chapter XII, § 13, certain new broad strands that have come into existence since 1929 to make this banking nexus still more effectively cosmopolitan. These strands are still too new for judgment; they are the Bank of International Settlements at Basle and its projected associates the International Trust and the International Mortgage Bank.

Here, because of the living interest of the subject, instead of motioning our reader towards museum galleries vanishing into imaginary perspectives and nonexistent encyclopædias, we will name a few recent books that he will find informative and stimulating if he wants to expand what is given here. There is no really comprehensive history and description of banking in existence, but the interested reader may be referred to *A History of Modern Banks of Issue* by C. A. Conant (6th edition, 1927), which is thoroughly good within its scope, and *Currency and Credit* by R. G. Hawtrey (1928), which deals very soundly with the general theory of money and the theory of banking. His Part II, "Historical Illustrations," describes most of the great banking crises from the Middle Ages onward. There is as yet no outstanding history of Central Banks or Central Banking. The history of cosmopolitan banking is being made but it is not yet being written. Kisch and Elkin (1930) give the constitutions of various Central Banks and the statutes governing them. *The History of the Bank of England,* by Andreades (translated from the Greek), is also well worth reading by the student.

These books will give methods of dealing and figures, but to make this part of our picture of human activities concrete and vivid something more is needed. How can we conjure up the visible manifestations of this banking network that now binds the vast complex of work and wealth together? At prominent corners, in busy streets, wherever there are towns and cities, rises the stout and handsome architecture of the banks. Within are the familiar bank desks and counters with their brass rails and guichets; altogether there must be miles and miles, hundreds of miles, thousands of miles of desks and counters; and clerks, clerks now by the hundred thousand, by the

million, busy, intent, entering up billions and billions of transfers of
purchasing power, sorting cheques, adding, subtracting, balancing.

Already the world's clearing-house for purchasing power, which may
ultimately supersede the use of all money but small change, is half
evolved.

This also we add now to the panorama of mines, plantations, factories, warehouses, docks, shipping, railroads, habitations, villages,
towns, cities we have evoked, culminating in those goldmines where,
with the use of the most skilful organization, the most efficient apparatus, the most beautiful applications of modern science and the toil
of many thousands of workers, gold is released from the quartz rock in
which it was disseminated countless ages ago, to start forth on its long,
indirect and solemnly idiotic journey to be sterilized in the vaults of
the hoarding powers.

§ 8. *The Modern Fragmentation of Ownership*

So far it has been simple and convenient to speak of the entrepreneur
as though he were a single person, a man of the peasant-townsman type
touched by imagination and larger ideas. That is what he was. But the
fruitful device of joint-stock enterprise, fruitful of evil as well as of
good, has long since made the entrepreneur no longer the organizing
owner of an enterprise, but simply the organizer of its ownership. A
very large and miscellaneous body of prosperous people, "the investing
public," now exists whose wealth consists partly or wholly of the shares
or obligations of enterprises over which they exercise no control, or of
loans made to governments or public bodies equally outside their range
of personal activity.

The expenditure arrangements of this comparatively novel class of
people are fairly uniform. They carry about with them a small amount
of ready money, which they constantly renew from the current account
they have open at the bank. This current account, according to the
fortunes of its owner, credits him with a few score or a few hundred
pounds. Any more purchasing power than that, waits in a deposit account bearing interest, from which usually it can be withdrawn at short
notice, either to be brought forward into the current account for actual
spending, or invested. Behind the current and deposit accounts come
the "securities" which constitute some or all of the investor's possessions. These may be stored for the investor in the bank's strong-room,
or in the investor's solicitor's bank, or in a strong-box, and normally

they can be converted into cash (at variable prices), in a few days. They
are from the owner's point of view a sort of money, a slightly con-
gealed purchasing power, which may be liquidated with reasonable
facility and which has the advantage of yielding higher interest than
the deposit account and possibly increasing in value, but which also
carries grave risks of deterioration.

Such is the typical investor's position; he is essentially a concentration,
small or great, of irresponsible purchasing power. To borrow a term
from biology, the body politic has *secreted* him as an oyster secretes a
pearl. But his reaction on the social body is much more considerable
than the reaction of the pearl upon the oyster.

The existence of this stratum of people, wholly or partly supported
by investments in businesses over which they exercise no control, or in
the loans made to governments and public bodies, at home and abroad,
is one of the most important differences between the social structure of
the modern community and any previous state of society. In every
preceding phase where there has been a concentration of wealth it has
been far less easily converted into kinetic purchasing power and far
more burthensome upon its owners. Securities are an abstraction of
purchasing power hardly less mobile and irresponsible than a cash
balance. That causes a great complication of the currency question. In
the preceding sections we have talked of monetary inflation sending up
prices and deflation sending them down. But easy credit and a rapid
movement of cheques are in their effect indistinguishable from inflation.
And so also is a general rise in the prices of securities during a boom
period. A phase of hopefulness among security owners and buyers—to
all intents and purposes *inflates*.

It would be an intricate task to disentangle the statistics that conceal
the relative importance of the income earner (individually and collectively) and the investor, as spenders. I am inclined to think we shall
find the investing public is now quite dominant in the exercise of purchasing power so soon as we consider any but the broad staple necessities. The investing public calls the tune for the rest of production. Its
demands and its refusals determine the forms and quantities of all that
production. It is the decisive customer in the world of work, the free
buyer.

There is no great freedom in buying below a certain level of individual prosperity. It is a delusion that individual buying gives the
freedom to get what you want. You get what the shops will let you
have. Unless you are very wealthy and will take the trouble to order

and have exactly what you want made, your buying is only a few degrees more free than if a socialist autocrat gave you what he thought good for you. You may buy model A or model B or model C. That is the limit of your freedom of choice. You are served out your necessities wholesale, and live by a definite standard. Your spending, at the middle class or any lower level, is dictated for you almost as much as your work. You *must* have this, you *must* have that, and by the time you have got this, that, and the other thing you cannot do without, your money has gone.

But as the individual earner's income rises above the demands of his standard of life, as he begins to "make money," he enters either partially into the investor class by purchasing securities, or he expends his money as his fancy dictates upon pleasures and an increased consumption of perishable goods, or he acquires material property for exploitation or enjoyment. The prevailing practice is probably, in the first phase, investment. The first impulse is to "put something by." The prospering money-maker does not immediately expend his surplus, but puts it out to earn interest or dividend and so supplement his own earning power. He withdraws this sum from the to-and-fro dealing of consumer and producer to increase the capital wealth of the country, and then he sits down to wait for the interest or dividend to come to him. Then, feeling safer, he readjusts his purchasing activities to his new scale. He launches out upon that new scale. He begins to signify now to the advertiser. Will he have a new automobile or a better automobile? Will he enlarge or refit his house? Or his wardrobe? Will he travel and see the world? Or will he reinvest and grow still richer? He has become one of those people who—in the measure of their freedom of initiative—command the world. The producer considers his wishes.

Let us ask how this investing and spending public, this most characteristic and influential stratum in the existing social order, achieved its present importance. It is not very ancient history. We shall need only to glance back to the sixteenth century to see a social system in which none but the actual holders of very real property, or people with money in pocket or strong-box, had any purchasing power at all. To own anything was a task. Rents, tithes and taxes formed the wealth of the rich and powerful, and they needed constant watching, collecting and administration. A mediæval strong-box, with its mighty locks and its key that had to be hidden, was a dreadful monster in comparison with a cheque book. The borrowing power of governments was slight. Partnerships were active and very personal, and only a few chartered trading companies had transferable stock. The free-spending investor was unknown.

It was not until towards the end of the seventeenth century that business corporations and trading and industrial companies appeared in any abundance in the world. They were simply partnerships with transferable shares and undefined liability. The great speculative storm of 1720 in France and England, the Mississippi scheme and the South Sea Bubble, marked the appearance of the investor as a serious factor in the world's affairs. Probably few of those who were ruined in these crashes were independent investors, people who had "made money" and were seeking a use for it; they were land owners, merchants, farmers and sinecure holders in a wild fever to grow much richer. They were people who sold their concrete property in order to invest; they brought their skins into the business. The mass of the modern "investing public" is not doing that.

There was a steady development of this new form of mobile wealth in stock and share, and a concurrent expansion of national debts, through the eighteenth and early nineteenth centuries, leading to the epoch of larger business organizations, of gas companies, railways, ship canals and town building, that followed the recovery from the Napoleonic Wars and the spread of invention and imaginative enterprise. We have traced already how this larger handling of affairs became mechanically possible, and now here we have to note how it became financially possible. The entrepreneur had insufficient credit for these enlarged undertakings, and so he had to call upon the credit of others. He had to form companies to share and realize his hopes. Company promoting became an art and a profession, businesses were merged, vast new adventures were contemplated, and the proportion of the economic apparatus in the country owned by company shareholders increased rapidly. This development was enormously facilitated by the device of limited liability, which with due legislative precautions gave a long-needed reassurance to the hesitating investor.

Within a few decades there was a great increase of the productivity of the world; a considerable expansion of population followed, and the rate of its increase rose to a maximum and declined; individual wages rose with relative slowness, but the numbers of the earning class multiplied greatly, and there was in particular an immense proliferation of the investing public and of the organization of investment. A new and growing system of purchasing power was arising, not in equivalence to, but in association with, and dependent upon, increased production, and it was diverting a large amount of the increased product both from the active earner and the genuine economic entrepreneur on the one hand, and, on the other, from the landowner, the rent receiver, into the pocket of the investor.

The contrast between the economic life of four centuries ago and life under the new conditions can be easily stated. The social-economic process of the sixteenth century distributed the power to acquire its product, that is to say, purchasing power, as wages, as profits of manufacture or trade, as rent, as interest upon incidental loans, and as taxes in support of the still very undeveloped State and such other public organizations as then existed. By the middle of the nineteenth century the same process had become much vaster and more highly organized, and in addition to the former recipients of purchasing power, workers, traders, landlords, usurers, tax-gatherers, there was now added this great and growing body of inert investors, receiving interest or dividends, and constituting a vast expansion of those formerly rare and minor items, the money-lender and the sleeping partner. The State and public bodies were now not only functioning in new and elaborate and expensive ways, but they were also carrying a great and growing burthen of debt, so that the share of purchasing power over the general product which was assigned to taxes was rising steadily, to be returned in part to the community in services, and in part paid to the State's creditors, the investing classes. The old social classifications had changed both in their proportion and in their nature because of the great expansion of this practically new class of investors.

That change continues. The war preparation of the opening years of the twentieth century, the Great War and its legacy of unsettlement, have enormously increased the public debts of the world, and the pressure to buy War Loan has, in America particularly, extended downward the disposition to invest to classes hitherto innocent of aught but petty hoarding. Beneath the body of investors who live mainly or entirely on their investments, comes a stratum, a multitude now, of earners, who may be, as regards a quarter, or a tenth or a hundredth part of their spending incomes, investors. The investor's income is taxed heavily, but so far as his money is directly or indirectly in public securities, a sufficient part of it returns to him to leave him now the dominant purchaser, albeit not the chief consumer of common needs, in the world's markets to-day.

In Socialist and Communist literature, that ill-defined term, the

Capitalist System, is abundantly used. Because of its confusing implications I have preferred not to use it here. What these thinkers of the Left have in mind when they say "Capitalism" is just this predominant presence of the investing public, the creditor public, in the social organism. But they seem to think the investing public exists through some inherent malignity of its own; they do not realize that it is an inevitable and necessary part in the confused evolution of a world economic system. There is a continual production for profits and a continual withdrawal of a proportion of these profits from consumption to investment and the creation of further capital demanding further dividends. The creditor mass, the debt burthen, increases steadily therefore until bankruptcy, inflation or—the Communist would add—revolutionary repudiation, relieves the economic body.

§ 9. Contemporary Investment Practice

The voluminous pages of that non-existent encyclopædia of Work and Wealth, would afford space for a detailed account of the current methods of company promotion and the flotation of public loans. It would explain the varieties of investment, in ordinary and preference shares, in debentures, in public loans. It would give a conspectus of the variations in company and corporation law in different countries, and the methods of subscription and sale. The reader would be taken in imagination to some of the world's stock exchanges with their supplementary outer markets, and be shown something of the manners and graces of these vortices in the modern economic process.

At these centres, from which financial stimulus or restraint radiates out to the material processes of world production, there is an incessant uncertainty and fluctuation of values, and a whole world of human activities concerned primarily with these fluctuations. An immense amount of human intelligence is being directed to the safety and "yield" of every item in the list of quotable and buyable securities, and beyond the acute professional practitioner, selling and buying to achieve a maximum of income and safety, is this whole vast "investing public" of ours, never altogether indifferent to the falling and rising prices and payments upon which it counts for its sustained purchasing power, and very prone to moods when better returns seems imperative, or when distrust chills the heart and panic impends. Climatic vagaries, bad crops and excessive crops, sudden revelations of mineral resources, new methods of production and unexpected inventions, fire, flood and political stresses, are all reflected in the plus and minus entries of the price list of stocks and shares.

But the stock and share market is not merely a barometer to register the unpredictable weather changes of the economic life of the world outside. It has also moods and pressures and storms of its own, originating within itself and having also heavy repercussions on the general life of the community. A study of company promotion reveals how great are the temptations to overestimate the price and prospects of any undertaking that is offered to the investing public. There is a natural disposition to "overcapitalize" undertakings and to exaggerate the permanence of profitable returns. There is so much hopefulness in man that, according to Mr. Mellon of the United States Treasury, as much as 1,000,000,000 dollars is lost annually in the too sanguine investments of American citizens. Much of this may be due to honest miscalculation, but a considerable proportion, it would seem, goes to support an interesting industry of deliberate investor exploiters, who deal systematically in unsound and bogus securities. There exists a very complete organization for this exploitation; there are even registers of "suckers" who may be trusted to subscribe to almost any rotten project that is put before them with sufficient attractiveness. A special study of the methods by which these trash dealers acquire their thousands of millions of purchasing power would make an entertaining and instructive section in our encyclopædia. There must be thousands of them and their families, rich but, one imagines, a little indisposed to "talk shop." If you are prosperous enough you may have sat beside some of these browsers upon the investment public last night at the theatre, or travelled very pleasantly with them in the train de luxe. Our sons and theirs may become great friends at college.

Hopefulness is a recurrent epidemic in America, and, as we shall show by a study of the 1929–31 boom and slump, it is possible to have a whole community overcredulous of values and prospects. While the mood lasts, everyone seems to be making a fortune, and purchasing power is used to stimulate industry to the utmost. The prices of securities rise— and bull speculators (buying for the rise) push them up still further. As we have pointed out already, this works almost exactly in the fashion of currency inflation. When a phase of disillusionment arrives, buying ceases, and workers are thrown out of employment by the hundred thousand and bereft suddenly of purchasing power. Their slackened demands further intensify the slump, and so the slump continues.

From these phenomena our encyclopædia of human activities would pass to the various methods of operating upon the exchanges. It would tell of bull and bear operations; of the way in which bear sellers of stock may be "caught short" and "skinned" and so forth. The fine question of how far a man may sell what he has still to buy cuts down to the roots of incessantly recurring financial situations. The foundation of considerable fortunes has been this dubious expedient of anticipatory selling. Some able but practically impecunious salesman has induced a seller or sellers to quote a price to him, or has secured an option to buy, and has then found either a purchaser at an advanced price or a bank willing to support him until he could put his proposition to the investing public. Such intervention, with a great range of variations, constitutes indeed a conspicuous part of contemporary "business." If the adventurer can keep his credit throughout the transaction he "gets away with it"; he becomes one of the New Rich, a Power in the financial world. If bankers become unfriendly, if they decide to call in his credit and he can find no friend to help him, he must unload what he carries, at disastrous prices. He is "skinned." There may be bankruptcy and suicide or effacement. Here too we find a system of inexactitudes and uncertainties that do not merely admit, but invite and provoke, the speculator and the cornerer, the seeker of wealth without work, the bold and brilliant parasite upon the sap and vitality of the economic body.

All the matter sketched out in this section will be so familiar in a fragmentary form to most readers that few will find it anything but natural and inevitable. It is, however, if we measure it either by former social conditions or by utopian standards, a very extraordinary state of affairs in which we are living. The modern world of work and wealth, with all its industries, cultivations and distributive organizations, has been evolved *pari passu* with the development of the investing and speculative public, as the desert camel was evolved with its hump, or the elk with its antlers; it has been all part of one evolution; and no one has ever yet speculated what changes of the environment, great or small, legal, political or "natural," might have developed the creature in a different form, with a smaller hump or a lighter burthen of bone and horn. Nor have we any measure yet of the extent to which, or the rapidity with which, this hump may not under changing conditions be reabsorbed into active nerve and muscle. Or whether the whole organism is so tied to its hump that it will perish rather than lose it.

§ 10. *Is the Investing Public More than a Transitory Excrescence upon Economic Development?*

A very natural enquiry arises here. This is the question: how far uncertainty is inevitable in economic processes, and how far a more scientific handling of the quantitative, distributive machinery of mankind may not eliminate most of the weaknesses of the system that renders this fungoid growth of large speculative fortunes, and the still larger growth of speculative fortune-seekers, possible.

After all, we have to remember that the present state of affairs is recent and novel. Our world has not always suffered from the superposition of a great creditor class "living on debt." Our civilization has been floundering about with experiments in partnership and joint-stock enterprise for only a brief century or so; limited liability dates from 1855. We have been realizing as yet only the crude possibilities of invention and science, and it is altogether too much to assume that the first adaptations of the old property-money-credit ideas to these new powers and their new range were anything but provisional.

Behind the adventurer, the speculator, comes that scavenger of adventurers, the statistician. He ends adventure and cleans up the mess. The method of trial and error will surely give place to analysis and the plan. Enterprise will then cease to look for support to the casual investments of ill-informed amateurs. Industrial projects will become more and more exactly calculable. *Pari passu,* the company promoter, will be brought under more effective control; there will be a more critical supervision of his acts and a readier jail for his delinquencies. And the "investing public" will gradually be helped and persuaded to avoid spasmodic investment, and its search for a safe return turned into new and less adventurous directions.

Perhaps it would not be a bad thing for the world's work if this swarm of amateur distributors of purchasing power were restricted altogether from direct investment in business enterprises. At present there is a very remarkable development of "investment trusts" which spread their clients' little capital over hundreds of securities. The small investors merge in one big investor, the Trust. This development, this pooling of small investors, may go on. It may be found possible, in the future, to confine individual investment absolutely to semi-public properly audited Investment Trusts.

At present the Investment Trust is in its early phase, and in making this suggestion we conceive of the Investment Trust evolving and rising to its possibilities and opportunities. It may seem an extreme suggestion that the freedom of the individual to throw away his savings should disappear. But it is at any rate worth while investigating how much of that 1,000,000,000 dollars per year, of Mr. Mellon's estimate, might not be embanked back by some such restriction from sustaining a horde of rogues and unproductive financiers, and directed into economically fruitful channels.

Dividends would, of course, fall as this was achieved, but the capital would be secured. High dividends are the reward of risk taking. High dividends are due to the uncertain profit of an exploitation, and where the exploitable value of anything can be calculated with certainty there is no need to pay unduly for the use of money. The enterprise can obtain its capital at the minimum rate of interest that is ruling at the time. In a perfectly safe, perfectly calculated social and economic system, the various directive and employing boards would do their bookkeeping with one another, and individuals would neither hoard nor lend their money; they would have no reason for doing so, and they would spend it. Consumption would equal production. Money then would have simplified out to its ultimate use as a check, giving purchasing power against a claim established or services rendered. Stock and share and all such interest-bearing quasi-money would have disappeared. A world economic control, evolved perhaps from the banking organization of to-day, would apportion purchasing power to the various world services, to experiment and research generally, and to bodies engaged in localized development. The existence of this investing public of ours would then become unnecessary. It would become an interesting past phase in the economic history of mankind.

There is nothing fantastic, and so far there is nothing Utopian, in these intimations of a world that will be largely released from the inconvenience of uncertain and fluctuating values. It is no imaginary "No-where," it is here on this planet that such an exact and unencumbered economic life is possible. Possible, in the sense that no absolute obstacle can be defined. People will be disposed to object that such completeness of organization is "incredible"; they will rake up the old vague rubbish about "human nature" being in the way, meaning ignorance and bad habits of mind; and they will attempt to substitute a confused vision of romantic incoherence, a distorted and foreshortened continuation of the past two thousand years of human life, for this plain prospect of a world with an adequate system of bookkeeping. But the movement of the last hundred years is all in favour of the statistician.

It is no good saying nowadays that "man has always been so and so and always will be so and so," meaning that he must remain forever an ignorant, limited, pitiful, disastrous fudger. Human biology knows better. We can trace our escape from dreams to ordered thinking. We can trace the spreading subjugation of life to ordered thinking. We see all about us the struggle of the human mind to escape from Realist delusions to Nominalist methods of thought. Science spreads into all human concerns, changing spirit as well as method. What science, with quite small resources, has done in a century or so in establishing a progressive order throughout a large part of the field of possible knowledge, all mankind in a century or so can do for all the affairs of earth.

This prospect of a proper accounting in human affairs presupposes certain things. It presupposes a vigorous extension of scientific enquiry into the field of business, the development of a powerful body of scientific workers in the social and economic field that such institutions as the London School of Economics foreshadow; it presupposes also an increasing honesty and broadening intellectual interest among business men, and a wide diffusion of the ideas and conclusions this gathering cloud of work and thought will produce. Further, it presupposes a correlated change in the business atmosphere where greed, rapacity, cunning and secrecy have played so freely hitherto. Every step that is won in ousting that tradition of hidden methods which is dear to the mediæval peasant and trader, and that other tradition of rapacious adventurousness which comes to us from the mediæval brigand-noble, in favour of the modernized intellectual tradition—the mentality, that is to say, of the self-devoted coöperative *educated* man—brings this prospect of a clear accounting in economic life nearer.

At bottom the dire economic stresses of our present world, its injustices and its vileness and the tantalizing uncertainty and irregularity of its progress, are due to the defective or pernicious education, mental and moral, of the vast majority of energetic people. It is not that they are bad at heart, but that they do not think sanely; they have no idea of what is needed, no image of conduct necessary to run the great machine of the world properly.

In Chapter VII, § 11, we discussed grades of organization and their relation to the moral and intellectual level of the community. To that idea we now recur.

As that scientific devoted persona, which must be the guiding object of modern education, is built up in more and more of the minds of active men and women, the face of our world will change. Things that are now impossible will become practicable, easy and "natural," and this dark and wasteful tangle, muddle, and obscurity in the counting house of humanity, this vast leakage of purchasing power, will no longer hamper the development of our racial life.

There is no essential reason why a world-controlled monetary system should not be continually draining away indebtedness by a steady gentle continual monetary inflation; why indeed it should be necessary to upset the balance of production development and consumption by individual "savings" and individual investment at all; why the creation of new productive capital should be possible only by the evocation of debts. The economic mechanism of mankind groans under a vast burthen of debt now, by habit and custom, and not by necessity. Debt prevents plenty, it is a restraint and a subtraction, but debt is no more essential to economic life than was human sacrifice to the building of a bridge or the raising of wheat. Yet for ages men were unable to disentangle the one thing from the other.

§ 11. *The Elements of the World Depression of 1929–34**

We have now put before the reader, in an orderly fashion, the main facts about the payment for, and financing of, human work at the present time. We have pointed out some manifest looseness in the machinery and some conspicuous weaknesses, defects and dangers. And lest this should seem to be mere carping at human and tolerable characteristics of the monetary and financial organization of mankind, let us now make a compact study of the machinery in a phase of bad results. This is a simple, unbiassed report upon the way in which the machinery has been grinding and stalling in the past five years. It recapitulates very conveniently many points already raised in this chapter.

Never has the industrial and commercial intelligence of mankind shown to such complete disadvantage as at the present time. Sum up the position calmly, and it remains unbelievable. All over the world are exceptionally large stores of the raw materials required for every type of manufacture. There are in the industrial areas more factories, better equipped and organized, than ever before. The knowledge and skill of workers, directors and inventors have never been greater. Our treasure of gold has reached the highest known level and is being steadily increased. The banks are choked with money which they cannot put to

---

*The elements of the story are to be found also in the Report presented to the Assembly of the League of Nations, 1931, *The Course and Phases of the World Economic Depression.*

profitable use. There is no war to speak of anywhere—communications are safer and speedier than at any time in history. Wholesale prices are back at pre-war level, and millions of decent, industrious people would be glad to obtain more food, clothing, houses, furniture and other goods which it would be well for them to have. Machinery stands idle everywhere; whole towns are stagnant and desolate; the manufacturer, unless he has already sold his product, hesitates to manufacture, and those who can afford it hesitate to buy. We have arrived at a deadlock.

Let us recall the main features of the story to the reader. We can begin most dramatically on October 24, 1929.

No one doubts that the proximate cause of this economic desolation is the crash which occurred on the New York Stock Exchange on that date. It is possible to put a finger on the calendar and show the exact moment on which the avalanche began to slide. But that was only the proximate cause—the Americans have speculated before without involving the whole world in industrial disaster. Their smash, bad as it was, merely widened and accelerated a downward movement which had been going on already for three years, worsening the position in countries which were already depressed, and laying open to the infection those, like France and the United States, which had so far escaped it. It is that downward movement which must first be examined if the great slump is to teach us anything worth learning.

One dominating influence can be indicated in a sentence: in an industrial world both trade and money seek to be international in their movements, while at the same time we have no international machinery, either physical or mental, for dealing with them. If our vast contemporary populations living in completely different climates are to be fed and maintained in reasonable comfort, goods must move to and fro across the earth, and gold, or its equivalent, must to some extent go out to meet them. And at present mankind is trying not so much to encourage or guide this process as to interfere with it from a dozen independent and hostile centres and on as many different principles. Some of the ideas now shaping economic policy date from the Middle Ages, some from the Roman Empire, some from before the dawn of history. Nowhere do we see conceptions based upon actual world conditions in operation. There is no authority to-day trying to promote world trade, or empowered to enquire whether the maximum quantity of desirable goods is produced and consumed. There are only partial governments trying to secure for their own nationals some opportunity, not of enjoying goods, but of making a profit which might otherwise have fallen to the citizens of a different country, whether or not this adds to, or subtracts from, the volume of their trade as a whole, or even contributes to the real comfort and welfare of the nationals concerned.

This state of affairs shows no tendency towards improvement—on the contrary it seems probable that there is less harmony to-day than there has been since the rise of modern industry. Before the war the financial side of international trade was in practice, as we have pointed out, controlled very largely from London, and the difficulties of the post-war period have been greatly increased because that no longer happens. It may be possible to produce all the goods the world needs and to distribute them in a rational manner while London, Paris, New York, Berlin, Calcutta and Shanghai are all in their greater or lesser degree empowered to take their own line, issue their orders that money is to be made scarce here or to accumulate there, that goods are to be refused admittance at one frontier or heavily taxed at another. But an examination of the policies and actions which led to our present stagnation does not encourage one to think so. If we are to avoid a recurrence of this slump, and if these separate powers are to be retained, they will have to be used in a very different way. The tragedy of the years 1929-31, in the last analysis, must be traced to suspicion and ignorance, to a flat refusal to use the accumulated knowledge of economic science, or to understand that even a nation cannot ruin its customers without suffering itself.

To illustrate this contention in detail would be a very complicated business and would take far more space than can be given it here. But it should be possible to make the main features clear and to indicate their importance and their interrelations. They will be found in the first instance to be rooted in economic nationalism. Whether such disasters can be avoided in the future while that background remains unaltered is for the reader to judge.

Economic nationalism, we say, is at the root of this, the greatest slump the world has ever known. But we do not mean that it is the only operating cause. Were all the world one, we should still have to face the distresses created by an ever-increasing efficiency in production, whereby output increases while employment and the general purchasing power under our present system of distribution diminish. But that problem, as we shall see later, would be altogether less formidable if the world were economically unified.

Plainly a chief cause of the trade depression which preceded the great slump was scarce and dear money. When the crash came there had been in the majority of countries and for several years a dearth of money for ordinary buying and the purposes of trade. Money is an artificial thing; its amount can be artificially increased or lessened, and it is as a result of monetary policies that consumers have been short of power to buy, while producers have been unable to afford the money they wanted either to reëquip their existing businesses or to establish new ones. To rebuild the world after the war, cheap money in adequate quantity was vital. And yet almost every step taken anywhere to influence its supply has been taken in the direction—and with the result— of making it dear and scarce. Each central banking authority has had its reasons for this—they have not restricted the supply for the sake of restriction—but the result has been that up to the day of the New York crash interest rates remained at a high level. The price of loans frightened off ordinary trade borrowers. And at the same time national incomes, instead of being increased to allow for the increases which have taken place in populations, have either been prevented from growing fast enough or have been actually contracted.

As Mr. J. M. Keynes has pointed out* there have been two main sources of pressure on the supply of money and credit. The first has been the financial distress of governments, aggravated in some cases by reparations payments. Unable to balance their budgets, states have been compelled to borrow, no matter what rate of interest they might be charged. If the money-lenders have made a good thing of it, the blame for that must go to the politicians. The other main cause is almost certainly the return to the gold standard on the part of Great Britain and the other important industrial countries. For one thing this meant that huge sums in gold had to be removed from active use in order that they might be stored away as cover to currencies—a policy which has brought about a wholly unnecessary scarcity of gold. By 1928 nearly two thirds of the world's monetary gold—almost £1,250,000,000—had already been locked away to perform a function which can better be filled by interest-bearing securities. Secondly, the various currency acts passed during the period of return have imposed upon central banks the statutory duty of protecting most of this gold, and thus forced them to check every sort of movement which might have led to the metal leaving the country. In England, where the Currency Act is elastic, the Bank of England refused steadily to make use of this elasticity and part with gold. The blame for the consequences which have flowed from this can hardly be escaped by Great Britain, for she, with her

*A Treatise on Money, Vol. 2, pp. 378 et seq.

dominant financial prestige, not only took the lead in returning to gold, but urged and encouraged other nations to follow her example.

In a little book, *Stabilization,* by E. M. H. Lloyd, published in 1923, the reader will find how clearly the evils of deflation were foreseen at that time, and how plainly the British and American authorities were warned by such experts as Maynard Keynes, McKenna and Professor Cassel of the mischief they were doing the world. To these warnings, the British bankers, speaking in the person of Sir Felix Schuster, replied:

"Countries which had departed from their pre-war gold standard must aim at deflating their currencies gradually so as to inflict the least injury, but with one object in view, a return as soon as possible to the pre-war gold standard. That would be the policy of the Bankers of the United Kingdom, and until that object was attained he thought they must adhere to a policy of gradual deflation—certainly in this country."

Looking back now, it is evident that the history of the decline began with this return. Before the gold standard could be restored, it was necessary for her financial authorities to raise English money rates and check supply in order to force the pound up to a pre-war parity with the American dollar, and so the Bank of England found itself committed to a régime of dear money and restricted credit, a régime which has led straight to the present débâcle. Owing to the extent of the British Empire and to the position of London as the centre of international finance, money rates and conditions in London still govern those prevailing in lesser centres, and the dominant factor making for world-wide depression has been the policy pursued in London. In 1925 the Bank of England's discount rate was put up first to 4½ per cent and then to 5 per cent, and these steps were accompanied by a serious contraction in credit.

Choosing a different aspect of the same facts, we may say that the pound was forced up in terms of other currencies and of goods, so that prices fell. British exports were reduced by £9,000,000 in nine months and the national output fell by £100,000,000 a year. Britain was unable to import so much or to pay so highly for what she did import, and there followed a depression in Germany, the United States and the British Dominions. France escaped by taking the opposite course— allowing the franc to fall in value and thus stimulating her exports and throwing the burden onto her rentiers and fixed salary-earners.

From then onward the economic vitality of Britain declined, and the diminished purchasing power of this great consumer of raw materials acted as a steady downward drag on world prices. The English bank rate may be taken as the mercury which registers monetary conditions, and until the present slump made money unusable it never fell below 4½ per cent, while at times it rose to 6½ per cent. As a corollary, during all this time credit was restricted whenever a demand for it arose. A progressive strangulation of business was inevitable under the conditions thus created.

The fundamental idea of the gold standard is that in certain financial centres, and particularly London, there shall be a free gold market, and the essential feature of that arrangement is that anyone who wishes to do so may buy gold from the central bank at a fixed price. The Banking and Currency Act of 1928 left the Bank of England provided with a very narrow margin of exportable gold, and there has been continual pressure upon that margin. The provision in the Act which allows the bank to relieve this position it refused to use. The position was that since the bank could not refuse to sell it was forced to prevent its customers from wanting to buy. This it was able to do, but only by the roundabout method of so decreasing the amount of money in the pockets of the public that everybody was obliged to buy less of everything.

There are three main reasons why individual purchasers require gold for export, and all of them in turn, during the period under review, exercised pressure upon the London rates. In the first place gold may be wanted to pay for imports. Where, as in the case of Great Britain, imports of commodities normally exceed commodity exports by large amounts, there is always a possibility that gold may have to be sent abroad to pay for imported goods. Other countries deal with this difficulty by duties which discourage their people from importing, but the central bank of a free trade country is fully exposed to the hazards of demand. And since it cannot prevent people from buying imports in particular, it must take the course of checking confidence and diminishing credit, and so discourage them from buying not only imports but anything at all.

A second and possibly a much more important influence during these years, is the traditional disposition of English investors to send their money abroad. Before the war Great Britain, in receipt of immense revenues from foreign investments, was virtually obliged to keep on re-lending the interest abroad, in order that other countries might continue to purchase her goods. Since the war the amounts coming in have been

THE WORKER AND THE CITY

A WORKER on the Empire State Building, which towers more than a
thousand feet above the streets of New York. In the background is the
Hudson River, and beyond it the New Jersey shore.

WOMAN IN INDUSTRY
A DELICATE step in the making of radio tubes.

smaller, and they have been set off in part by a larger adverse balance
of imports, yet the country has continued to lend abroad in excess of its
real power to do so. Custom plays a considerable part in these arrangements, and the machinery for foreign lending in London is planned on
a large scale, and, so to speak, draws in its own supplies. Borrowers are
accustomed to come to London, and London is accustomed to lend.
From a world point of view that function should now be shared by
Paris and New York, the money centres of the two other great creditor
countries. But the French fared so badly over their pre-war Russian
investments and the Americans show such a preference for investing
in their own industries, that large though the loans from the United
States have been in particular years, neither of these countries has in
fact played the part which international trade now demands of it.
Even had the French wished to invest they would have met with
legal difficulties for France, in her inveterate nationalism, taxes both
issues of foreign loans and dividends received from them by as much
in some cases as 25 per cent. As for the private investor in England, his
motive was the reverse of his American brother's; he wanted to get his
money out of the depressed industries of his own country. The worse
conditions became at home, the more reasonable it seemed to him that
he should seek his profit abroad. Political fears have accentuated this
tendency, and it has been further increased by the discovery on the part
of wealthy citizens that there are ways of placing money abroad which
enable them to escape income tax and surtax.

These were influences which affected long-term investments. Another cause of the drain on the British gold supply was the movement
about the world of what is called short-term money—funds which are
lent for days, weeks or months on money markets and stock exchanges.
Money of this sort is very mobile; it follows high rates of interest from
one great financial centre to another, and there is always a danger that
when it comes in paper it may be taken away again in gold. To prevent
those persons who are accustomed to lend money in this way from dislocating monetary conditions, money rates in the various centres have to
be kept in step, and the country which is in need of cheap money must
forego it whenever a leading foreign central bank thinks well to raise its
rates. Thus as long as countries consider it necessary to maintain large
reserves in gold while selling gold freely at a fixed price, the mobility of
this form of capital is a continual reason for keeping money dear, and
again and again during the period with which we are dealing it had
this effect.

Further, both these factors combined to aggravate a third—that storing away of money in central banks to which reference has already been made. Both France and America in one way and another were receiving more gold than they could use. During 1930 alone they added to their already swollen reserves more than twice the annual output of the mines. France, as we have already noted, held over £500,000,000 in 1931, and the United States nearly £1,000,000,000. As against this the whole British Empire possessed only £250,000,000, of which something like £150,000,000 was held in the Bank of England. And since these two great hoards had been accumulated faster than new gold had been produced, all other countries were in constant fear of losing their own reserves, and Britain especially tried continually to tempt money to London or to keep it there by the offer of exceptional rates.

All these modes of human behaviour, the buying of what in the circumstances were too many foreign goods, the desire to invest abroad, the wish—expressed through central banks but reflecting a profound instinct in peoples—to amass as much gold as possible and part with as little, helped to make the British system unworkable except at a monstrous cost to its industry. Taken by themselves alone they would have formed an adequate explanation of bad trade and unemployment. No country could have flourished under the monetary conditions which have been considered here. But in all their badness they were aggravated by another influence, that of the high tariff walls erected by both France and the United States. It is argued on behalf of the gold standard that if gold flows into a country, goods will flow in after it and bring the gold back again. That is how things ought to work. Under a system of free trade, if France and America had used their gold either directly to increase the money in circulation, or as a basis for fresh credit, or both, demand would have increased, prices would have risen, and goods would have been sent from all over the world to take advantage of the higher prices. In this way prosperity would have spread from the centres where trade was brisk to other producing countries. Purchasing power would have risen there in response to the intelligent exercise of purchasing power by these creditor countries. But by means of higher and higher tariffs foreign goods were in fact shut out from these two prosperous areas, so that nations buying from them, unable to pay their debts in goods, found themselves obliged to remit yet more gold to markets already gorged with it. Great Britain especially, unwilling to prevent her own nationals from buying from France and America, suffered by being refused a market for her own merchandise. From a world point of view the countries which should have admitted goods freely were the most determined to shut them out, and the nation which could perhaps least afford to do so—having regard to its monetary system—bought too much from abroad.

To these main factors of the world's distresses—dear money during a period when cheap money was most urgently required, faulty working of the international loan machinery and maladjustment of tariffs —other causes of adversity must unfortunately be added. The war-debt arrangements increased the flow of gold to the United States, which did not need it, from Europe, which needed it very badly indeed. The position of Russia, with her depreciated currency and inadequate foreign credit, was another source of weakness. She had ceased to be a customer on an adequate scale, and in order to buy even the equipment vital to the success of her Five Year Plan, she was forced to be a constructive seller, throwing wheat, furs and timber into the market for what they would fetch, and dislocating the trade of the countries which took advantage of her necessity.

Lastly, all over the world a series of plentiful harvests occurred, and agricultural countries made unprecedented efforts to recover prosperity by increasing and improving their production. Had world trade been good, these additions to real wealth would have been absorbed and added to human well-being, but coming at a time when prices were already being forced down by monetary influences—when less and less money was available for buying—they caused the prices of raw materials to fall yet further and increased the distress they would otherwise have alleviated.

These are the fundamental causes which had been operating to prepare ruin in the midst of potential plenty. The last touches were added to the picture by greed, folly and mismanagement. In 1926 one effort was made to stop the decline. When the Federal Reserve Board of the United States found that Great Britain's return to the gold standard was preventing the sale of American harvests and producing a depression, it took the wise step of releasing money and keeping its rates of interest low. This enabled trade to recover, and a period of prosperity in America ensued. It even led to a certain amount of gold being withdrawn from New York in order to take advantage of the high money rates in Europe. Had this been followed by a lowering of tariffs so that some of the fresh money could have gone abroad in payment for goods, prosperity might have spread across the Atlantic and the balance been restored. There was a potential world recovery in the 1926 situation. So much sanity was still too much to expect from the current American ideology. Moreover, the spectacle of European indigence side by side with American plenty led the American investing public to tip the scales still further by decreasing their purchases of foreign loans and using their money at home. And so we come to the American boom of 1928, when it still seemed to the ordinary man in America that his favoured continent was to be exempted from the malaise of the rest of the world and that an era of abundance opened before him. Everyone was to buy hopefully. Prosperity was assured.

The prices of stocks soon answered to this feeling, and as they rose the gambling instinct of that great adventurous people awoke; the plentiful bank credit which had been created in order to help agriculture, was lent to provide money for speculation, and there followed one of the worst Stock Exchange booms in history. America went through a phase of violent inflation—not currency inflation but inflation of security values. A man's bank balance remained the same but the negotiable securities, which formed his next line, mounted to astonishing levels. America passed into this phase of inflation by security values, while the world at large was in a process of steady currency and credit deflation. Prices of commodities did not rise in America, but they did not fall as they were doing elsewhere. But an immense rise in production and profit was *anticipated*. There was consequently a fantastic exaggeration of the value of all but fixed-interest-bearing securities. There was a boom in hope. People became giddy with this rise. You bought, you sold again; you got out with your profit as the rise went on. You were sorry you had not stayed in—just a little longer. So you went back to it. Attention focussed on the Stock Exchange. People did not spend their profits at once; they reinvested. No such expansion of trade occurred to justify the mounting prices of industrial shares. Nothing real was responding to all this hopefulness.

All America rang with a new gospel, the gospel of wealth by consumption. It seemed possible to evoke prosperity through a mere imaginative effort. "Every day, in every way," said the American investor, following the Coué formula, "we grow richer and richer."

By the middle of 1928 the Federal Reserve Board began to feel alarm. It had already been fiercely attacked in the Hearst papers for its policy in allowing gold to leave the country, and it now decided, as Mr. R. G. Hawtrey has put it, "to stop speculation by stopping prosperity." During 1928 the rediscount rate was raised by steps from 3½ per cent to 5 per cent, securities were sold by the banks in the open market, and other action was taken to reduce the supply of money. Trade began to suffer at once, but nobody was paying any attention to trade. The upward gamble continued. The results were that the rates for call money in New York rose to extraordinary heights—in March, 1929, they touched 20 per cent.

It takes time to stop a gambling fever; people will pay whatever they are asked to pay for loans so long as they imagine that they can make a profit with the borrowed money, and money was, of course, rushed in large amounts from Europe to earn this preposterous interest, in spite of the fact that European banks had raised their own rates to check such adventures. In August the New York Federal Reserve rate was put up to 6 per cent, in September the London rate went to 6½ per cent. These figures foreshadowed a crash, and doubtless operators of sufficient intelligence recognized this and got out of things.

On October 24th the crash which we have made the starting date of the world slump came, and on the 31st of that month the bank rates began to go down. But instead of attempting to offset the inevitable wave of depression by a decided policy of cheap and plentiful money, the Bank of England brought its rate down slowly and reluctantly and did nothing whatever to expand credit. This was probably due to nervousness engendered by the behaviour of the French, who were characteristically engaged in turning everything they could lay hands on into gold or notes and hoarding it away. A currency shortage in France could only be avoided by the issue of notes to replace those hoarded, and the Banque de France, under its charter, is obliged to cover in gold every such fresh issue whether its gold stock is already too great or not. In any case it was May, 1930, before the London rate fell to 3 per cent, and by that time the effect of widespread losses, combined with that of the Hatry scandals (a forgery of securities on a large scale), had conspired to establish an atmosphere of dismay and hopelessness.

During the year that followed nothing was done to relieve the gathering stresses. Wholesale prices fell almost week by week; gold continued to flow into France and the United States to be sterilized by their central banks. Economists were at one in pointing out that this could not continue without dislocating the finance of the whole world, but as the debtor countries did not wish to default, only the two great world creditors could take any steps to arrest the process, and neither in France nor America was public opinion thought to be ready for a change in policy.

Attempts were made here and there by producers to hold up this or that particular commodity in order to check the fall, but the knowledge that accumulated stocks were overhanging the market if not actually on it served only to depress the price still further. Moreover, it was known that Russia was enormously increasing her acreage of cotton and wheat and everything else that she could grow. Most of these projects to restrict sales ended in disaster, and by the summer of 1931 producers were planning actually to destroy crops, throw them into the sea, burn them or hoe them in. The problem of wheat prices was considered so pressing that a series of international conferences was held to devise some means of getting rid of the stored-up American wheat and checking new production, but all these conferences failed. The interests of Russia and the older producing countries were completely antagonistic, and there was no supernational authority to force an agreement, no representative even of the world interests which should have been paramount. Those were left to the consciences of the delegates. By the summer of 1931 Brazil and the United States were actually bartering wheat for coffee because of the difficulty of monetary payments.

The complete failure of concerted international action, left each country faced with its own problems. There were two solutions of the riddle conceivable: either to make a resolute attempt to check the fall in prices by spending money on some programme of development, or else so to cut costs that production would become profitable once more at the lower level of prices. The first involved State action, for private enterprise cannot in the nature of things be expected to incur heavy expenditure without even a reasonable expectation of paying its way, much less of profit. And State action meant either additional borrowing or further taxation—at a time when people were already crushed by taxation. Moreover any single nation which adopted this course while its competitors were taking the alternative path of cutting costs, placed itself at a disadvantage in the world market. "To cut costs on the other hand seemed to offer some hope of underselling competitors even though it depressed the standard of living of the working class and thereby increased unemployment."

It was to the competitive expedient that the continental nations turned. Wages fell everywhere—sometimes by as much as 30 per cent. This drove prices lower and increased both the burden of the external debt and the proportion of wealth automatically received by the *rentier* classes. In Italy the Dictatorship was able to ease the adjustment by enacting—and securing—that retail prices should fall *pari passu* with a 10 per cent drop in wages. In other countries this was not done and the poor were left to manage as best they could. In Great Britain alone wages did not fall, but because they were buttressed by her system of unemployment insurance (the dole). But unemployment increased as her export trades found themselves less and less able to hold their own in the world market, owing to their disproportionate bills for wages. And though Great Britain's exports fell, her imports rose in quantity—a fact masked by the continual fall in prices—because her masses still had purchasing power through the dole.

In February, 1931, Mr. Snowden, her Labour Chancellor, warned the country that it could no longer hope to maintain the existing level of public expenditure, and an "Economy Committee" (the May Committee, named after its chairman, Sir George May) was set up inspired by the idea of economizing in every possible direction.

By June, Austria was unable to bear the gathering strain of the situation any longer, and banking failures occurred there which dragged some important German banks down with them. Germany since the war has been obliged to carry on her economic life by means of loans, and in particular she has been forced to borrow the money for her reparations payments.* According to the Midland Bank Review for June–July 1931 her debts by the end of 1930 amounted to nearly £400,-000,0000 on long-term and £300,000,000 on short-term account. The American crash abruptly dried up the chief source of these loans, and as they ceased and the true situation became clearer to the mass of the German people, the Nazis came into being, pledged to repudiate reparations payments. At the General Elections in September, 1930, the Nazis gained enough votes to weaken the confidence of foreign investors. Loans except for very short periods really did become very difficult to obtain, a new "flight from the mark" began, and the German government was forced to confess that it could no longer maintain its foreign payments.

At this point the United States, whose citizens held over half the German loans, came forward with a constructive offer in the interests of German solvency. President Hoover, acting on the advice of the leading American bankers, announced that if all the other creditor countries would agree to follow her example America would for a year excuse her debtors from the payment of their war debts. It is said that he had

---

*A brilliant analysis of the German position and the position of debtor countries generally under our existing financial system will be found in Chapter IX of the Macmillan Report—Report of Committee on Finance and Industry. Command Paper 3897, 1931.

intended, had this offer been accepted immediately, to make the improved situation so created, the occasion for an attempt to release money
from the United States hoard and so send up commodity prices.

Great Britain accepted, so did all the other creditors of Germany,
with the vitally important exception of France. France, alas! has still to
disentangle finance from foreign policy. She held out, on the grounds
that Germany's position was due to her own extravagance, that she was
still finding enough money to build ships of war and that France owed
it to herself not to give up her just rights. It is unnecessary to recount
here the hasty meetings, the goings to and fro, the haggling, the marvellous diplomacies which followed. An arrangement was finally patched
up, but not before Germany had had to close her banks while she set
up machinery to ration imports and prevent the export of currency and
gold. Under this arrangement she was relieved for the moment from
repayment of her foreign debts, and it was immediately clear that this
must have serious effects in England. The City of London found itself
with £70,000,000 locked up in Germany, much of which had unfortunately been borrowed on short-term account from France. At a time
when every economist was explaining the imperative need for the
richer countries to lend freely to the poorer, it is perhaps unfair to
blame the City for carrying on business in this way, but use was certainly made of the fact to carry on anti-British propaganda in France,
and the heavy French deposits in London began to be withdrawn in
gold. We have pointed out already that these short-term French deposits have been a grave nuisance to world finance throughout the whole
post-war period. Whenever the English bank rate went up they flowed
to London; whenever it fell, the bank was under the threat that if the
short-term lenders chose to withdraw, London would be pulled off the
sacred gold standard. So long as London was obsessed by the gold
standard it became possible to provoke a rise in the bank rate by withdrawing a due amount of short-term money, thus enhancing the interest
on what remained. For a certain type of big operator abroad this had
an irresistible appeal. But now the end of this process seemed to be in
sight and the successful operators began to take away their gold and
their gains for good.

The outward movement began on July 13, 1931, and proceeded so
fast, that to protect its gold the distressed Bank of England arranged
credits of £50,000,000 in Paris and New York. And at this most inop-
portune moment the May Economy Committee which had been ap-

pointed in the spring presented its report. This document informed an already uneasy Europe that there would be a British budgetary deficit in the current financial year of £70,000,000 and a further deficit of £120,000,000 in 1932–33, and proposed to meet these deficits by drastic retrenchment on education, housing and the salaries of all State employees, whatever the nature of their contracts, and by reducing the amount of unemployment benefit. Military preparations were left practically unchallenged by this mischievous report, nor was any suggestion made for scaling-off from the *rentier* the advantages which had accrued to him through the fall in prices.

The report was seized upon in the usual way by persons and parties opposed to the government, regardless—or perhaps not altogether regardless—of the effect their propaganda must have upon opinion abroad. For party ends the Labour government was denounced as insanely spendthrift. These denunciations lost nothing by translation in the continental press. The foreign panic intensified and the drain of gold increased—one alarmist article in a leading London journal is said to have been directly responsible for the withdrawal of £11½ millions in one day—and by the middle of August the £50,000,000 credits were exhausted. The Bank of England informed the government that it must raise further credits and that these were obtainable to the amount of £80,000,000, but only under certain conditions. These conditions, as laid down by the New York bankers, were firstly that the budget must be balanced, and secondly that a cut must be made in the rate of unemployment insurance benefit. Such conditions may seem peculiar, coming as they did to one of the greatest "sovereign" countries in the world from a group of private bankers, more particularly when it is borne in mind that Washington displayed no intention of balancing its own budget, though faced with a very much larger deficit. But Great Britain had apparently always made it a condition of loans that the state receiving them should balance its budget and the Americans obviously had this precedent in mind.

The Labour Cabinet agreed to balance the budget but could not agree to reductions in the rate of unemployment benefit. It resigned, and at the personal request of the King a "National" Government was formed on August 25, 1931, composed of the two opposition parties, the Conservatives and the Liberals, plus the Labour Prime Minister, his Chancellor and a dozen of their followers. It proceeded without delay to carry out its pledges—that is, to reduce the national income, pile fresh burdens upon industry, check consumption and thrust prices down still further. The *rentier,* like everyone else, was to submit to a 10 per cent increase in his income- and sur-tax, but he was not specifically taxed as a *rentier,* nor was any attempt made to relieve the burden of internal debt, lest he should take his money out of the country if this were done.

The British public under the guidance of its press and politicians, rallied to this programme. An heroic struggle to save the gold standard was staged, a struggle which lasted exactly twenty-six days. The British people had come through a previous crisis, the war, by going without, in order to provide goods and money for the army and munitions, and it was apparently prepared to accept the suggestion that it was right to tackle this new problem of a world impoverished in the middle of unconsumed wealth, in precisely the same manner. The Labour party adopted this view as well as the other parties—and quarrelled merely over the details of its application. There was much enthusiasm for economy in the correspondence columns of the *Times.* The King made an exemplary reduction of his civil list by £50,000, and many people sent voluntary offerings to the Treasury.

But the run on gold, though checked for a day or two, increased again. Britain was still paying—heroically—and there was a scramble for its final outpour of gold. Holland and Switzerland were now drawing on London as well as the United States and France. Both the Federal Reserve Bank and the Banque de France did what they could, now that it was too late, to staunch the flow. The Americans left their funds in London and the French stated that they would follow the American example. By September 20th the Bank of England had lost £200,000,000 in ten weeks, and gold was still going at the rate of over £10,000,000 a day, and the Bank had no alternative but to ask that it might be relieved of its obligation to sell gold at a fixed price. This was done and the statesmen who had been saying only a month before that the suspension of the gold standard would mean unchecked inflation and social disaster and had to be fought at any sacrifice, set about explaining that a fall in the exchange value of the pound would really be of considerable benefit to the country. So long, of course, as they themselves remained in office.

That the pound had stood too high on the exchanges was true, and had they understood what had happened, or what they were doing, or what they had said themselves, the worst phase of the depression might have passed. For the chief factor which was prolonging the world-wide trade depression was that the costs of producing manufactured goods were not falling as prices, and especially the prices of agricultural products had fallen, with the result that the world in general, and agricultural countries in particular, were no longer able to buy manufactured products. This was due to the comparative rigidity of wages, rents and other fixed charges. All over the world efforts were made to deal with it by piece-meal reductions of wages—with the effect that purchasing power diminished further and prices were depressed to still lower levels. But had the value of the pound been allowed to fall sufficiently a point would have been reached where the fall in the exchange would have compensated for the rigidity of the British wage-scale. British exporters would have been able to sell at a profit and to increase their sales while the increase of purchasing power thus provided would have stopped the fall in the wholesale prices of food stuffs and raw materials, even if it had not reversed the movement. And since the goods with which the British Empire provides the home country are largely either the one or the other they would have continued to flow in to Britain even if higher prices made foreign luxuries too dear to buy. As it is the average net fall of 25% in the value of the pound which took place in the twelve month after the suspension of the gold standard has maintained, though it did not suffice to increase, the British export trade, in spite of the strangulating effects of the new tariffs.

Moreover with an unrestricted fall of the pound the balance of trade would have redressed itself, for under a system of fluctuating exchanges whenever imports enter the value of the currency falls, and whenever the value of the currency falls imports become dearer, so that less of them are bought, while exports are subsidized. This would go on until the payments for the exports and the dwindling of the imports, sent up the value of the currency again. So that unless movements of money for purely financial purposes upset the exchanges, as they will do under any fiscal system, the trade in goods would balance. Thus Britain could have secured, automatically, without any bargaining and sacrifice of sentiment, both a higher price level and a certain discrimination in favour of Empire trade. The burden of wage-payments would have been reduced, without political action, concurrently with a rise in prices that would have revived trade and increased employment. A fall in the value of the currency when it is brought about naturally and not as a result of an artificial inflation, has all the advantages claimed for tariffs and tariff increases, while it stimulates exports instead of reducing them. And it is harder to retaliate against currency movements than against the clumsy, definite and comparatively permanent barriers set up by tariffs. The only effectual rejoinder which other countries could have made to such a natural readjustment would have been to let their own currencies sink in terms of gold i.e. to start that much desired international reflation which we are told is impossible through negotiation.

But the National Government was not prepared to wait upon events. It wanted to hold a general election and take advantage of the wave of favourable sentiment which then existed. As the government which came into power to save the pound it could hardly have gone to the country on a programme of letting the pound sink, even had the majority of them understood what the effects of such a movement must be. So it came forward instead with a policy of still more rigorous "economy" and tariffs, and were returned to power by a frightened and confused electorate with an unexampled majority.

Returned, they at once set about undoing the good effects which had been produced by going off the gold standard. Undeterred by the fact that every other nation in Europe had had recourse to such expedients and had found that they only accentuated its difficulties, the National Government proceeded to cut down purchasing power all round. It imposed higher taxation, it reduced all public expenditure except expenditure on armaments and it lowered wages and salaries both by influence and example. And finally it set about restricting imports by a system of tariffs and quotas. So as the phrase goes it "improved the national credit" and forced up the value of the pound by every means in its power and at the same time made the expansion of internal trade impossible.

At the time of the general election the British electorate had been told that these restrictions were to be but a prelude to "Empire Free Trade" or at any rate to a lowering of tariff walls within the Empire, and in October 1932 an attempt was made to honour this pledge at the Ottawa Conference between members of the British Commonwealth of Nations. During these negotiations a number of bargains were struck which involved both reductions in inter-Imperial tariffs and the erection of fresh barriers against foreign goods. The actual details are complicated, and it is too soon yet to pronounce on their effects. In the matter of duties on goods it appears as though the Mother Country has conceded rather more than she has gained but that does not necessarily mean that she will suffer in the result. The sums invested by her in her overseas Empire are so large that the restoration of colonial prosperity is a matter of the greatest importance, at any rate to her investing classes. On the one hand the flow of dividends would be augmented or restarted, on the other it would be possible to find employment for some of the money now earning ½% in the British banks if profits could once more be made in colonial enterprise.

In the meantime the monetary situation was left to the Bank of England. A long overdue conversion scheme reduced the rate of interest on much of the internal debt to 3½%, but that is unfortunately only a measure of the general trade stagnation. Not the slightest attempt was made to formulate a monetary policy—as indeed is natural in a country where the majority of the governing classes want the pound both to rise and fall without being clear as to the results which would follow in either event. The conflict of voices was remarkable. The Governor of the Bank of England signed a report of the Bank of International Settlements in favour of yet another return to the gold standard. The Chancellor of the Exchequer, on the other hand, stated that this could not take place until the situation had changed entirely. In the meantime unemployment increased by over 200,000 in twelve months (though this number was masked by certain administrative changes) and as still further measures of "economy" are promised, at the time of writing, it seems probable that it will presently increase still more. The figures of employment are down, though production remains about the same—showing that what is called "rationalization" is also contributing to the contraction of welfare.

The state of public confidence produced by these measures may be judged by the fact that in spite of a London deposit rate of only ½% the deposits in the joint stock banks rose by nearly £70,000,000 during the year ending October 1932, while their advances to borrowers fell during the same period by £114½ million. That is to say, the money which was being withheld from public expenditure was not being used by the richer classes either for investment or private use. Production was not being stimulated though wholesale prices continued to fall.

While the economic situation in England was thus sliding gently from bad to worse the standard of life was falling even faster in other countries. America attempted a policy of reflation, but confidence in any real revival of trade was so lacking that the additional money was used mainly to finance a small stock exchange boom, which presently died away again. By the fall of 1932 the number of unemployed in the United States is said to have reached 12,000,000, and to have included men and women of the highest character and of every social class. Extraordinary efforts were made to provide these unfortunate people with food and some kinds of clothing, but it was estimated that only about 10% of what was really needed was distributed. In Germany there was a severe deflation, imposed by the Reichsbank in order to maintain the exchange value of the mark after an iron system of exchange restrictions had failed to achieve this end. The restrictions stifled her international trade and according to the official British Report on Economic Conditions in Germany Sept. 1931–Sept. 1932, the deflation produced "a terrifying increase in bankruptcies and compositions." The amount of capital reductions in the first half of 1932 amounted to 965,000,000 marks.

All over the world indeed as 1932 drew to its end, producers were going bankrupt. Sheep were selling for 1/-apiece in the south of England—or could not be sold at all—wheat was fetching 10 cents a bushel in some parts of the United States. And still no concerted action whatever was being taken to deal with the crisis as a whole unless we may include under this head a request to America from her debtors that the Hoover moratorium should be continued and the postponement of the World Economic Conference from 1932 until the late Spring of 1933.

Meanwhile France, Belgium, Holland and Switzerland went on increasing their hoards of gold, so forcing up its price and still further and still further lowering the prices of goods. By October 1932 the French held no less than £662,000,000 and manifestly they contemplated a prolonged possession of it, for among other fortifications of this hoard they surrounded the vaults of the Banque de France with a subterranean lake. This last increase in their gold reserve was effected in part by selling the French holdings of dollars in New York, and so abruptly was this done that at one moment America was almost sucked off the gold standard. The Belgian gold hoard increased in a year from £46.4 million to £74.8, the Dutch from £54.3 to £85.2 and the Swiss from £47.1 to £104.8—again by the sale of foreign exchange.

Thus we see how completely the recommendations of the Genoa conference and of every international gathering since held were disregarded. Instead of attempting economies in the use of gold so as to keep its price stable the Central Banks as a result of the prevalent spirit of financial distrust, struggled on against one another to secure larger shares of it and so raised that price still higher. The disproportion in the world's gold reserves became more marked than ever (the English figure for Sept. 1932 was under £140,000,000) with all the possibility of sudden and violent gold movements which that disproportion involved.

But we will not go on with this intricate history of divided and conflicting policies. The gallant struggle of President Roosevelt to stem the tide of disaster in America is too contemporary and too complex for detailed treatment here where we are concerned rather with general principles than policies. What leaps to the eye is the manifest impossibility of any local solution of the world's difficulties and the apparently incurable disinclination of mankind to attempt anything but local solutions. Everywhere barriers are rising between nation and nation and it is becoming more and more difficult for money, goods, or human beings to move about the world. Along every frontier there are embargoes, restrictions, taxes, interference. The poor nations are growing still poorer, becoming less and less eligible as borrowers as the need to redistribute money grows more and more urgent. They are sinking deeper into discontent, until it only needs a demonstrable rise in the Russian standard of living to make communism a vivid issue in half the cities of Europe. An immense amount of misery is being caused during these slow blunderings towards adjustment,—if indeed they are towards adjustment—and it is still an open question whether the world conferences in which alone lies any hope of restoration for the ebbing economic life of mankind can now be assembled and made effective, before the intolerable vexations and sufferings of the generality produce a world-wide series of social catastrophes. What Mr. W. Wylie King has called a "Grand Audit" of the world's affairs is an unavoidable preliminary to world action, and such an audit would take time. Yet concerted devalution of money by America, Britain and France with a stringent repression of speculation and (as we shall show later) a vigorous policy of public employment, may still give the existing order of things a new lease of life.

Organized devaluation of money, however, the systematic arrest of the process of deflation by increases of currency, bold public expenditure and a raising of the common standard of life cannot be achieved by any single country or group of countries while trade is still going on with other states which refuse to collaborate in these operations. It can no more be done than can the level of water in one part of the sea be raised without an equal elevation of the rest of the sea. World trade needs a world currency. Given, however, a belated recognition that this is fundamentally a world problem, and there are no insurmountable obstacles to its solution. There remain problems and possibly very intricate problems of adjustment, but none, for example, beyond the standard of difficulty encountered time after time by the human intelligence in the addition of the aëroplane or submarine to human resources. But concerted world action is essential. Without that the economic dégringolade and social dissolution will continue, down to some point when with a sufficient dwindling of population and vitality, a sort of barbaric stabilization will be achieved.

CHAPTER THE TENTH

The Rich, the Poor, and Their Traditional Antagonism

§ 1. *Short Studies in the Acquisition or Attempted Acquisition of Wealth*

IN THE preceding chapter we have had to display the financial organization of man's economic life as loose, vague, experimental and extremely dangerous. We have had to show that money is still a most imperfect counter for social service, and that the getting of money, which for the most obvious reasons should be the correlative of productive exertion, becomes in many instances and very easily, a process parasitic upon, rather than contributory to, the progressive development of the economic organization. We have seen how badly the machinery as a whole is working at the present time. We now propose to show how it has worked in recent times in certain individual instances. We are going to put before the reader a selection of individual accumulators for his consideration.

Our studies will be chosen chiefly to illustrate the working of generally accepted property and money ideas and conventions. But one or two of our cases will anticipate certain issues about legislation and administration that we shall deal with in Chapter XII.

The study of individual instances of wealth-getting is a department of social research of growing value and importance. A number of scattered writers* have directed their attention to these enquiries, but so far they have scarcely got beyond the anecdotal stage. Their studies are not yet numerous enough and searching enough for even a pretense of scientific treatment. The subject is at a stage comparable to that early phase of natural history when the collection of "curios" was preparing the way for the systematic marshalling of specimens in museum galleries. We shall marshal our "exhibits" and draw conclusions where

*For example, Richard Lewinsohn with his *A la Conquête de la Richesse, Zaharoff,* and *Histoire de l'Inflation.* A more comprehensive study which Professor Laski recommends is G. Meyer's *History of the Great American Fortunes.*

that seems reasonable, but in many respects we cite these cases rather to inform and suggest than to demonstrate.

HETTY GREEN AS AN UNCREATIVE ACCUMULATOR

For our first exhibit, a very wealthy product indeed of the current phase of financial organization, we will take Mrs. Hetty Green, who was born in 1825 at New Bedford and died in New York at the age of eighty-one worth a fortune of certainly over thirteen million pounds and probably of half as much again. She may be described as a pure accumulator. Her life has been written very ably by Boyden Sparks and Samuel Taylor Moore, to whom I make my acknowledgments, and it is essentially the history, as they put it, of a woman with a genius for acquiring and making money and an inability to spend it. She is therefore a very good test of the social value of the money incentive under modern conditions.

Apart from her passion for acquiring and holding money she seems to have been a humorous, industrious woman with a certain personal attractiveness, considerable homely skill in nursing and a taste for domestic drudgery. But she was by nature self-centred and acquisitive, and all the circumstances of her education developed a vindictive persona. Her habits were miserly from the beginning, and they became more so; in her phase of maximum business energy she wore newspapers in winter to avoid buying warm underclothing, and she lived in cheap lodging houses, moving from one to another in order to evade taxation. Her only luxury was hatred. Her self-esteem took the form of revenges of which she was proud. She liked to get equal with people who had thwarted her in her more questionable projects. She was one of those people who nurse grievances and pursue them, and she succeeded in ruining several men and in worrying one unfortunate trustee to death. These were her greater passions. She loved her son—to what extent we shall see—and she gradually dispossessed her husband of his property and separated herself from him on account of his habit of expenditure, in spite of her undeniable affection for him.

She was the daughter of a hard-fisted shipowner and trader, who followed the fashions of New English Puritans in leading a life of successful acquisition; she was at first a bold, handsome girl, whose face hardened quickly; she bullied her mother; perhaps she learnt that from her father; and when she was sent to New York for the winter with $1,200 to spend, she invested a thousand in bonds and went on investing thereafter. If she had the passions and vanities of a girl, she had them well under control. Her hostess in New York, being ashamed of her guest's dowdiness, bought smart and fashionable clothes for her, which Hetty put aside as too valuable to wear. After the death of her mother she lived with an invalid aunt whom also she bullied, making stupendous scenes on the slightest occasion—generally on such scores as the rate of domestic expenditure or the denial of access to her aunt's private papers.

Hetty was heiress both to this aunt and to her father. Her father left her nearly a million dollars as well as other property in trust; her aunt, who died worth about $2,000,000, had covertly made a will devoting about half of this sum to various charitable purposes and giving Hetty only the income for life of the residue. Hetty attempted to set this will aside in order to secure control of her aunt's entire capital, and she seems to have committed forgery, perjury and fraud in her unsuccessful attempts to do this. Then, being married to Mr. E. H. Green, who was also worth at least another million dollars, she set herself single-mindedly to the task of increasing her wealth. The tangle of litigation about the will ended in a compromise that left her with an income of 65,000 dollars a year from tied-up capital, and free cash to the value of about 650,000 dollars. Already before that she had been operating on an original fortune of a million, inherited from her father.

She and her husband lived for a time in Europe to escape the disagreeable atmosphere (and perhaps even the possibility of worse consequences) created by the will case, and in London—for their headquarters at the then most famous and splendid Langham Hotel—she and her husband engaged in discreet but successful speculative operations. He was an able enough business man, and at first he had considerable influence over her and gave her valuable advice. It is evident from her subsequent history that the choice of that particular hotel was his. He had none of her retentive acquisitiveness. He speculated to spend; he did not know how to hold, and while he consumed what he had and made, Hetty acquired and acquired. In one year she made more than a million and a quarter dollars through the purchase of United States gold bonds. London knew little or nothing of American conditions; there was considerable doubt whether the Washington government might not break faith in regard to these bonds, and at times the uncertainty deepened to panic. There came the sort of opportunity for which Hetty lived.

The Greens returned to America in 1874, by which time the statute

of limitations made any further annoyance on account of that will impossible, and they returned in a period of depression when buying
cheap was easy.

Sparks and Moore (*op. cit.*) quote her own explanation of her
method:

"I believe in getting in at the bottom and out at the top. I like to
buy railroad stock or mortgage bonds. When I see a good thing going
cheap because nobody wants it, I buy a lot of it and tuck it away. Then
when the time comes they have to hunt me up and pay me a good
price for my holdings. I own a lot of city mortgages in crowded sections. They seem to me as good as anything.

"I don't much believe in stocks. I never buy industrials. Railroads
and real estate are the things I like. Before deciding on an investment
I seek out every kind of information about it. There is no great secret
in fortune-making. All you have to do is buy cheap and sell dear, act
with thrift and shrewdness and be persistent."

She pursued that system of buying, add our authors, in every transaction in which she engaged, whether she was buying a mortgage, a
peck of potatoes, a house or a horse. In the spending of money she
might have been compared to an athlete who never broke training. She
spent nothing. In Green she possessed a steward who did not charge
for his services, who supplied her with food, shelter and clothing, as
any husband is required to do. Also in the earlier stages of their married life he gave her some very sound and shrewd counsels. Consequently there was not the slightest drain on her own fortune, and it
grew monstrously. A time came when she separated her life and estate
from Green's altogether, and he ended his days an elderly, impoverished loafer in a New York club.

She became a grotesque, familiar figure in the financial world of New
York, a dingy, alert old woman in a hackney carriage, flitting from
bank to bank, with bales and valises of securities. She would invade
bank premises with her auriferous litter to save herself the expense of
offices; she would borrow clerks and so recoup herself for the charges
the banks made for the business they did for her. She would scold
and weep and make a terrible fuss if things were not done as she desired.

The reader must go to the biography I have quoted for a fuller account of the habits of this astounding creature, of her gradual

effacement of her husband in the conduct of her affairs, and of how she sacrificed the leg of her son, whom she certainly loved very greatly, to her hatred of paying doctors' fees. The leg was injured in a toboggan accident, and failing proper treatment became so bad that at last it had to be amputated. She used to dress herself and her son in their shabbiest clothing in order to get advice and treatment in free clinics. But the doctors knew her. The clinics were warned against her. She grudged the cost of a competent specialist until it was too late. And yet they say she nursed that son, skillfully and devotedly.

Enough has been said here to show the quality of her life. The aspect that most concerns us is that she was able to lead such a life and keep her self-respect. She was proud of herself. Her persona sanctioned these things. The system of ideas in which she was reared, and which prevailed in the world about her, justified her career.

She had grown up in a community which held the getting of money to be the test of a satisfactory life, and where want of money was considered more hideous than any deformity. She was ego-centred, responsive to the standards about her, and capable of great sacrifices, so far as immediate satisfactions were concerned, to the ruling ideas in her mind. In happier circumstances she might have had altogether different ruling ideas; she might have been a fanatic of faith or works; or if money had really been a fair measure of public service, even her avarice might have become an incentive to vigorous efforts for the community. As it was, she became a morbid accumulation and an arrest of spending power. She stimulated no wholesome human activity.

She was misguided. It is the way in which she was misguided that concerns us. She was misguided by our monetary-credit system and by our reliance upon competition in getting as a test of worth. Her significance in this study of human work and wealth lies in her demonstration of the entire ineffectiveness of that money-credit system. The money-credit system should be a system for stimulating and rewarding productive energy. Here we see in the plainest way how its fluctuations can be diverted entirely to unproductive accumulation. That is the fundamental unsoundness of the money motive. We see the surplus profits of the activities of city and railroad converging upward to this sordid, clutching old woman, who desired no progress, imagined no increase in the grace and sweetness of life, opposed any development that touched her monopolies and securities.

Slowly, inevitably, her fortune grew. She was a patient, implacable creditor. Only her death arrested the growth and concentration of her property. An immortal Hetty Green would have become step by step, and in strict accordance with the rules of the money credit game, the owner of an economically arrested world.

And it happened as a further mitigation of her activities that, as her hoard accumulated, money cheapened. She added million to million and became a legendary figure in Wall Street, but all the while something else was happening in the world on a larger scale than any of her operations. New sources of gold had been discovered and were yielding abundantly; cheques quickened and multiplied payments, production increased immensely, and the gross increase of wealth in the world was out of all proportion greater than her individual gettings. In a world of falling prices her strangulating influence would have been a very serious thing, but that abundant later nineteenth century, with its amplifying financial resources, could carry Hetty Green without much discomfort.

THE LANDGRAVE OF HESSE-CASSEL, THE ROTHSCHILDS AND NATIONAL LOANS

Mrs. Hetty Green is a single specimen, a solitary acquisitive individual reacting to the ideas current in her time and circle, of ownership and success. She succeeded, and the world that had made her disliked her. How many minor Hetty Greens, male and female, there are in the world, individual centres of sterilizing ownership, it is impossible to estimate. So it is impossible to estimate their arresting action upon the general economic process. There may be multitudes of minor hoards of the same moral quality.

We will turn now to a larger system of acquisitions, to that great family of money accumulators and operators, the Rothschild family.

The beginning of the story goes far back beyond the beginnings of Hetty Green. It goes back into the period before railways and the gold discoveries of the middle nineteenth century, to the days when the supply of gold was restricted, and almost the only way to wealth and power lay through the acquisition either of land or of the key-metal. Land aggregation, saving and usury, were the older ways in which one grew rich. You saved, you tried to monopolize, you squeezed the needy. The story opens with a territorial prince selling men and lending money, and a Jew trader selling jewels wisely. It brings us into the modern period, when the finance of great industrial undertakings was beginning to overshadow the loans of militant states.

The Rothschilds were shop-keeping Jews in the Frankfort ghetto, general dealers. It was a prosperous but not conspicuously rich family, until the days of Meyer Anselm Rothschild, in the latter half of the eighteenth century. He was interested in coins; he became among other things an expert dealer in medals and jewels, and in those days of small states and diverse coinages his knowledge and advice were useful to his contemporary, the Count of Hanau-Nunzenburg, who presently became Landgrave of Hesse-Cassel. The landgrave was a seller of men. Human flesh was one of the chief exports of Hesse-Cassel. He took his subjects, made soldiers of them, and sold them by the regiment to various foreign powers, particularly to the English government, at that time in conflict with its North American colonies. When any of his men were killed or maimed he received compensation from the hiring government. There is no record of the payment being handed on to the wounded men or the families of those who were killed. He inherited very considerable wealth by the standards of that time, he was insanely avaricious, and he had marked financial ability. Rothschild, who had won his confidence steadily, became his "Agent General" and ally, and in various transactions his partner. Loans were made to the rulers of Denmark, Hesse-Darmstadt and Baden. Rothschild was already in possession of a respectable fortune in the dawn of the Napoleonic age. When the landgrave had to flee before Napoleon in 1806, Rothschild, in association with friendly bankers in Frankfort, was able to save the larger part of his fortune for him.

This Meyer Anselm Rothschild died in 1812, leaving a widow of vigorous character and five sons. The old general shop still flourished beside the new and growing bank. The unmarried daughters, the sons and the daughters-in-law, says Lewinsohn,* all took a part in the shop; one was cashier; the sons travelled to deal personally with the more important transactions of the firm.

A year or so before his death old Meyer Anselm sold his business to his five sons for a sum which he then bequeathed to his wife and daughters. This was done in accordance with one of the fundamental principles of Rothschild policy—all money, and the sole control of the business, must be kept in the family. To this end he shut out his daughters' husbands from the common interest, and to this end the third and fourth generations intermarried, but without any intensification of the ancestral business ability.

At the time when their father died the sons had already begun to spread themselves in Europe. The most talented, Nathan Meyer Rothschild, had established himself in England, and in order to facilitate his

*A la Conquête de la Richesse.

transactions with the continent had arranged that another brother—
James—should settle in Paris. It was this willingness to adventure themselves in foreign countries, together with their strong family sentiment,
which gave the Rothschilds both their strength and their opportunities.
Through all wars, invasions, blockades and changes of government, they
could trust one another in a manner impossible to the mere groups of
banks and merchants who were their rivals. They could supply one another with the most dangerous and intimate information, information
the collection of which they organized with the greatest care. Later
they instituted a special system of couriers. In spite of the enormous
expense, they found this worth their while, for they not only secured
for their business a privacy which could not be counted upon by any
other firm in Europe, but they left themselves free to send through the
post or in embassy bags any documents which they wanted the governments of the moment to read. Further, on the basis of this entire confidence, they were able to let themselves be absorbed each in the life
of his own adopted country, naturalize himself, and work in the interests
of its government, as long, of course, as it did not threaten Rothschilds
in particular or Jews in general. They knew that, under this scheme, if
all the Rothschilds could not be on the winning side, at least one must
be, and in a position powerfully to assist the others. It is said moreover,
that no one of them ever criticized another's business policy.

The most dramatic example of this international coöperation was perhaps the system by which Nathan and James in London and Paris were
able to keep Wellington in the Peninsula supplied with money for his
armies. Nathan had already made a considerable fortune by ordinary
trading when he was entrusted, through his father's influence, with the
making of some important English investments on behalf of the Elector.
This gave him the command, if only for short periods, of large sums
of money, and he used them to buy gold and silver and smuggle them
across the Channel into France. This in itself was extremely profitable
so long as he could be certain that the French would give a passage to
his consignments, and to secure consent he arranged that James should
go to Paris and interview the authorities. The Continental blockade was
in force, but Napoleon had found that he must either allow his allies a
certain amount of permitted smuggling into, and out of, England or
lose them as allies; and James, by representing that the English were
extremely anxious to prevent the precious metals from leaving their
country, was able to obtain permission to receive his parcels from
Nathan. The English were, in fact, most anxious to get money through

to Wellington, and this, James, by using Rothschild connections to buy bills on bankers in the south of Europe, could do with uninterrupted success.

Later England herself ran short of gold, and Nathan was able to make very large profits, first by knowing where to buy gold, which he sold to the English government, and then by undertaking its transport to the troops abroad. He succeeded also in getting across to Holland, where he bought up the French money with which the Continent was flooded, and again through his brother in Paris conveyed it to Spain.

His services to the English were fully recognized by the Chancellor of the Exchequer, and he made use of his new credit to suggest at once that the Rothschilds should be given part of the work of transmitting the British subsidies to Austria. At this time the expenses of handling these subsidies from Britain were very high. Metternich reckoned that what with loss on the exchange, commissions, and bankers' charges, one third of the money—two millions out of six—would disappear before it reached his hands. The British government naturally desired that as much of its money as possible should be spent on the upkeep of the Austrian armies and it was glad to support the advances of the Rothschilds when they offered to undertake the work without upsetting the exchanges and to guarantee the money's safe arrival. But the Austrians at that time preferred to have their affairs mismanaged by Austrians and Christians rather than that they should be handled prudently and honestly by foreign Jews.

In spite of this check, however, the reputation of the firm was spreading all over Europe. The renown of Nathan in particular was growing, and it assumed a legendary tinge when one of his agents brought him the news of the victory of Waterloo a day sooner than the official despatches reached the British government. It was said that Nathan's information had been obtained by a special secret pigeon post, and also that he himself brought it across the Channel through a raging storm, and laid the foundations of his incredible fortune by utilizing his knowledge on the London Stock Exchange. If, as is highly probable, he did use his early information in this fashion, he can have made only a small amount in comparison with the enormous sums he had already earned. What in fact he did with the news was to take it at once to the government, which refused to believe it, and was correspondingly impressed when it was confirmed next day.

The financial readjustments which followed Waterloo were the perfect opportunity for the Rothschilds. To begin with, the war indemnities imposed on France had to be conveyed across a distracted Europe. To every other agent this meant the physical moving of cash and bullion in large amounts, with its attendant risks. The Rothschilds alone were in a position to give an absolute guarantee against losses, for they alone could raise the money where they wanted it without any movement of cash at all. They were, in fact, immediately entrusted with the handling of over £20,000,000; and they received for their successful conduct of the business a commission of 1½ per cent, the warm thanks of the English Chancellor, and their longed-for opening in Austria. The government of that country, heavily in debt to its own bankers, not only now consented to receive its share of the indemnities from their hands, but also allowed them to advance large sums on account of future payments. These transactions went off so well that the Emperor —after a good deal of solicitation—granted titles of nobility to all the brothers except Nathan. In fact, so convenient did the Austrian ministers find it to deal with this family, who kept their engagements, who carried through their business with the minimum of disturbance, who took the trouble to have their letters written in a hand which ministers could read, and phrased in a manner which laymen could understand, that in complete reversal of their previous most Catholic attitude, Solomon was invited to set up a branch in Vienna and entrusted with the issue of a lottery loan of 20 million gulden. In the meantime Meyer Anselm (Meyer Anselm II), the eldest brother, who had remained in Frankfort, had lent several millions to Prussia, and the new Viennese branch was soon to finance a loan of £6,000,000 to Russia. All governments at this time needed money even more urgently than usual, and for the Rothschilds it was for a time a question of naming their own terms and picking and choosing among their possible debtors. The nobility of Prussia and Austria were equally in need; so that both the Viennese and Frankfort branches of the firm were also able to build up a lucrative business in making private loans.

The partition of Europe between the brothers was now completed by Metternich, who sent Carl Rothschild to Naples where the Austrians had been crushing a revolution. It was Carl's business to manage the loans forced on the people of Naples by their conquerors and to represent the Austrian interest. A true Rothschild, however, financier rather than partisan, he began to identify himself with the country in which he settled, to oppose the continuance of the Austrian occupation, and to stand out against the more outrageous of the Austrian claims. In order to reëstablish Neapolitan finances he lent the little kingdom very large sums on his own account, and when its rulers proved incapable of prudent administration, he forced them to accept his nominee as Minister of Finance, got their affairs into some sort of order, procured a loan for them from England, and so improved his reputation that he achieved finally the unexpected position of banker to the Pope!

In the meantime James had opened a bank in Paris, where loans were as much in request as everywhere else. It was an immediate success. He soon became, after the King, the richest man in France, and Metternich said to him: "The house of Rothschild plays a much more important rôle in France than any foreign power, with the possible exception of England." The Rothschilds were now the greatest financiers in the world, and for the next twenty years, at least, their fortunes continued to increase.

It is unnecessary, for the purpose of this book, to trace the remainder of their careers in further detail, for they did not alter their policy, the third and fourth generations produced no dominant figures, and on the whole they held aloof from the real business of the new age, the industrialization of Europe. Solomon in Vienna financed Austrian railways indeed, and interested himself in mines and blast-furnaces. But he supported these enterprises solely as a financier—the organization of a great industry, its technical side, made no appeal to him. The French Rothschilds bought oil-fields in Russia, but sold them in 1911 to the Royal Dutch Shell group. First and last the Rothschilds have been dealers in money, with only one other spontaneous interest. If they begged for titles and pushed their way into the social life of the capitals of Europe, it was because that method of approach was forced upon them. Without titles they could not have entered into the personal relations with the nobles who held what was almost a monopoly of offices of state. Old Meyer Anselm had made his way by his knowledge of coins and jewels; his sons patronized the arts in the same spirit —it helped them to obtain what the Americans call "contacts." The head of the firm in Frankfort led a simple bourgeois life—if James in Paris threw money out of his window he did not throw it for the fun of the thing, but as means to an end. Their descendants have acquiesced in wealth—they have never produced a new idea for the handling or spending of it.

They ceased to dominate the finance of Europe, not because of failure or disaster—they have saved themselves from that with remarkable skill—but because the gold discoveries of the last century, flowing into the new channels provided by the growth of industry, went to build up not only great accumulations but millions of small middle-class fortunes, and thus made possible our joint-stock banking system and its towering structure of credit. There is too much money in the world to-day for the resources of one family to be any longer of dominating importance. The Rothschilds are said, by refusing a loan, to have prevented Metternich from making war upon Belgium. In 1930 ten million small investors would rush to take their place.

To return to the one great unmercenary activity which has been mentioned—the assistance of their fellow-Jews. From the beginning they used both their money and their interest on behalf first of the Frankfort Jews and later of Jewry wherever it may be found. To the present day that tradition holds them. It is easy to set this down to calculation, to say that when they freed their fellow-Jews they freed themselves, and that the money expended came back to them in grateful coöperation. The letters they wrote, the way they went to work, do not give that impression. Racial loyalty seems to have been as much part of the instinctive make-up of these remarkable men as their family solidarity or their persistence in business.

If the Rothschilds had never lived, would the world have been worse or better off? There is no decisive answer to the question. They accumulated enormous fortunes—constellations of enormous fortunes; their rate of profit was extremely high, and the states which harboured them paid dearly for their assistance. On the other hand, they worked very hard for what they earned, and rendered what are called "distinguished services." We may say a great deal against them. They charged too much. Though they turned their coats when governments changed on the whole they supported reaction. They deteriorated under the strain of wealth. They used their wealth and intelligence to set an example of ostentation, and supported no great principle or cause but the grievances of their own race. They were the first to manipulate the Stock Exchange on a large scale. Finally, they were and are, in respect of their own jobs, totally unscientific. In the financial welter which followed the present war, no single Rothschild came forward to unite the enormous fund of information which the family must possess with the theoretic knowledge now at the command of economists. One such man might have saved a thousand blunders and been of incalculable service to the world.

To their credit one must place this—they were honest. To arrive, they made use of the methods of the age, but what they promised they performed. No one had ever been honest before on so large a scale, in respect of transactions passing through so many hands and in such troubled times. They not only honoured their own obligations, they introduced financial integrity and sound financial methods into courts and places where such things had never been seriously thought of. Dishonesty is one of the most wasteful and destructive of anti-social vices, and the prestige the Rothschilds gave to probity in finance was a very great contribution to the economic development of the new time. Whether that contribution could have been made at a lesser cost to the community is now only an historical speculation. All that they did was just and justifiable by contemporary standards.

CORNELIUS VANDERBILT, JAY GOULD AND RAILWAY DEVELOPMENT

We turn now to two men whose money-getting lives are best considered together in contrast and conflict. They lived in the same financial world; they played their games on the same board, but while Gould was essentially a maker of money, Vanderbilt was a man of a more complex intellectual and moral quality. Both were fairly unscrupulous when it came to bribing a legislator or a judge. Neither of them amassed his fortune simply by buying cheap and selling dear and by loans and usuries. They won their gettings by much more active and aggressive proceedings. They played a complicated part in the process of replacing old methods of transport by new—the cardinal fact of human history in the middle of the nineteenth century.

That period saw a very great stimulation of productive industry by the discovery of new supplies of gold in California, Australia and other regions. This meant, as we have already pointed out in our discussion of money and credit, a rise in prices, a fall in the real value of debts, and so a relief of debtors and an unburthening of business. Everywhere enterprise found money easier to obtain, became brisker; in particular, the spread of the new railroads and steamships was quickened.

Material forces and social needs were all on the side of a rapid extension of the new transport over the whole United States. On the other hand, as we have noted in Chapter III, the early disposition was to use railways only for heavy traffic of not very long range, and it was only slowly—and too late to get wide gauges—that men realized the immense possibilities of long-range trains and continental railway transport. Consequently, the story of railway development in America begins with the appearance of a miscellany of petty lines. The linking of these into systems of wider range involved huge operations and bargainings, struggles to "capture" railways and so forth of the most extraordinary sort, made all the more extraordinary by the feeble grip of the legal and police organization, in many of the states, upon bold and resolute men who knew when to employ violent methods. With this linking up of the American network is associated the rise of such names as Morgan, Harriman and others, but it is on Jay Gould and Vanderbilt that we will focus the light for our present study.

Vanderbilt was the older, abler, and greater man but it suits our present purpose better to make Jay Gould the *jeune premier* of our display.

Jay Gould was born in Roxbury, New York State, in 1836. He came of a respectable English family. The Christian names of his forbears included Nathan, Abel and Abraham, and his build and appearance were Hebraic, but according to his biographer, Mr. Robert Irving War-show,* there is little other evidence of a Jewish origin. His parents were extremely poor, and his health suffered all his life from the privations he endured as a child. And, for an American millionaire, his religious training seems to have been superficial.

He was obliged to work far too hard on his father's little farm, and when, after only a year's schooling, he got a job in a country store, his hours were from six in the morning until ten at night. He said afterwards that he used to get up at three in order to study mathematics and surveying, and that during this time he arrived at the hard and permanent realization that one must look after oneself and let others do the same. At seventeen he obtained a post as a map-maker, working first for a firm that went bankrupt and then on his own account. He was more or less successful, and local people began to talk of him as a promising young man, but the chief advantage he gained from his surveying work was that it took him from one area of exploitation to another and introduced him to wealthy people. With one of these, a rich retired tanner named Zadoc Pratt, he managed to establish a friendship so close that the old man finally offered to set him up in a tannery. The two were to be equal partners, Gould was to do the work, and Pratt to furnish the capital of $120,000. Gould seized his opportunity, made a success of his tannery, and was soon recognized as an able man of business by the leather merchants in New York. Unfortunately for Pratt, he was also one of those men who find it impossible to be honest. He could not keep his fingers off money, and within a year the old

---

*Author of *Jay Gould. The Story of a Fortune,* from which many of the facts in this account are taken.

tanner found that his protégé had been falsifying the books. He did not prosecute, but merely told Gould that he must either buy his, Pratt's, share in the business for $60,000 or be bought out himself. Gould went to New York, where he soon found financial backing in a wealthy and respected leather merchant called Leupp, and Pratt retired, having lost $60,000 through his generosity.

Leupp did not live long to regret his bargain. Three years later a wave of depression swept over the country, and in the middle of the business anxieties occasioned by this he discovered that Gould had been using his name to make large purchases with the idea of arranging a corner in hides. Overwhelmed by the fear of disgrace, this second benefactor shot himself, and Gould was left to struggle with the heirs for the control of the tannery. In the end it came to an actual fight between two bands of armed men. Gould apparently tried to best Leupp's son-in-law over some detail of the negotiations, and both sides tried to secure possession of the tannery by force. Gould's army of fifty men were victors in the battle, but his opponent managed so to tie up the business by litigation that Gould abandoned it and set off for New York with the few thousand dollars he had been able to retain.

In that city he found almost at once another wealthy man to befriend him. This time it was a grocer named Philip Miller, upon whom Gould made so favourable an impression that he was soon accepted as a son-in-law. The marriage seems to have been completely happy, for Gould, it seems, possessed an affectionate and gentle side, which he reserved almost exclusively for domestic use. At that time Miller owned a large block of worthless shares in a derelict railway—the Rutland and Washington—and Gould, who appears to have had no particular occupation, suggested that he might be sent to inspect and report on the line. It ran through country he had covered during one of his surveys; he knew the railway had possibilities and advised his father-in-law to purchase control. This was done, Gould was made president, secretary, treasurer and superintendent, and succeeded within a few months in selling his own share of the railway to a neighbouring line for $130,000.

With the profits from this he purchased control of other small lines, pulled them together, or made a show of doing so, and then sold them to the big railway combinations which were forming at that time. He had a quick eye for the potentialities of these little railways, and in less than a year he had made a profit of $100,000. If in fact he reorganized these lines before he parted with them, it was the last constructive work he ever did. He used his winnings to set up in Wall Street as a partner in a firm of brokers, Smith, Gould & Martin, and from that time forward, whatever he may have said he was doing, he devoted himself to the manipulation of share values.

Little is known about this firm, or about Gould's transactions while a member of it, but neither of his partners came to a good end, and both became his enemies. Martin died bankrupt in an insane asylum, and Smith was ruined by Gould. From the first Gould seems to have worked on his own account rather than in conjunction with the firm, using his connection with it principally to bring himself to the notice of bigger men. The great event of this phase—which covered the period of the Civil War—was that he came into touch with the once notorious Daniel Drew.

Drew was the treasurer and director and virtual controller of the Erie Railroad—the most important of the growing and extending railway systems which connected the Middle West and the Great Lakes with New York. He had got himself on to its board of directors first by spreading rumours about its financial stability at a moment when it needed money, and then himself, for a very high price, lending it the funds required. He was by origin a circus man and cattle drover who had "got religion" and subsequently made a large fortune out of steamships on the river Hudson, and after that another large one on Wall Street. He was now using his position—with an entire disregard for the interests of the shareholders—to cause movements in the price of Erie shares. He could, apparently, make them rise and fall as far and as quickly as he chose, and though the line was a valuable property and doing an excellent business Drew was making more from it on the Stock Exchange than the railway itself made from its total traffic receipts. When he met Gould he was in need of an ally. His hold on the Erie was threatened by New York's greatest financier at that time, Cornelius Vanderbilt, and he felt himself inadequate for a single-handed struggle. Vanderbilt was proposing to rescue the Erie Railroad from Drew's unrighteous hands.

So we bring Cornelius Vanderbilt into the picture. Let us explain who he was and why Drew should have found him too formidable to resist alone. Drew had already had some disagreeable experiences of Vanderbilt. Vanderbilt at this time (1869–70) was over seventy years old. He was born in Port Richmond, Staten Island, and—with his possibly abler son William—he occupied a dominant position in the railway world.

He was essentially an improver of business; Gould essentially a

A FASTNESS OF THE MONEY SYSTEM
THE New York Federal Reserve Bank at 33 Liberty Street,
New York City.

A FINANCIAL NERVE CENTRE
WHICH MAY STIMULATE OR INHIBIT

THE three small windows belong to J. P. Morgan's office, 23 Wall Street.

plunderer and wrecker. Throughout his life Vanderbilt had been taking hold of things and making them go better—with very great profit to himself and his family.

His father was a poor farmer, and as a boy of sixteen he left the farm and started a modest ferry-boat service of his own between Staten Island and New York. These ferry-boats then were small sailing boats. It needed little capital to start such an enterprise. By efficiency and ruthless overwork, and by equally ruthless economy at home, he made his service trustworthy and respected. By the time he was twenty-three he had got together three boats and $9,000,—as well as a wife and family. The boats were bringing in a steady income, and most men would have settled down at that in gradually expanding contentment. But steam was now appearing in the world, and he sold out his ferry service and began life again as an employee, as captain on a rackety primitive steamship, in order that he might study and follow up the possibilities of the new power.

At that time the state of New York had granted a monopoly of steamboat traffic to two men, Fulton and Livingston. But this monopoly applied only to the New York landings. The boat Vanderbilt commanded was a "pirate," dodging between the state of New York and the state of New Jersey, and he had not only to secure punctual running with thoroughly unreliable engines, but also he had to protect his boat and his crew from the sabotage and persecution of his competitors and himself evade arrest whenever they stopped within the New York jurisdiction. In spite of the handicap of these conditions, he built up a service, and made it pay so well that to break the competition Fulton and Livingston offered him four times his salary and the command of their largest steamer, if he would abandon his employer and come into their pay. He refused, for he intended to become an owner himself, and to make that possible it was necessary to break the New York monopoly. He remained therefore the manager and inspiration of his original employer in the legal struggle that followed. The details of it may be read in *Commodore Vanderbilt,* by J. A. Howden Smith. In 1824 Chief Justice Marshall, in the Supreme Court of the United States, decided that any shipowner might take his vessels to any landing in the States so long as he possessed a coasting license. So the New York–New Jersey service won its freedom. Steamboat traffic was increasing rapidly on all the American rivers, and Vanderbilt next organized a service for his employer between New York and Philadelphia (25 miles in 22 hours for $3.00), which was the cheapest, fastest, and most comfortable in the country. By 1829 he had $30,000 saved and felt able to set up for himself, move to New York, and build up a fleet of his own.

His driving force, his courage, and the quickness with which he seized upon new developments—such as the water-tube boilers stoked with anthracite which were everywhere displacing the old wood-burning engines—enabled him to cut prices and drive out competitors, and in the years which followed he became a wealthy man, the owner by 1848 not only of some of the finest ships in the country, but also of ironworks and shipyards. At that time Daniel Drew was also running steamships; the two men made friends and together bought the Boston & Stonington Railway, which, with their steamers, gave them a through route from New York to Boston.

It was the Californian gold-rush of 1849 which enabled Vanderbilt to take his next step towards financial greatness. At that time transcontinental railways were undreamt of, and the shortest route to the gold-fields was via Panama. He saw that if he could run boats up the River San Juan—which flows between Nicaragua and Costa Rica—organize a steamship service across Lake Nicaragua and make a canal of a few miles to the Pacific, it would give him a route 500 miles shorter and far less expensive to work than the one in use. He travelled to London to get money for this scheme, but without success, for not only was the San Juan River considered to be unnavigable on account of rapids, but Lake Nicaragua lies so high above sea level that a canal would involve the construction of extremely extensive locks. Not to be discouraged, Vanderbilt went to Nicaragua himself in a small boat with a wooden bottom, determined to steam up the river anyhow. He took command himself, and said afterwards that when they reached the rapids, "I just tied down the safety valve and jumped the damn rocks." He did finally organize his "Transit," taking the passengers as far as the worst rapids in iron-hulled boats "which used to clang merrily as they jumped from rock to rock," and then sending the traveller on by a porterage, another stretch by steamship, and finally a coach service. The scheme succeeded, for the journey was shorter by two days than the Panama route and cost only $300 as against $600. This achievement both made him famous and brought him a fortune; by 1853 he was worth $11,000,000. When he went to Europe again in an immense yacht of his own building, he was received by the Lord Mayor of London at the Mansion House and by the Czar of Russia.

When he got back he found the "Transit" involved in a filibustering war, and he seems for some years rather to have enjoyed taking a vicarious part in it by means of agents, subsidies and political intrigues. But he finally abandoned the enterprise when he sold his ships in 1859. At that time he was running an Atlantic service and was able to compete successfully with other American lines, but taxes placed by Congress on hulls, engines, iron, steel, copper, lead, spars, sails and cordage made it impossible for American boats to hold the sea against the French and British. He decided, therefore, to leave shipping and concentrate on railways.

A large number of railways had already been built in New York State, but they were short, wastefully planned, and over-capitalized, and many of them had gone bankrupt or almost bankrupt in a financial panic which had swept America in 1857. Yet the need of great trans-continental lines, the great future of American railways, was becoming more and more plainly manifest.

And now Cornelius was to find congenial help in his own household for his new creative task. During the Civil War his eldest son William had asked him whether he might be made receiver of a small derelict line in Staten Island. He wanted to try out his administrative ability. He reorganized and reëquipped this line so successfully that in five years its shares had risen from a few dollars to $175. Manifestly, then, this might be worth doing on a larger scale. In 1862 Cornelius began to buy stock of the New York & Harlem Railway, when it stood at $9.00. He got control, gave the line to William to reorganize, and the stock rose to $50. A year later he did the same with the New York & Hudson River. During these operations he was twice assailed by Daniel Drew, and twice defeated him. On the first occasion Drew persuaded the New York Common Council to sell Harlem Railway short, and then break its price by suddenly rescinding an ordinance which give Vanderbilt permission to run a tramway line in conjunction with the railway. The councillors sold at $100 thousands of shares which they did not possess, only to find that Vanderbilt was the purchaser, and that all the real shares of the company were also in his hands. The bears were ruined, all but Drew, who persuaded Vanderbilt, apparently for the sake of their old association, to let him off for half a million dollars.

The next encounter was of similar character. Vanderbilt had brought before the State Legislature a bill allowing him to amalgamate the two railways. To do this he was obliged to bribe legislators, and he bought enough promises to get a majority. Drew, however, arriving later at Albany, persuaded the people's representatives that they were missing a chance of making large profits. Hudson Railway shares, he explained, stood at $150; if they sold short and then defeated Vanderbilt's bill they would be able to bring the price down to $50. But again the same thing happened. Vanderbilt, with the support of his friends, was able to buy up all they dared sell, until finally he had bought 27,000 more shares than in fact existed. When delivery became due the price rose to $285—it could as easily have gone to $1,000, but Vanderbilt's friends begged him to settle in order to avoid ruining every broker in Wall Street. Drew, this time, is said to have lost $1,000,000. Even without his bill Vanderbilt was able to effect a practical consolidation of the two lines.

After that he set out to acquire the New York Central, a line running from Buffalo down the Hudson to Albany, where boats or the Hudson Railway carried on to New York. It was not until 1867 that he was able to effect this, and to hand over the line to William Vanderbilt, so that its rails might be relaid, and its engines and cars replaced. In 1869 he secured a Consolidation Bill for all three lines, which now became an efficiently worked and exceedingly valuable property. He was strongly blamed for increasing the stock of the combine from $44,000,-000 to $86,000,000, which with a profit in cash of $6,000,000 was said to be an excessive reward. But the service rendered was great, and the shares of the combined enterprise rose ultimately to $200.

And here we take up the story of Jay Gould again, for it was at this point in his career that Cornelius Vanderbilt came into collision with Drew and with Gould his ally, over the control of the Erie. If once he could add that line to the other three his hold over the traffic of New York would be complete. It must have irked his efficient, constructive mind to see a great railway allowed to fall into an almost derelict condition—its rails rusting away, its rolling-stock in shocking disrepair, its service untrustworthy—while men whom he regarded as common thieves gambled with its stock. He announced publicly that he meant to clear out the whole pack of them, and he set confidently to work to secure the election of sufficient of his nominees as directors to control the line. It could not have seemed a difficult undertaking. Drew was not popular with the stockholders; proxies (the power to vote in elections of directors) were usually purchaseable, and Vanderbilt must have thought that it would be easy to buy enough of them to enable him to win the forthcoming election, do what he wished about its reorganization, and save himself the expense of actually buying the line.

Daniel Drew was fully aware of his danger, and he invited Gould onto the board in order to strengthen his position. From that moment Gould wielded an increasing influence over the policy of the Erie Railroad. For some time Drew remained as the figurehead, but he was by nature treacherous, and Gould found that his natural ally on the board was not its treasurer, but another director called Fisk, also a protégé of Drew's, and also invited to the board by him in order to defend the railway against the purifying domination of Vanderbilt. These three, Drew, Gould, and Fisk, acted in common throughout the struggle which followed.

It was long and complicated, and its ins and outs are described in a confused but extremely amusing series of articles written at the time by the two brothers, Charles Francis and Henry Adams.* It appeared probable that Vanderbilt's nominees would win the election and get control, and Drew, Gould and. Fisk decided to provide for this contingency. Drew, by arrangement with them, went to Vanderbilt and offered to cease certain of his market operations, and in particular to send Erie shares up instead of down, in return for an agreement that if he were defeated he should be reinstated on the board after the election and sit there in the Vanderbilt interest.

There is really no reasonable explanation of the fact that Vanderbilt accepted. He knew Drew, he knew the man was incapable of an honest intention, much less straightforward conduct, and yet, after the election had resulted in a victory for Vanderbilt's side, he replaced his old enemy on the board. Then he began to draw up plans for an amalgamation of all four railways.

This was the last thing Drew wanted, for it would have put an end to his manipulation of Erie stock. Quietly, therefore, behind Vanderbilt's back, he began to agitate against the proposed amalgamation. Its actual terms when they were stated gave him an excuse. Vanderbilt intended to divide the profits of the new pool between all four lines in such a way that Erie, which earned more than half of the total, would receive only one third. The Erie directors joined together to refuse this, and Vanderbilt found himself defeated.

There was no doubt that he had been betrayed by Drew, and he was extremely angry. In addition, he had been made a fool of in public. He announced, therefore, that he intended to buy up the line and ordered his brokers to purchase enough Erie stock to give him and his friends control.

At that time there was in existence about $86,000,000 worth of shares.

*Reprinted 1929 and published as *High Finance in the Sixties*, Yale University Press.

A large amount of this was held in England by persons not favourable to Drew, the whereabouts of the rest was pretty well known, and Vanderbilt felt confident of his ability to carry out his purpose. Only one danger seemed to him serious, and that was that the Drew party might issue more fresh stock than he could buy. Once before Drew had sold short of Erie and then produced, at the last moment, 58,000 fresh share certificates printed to meet the occasion. Now again Drew's game was trending in the same direction. Under a statute of the state of New York, a railway company might create and issue its own stock in exchange for the stock of any line which was under lease to it, and Drew and his friends had recently bought and leased to the Erie a little railway called the Buffalo, Bradford & Pittsburgh. By creating and issuing new Erie stock in exchange for the Buffalo, Bradford & Pittsburgh stock, the Erie gang could greatly increase the load of stock Vanderbilt would have to buy.

To prevent this manœuvre Vanderbilt decided to litigate. His lawyers applied to the Supreme Court of New York, and, on the strength of some of Drew's past transactions, asked for a series of legal injunctions which would suspend Drew from his office of treasurer, order him to return to the Erie Railroad 68,000 shares of its stock said to be improperly held by him, and debar the directors from adding in any way to the amount of the company's stock then in existence. These injunctions were granted by the judge—a certain Judge Barnard, who was destined to be turned off the bench at a later date for his activities on behalf of Gould and Fisk—and their effect should have been to lessen the amount of stock which Vanderbilt would have to buy by one fourth of the whole amount.

Drew, Fisk and Gould, who were all selling short, seemed to be heading for ruin. Nevertheless, they continued to carry on business and to sell to Vanderbilt, day after day, stock which they did not hold. As for the injunctions, they went to another judge who, under the American legal system, had coördinate authority in New York State with the first, and from him they obtained another injunction suspending one of the directors who was a friend of Vanderbilt's and his channel of information, and staying all proceedings in the suit commenced before Judge Barnard. Vanderbilt replied by getting the latter to forbid any meeting of the Erie Board or the transaction of any work by them, unless his director was at liberty to participate. The Drew, Gould and Fisk group thereupon applied to yet a third judge, before whom they accused

Judge Barnard of having entered into a conspiracy to speculate in Erie stock and of using the process of the court in order to aid his speculations. Thereupon this third judge issued an injunction restraining all parties from committing any acts "in furtherance of said conspiracy," and ordering the Erie directors, other than Vanderbilt's nominee, to continue in their duties and in particular not to desist from converting bonds into stock. In the meantime Judge Barnard was "issuing half a dozen injunctions a day," but being now commanded by the law both to do and not to do everything possible Gould, Drew and Fisk left the judges to fight it out while they perfected their preparations for their final struggle with Vanderbilt.

Before the first injunction they had held a meeting of the directors which authorized an issue of convertible bonds for $10,000,000 for "completing, finishing and altering the road." They said that it was to be spent in replacing the company's worn-out rails with steel rails and in laying a third rail which would enable trains of standard gauge to run over the Erie's permanent way. Ten minutes after the meeting closed they had a second secret meeting and agreed to sell these bonds to Drew and his friends at 72½ per cent. Half of these bonds were at once converted into stock and sent to Drew's brokers. As for the rails, Drew gave orders that the old rails were to be relaid inside out, so as to present their unworn edges to the wheels; of the third rail nothing more was heard.

Then the first injunction came into action, and the price of Erie rose, for the public seems to have imagined that the Erie directors would be deterred by it from adding to the amount of stock on the market. They did not know their men, for the vice-president of the company immediately signed fresh share certificates for the whole of the remaining $5,000,000 worth, stating that he did so "in case a modification of the injunction could be obtained." The secretary then told a messenger to take the books containing these signed certificates and lock them in the safe. A few minutes later the messenger returned, saying that Mr. Fisk had met him, taken the books away from him, and carried them off. That meant that, unknown to Vanderbilt, another $5,000,000 was interposed between him and the control of Erie.

On the day after that, these new shares were placed upon the market. At first Vanderbilt's brokers and friends continued to buy, and the price of Erie continued to rise. Then somebody noticed the dates on the new certificates. It was realized that the Erie directors had disregarded the injunction, but nobody could tell to what extent. The price fell from

80 to 70. Vanderbilt went on buying, but when night fell it was clear that he had failed to obtain the control he desired.

On the contrary, the Erie directors had obtained $7,000,000 in return for practically worthless stock, at least $4,000,000 of which came from Vanderbilt. This $7,000,000 had been obtained in despite of injunctions, and the Erie gang was subject to all sorts of pains and penalties in the sovereign state of New York. But before warrants for contempt of court could be issued the offenders were over the Jersey ferry, safe in the sovereign state of New Jersey.

In Jersey City these financiers took up their quarters in a hotel, surrounded themselves with an armed bodyguard, mounted three 12-pounder guns on the waterfront, filled patrol boats with riflemen, and announced that Vanderbilt and Judge Barnard were trying to have them kidnapped. They were said to have taken with them in a cab $6,000,000 in notes; at any rate, they had with them enough money to secure the passing of a bill by the New Jersey legislature in two hours, making the Erie Railroad a corporation of New Jersey. Then they set on foot a newspaper campaign against railway monopolies, reduced the Erie rates and fares in order to embarrass Vanderbilt still further, and squabbled over the division of the spoils. For a while they were safe, and as arrests could not take place in New York on the Sabbath Day, they could even visit their friends from time to time.

But they wanted to go back to New York for good, and Gould drew up a bill which he proposed to pass through the legislature of New York State, legalizing the recent transactions and making it impossible for the Erie Railroad to be absorbed into Vanderbilt's group. The first time it was introduced the bill failed to pass, and Gould was obliged to take the risk of going himself to Albany where the New York State legislature has its seat, in order to interview members of the legislature. He was arrested, but succeeded first in getting bail and then in giving his custodian the slip. He had taken with him $250,000 of the money recently acquired, and Vanderbilt's papers soon began to bring against him charges of corruption. He was never prosecuted, but subsequent inquiry proved that while in Albany he signed a large number of cheques for large amounts and distributed them among senators without—according to his own statement—being able to remember why he paid them or what he did with them. In any case, he spent enough in the town, in whatever manner and for whatever reason, to make Vanderbilt feel that opposition would be likely to fail. Vanderbilt at this moment was not in a happy position. The carrying off of the

$6,000,000 had brought about a monetary stringency and forced down the prices of all stocks, and he was loaded with Erie shares whose price he was only just able to maintain. The price of the legislators at Albany on the other hand was high, and when Senators disembarked from the special trains which it had seemed worth hiring for such an occasion, they found that Vanderbilt's agents were not in the lobby to buy them. Their disappointment and spite were such that they passed not only the Erie bill, but two other railway bills which they hoped might prove harassing to the Vanderbilt railroads.

Soon after this Drew opened secret negotiations with Vanderbilt, hoping no doubt to make something for himself at the expense of Fisk and Gould. But his partners got wind of it, appeared themselves at the rendezvous, and insisted that any settlement must include Drew's retirement from the Erie Board. Terms were arranged. As Vanderbilt said, he could buy up the Erie Railroad, but not the bond printing press. It was agreed that all suits were to be dismissed and offenses condoned; Vanderbilt got $4,000,000 back in return for Erie shares, various of his friends got money—the property of the railway—Drew retired with a certain amount of plunder, and Gould and Fisk got the line.

This settlement cost the Erie treasury $9,000,000 and left the company burdened with 150,000 additional shares. Gould and Fisk held themselves out as exceedingly indignant—"thunderstruck and dumbfounded" was the way Fisk put it—and stated that in their opinion the line was likely to go bankrupt. But it was all they could get, and they proceeded to make the most of it. They turned all but their own friends off the Board and brought on instead Tweed and Sweeny, the bosses of Tammany. Tweed had been an ally of Vanderbilt, but he had been rewarded for his services to that financier with Erie stock, and he therefore thought it better to go over to Gould, taking with him control of the politics of New York City and the services of certain of her judges. Among them was Judge Barnard, and from that moment his injunctions were as freely at Gould's disposal as they had been at Vanderbilt's.

Thus protected, Fisk and Gould started once more to manipulate Erie stock. In the course of the next few months they manufactured another 250,000 shares, broke the price from 80 to 40, and then—when they had bought all they wanted and desired to force a rise—obtained from Judge Barnard a ruling authorizing the railway to buy the new stock back at par. This ruling directly contravened a law forbidding railway companies to traffic in their own stock, and it led to the bringing of various legal actions. At one time no less than six judges were issuing contrary injunctions in different courts on behalf of different parties, and no less than three different receivers and a referee were judicially appointed to control of the railway on behalf of different applicants. But Gould and Fisk were not, in the end, dislodged. Gould stated in evidence before one committee of enquiry that he thought himself entitled to issue as much stock as he wanted when elections were pending, in order to keep the railway out of Vanderbilt's hands, and this argument is said to have made a favourable impression on the committee. In any case, they came to another agreement with Vanderbilt, by which he was to have a bill he wanted to consolidate the lines he owned already, and they were to have a bill allowing them to issue as much stock as they pleased, and be subject to reëlection only once in five years instead of every year. After that they were the undisputed masters of Erie.

One more brush with Vanderbilt took place before hostilities between the two parties ceased. The rate for a carload of cattle from Buffalo to New York was at that time $125. Vanderbilt cut his rate on the New York Central to $100. Gould reduced his to $75; Vanderbilt went down to $50. Gould retaliated by offering to carry at $25 the carload, and Vanderbilt went down to $1.00. Gould, apparently, was beaten, and the whole of the cattle-carrying trade went to the New York Central. In the meantime, however, Gould had been buying all the cattle west of Buffalo, and he now made a very large profit out of what was practically free carriage to New York. It is said that when Vanderbilt heard that he was carrying Gould's cattle for a dollar a load he resolved never to try conclusions with him again.

All the same, the two men, from policy and conviction rather than from personal feeling, were usually to be found on opposite sides on Wall Street. Vanderbilt worked for prosperity, he took control of enterprises in order to make them flourish; Gould's method was to manufacture disaster in order that he might pick up shares cheap. When Gould and Fisk in 1868 and 1869 respectively, cornered bank notes and attempted to corner gold, it was Vanderbilt who steadied the market and saved numerous firms from ruin. In those days it was easy to corner bank notes. The supply was inadequate to the needs of an expanding commerce, in the autumn when crops were being moved there was always a shortage, and the banks were obliged to keep a cash reserve of 25 per cent against their advances. When Gould and Fisk, together with Drew, managed to raise $14,000,000 and turn it into notes which they then withdrew, the banks were obliged to call in loans to the extent of $56,000,000. There was an acute crisis; prices fell, shares slumped heavily; the confederates who had been selling short for months made enormous profits, and numbers of innocent people were ruined.

Of the unsuccessful attempt of Fisk and Gould to buy up and corner gold we will not tell here. By a treacherous manœuvre Gould managed to sell most of his holding to Fisk, while Fisk, under an agreement with him, was continuing to buy at top prices, and harmony was only restored between them later after Gould had assisted in an ingenious plan for shifting the liabilities Fisk had incurred, to a man of straw. In the later days of their association Gould and Fisk established themselves very sumptuously in New York. They had an office in the buildings of the Grand Opera Company, and Fisk had made for himself a private banqueting hall and a private passageway connecting his apartment with the stage. The troupe of the opera kept him supplied not only with mistresses but with a permanent attraction for his business associates. He is said to have remarked of them: "I travel on my shape, and I like these scarlet women: they're approachable!" Gould took no part in such activities, he stuck to the office, he preferred in the intervals of his piracies to cultivate flowers and lead a peaceful domestic life. His preference was wise—Fisk was murdered later on by the lover of one of his mistresses; but in the meantime the two men worked very well together.

To Gould the murder of Fisk was a great loss. Fisk had been liked by the shareholders and the railway employees, and was useful when it came to a rough-and-tumble. After his death the English shareholders —of whom there had always been a surprisingly large number—decided to get rid of Gould. They organized an opposition on the Board, and when he refused a directors' meeting the English party held one, marched to the Opera House, broke through its guard, held their meeting in the face of an assortment of warrants, and elected a new Board. Their hands were strengthened by Gould's old partner Martin. He had been brought near to ruin by one of Gould's corners, and now he offered his enemies the firm's old books, knowing that they contained evidence which would have sent the great financier to prison. For once Gould could do nothing, and he retired from the Erie followed by a suit on behalf of the company for nearly $13,000,000 and various criminal charges. He was again arrested, but even out of that he made money. By stating that he intended to make restitution, he sent up the price of Erie stock; by denying it, he brought the price down again. When he had done this two or three times he had got rid of all his shares and made enough to indemnify himself against pretty nearly anything that might happen. In the end he did actually hand over a number of securities with a par value of $6,000,000 in return for a withdrawal of the criminal charges, but these papers were found later to be worth practically nothing.

Gould left the Erie Railroad with $86,000,000 of stock and funded debt as against the $22,000,000 it had carried when he joined the Board. Not one dollar of the increase represented any real improvement. Erie, like all Gould's lines in his later life, remained notorious for its mismanagement, inefficiency and dangerous state of neglect. It did a magnificent business, but it was a long time before it emerged from the receiver's hands, and nineteen years after Gould left it before it was able to pay a dividend.

We will not deal in detail with any of Gould's other enterprises. Our story is already too long. A consolidation of the various "elevated" lines in New York brought him fresh unpopularity. Part was due to his having acquired control of the Manhattan by a bear campaign in the course of which, speaking as one of its directors, he made a sworn statement that the line was "hopelessly and irretrievably insolvent." Shortly afterwards it became known that he had been purchasing a majority of its stock, and as soon as this was done the price returned to the point from which he had depressed it. Further, by posing as a friend, he deliberately ruined Cyrus Field, one of his associates in the transaction, for suggesting that the Elevated Railways ought to be a public service.

From that time forward he became less active. In 1884 there was a Wall Street panic in which he is said to have lost very nearly $20,000,-000. Whatever his losses he was able to leave to his descendants one of the largest fortunes in America. He was not and had never been a man who gave to charity. By this time his health was failing—although he could not bear to admit the fact, he had developed tuberculosis. In 1892 he died. When the news of his death reached Wall Street, all the securities in which he was known to have large holdings went up.

The nomad, the pirate, was written all over the life of Jay Gould. He played a rôle in the spreading American community parallel to that of the early nomad raider towards the early agriculturalists in the alluvial plains of the Old World. He plundered and he devastated. Were he taken as the test instance for freedom of private enterprise and the contemporary cash and credit system, they would stand condemned for having produced and tolerated him. In the conflict between the State in the person of Judge Barnard, for example, and this anti-social individual, the latter seems to be given all the power and freedom, and the former is a mere weak bribable piece in the game. But the Vanderbilt story throws its light on our problems from a different angle. This is even more the case with the Rockefeller history to which we shall next proceed. We find Vanderbilt and Rockefeller the instruments of very broad economic reconstructions, which it is hard to imagine achieved in any other fashion. Reactionary and conservative-minded thinkers would argue that Jay Gould was an unavoidable evil, that he was the shadow of the freedoms in which alone progress could occur. But progressive and socialist would dispute this. They would maintain that all the good and little of the evil of the Vanderbilt-Rockefeller type could be released in quite a different fashion.

J. D. ROCKEFELLER AND THE ORGANIZATION OF OIL PRODUCTION

In our second chapter (§ § 6, 7, and 8), we have described the amazing increase in available substances and the development of new sources of power that are making over man's world anew. Each extensive exploitation of new substances, and each new utilization of power since the onset of this period of science and invention, has had for its correlative the development of great fortunes. We may take as the typical story of this species of wealth the history of oil and the Rockefeller fortune.

While Vanderbilt was extending his railways, J. D. Rockefeller was building up that "Mother of Trusts," the Standard Oil Company, and amassing what many people believe to be the greatest single fortune in the world. The life history of Rockefeller is the history of his trust; he made it, and equally it has made him; he has grown and adapted himself to it as it grew, so that apart from its story it seems hardly necessary to detail his personal life in chronological order.

A fact outside his business life on which hostile critics have laid stress is that he is unquestionably a sincere Baptist, that he attended his church every Sunday until age forbade, and brought up his family as believing Christians. They found that inconsistent with many of his business acts. There is, for example, legal proof, in judgments and accepted evidence, for the statements that his business methods have included lying, perjury, the bear of false witness against his neighbours, widespread bribery, the corruption of other men's servants and of public officials, the use of threats, and the obtaining of illegal drawbacks and rebates. His whole career indeed has displayed a very complete disregard for the rights or interests of anyone opposed to himself and his projects. "The little revolutions" he has stirred up in Mexico and South America have cost many lives, and he has ruined by the thousand not only the fortunes of his fellow-citizens, but what—if we are to hold to the precise teachings of his sect—he should regard as their immortal souls. But while doing all this, he has been accustomed to collect money for his church with great energy and ability. He also gave abundantly and freely; and he has certainly always been a charitable man. Such apparent inconsistencies of doctrine and method may be due to nothing more than intense preoccupation with his main concern. A man concentrated upon an accumulative effort that rapidly developed vast creative possibilities may have had no time to turn back on his upbringing and scrutinize the precise formulæ of his faith. And there is a sort of constructive excitement, an intensity of conviction, that can make men extraordinarily ruthless and unscrupulous in their dealings with antagonists and obstacles. Theologically J. D. Rockefeller has remained what he was as a boy; in substance and effort he has changed with his times, his successes and his opportunities.

All his life he has given generously. It is estimated that his benefactions must by now have amounted to £600,000,000. And they have been made—we have had occasion to note it already in this work—with distinguished wisdom and ability. They have left a perceptible mark on the advancement of science. A "perplexing psychological dichotomy," say some observers, a man whose right hand is abnormally unaware of what his left hand is doing. But before we dismiss the personal make-up of J. D. Rockefeller in this way, as a monstrosity, we have to bear in mind the standards of honesty and enterprise, the legal and political unscrupulousness, the ready resort to violence, prevalent in the American community at the time of his ascent. He bore false witness perhaps in a crisis, but what was the tangle he was pushing through? He stirred up revolutions in little states, but what had the governments of those little states done to him? We have already had a sample of those standards in our study of Jay Gould as a money-maker.

The importance of J. D. Rockefeller in the development of modern economic conditions is very great. Two great achievements are his. In the first place, he organized the collection and marketing of mineral oil and the comparative stabilization of its price throughout the world. In the second, he inaugurated, by his immense success, the era of Big Business.

Even now it amazes that from his first entry into the oil business until he attained virtual control of the entire industry was less than ten years. At the end of that period he was in such a position that he alone could fix the prices of both crude and refined oils. When he went to the oil-fields, an unknown man of no particular wealth, he found that every section of the trade was suffering from overproduction, wasteful methods and confusion. The getting of the oil to the surface was carried on by that type of greedy, emotional, optimistic pioneer which is attracted by risky enterprises promising enormous profits. These men were in many cases able and ingenious, but one fact always defeated them—the fact that if a man refrained from drilling for his own oil it might be drained away from under his land by the drilling of his neighbour. The "oil men" were never able to overcome the suspicions to which this gave rise and combine to restrict their output when some hitch occurred in transport or marketing. Only once did they stop the drills and for only a few months. They would let the oil run to waste on the ground rather than not drill. Any accident, therefore, might break the price of oil, and with production continually pressing upon storage capacity, new oilfields being discovered and old wells running dry, prices fluctuated from dollars to cents, and individuals alternated between wealth and ruin.

The refining section of the industry was run by ordinary business men, but as in the early days it had been impossible to get their machinery and materials to the wells, the stills had been started wherever transport conditions made it feasible. As the railways built branches to the actual oil-fields, these refineries found themselves being undercut by new enterprises starting at the mouth of the wells. As for the railways—the four roads in question were in a state of what almost amounted to open warfare. As will be evident from the section on Gould, they were precluded by the personnel of their governing bodies, and the fraud, violence and treachery which had characterized their relations, from entering into any durable or trustworthy agreements. Their officials, though probably less corrupt than their directorates, seem to have been incapable of refusing bribes, and various oil refineries had already found it practicable to extort illegal rebates on their cargoes. And all these causes of difficulty and uncertainty were accentuated by the activities of speculators.

It was the refining section of the industry which Rockefeller entered when he turned from a mixed transport and commission business to deal with oil. Within three or four years, through sheer ability, he had become the largest refiner in the country, only to find himself faced with falling prices due to reckless overproduction on the fields. He had every reason to desire that some sort of order might be introduced and some attempt made to limit production and to stabilize prices, and the plan he produced was always stated by him to have been drawn up solely for the good of the industry. There is no reason why we should not take his word for it. For good or evil, had the plan remained secret it must have succeeded. First he persuaded the leading firms of the Cleveland district to enter a common company and allow him to arrange for their buying and selling. This made him by far the railroad's largest customer. Next he used this position to bully and bribe the railways and extort from them concessions which would involve the ruin of his competitors. The scheme took some time to arrange, for he had to convince the railway chiefs (or so they swore) that his company intended to take in all the existing refiners, but in the end he secured three things: a heavy rebate on all his own oil, a cash payment for every barrel of oil carried for a firm outside the company, and a promise of the fullest and earliest information of any moves on the part of his competitors. Armed with this agreement, he was able to go to the refiners who had not already joined his company, and make it clear to them that if they would not sell out to him at what he considered a reasonable price, they would have to go out of business.

As far as the refineries were concerned, his plan succeeded—he was able to buy up on very advantageous terms all the remaining stills in the district. He shut down the less efficient and less favourably placed, and limited the production of the others; he introduced improved methods and took over the buying and selling for the industry. In fact, he rationalized the industry on the refinery side.

For a time, however, as far as the producers were concerned, his scheme failed. His secret leaked out, and when they found their transport charges being raised, the oil men organized to attack him. The story of this struggle is extremely interesting and very valuable to anyone who wishes to understand the social behaviour of human beings, but there is neither space nor need to tell it here. With the rest of the early story of Standard Oil it may be found in Ida Tarbell's well known indictment *The History of the Standard Oil Company*. It is enough to say that the organized oil men so far won that they got Rockefeller's company condemned in the courts as an illegal conspiracy in restraint of trade, forced him to dissolve it, and made him sign an undertaking to take no more rebates from the railway companies. For some months they boycotted him, and they succeeded in rousing a great deal of sympathy. In fact, they won the first engagement in that prolonged fight between the Standard and public agitations which was to continue until the Great War. By then, on the one hand, Mr. Rockefeller's benefactions had for more than a decade maintained their exculpatory flow, and on the other, the importance of a steady, efficient production of petrol to mechanized armies and navies had placed the great oil companies under the protection of their governments and beyond the reach of newspaper criticism.

This initial check, however, did not frighten Rockefeller in the least, or succeed in changing even the details of his procedure. By this time he had made up his mind to obtain, through control of transport, effective control of the whole industry, and he did it. He bribed his way through the boycott, bought up some of his chief enemies, and had concluded a fresh arrangement for railway rebates some days before the date on which he had promised to forswear them forever. It was his pull with the railways which made it impossible to defeat him. He kept to himself the names of all the firms he had bought or brought in—he could tell every railway in turn that he would withdraw all freight if they dared to disoblige him, and none of them knew that he was, in fact, dividing it between them all. As long as cars were the only means of moving oil, he could undercut everyone else on account of his rebates, and if that did not force his competitors to sell, he could either see that they were refused cars or storage, or he could tamper with their supplies of raw material. Whenever the producers organized against him he had only to wait, choking their outlets, until they could hold up oil no longer, or at worst to buy enough men among them to defeat the others. When judgments were given against him in the courts, ordering him to dissolve his trust, he pretended to obey them, changed a name or two, and went on conducting his affairs in all other respects precisely as he had before. When he was personally indicted for conspiracy, he contrived to get the suits withdrawn at the cost of a bargain which he did not keep.

The railways themselves were able to do nothing against him. When one of them, the Pennsylvania, dared to resist his demands in order to protect the rights of the last considerable group of independent refiners, an all too manifestly arranged strike broke out on their line which crippled its working, and a drop took place in the price of oil which forced the refiners to sell out.

When it became clear that the pipe line would supersede the railroads as carriers of oil, Rockefeller extended to pipe lines the methods he had adopted with refineries. When the producers attempted to construct a line of their own to do what was supposed to be impossible— to pump crude oil over the Alleghany Mountains to the sea—he obstructed them at every step. His newspapers attacked the characters of the chiefs of the enterprise in order to damage its credit. His agents frightened the farmers over whose lands the pipes must pass, by stories of poisonous leakages and unquenchable fires, and gangs of railway employees attacked the workmen laying the pipes.

The first attempt to get a free pipe line past him was killed by this sort of opposition. A second succeeded, only for it to appear that a third of the company's shares were in Rockefeller's hands, and that his nominees were so strongly entrenched in its councils that he was able to impose a working alliance upon it.

As he monopolized the pipe lines, he also reorganized them. That is a very important point on his credit side. He did not monopolize to extort and stagnate. In his hands the pipe-line organization became a service of extreme efficiency. When in 1878 a new oil-field was discovered, in three years United Pipe Lines created a whole new system of pipes to carry this fresh oil. But the cost of this extraordinary achievement was recovered from the men in possession of the fields by Rockefeller forcing down the price of crude oil while he kept up the price of refined. It was complained that at one time he was eating up the whole of their profits by his charges for transport and storage. Perhaps it is truer to say almost all. They could do nothing effective against him because he was the only carrier and also the only purchaser for their oil.

While he was completing his control inside the industry, he was carrying on a tremendous campaign for markets, not only throughout the United States, but in every country in the world. As always, his method was to make his own enterprise extremely efficient, to insist on the highest skill and integrity among his own people, and to take every possible advantage of the timidity, greed or dishonesty of everyone else. By the end of the century he had built up in his own country a system of espionage and corruption so complete that he was said to receive information about every movement of every barrel of independent oil. If a peddler hawking paraffin on a barrow purchased a gallon from an outsider, he was confronted by a Standard agent and bought up or intimidated or systematically undersold.

Standard Oil was also engaged throughout this period in fighting anti-trust legislation, as well as the private bills by which the dwindling number of independents sought to secure way leaves or charters. Rockefeller was said to have bought a seat in the Senate of the United States for the uncle of Standard's treasurer, and his agents were familiar figures in the lobbies of all lesser legislatures.

Gradually the knowledge of these methods leaked out. It did not simply leak out, it came out presently in a blaze of denunciation—perhaps of exaggeration. Whenever, as happened frequently, a suit was brought against the Standard Oil Company—and it was a rich corporation to bring suits against—the evidence given would be published as loudly as possible in the press and more than once it roused—or was used to rouse—a great popular campaign against trusts. At every step in his career Rockefeller had engendered envy and resentment, and every corner grocer by now was feeling that although he was living in the land of the free, the Standard would break him if he did not knuckle under to its regulations. In those prosperous days there seemed to be enough wealth for all—men might easily believe that only wanton rapacity could spread far-reaching frustration in order to organize a trade. And in fact the success of his methods had been so great and manifest that nobody felt safe; small men in every industry wondered when they went to bed whether they might not wake to find their independent livelihoods menaced by such another frustrator, and the ordinary consumer was induced to believe that the Standard kept up the price of oil systematically, except when it was undercutting to ruin someone. A campaign against the trusts became a leading issue of party politics; there was a burst of legislation, and in 1907, at the end of a tremendous lawsuit, the Standard were ordered once again to be dissolved and to pay $29,000,000 in costs and penalties to the State. Rockefeller is said to have received this news while he was playing golf, to have paused, observed: "It will be some time before that judgment is carried out," and to have gone on with his game.

In fact, the fine was never paid, nor was the judgment ever made effective. In 1911 there was a show of dissolution, but nobody supposed for a moment that either the direction or the policy of the Standard would be changed. It was rumoured that Rockefeller had made another fortune on the Stock Exchange by anticipating movements in his shares. Nor did anyone credit his statement that he had retired from control of the Standard in 1895—when the first dissolution was supposed to be taking place—and was living now as a private citizen concerned only with his family and his charities. In fact such was the public state of mind that nobody believed a word to which the Standard officials swore unless it served to condemn them. When on one occasion a man brought to trial for tapping one of the Standard's pipe lines admitted that he had stolen a considerable quantity of their oil, the jury acquitted him forthwith.

The hatred that was felt for Rockefeller seems to have died down. That may be due in part to his age and in part to his liberality. But much more is it due to changing views of the utility of his achievement. In the days of his ascent the social ideal in America was a mosaic of small independent, prosperous undertakings. It was a jostling conflict in which no doubt many failed, but wherein also with a certain smartness but with no steadfast wickedness, and with loud protestations of "live and let live" and "give everyone a chance," everyone might expect to do as well as his neighbour—and perhaps a little better. The reality to which this ideal led was a clumsy, socially wasteful life of petty competition, keen rivalries and mean triumphs. Politics were profoundly corrupt, the law courts untrustworthy, the press blatant and unscrupulous. There was no living spirit of public service, no "sense of the State," no coöperative end. It was an Individualist's heaven, Babbitt land. That was the world into which J. D. Rockefeller was born, with a relative steadfastness of purpose and a power of organization greater than he knew. In a muddle-headed and unscrupulous scramble he was clear-headed, creative and unscrupulous. He did not play a much wickeder game than everyone about him was playing, but he certainly played that wicked game better. And so the world about him was filled with the resentment of the defeated and the protests of besters outbested. Most of the literature against him is saturated with the paradoxical implication that in a competitive world one should not compete too much.

No one who understands anything of the conditions out of which he arose can believe that this organization of business on a new scale, the elevation of a private business to the dimensions of a world power, could have been achieved by generosity or scrupulous fairness. Generosity in his dealings would have been exploited and fairness misunderstood. He competed after the patterns of competition all about him, and so—to the great economic advantage of mankind—he killed competition. If his success was a scandal, then the competitive system in business is responsible for the scandal. He is the supreme individualist working out individualism to its logical end in monopolization. And of all the base criticisms his career has evoked, the charge that his magnificently intelligent endowments have been planned to buy off criticism or save his soul from the slow but sure vindictiveness of his Baptist God is surely the most absurd. It is made a grievance .against him that, unlike most of the successful financiers and industrial adventurers of our time, he has not bought yachts and palaces and women, run theatres, gambled, been a "good feller," and bred a family of spendthrift sons. His worst enemy cannot accuse him of a trace of the normal snobbery of the *nouveau riche*. He has deposed and bought legislatures, but that was because they were not for public service but for private sale. Manifestly he has grown and broadened at every stage of his career. He has changed as he has lived. The young man born into conceptions of Protestant virtue and self-help, saving his few dollars weekly and gripping every opportunity with all his strength, developed consistently into the great business chief whose thoughts and influence have spread out from the organization.of.pipe lines to the organization, with the same unsentimental thoroughness, of scientific research.

We are trying here to state the facts about this extraordinary .man. He is put here for the reader's consideration and judgment. It has been urged against him that he debased business standards in America, and certainly that is unforgivable. But did he do so? He was living in the world of Jay Gould and Hetty Green. He did not raise standards as the Rothschilds did, but did he lower them? Something in the nature of J. D. Rockefeller had to occur in America, and it is all to the good of the world that he was tight-lipped, consistent, and amazingly free from vulgar vanity, sensuality and quarrelsomeness. His cold persistence and ruthlessness may arouse something like horror, but for all that he was a forward-moving force, a constructive power. Like begets like, and he did not so much seek to found a family as to create a great research organization and devote his family to it.

J. PIERPONT MORGAN AND THE OLIGARCHY OF CREDIT

Let us turn now to the rise of the great firm of J. P. Morgan and Company and its bearing on the financial organization of the world. On one facet this great agglomeration of monetary power has been associated since its beginnings with the adventurous story of American railway exploitation, on another it marches with the mighty organizing abilities of J. D. Rockefeller and the attempt to link the whole monetary and industrial life of America and perhaps of the world into an aggregate of coöperating non-competitive trusts. This attempt was fought

and thwarted, on sentimental and democratic grounds, by Theodore
Roosevelt. As it developed, as J. P. Morgan the First aged and passed,
the Morgan organization took on more and more of the character of a
responsible institution, becoming aware, to a certain extent, of the implications of its opportunity. The War made it a power capable of dealing upon more than equal terms with states and governments. Whether
it is as yet fully aware of the implications of its opportunity we cannot
say. It is still to-day a cardinal reality in our debt-strained world.

There is no authoritative life of J. P. Morgan, the virtual founder of
this creditor organization, but J. Kennedy Winkler has produced a vivid
and convenient sketch of his career (*The Life of J. Pierpont Morgan.*
1931) to which we are considerably indebted in this summary. He was
the son of an already prosperous banker who had begun as a dry goods
merchant, and from the first he moved in an opulent atmosphere. He
was born in 1837. At school he was "the richest boy in the school" and
he completed his education at Vevey and Göttingen. He was, he held, a
"gentleman," and bound to observe certain standards of veracity and
honour. His contempt for contemporary democracy was profound. At
Göttingen he distinguished himself in mathematics and played a leading
rôle in his students' corps, with cap and feather, long porcelain bowled
pipe, sword and leather breeches all complete. He went to London in
1856, when he was still only nineteen, and was at once taken into the
Anglo-American firm of Peabody and Co., in which his father was a
leading partner. He returned to New York the following year, and
found America in a state of panic following upon a phase of world
optimism and expenditure, that had arisen out of the over confidence
and excess of enterprise produced by the Californian gold discoveries.
He saw a suspension of gold payments and all the distress and tragedy
of a financial tornado. It was the first of a series of devastating panics
that have followed the gold discoveries of '48 and onward. He seems to
have accepted these successive panics without any attempt to probe
their nature or avert them. Later on he was to find them seasons of
opportunity for a wary and conservative financier.

After the panic came the Civil War, and the young speculator seems
to have burnt his fingers and involved himself in a manner difficult to
explain over the purchase and resale to the government of 5,000 condemned carbines. He never did explain. He was too much of an aristocrat. Apparently he was misled and blundered and learnt a lesson and
went on stoically to live the story down. He was presently actively engaged in the manipulation of gold on behalf of Peabody and Co.

In this phase and in certain of its later characteristics, the story of Peabody and Company and the Morgans recalls the Rothschild story. Peabody set out to be trustworthy. His firm manipulated situations, they charged as high interest as they could exact from a government in trouble, but they were scrupulously exact and honourable in the conduct of their transactions; they never lied nor cheated. All this was according to the highest financial standards of their time. They backed the Union Government in the Civil War, when the confidence of the over-cautious Rothschilds was failing, and the reward was great. At one time, they were getting gold for the government from Europe at twelve per cent interest. Peabody and Co. possessed the complete confidence of the British investor at that time, and the Morgans came into the irresponsible Wall Street of Drew, Fisk, Jay Gould and Commodore Cornelius Vanderbilt, to inaugurate a new phase of integrity and stability. But their ethical code was strictly individualist. The necessity of the community was the investor's opportunity.

We have told already of these early days of railway development. "Gould," says Winkler, "picked up railroads as one might collect old coins, manipulated their stock and unloaded on the public." He victimized the investor. But the Morgan code required that the financier should be loyal to the interests of his supporting investors. The promises of a prospectus must be observed. Morgan came into the railway business with the intention of making the properties pay. This improved upon the spirit of Vanderbilt which was chiefly to make them work, and Morgan's first fight was with Gould for the Albany and Susquehanna Railroad which Gould was trying to acquire and use against the Vanderbilt interests. It was a rough struggle after the early fashion. There was actual fighting for this line, head-on collisions of trainloads of toughs, wounds and bloodshed. Morgan emerged triumphantly with the prestige of having "beaten Jay Gould." This was his introduction to the world of American railroad adventure, to which he was to return with enormous effect in the eighties.

But the Morgan story is not only a story of increased integrity and a growing sense of efficient performance, it is also one of associated action instead of purely personal aggrandizement. Both Junius Morgan and his son were pioneers in financial combination. In October 1870 France was in the throes of her defeat by Germany, the army of Sedan had surrendered, the Emperor Napoleon was a prisoner, Paris was besieged and the government had fled to Tours. John Morgan was asked to raise a loan of 50,000,000 dollars for the French Government. He offered to do so in the form of a six per cent bond issue at eighty. These were hard terms for France but the need for cash was urgent. The bonds were offered to the public at eighty-five and were presently selling at par. In order to raise the money promptly a group of financial houses had to be assembled. This "Syndicate"—it was the first appearance of the word in British and American finance—was the beginning of a series of alliances centring upon the Morgan firm. The next was a big group concerned in funding the American War Debt. Thence Morgans—now completely under the personal direction of J. Pierpont, for his father Junius had retired at the early age of sixty-four—entered upon the work of underwriting American railway stock. So we come to the next chapter in the history of capitalist finance; the struggle—less planned perhaps than necessitated—for the consolidation and control of economic life by an oligarchy of banking organizations. It is a struggle—or a drive, shall we say?—which is by no means at an end.

We must refer the reader to J. K. Winkler for the particulars of this intensely interesting process. We will not attempt even a brief summary of the battles of Morgan, Hill, Harriman and the other financial barons in this internecine war. The characteristic and essential rôle of J. P. Morgan was reconciliation, combination, the elimination of conflict, the identification of financial interests. He persuaded or he compelled the men of money to cease from bickering and work together for the common end of profits. He was the bully of peace. We have shown already the inherent need there was in the case of the American railroads for a consolidation of the fragmentary and mutually injurious companies which first exploited the transport possibilities of the continent, and we have shown something of the adventures, robberies and wealth-grabbing that occurred almost inevitably because of this planless drive towards larger and more efficient systems. There was no effective economic government in existence; there was no "competent receiver" (see Chapter VIII Section 6) to take these things out of the hands of private profit-seekers. The so-called democratic institutions of the time were ridiculously unfitted for the job. It had therefore to be done in this fashion or not at all. There were intelligent and vigorous American bankers who were attempting to bring order and a *paying* efficiency into the continental transport system, were in fact blundering towards a public service which was otherwise not attainable, blundering from pure piracy to a more and more centralized profitable administration, hardly knowing what they did. By way of steel rails and the like the financier of transport must presently come into the iron and steel industry. Coal concerns him primarily. Indeed he finds himself, almost unawares, exercising an unanticipated power over every type of distribution. Necessarily the expanding Rockefeller system was early involved in these railway concentrations. J. D. Rockefeller was a man of far greater inventiveness and adaptability than even Morgan, and his Standard Oil organization supplied patterns for Morgan's own interlocking devices. But while Rockefeller absorbed and grew, Morgan accumulated subservient allies. Morgan, says Winkler, hated Rockefeller. He found him cold-blooded and in a way terrible. He was a Puritan; he had no taste. Moreover Morgan detested Andrew Carnegie, who called him "Pierpont" to his incessant annoyance. Carnegie seemed, to this fastidious and self-conscious "gentleman," the quintessence of familiar democratic vulgarity. But this did not prevent Morgan from dealing with both Rockefeller and Carnegie until they had brought together a vast multitude of metallurgical plants and accessories into the one vast property of the United States Steel Corporation (1901). Its structure was frankly modelled upon that of the "Mother of Trusts" Standard Oil. It was evolved by the same forces; its natural ally and associate.

In the closing decade of the century there arose a counter movement to this drive, of which Rockefeller and Morgan were the exponents, towards a vast economic organization that should eliminate waste and competition, and comprehend at last and control the entire material life of the community. The steady getting together of the great property concerns of America was making the politician, the minor economic adventurer and the common man uneasy. Although none of these consolidations had led to any deterioration in public services or any rise in the price of commodities, it was felt that they involved these possibilities. And their treatment of labour was unsympathetic and stupid. The fact that an economic system with definable headquarters—even if these headquarters are not politically responsible—is far more amenable to public opinion than an unorganized chaos, was ignored. The public was alarmed by the suggestion that so soon as monopoly was established prices would be raised to an unendurable level, and the minor producers and traders were rallied to an attack on this "octopus" of the confederating trusts. Washington had already measured itself unfavourably against the new money power. There had been another monetary crisis in 1895 and the government had had to accept hard terms from a combination of Morgan and Belmont, who represented the Rothschild group in America. In 1901, through the assassination of President McKinley, Theodore Roosevelt had become President, and he set himself without delay to a trial of strength between the formal government of the country and this new oligarchy which threatened to take control of all the more vital interests of its citizens.

Already in 1890, Congress had passed the Sherman Anti-Trust Act to prevent the elimination of competition in business, and this Act Roosevelt applied to a merger of the hitherto competitive Northern Pacific and Great Northern railroad companies in the Northern Securities Company. Morgan was outraged by the attack. He raved at Roosevelt as "worse than a Socialist." "If Roosevelt had his way," he said, "we'd all do business with glass pockets." These are the phrases of a conspiring plutocrat and not of a public servant. Morgan manifestly did not understand the forces that had evoked him. The litigation went in favour of the government and the Northern Securities Company was dissolved. It was the first serious check in the growth of the octopus. Roosevelt was triumphantly reëlected in 1904, and proceeded to prosecute Standard Oil and the Harriman group of railroads as conspiracies in restraint of trade. He also carried through the Hepburn Law empowering the Interstate Commerce Commission to fix railroad rates.

The whole spirit of Roosevelt's work was boldly constructive, and in spite of certain personal limitations he posed the main issue of modern political life quite plainly to the world. The higher organization of the economic life of the community under the confederated activities of an oligarchy of irresponsible and adventurous money barons was confronted for the first time in America by the idea of the modernized administrative state. That issue remains undecided to this day.

The issue remains undecided because of the unpreparedness, incompleteness and inefficiency of the contemporary governments. There was no modernized administrative State behind Roosevelt. Only in his more exalted moments did he imagine there was. He felt that the community should control its economic life, make and enforce just laws, conserve its resources and plan its future. But his intelligence was not on the level of the vigour of his personality. He had no sense of the complex educational processes that must underlie a public organization adequate to modern needs. The political structure of America—the political structure of the world—was not responding to the demands of the time. This gave—and gives—the barons of finance their opportunity and their justification. It is still open to them to steal a march upon democracy and reconstruct and modernize the world. Moreover Roosevelt was a strong patriot. In that he was less enlightened than the financiers. He saw his administrative state as pure American. But though he disavowed

Socialism he sustained the railroad workers and miners against the illiberal methods of the profit making trusts.

We have no space here to analyze the causes of the great American panic of 1907 which foreshadowed in many of its incidents the great slump of 1929–31—the slump of which we have given a summary in Chapter IX Section 11. Morgan appeared as a supporter and saviour of tottering financial institutions. But at a price. He forced Roosevelt to acquiesce in the purchase by the Steel Corporation of the Tennessee Coal, Iron and Railroad Company, one of its chief outstanding competitors, before he would bring his forces to the restoration of confidence. Then for a brief period he was a great popular figure.

This was the last important phase in his financial career. He was over seventy. The war of the government against the big trusts went on, but he was already dead, and Roosevelt was dead, when—in 1919—the Supreme Court decided in favour of the United States Steel Corporation. His last public appearance was before the Pujo Committee of Congress "to Investigate the Concentration of Money Control of Money and Credit." This Pujo Committee, says Winkler, "showed that a definite community of interest had been established between Morgan and Co., the First National, and the National City Bank. Figures made plain the enormous power of these groups in banking resources, transportation systems, producing and trading corporations, great public utilities. Firm members or directors of the three institutions, it was disclosed, together held 341 directorships in 112 corporations having aggregate resources or capitalization of no less than 22,245,000,000 dollars."

Morgan died in Rome in March 1913. His bank has passed into other hands and has changed its manners and methods. In recent years it has played a similar rôle to that of the Rothschilds a hundred years ago. It follows the laws of its being. It is on the side of the creditors in a debt-strangled world. At the outbreak of the War, the City of New York found itself unable to meet its obligations in London and Paris amounting to 80,000,000 dollars, and was assisted by a bankers' syndicate organized by the firm. Then J. P. Morgan and Co., became the official purchaser in America of foodstuffs and munitions for the British and French Governments. Before America entered the War the firm had arranged loan issues to the British and French Governments amounting to 1,550 millions of dollars and during the War and after the conclusion of the War up to 1926, loans amounting to 1,700 millions were issued to Britain, France, Belgium, Italy, Austria, Japan, Switzerland, Argentina, Australia, Cuba, Canada and Germany. A second J. Pierpont Morgan replaces his father at the head of the firm, but the organization is not like the Rothschilds, a family concern; it is a constellation of associates and still extraordinarily vital. It has lost any quality it ever possessed of autocracy. J. P. Morgan and Co., like Standard Oil, is not a man's creation, it was a necessary growth of the economic conditions and financial arrangements of the later nineteenth century. Something in the form and nature of these organizations would have come about had J. D. Rockefeller and J. P. Morgan never been born.

In this account we have said little of the personality of J. P. Morgan outside his financial career. For that and for portraits of him we must refer the reader to Mr. Winkler's book. There one may learn of his art collections and his interest in church affairs and beautiful women, often oddly interwoven, of his gusts of passion, of his black cigars and his trouble with a strange disfiguring growth of his nose and how he was obsessed by the resemblance of his life to that of a nobleman of the Renascence, and many such things, entertaining and instructive in themselves but bearing little upon the attainment and use of his wealth —which is our concern with him here. He was an extraordinary man but he does not seem to have been a great man; he was the creature of our methods and his time. It is the money power, and his abnormal arithmetical intelligence, and not the man, which will figure in history.

THOMAS ALVA EDISON

Except perhaps George Stephenson, who invented the locomotive, no human being can have created more wealth than Edison, for his was certainly the most ingenious mind that has ever devoted itself to the commercial application of science. He was born in 1847 at Milan, Ohio, and his formal education was limited to three months in the common school of Port Huron, Michigan. Reading and writing he had learnt at home. The rest of his finally immense scientific equipment, he got for himself, driven by an indefatigable curiosity. His first patent was a device which nobody wanted to use—an instrument for enabling an assembly to vote by pressing buttons and for registering and counting the votes. It worked very well, but was refused by Congress on the ground that it counted the votes too accurately. That refusal made a deep impression on the young inventor. He resolved that henceforth he would produce what people wanted instead of what he thought they ought to want. The fruits of his resolution were to build up half-a-dozen new industries, to provide employment for millions, to extend the reach of civilization, and to enlarge the life of almost everyone who lives within it. Henry Ford says of him that he doubled the efficiency of modern industry—that it is due. to Edison that America is the most prosperous country in the world.*

The list of his inventions is too long to give—he took out 1,500 patents. They astonish by their variety as much as by their importance. Edison made the telephone possible and turned the telegraph into a general means of communication. He invented an incandescent lamp (following Sir Joseph Swan) that would give the amount of illumination needed in a building—the incandescent lamp—and in order to make it useful he worked out an entire system for the generation and distribution of current. He himself says: "It was necessary to think out everything: dynamos, regulators, meters, switches, fuses, fixtures, underground conductors and a host of other detailed parts, down to the insulating tape. Everything was new and unique. The only relevant item in the world at that time was copper wire, and even that was not properly insulated."

Existing dynamos were only 40 per cent efficient: Edison's dynamo gave an efficiency of 90 per cent. This made possible the line of advance which emancipated industry from the belt and shaft and led to modern high-speed tools. He made the typewriter into a practicable instrument and contributed to the development of the storage battery. He invented a microphone, the phonograph and the kinetograph, which was the beginning of the cinema. The first electric cars were made possible by his work, and he also constructed an electric railway—though there the Germans had been before him. He devised methods for making and handling cement which brought it into the field as a material for building construction, and a technique for separating and smelting the iron which is found in sand. He introduced paraffin paper and the mimeograph, which multiplies copies of letters. During the war he worked out thirty-nine inventions for the Navy Department of the United States, but although his country had already recognized him as one of the greatest men alive, he was forced to complain that the Navy Department paid little attention to what he offered them.

This is a formidable list, even though in almost every case the theory of the subject had been worked out and the first practical applications made by others. The principle of the telephone, for instance, had been established seventeen years before by Reis of Frankfort. Professor Bell,

*Henry Ford: *My Friend Mr. Edison.* See also Dyer and Martin: *Edison, His Life and Inventions.*

of Boston, succeeded in producing a system which would carry for twenty or thirty miles; it was Edison who turned it from a brilliant experiment into a commercial success.* In the same way with his incandescent lamp. When he began to work on that, the now obsolete arc lamp, with its sizzling carbons and fluctuating glare, white with occasional violet blushes, held the field; the incandescent thread of imperfect conductivity, the metal thread that would glare or fuse, was known, but not the carbon filament which glared but did not fuse. The task of Edison was to find a filament which was reliable and would burn for long periods, and a lamp which could be handled by the public and would be cheap both to produce and to maintain. His chief original invention was the phonograph, which he was inclined for some time to consider as a toy. The principle of the kinetograph—that successive images superimposed upon the retina at more than a certain rate of speed produce an illusion of movement—had been known for nearly two centuries. The invention of the celluloid film by Eastman synchronized with his own work on the subject, but he was never sufficiently interested to join the host of experimenters who were trying to find a way of projecting the images on a screen and who did ultimately produce the cinema world.

In the beginning, it was accident which directed his attention to electricity—the branch of science which seemed especially waiting for a man with just his gifts. His first interest was chemistry. As a boy he was continually starting fresh enterprises in order to earn the money he needed for books and materials for experiment—he liked to read everything that had been written on each point and to work out every experiment for himself. For he found that he was able to learn more from the actual sight of them than had been gathered, or at any rate recorded, by their originators.

This was an expensive way of working, and his parents were poor. His father dealt in grain and wood; his mother had been a schoolmistress. He disliked school—she gave him the elementary training which enabled him afterwards to teach himself. At twelve he took a job as newsboy on the Grand Trunk Railway which runs between Port Huron and Detroit, and he added to this occupation a number of others initiated by himself. He opened stores in Port Huron, he employed other boys to sell vegetables in Detroit and provisions to emigrants in passing trains. He published a newspaper of his own which he printed on the train itself in a laboratory installed in a baggage car. He would

*The microphone again was first invented by Professor David Hughes F.R.S.

have made a success of it if he had not set fire to the car with some phosphorus and so been deprived of his laboratory and turned off the train.

After this setback he became a telegraph operator—he was one of those men who seem able to learn anything they choose and become expert at everything they learn. As a skilled telegraphist he could get a job wherever he liked, and for some years he wandered about in Canada and the northeastern states, either on railway telegraphs or reporting the proceedings of Congress—work which included filling in the gaps in the speeches caused by the faulty apparatus of those days. As he went he seems to have left a trail of small inventions behind him, but none brought him in any money, and one at least got him into serious trouble.

He was engaged to send signals at intervals through the night from the station where he was working to the next along the line, and he invented an automatic which would do it for him. One night an unusual call was made. He did not reply, so a party went to look for him and found him asleep in comfort beside his apparatus.

It was in New York that he got his first real chance. He had gone there from Boston—where he had invented the vote recorder—in order to sell an idea for a telegraph cable which could be used for two messages at once in opposite directions. The Pacific Telegraph Company adopted it, and are said to have made a great deal of money by it, but to have refused to pay the inventor anything. Certainly he was almost stranded when he noticed one day a noisy crowd outside an office. There had been a breakdown on the Stock Exchange telegraph, and the crowd believed that the apparatus had been wrecked by speculators who wished to prevent the arrival of news. Edison walked in at once and offered to repair the damage in an hour. He carried out his promise, and received in reward the post of technical director of the Gold Reporting Company with a salary of $800 a month.

It was his first good position; he not only saved money there, but met men who were impressed by him and afterwards became his clients. He was soon able to start a small company, "Pope, Edison & Co.," and set up a workshop where he could spend most of his time experimenting. There he devised an improvement in the Stock Exchange ticker which he was able to sell for $40,000, and from that moment the flow of his inventions never ceased.

At first he seems to have had great difficulty in getting paid for them. For our present purposes that is a very interesting point to press. We have been studying money-getters hitherto. But here we have something else, a creator who was forced into money-getting. It is not only that this man did his work from quite other motives than the money motive, but that he was impeded in doing it by money-getters. They bested him, time after time. There are stories about an English company who bought some automatic telephone apparatus and never paid for it at all, and about American companies who involved him in litigation and paid him reluctantly and on a niggardly scale. But he had become well enough known for telegraph companies to bring him their problems for solution, and in four years he managed to save nearly half a million dollars. It was then that he built the laboratory, workshops, library and houses at Menlo Park which were afterwards to become world-famous.

From that time his course was fixed. He had already married, and though afterwards he moved from one set of buildings into another and made occasional voyages to Europe to introduce inventions or receive homage, his real life was spent in the laboratory, among his workers and collaborators. There he took most of his meals, received his guests, and in his spare time held singsongs with his men. His methods of work were still extremely thorough—to start from the beginning, have everything read, worked out, noted up and tried. But he knew how to surround himself with able men and how to coöperate with other minds. He himself could work for days and nights on end if he wanted to, and sleep when he had finished. Time meant nothing—the clock in his laboratory had no hands to its face. He expected his staff to work in the same heroic fashion, and such is the appetite of human beings for interesting work of any sort, their passion for machinery and their capacity for hero-worship, that most of them seem to have enjoyed the life and accepted the régime. If anybody, thinking himself indispensable, tried to impose conditions, Edison would do a little inventing and work out a method which got rid of him.

For his work the man grudged nothing as too costly. He would experiment for years and get deeply into debt in order to try out every possible combination. He recently examined more than 15,000 plants in order to find one which would grow in the United States and assure her supply of rubber in case of war. He spent $40,000 on his electric-light experiments before he got his first crude carbon filament. It burned for 45 hours and was made out of a piece of suitably treated sewing thread. On the other hand, he gathered in great pecuniary rewards. He manufactured many of his inventions himself instead of selling the rights, and he became under necessity a good man of business. In order

THE RUSSIAN WORKER

TIGHTENING bolts preliminary to permanent riveting on one of the water distributors of the Dnieper Dam. The distributor is in the substructure of the power house and will be the largest in the world. According to present plans, the dam, with nine such distributors, will be completed in 1933.

OIL TO–DAY

OIL storage at Bayonne, New Jersey. In the foreground are distribution pipes leading to a great variety of stills and tanks.

to popularize his lamp he contracted to sell at first for 40 cents, although it was costing him 125 cents to make. For three years he lost money—the cost of manufacture was coming down, but sales were increasing rapidly. In the fourth year the cost was down to 37 cents, and he made good all his losses. Finally he invented machines which made a lamp for 22 cents, and then he sold the business.

Edison was manifestly not a man who cared for money for its own sake. Why should he? The acquisitive instinct is plainly something quite different from such gifts as his, and the delights offered by the luxury trades must have seemed extraordinarily stupid and simple to an inventor of his calibre. He had no time to waste in spending and no need to surround himself with visible reminders of his success. All he asked for was the money he wanted to carry out his work—work which has opened to mankind inexhaustible possibilities of wealth. Not all of his inventions have been developed—as the world is organized to-day it does not follow that the man who buys a patent will make the best, or indeed any, use of it. A firm may think it worth its while to suppress a novelty rather than to produce it or to compete against it. It would pay a World State over and over again to buy, not the inventions of men like Edison, but the men themselves—to allow them whatever they want to carry out their experiments, give them the freedom of the planet, and then make the results as they came available to the world at large. That is manifest. Also, as we shall show plainly in our studies of government (Chapter XII) and education (Chapter XV), it is at present manifestly impossible.

HENRY FORD

Ford, like Edison, is a man of higher intrinsic quality than the examples we have taken before these two. His also is a mind dominated by constructive motives, by the desire to invent, and to invent in such a way as to lessen human labour. He was born on a farm, and he says himself: "My earliest recollection was that, considering the results, there was too much work on the place. That is the way I still feel about farming. . . . That is what took me into mechanics."

As a matter of fact, though this may have been his conscious excuse for withstanding his father's wishes, he was instinctively and from the first a lover of machines. His toys were all tools; he says: "The biggest event of those early days was meeting with a road engine. . . . The second biggest event was getting a watch." These three impressions are quoted because they determined the course of all his future energies. He is not by nature a money maker. He is a born engineer, and that stands as the root of his success. In his workshops the technician is king, and as Mr. Ford happens also to be a great organizer, his shops get ahead of those whose owners are less interested in the work being done than in the profits to be made from it.

To this main purpose of saving toil he has added another—that of using his enormous undertaking to build up prosperity where he wants customers. The acquisition of a personal fortune really seems to count for nothing. He puts his money back into the business, where he spends it in improving his factories, raising his wages and lowering the price of his products. His business, to him, is "almost sacred." He has devoted his life to it, and it is the axis of the philosophy which he expounds in his books. In this doctrine, too, he believes with the faith of a man who has started life with a few simple ideas, carried them out, and found that they made of him the world-famous head of a great industry.

His mechanical training he began himself, with the help of the watch. By the time he was thirteen he could take it to pieces and put it together again so that it would keep time. At seventeen he persuaded his father to let him become an apprentice in a machine shop, and in his evenings he worked with a watchmaker. There he decided that, as watches are not universal necessities, he would not devote himself to making thirty-cent watches, but would invent a mechanical tractor which would do all the hardest work of a farm and especially ploughing. To this end he took a job with the Westinghouse Company, where he would have a chance of working on road engines, and in his spare time, in a little workshop at home, he endeavoured to build a steam car that would run. He built it, and it did run, but he soon realized that steam vehicles, to be safe, must be far too heavy for the existing country roads, and too expensive for any but the richest farmers. Moreover, the public showed no interest in agricultural machinery—it was only through the success of the motor-car that the farmers came to see its possibilities. So he turned his attention to road cars and began his search for something light, something cheap, something that could be used by everyone. The Westinghouse Company could not help him with this, so he left them and "looked around for another sort of motive power."

The single cylinder petrol engine had already been developed in England, and in 1885 Ford was given one to repair. He then built one for himself, to make certain that he understood it, and began to experiment on double cylinders. He moved to Detroit, took a job with the Detroit

Electric Company and worked half the day and all night long on Saturdays at bringing out a car of his own. His main difficulty was that though he knew that other people were working on horseless carriages he could not know what they were doing. His main support was: "That my wife was even more confident than I was." In 1893, when he was thirty years old, this first car "ran to my satisfaction." It was built of bits and scraps, its wheels were bicycle wheels, and it was not cooled at all, but he drove it a thousand miles and then sold it for $200.

About this time he met Edison—an important meeting partly because it influenced the trend of his ideas, partly because he received encouragement on the subject of his car. He even refused the position of general manager to the Edison Company in Detroit because it was coupled with the proviso that his car must be abandoned. But Edison became his lifelong friend. By 1899 he felt that he could do something with his car; he threw up his other job and "went into the automobile business." He had saved money, but he was not in a position to finance a whole undertaking by himself, so he formed the Detroit Automobile Company in which he was chief engineer but holder of only a minority of the stock. This arrangement was not successful. The creative man and the financier were almost immediately in conflict. Ford wanted to make better cars as a step towards a wider market, the company wanted to make immediate profits. To the man obsessed by his idea, the man of nearly forty who had given up his life to the solitary accomplishment of his task, this attitude was shocking. Nor was it financially successful. He resigned in 1902, "determined never again to put myself under orders." From that day to this he has been unable to tolerate either the ideals or the methods of financiers. He is, indeed, one of our most striking witnesses against the value of the money motive.

In 1903 he founded the Ford Motor Company. First he built a car fast enough to win in a race against the track champion of America; then he founded the company on the advertisement this gave him. In the new concern he was vice-president, designer, master mechanic, superintendent, general manager and owner of 25½ per cent of the capital of $100,000. Only $28,000 of this was ever paid, and this $28,000 is the only money the company has ever received from other sources than sales of cars. From that time, he says, he was never short of money. In 1906 he bought his holdings up to 51 per cent; a little later he was able to increase this to 58½ per cent. In 1919 his son, Edsel Ford, bought up the rest of the stock at a price of $12,500 for each $100 share. This seems to have been done in order to reaffirm once again Ford's dislike of sleeping partners in business. He has no use for the investing public, and that, in view of what we have said in Chapter IX, § 10, is very interesting to us. The other stockholders had brought an action against him, in which they demanded that a larger proportion of the profits should be distributed in dividends instead of being put back into the business. Ford won his case by convincing the court that the best possible use had been made of the shareholders' money, but he did not care for a fiduciary position when that meant running his business to profit other people instead of to justify the creative drive in himself, and he solved his difficulty by getting rid of them. The only outside shareholders now are understood to be those of his own workpeople who have bought shares offered under a special scheme.

From the beginning he ran this new company on his own lines. As what he wanted to produce was not a luxury but an article for general use, he determined to "concentrate on the best selling product," to produce the smallest number of models at the lowest possible price, to make them as light as possible, foolproof and perfectly reliable. He announced that what he was selling was not a machine but a guaranteed amount of service, and that if anything went wrong it was up to the company to see that the purchaser suffered as little as possible. This brought him customers in large numbers at a time when buying a car was considered to be a rich man's gamble, since it might be expected to break down at any moment, and there were no arrangements of any kind for service or repair.

In 1909 he carried this policy to its logical conclusion and decided to sell only one model, Model T, of which he said: "'Any customer can have a car painted any colour that he wants so long as it is black." But though only one model was on sale at any given moment, the car itself was always changing, continually having put into it, the maker claims, better workmanship, better material, and better design. That model ended, for instance, by using twenty-four different types of steel.

When he had decided on the form of this model he turned to build up his marketing. That in itself must have been an undertaking sufficient for the ambition of most business men. Ford's idea was to sell through a network of agencies which were to cover the United States. Every agent was to have clean, attractive premises, carry a complete stock of spare parts, be able to offer a reliable repair service, and know every potential customer in his district. When this was on its way to accomplishment, he turned back to improving the efficiency of his system of production.

This system of production has received as much criticism as the car; it has been as successful. Its master idea is the elimination of waste. Not an inch of factory space is to be wasted, not a moment of time, not a fragment of scrap, not an ounce of physical strength nor of mental effort. Ford has built an electric motor into every machine in the engineering shops in order that their alignment might not be restricted by the possibilities of pulleys and shafts and belts. It is wasteful to employ engineers simply as pedestrians and carriers, so the work, with all necessary tools and materials, is everywhere carried by machinery to the hands of the men. He will not have a man obliged even to shift his feet if it can be avoided. . . . It is wasteful for able-bodied men to do work which can be carried on by disabled men, and he therefore employs considerable numbers of blind, deaf and crippled men. They are paid the usual rate of wages, and he says that they are worth more to him than normal men, for they are glad of the work, and not so worried by its monotonous or trivial nature as men who look about and hear outside noises would be.

It is wasteful to spend human labour hewing and hauling coal when we all, in the course of our ordinary lives, produce combustible refuse without devoting any particular time or thought to it. He therefore, where refuse is available, builds power plants which are able to consume it—his new Dagenham works will be run largely upon the rubbish of London. . . . It is wasteful to ship cars (and pay import duties on them) when parts can be packed more compactly and more conveniently handled. He therefore ships parts and has them assembled wherever in the world they are needed for sale. This involves the complete interchangeability of every part, and that means that many of them must be accurate to $\frac{1}{10000}$ of an inch. To control this the gauges, themselves ten times as accurate, must be tested to something like a millionth of an inch. In order to achieve this degree of accuracy Ford became himself a manufacturer of gauges.

But his greatest struggle has been devoted to the saving of time. When he started mass production it took him twelve hours and twenty-four minutes to assemble a chassis. By subdividing every operation and studying every movement he cut that down to one hour, thirty-three minutes. Dies, again, required seven hours to make and could only be used about 40,000 times. He devised a method which would produce in two minutes a die which can shape from 80,000 to 100,000 pieces. The same story has been, and is, going on at every point in his factories. He never ceases his search for machines which will carry out a process faster or with less human labour. By the time he had exploited to the full the process of subdivision, the invention of the turret enabled him to build machines each one of which performs several operations on a part before returning it to the worker. When electric welding became practicable on a large scale, .he decided to dispense with all casting as fast as his staff could invent machines to do each particular job by welding instead. So he gained in strength, lightness and simplicity, in the elimination of faulty castings and in the supersession of that machining which all finished castings require. In fact, Ford's principle is that while every operation is standardized for the time being, no single operation, material or product is ever standardized in the sense that it is considered incapable of improvement.

"Years ago," says Lord Melchett in *Why the Crisis* (1931) "the power plant of the ordinary factory consisted of Lancashire boilers where rows of sweating men, black with coal dust, stood shovelling coal into the fires by hand, very often working in the open and usually stripped to the waist. A modern boiler plant is attended by a couple of intelligent men in white coats, who walk about watching their recording instruments, occasionally turning a tap or so, and drawing a great deal more than the pay of one of the sweating hand stokers of the old days." In the Ford plant this emancipation of the stoker is carried to its extremest limit and the coal flows from the River Rouge lighters to the blast furnace without staining a human hand. But it occurred to Ford that there was something improper in a furnace room without either shovel or barrow or iron pokers, and so at the end of the white and silvery arcade there is a sort of trophy of the bad old times, shovel and pokers and barrow of silver, resting for ever on a crimson cloth.

To obtain the incentive for his unceasing, relentless pursuit of economy, Mr. Ford relies on his basic principle of constantly raising wages and lowering prices. He believes in the theory that it is the function of industry to create the prosperity which will enable the public to buy its products. If these are to be sold all over the world, money must be distributed as widely as possible. More than once he has cut prices and raised wages, not because it was justified by the figures of his actual business, but on the promise of the increased sales which he anticipated as a result of this procedure. When, on one occasion, the new sales did not mount quickly enough to prevent a loss, instead of putting back the old price he made a further cut, and this brought him the result he wanted. His own explanation is that the whip laid to the backs of the staff by increased charges resulted every time in new economies which more than counter-balanced the new burdens. The whole thing happened, however, at a time when there was a sharp deflation going on in the United States, so that in real value his new price was very little smaller than his old one. In the nineteen years during which it was producing the famous Model T, the Ford Company paid out wages and salaries to the amount of almost two thousand million dollars. If the rewards of agents and outside workers in garages and repair shops generally are added, the total comes to nearly five and a half thousand million dollars. This does not include the pay of the workers on his railway, oil-fields or rubber plantations or in his mines. The sums distributed by the company in purchases fall little short of five thousand million dollars. He may well claim that this is a substantial contribution to international prosperity.

It is in pursuit of this prosperity, as well as to save the heavy costs of transport, that he has placed his factories and assembly shops all over the world. He likes to balance the drain of money into the funds of the company by the provision of work and a corresponding outflow of wages and salaries. But he goes further. He thinks that work should be so planned as to provide the best possible life for the worker. The great industrial cities he regards as evils—the normal life seems to him one which allows a man to work on the land in summer and come into the shelter and light of the factory in winter time. He has several factories of this type established in the United States. In Kentucky and Virginia he is said to be taking factories to the mouth of his mines so that the miners may be able to spend only half their working hours below ground and for the rest of their time earn their living as machinists.

While all the work of carrying out this system was being done, Ford was extending his business. During the war he added to the manufacture of Model T that of farm tractors for the English government, and many smaller products for the government of his own country. These tractors realize a very early ambition. They are designed to lessen the heavy work as well as the cost of farming—each is in reality not only a tractor but a light and portable power plant. Since the war he has scrapped Model T—of which 15,000,000 had been sold—and substituted a car built on more modern lines; he has also undertaken the manufacture of a luxury car—the Lincoln. His aëroplanes are among the most trustworthy of American models. In addition, stoppages in his supplies of raw material, some due to accident, others to business operators, have forced him to buy a railway (which paid for the first time after he took it over), mines, rubber plantations and oil-fields and to manufacture for himself glass, cloth and several other materials needed for the manufacture of his car.

He is now, in fact, by himself a gigantic "vertical" combine.

It does not fall within the scope of this book to discuss Mr. Ford as a pacifist, as a denigrator of Jews and bankers, as an admirer of the arts who presented the "homey" Detroit patriotic poet, Mr. Guest, with a Ford car every year for several years, or as the nature lover who has had his garden fitted with birds' nests suspended on flexible steel springs so that his wrens may use them undisturbed by sparrows. It is more to the point that he has created and maintains a large model hospital specially organized to check the professional failings of doctors, and that he runs schools for boys in which the pupils are trained in several skilled crafts and earn from the first a good rate of wages. He has given the world these, and a car and a tractor which have reduced labour for millions. He has given it also his great business, a heavy item to the credit of the individualist capitalist system. His museum of technical history at Dearborn promises to overshadow Munich and South Kensington. It is a vast and necessary educational assembly. This is what the profit-making system can do—run at its best, with the spirit of greed eliminated and a real desire to help mankind put in its place. Even so, his productive organization has been attacked—bitterly attacked—on the score that it is a despotism, that it is harsh and that it wears out its men. A despotism it is—that is what makes of it so illuminating an example. Ford is not primarily a humanitarian or a philanthropist. He is an excessively ingenious mechanic, with a divine passion for putting things in order and making them "go," and on that level he must be judged. His psychological insight is inferior to his mechanical insight. As a politician he has shown himself ignorant and naïve. The Peace Ship story makes it clear that his pacificist ambitions were cloudy and insubstantial when the concrete future of his factories was at stake. (See *America's Don Quixote* by L. P. Lochner.) As for the other charges—that sort of thing is a question of more or less which cannot be weighed here. An admirably temperate indictment will be found in Edmund Wilson's *Devil Take the Hindmost*. The figures Ford gives of average length of service seem to prove that his men are not physically worn out. The criticism seems to boil down to this—that his workers are completely absorbed, capable away from work of only the crudest recreations and unable to play any extra part as useful citizens. That is a criticism which can truthfully be made of whole classes and communities of business men in every country, and it leads us again to the connected problems of education and the use of leisure.

In summing up Mr. Ford's work and its rewards the question of desert seems hardly relevant. However much he has, and whether he deserves it or not, his is a mind which can be trusted with money. Let him make as much as he can—it will be used for important purposes and in a stimulating and individual way. The essential point is that he does not want money for its own sake, and money has never been his main incentive. For him money is opportunity to make, and if he could have had opportunity in any other form he would probably have been equally satisfied. His approach to financial discussion has always been that of an irritated man.

ALFRED LOWENSTEIN

We now turn back again from these processes of wealth accumulation by creation, to the more purely acquisitive type of accumulators. While the great forces of invention and accelerated communication embody themselves in such great industrial forms as Standard Oil, Imperial Chemical Industries, United States Steel and so on, there runs by the side of these huge organizing processes a great multitude of people intent merely on getting rich by virtue of the opportunities they afford. We have studied old-fashioned forms of accumulation in the cases of Mrs. Hetty Green and the Rothschilds. Essentially such types are "wealth-grabbers." The wealth was there, anyhow, and they did nothing to increase it. They merely accumulated it. Let us see now how wealth-grabbing can be practised under more recent conditions, with the aëroplane to replace Nathan Meyer Rothschild's corner in fishing boats, and with all the bold precedents of the railway and oil kings to follow. Alfred Lowenstein, whose life was ended accidentally or deliberately by a fall out of an aëroplane while crossing the English Channel, can be taken as the crowning instance of the modern financial adventurer who neither evokes wealth nor buys existing wealth, but who seizes upon it as it struggles into being.

There remains an element of mystery about his end. A preliminary enquiry returned a verdict of accidental death, but his body was recovered a week or so later and Dr. Paul, the French pathologist, examined the body and reported the presence of "toxic matter." Lowenstein seems to have been in the midst of very extensive financial operations in which he was losing considerably, and there is no very clear account of his actual position at the time of his death. He may have been mortified and tormented by his situation at that time, but he was certainly not a ruined man. Very naturally, the tragedy was followed by a slump in the securities in which he was interested, but the mere fact of his death while the market was in a nervous state would be sufficient to account for that. Here is a man who appeared suddenly in our financial skies, buying and selling on a scale of romantic enormity.

He was, it seems, the son of a small banker in Belgium; he was born in 1874, and when his father went bankrupt with 1,800 (pre-war) francs of debt in 1892, the son reconstructed the firm, accepted his father's obligations, and became a broker in Brussels. For some years he worked in partnership and without any great distinction. He was propagandist of the geographical distribution of investments and showed himself skilful in guiding the investing public to new fields of risk. His first considerable opportunity came in 1906, when he was able to raise capital for the Rio de Janeiro Light and Power Company. Investments in Brazil were not well known at that time, and he earned his money by a very vigorous pushing of the new securities. He proceeded to other South American flotations. His methods did not pass without hostile criticism. He was already a multi-millionaire (in francs) before the war. The war perhaps retarded his development for a time; he joined up and served his country in England (where he bought remounts for the Belgian cavalry), and in America, but he still found opportunities for profit. The relative value of railways, tramways, power companies and so forth in South America increased with the destruction and exhaustion in Europe; the French and Belgian francs staggered at the end of the war and every ordinary investor was assailed by doubts and fears. Wealth offered itself to the alert, and Alfred Lowenstein was one of the alertest men alive.

It was after the war that his phase of conspicuous magnificence began. Then he became a speculator on a vast scale, interesting himself chiefly in hydro-electric undertakings and the new great industry of artificial silk. He clambered to the position of the third richest man alive. But all he did was to "find money" for these enterprises, and he found it in the most expensive way for both the enterprises and the primary investors. It is hard to avoid the conclusion that even at the best phase of his career he was only in a very limited sense an operating organ of the economic body. Possibly he irritated a too sluggish banking world which was retarding new developments into greater activity. That is very doubtful. Essentially he was a boil on the face of business, and a very conspicuous and dangerous boil.

Privat* gives some glimpses of his life in its brilliant phase. He moved between a suite of rooms he possessed at Claridge's in London and a suite he took by the year at the Ritz in Paris; he had a palace in Brussels, a great estate at Melton Mowbray, where he entertained the Prince of Wales, and a great villa at Biarritz. He was surrounded by an army of secretaries and stenographers. He had private aëroplanes for the use of himself and his special messengers at Croydon, Le Bourget, Brussels and elsewhere. When the Belgian and French franc went through a period of rapid devaluation in 1925 he offered, upon certain conditions, a loan to these governments at 2 per cent sufficient in amount for an immediate stabilization. It was refused. His ambitions were boundless. He seems to have aimed at a control of the entire electric supply of the world. He was caught by a sudden restriction of his credit through the concerted action of a powerful group of banks, and shorn of a considerable part of his incredible fortune. He tried to regain what he had lost, too hastily and rashly; his operations were ill-judged and unsound, and he was certainly in the grip of a second shearing operation at the time of his death. How far he was a mere gambler and "operator" it is hard to determine. His anticipation of the future of electric-power enterprises and of artificial silk was certainly intelligent. Privat says he consulted fortune-tellers and was guided in some of his decisions by communications made to him through various "mediums" by a spirit "Phlogiston." By the scale of payment of ordinary human activities, the wealth he came to handle was fantastically vast. It was somewhere in the region of twenty million pounds or so. In 1928 the 430,000 shares of his International Holdings Company stood at £31,000,000 and receded to £18,500,000. On the news of his death in July this fell further to £12,500,000.

It is very remarkable how poorly documented all such careers seem to be. There is nothing about Alfred Lowenstein in the New Encyclopædia Britannica and nothing about him in the 1928 Who's Who. I have quoted already from an able little book about him by Maurice Privat, but it is improbable that his life will ever be exhaustively studied. While the poor little affairs of obscure, industrious men of letters are made the subject of intensive research, and while every scrap of their entirely unimportant private correspondence commands the money of eager collectors, the far more romantic, thrilling and illuminating documents that must be scattered abundantly through the world, about these seekers and makers of great fortunes, are neither gathered nor cherished.

*La vie et la mort d'Alfred Lowenstein.

When at last the scientific historian of the economic processes of our times sits down to his task, he will have small reason for thanking the collectors of letters, diaries, private account books and personal memoranda. Beautifully preserved First Editions, autographs, and the self-conscious love letters of a thousand insignificant scribblers will leap to his hand, while hardly a scrap of early Harmsworthiana or Zaharof-fiana or Lowensteiniana will be forthcoming.

MEN WHO HAVE GONE BEYOND THE PERMITTED LIMITS

If, however, we descend to the next lowest grade of wealth-seekers, we come immediately to a soundly documented record, because we have the reports of their trials or of the public enquiries after their suicides. These are the quite illegal wealth-seekers, the men who did not restrain their acquisitive effort within the limits of the law. They were too impatient or too clumsy or not lucky enough to avail themselves suc-cessfully of the permitted ways of acquiring large sums suddenly. They blundered into tight corners, and then, by the rules of the game, they cheated, or else they set out to cheat from the outset. Such "operations" as those of Jabez Balfour with his Liberator Society, which flourished in appearance for fifteen years after it was bankrupt, or the London and Globe Company frauds of Whitaker Wright, may serve as classical in-stances of financial affairs below the threshold of permissible enter-prise, and from such cases we pass down to a consideration of such simpler abuses of confidence as the creation—the forgery, to be more exact—of fictitious shares. This has been occurring periodically on a large scale throughout the last hundred years, and it has taxed the economic process to the extent of many hundreds of millions.

One of the outstanding instances of money getting, in recent years which passed beyond the legal limits, is the Hatry affair. Clarence Hatry was a good-looking attractive energetic young man, whom at the outset probably did not seem to differ from, let us say, the young J. Pierpont Morgan, whose story we have already told. Internally he did differ, in the facts that he did not understand the art of building up confidence in his fellow creatures and that he imagined himself clever enough to break the rules without being found out. But both were getters. Both followed the ruling conception of our business life that success is to get. And throughout his career and even after his collapse, Hatry had many sympathizers and even admirers in the financial world.

The City had had an early intimation of a certain—shall we call it unsoundness?—in his quality. He had as a very young man been as the *Economist* (Sept. 28th, 1929) put it, "an exponent of rationalization in its most irrational form." In 1919, he organized various glass concerns into British Glass Industries with a paid up capital of £3,659,709, and after a series of operations, from which he seems to have derived no personal profit, the capital value was reduced to one quarter of this amount in 1924 and the company was finally wound up in 1926, when the shareholders found themselves with ninepence for every five shilling share they had in the already reduced enterprise. There were other parallel experiments with jute and other businesses and a "Commercial Corporation of London" went into liquidation in 1923 with a loss of over two millions.

This the City regarded as brilliant but unsound finance. It was all accomplished without any breach of the law, and apart from his shareholders' money, Hatry lost little but a reputation for success and trustworthiness by these evolutions. However, in 1925 he succeeded in achieving what is called in this City in which our money and credit are manipulated, a "come back." "We thought," said one financial wiseacre in telling me about him; "he had learnt his lesson and most of us believed he was a very very clever fellow. Not all of us, but enough of us to let him get going again." This time an "Austin Friar's Investment Trust" with a capital of £300,000 appeared and resumed the business of "irrational rationalization," this time with drapers' shops, the Drapery Trust and other retail trades and later automatic photographic shops. In 1926 Hatry opened up a new field and founded a Corporation and General Securities Limited to float loans for corporations. Wakefield, Swindon, Gloucester and Melbourne trusted this new-born company as though it was a bank. And in 1929 he attacked the wider and greater field of the iron and steel industry with his "Allied Ironfounders." For the greater convenience and privacy of his operations he established "Secretarial Services Limited" which acted as secretaries and registrars for his undertakings.

And then it became more and more evident that something was wrong with this spreading Hatry octopus. It was in difficulties. It was in such grave and complicated difficulties that the Stock Exchange suddenly stopped dealings in a whole list of "tainted" stock and shares. It became more and more plain that Hatry and his associates, entrusted with the power of printing scrip certificates for these various loans and receiving the money for them, had succumbed to two obvious temptations. They had printed more than they were entitled to print; they had sold these forged certificates or obtained loans by depositing them as securities. There were other offences but this was the typical offence. The little group of financiers passed into the dock. They were charged with obtaining by false pretences and with intent to defraud nearly two million pounds. Hatry won the admiration of the City by taking most of the blame for these irregularities upon himself and he was sentenced to 14 years imprisonment. Whether he will ever achieve a second "come back" is still hidden in the obscurity of the future. The total default of the Hatry group was about £13,500,000, but the loss caused less social disaster than it might have done because a large part of it fell upon big banks and kindred financial concerns and upon jobbers rather than on the small private investor. The whole affair was so rapid and novel that the Stock Exchange had not unloaded upon the general public.

The Hatry business was impressive because of its magnitude and if it did not ruin a very great number of homes, it nevertheless distressed the Stock Exchange by chilling the confidence of the ordinary man. There was a check upon the hopefulness of investment, which aggravated the effect of the American slump we have already described in Chapter IX. But presently a new figure of deception and collapse appeared and cast the financial enterprise of Clarence Hatry completely into the shade. This was Ivar Kreuger, the crowning instance of the evil of privacy and private enterprise in the machinery of credit. We have noted in our account of J. P. Morgan, his bitter outcry at President Roosevelt for wanting financiers to "do business with glass pockets." If the firm of J. P. Morgan does not in itself supply a sufficient case for the urgent need of universal glass pockets in high finance, then the story of Ivar Kreuger does. Ivar Kreuger was a man of great imaginative and general intellectual power; he was far above the level of Morgan and at least the equal of J. D. Rockefeller, Henry Ford and Edison in these respects; but he had the weaknesses of the artistic temperament and that conceit that makes a man believe in his power to cheat and go on cheating his fellows. It is perhaps the relative bad luck of his circumstances rather than any profound moral inferiority, that puts him here not among the men who have grown colossally rich but among those who have gone too far. His total default was beyond all precedent vast. It rose above the hundred million pound level. There was never anything of the sort so big before.

Here again the sources of information are poor. On the one hand is material rather of the quality of the gossip correspondence in a smart popular paper; on the other the cold report of the accountants' investigations. The former is evidently a vulgarization and the latter a numerical abstraction. Between the two the man eludes us. He was a reserved, rather pleasant mannered man, not very effusive nor very persuasive. I have met some score of men and women who had seen something of him and it is extraordinarily difficult to get any really outstanding living impression. Maurice Privat (*Ivar Kreuger*) does his best to materialize him, but I do not feel any conviction from that portrait.

He was born in 1880 in a small town in Sweden. There are stories of dishonesty at school and tricks at examinations but they do not seem to have affected his reputation very seriously. At the age of twenty he left the Technical University in Stockholm and spent the next seven years abroad, working in various capacities in New York, Illinois, Mexico and finally in Johannesburg, where he made several thousand pounds in a business deal. In 1907 he returned to Stockholm and with Paul Toll, started a constructional engineering firm. In 1911 the firm became a limited company. His family was associated with the match industry and in 1913 Kreuger and Toll acquired their first shares in a match manufacturing company, and by 1917, when the Swedish Match Company was formed, they had achieved the feat of amalgamating all the main Swedish match manufacturing companies. Kreuger was managing director of both the Swedish Match Company and Kreuger and Toll. Sweden in those days was already the leading match manufacturing country. Ninety per cent of the products of these companies was exported and Kreuger set himself to explore and expand their foreign markets. That exploration was to take him far—to world wide influence, to an immense prestige, to overwhelming difficulties, to fraud and at last to suicide on March 12th, 1932.

He himself may have been taken by surprise by the vast expansion of which his marketing was capable. It spread until it overshadowed the world. At the time of its collapse his combine was connected with about four hundred subsidiary or allied companies, of which the most numerous were match companies and telegraph and telephone companies, but which also included banks, mortgage interests and industrial companies. His firm operated Government match monopolies in ten European countries and in Peru, Ecuador and Guatemala, and it had an arrangement with the French government (which operates its own monopoly) for the supply of machinery, raw material and additional supplies of matches. In addition it controlled or was linked with the most important match companies in countries which like England and

Japan had no state monopoly. It was Kreuger's policy to obtain government monopolies for the manufacture and sale of matches in return for loans to the various governments, the interest on which was usually a first charge on the royalties payable to the state by the subsidiary companies operating the monopoly. The growth from pure match peddling to state finance was extraordinarily swift. He found himself great and dominant unawares. He awoke to find himself a Great Power. In his last magnificent years he would occasionally make loans to governments without any specific security, for instance a loan of $125,000,000 to the German government, which undertook to make provision for its service in the annual budget. He was regarded as an important channel for the transfer of capital from one country to another. Said the *Economist,* writing after his suicide but before the revelation of his forgeries and frauds: "In the rôle which he played as the financier of Governments, Ivar Kreuger differed from such of his predecessors as the Fuggers and the Rothschilds, and even the House of Morgan, in that he was primarily an industrialist seeking assured markets with stability of prices for his product—the humble but universally needed match. The loans which he made to Governments—and they ran into enormous figures—were made for the purpose of securing match monopoly concessions. . . . Technically this conception of wedding the acquisition of markets to the provision of capital for borrowing Governments was an inspired notion, which seemed to hold all the 'inevitable simplicity' of great ideas; politically, as a citizen of one of the ex-neutral countries and as an individual for whom the game of politics and statecraft meant nothing, Kreuger was well placed to bring his policy to fruition.

"But this description of his financial activities does certainly less than justice to the motives which inspired it. Quite apart from his absorbed interest in the development and organization, first, of his matchmaking and, finally, of his telephone enterprises, Kreuger undoubtedly conceived it to be his function to play what part he could in acting as a medium between nations with surplus reserves available for lending and countries in desperate need of such resources. The last annual report issued by the board of Kreuger and Toll deplored the fact that Great Britain had had to restrict her foreign lending, while other creditor countries had been unwilling or unable to fill the place of Great Britain in this respect. Again, it noted with great regret the disappearance in the modern world of the great merchant houses and private bankers who had a wide latitude in the choice of their investments and the substitution for them of large deposit banks and other institutions all more or less restricted in the use of their funds to clearly specified investments—with the result that the whole economic structure of the world was more rigid than previously. In his policy of granting State credits, supplemented since 1930 by his participation in banking institutions formed for the purpose of financing mortgage bonds, Kreuger was entitled to claim that he sought to make good shortcomings which he saw in the world's borrowing-lending mechanism. His financial organization functioned, in fact, in a manner complementary to and comparable with that of the Finance Committee of the League of Nations."

Such at last were his dimensions. This policy of foreign loans involved the handling of vast sums of money. He was forced to adopt very complicated procedures in order to raise them. They became more and more complicated, more and more nefarious. At first this was not suspected. At first it was supposed he had been "destroyed by the impinging of forces that even the League of Nations had been unable to withstand" (*Economist*). He had been crushed wrote Mr. J. M. Keynes "between the icebergs of a frozen world that no individual man can thaw and restore to the warmth of normal life." It was generally believed before his death that the huge sums he was able to produce were obtained from legitimate and properly secured borrowing or from the proceeds of his various share and debenture issues. Between 1928 and 1932 shares and debentures to the value of £103,000,000 (1,650,-000,000 kronor) were issued by Kreuger and Toll, the Swedish Match Company, and the International Match Corporation, and it was not realized until after the tragedy that many of these were not bought by the public at all but by Kreuger and Toll itself in order to force up prices. High dividends far exceeding the actual earnings of the companies had also been paid to sustain quotations. Such confidence was reposed in Kreuger by the investing public that his shares were usually sold on a 4% dividend basis, even at the time when dividends were being paid either from bank loans or out of the proceeds of new issues.

And further, a systematic falsification of accounts and balance sheets had been going on for years. There was the usual playing off of main and subsidiary companies. Assets were created and liabilities extinguished by posting items from one set of books to another. The assets finally appeared in the balance sheets of Kreuger and Toll, the Swedish Match Company, and the International Match Corporation, and the liabilities disappeared as sums owing by Kreuger personally.

A large loss on matches sold below cost to meet Russian competition was capitalized, and finally shown as an asset under a misleading classification. Three subsidiary companies were formed for the specific purpose of facilitating the fraudulent transfer of funds, and used to hide losses incurred by other members of the group. The accounts of the Dutch subsidiary were never audited. Lange, Holm and Huldt, three of Kreuger's colleagues who were arrested during the course of the investigations, all admitted to having prepared false documents and receipts on Kreuger's orders for the use of the auditors. Anton Wendler, the auditor since 1930 of Kreuger and Toll and the Swedish Match Company, was also arrested. The most amazing discovery was that of forty forged Italian Treasury Bonds, each for £500,000 sterling, £9,-000,000 of which appeared as assets in the 1930 balance sheet of Kreuger and Toll and the remainder in that of the International Match Company. Five forged bonds of £1,533,700 each were also found, all marked as having been issued by the management of the Italian Government Monopolies. The bonds it seems were printed in a small stationer's shop in Stockholm, and the signature of the General Director of the Italian Government Monopolies, was forged by Kreuger personally. He had a private apartment of his own in which he "meditated," a great bare beautiful room. The study of signatures seems to have been an important part of his meditations.

We will not multiply details of this amazing complex of swindling. Nor will we dwell on the psychological interest of this secretive, lonely man, spinning these vast webs of illusion in the untidy world of finance. Like most men he had moods of sensuality and he was interested but not overpoweringly in women, but he does not seem to have been exceptionally dissipated or extravagant. He had considerable "taste" and built some splendid houses and offices for his concerns. But the things of interest for us here are the conditions that let him loose, unchallenged and unwatched, to clamber to so enormous a position and achieve so colossal and world-shaking a smash. The shares of Kreuger and Toll were distributed among the small investors of the whole world; everywhere his disaster spread loss and ruin. Following the Hatry experience and the world boom and crash in America it gave the common man a shock from which he will take long to recover. He has become suspicious with his savings and panicky with his investments. He begins to see the spectre of Hatry and Kreuger behind every bank counter and in every prospectus. There has been a great increase in simple hoarding in the last few years.

These cruder frauds are due essentially to a fundamental looseness of checking in the business machine, and so of course is plain embezzlement, which also recurs with a certain regularity and is a calculable and insurable risk. Many cashiers, many bank managers, many bankers, many chairmen of boards get a feeling that no one is watching them closely, and under various stresses a certain proportion succumb to this appearance of opportunity. It is often a very justifiable feeling, and some perhaps go undetected. They snatch a profit somewhere and put the money back in time and cover their traces. The embezzler, the criminal operator, the bold but just tolerated operator, the brilliant and accepted operator, the pushing and promising young "giant" in the City, the admired financial magnate, and the triumphant amasser of wealth can be brought all together into our picture because they have this in common—they are possible through the general defectiveness of our methods of accounting in the distribution of purchasing power. They are produced by the imperfections of an involved and still tentative system of defining economic relationships. It is not acquisitive, speculative or dishonest individuals, but a system of hidden operations and uncertain values that has finally to be arraigned if anything has to be arraigned.

But the best plan for mankind is to arraign nobody, declare a general amnesty and get on with the task of so reorganizing our methods of direction and payment that all this juggling in the counting-house of human affairs, legal or illegal, to the detriment of worker and consumer alike, may become impossible. We want light, more light and more light on all these businesses and the sooner J. P. Morgan's nightmare of glass pockets for financiers is realized the better for the whole world.

§ 2. The Contemporary Rich

We have shown how arbitrarily purchasing power is distributed in relation to productive activity because of the extraordinary looseness of the world's financial machinery. Wealth today has become largely financial. It is no longer mainly a directive ownership of actual property but a monetary claim upon production. The owner-producer, after the fashion of Henry Ford, is the exception, not the rule. The majority of the rich belong to the investing public. They are the upper stratum of the investing public.

We have shown by some typical instances how the financial system works. For the real creators of wealth, finance is an embarrassment; but it is the normal way to wealth, nevertheless. The intervention of a highly speculative and adventurous stratum of financiers and business operators of various sorts between the producing and consuming activities of the community, diverts and intercepts a large amount of the world's production from what an increasing number of people consider its only legitimate destinations. They hold that the gross product of our collective activities, or rather the power to purchase that product, should be the reward for definite services rendered and for contributions to the collective welfare. There is this interception and concentration of purchasing power. A considerable section of the "well-off" and rich classes in the community represents this intercepted purchasing power in action. Dominant purchasing power means the right to "call the tune" for social life, and not only the way in which this intercepted purchasing power is accumulated, but the way in which it is expended, is a matter of primary importance in a comprehensive study of economics.

The way of living and spending of these financially successful people, the new rich, must affect the general operation of demand and supply in the community very profoundly, but whether their purchasing power is dominant and whether they are really "calling the tune" is a very different matter. If they spend variously and discursively they may not in the aggregate make much of a demand in any special direction.

All rich people, be it noted, are not to be regarded as the result of the interception of purchasing power by speculative operations. The big new wealth is largely that, but it is only one of the possible types of wealth. There are old fortunes as well as the *nouveau riche*. There are social types of an older tradition who share the privilege of irresponsible spending with these comparative newcomers. Such are the recipients of the exaggerated rents due to modern urban developments, of the royalties upon coal and other mineral wealth discovered underneath landed estates, and the like. And for the purposes of this economic analysis we must also include the British, Dutch and Scandinavian royal families—almost the only royal groups which have had the good sense to abstain from those stock-exchange adventures which send kings into exile. Akin to this special rich type is the mediæval wealth of the protected princes in India and various other Oriental rulers. Such relatively unacquisitive rich people trail a picturesque tradition of honour, titles and precedences into the world of modern wealth. They give it a dignity it would otherwise lack, and in a partial traditional way they give it a direction. They supply the framework of a social organization, a discipline, an aspiration towards social solidarity, that would otherwise be wanting, to the great accumulators of the present time. The proportion of new wealth to old in the modern community is probably very large. There are no exact figures. The question is discussed very interestingly by Sir Josiah Stamp in *Some Economic Factors in Modern Life* under "Inheritance." In the past a vast part of the wealth in the world was inherited, and there was a permanent wealthy *class* with a rôle and tradition of its own. But wealth is not the same thing in the modern community as wealth in the eighteenth century. Its dispositions are different; its reactions are different; it is altogether less stable.

In the wealthier life of most European communities there is evident, or at least there is still traceable, a seasonal social routine, typically or, originally centring on the movements of a court or the assembly of a legislature, and deriving many of its observances from the pre-railway era. Its observances still preserve a faint association with current political and social functions. Because it was, in fact, once functional and responsible. Even in the United States of America there is a certain limited movement of wealthy people to and from Washington, but the life of the rich in America is far less centralized and far more highly individualized than in Europe. There is not the same association with social and political responsibilities. American wealth, throughout the continent, is almost entirely modern wealth of the modern type, arising without any tradition of political or social responsibility whatever, out of the financial and industrial events of the last hundred years. There is no such rendezvous of political, intellectual and artistic life as the London "Season" used to be, and still to some extent is. There is nothing to equal the desertion of Paris in July and the return to Paris in October. But even in the countries of old established routines, these routines are manifestly undergoing a process of effacement. The convergence upon court, Ascot, and Goodwood, is less and less obligatory and general, and the rich tend now to follow their own devices as they were never disposed to do before. In other words, their solidarity is disappearing. They are free and individualized beyond all precedent.

We have already dealt in a general fashion with "How Mankind is Fed" and "How Mankind is Clothed and Housed." We can but glance here at the way in which the rich are fed, clothed, housed—and amused. The conjunction of leisure and great purchasing power involves a very vigorous demand for amusement on their part. Perhaps it will be best to begin with housing. The story of the household of the contemporary rich, takes up from the household of the rich family of the old régime possessing at least one great country estate, almost self-supporting, and a big town house. To these were added shooting estates, houses in hunting country, stud farms, with a very numerous staff of servants and estate men. The new wealthy were at first disposed to fall into this pattern. Many of the earlier *nouveaux riches* were indeed completely absorbed into traditional "society," and their descendants are among the most conservative of those who continue the country-house tradition.

The country house, however, even when it is still in the hands of the old type of rich people, is, under the stress of new facilities for provisioning, becoming less and less autonomous, and with this departure from actuality there is an increasing development of toy farms and dairies and the like, a playing at utility after the fashion of the Petit Trianon. A sort of "out-of-town" house has gradually replaced the great house, the château of the old order; it is smaller, more luxurious, better fitted to save labour and trouble, less and less a centre of local life and more and more dependent on exterior supplies. There has been a tendency to go abroad, to the French and Italian Rivieras, for example, in the case of British, Germans and Americans, and there to build and occupy beautiful toy villas and garden villas, inhabited only for a part of the year. Now such pleasant houses spring up in South Africa, Florida, California and wherever there is any exceptional charm of climate. The rich become more and more delocalized and cosmopolitan.

The country house, in the homeland where it is still used, is no longer central and self-sufficient socially. There is a golf club or a country club at hand for informal social mingling. The country house is not, as it used to be, a centre of continuous living. Parties gather for the weekend and vanish again. The "letting" of both town and country houses has increased; they are, generally speaking, less personal than they were, or else in exceptional cases they are much more personal, the "creations" of their owners, intensely individualized. Most of us have heard and seen something of these latter very personal houses in America and Europe. They are what a Cockney would call "fancy" houses—on the analogy of "fancy ladies." But the distinctive habitat of new wealth is now not a house possessed, but a great hired house, the pleasure villa without any tributary "estate" or with merely sporting "grounds" attached, or it is the hotel de luxe. The new wealth does not settle; it goes now here, now there. It does not root locally as the old wealth did; it produces no type of home of its own; it seems to be conscious of its own impermanence.

Here we need give no detailed account of the modern life de luxe in all its irresponsible glitter. The contemporary society papers, the large illustrated advertisement-carrying weeklies give and renew a constantly changing picture of these activities. Marvellously dressed people stand about in groups. They do not seem to be up to very much and in fact they are not up to very much. They do not appear to be actively oppressing mankind or to be doing anything active at all to avert a possible catastrophe from the system that has produced them. They do not know how they were produced, and they do not understand what threatens them. A large part of the energy of the new spending goes into a search of pleasure, sensuous pleasure, or it seeks the mere gratification of vanity or the stimulus of personal danger. Many of the new rich, if they employ fewer servants, have, nevertheless, larger retinues than the older kind. It would need a little band of novelists to describe many of these retinues. The extremely rich have actual courts. Service passes on the one hand into friendly help and on the other into actual prostitution. So far as published letters, law reports, scandal and the contemporary novel admit the student to this side of life, the adventuress appears to be playing a larger rôle in an increasing number of personal dramas than ever before, and the satellite systems of flatterers and illegitimate dependents of every type develop thickly and readily about almost all holders of preëminent purchasing power. These satellites again collectively furnish employment for a large class of purveyors of their own.

The beauty specialist and the parasitic doctor of the rich merit the attention of the modern playwright. The parasitic doctor is a convenient dealer in the stimulants and drugs his professional qualification enables him to supply. To be a patronizable artist, writer or critic supplying intellectual and æsthetic reassurance, supplying drugs for the mind, or a religious teacher, supplying drugs for the soul, is now also a métier, and at a slightly different level comes the exclusive dressmaker.

From these intimacies we pass to the rich man's architect and decorator, the rich man's landscape gardener and the builder of the rich man's automobile. Here to a large extent we pass beyond the range of prostitution. We find an increasing factor of technical ability and technical conscientiousness. And this applies also to the household and estate servants of the rich man. "Things have to be right," so far as these people are concerned, and the seductions of flattery and self-abasement are no longer of primary importance. They retain their backbones. In the hotel de luxe and the great restaurant which have to cater not only for the very rich but for the merely rich, this is even more so. The standard of performance in all such places has to be a very high one and their control must be in the hands of able, if cynical, men. There is a continual unpremeditated struggle between the rare and fickle rich and the vast and calculable multitude of people with mediocre fortunes, for the services of this type of organizer and director. And the same struggle occurs in the continual development of new and more agreeable forms of de luxe travel and its rapid cheapening down to middle-class requirements, less lavish but more certain.

Few of the rich, and very few indeed of the new adventurous rich, are content to be merely sensuous and flattered. They want to go on happening. They come out—and particularly their young people come out—of their securities to flirt with danger, danger de luxe, in aëroplanes and hydroplanes, in travel in unsettled countries, in destroying such big game as survives in the world, in riding to hounds across cultivated land, in the desperate driving of powerful cars. Still more of them, as patrons, spectators and backers, taste the delights of dangerous exploits and athleticism at second hand. Others, returning to tease the risks that might once have ended them, gamble frankly. Gambling is socially much more mischievous in the rich than in the poor, but our laws seem to be based on the reverse idea. There is nothing to prevent the active entrepreneur, on whose stability some great enterprise and the employment of thousands of people may depend, from hazarding the welfare of the whole organization upon the chances of the tables. Just as there is nothing to prevent him from gambling as desperately upon the Stock Exchange. Abruptly his business may have to be transferred to other hands, sold up possibly to his former competitors, managed by some inexpert trustee, or closed down altogether.

An account of rich leisure would not be complete without a glance at the worlds of sport and gambling. The Turf survives from antiquity. In Great Britain it is part of the traditional monarchy, and the king by right divine still goes to Ascot and Epsom very much as the Son of Heaven used to go to the great Temple in Pekin to sacrifice and inaugurate the seasons. The race meeting is a very ancient function in the life of man. It was once a really vital social function, a parade of the entire community. There were seasonal races at Stonehenge before the beginnings of history. I do not know if Newmarket derives from some East Anglian Stonehenge or Woodhenge, through an unbroken tradition, or if it was Stuart revival. Horse Show week in Dublin seems more certainly the survival of an ancient gathering.

It would be an interesting thing if in our still unrealized encyclopædia of Work and Wealth we could have a history and social description of the Turf—for the non-sportsman. Had we the time and resources available, we would go into the racing stables and consider the code of honour prevalent there. We would discuss the science of form. We would gather our material for a psychology of betting. Here too the initiatives of the rich spread their influence far and wide throughout human affairs.

There is a little world of people whose way of living is to bet. Many there are who "do quite well by it." They live in not unpleasant places, their days are passed in a pattern of sunshine under trees, white rails, green turf, amidst holiday crowds, to the accompaniment of the swift, thudding crescendo of the racing horses. Wealth flows into this bright little world from the casual betting of the outsider and from the deliberate spending of the sporting rich. Our present economic system can carry it, just as it can carry the innumerable thousands of grave quartettes who are at this moment playing auction or contract bridge. No one has ever attempted to measure the proportion of human intelligence and energy absorbed by betting. There are great offices, beautifully organized, with polite clerks and managers and small regiments of typists working upon this quite sterile activity.

The outward radiation of the mentality and example of the contemporary rich calls for a very close scrutiny. Their concentration of purchasing power is by no means all-powerful in economic life. It is not even all-powerful in evoking styles and fashions. Its prestige is very great, but not so great relatively as was the prestige of the nobility and gentry of France and England and the small royalties and princes of Germany and Italy in eighteenth century. They constituted an organized system, and modern wealth does not do so. Modern plutocracy is an indeterminate pressure of purchasing power, it sets perhaps certain standards of smartness, it may give a direction to gambling and many of the more expensive sports; its individuals can bribe enormously, can subscribe to pay the debts of reckless "statesmen" in difficulties, or splash about ignorantly and mischievously in public and international affairs; but in regard to commodities in general I doubt if the new rich have anything like the directive purchasing power of the middling mass of people, whether these people be rentier, in business or employed.

Except for the rentier section which may be, and probably is, shrewdly discriminating in its expenditure, this class of middling people, this great main mass of the modern community—so far as purchasing power goes—though it has neither the leisure nor the breadth of experience to buy with acute directive force, has broad essential requirements that must be respected and obeyed. Its want of discriminatory leisure is supplemented by the modern development of the advertiser. It has to be flattered and tempted and induced to spend by the advertiser. The advertiser has to explore the mind which the class as a whole has not the freedom to make up. The advertiser studies and guesses, and the nearest guess, the one that crystallizes the unformed wishes of the prosperous mediocrities, wins. It is certainly this middlingly prosperous class and not the rich which sustains most of our theatres, evokes such things as broadcasting and the cinema, suffers the modern press, accepts and is the medium for the propaganda of the less expensive sports like lawn tennis and golf, and tolerates the contemporary café and restaurant and ordinary travel conditions.

I am inclined to think that it is increasingly the advertising producer who determines changes and fashions in the consumption of people of middling fortune, and that the mere snobbish imitativeness and life at second hand which formerly prevailed in this mass are becoming relatively unimportant. In the past the middle class had no patterns for social behaviour except the ways and equipment of royalty and the nobility and gentry. The nobility and gentry indeed played the rôle of an advertisement system then for purveyors. In London the Royal Arms over a shop, and the words "By Appointment," were of immense value to shopkeepers. I doubt if they are now. The modern rich by comparison have neither the uniformity, the prestige nor the desire to impose their standards. They do not want to lead and dominate morally; they have no sense of responsibility for the general behaviour; they want rather to be free and uncriticized or admired and conspicuously different. They are not so much a class now as a number of miscellaneous experimenting fortunate individuals. They arouse envy rather than emulation, and the immense publicity given to some of their more remarkable feats of expenditure probably evokes not merely curiosity and admiration in the ordinary beholder, magically inhibited from anything of the sort, but personal humiliation and envious hostility.

The very rich are now a criticized phenomenon in the social scheme. They are stared at like strange large wonderful animals, but they are not loved. There is no element of affectionate ownership in the feeling of the public for any of them, except (in Britain and the Scandinavian countries) for royalty. And even the prestige of royalty is difficult to measure. It collapsed very suddenly in Russia and Spain. Setting royalty aside, few people, outside the parasite systems the very rich have collected about themselves, would move a hand to save them from extinction. They are easy to tax. Income tax, super tax, surtax, death duties deflate their accumulations, and they seem unable to prevent it, while the steadying of productive enterprise by changes in company law and the spreading exactitudes of the statistician, may presently limit the scale of new speculative gains and check the appearance of fresh great fortunes. If we are right in our supposition that the loosely investing public is a transitory phenomenon in economic development, we are probably still more right in anticipating the passing of these large wild fortunes which now move so portentously, so like the hurrying tail of a belated carnival procession at nightfall, across the accumulating uneasiness of the contemporary scene.

§ 3. *The Alleged Social Advantages of a Rich Class*

There can be little question that the existence of this irresponsible rich class, so conspicuous in contemporary life, involves a very considerable waste of human resources, a vulgarization of youthful imaginations, and a widespread demoralization of potential producers. Moreover, it carries with it the possibility of powerful, irrational interventions in the political and general mental life of the community.

But that is only one side of the case for and against the "idle rich," and our survey will be a very inadequate one if it does not take the other side into account. We have to consider very carefully what case for the defense can be offered on behalf of the free spending and the free initiatives these great fortunes afford.

It can be urged that although a very large part of the spending of the contemporary rich is, in a word, waste, that is not true of all of it. Some of it produces things that are vitally important, things which as yet we do not seem able to produce in any other way.

We have already foreshadowed this line of defense in the treatment in Book II of the development of Science and the release of Invention. There it will have been shown how the intellectual emancipation of mankind has been sustained through all its phases of vigour by the existence of people with leisure and liberty of movement, people we may best describe as independent gentlemen. In the gratification primarily of their own curiosities, such men lit that lamp of Science which now illuminates the whole present and future of mankind. Movements of searching criticism and ideological reformation have, it is true, come mainly from the dissentient priestly type, but the positive establishment of these new idea systems and the accumulation of new facts have generally demanded a greater freedom and purchasing power than the intellectual rebel has had at his command. Roger Bacon, in an impoverished world without any rich leisure class, cried out and was extinguished, but the Academies of independent gentlemen in the easier circumstances of the Renascence experimented and printed and distributed their observations and made the modern world possible.

In this survey of human economics we have classified the royal and noble as an older section of the rich, and it is inconceivable how the earlier phases of the scientific movement could have occurred without the patronage and endowment of these stabler rich people in the past. Right down to the present, it is to the free rich that men of originality have had to turn to realize a great multitude of projects that would otherwise have lain dormant; explorations, great laboratories, bold innovations in apparatus, which made no appeal to the common voter or the political boss. The enormous debt of the world to Mr. J. D. Rockefeller alone, is a powerful argument against any too hasty conclusion that the great lumps of riches in the social organism are essentially or even mainly morbid growths. We must take the Rockefeller endowments in one hand, weigh them very carefully against the extravagances of other families as fortunate but less intelligent. The name of Rockefeller is not alone. There are a score of conspicuous names which stand like pillars to sustain the work of modern research. Wealth is not always reactionary; often it is not even self-protective.

It is not simply in the field of science that the rich have a reasonable claim to functional value. They have also played an as yet quite unassessed part in the development of the arts and the protection of intellectual freedoms. The free rich have been the informal protectors of free speech. A very considerable proportion of the more influential and less popular organs of critical and philosophical discussion are still subsidized by relatively rich people, and it is difficult to imagine how their practical independence could be sustained in any other way.

People of smaller means, it may be urged, might form societies and subscribe small sums that will be effective in the aggregate. But the really rich man of understanding and leisure can see that he gets what he pays for, and that is exactly what a crowd of well-off but busy people putting up guineas and five-pound notes never does. They fall a prey to secretaries and such like "organizers," and once a society has given itself over to a secretary it is usually very difficult to come together to call him to account. The waste of money through the impotent subscriptions of people of moderate fortunes, runs parallel to their haphazard investments and is due to the same reasons. They are attempting things outside their scope of direction and control, they are attempting often vitally important things for which they have insufficient time and specialization. A middle-class association is a very inferior substitute for a single intelligent rich patron.

It is even more difficult to imagine politicians directing public money carefully and intelligently into a channel which is as likely as not to repay them with corrosive comment, and will certainly never repay them by a vote. The bad side of rich leisure, the side of luxury and waste, we must remember is its most conspicuous side. There are, collectively, a very considerable number of less obtrusive rich people going about businesses that are necessary to the progress of mankind. Just exactly what proportion these redeeming functions bear to the pure waste and social mischief of free wealth nowadays it is impossible to say. There, beyond all denial, are these redeeming instances, these salvagers of spending power.*

Here, at any rate, is a considerable justification for the existence of a relatively rich class in modern life, but it does not follow that there is any justification for the sort of rich class that has been produced by the financial confusedness of economic life during the past hundred years. But why presently should there not be a different sort of rich class? There might easily be a rich class with more responsibility and less vulgarity. Much of the life de luxe which flaunts itself before the worker is a very vulgar and wasteful life indeed.

But since, as we have seen, wealth can change its character in a couple of hundred years, from concrete possessions to entries in share lists and bank credit, why should it not go on to still more abstract and much more controllable reservations and allocations of spending power?

All the good and less of the evil of free spending may be obtainable, we would suggest, by some other class of free spenders, not yet clearly defined. There is, for instance, no reason why great loyalties and public grants should not still be paid to inventors and artists and men of con-

*But for a criticism of rich man endowments see Professor Harold Laski's *Dangers of Obedience,* Chap. VI.

spicuous creative ability. True, that creative ability is not always associated with organizing and directive ability. But a world of vigorous productivity, with a high standard of general comfort and behaviour, will not only be able to afford experimental-minded and intellectually active rich people, but it will realize the need for them. It may even choose and appoint men and women to spend great sums of money as they think fit. It is amusing to think of a rich class, rich by achievement, election and appointment, and not through acquisitive concentration—people whose wealth has been given to them and not grabbed by them.

A sort of foreshadowing of the kind of thing that might be done more extensively in the future, is to be found in the recently established "Pilgrim Trust" which has assigned to five men (Mr. Baldwin, the Rt. Hon. Hugh Macmillan, Sir James Irvine, Sir Josiah Stamp and Mr. John Buchan) a practically unrestricted freedom to spend two million pounds in any way they think proper for the benefit of English people. The donor in this interesting experiment with wealth is Mr. Harkness of New York. His modesty makes him doubt his ability to spend his money to the best advantage, and so he has decided to delegate the task to these others. He washes his hands of the money. He insists on the freedom of his trustees. But manifestly a rich world in the future could play the rôle of Mr. Harkness and give a popular man or a group of competent people the free disposal of large sums of money.

§ 4. *The Ideal of Equal Pay for All*

The Communist ideal that everyone in the community should have equal pay has recently been widely popularized by Shaw in his *Intelligent Woman's Guide to Socialism and Capitalism*.

Everybody has heard of that idea now, even if there has been little or no discussion. It is an idea that was always in the background of nineteenth-century Socialist thought; it is the idea of Ruskin's *Unto These Last,* and it seems to have been the idea of Jesus in that parable of the Workers in the Vineyard to which Ruskin's pamphlet owed its title. It is the ideal, if not the reality, of Russian social administration. It is the statement of a moral attitude, and not a biological or economic conclusion.

There is a marked strain of unresolved mysticism in the naturally very clear and critical mind of Shaw. It is an essentially scientific type of mind that has never undergone any mental discipline, it is a scientific mind that was found and brought up by musicians and artists, and it has been greatly depraved by his irresistible sense of fun and his unsurpassed genius for platform effect. His is a fine intelligence which is always going off on the spree. No men can be mentally energetic all round, something everyone must take for granted, and Shaw is no exception to this rule. His indolence is about fundamentals. He betrays an unwillingness to scrutinize the springs of his opinions, and these springs arise, more directly than is usual among minds of his calibre, from personal attachments and reactions. He has never freed himself from the dispositions of nineteenth-century radicalism and equalitarianism. Equal pay for all, equal purchasing power for all, is really the logical extension into the sphere of material things of the pretensions of nineteenth-century democracy. Equal pay—so soon as the immediate personal needs of a human being are satisfied—means an equal share in the direction of the world's productive activities. For that end, the present mental equipment of a normal man is at least as insufficient as it is for the exercise of political controls.

It has already been pointed out in this survey how deeply the socialism of Marx was coloured by democratic obsessions, and how, in the presence of modern conceptions of economic organization, this quality in his doctrines has given a curious double face to the great experiment of Soviet Russia. The consequence in Russia is, and the consequence in any attempt to realize the proposal of Shaw would be, to make a fraternal communism of the extremest kind the common profession of faith, while at the same time—under the pressure of modern inventiveness and large-scale production which demands skilful direction—vesting practical direction in a highly concentrated body, holding power in some questionable manner, claiming to work for the "general good" and restraining all criticism and divergent initiatives. The practical realization of "Equal pay for all" can work out only as a dictatorship giving the individual citizens, in roughly equal amounts, what it considers to be good for them. The loss of variety, liberty and above all, initiative, involved by this equalitarianism, may easily be too high a price to pay even for the elimination of the luxuries and wasteful rich from the social process.

We must insist here that it is unsound to assume that wealth is the *cause* of poverty. That is, we hold, one of the popular delusions of our time. The position to which our studies in this book bring us, is that both irresponsible wealth and poverty are produced by a faulty, in-

accurate economic mechanism, as smoke, noise, dirt and delay are produced by a badly adjusted motor-car. But the noise does not produce
the stoppages, or vice versa, and one may be eliminated without the
other.

Equally unsound is it to assume, as the "equal pay" idea implies, that
any economic organization will grind out the same amount of wealth,
and that it is only a question of the equal or unequal division of a fixed
total product. The sterilization of wealth by the Hetty Green type of
accumulator does far more mischief to production than would be represented by the deprivation of millions of workers of a contribution
merely equivalent in the aggregate to her accumulation. The Hetty
Green type holds up creative exploitation; it not only makes off with
wealth but it misdirects wealth and obstructs the creation of fresh
wealth. Hetty Green is only one case of the immobilization of natural
resources and economic possibilities under uncontrolled private ownership. It is an unscientific theory of property that is to blame. Restrictive
property is only one form of "riches." "Operations" of the Jay Gould
type, again, work like bombs thrown into the engine room. But such
operations are preventable. Riches can be evoked as well as acquired.
The enrichment of Ford and Edison enriches everybody.

Is it impossible to readjust affairs so that service may become a necessary associate of enrichment? The trend of the facts we have accumulated and arranged in this and the preceding chapters is towards an
affirmative. It is manifestly childish to suppose that either an efficient
monetary or an efficient credit system has yet been worked out, much
less tried out. The world has hardly begun to think intelligently about
money. Our classifications of property and our legal control of its use
are infantile. The science of social motive has barely dawned. The
problem of leaving freedom of initiative in an organized world remains
untouched. Much thought and trial, dispute and disappointment lie
ahead. We are faced with periods if not ages of conflict and confusion
in which the victory of constructive forces is by no means assured. It is
the purest fantasy to imagine that we can leap at one bound from all
the complexities of the contemporary system to an equalitarian Utopia.
Even if anything of the sort is socially or biologically desirable.

§ 5. *Do the Modern Rich Want the Poor to Be Kept Poor?*

Here it will be interesting to discuss a paragraph in a recently published book on monetary questions, Professor Soddy's *Money Versus*

Man. It is a very significant sign of the times to find so distinguished a figure in physical science as the Nobel laureate for 1921 drawn by the urgencies of the subject into a scrutiny of finance. His approach is extraordinarily fresh and vigorous. He has already published *Cartesian Economics* (1922), *Wealth, Virtual Wealth and Debt* (1926), and *The Wrecking of a Scientific Age,* and he has declared himself in Who's Who to be "interested in Postdiluvian Economics." He is certainly a welcome leader in the attempt to put orthodox political economy into the palæontological museum. There is an inspiring riotousness in his style of attack. He is not a solitary phenomenon. He is a pioneer. The banker's parlour, the stockbroker's office and the board room are going to be invaded by an increasing number of highly intelligent and highly sceptical enquirers, resenting bluff and mystery, using unflattering words like "antediluvian" and "dishonest old fumblers" and suchlike phrases with a startling readiness, and very resolutely "wanting to know."

We can represent Professor Soddy as saying on behalf of physical science: "We men of science have abolished toil and people are still toiling; we have created plenty, and everywhere there is want. What has got between us and them?" And then sharply: *"What the devil are you money-fakers up to?"* These are not his words, but that is his manifest temper.

Here, however, we are not dealing with his temper, but with a very vital issue he raises. He raises it as a side issue, but it is indeed a fundamental issue. What he says in the particular matter we now want to discuss, follows. It is a bold assertion of the malevolence of successful humanity. He says in effect that most energetic men live for power and to triumph over their fellow creatures. Here is the passage:

"Now it is one thing for science to make some relatively much richer than others, and quite another, without even a by-your-leave, for science so insidiously to undermine the established order of human society as to put all beyond the persuasive influence of want. There are many neither unimportant nor over-scrupulous people, if not the majority of the most forceful and successful people in the community, who would probably quite openly side with no civilization at all rather than a, to them, so thoroughly uninteresting and objectionable one. Some have, in fact, already scented the danger. It used to be only the genuine artists and æsthetes who railed, quite ineffectively, at the growing mechanization of the age. But when the tide turns, and science by making the poor richer makes the rich relatively poorer, the movement to break up the machines and revert to hand and serf labour is likely to receive some very unexpected and effective recruits."

In fact, he would add to our three main groups of personas, the peasants, the nomads and the educated types, a fourth, the modern money manipulator, a new type whose primary delight is domination and oppression through relative gain.

How does that square with the psychological analysis of social and economic relationship we have been making in this work?

I think we shall have to recognize that there is nothing in the story of the development of the current economic financial system as we have unfolded it, to rule the plain accusation of Professor Soddy out of court. The old system, before the industrial and mechanical revolutions, was quite frankly repressive. It had the excellent excuse that human society could not exist unless people were kept down. The priest kept himself down, helped to keep the peasant down, and all the surplus of good things in life, the pride and the glory, fell to the gentleman, the aristocrat, and the prince, the successors of the nomad conqueror. These upper-class people had the colour and high places of life, and to them fell such women as they desired. It is impossible to ignore the rôle of women throughout the past of mankind as prizes, incentives and rewards. They have always fallen into that rôle with extreme readiness, accepted the jewels and dresses and played the hostess queen to the triumphant robber. Through the long ages of insufficiency, women have always been the demure receivers of the captured joys and displays of life. And the society these ladies adorned, the young they educated, understood quite clearly that the toiler had to be kept under—there was no need for anyone to stipulate that the poor should be kept poor, for that followed as a matter of course. The priest went about the human battlefield mediating between the parties, persuading the rich to be charitable and the poor to be grateful and resigned, and doing his best (the more intelligent of him and when Statutes of Mortmain and the like did not prevent him) to get what he could of productive property out of private hands.

The development of modern industrialism, subtly associated with mechanical invention and following on the mental releases of the Reformation period, changed a world of insufficiency to a world of potential universal plenty, but it found no ideology ready for such a state of affairs. So it went on with the old. The personas of the people engaged in it arose out of the long established main types. The "educated" personas were creating opportunity but did not themselves exploit opportunity. The scene for the new act in the human drama opened therefore with getting and grabbing. It need not have opened in that fashion, but it did. The industrial entrepreneur was essentially the child of the grasping, hoarding, economizing, close-working peasant type; the financial adventurer was essentially predatory. The two intermingled with each other to become the New Rich as we have studied them in § 1, and to associate themselves with, and largely buy up, the Old Rich, so far as prestige and claims to essential dignity were concerned. They were New Rich in Old Rich traditions. The elements of triumph, display, the buying of splendour for women, the buying of feminine adoration, contempt for the generality and a certain jealousy of any competition, rivalry and comparison on the part of the generality—they took over all these things as a matter of course and found them very congenial. What fills our fashion papers to-day, amidst the pages and pages of luxury advertisements, but the photographs of successful people displaying their triumph for the admiration and envy of mankind and, more particularly, for the incitement of womankind?

That the modern rich generally do not feel any strong desire for the poor to be less poor—so long as their poverty does not make them dangerous—is manifestly true. So far we go with Professor Soddy. They are evidently prepared to endure the sufferings of others with smiling courage, and even to repay envy with a certain exhibitionism that rouses its interest even more vividly than its resentment. But is it true that there is any strength of will behind these naïve products of our present clumsy financial mechanism? That is where we part from Professor Soddy. Let us admit that the modern rich cannot be expected to help in the monetary and financial reconstruction of human affairs. Let us recognize that they will even encumber and hinder. They will appear, they do appear, lumpishly auxiliary in all sorts of reactionary and obstructive movements. They will be supporting romantic monarchy here and patriotism and religious intolerance there, if only for the sake of the titles and reassurance they can get, the coronations they can attend, the patronage they may exercise. All that much is true. They cannot be expected to be very much more than a stupidly consuming and resistant mass. But what is an altogether different matter: are they likely *in any effective and organized form* to put up a fight against the steady development of one genuinely conceived economic state in the world?

Now there it is we have to join issue with Professor Soddy—and others. His clear and vigorous mind is irritated at the dragging distresses, the baseness and injustices of our world when he has the sure knowledge that it might be energetic and happy; he assumes social good-will as a duty, and then very naturally he hits out and hits round

in an ecstasy of indignation. But there are things about life that so far
he ignores; his biology, his psychology and his philosophy of living are,
if we may say so, not as serene as his physical science. To him the
world is an exasperating spectacle of reasonable creatures behaving
unreasonably and wickedly. But the fact is they are not yet very reasonable creatures. And they do not admit that social good-will is a duty.
They do not pretend it is. They have not the idea of service in their
personas. Let him look at the spectacle again and look at it whole, as
we are trying to do in this work; let him look at it as a species of about
nineteen hundred million individuals, descended from rather ferocious,
ego-centred, ape-like ancestors, not very greatly modified yet, and modifying very slowly, and only very slowly muddling their way to knowledge, reason and efficient coöperation. He can never see the absurdities
of the situation better than he does now, but he will find then that he
has a better grasp upon the obstacles he is up against and the nature of
the remedial processes in which we have to put our trust.

He will become less impatient and more constructive. He will give
us more explicit plans and fewer scornful witticisms at the expense of
—everybody. He denounces a burthen and embarrassment of rich people
who live, not only idly and luxuriously, but obstructively, on the exaggerated debts they have imposed upon the community. He denounces
our banking system. So far as these are indications for reconstruction
they are of immense value. But he finds much more deliberate plotting
by the rich against the poor than our survey has revealed. He finds
plots where we find instincts and traditions. He thinks entrepreneurs
and bankers are anti-social men, and we have found reason to suppose
that they are becoming, and likely to become, less and less anti-social.
He does not concede that many of them are routinists who can be
turned into different routines, and that a certain leaven among them is
as anxious to achieve what he wants as he himself. He does not envisage the possibility that the present enormous and preposterous debt
charge of mankind, like the almost universal preëmption of natural resources by private owners, may constitute as inevitable a phase in
human development as slavery or the primitive taboos, and that it may
already be at its maximum and be quite easily amenable to a tremendous reduction and writing off. He thinks, for example, that the
present struggle to arrest the hopeful expansion of human affairs for the
sake of the gold standard is due to a conspiracy of powerful, aggressive,
able men. We think that it is due to a blind convergence of fear, habit
and traditional stupidity. He cannot wait for the steadfast unfolding

of our release from tradition. He turns, in his passion, to governments to take this, that and the other profit-making privileges out of the bankers' hands—now. But even as he turns to governments he remembers what they are. He turns to "democracy," and the thought of the daily newspaper rises hideously between him and that ideal rescuer. Crowd action is no remedy. And then he shows his bad temper. It is, we find, a most sympathetic bad temper he displays. But it is no use for constructive purposes; it has to be controlled.

That is why it is so interesting to quote him here. In response to his indignant outcries we are enabled to underline the more deliberate impression our survey evokes. We do not believe that any large proportion of bankers are plotting to keep the world poor. There is a number of honestly perplexed men among them, men who are dismayed and distressed by the turn things are taking. They are often business men unaccustomed as yet to the scientific method of thought, but they are picking it up steadily.

And, further, as to the rich generally. There are only a minority of rich people, we suggest, who clearly and definitely want the poor to be kept poor, and they are not among the "forceful and successful" types. Progress is encumbered by the relative barbarism of women, but even among women education is spreading. The people who really change things are not the luxurious receivers in "society," not the men who want outstanding power and triumph—they are men like Edison and Ford. Professor Soddy, in the passage we have picked out to make the text for this section, seems to forget men of the Edison-Ford type, just as he forgets the existence of men like himself. Where did *he* get his social passion? Whence comes his indignation? Why is he not on the other side?

He is actually writing book after book to change men's ideas—that is to say, their minds and their personas about these things—and yet, all the while, he does not seem to take into his reckoning the great and growing body of other excited and disinterested men engaged in unorthodox extra-mural educational activity; nor does he show any sustaining disposition to coöperate with other workers in the same field.

The way to the new world economy, when everyone will be prosperous, is likely to be hard, difficult and dangerous. But the best brains will be on our side. They will not be against us. We may have to wade through morasses of foolishness and fight stampedes of boorish plutocrats, but that plotting of a "majority of the most forceful and successful people in the community" against progress, is a nightmare of

Professor Soddy's bad hours. It is a nightmare to be exorcised, because such things rankle in the brain and make us violent and bitter, just when, if we are to be of any real service to mankind, we should be most careful in our adjustments and accusations.

If Professor Soddy is right and the interpretation of current fact in this book is wrong; if it is true that the majority of able spirits among the contemporary rich are, for the sake of power and preëminence, deliberately impoverishing a community, which need not be impoverished, then the conception pervading this book of the progressive construction of a universally prosperous economic world community out of the current social order, is unsound. There is nothing to be hoped for along that line. There is nothing for it but, as the Marxists teach, a class war against the rich and the able, social insurrection, the breaking-up of the whole contemporary organization of mankind in wrath and disgust, and beginning again upon a different ground plan, with whatever hope is left to us, amidst the ruins.

§ 6. *The Poor*

Abandoning for once any resort to our encyclopædic *Science of Work and Wealth* or our imaginary museum collections, we have, by merely flapping at the reader the familiar smart illustrated periodicals, *Vogue,* the *Graphic,* the *Sketch, Punch, La Vie Parisienne* and their kin, added the Turf and sport generally, the gambler in the Casino, the brilliant crowd at a levee, the smart prostitute, the hotel chef, the fashions and the palace, to our enumeration of human life patterns; and we have linked all this brilliant swarm and their motives and what they are doing and why they are doing it with the worker in the factory, the miner in the seam, the peasant among his vines, the shepherd on the mountain side and the spray-wet fisherman hauling in his nets from the heaving sea. We have shown the strands of this relationship running through mint, bank, office and stock exchange. This futile, expensive existence of the rich is a surplus product of the economic machine.

By the time these rich people have been brought in, our spectacle of activities will have extended to more than a thousand million living souls, each conducting itself according to a persona of its own, each with its own idea system and its separate vision of the world about it, and yet all reacting mutually in one economic ensemble. But still something very grave and essential remains to be explained and considered. There is a deep shadow into which we have now to go, a gathering multitude which can neither work contentedly nor play happily, the unemployed without purchasing power, those who mingle want with a joyless leisure, the apparently superfluous poor.

How do they stand in regard to the rich? We have already pointed out that the one mass is not directly and quantitatively dependent on the other, that it is unsound to assume that if there were no rich there would be no poor. It is too hastily believed that the poor are poor *because* the rich have taken something away from them. That is not the truth of the case. The relationship is much more subtle and complicated.

The very variegated class of rich leisure is held together by the common characteristic of a purchasing power enormously exaggerated by traditional conventions about property, or by the loose working of the financial parts of the economic machine. Now in contrast we have to consider a great, and it would seem a growing, mass of nonproductive or insufficiently productive people whose purchasing power is either slight or nonexistent. Certainly the machine gives here and deprives there. But that is not by any means the same thing as taking from one and giving to the other. It is not a process that can be remedied by selling up the rich man and giving all that he had to the poor. The faults of the machine are by no means so simple as that.

Always in the world there have been the poor. Poverty is not a thing confined to the species *Homo sapiens;* it is a phenomenon throughout all the orders, classes and kingdoms of life. It may strike some readers as an odd phrase, but it is true that most animals and plants live in extreme poverty. They have no reserves, that is to say, they live from hand to mouth. *Homo sapiens* is alone among living creatures in the possibility that he may abolish *want,* for himself and perhaps for many plants and beasts. All other species exist in almost continuous contact with a margin of starvation. If by some splendour of fortunate chance a species is lifted into abundance for a time, straightway it increases and multiplies until the margin of hunger is once more attained. The only qualification of that law is when some other hungry creature, great or small, hunter or parasite, preys upon a species abundantly enough to bring the increase of that creature below the resources of its .food supply. A living species must be devoured, or it will multiply until there is an internecine struggle for food, with famine destroying the defeated. A species must live in constant danger, or in constant need. Hunger or the hunter is the common alternative of life. We win the hearts of nearly all inferior creatures and persuade them to subdue their instincts and belie their natures, by feeding them.

"The poor ye have always with you." That has been accepted too readily as a divine assurance that the prevention of poverty is impossible. But there can be no denial that hitherto want has always dogged the footsteps of life. The life of the ordinary savage and the ordinary barbarian is an extreme poverty. Savages will abandon the infirm and put an end to "useless mouths" with a brutality that outdoes Napoleon. And this they do in the midst of potential wealth the nearness of which they do not suspect, and which they have no means of exploiting.

A short history of destitution through the ages would make a grim and painful book. It is hard to get an idea of the proportion of the population at various periods of the world's history which died of starvation, or through the weakening of resistance to disease by undernourishment or exposure. I am inclined to think it was a very considerable proportion indeed. Few districts of the world in past times got through threescore and ten years without actual famine, and up to the middle of the nineteenth century people still wandered about the cities of western Europe in actual immediate need of bread. There is real starvation happening now in China, India and Russia. The state of affairs in such countries as England, France and the United States—the rarity of extreme hunger—is abnormal and altogether modern.

The growth of the sense that the existence of poverty is discreditable to the rich and the ruler, and that they ought to do something about it, is comparatively recent. I believe that up to the beginning of the nineteenth century the general feeling was that the poor were very much to blame. One threw them crusts and gave them old clothes and permitted them to sleep in outhouses, insisting relentlessly on "gratitude." One did that as a virtuous exercise with very little sense of any converse obligation. The Elizabethan poor law was a law in restraint of wanderers; a device for maintaining social order; it was not primarily to abate distress. The charities at the convent gates of pre-Reformation times accepted the perennial fact of restitution unquestioningly.

But through the ages there has also been an undertow of protest. In Egypt, long before the Hebrew prophets, there was a literature denouncing the exactions of the rich and complaining of debts and labour conditions. That seems, however, to have been a protest against types and individuals rather than against the system. The bad rich man ground the faces of the poor, but the riches of the good rich man (how rare he was!) and the existence of the poor were hardly challenged.

It was only, I believe, with the radiation of humanitarian ideas and feelings in the middle and late nineteenth century that the protection, not only of human beings, but of the larger beasts, from starvation and even from conspicuous undernourishment, came to be considered a public duty. A skinny foreigner, a quaint beggar in rags, a miserable horse, were fair fun for the caricaturists until less than a hundred years ago. Since then there has been a steady development of the organized mitigation of want. There has been a sustained and increasing effort in all civilized countries to make deaths from exposure and under-nourishment impossible, to rescue and reinstate people who have fallen into destitution, and to assist those who are slipping down towards that state. Unemployment, which was formerly regarded as a marginal condition necessary for the proper working of the wages system, is now considered an evil not merely to be alleviated, but to be fought and overcome.

The *Science of Work and Wealth* when it comes to be assembled in its encyclopædic form, will have to review contemporary methods of dealing with this stratum of uncertain, diminishing or nonexistent spending power. It will have to give a general vision of the life of the underproductive. It must amplify its description by photographs to show how the poor live, not only in the dismal back streets of America and Europe, but in the poor quarters of Chinese and Indian cities, and it must give pictures of famine relief work and sanitary missions invad-ing kraals and tents and hut villages. It will have to go far beyond mere industrial unemployment; it must give a panorama of poverty through-out the world. Then it will show us more particularly the Labour Ex-change, the Workhouse, and the Casual Ward of the more highly organized communities. It will explain the regulations of Old Age Pensions and Unemployment Pay. It will note the varieties of poor-law method following the variable temperaments and economic ideology of typical states.

The broad fact underlying the whole spectacle of the alleviation of distress that we glance at in this fashion is that the modern community has been gradually recognizing and accepting the responsibility for the maintenance of every one of its citizens at a certain low minimum standard of shelter, food and clothing, irrespective of the productive activities of the particular individuals concerned. It does not compel them to work in return. It does not even afford the opportunity to work in return. That is the worst aspect of this sort of relief. What the community offers is dull, dreary, and undignified, no doubt—"pauper-ization," to give it its proper name—but, nevertheless, life and con-tinuation. This is an absolutely unprecedented state of affairs. It is a biological revolution. In all the rest of the kingdoms of life defeat, whether through defect or ill luck, has meant death. So hitherto life has been driven up the scale of efficiency. *Now,* what does defeat mean in the modern community? Stagnation. A dingy and unhappy stagnation.

The immense increase in the total of human productivity under modern conditions renders this possible. There can be little doubt that a few hundred million economically active people could now feed, clothe and house all the rest of the race—as nonproductive paupers, that is—at a base, dullish but endurable level of existence, and still have a surplus for a fairly pleasant type of successful life. And it is plain that the stratum of intermittently productive, insufficiently productive and nonproductive people is under the present conditions of concentrated production and of maintenance for the unemployed, increasing in proportion to the whole community. More and more people are coming out of employment, are being superseded; the modern organization has no jobs for them and no use for them. As industrialization spreads over the world, the supersession of the small producer and the diminution of hands needed for any given product go on. Nothing like the possible ratio of inactive dependents has yet been reached. This relative stagnant mass can go on growing. There has been much exaggerated writing about the Rapid Multiplication of the Unfit, for it does not follow necessarily that the people who are coming out of employment are inferior in quality to many who remain at work, or that their superfluousness is a consequence of relative breeding rather than a supersession; but the fact nevertheless confronts us that this perplexed and perplexing lower stratum to the economic edifice may continue to expand, and probably will continue to expand for some time, relatively to the whole human population.

The economic world machine is rapidly coming to resemble an unhealthy overgrown body which is accumulating two sorts of unwanted secretion. On the one hand, it has been accumulating the new, generally functionless rich, the Consuming Unemployed, a sort of plethora, and on the other it is developing a morbid mass, a huge tumour now growing very rapidly, of Penniless Unemployed. These two developments are so independent that it might be quite possible to eliminate one and still leave the other increasing formidably. We have already pointed to possible processes that may lead to the resorption of the irresponsible rich. The graver riddle is certainly this New Poor, this menace of the unemployable expropriated.

What is humanity doing about it, and what is it doing for humanity?

§ 7. *The Paradox of Overproduction and Want. Community Buying*

Let us turn this business about and look at it from another direction. It is not a simple matter, and its problems do not admit of simple solutions. Several processes are at work concurrently, and any single simple solution will be true only of its own process. The poor are not a class, but a miscellany with scarcely anything in common but deficient purchasing power.

First there is the product of the immemorial comprehensive process of the struggle for existence: the real failures. These are people definitely and manifestly below the average. They have inherently feeble bodies or minds. Biologically it is bad that they should survive and reproduce. Our world is wealthy enough for them to live out their lives as pleasantly as they are capable of living them, but the persuasion spreads steadily that by birth control in some form, by humane sterilization— now a proven possibility—such strains should be brought to an end. The problem is not quite so simple as those unfamiliar with genetic science may suppose, but for all its complexities, there is no reason to doubt its ultimate solution. It seems that a progressive extension of genetic knowledge, medical science and organization and hygienic control, will suffice to meet this biological aspect of the problem of the poor.

And then, always since society began there has been the correlative of the man who grabbed the lion's share; there has always been the opposition of the "have's and have-not's." There are the poor of the old social inequality. They too are commonly of the weaker sort. They have been living their distinctive lives in contact with their "betters" for many generations. They are hereditary inferiors. Tradition mixes with heredity perhaps in many of those who fall into this class. They were poor because there was not enough to go round. They came late or they had been pushed aside. They were the outsiders of the crowd round the rice bowl.

But there is a third sort of poor to-day. There are the poor by sheer chance, the poor with as good heredity as any other class of people. It is difficult to maintain that the majority of the people one meets, inadequately employed or out of a job, or that the populations of impoverished regions beyond the more highly civilized areas, are all individually inferior to the people who are busy and prosperous in the more active parts of the economic system. There are defectives in the crowd and poor creatures in the crowd, but they are only ingredients in the crowd and not the whole of it. The others have been born at a disadvantage, in a declining district or a shrinking industry; they have been involved in the misgovernment of some reactionary State; their parents or grandparents were sufficiently prosperous at home not to emigrate to some new land of hope, which presently gave their defeated and departed neighbours all the opportunity that was receding from their own native country. The incidence of education is still the most uncertain element in life; here a fine family may live in a reactionary district that will not suffer an efficient school or a modern factory; there the best of teaching, training and employment may be forced on every mediocrity. That this man in a modern community is illiterate, limited in his outlook, inapt for any new job, badly nourished, angry, resentful and unwilling, and that man, well informed, hopeful, readily useful, may have nothing whatever to do with their inherent quality. The forces that have determined their fates are too wholesale and remote to have tested it. Very exceptional individuals are known to have triumphed over the most desperately discouraging circumstances, but generally they have done so at a price, and their careers are no disproof of our general proposition that the main, mediocre mass of mankind is in no way being sifted and selected by the relative increase in unemployment throughout the world. This second sort of poor—the poor of economic fluctuations—is being deprived of purchasing power not as individuals but as units in a group. There is no selection at all among them.

And very plainly one cause—though not the only cause—is that production is being run primarily for the profit of entrepreneurs and their financiers, and not for the good of the mediocre mass. The profit side has the first call on economies. Every economy in production which diminishes the amount of work needed generally diminishes in the same proportion the amount of wages paid relative to the total output. But if profit was not a primary end and things could be so adjusted, by a reduction of hours of work per day, or weeks of work per year, or years of work per lifetime, there need be no such ejection of workers as occurs from the employment in question. The industry would continue to create as much dispersed purchasing power in the community as it did before, instead of skimming more of it off in a concentrated form for the financier and entrepreneur.

Since concentrated wealth is apt to run into special channels of luxury and waste, there is a wide and well founded feeling in the world that it is less desirable socially than a more diffused spending power. In the end economy of production that leads to restricted employment must be bad for industry itself, because in the case of anything but a commodity de luxe it means producing more for a community less able to buy. We are faced indeed with the spectacle of industry, through sheer progressive efficiency, producing more and more, and killing the demand for its product as it does so. That seems indeed to be the essential fact of current economic troubles. There is too much wheat, steel, coal, copper, rubber, oil in the world, too many motor-cars, too many gramophones, sewing-machines, and radios, and there is a gathering multitude of people, not defectives, not intrinsically inferior people, but people at a quite chance disadvantage, who cannot buy this accumulation of unsold commodities.

Prices fall, production declines; that does not solve the problem, because it only increases the multitude which cannot buy. Economists tell us that if by a miracle everyone alive could wake up the recipient of sound bonus shares worth £100 a year, the whole world would be transformed for a time at least into a busy hive of well paid production. Our present anæmia, our lassitude, would vanish. The problem of restoring purchasing power to this new poor, these modern poor evoked by the economic fluctuation, is exercising a great number of extremely ingenious minds. Their findings lack unanimity and assurance, but their general idea is the same.

One school assures us that production for profit is at the root of the evil. Among other things it is. That is the central idea of the Socialist. But the abolition of production for profit is not to be done in the twinkling of an eye. The whole modern economic process has grown up on production for profit, and the redoubtable attempts of Soviet Russia to produce an industrialism upon different lines in one swift revolutionary change merely expose the complex difficulties of the task. The peasant persona with its diverse modifications, which is still the prevalent persona in our species, is all against it. The less abundant but more energetic and influential adventurer type is equally against it. We have shown how the gradual subjugation of business finance to scientific control, may mitigate many of the wilder fluctuations of business enterprise, but that is a comparatively slow and intricate subjugation which gives us more hope for the next fifty years than for to-morrow. Meanwhile the squeezing out of fresh unemployed goes on.

Restriction of hours of employment, the relief of the labour market at either end by giving old-age pensions and raising the school-leaving age, the deliberate raising of wages *à la* Ford above competitive rates, are admirable palliatives—and something more than palliatives. The workers still in employment may develop new wants as their standard of living rises, and this may attract a certain proportion of the out-of-works into new industries and make buyers of them again, and so again increase demand. But such measures alone will not arrest the secular restriction of organized and rationalized industries to a dwindling staff of increasingly efficient and no doubt increasingly better paid workers. And, moreover, against the vigorous application of such measures to shorten hours and take the young and the old off the labour market, fights the traditional spirit of international competition. "This will put us at a disadvantage against the foreign producer" is a deadly objection. The British workers have a limit set to their progress by Indian, Egyptian and Chinese workers. There is no world authority yet to handle labour conditions as one single world-wide problem.

Another school of thought lays greater stress upon what is practically a distribution of buying power to the unemployed in the disguise of public works. The prosperous classes are to be taxed either directly or by the indirect method of currency inflation, to provide the means for a comprehensive rehousing of the community, a replanning of town and countryside, new roads, bridges, harbours, parks, schools, hospitals. There will be no attempt to secure a bookkeeping profit on the transaction. The profit will be social. Since admittedly the modern community has to support its poor at some level of comfort, it may just as well, it is argued, give as large a proportion of them as possible, work and active buying power, by such great public undertakings. Instead of just carrying on, it will stimulate. The gross wealth of the community will be increased. Concurrently with the restoration of purchasing power to the people thus actively employed by the State, there will be a restoration of general industrial activity. As employment increases the State will slacken its operations; as it falls, it will put new energy into its public works and adornments. This is the "Plan" of Foster and Catchings in their *Road to Plenty* published by the American Pollak Foundation. It was also suggested in the Webbs' great achievement, the Minority Report of the Poor Law Commission. All these proposals will shock the minds of such Victorian individualists as still survive, those fundamentalists of economics, profoundly, but they will be accepted as a matter of course by the new types of scientifically educated business, banking and public officials, who seem to be ousting slowly but steadily the crudely acquisitive business men of the old régime from the control of our economic destinies.*

How far our world has gone already in the free distribution of food and services to producers out of action, how far it has gone in the distribution of purchasing power in doles and pensions, and how far it is committed to public enterprises to take up the slack of unemployment we cannot yet tell in detail. The facts have still to be gathered together and put in order. The total already attained is likely to be a surprise to many. And we have to remember that if there is anything whatever to be said in defense of armaments, it is that they distribute a very large amount of purchasing power to skilled workers and trained and fit men who might otherwise stand out of employment. A sudden world-wide disarmament, unless it was accompanied by colossal housing and transport schemes and the vigorous reëquipment of civil life, might enormously increase the world's economic difficulties. The thought of this possibility is one of the obscurer obstacles in the way to the abolition of war. It is one of the many reasons why merely negative pacificism is futile. Men will not be able to give up war preparation *until there is something else to do in the place of it.*

A colossal increase of public or quasi-public constructive works throughout the world seems therefore a necessary condition for both the establishment of world peace and the control and reduction of unemployment and poverty. It is not that man *may* plan and make a new world for himself; he *has* to do so or be overwhelmed by his own undisciplined devices and impulses. Work and wealth or disaster are the alternatives of his destiny. The present system has to pass on to this phase of organized collective enterprise or break down. This is no dogma; it is the plain and inevitable conclusion to the considerations we have put before the reader.

A prominent American business man recently put the ideas we are suggesting here into a phrase that is capable of considerable enrichment in its interpretation. He was discussing the paradox of overproduction. He said that while this current system, the profit-motive system, our so-called capitalist system, had been able to evolve the most efficient mass production, it had still to solve the secret of "mass consumption." In itself the phrase has scarcely more in it than "rationalization" when it

---

*The reader interested here can expand this section further by looking up the publications of the Pollak Foundation (Newton 58, Mass., U. S. A.). Another book he may find stimulating and suggestive is F. Henderson's *The Economic Consequences of Power Production.*

was used by the late Lord Melchett as a counter catchword to nationalization, but if we confer upon it the cognate idea of the "community-
buying" of peace-time material as well as of war material, we find it
at once germinating in a very suggestive and profitable manner. We
shall see later how the community-buying of armaments was forced
up during the last half century by armament salesmanship, and there is
no apparent reason why a similar procedure on a larger scale on the
part of architectural and transport salesmen, should not presently come
to the relief of the present paradoxical deadlock in economic life. The
cathedral building of the Middle Ages was, as we have noted, a form
of community-buying. Not only the remaking of roads (already going
on in Great Britain, for example) and the comprehensive replanning of
the entire transport system, but the deliberate rebuilding of entire
towns with modernized sanitation and public services, the continual
modernization of our rationalized industrial plant and the entire reconstruction of the layout of the countryside for production, health and
pleasure, may be made collective communal enterprises. If we can build
magnificent jails and asylums out of our common resources, why should
we not build great housing quarters for common people to prevent
their becoming recalcitrant and criminal? If punitive comfort, why not
preventive comfort?

There need be no violent revolutionary transition to such a new economic phase. The idea of collective buying has indeed been tried already
to assist distressed producers. It is not a new idea. Brazilian coffee, for
example, and Canadian wheat have been dealt with in this fashion. The
risk of loss, the actual loss in an overstocked market, is thrown upon the
public credit. These are instances, and not very successful ones, of collective buying for resale, but there can be also collective buying for
communal use. Then there need be no risk of loss. Existing methods of
buying and distribution are in fact extremely plastic, and amenable to
unlimited progressive adjustment. But such adjustment demands for
its achievement a very considerable change in the spirit of financial and
industrial enterprise, and a general rise in the intelligence and understanding of the community. It involves almost necessarily certain measures of currency inflation. Inflation is dangerous to all but very well
informed and well disciplined communities. We are brought back to
what has been said already about grades of organization (in Chapter
VII, § 9), and to the fundamental importance of educational level, in all
these matters.

Let not the reader unfamiliar with modern economic discussion, imagine that there is anything novel or indeed anything unorthodox in this suggestion of collective employment in rebuilding cities and the like great undertakings. I turn over *Some Economic Factors in Modern Life,* by Sir Josiah Stamp, and I find him quoting Professor Lethaby with approval as saying: "Except for a hundred or two buildings, London needs to be rebuilt from end to end. No writer on Economics has yet told us what are the limits to expenditure on public arts, whether a beautiful city is an investment or an extravagance." I turn from Sir Josiah's luminous page to my newspaper, and I read of two million unemployed in Great Britain, most of whom are being paid a dole for very miserably doing nothing. Then comes a communication from Professor Miles Walker, F. R. S. He is a professor of electrical engineering and an inventor of distinction, and he and a few friends have drawn up a scheme—a perfectly reasonable scheme, if we disregard the psychology of a profit-seeking community—for setting the unemployed to work to supply the needs of the unemployed. Nobody is going to dismiss the controller of the London, Midland & Scottish Railway, or a Nobel laureate in physics, or Professor Miles Walker, as dreamy Utopians or impracticable propagandists, and yet this is how they are thinking. These are men of the facty sort; men who can count. That unemployment and every form of poverty are avoidable is for these authorities not a mere opinion: it is a straightforward statement of fact. It would seem impossible to them for any review of human activities to omit that statement.

§ 8. *The Attempt of Soviet Russia to Abolish Rich and Poor Together**

At present the readjustment of distribution to modern methods of production is being attempted on a quite heroic scale in Soviet Russia. We have already discussed certain aspects of this great forward effort in human affairs. For indisputably it is an effort to go forward. An ultra-modern ideology involving a grade of organization higher and more

*G. T. Grinko's *The Five Year Plan of the Soviet Union* is authoritative and more or less official. Michael Farbman's *Piatiletka, Russia's Five Year Plan,* is like all his work, clear, scientifically impartial and illuminating, and another very sound book is H. R. Knickerbocker's *The Soviet Five Year Plan.* For a vivid picture of human life during the phases of this monumental experiment in social reconstruction, the general reader cannot do better than read the books of Maurice Hindus, *Broken Earth, Humanity Uprooted* and *Red Bread.* There are many other very competent and interesting books, and a veritable flood of superficial and inferior productions upon the Russian effort. We make no attempt here to adjudicate upon them, but we can certify to the excellence of those we have named because we have made a liberal use of them.

elaborate than any that has yet existed in the world is being imposed, with how much success it is still impossible to say, on a great region of the earth where the normal culture remains in essence mediæval and where many vitally essential industrial organizations are still undeveloped—and this in the face of the hostility of foreign governments and world-wide distrust. At every stage in the process, the difficulty of insufficient understanding by the public and inadequate directive power have had to be faced by the adventurous fanatics who seized upon Russia after the exhaustion and social disorganization caused by the Great War of 1914–18.

In Chapter IV, §5 we have considered the Russian attempt to pass at one stride from peasant cultivation to agricultural production upon big estates, but so far we have had very little to say about the industrial development of Soviet Russia. But there many of the things that we have been suggesting as probable developments of contemporary business conditions in the Atlantic world have already been anticipated. It is hard to decide whether Soviet Russia is rather desperate, inspired and heroic or presumptuous and headstrong. Her forward thrust is unprecedented in history. With political institutions of the most provisional sort, without even the skeleton of an efficient civil service, without freedom of criticism and suggestion, using indeed to this day terroristic methods of the crudest and bloodiest sort, she has attempted to evoke an exhaustively planned economic organization of more than a hundred million people which shall buy and sell as one merchant. She has attempted to eliminate that individual buying which is still the general practice of contemporary civilization for all but war material, highroads, educational appliances, and a few other common needs. Her Communist professions, as Knickerbocker points out, are absurd. Her system is an ultra-modern State Capitalism.* She has made the State the universal buyer and seller, she buys machinery and staple imports collectively, and whatever the outcome of her effort, it is impossible not to believe that the most valuable lessons, examples and warnings are to be found in her expedients. Towards the ends her government seeks so passionately, hastily, bitterly and clumsily, the economic order of the whole world is moving slowly but surely, if only on account of the economic paradox between increased output and diminished consuming power that evolves from capitalism. It is rather the luck than the merit of the Atlantic systems that they may go more circumspectly and comfortably towards the common goal of a planned and measured reorgan-

*See also Gide and Rist: *Histoire des Doctrines Economiques* (1922).

ization of economic life, in which the motive of profit will be replaced almost altogether by the motive of service, and goods be distributed as common needs rather than as industrial and financial prizes.

Chief among the difficulties of Soviet Russia is the fact that her economic development was conceived as a world system a score of years in advance of any general recognition of the necessity for developing economic life on planetary lines. It was conceived rather than planned, and her painful history is largely a record of convulsive improvisations as this or that vast unanticipated obstruction has become apparent in her path. With an educational standard far too low for effective working, and in a state of extreme industrial underdevelopment, she has from the beginning found herself out of step with the rest of the industrialized world, and in unconcealed antagonism to all other governments. This has necessitated, among other intricate extra arrangements, the building of a wall between her internal currency and that of the world outside. Internally she has inflated, and it is hard to see how any increase of State or individual production can be managed without inflation. The elements of modernity in her experiment are mingled with an impatient dogmatism. Hence her perpetual trouble about social and political propaganda abroad through her attempts to bring some classes at least in the populations of the world outside her into sympathy with her leading ideas. It is reasonable that she should persist in propaganda; her very existence is a propagandist demonstration; and it is logical that the separatist national and imperial governments her effort threatens by example and precept alike, should resist her implacably. She is premature. She is progress entangled with a pronunciamento. She crushes recalcitrant workers and shoots disingenuous or inefficient officials. The immense tragic sufferings and sacrifices of her people, the blunderings, harshness, obduracy and cruelties of her overworked administration, the internecine angers and tyrannies of her dictatorship, must not blind us to the greatness of many of her efforts and achievements. Dogmatic, resentful and struggling sorely, crazy with suspicion and persecution mania, ruled by a permanent Terror, Russia nevertheless upholds the tattered banner of world-collectivity and remains something splendid and hopeful in the spectacle of mankind.

A complication of the Russian situation is the present rapid increase of her population. She is now, if we may rely upon her very questionable official statistics, adding about three and three quarter millions annually to the population of the world. Although her birth rate has fallen from 46.8 per thousand (pre-war) to 40, her death rate has come down from 30.5 to 17.4. So that her effective rate of increase has risen from 16.3 to 22.6. The significance of these figures will be perhaps better appreciated after the reader has gone through Chapter XIII, but it is foolish to ignore the advance in the quality of domestic life they imply.

In our review of human activities these scores of millions of per- plexed peasants in Russia, and the ill fed and badly housed workers in her impoverished towns—150,000,000 altogether of peasants and workers —are an extraordinarily important item. However ill fed and badly housed they now are, the vital statistics we have just given show that they are cleaner and better cared for than in Tzarist times. Our survey must not ignore these millions of babies.

And it must display also the peasant with his highly individualized fences broken down to make the great fields of the Kolkhozy, and his family, its most intimate ties broken, entering a community house. Moreover, we must picture the workers in the newly erected factory, all bought complete in America to be set up in Russia, listening to the exhortations of some revivalist from the Communist party sent to keep up their spirits. They are poor. They are inept at this new job. They blunder humiliatingly and are reproached ferociously and punished without pity. They go short of clothing and they feed badly. Poverty still broods over all things Russian. Nevertheless, they are busy; they are not expropriated and defeated and aimless like the gathering ac- cumulating unemployed of the Atlantic civilizations. They are sustained by a flickering enthusiasm that can be blown up at times into passion- ate hope.

Our more intricate Western world may solve piecemeal and day by day the complex riddle of industrial stagnation in the midst of wealth that confronts it now. It may have its local political and social troubles and convulsions, and yet never pass formally through the social revolu- tion foretold by the prophet Marx. But self-sufficiency in response to Russian self-sufficiency will hamper our Western world enormously in its systematic reconstruction. Russia is in sore need of coöperation with, and understanding from, the Western world, but the Western world has also much to learn from Russia, and much to unlearn also of its prejudices through the sacrifices of Russia. We can learn much of how enthusiasm can be raised and of what it can do. We can also get some idea of what enthusiasm cannot do, without an educated, self-disciplined service of directors, officials and industrial officers.

We have described in Chapter IV, § 5, the violent reconstruction of Russian agriculture. We have noted the difficulty of mechanizing farming, with a population untrained in large-scale production and the handling of machinery. This difficulty reappears in a magnified form in the attempts of that super-individual, the Soviet State, to create, out of the earth, so to speak, with a minimum of imported machinery, great modern industrial plants. The Moscow correspondent of the *Manchester Guardian* (May 23, 1931) draws an impressive picture of the state of affairs at the huge new attempt to out-Ford Ford in the production of tractors at Stalingrad. He tells of the clumsy handling of the machine tools, of six thousand breakages to three thousand machines in ten months. The output has not yet reached a twelfth of its maximum possibility. He quotes Ordzonikidze, the head of the Supreme Economic Council, who visited Stalingrad to find out why the Five Year Plan was not producing its promised results there, and why only 3,000 not very good tractors were forthcoming instead of an estimated 37,000. There is a reassuring frankness about many of these Russian reports, and this is what Ordzonikidze discovered, among other troubles:

". . . complete absence of accounting; factory buildings filled with waste products and the courtyard piled with filth and damaged products; complete absence of control over the coming to work of the workers; foremen and engineers not at their posts; uncontrolled starting and stopping of conveyors, absence of suitable care for equipment, an absence of persons responsible for the correct course of production in individual departments." . . .

These are the words of one of Stalin's most intimate and trusted helpers. When presently our survey brings in the organization of government and administration in the modern State, we shall be the better able to understand how inevitable were these wastes and confusions in the Russian improvisation.

But the frank admission of difficulty and disappointment is not the only virtue of the Bolshevik. There is also great boldness and courage in changing methods directly they disappoint. On June 23, 1931, Stalin addressed a conference of economists in Moscow and announced a new phase in this great experiment. He said that progress had been hampered by the cessation of the voluntary flow of peasant labour into industry, particularly into the timber, coal, building, transport, and iron industries. The countryside, therefore, must be constrained to deliver to industry sufficient supplies of labour based on a system of contracts between the economic organizations and the collective farms. He rebuked those economists who "sigh for the good old times when labour came voluntarily," and admonished them to recognize the new conditions requiring new methods. But economists, he continued, must realize that the conscription of labourers was not the whole task. Labourers must be bound to enterprises to which they were indentured and "labour flux" combated by a system of differential wages to increase productivity. Hitherto there had been hardly any difference between the earnings of skilled and unskilled workers and therefore the unskilled had no incentive to improve their qualifications. That evil could no longer be tolerated. The Soviet State required from the workers hard work, discipline, and mutual emulation. A system of payment according to the worker's need could not be allowed, and workers must be paid strictly according to the amount and the quality of the work they performed. One of the most important tasks would be the creation of a new "productive, technical *intelligentsia.*"

The economists, Stalin declared, must not be afraid to face the truth, and should openly admit that the system of an uninterrupted three-shift day had not everywhere been justified. Many enterprises had introduced the uninterrupted day on paper without enough preparation. Those enterprises must boldly throw away their paper reforms and return temporarily to the one-shift day, as the tractor works at Stalingrad had already done, and cease the practice of "charming away difficulties" by high-sounding phrases and heroic resolutions which accomplished nothing. Further, the one-man system of management must be established everywhere. Unwieldy combines must split up into smaller units. Instead of a board of directors one single director must be charged in each small combine with full personal responsibility for the conduct of affairs. . . .

So much for the internal difficulties of the Russian experiment. Let us now consider how the difference in phase with the rest of the world affects its external relations.

In every country where trading with the Soviet Republic is permitted, this gigantic super-individual is represented by a buying organization, such, for example, as the American "Amtorg." This negotiates credit, gives orders, sells produce, it is the commercial representative of Russia Unlimited.

Russia Unlimited has one single purse against the foreigner. Its internal monetary system is protected by elaborate barriers against confluence with that of the external world. But it has a continual need of foreign money to buy vitally necessary imports. Its efforts to get something to sell for that money are amazing. William C. White (one of the first scholars to be sent by an American university, the University of Pennsylvania, to study Russia at first hand) describes the intensive effort to produce salable exports to meet Russia's needs of machinery. There are "drives" to collect waste—old rubber, for instance, and scrap iron. "A municipal order in Moscow," he says, stated "that deposits would not be paid on empty vodka bottles unless the original cork was returned with them"—a foreign market had been found for second-hand corks. "Prizes are offered, which included at one time that most desired of all premiums, a trip abroad, for those who were able to suggest new products for export." There are expeditions exploring the White Sea for iodine-producing seaweed; the Caucasus is experimenting in tea-growing to cut down the Chinese import; Turkestan cotton ousts American. In order to keep up his payments abroad, the super-individual tightens his belt, exports goods—wheat and even manufactured cotton goods that are badly needed by his people at home. The Russians suffer amidst hope and exhortation, and the limit of their endurance is unknown.

Every "capitalist" country is divided within itself about dealing with this super-individual. There are the trades which sell to Russia and the trades which Russian produce undersells. The former are naturally pro-Soviet, and the latter are all for the prohibition of trading. The super-individual is making a remarkable fight for it. He betrays many signs of intense strain, but he keeps on. If his factory organization lags, his agricultural production is exceeding expectation. If he wins through, as he hopes to do, Russia will become an exporting country, underselling the produce of profit-seeking agriculture and industrialism, with a rising standard of internal comfort and no unemployed. That is the goal of the Russian effort, and even if it is not completely achieved, its partial realization is bound to compel very great readjustments in the economic organization of the rest of the world. These readjustments are bound to be also in the direction of comprehensive planning, and that again must involve either a voluntary or an imposed directive control. The enterprising individual must become more coöperative or he must be made more coöperative. And so we come back again here to the need for a high educational level in the community to make the large coöperations of a new age possible.*

*In *Stalin,* by Isaac Don Levine (1931) the reader will find a vivid account of the current phase of the Five Year Plan and of the strange personality behind that plan.

§ 9. *The Race between Readjustment, Disorder and Social Revolution*

Let us consider now how far we have come towards a comprehensive review of human activities. The panorama we have evoked up to this point is world-wide but still incomplete. We have as yet given no direct attention to the governments of mankind, or to the education of man-kind, and very little stress has been laid as yet on the differences of the masculine and feminine rôle in economic life. We have disregarded race and rank and many ancient pieties and loyalties. Our spectacle, thus simplified, exhibits a great confused variety and mingling of world production, distribution and consumption, plantations, mines, factories, transport, commodity markets, stores, shops, stock markets, banks, full of busy human beings, guided each one of them by a complex of motives, which, for most of the ordinary acts of economic life, are symbolized and presented in terms of money. It is as if society said to the individual: "Do this and you get so much." We have spoken of money therefore as the blood, the vital fluid in this contemporary economic body. The financial world, the banking system, mints, treasuries, play the rôle of the glands and nerves that control, increase, or restrain and purify the animating flood. And further we have traced how loosely that circulatory system and its controls are working, so that chief among our distresses we have on the one hand an excessive concentration, a congestion of wealth in the hands of an unhelpful and even obstructive minority, who have got it and who grip it, and on the other a morbid increase of undernourished and encumbering multitudes of human beings. We cannot therefore compare the economic life of the 1,900,000,000 human beings now alive to that of a healthy animal body. It is a sick body if it is to be considered as any organized body at all. It is indeed more like a body struggling to come into being and failing in strength and determination. It is manifestly in need of treatment, pos-sibly of very drastic treatment. It may be in need of surgery.

We began this work as a survey of productive activities. It was only as our study became closer and more searching that this contrast of the rich who have got the money and the poor who have not, came, almost in spite of our design, athwart the spectacle. Gradually we have been forced to recognize that in the course of twenty-five centuries or so, the ancient rules, servitudes and tyrannies of mankind have given place, step by step, by the substitution of money for other methods of compulsion, to the rule of wealth. The latter steps in this transition, made in the past three centuries, have been the most rapid, so that now the cash nexus reaches from the jungles to the mountain tops, and the rich are the potential, the inadvertent rulers of mankind. The pen (with a cheque book) is mightier than the sword. A sense of price is the secret of power. The rich man may not actually rule the world, but outside Soviet Russia no rule seems possible without him.

We find ourselves therefore describing not the working of a world-machine, planned and efficient, protecting and expanding human life, but a fortuitous concurrence of unplanned, unforeseen economic inter-actions, which has developed very rapidly and wonderfully in the past century, but which now betrays an alarming and quite unprecedented instability. It is not, we find, an economic order we are dealing with; it is an arithmetical crisis in the affairs of the human species. What promised to become a world-wide economic order is threatened by disaster in the counting house. Our work is inspired by the hope and belief that our world will yet develop into a real economic order, but we can give no certain assurance for that hope and belief.

Our analysis, in the preceding chapters, of social motives and of the money-credit system of the world enables us now to state the main factors in the present world crisis in elementary terms. There has been a stupendous increase in human power and productive ability during the last hundred years, and such an "abolition of distance" as to bring all mankind into close and rapid interaction. But there has been no sufficient corresponding adjustment of the monetary system and the system of ownership, so that humanity is entangled at every turn by obsolescent barriers, burthened with a constantly appreciating load of debt, and debarred from access to land and natural resources generally. The production and distribution of real wealth on anything like the scale of scientific possibilities is prevented by the concentration of financial wealth in the hands of a restricted, miscellaneous class of acquisitive and retentive people, the modern rich, enterprising only in acquisition, a class which has, so far, shown no signs of realizing either the possibilities or the dangers of the present unstable and unsatisfied state of mankind.

In Chapter VIII we ventured upon a broad and what we believe to be a very serviceable classification of human personas. There we made it clear that the ideology of the rich and influential, as we know them to-day, is very largely a mélange of ideas and dispositions derived from peasant and predatory types of mentality. With some exceptions the rich have done little to create the wealth they control. They have ac-quired it. Whenever business magnates or financial leaders are gathered together, there the boor and the brigand appear. The idea of creative service is there too, no doubt—and in increasing measure—but we have to remember always that the conduct of human affairs, when it is disinterested, is disinterested in spite of great inherent internal resistances. Every step towards a clear-headed, clearly understood control of economic life in the general interest of the race is made against the resistances of these baser factors present not only in the dominating rich but in ourselves and in everyone concerned. It is generally made, therefore, clumsily, ambiguously and slowly, and the present situation seems now too urgent for slow, clumsy or ambiguous measures.

The rapid accumulation of a great mass of superfluous poor people in our Western profit-organized civilization is now a continuous process; the ratio of that mass to the general population rises steadily, and there is all too great a possibility of effectual obstruction to any scientific alleviation of its stresses. A conflict develops steadily between the needs of this mass and the less intelligent and creative of the rich. The boor element in the wealthy and influential stratum is disposed to resist all attempts to alleviate the lot of these unemployed, to resist the giving of doles and any assistance in kind, and also any shortening of the working week, any increased superannuation of workers, any restrictions upon the employment of the young, of women or of old people, that might reabsorb many of those out of work. The masses in Russia, we are assured by most observers, *hope*. The supreme ambition of the boorish element among the modern rich seems to be to destroy hope. And this boorish spirit above will also appeal to patriotism, to that international competition which is based on the sweating of a working class, as an excuse for the unmerited privations and repressions it will want irrationally and instinctively to thrust upon its inferiors. This resistance of the casually and adventurously rich to scientific readjustment and to the scientific amelioration of change, will go on in the sight and knowledge of the expropriated and will deepen the natural antagonism of the have's and have-not's. The cinema, the popular press, the ever increasing *visibility* of modern realities, all tend to bring inequalities of fortune more and more vividly before the minds of the have-not's. The delusion of a fated subjugation to the wealthy nobility and gentry is continually more difficult to maintain. Yet the stupider elements among the modern rich are doing their utmost to sustain it. We have here the necessary elements for an intensifying class war.

Can the insurrectionary side in a class conflict between rich and poor supply the directive will and intelligence needed by the modern economic complex? Faced with an imminent class conflict, this question becomes imperative.

It is surely too much to expect people who have been deprived by the boorish element among their rulers from adequate knowledge and education, and who have no experience whatever of the directive side of economic life, to understand or sympathize with the constructive forces in a modern State. The poor, the "proletariat" in particular, as we have shown (Chapter VIII, § 2), also inherit their own distinctive modifications of the narrow peasant psychology, and their reaction is likely to be in the main not so much an effort to readjust as an unintelligent resentment not only against the rich, but against the methods and machinery of modern production, against social discipline and direction. They can hardly be expected to revise and improve what they have never been permitted to understand. That would be too difficult. Their education, such as it is, has been deprived of any constructive and directive ideas by the reactionaries above. So they are likely to show themselves much more disposed to hamper and break up the contemporary organization altogether than to reconstruct it. They are living shabby, anxious, undignified lives on the margin of subsistence. By that they judge the system. "Anything," they will say, "is better than this"—ignoring the fact that much might be worse.

If Soviet Russia succeeds and begins to prosper, or even if it can survive and make a fair appearance of success, this inevitable insurrectionary tension in the Atlantic populations will increase, and the resistance of the property-owning classes may be hardened by incipient panic. It may be. Or it may be mitigated by an intelligent realization on the part of some of their number of the need for extensive economic readjustments and sacrifices. How far rich and influential people will consent to learn and lead, and how far they will merely resist and suppress, is only to be known after the event, but on that depends the whole issue of progress or disaster. Some resistance to adjustment there will certainly be. We have no statistics to show us how far the modern rich man belongs to the educated class and how far he is a boor. So far as he is a boor, he will simply hold tight and resist and provoke the multitudinous boor below. We can count with some certainty, therefore, for some decades ahead, on the presence of very active, chaotic, revolutionary stresses in the world outside the Russian experiment. The boor above, afraid for his gettings, will be disposed to use to the extremest limit whatever advantage he may have with the legal, police and military organizations of the community in defense of his mean accumulations. He will be using all his influence for suppression and more suppression, and when he finds the spirit of the public services and the legitimate political system too fair, reasonable and temperate for his purposes, the brigand who is also in his composition will come to the surface and resort to illegal violence. He will seek a "strong man" to seize on power, lead the *Jeunesse dorée,* and keep the resentful and threatening multitude in order. The boors of good fortune above are no more likely to show compunction than the millions below in smashing up the slow-won methods of order and law. Reasonable and constructive-minded men will find themselves in a cross fire of misunderstandings, suspicions, panic and class hatred. That cross fire will be the atmosphere in which the building up of the modern world state must be achieved. Even though we dismiss Professor Soddy's suggestion that able men are generally wicked, we are still left face to face with the fact that many rich and powerful adventurers are as stupid and incurably dangerous as the departed Romanoffs.

The possibility of an arrest and even a retrogression of material civilization outside Bolshevik Russia, as grave or graver than the indisputable setback that occurred between 1914 and 1918, has to be faced. Confidence in public justice, faith in the law, is a slow and sensitive growth. When it is destroyed, human affairs sink to a lower level. When the law does not command respect, the lawbreaker becomes a hero. When the law does not give assurance of well-being, everyone drifts towards lawbreaking. The day of the sentimental gangster who robs only the rich dawns, and the epoch of dictatorships and popular "saviours" arrives. The gangster of the hired bravo type is confronted by the gangster of the Robin Hood type. Gangster and politician assimilate. It becomes more and more difficult to sustain firm and balanced government and to preserve the general liberty of discussion and initiative.

In various parts of the world we have, already, a number of more or less illegal dictatorships made possible by this antagonism of the ignorant and base-spirited rich above and the ignorant and base-spirited masses below. Usually it is the rich and privileged of the old and new types who have saddled themselves and their country with a military dictatorship. In Russia only has it gone the other way about, and the "proletarian" (or Stalin in the name of that mystical being) has become autocrat. In many cases the dictatorship is more or less controlled and steadied by an organization, the Fascisti in Italy, the Communist party in Russia; in others it is more frankly a brigand dictatorship. The persistent weeding out of his rivals and critics by Stalin is rapidly reducing the party control of Russia to a personal absolutism. In China an organization, the Kuomintang, with its variants and derivatives, struggles to keep its mind clear and maintain a constructive nationalist ideology against brigand adventurers and ruthless foreign exploitation.

Besides these broader displays of illegality, these seizures of whole nations and provinces, there is manifest throughout the world a wide-spread change in the popular attitude towards criminality, based on the deepening distrust of the expropriated masses in the spirit and intention of the existing legal order. This is due not to any intensified unfairness in the law, but to an acuter, less acquiescent criticism by the ordinary man. Indeed, the law has not gone back; it is more enlightened than it was, but it has not kept pace with the increase of scepticism and impatience. Its developments have not been sustained by public opinion because there is no general understanding of, or participation in, its modifications. The law does not advertise its modernity. It should. It should get out of sham Gothic buildings and sham dignity, antiquated wigs and fancy dress, and demonstrate its beneficent workings in the light of day. It should associate itself with modern concepts of society and bring its problems into line with everyday discussion. It is absurd that the only legal proceedings that are made interesting to the contemporary public are in the criminal courts.

The masses are losing any belief they ever had that the social organization embodied in the law is on their side. They are also losing faith in the value of money, the honesty of banking, and the security of any savings and investments. They are, in brief, being disillusioned about the social system to which they have hitherto submitted. The immediate loss of confidence, the diminution of confiding honest living caused by recent displays of monetary and credit instability, has been enormous. Fluctuations in money values leave the masses with an impression that governments can and will cheat. Then everyone, to the best of his courage and ability, begins to cheat and snatch also. The idea spreads that one is a fool to be conscientious. Concealment of all sorts increases. Economic morale is destroyed.

Across our broad picture of the world's expanding social and economic life we have to bring these shadows and symptoms of social disintegration. We add to our representation of the rather foolish and incoherent spending and waste of the modern rich, a multitude of mines and factories closing down, fields and plantations relapsing from cultivation, and gatherings of more and more unemployed workers, listless and dissatisfied, at the street corners. They trusted the property owners to keep things going, and the property owners have let them down. Criminal gangs multiply, and the forces of order lose energy and confidence. These are the outward and visible signs that profound changes are going on inside hundreds of millions of brains. There is manifestly a fading sense of obligation, loss of faith in the "honest" life, a growing sense of undeserved frustration, an increasing disposition to snatch pleasures and satisfactions while they are still within snatching range. These may not be all or most of the change that has occurred, but they are the changes that produce the most disquieting symptoms. There has been a world-wide seeping away of the beliefs, assurances and confidence on which the steady working of the traditional social organization has depended, and by which it has been able to carry on. We have therefore to balance this current degeneration of social morale under the stresses of our economic monetary and financial maladjustments, against the huge constructive achievements of the last hundred years.

What is happening may be a necessary parturition before the birth of unpredictable mental harmonies. These millions of brains, perplexed, anxious, greedy, planning, angry, resentful, vindictive, aspiring, this teeming ocean of gray matter, may be traversed by currents and stirred by tides whose movements we scarcely begin as yet to apprehend, much less to measure. The printing press, the cinema, the radio, stand ready to be used by anyone with the power and courage to use them upon this reservoir of will. We have all the means—and we have now the ideas and knowledge—needed to orient all these hundreds of millions of minds towards the undeveloped abundance, the clear and splendid possibilities of life at hand. We can set that tide going. We are surely in the dawn of an age when human motives and wills mingle and modify and combine, with a power and perhaps a violence they have never known before.

In our penultimate chapter we shall study the educational processes of the modern community, and we shall then be better able to weigh the factors in this crisis in social morale. We may then form a better conception than we can now of the profounder readjustments demanded by the present situation. We may realize how immense and rapid, under modern conditions, may be the readjustments in those hundreds of millions of brains.

Before we come to that, however, we have to consider two other systems of mental disturbance, the very great changes that are going on in the relations of women to men and of women to the community, and the tragic complication of all these problems we have opened up, by the impact of material progress upon the political and racial divisions of mankind. Then our outline will be completed. Throughout all these aspects of human life, as we pass from one to the other, runs one common theme, the theme of unforeseen and uncoördinated expansions of human power and possibility, and the consequent conflict of crude and novel opportunities and dangers with things outgrown. Things come out of the past and change in their nature under our eyes. The ancient antagonism of the rich and poor resembles the present antagonism of the rich and poor, but nevertheless, it is not the same antagonism. The old-world rich were real masters; the old-world poor were real slaves and serfs. The old-world civilization was only possible with that dominance and that subjugation. That order of things seemed inevitable. But the new-world rich are no longer essential to the productive scheme, they have become curiously detached from its administration, and their relations to the poor are indirect and complex. Possibilities of release and liberation open before our species, undreamt of before the Conquest of Power and Substances began.

CHAPTER THE ELEVENTH

The Rôle of Women in the World's Work

§ 1. How Far Sex Need Be Considered in This Survey

WE HAVE now brought our survey of human activities to a fairly comprehensive stage; we have got the whole ant-hill working, we have shown the workers busy and we have studied their motives and incentives. But still the spectacle is an extremely simplified one. Governments and politicians remain to be considered. No national flags have appeared. We have not yet brought the custom house and the barrack yard into the picture; we have indeed set aside the whole complex of national rivalry and war. The numbers of this human multitude and the increase of populations have yet to be studied; we have not mentioned crime and prison, and though we have alluded constantly to education, nevertheless the schools, colleges, instruction books of the world have still to be displayed.

And not a paragraph has been given yet to that intimate human activity, the relations of the sexes. That we will now take up.

While we have noted the progressive supersession of the autonomous home by collective services, we have refrained from considering how this has changed the mutual relations of man and woman in the ménage. Even in Chapter VIII when we set out the broad types of persona as the basis of our study of social interactions, we did not trouble ourselves with the fact that there are a feminine peasant and feminine nomad and (less important hitherto but not necessarily less important now) a feminine educated type. We would justify that simplification by saying that, roughly speaking, for the broad social ends of that chapter, the woman goes with the man of her class, that the peasant's woman shares his outlook on the world and has the feminine to his persona, and that the nomadic autocratic woman agrees also in all its main essentials with the ideology of her male.

"Roughly speaking," I write. But now let us try and speak and think a little less roughly, and take into consideration that every human affair is two-sided, that from the hut of the savage to the palace of the king

478

or multi-millionaire the woman is thinking and acting with certain differences—perhaps ineradicable differences—of her own. Hitherto we have considered the net result, the common denominator, economically and socially, of male and female. Now we are admitting that this human drama may have been played, and may always have to be played, by two series of non-interchangeable actors. Each may have a kind of rôle which is inseparable from the drama. Through the looms of our world of work and wealth may be running two systems of lives, about nine hundred and fifty million individuals in each, having different dispositions and different ends.

We write "may be" and not "is." We are posing a question here. By way of reply we offer the suggestion: that there are indeed such differences of disposition and end, but that they are the slight differences of essentially similar as well as kindred beings. They are coöperative and not antagonistic differences. They can point to a common destiny. To the end of time there are things that will be better done and rôles that will be better played by women than men, there are things women will think more desirable than men do, and *vice versa,* and a large part, if not the larger part, of human operations are, and will remain, definitely assignable as men's jobs or women's jobs.

But let us ask first, how far does sex extend into the being of a man or woman? Are we male or female to our finger tips? Many creatures are sexed, so to speak, only as far as reproduction goes. A herring has a soft roe or a hard roe, and that is as much sex as a herring seems to have. Nor is there anything particularly virile or ladylike about the male or female ostrich. It is only when incubation or suckling and the care of the young come into the life cycle of a species that we remark any wide structural or temperamental divergences. All these divergences are related to the reproductive specialization of the female. The Hominidæ do not present as much sexual divergence as most varieties of cattle; there is with them neither an all-round mental nor physical ascendency of either sex; while, for example, a man is able to hit harder, run harder and toil more heavily than a woman, she seems to swim better, is quicker to learn the balance of a bicycle, and has more endurance for continuous low-pressure work. There seem to be very small odds against her when it comes to the handling of an automobile or aëroplane. The conquest of Power, the abolition of toil, is relieving woman of many economic disadvantages. The light machine has put her upon terms of equal competition with men in many once masculine trades. The progressive socialization of the household is detaching her

more and more from traditional household drudgery, and birth control
minimizes her ancient specialization as the reproductive sex. Our
species, never very highly differentiated sexually, is now, it would seem,
undergoing a diminution of sexual differentiation.

§ 2. *Women as Workers and as Competitors with Men. The Keeping
of Wives and Families by Men in Relation to Feminine Employment.
Social Neuters*

Let us now review very briefly the work of women, and particularly
woman as an industrial worker, side by side and in competition with
man.

Before the war there was a polite pretence, maintained by at least the
middle and upper classes of the Western world, that women were incapable of doing ordinary industrial work. They could work in the
household, but they could not "work for a living." Cooks, for example,
were supposed to lack the intelligence needed for minding a machine;
and housemaids, "up and downstairs all day," the strength required for
climbing the steps of tramcars. When, during the war, women appeared
doing these things quite successfully, everybody expressed astonishment
and admiration. Women themselves seemed to be as astonished as anybody. The newspapers were full of it. People wrote books about it. And
yet in Great Britain alone, before the war, nearly five million females
were working outside their homes for wages and over one hundred
thousand of them were in the metal trades.

It is this sort of mass illusion and mass convention about women that
makes it difficult either to estimate what they can do or to find out
what they are actually doing. Nobody seems able to think about them
without feeling strongly in the matter and being moved to pretenses and
concealments. Everything undergoes a conventional dramatization.
Women themselves dramatize their behaviour in one way and men
dramatize it for them in another. Cold, clear statements of fact are rare
—we have only partial information, and statistics so incomplete that
they cannot be compared one with another.

The industrial life of women goes on against the opposition of these
conventions. In no period have men approved of their women working
for money. To do so reflected upon the social position of the head of
the family and implied a threat to his authority. The rich, from a mixture of good and bad motives, do not like their women to work at all.
Even the poor resent their working away from home. It was only when

engineering became coloured with patriotism, so that women in the factories became a credit to their country instead of being vaguely shameful, that the average citizen was prepared to realize what they could do there. And now that the war is over and its glamour gone, we are again at a stage when nobody seems to know or to want to know, fully and exactly, to what extent women are employed in industry, what they are doing, what they are being paid or the conditions under which they are working.

Women, as far as their work goes, may be divided into two main sections: those who work in and about homes, and those whose employment takes them into the outer world. The first group is engaged all over the planet in domestic tasks and crafts and agriculture. It is the huge majority of womankind. It includes, indeed, the American housewife with her heating from the main, her electric refrigerators and her country club, but also the savage wife—who, besides cooking and taking care of her children, builds huts, cultivates the ground, spins, weaves and makes baskets and pottery—and the whole multitude of domestic slaves and servants. It includes nearly all the women of India. Among these are scores of millions of Hindu wives, married before they are nubile, slaves not merely of their husbands and mothers-in-law, but of a rigid system of custom and superstitions, that makes the cardinal phases of life horrors of helplessness and uncleanness. Millions may never leave the homes and are thrust into solitary huts to bear their children. Most of these domesticated women workers are not paid in money, though money may be given them; where they are paid they are not paid very much. And in spite of the vacuum cleaners and gas cookers of the Western world, the bulk of this work is still done under conditions and by methods which are centuries out of date. The work is monotonous, lonely and imprisoning; it is set about with class distinctions; the performers have often no taste for it and have not been trained to do it, and they leave it whenever they get the chance. Woman may be a domesticated animal, but she certainly has not a domesticated soul. She loves toil and restraint no more than man. Housekeepers buy bread and send the wash to a laundry; the cook's daughter takes a job in a tea shop, and the intellectual young school teacher refuses to marry at all. In Russia, the Bolshevik authorities tell us, it is the women who take eagerly to the collective farms, who vote for "going collective" in village after village. What are supposed to be their deepest instincts disappear promptly when the chance of getting away from housework appears. According to the official figures there were over 13½ million

Russian women working on collective farms in March, 1931, and the figure was then said to be increasing. The proportion of domesticated women seems to be falling, all over the world.

Manifestly there must be a corresponding increase of non-domestic women. One group of non-domestic feminine employees, however, is almost certainly shrinking. These are the mere poor drudges, the sweated, the exploited women, in corners or on the fringes of the industrial world, toiling at work so badly paid and disagreeable that men refuse to do it. Factory acts and laws dealing with public health are abolishing this type of employment in civilized countries. Filthy jobs like gut-scraping have been cleansed and disinfected; the beer-bottling and rag-sorting that used to be carried on in insanitary cellars are now performed in dry and properly ventilated workshops, often with the help of machinery. In the opinion of a high official in the Factory Department of the English Home Office real driving and oppression of women, so far as the modern communities are concerned, are now only to be found in domestic service, where in rare instances a little slavey has not spirit enough to leave a tyrannical mistress. As industrialism spreads into backward countries where there are no trade unions or restrictive laws, exploitation reappears for a time. Dame Adelaide Anderson's report on the employment of children in Egyptian industry describes cotton-ginning sheds filled with irritating dust where boys and girls of seven are kept at their work by whips. Women still coal ships in Japan. But international control in these matters is increasing, and unless there is some sort of world collapse, our great-grandchildren may very well live in a world completely cleansed from the barbarous industrial consumption of women drudges.

But the bulk of non-domesticated women now, the real modern women workers, are the product of education acts, trade unionism, and the light machine. It may be a lathe or a typewriter, but where a machine can be made light and easy they are drawn to it to perform, generally speaking, the less responsible kinds of work of which it is capable. In comparison with men they take down letters but do not dictate them, they mind machines but they do not set, mend, improve or invent them. And they receive, as a rule, from rather over half to two-thirds of what a man would get for doing a similar if not identical job. They are young (Sir Josiah Stamp has estimated that half the women in industry in Great Britain are under twenty-three), and they are badly organized.

A want of organization of women workers is a world-wide phenomenon. In Japan, where the number of men and women in the factories is almost equal—rather over a million of each—there are three men in the unions for every woman. In England 32 per cent of the "gainfully occupied males," as the census returns call our men workers, are organized, and only 15 per cent of the smaller total of gainfully occupied females. The cause of this abstention does not seem to be hostility towards trade unions, but low wages and adolescent amateurism. The younger women regard their time in the factories as an interlude preceding marriage, and they want every penny either to collect a dowry or to pay for the clothes and outings which ensure a wider choice of husbands. When women's wages rose during the war and marriage seemed less certain, they flocked into the unions: since then they have lapsed into their old indifference to industrial organization.

It is claimed that the influx of girls into industry has had on the whole a civilizing influence upon working conditions. It was probably their appeal as unprotected minors to Victorian sentiment which passed the first factory acts, and when under pressure of foreign competition that sentiment hardened, its place was taken by a growing biological conscience. The presence of women in the factories seems to have raised the standards of cleanliness, decency and comfort there. And as soon as their working conditions ceased to be hopelessly degrading, their greater desire for colour in life, pleasantness, romance, their views on the subject of manners and conduct, have had a decisive influence on the industrial atmosphere. Filth and brutality have retreated before them. The general amelioration of life in the past half century may have had its share in these improvements, but the industrialization of women was the main progressive force.

What is the present outlook for women in industry? They seem likely to remain an important industrial factor—possibly in increasing numbers—but not as life workers. That girls should have somewhere to go between leaving school and entering into marriage is under contemporary conditions an obvious social convenience. But whether they will ever occupy more than the lowlier positions in industry is another question. Apparently, as a sex, they lack both a man's ambition and his disinterested mental curiosity. They do not mean to remain at the work and they are not willing—except in a few trades here and there like the Lancashire cotton trade—to train for skilled or responsible positions. Moreover, employers, because of the possible transitoriness of their engagements, are unwilling to train even those girls who ask for the chance to qualify themselves for higher posts. It is difficult, therefore, to estimate the force and soundness of their disposition to take and use such a chance. The matter is further complicated by the fact that in the factories of Great Britain, trade-union regulations shut women out from entire industries and from the cream of the skilled jobs in most of the rest. In America the wages for unskilled labour have been so good relatively that it has been difficult to induce even men to train for the best positions, which to a surprising extent therefore are filled by skilled craftsmen from Europe. In Russia, where there are now no such barriers, 150,000 women, we are told, are being specially trained for skilled work, but it is too soon to say whether they will prove as valuable as men. In Latin countries an exceptional woman may be found doing anything—but she remains exceptional. At present, indeed, it is only in Scandinavia that women as a sex seem to be demonstrating any aptitude for the more skilled branches of technical work, and obtain employment to any perceptible extent on equal terms with men.

THE KEEPING OF WIVES AND FAMILIES BY MEN IN RELATION TO FEMININE
EMPLOYMENT

The industrialization of women on anything like equal terms with men goes on not only against trade-union bars and the distracting competition of the marriage market, but also against the long established prejudices of our race. The belief in woman's inferiority as a worker still prevails. This inferiority is not proven up to the hilt, because the handicap of the bars and distractions we have noted prevents a fair try-out, but it remains the established impression. Without bars and handicaps it is felt that she would still be inferior. This persuasion may be due partly to the fact that she is paid lower wages even on work she is better able to do than a man. To get 60 per cent of a man's wage means in effect only 60 per cent of his food, freedoms and self-assurance, and girls, from the first day they go to work, are accustomed to this attitude of inferiority to their brothers and accept it without demur. And because they accept it they are now being employed in many types of work instead of men. They have not actually driven men out of men's own jobs—they are generally prevented from doing that by trade-union agreements—but either they have followed domestic trades, such as sewing, cooking and laundry work, out from the home into the factories where they are now very largely carried on, or a skilled trade carried on by men is changed into a trade where the skill goes into machines which can be managed by young women—though this very possibly would not have been done if it were not for the woman's lower wage. This question of relative wage rates is likely to become more acute in the future. At present both working men and working women seem to accept the proposition that man, as woman's superior and as the potential keeper of a woman, is entitled to be paid more for what he does. The man protects his standard of living not by forbidding the woman to undersell him, but by shutting her out completely from this or that particular pool of work. The result is that new trades—such as electrical work for wireless apparatus—get very largely handed over to women, and there is a constant inducement to break up skilled jobs in this or that part of an old trade and get the rearranged operations classed as women's work. An intensification of this might at any time cause the present discrepancy in rates to be felt as intolerable, and men might then insist upon a uniform rate of pay for both sexes. That might check the increasing relative employment of young women for some time, though it might ultimately increase the proportion of skilled women who meant to make their jobs their life work.

At the back of the disposition to underpay women relatively to men is the old tradition that the man has to "keep a family." This is what the trade unions are defending when they bar women from the better paid types of employment. Modern industrialism knows nothing and can know nothing of marriage so far as its pay sheets go. If a factory were obliged to discriminate between married and single, put up the pay of each worker whenever he chose to marry, and give him a rise whenever his wife presented him with a baby, it is plain that in this world of competition it would have to restrict its employment to guaranteed bachelors or go into an early bankruptcy. The present state of affairs is a rough adjustment to social conditions under which young men leaving home and going into employment are strongly impelled to marry. The normal state of mind of the adult male in a trade union is that of an actual or potential family man. He does whatever he can through his union to prevent the girl underselling him by her unskilled labour, or getting beyond his reach by winning her way to skilled employment on equal terms. She does the former, but so far she has shown very little energy in doing the latter. And he tries to keep his wages up to a level at which he can "keep a wife."

It has frequently been asserted in the British press that a serious factor in unemployment is that women are driving men out of work. That is not true. Certainly, while the number of men employed has increased, the increase of employed women has been sensibly greater. But it has not been enormously greater. The gross difference between 1923 and 1930 shows a steady increase in the number of women employed in the industries covered by the British unemployment insurance, from a little under three million to three million and a half. If the pre-war rates of employment held to-day there would be about a hundred thousand more men and about a hundred thousand less women industrially employed. That is all. A large part of the increased industrial employment of women has nothing to do with the unemployment of men; it is a transfer of women from domestic to industrial life, because work that was formerly done in the home, laundry work, sewing, baking, urban lunch and tea service, is now supplied outside. Also the nursery has fewer children and needs fewer nursemaids. There were a quarter of a million fewer domestic servants in 1921 in Great Britain than in 1911. Nor, so far as Great Britain goes, is feminine employment responsible for male unemployment, which is greatest in the heavy industries where women do not compete with men.*

We may therefore dismiss this suggestion that the industrialization of women is to any considerable extent the cause of masculine unemployment. It is the ancient tradition for a woman to look to a man to keep her, and that in effect is what ninety-nine women out of the hundred, even in most "advanced" circles, still do. The modern woman likes to keep free and own herself, but she finds it as a rule more practicable still to do so at the expense of someone else. What is of far more importance in a study of womanhood under modern conditions, is the vast masses of unemployed men which are now appearing in every modernized community, who have little or no earning power at all. Instinct and tradition conspire to make nearly all of them want to "keep a wife," but a vast proportion realize that they will be quite unable to keep children. An increasing proportion of men workers, workers of the black-coated class as well as manual workers, must marry women with a certain apologetic air therefore and with the agreed intention of evading offspring. There is a steady increase in the number of childless ménages. A new sort of marriage and a new sort of home have come into existence unobtrusively but surely; a marriage which does not ensue in a brawl of children. It ensues, however, in a dreadfully unoccupied woman, whose leisure becomes a grave problem to the community. She lives a life of small economies. She feels her use-

*The British health insurance figures show 70.5 per cent men to women in 1912 and 68.2 per cent in 1928. The percentage of males in the British Civil Service was 88.6 in 1913 and 77.6 in 1929.

lessness in the measure of her intelligence. At the side of that fruitless type of ménage there is also an increase of "bachelor women" on the one hand, maintaining themselves on their pay, and on the other, an increasing number of men at a level of pay and employment below the possibilities of even keeping one woman.

SOCIAL NEUTERS

Deliberately sterile ways of living have existed for a long time. In France, for example, it has long been customary in a great number of bourgeois households to employ man and wife, often quite young people, on the distinct and carefully observed condition that they have no children. Such callings as that of the shop assistant, having gone on for a hundred years or more, imposing a practical celibacy upon the majority of those who followed them. But the self-subsisting woman is—as anything but a social exception—practically new, and what is more significant is the rapid increase and wide dispersal of these hitherto exceptional types of life, which have no reproductive value in the community. In Roman times the proletary was that impoverished section of the community which contributed nothing but children to the commonweal. These new types constitute a sort of negative proletary which contribute few or no children at all.

Our mechanized civilization is thus producing, in increasing quantities, individuals whose sexual life is of no social importance whatever. That does not mean that they are not making love and leading a very full emotional and physical sexual life; many of them are. But this part of their existence produces no results that justify any sort of control of the sexual life by the community. From the biological point of view they are as neuter as the worker bees.

In Chapter XIII we shall deal with the main facts of the population question and then the high probability that this mass of neuters in our species will increase will become very plainly apparent. The time may be quite close at hand when only a half or a third of the adults in our world will be producing offspring.

The social and economic utilization of the women of this neutralized mass is a much more serious problem than that of the men, because of the greater relative importance the reproductive (and not simply the sexual) side of life has had for womankind. At present this problem of feminine frustration and lack of rôle outside domesticity is overshadowed by the far more serious economic and political difficulties in which our world is entangled. But whenever those difficulties are cleared away this problem will emerge to primary importance. So far from the relative increase of feminine to masculine employment being a serious and threatening phenomenon at the present time, the much more serious fact is that so few women relative to the numbers who are now unproductively dependent are striking out for a social and economic independence of their own.

§ 3. *The Inherent Difference of Physical and Mental Quality between Men and Women*

It was only after the writer had set himself seriously to summarize the differences of man and woman that he realized how vague, vaporous, and useless is the enormous literature of the subject. It is like a wide, warm, damp, haze-filled gulley between science and literature, choked with a weedy jungle of pretentious writing. One has not so much to summarize as to mow down and clear away, thousands of volumes that in the guise of general discussions express merely personal prejudices and aspirations. The substantial matter of even profoundly "scientific" works is not so much a record of controlled observations as a series of casual remarks.

No really definite attempt has yet been made to discount the enormous subjective factor that enters into thought about the business, or to make allowances for the variations in the amount and nature of that subjective factor at various stages in the sexual cycle of the observer's life. Inherent and imposed qualities are recklessly jumbled by everyone. No clear recognition is made of the varieties of human type and race. No account is taken of age phases. A Bengali woman, a Patagonian woman, a Norwegian fisher-girl or a Hottentot woman, has each a definite difference from her associated male. She has an innate difference and an acquired difference. There are an innate difference and an acquired difference in Bengal, and they are not at all the same differences as those in Norway. And the woman passes from phase to phase in her life orbit—as her man does also—according to her type.

But in nearly all this sex literature these differences are assumed to be, if not the same, at least of the same nature. People write of "virile" and "feminine," of what men and women are and will do, regardless of pattern or phase. So far as one can generalize about these "studies," by "man" is meant a male of middling class and some education in one of the European or American communities, round about the age of forty, and by "woman," a female in the same social stratum, of from twenty to thirty-five. About whom the pens scribble uncontrollably.

Our task here is not to swell this already overwhelming literature of provocation, excitation and complaint. We have to state the material facts of the case as compactly and clearly as we can for the purposes of our spectacle. The rest matters no more to us now than—love poetry.

We may add a few observations upon the question of physical difference already posed. In all varieties of *Homo sapiens,* over and beyond the differences of the actual reproductive organs, we note that the female pelvis is relatively more capacious than the male, the upper parts of the legs are set differently, the breathing is more costal and less abdominal, the whole build is lighter, softer and finer. The difference is not so marked in some races as in others, but it is always a difference in the same direction. As with the other Primates, the fully developed human male is heavier than the fully developed female. On these points there can be little or no dispute. The relative fineness and lightness of the female extends to the head, neck and brain. The differentiation is obviously less wide in man than in the gorilla. And all these differences seem liable to great exaggeration through custom and social condition.

As Metchnikoff pointed out long ago in his *Nature of Man,* natural human life is full of incongruities. The human female is capable of sexual intercourse and excitation ten years before she reaches the age when she can bear children to the best advantage; she can have sexual intercourse forced upon her against her will as very few female animals can; she cannot resist as effectually; and in many savage, barbaric, and even civilized societies, the complete development of a large proportion of women seems to be greatly retarded by their premature subjugation to sex. They do not really grow up. Presently their stock of vitality is put under contribution for child-bearing. Or if they do not marry young they do not marry at all, and so go on to what may perhaps be considered another type of underdevelopment. The sexual life of the human male seems to be more passionate and violent but more transitory and incidental than that of the female. The storm passes, and he is quit of the urgency for a time. He returns to the work he was doing. He gets a better chance therefore of maturing according to his innate and individual possibilities.

These essential differences and these natural disadvantages have been greatly masked, distorted and exaggerated by custom and tradition in all human societies. We do not know, with any certitude, anything that we can call the "natural" sexual disposition of either man or woman at any stage of development. So great has been the masking that in Britain and North America, for example, it was commonly assumed until a few years ago that the majority of women were, as the phrase goes, "cold"—devoid, that is, of strong sexual appetites—and that the minority who sought pleasure in sex were abnormal and reprehensible. This assumption prevailed during a period of repression, and it was only an intensification of an almost world-wide mental disposition. But it was no more than a convention. Now, simply through the annulment of various prohibitions and the lifting of a veil of secrecy, this assumption of feminine frigidity is no longer accepted. Now, it would seem, a great multitude of women are as sensuous and excitable, if not more sensuous and excitable, sexually than men. There is a difference in the tempo rather than the quality of their desires.

These again may not be permanently valid observations; we may be witnessing only the release and sur-excitation of feminine desire through the lifting of old repressions and the realization of new opportunities and novel systems of suggestion. Yet it is plain that until we have more definite knowledge in this field we are unable to decide upon almost fundamental issues in social life—such as our treatment of prostitutes—or in education. Our estimate of good or bad conduct must remain in many respects provisional.

It seems at least clear that women are more selective in their sexual conduct and more easily subdued to self-control. Sex in the normal male is more resentful of control and more forcible in achieving its ends. Yet here again, while the male is more disposed for open rebellion against prohibitions and lapses easily into a rude, clumsy, aggressive, mean pursuit of reliefs and satisfactions, the subconscious urgencies of the female may in the end be a slower but more effective drive. He can be more easily put off with crude gratifications than she. It has always been possible to separate parenthood from sexual relationships in thought, and it is becoming possible to do so in practice. Traditional morality sets its face against such a separation, but modern ideas are changing that. It is asserted by many now, asserted but not proved, that through the larger part of adult life, physical and mental health is only possible while the stir and satisfactions of sexual relationships are going on, and that parenthood need not be involved in that emotional system. The sexual life of a woman earning a living for herself, if it is conducted in this spirit, approximates very closely to the sexual life of a man living under the same conditions. She is more in conflict with tradition, but beyond that there is no other important difference between the two.

On all such questions the physiological and psychological sciences give us as yet scarcely any clear, assured and measured information. They ought to do so, and presently, no doubt, they will. But as it is we are left rather to the immediate and superficial appearances of the case, and to guesses and intuitions. It is manifest that in the relations of men and women we are dealing with plastic mental material which can be moulded into a great variety of fashions by suggestion, law, custom and accident, but we are still incapable of stating the limits and conditions of that plasticity.

On the whole there seems to be a rapid and considerable assimilation of qualities and conditions going on, women are gaining freedoms, enlarging their scope, and men are losing privileges, authority and personal prestige, but it does not follow that that assimilation will go on indefinitely until we return to the herring's immunity from all secondary sexual characters. Men and women may readjust to new and progressive conditions, retaining and even intensifying certain male and female characteristics. And we may find that there will be a definition and recognition of many more rôles than the traditional two, between various sexual types. The private sexual life is not our concern here, but we are concerned with all varieties of sexual rôle that affect the general social and economic process.

§ 4. *Motherhood and the Dependence of Women Because of Motherhood*

The life of the ordinary mammal, up to and including the more primitive human types, is almost entirely taken up by growth, sleep or basking, the search for food and reproduction. That fills the year. Up to our own times that was as true for human beings in the mass as for their humbler relations. They worked, they paired, they brought up a family. There was little margin to their days and by the time the family was completed and launched life was nearly consumed.

Men and women were pressed forward by custom and daily necessity from the cradle to the grave. Since the number of female births is roughly equal to the male, the normal state of affairs has been monogamy, with a certain amount of polygamy superimposed whenever exceptional men as chiefs and so forth got a chance of monopolizing more than their share of the supply of women. This was balanced against the greater liability of males to violent death, and the lesser resisting power of the male to many forms of illness. (The proportion of females to males is somewhere about 21 to 20 in western Europe.)

A certain obvious division of labour established itself therefore (with a variety of interpretations and minor variations) throughout the world. The frequent pregnancy of the female, and the young children's need of protection, made it natural and proper that the male should do the more heavy, active and adventurous part of the food-hunt or food-production, and that she should keep house and cook and stay with her offspring. Upon the basis of these necessities (which are necessities no longer) the whole tradition of feminine dependence was established.

But the business of parentage is as much the male's concern as the female's. It is as much the business of life for one as the other. The natural social man, as we find him expressing himself in the peasant persona, is benevolent and responsible, but tyrannous and possessive, towards his woman and his children. He is the captain of the home, and she is the mate. All mammals and all incubating birds make great sacrifices of personal freedom to the production and welfare of their young; man makes greater and more prolonged sacrifices because his young need protection for so long, and woman has made even greater sacrifices than man. Throughout the ages she has been obliged to concede leadership. If it is not in her nature to concede leadership it is woven now almost inextricably into her persona by the power of tradition.

This convention, the thrusting upon her of rather more than a fair half of the toil of the household, premature conception, the worries of children, have used up the majority of women rather faster than their men. In the past women *aged,* and where old-fashioned conditions prevail women still age, sooner than man. The man, when he has had the power and authority to do it, has therefore tended always to supplement his first mating and bring in younger wives. For many thousands of years there has been the urge towards the possessive polygamy of energetic and powerful men, either imposing itself openly as in black Africa and much of the Orient, or working beneath the conventional arrangements of society, against the necessary habitual monogamy of average men and women. Polyandry, on the contrary, is a Tibetan rarity, and is rather a fraternal shareholding of women than any equivalent to the possessive polygamy of the influential male. Where women have had great power and opportunity—the Empress Catherine the Second of Russia, for example—it is true that they have shown themselves as polygamous as men, but such occasions have been rare. Of prostitution we will speak later. None of these exceptions does very much to alter the fact that motherhood has been so great a disadvantage to women as to impose upon them a dependence and defenselessness that are almost inextricably woven into our social tradition.

But now very rapidly, in the countries affected by the Atlantic civilizations, a conspiracy of circumstances has been changing and destroying all the foundation facts upon which that tradition was based. The chief elements in this conspiracy have been, first, the restriction of births and such a hygienic prevention of infant mortality that physical motherhood becomes a mere phase of a few years in a woman's life; secondly, the socialization of education and of most domestic services; and thirdly, the supersession of any protective function on the part of the male by the law and the police. Women is left almost abruptly released and exposed. But the tradition of countless generations of disadvantage and real dependence clings about her.

§ 5. *Some Consequences of the Traditional Inferiority and Disadvantage of Women. Feminine Acquiescence and Disingenuousness. Prostitution. The White Slave Trade. The Gigolo*

The quality of the life of women throughout our changing world today is determined by two main factors. First there is the mechanical factor in economic progress; the supersession of toil, particularly of heavy toil, and the socialization of many of the more important tasks that were once distinctively feminine. This mechanical factor makes for an equalization of economic importance and a release of women from the implication of inferiority. The only remaining physical differences between man and woman are becoming horizontal, i. e., differences between individuals in the same class, and not vertical differences, in which all women are put below all men, or vice versa.

But secondly there is a huge mass of tradition still operative by which the man is incited to take the overmastering and responsible rôle, and the woman tempted to accept and make the most of the old-time subservience, instead of insisting upon the logical consequences of the new conditions. She finds she can get most of the traditional advantages and concessions, won for her by her past devotion to maternity and domesticity, while being in fact relieved of most of the burthen of that devotion. She finds this the more easy and excusable because the pride of the men with whom she has to deal in business or professional life is easily roused against her; it makes things difficult for her as an equal or antagonist; it makes it harder to play a man-like rôle than if (all other things remaining equal) her sex were male. On the other hand, it wins her unjustifiable "chivalrous" concessions.

Ancient tradition makes it seem right and proper to a man—even if he is an economically incompetent man—that he should have a woman of his own, under his control. The feeling is very widespread that every man should have a woman of his own, and there is plainly a sex consciousness like a class consciousness in the matter. There is sex solidarity. There is a widespread psychological resistance on the part of both men and women against the economic equalization that material changes are bringing about. A woman working on her own behalf does not get a fair deal from either men or women. Municipal authorities in Great Britain usually dismiss their women doctors on marriage, even when they are running maternity clinics. But a male doctor may marry, and marry again after the briefest widowerhood, and no municipal authority will take cognizance of the matter.

There is more here than an envious prejudice against seeing two incomes flow into one home. Nobody minds how many incomes a man earns, inherits and marries. What almost nobody really believes is that a grown-up woman has a right to manage her personal life as freely as a man. Not only is she expected to live more timidly, but large sections of the population feel that they have a right to compel her to do so. And the forbidding of outside work to married women, the shutting of them up in their homes, is bad for the home, where it produces a combination of restlessness and mental stuffiness, and bad for the reputation of women as workers. They are accused of emotional instability, of "bringing their feelings into their work," of lacking ambition, breadth of mind and human understanding. The traditional influences of which we have been speaking are powerfully reinforced by financial factors. Under all the talk about women's emancipation, and in spite of the considerable steps that have been taken towards legal freedom, there remains the fact that the overwhelming majority of women in the world are economically dependent—have no money of their own at all. Hundreds of millions of them are not allowed to own money or any property but personal jewelry. Over most of the world the husband has control of his wife's property: we find this state of affairs not only in backward countries, but in France, Switzerland, Belgium, Spain, the State of Florida and the Province of Quebec. Where they may own it, custom—and the sincerely held belief that a man needs money more than a woman—diverts the flow of inheritance into male hands. Where money is left to women it is, more often than not, tied up so that they are not free to use the capital. We have already seen that as wage-earners they earn less for the same work than would be paid to a man. As a sex, when it comes to money of their own, they are poor.

The effects of this comparative poverty are so far-reaching that it is difficult to determine where they end. For one thing, it means that women on the whole are not educated to deal with any aspect of money but spending. They do not realize, imaginatively, its industrial and financial functions. They are urged by every magazine and paper they pick up, by the implications of almost every book, to regard themselves as spenders, as elegant or beautiful, or, at the worst, subtle creatures, for the maintenance of whose elegance, beauty and subtlety an immense mass of spending is necessary and justified. We have already seen in our section on Cosmetics how this works out in detail. So when money falls unfettered and in large quantities into the hands of a woman, she is likely to be someone with no ideas about money but that it can be spent in amplifying and decorating her personal life—with a certain minor flow towards charity and the support of art and music—and she will receive far more admiration, gratitude and press publicity for doing that with it than for using it in any fruitful or constructive manner.

As for the women who have no money—or less money than the corresponding men of their class—they are hampered at every turn. It is not worth while spending so much on their education as on that of boys, because they cannot be expected to earn so much. The ordinary English parents may be as willing to make sacrifices for their daughters as they are for their sons, but if one or the other must be preferred, it is only common sense to invest in the boys. Then there is the question of capital—women, because of their customary poverty, cannot buy practices and partnerships or stock or premises; they have to remain as employees, assistants, secretaries. Even in a profession newly opened to women, like medicine, we find groups of doctors joining together to run a practice and taking in a fully qualified woman, not as a partner, but as a mere salaried assistant, to do the work they most dislike. And in such positions—partly because they are paid less, partly because there is the risk, if they are young, of losing their services on marriage—they are generally regarded as less valuable than men. This may not be true of the individual employer, who will readily admit that the women in his own office do their work as well as men would do it. But that does not prevent him from considering them inferior, as a whole, to the same sort of men.

The result of all this is that while the conventional relations between men and women are weakened, the much advertised new relations which are arising to replace them do not correspond to economic fact. Marriage and dependence still provide the most dazzling social and monetary prizes for women. Except for those born rich, prettiness, suitable clothes and pleasing manners are far more likely to lead to success in life than ambition, knowledge and intelligence. Women want children, homes, love-making, and on the other hand travel, entertainment and ornamental backgrounds. Men alone can give them these, and men prefer as a rule to give them only for personal and emotional reasons. "Emancipated" women at the present time are therefore likely to be inconsistent. They value freedom, and they claim equality, but unless they are prepared to give up every other side of life to these, they must not behave as equals except after they have got what they want. This may be as unfair to the man involved as the original predicament was unfair to the woman—it is not surprising that there is a great deal of talk about the relations between the sexes and a good deal of open hostility. But that does not mean that there is more sexual unhappiness. On the contrary, it seems likely that there has never been a time when there was so little.

Economic inferiority—not of actual gross earnings, perhaps (on account of the number of women who cease to earn after marriage), but of status and opportunity—will probably diminish. It is more difficult to see what will relieve the almost complete dependence of the married woman. Increasingly, parents are unwilling to provide dowries even in countries where they are under considerable social pressure to do so. The system which is proposed in lieu of them is that of endowment of motherhood or children's allowances. There are several ways of securing such payments—they may come from the State, or from the industry in which the husband is employed. But they presuppose a high degree of national organization. They would benefit women—there would be a considerable transfer of wealth direct from men to women—the mother would no longer be wholly dependent on her husband, the unmarried woman worker would find it less difficult to establish the principle of equal wages for equal work. On the other hand, they would almost certainly involve the lowering of the wages of single men, and in most of their forms they extend the dangerous principle of distributing public money whose expenditure is not subject to control.

In the meantime the majority of women are not yet insisting with serenity and steadfastness upon their legitimate autonomy. It takes a

Hetty Green, for example, to keep a woman's fortune from the exploitation of her man. Few women with property have as free an enjoyment of their property as men have, the law and sentiment notwithstanding. They give way. They cannot, as they say, "endure a row." Nor do women insist as plainly as men do on their own tastes and desires. They have to "get round" the man. This is the story the modern novel and play have to tell over and over and over again in thousands of forms, the story of a compeller and an outwitter.

The testimony of contemporary literature seems to be that on the whole the outwitting defeats the compulsion. But it may be that the dominance of the male decision gives us neither plot nor drama, and yet in reality is the more widely prevalent state of affairs. A struggle for the "upper hand," as Samuel Butler describes it in *The Way of All Flesh,* occurs in a great number of pairings. In the past probably a greater proportion of women lost that struggle than at the present time, and it may have occurred more generally. A more intelligent education of children for adult life and sexual relationship, the progressive alleviation of mutual pressure in a broadening social life, and greater facilities to escape from marriage, may go far to eliminate any need for such a painful and intimate struggle in the future.

In a complete summary of human activities it is necessary to bring into the picture that ineradicable class of women, the oldest profession in the world, the prostitutes. The peculiar conventions of the pre-war age required writers to mention this trade only in terms of exaggerated horror. It flourished everywhere, and everywhere there was a pretense that it did not exist. It was outcast, unspeakable, untouchable. Moreover, in all ages the peculiar circumstances of these women have subjected them to legal extortions and illegal exploitation, and in default of the normal male husband-protector, they have had to resort to a variety of illegal defenses. A type of man has been evoked to organize and profit by their necessities. And they have been less able to escape their special disadvantages because within, in their own minds, they were trained and prepared to acquiesce in the traditional standards of feminine conduct.

Let us consider dispassionately what a prostitute is. A prostitute hitherto has usually been a woman, though, as we shall note in a moment, this is not necessarily the case. And her rôle through the ages has been to sell feminine companionship to men who were in urgent need of it for limited periods. Excited moralists have been prone to exaggerate the purely physical side of her existence; those who are bet-

ter acquainted with the realities of life know that the common prostitute has no particular skill or charm in her caresses, and that the element
of sensuous gratification is of hardly more importance to her intermittent relationships than it is to permanent wifehood. If one notes the
districts which prostitutes frequent, the social aspect of prostitution
becomes apparent. Such women have abounded in seaports since the
beginning of time; they walk near railway termini; they are in evidence
wherever business brings men up from the country for a stay at some
commercial centre; they hover where unmarried men are gathered.
Loneliness, loose intervals of time in a friendless place, these call for
the prostitute quite as much as gross desire. Prostitutes not only go with
these lonely, comfortless men, but they hear their talk, they flatter and
console them, they give and receive real friendship and affection. They
do not in their normal rôle minister simply to lust; what they sell and
give into the bargain is much more than that. It is womanhood. They
witness in fact to the inherent dependence of the male mind upon
women, of one sex upon the other. They are temporary wives.

But our world has never accommodated itself to this institution of
temporary wives, much less has it made any effort to protect them, and
so this type of relationship—so inevitable that never in any part of the
world has it been stamped out altogether—has been subjected to every
possible type of degradation. These women are tolerated and assumed
to be intolerable, they are exploited both legally and illegally, prosecuted
and persecuted; they are forced down into a festering obscurity where
the thief, the bully, the blackmailer and the cruel coward, make life
horrible for them. They take a colour from their surroundings, they
succumb to the suggestion of their shamefulness; dissatisfied by a perpetual truncation of their friendships, they evoke vile male dependents,
and often they themselves become mentally distorted. And across the
disorder of their lives is drawn the threat and darkness of those con-
tagious diseases lust transmits. The stigma upon them is so widely
appreciated, their dangers are so great, that very few girls or women
take to the life voluntarily. They fall into it. So that there has always
been a calling, a trade, quasi-illegal, the White Slave Trade, to provoke
and tempt and cheat young inexperienced women into it, and to find
out, help and exploit those who have offended the established code of
good behaviour and so are ripe for enlistment. And naturally the White
Slave Trader is active wherever underpaid and insecure feminine labour
is to be found.

In our interminable encylopædia of work and wealth there would be space to discuss in detail the treatment of this persistent social element throughout the ages and in various parts of the world at the present time. It would be an intricate story of confused aims, general muddle-headedness, intolerance, jealousy and cruelty. Almost all its uglier and viler aspects would be directly traceable to the tradition of feminine subjection, and the necessary dependence of women upon some powerful protector. It is possible that in the future, as the equality of men and women ceases to be a mere sentiment and establishes itself in usage and law, there may be a relaxation of interference with the private sexual life of women, and the harsher and socially more injurious aspects of intermittent sexual associations will disappear.

Prostitution in the past has been chiefly feminine. That is not due apparently to any inherent sexual difference. It is a difference in rôle which puts men more in need of casual women. In the past women have stayed at home more than men and have been more firmly kept at home. It is the man, especially the man as traveller, sailor, merchant, soldier or student, who has been driven by the stresses of loneliness and boredom that lie at the base of this business, and who has had the freedom to solace himself. His womankind were driven to obscurer consolation or none at all. But now that types of free and prosperous women are developing, who can travel and get away from the observation and moral support of their own community, the parallel need evokes the parallel supply. The dissipated middle-aged woman is becoming almost as common as the dissipated middle-aged man. In the pleasure resorts of Europe and North Africa one meets now the wealthy lonely American wife or widow, looking for the consolations of masculine intimacy and picking up the "gigolo," the dancing partner, as a protégé, a companion and often a venal lover. She is almost as abundant as the Americans who visit Europe to get drunk. But the drifting, prosperous women are by no means all Americans. The gigolo is entirely the equivalent of the prostitute adventuress at the same social level, but because of the difference in his sexual tradition, no one has yet set about pursuing him with a *police des mœurs,* segregating him in brothels, banishing him from ordinary life and legislating against him. He does not seem in need of protection from Geneva, and the White Slave Trader finds him an unsuitable commodity.

But if he can take care of himself, surely the ordinary adult woman, if she were given proper treatment as a citizen like any other citizen, could do likewise. The difference in the world's treatment of male and female prostitutes is a very interesting and significant consequence of the age-long traditional disadvantage of women. And of a changing attitude towards the personal sexual life. In that saner, better instructed and franker world to which we seem to be moving, when women will be able to fend for themselves, and will be as free to come and go and do this and that as men are, the peculiar needs, tensions, shames and distresses that have maintained the prostitutes' quarter, the red-lamp district, the Yoshiwara, throughout the ages, may be at last alleviated, and prostitution as a special and necessary aspect of social life, that enduring scar upon the mutual kindliness of the sexes, may be superseded and disappear altogether.

§ 6. *The Power of Women through Reassurance and Instigation. Women's Rôle in Determining Expenditures*

Let us turn now to another aspect of the contemporary relations of men to women which is also of very great economic importance. We have dealt hitherto with the disadvantages of women in relation to men. We have now to consider their very real power over men.

It is not exact to say men and women have a need for each other. They have all sorts of needs for each other. It has already been suggested that men resort even to prostitutes for much more than mere sexual gratification. They have a strong need for a general association with women. Their imaginations require that, perhaps more than the feminine imagination calls for the companionship of men. In many cases that desire may change over to repulsion and misogyny, but hardly any men are indifferent to women. Normally they want to be approved of and liked by women; they want their acts and successes to be sanctioned by women; women are the custodians of their self-respect. Women will observe men and attend to the demands of their personas, keep them in heart, keep them in countenance, in a way no man will do.

We write "normally." We are dealing here with the average commonplace human being, who makes up the body and substance of the economic process. There are exceptional instances, there are perhaps exceptional races, where the man will watch and sustain the woman's idea of herself and so determine her actions in a manner entirely feminine. And many women nowadays woo and flatter other women. But the general situation is that the woman throws the qualities of bravery, brilliance, cleverness, generosity, dullness, stupidity, elegance or inelegance, meanness, baseness or foulness over the various acts of the man. She owns the moral box of paints. The determination of the values of an extraordinary number of things rests with women. Even when they are slaves they are appraising slaves.

This appraising function of women, their power over masculine self-esteem, combines with their real practical ability to control his social and physical comfort to give them an ecomonic importance out of all proportion to their legal ownership of purchasing power. The greater part of the wealth of the world is still in masculine hands, but a very considerable proportion of that spending power is controlled by or actually delegated to women. What, outside actual business needs, purchase of stock, material, premises, general investments and so forth, do men buy? They buy, one may say, railroads, war material, shipping, aëroplanes, public buildings. They buy their own clothes and their sporting outfits. But even when it comes to the railway and steamship, was it the male or the female demand that evoked the train or cabin de luxe? That we will leave an open question. But so soon as we come to actual living conditions, the woman's influence appears. Men may buy the sports car, but the comfort of the ordinary car is the woman's affair. In domestic architecture it is mainly her taste and needs, her consideration for herself and her consideration for her domestic servants, that have to be respected, and still more is this the case when it is a question of furniture. Household equipment and material, all food and her own steadily increasing wardrobe, are almost entirely in her hands. According to some rather sketchy statistics from America, 80 per cent of the shoppers in a large city are women.

This means that women, and especially the women of the more freely spending classes, exercise a great and perhaps a predominant directive influence on productive industry. They call the tune for most perishable goods. Textiles, furniture, building material, catering, are all manufactured and marketed with a view mainly to their satisfaction. They rule the tea shop, they now invade and change the spirit of the restaurant, and in America, where custom closed the drinking saloon to them, they voted and shut it down. The colours and fabrics, the tones and tastes of daily life and who men may meet outside their business and their clubs, and what shall be permitted in social life, are in our Western communities dependent upon their decisions.

So far women have exercised their enormous influence over the quality of daily life, with very little sense of any collective responsibility. It has been done individually with no perception of an aggregate effect. They have set about making homes and making up personalities, and have not thought that they were thereby making a world. Even with regard to their children, they have directed attention almost entirely to their present happiness and personal well-being, and disregarded as entirely the way in which social life as a whole would be affected by their upbringing. I think, if educationalists were consulted, they would say that in spite of the immense debt of educational progress to particular women, the general influence of the ordinary mother is often tiresome and rarely directive. Her ideas are limited to immediate things; she notices health, feeding and good manners. The rest she leaves uncritically to the school.

She leaves it uncritically to the school because she has never been taught to ask what the school is for.

This is directly due to the fact that a great majority of women of the spending class are relatively uneducated. They have not learnt to ask what anything is for. So far, the ordinary girl of the more prosperous classes has not been educated as well as her brother, she has not had the stimulus of a professional career, and her instruction has been sooner discontinued. The men and women of the labour classes of the Western world are now fairly on a level in the matter of education, and have for the most part what we have termed in this work a peasant persona or an urbanized or industrialized peasant persona. But when we consider the class which prolongs its education beyond the elementary school stage, we get a much greater number of males who are educated to the level of what we have styled variously the "service" or "clerical" or public-spirited persona. There are more men infected with ideas of service, of professional and class honour than there are women. The woman's persona in the middle and upper classes still falls in most cases into the more primitive classes of peasant or predatory or a mixture of both. The woman of a good social position is peasant-predatory much more often than the man, and she sets the pattern for the main mass of women. Probably we are not dealing with innate sexual differences here, but only with a wide divergence of tradition and a long lag in woman's education. The experiences of the Catholic Church would seem to show that women can be educated to a service ideology as completely as men.

This lag in feminine education which leaves a dominating majority at the peasant-predatory level, is manifested most strikingly at the milliner's, the costumier's, the jeweller's, and the beauty specialist's. The tradition of service, the process of "impersonalization" through education in the Western world, has made men deliberately inaggressive in their costume, made them at least ostensibly public-spirited, and

more and more amenable to official and business and creative preoccupations. This is not a natural thing: it is the result of formal and
informal educational influences. The illiterate ancestors of these same
preoccupied and creative Western men were more gaudy and splendid
in their costume than their contemporary women; they wore conspicuous jewels, dyed their hair and beards, and had little sense of
loyalty to anything but a person, prince, king or other leader. Their
women had neither the same opportunities for a show or the same
chances of getting the stuff. To-day a great proportion of Oriental men
retain that disposition of mind, and most Western women are still, as
a sex, at the same barbaric stage. Quiet clothes and unobstrusive
uniforms are to be endured only under protest, as acts of extreme self-
mortification. And as a consequence, if the Western world were all
men and the only buyers in the world, the pearl diver and the pearl
imitator might now cease from their labours altogether, the dealers in
jewelry and precious stones shut up shop, the trapper and hunter wear
their furs themselves or go out of business (leaving a happy remnant of
fur- and feather-bearing creatures to survive), and the whole great
industry of cosmetics and all the costumiers and milliners would tumble
into bankruptcy. The sale of splendid furniture for display and of
architecture for great gatherings would also cease almost altogether. A
few court officials and professional soldiers might still betray a craving
for furs, decorations and cosmetics, the secret indulgence of the gorgeous dressing-gown and the vivid pyjamas might intensify, but these
demands would be too infinitesimal to sustain all that multitude of
workers and arrest the ruin that the disappearance of Western femi-
ninity would entail.

And although there is no possibility of Western women disappearing, there is a very strong probability of their standard of education
rising to the masculine level and of a general westernization of their
world. This opens a prospect of women more gravely dressed and
more gravely occupied than at present. Women may presently want
to outshine other women as little as contemporary men do, and that
conception of jewelled, painted and triumphant gorgeousness which
rules our own social life now only so far as women are concerned, but
which still rules the lives of men and women alike in the courts of most
Oriental princes, will disappear altogether.

Yet to think of gorgeousness disappearing altogether from social
intercourse is almost as painful as anticipating the extinction of
humming-birds. Men, under the influence of science, puritanism and

practical convenience, have taken to costumes as undistinguished almost as modern service uniforms, but those dressing-gowns and pyjama suits in their outfitters' windows betray how near to the surface the craving for gorgeousness remains. The popularity with them of "fancy-dress" balls and entertainments and of "dressing-up" parties confirms this testimony. Academic costume, the nodding plumes of the deputy lieutenant and the insignia of various American "orders of chivalry"—voluntary and unsolicited chivalry—give it further support. Perhaps the typical modern professional woman already approaches a quasi-masculine compromise, dressing with the greatest severity during business hours, and upon occasion expanding magnificently into an evening costume. But these half private and occasional relaxations into splendour of serious men and women involve preparations and purchases of a much more incidental sort than does that sedulous, untiring hunt for elegance of the essentially barbaric women of to-day.

It has been asserted that a man's conception of his importance to himself and others seems to be more in his *doing* something than in his *being* anything; while on the contrary the form in which women seem to see themselves lies rather in being something than in getting anything done. There is a certain truth in this if we may judge by the famous figures of our world. The famous men of our time have done this or that; the famous women are "personalities." They are ends in themselves; they exhibit, and it carries nothing forward. If anything is done by them it is a display stunt. They do something a man has done before—charmingly, I admit. These are persons released to some vigour of expression. In ordinary life both man and woman must live under the restraints of common usage, but there is sound reason for assuming that famous people are, in all things except their especial distinction, just ordinary folk let loose. They are fair samples of what most men and women would be and do if they had the same opportunity.

But this difference of doing and being between men and women as it is displayed to-day may not be a real difference between men and women at all; it is much more probably another aspect of the difference between the barbaric and the educated disposition. If that is right, then the reactions between men and women must be undergoing a change now. If woman is to become less of a gaudy incentive to man and more of a companion and collaborator, then her particular rôle of scrutiny, appraisal, encouragement and reassurance is likely to be played far more subtly and penetratingly than ever before. As she becomes less of a prize in a competition, she will become more of a judge of effort. She will have a different influence upon spending and the spirit of spending, and that means she will exert an increasing influence upon getting and methods of getting.

In our study of the working of contemporary financial arrangements we have shown by a concrete instance or so the immense mischief caused by the financial adventurer. Most of our readers know well enough, if only by repute, the sort of individual who flounders through the world of finance to bankruptcy or the jail, leaving ruin in his track. What is the vision that justifies his risks and toil? Essentially it is success in a world of vulgar display, a world ruled by peasant-predatory standards in which the approval of women and power over women play a large part. For them he becomes a divinity distributing the coveted means by which gorgeousness becomes possible. And that woman-made apotheosis enables him to dismiss all compunction about the method by which he has filched, sneaked or bullied his way to wealth. If he has arrived at divinity, he can afford to forget that the means of arrival were in no sense divine. An extensive infiltration of womankind by educated types would make much of the successful adventurer's gorgeousness seem tawdry and its methods of attainment unclean. Such women would bring a new set of social values to bear upon their estimate of personal quality. They would regard the successful peasant-robber not as a hero who had stormed the golden gates of opportunity, but as a greedy and extraordinarily tiresome and destructive parasite upon economic life. They would reveal his affinities to the gangster, pure and simple. All the money in the world in that colder light would not suffice to make him anything better than Clever Alec, the spoiler of things. They would tilt the balance of his self-esteem against him.

§ 7. Is a Special Type of Adult Education for Women Needed?

It may be that the pattern of man's education has been followed too closely in the planning of the feminine equivalent. Because men can be most conveniently trained and educated continuously and progressively from five to twenty-five or so onward, it does not follow that women can be educated in the same continuous fashion. Their phases of maximum educability may occur at different periods of their life history.

Since this idea arises naturally out of a comparison of the masculine with the feminine quality and life cycle, we may perhaps anticipate our Chapter on Education and discuss the implication of this particular suggestion here. The suggestion is that it may prove a better arrangement to have a resumption of definite study by women and the taking on of new tasks and new responsibilities by them round about the ages between thirty-five and fifty. A girl should, of course, be educated from the beginning to look beyond the romantic phase of life, to regard that phase as partial and terminable, to consider the concluding years of life not as a process of growing old—growing out of things, but as a going on to a new system of activities. The loss of youth should not be the tragic thing it is for women; it should at most be no more tragic for them than it is for men. But it is a less gradual change in one case than in the other, and their transition to the really adult phase needs to be more definitely recognized and made than is done at the present time.

Even where women are not constrained by custom to the premature acceptance of a sexual rôle, the emergence of sex seems to affect their lives in the opening phase of adult life much more fundamentally than it affects the lives of men. It is hardly too much to say that in the alert and curious-minded girl, possibly more eager for knowledge than a boy of her age, a new personality is born at adolescence. The change is greater and more revolutionary than it is with the ripening male. Its onset is relatively catastrophic. The new personality that emerges may be domestic, maternal, erotic, or religious, or a mixture of any of these —the choice will be determined partly by type and partly by circumstances—but it will be typically an acutely self-conscious personality and given to dramatizing its performances. In the course of two or three years this new-born personality seizes upon its rôle. In the average woman we may go so far as to say that the new system of interests and emotions for a time takes charge of her life altogether, thrusting the wider interests of a human being aside, or rather, making of them a mere background to this intensified individual personal life.

It may be biologically desirable that women should for a phase lose touch with broader interests and take themselves thus seriously and intensely as persons, both as lovers and the recipients of love, as wives and then as mothers; it may be altogether good that their minds should undergo this narrowing down to and concentration upon the personal life. In all these intimate rôles more is required of them to-day than has ever been asked before, and more still will be required as the level of civilization advances. The mothers of young children, at any rate in the more forward races, are generally aware of the new responsibilities placed upon them by modern advances in infant management, general hygiene, child psychology and educational practice. They are genuinely anxious to improve themselves. All over England and America there are circles of women, from the poorest wives of agricultural and casual labourers upward, who are studying these subjects and finding them enthralling. In fact, this seems to be the most important result so far achieved by the spread of education among women. Whatever else may be said in this chapter on their technical and professional performances compared with those of men, there can be no doubt that their mental emancipation has resulted in happier and healthier nurseries. The little children of 1931, class for class, are better grown, better looking, more scientifically fed and clothed, than children have ever been before, and their minds develop more freely. Let any reader whose memory goes back to the parks of one of our great cities thirty years ago, compare the uncouth and ragged hordes which poured into them when the schools of the poor closed for their holidays, with the friendly and intelligent little creatures who appear to-day. The change is startling; it is due, of course, to many factors, but it could not have taken place without the devoted efforts of the mothers of these children.

What we are now considering, however, is not the children but the mothers. The management of a nursery has never been such a highly skilled job as it is to-day, but it does not go on being a job for nearly as long. In almost all families the girls as well as the boys now go to school—the family itself seldom exceeds four—and by about thirty or thirty-five the modern mother is more or less out of work. The personal life has called her, and the urgent demands of her personal life have been satisfied. And now what is she going to do with the rest of her life, the thirty or forty years which remain?

The answer to this question is naturally dependent upon economic circumstances. If times are hard she will be obliged to dismiss the maid and do her own work, and even though this may leave her with time on her hands, there will be no money for books or fares or subscriptions; she will not be able to get about as one must get about if one is to fill any function outside the home. But if her circumstances are prosperous, then there are two possible roads before her. The majority of middle-aged wives can be carried by the community as parasites or semi-parasites, for the most part either sunk into nonentities or "developing their personalities" by spending as much money as they dare and snatching at their diminishing chances of sensation, or, on the other hand, some rôle, some sort of useful part can be found for them.

At present there is no such rôle for most of these women in the forties and fifties. Their old jobs, if they had jobs before marriage, do not want them back, and there are not nearly enough fresh openings.

Individuals of an original turn strike out for themselves and take to charity, religion or politics, but no one who meets large numbers of middle-aged women can doubt that such occupations fail to absorb more than a few of this surplus. Some months ago a leisured woman wrote to the "Home Page" of a London evening paper and asked its readers: "Is there, after forty, any alternative to bridge?" They replied in large numbers, but the only alternatives they could offer were that she should feel ashamed of herself, or count her blessings, or find some blind neighbour to whom she could read aloud.

The instance sounds trivial, but the problem is profoundly important in the developing social life of the world. These millions of under-occupied citizens have votes, control expenditure and exercise great influence on the general body of opinion. If they are to be left to themselves because they are uninteresting, left to a narrow and frivolous personal life, the world is creating for itself a force of ignorance, prejudice and self-satisfaction, an atmosphere of mental stuffiness and sluttishness, which will impede all efforts to clear and widen thought and to build the future upon a controlled and courageous use of knowledge.

Here, it seems, a new development of our educational system is demanded. Here is a remediable waste. Here are great numbers of citizens, emerging from a score or less of vivid years of intense personal pre-occupation, anxious to find new systems of interests, desirous as a rule both to be of use and to improve themselves, but failing for the most part to satisfy these wishes. A considerable proportion of these released women, released to complete triviality and ineffectiveness, are extremely unhappy. The widespread nature of their need is indicated by the existence of Women's Institutes of Canada and Great Britain and the Women's Clubs of the United States. These give some social relief. But there is need for something more systematic and scientific. It should be possible for a middle-aged woman, without feeling that she is not wanted, or making herself ridiculous, or getting in the way of young people, to reëducate herself. She may wish to take up again interests which she has neglected since her marriage. She may wish to extend her range—probably in the direction of some science dealing with human life—politics, economics, education, psychology, hygiene or history—or she may simply want to have some sort of interest taken in her by somebody, to find other people who feel as she does, to be shown how to use her leisure. Even at that, she constitutes an opportunity, she is unused raw material for social organization. She is a citizen, and there is work to be got out of her. She needs, as the automobile people say, "reconditioning" so that she can return to the open road of life afresh.

In the next section we will discuss the possibilities of distinctive work that present themselves to women in the continually more intricate weaving of the modern community, and in our Chapter on Education the nature of the moral and intellectual effort towards a more scientific organization of human society will be examined. In Chapter VIII we have defined what we call the educated persona. As our survey of the mental life of our world develops, the reasons will become more and more manifest why women should regard the highly sexualized and personal years that follow their adolescence as only a phase in their development, and find, in the later acquisition of the educated persona and disinterested work, an escape from this living death so many of them lead now as mere waste products of the social body.

§ 8. Possibilities of Distinctive Work for Women in the Modern Community

In the excited days of feminine emancipation at the close of the last century there was much talk of the changes and marvels that would happen when this ceased to be a "man-made" world. Women were to come into their own, and all things would be the better for it. As a matter of fact, the enfranchisement of women, the opening of every possible profession to them, such legislation as the British Sex Disqualification (Removal) Act of 1919 meant that women were not coming to anything of their own, they were merely giving up their own— or, if you will, escaping from it. And now sufficient time has elapsed for everyone to see quite plainly that women had been not so much emancipated to a new and wonderful distinctiveness as—*despecialized*.

Certain distinctive types of work for woman remain. Everything that cannot be socialized of motherhood; certain forms of work such as nursing, where there is authority without initiative, remain especially hers. She has her distinctive beauty and that power of exploiting the elements of personality which reaches its climax in the great actress. These things are forever hers. For the rest, she is free now to do what she can and find her level. She writes novels and plays, and when she restricts herself to the subtleties of social behaviour and domestic relationship she does better than any man. She pilots aëroplanes and hunts big game with due assistance. She does scientific work; she practises medicine, pleads in the law courts, owns and runs businesses, farms, and the like; there are very few things she does not attempt. A woman captain of a Soviet ship recently came into the port of London. The level of feminine achievement is often high, higher than that of second-rate men, but in none of the open fields, except domestic fiction, can it be claimed that any women have yet displayed qualities and initiatives to put them on a level with the best men in any such department of activity. Outstanding women may presently emerge, but they have not yet emerged. In literature, in art, in the scientific laboratory, they have had a fair field and considerable favour. They suffer under no handicap. But so far none has displayed structural power or breadth, depth and steadfastness of conception, to compare with the best work of men. They have produced no illuminating scientific generalizations. The most successful feminine criticism so far has consisted of temperamental responses and brilliant flashes of personal comment.

It seems fairly certain that women are not going to outstrip men or even to equal them, in the fields in which men are certainly successful. Is there any chance that they may make a special contribution in those directions in which men have so far fallen short of their own feats of mechanical invention and creation—the social fields, politics, administration, education, where interest is concentrated on human life and personality rather than on machinery or abstract thought? *Prima facie,* these are the matters in which one would expect women to display distinctive aptitude. They may have an instinct for management, and their curiosity seems to be naturally inclined towards the practical problems of life rather than mechanisms. Where they exercise political power—as opposed to personal influence over politicians—legislatures have found themselves obliged to take a greater interest in social questions. On governing bodies—in spite of the fact that women are hardly yet placed in such positions for their own sake, but only too often because they are the wives or daughters of some influential man—their work is admittedly of weight. Even if their share in the world movement for peace (see Devere Allen's excellent *Fight for Peace,* 1931) has proved a feeble one, there can be little doubt that Prohibition (with its still unfolding consequences) followed in the order of cause and effect upon their enfranchisement. In politics, as in factory life, they seem disposed to make things cleaner and to throw their weight in favour of open and decent conduct.

Nevertheless, it is only in one country that they seem to be rising to the most responsible type of position, and that is a country where conditions are unusual—Russia. Nearly all facts as to Russia are dis-

THE HANDS OF THE MODERN WATCHMAKER

THEY are the hands of a woman. In the past they would have been the hands of a man.

A MODERN SILK MILL

THE operator is engaged in one step in the manufacture of stockings. In the background are the weaving frames.

puted, but there does seem to be a consensus of opinion that under the stimuli provided there—if the reader pleases he may regard them as monstrous and abnormal stimuli—women are losing some of the characteristics which lessen their usefulness in other countries. They are said, there, to display an intellectual curiosity, a mental energy, as great as that of men. Nobody shrinks from appointing a woman to any position for fear that as a woman she will be timid, personal, unscientific, limited in her outlook. Between the young women and the young men there is said to be no difference in these respects. Women are as free as men to choose what they will do, and they are, in fact, entering everywhere into the administration of the country. In the villages the peasant women sit on the local soviets and, as we have said, serve on the coöperative farms. In the towns they are largely employed as inspectors, welfare supervisors, and assessors and collectors of taxes. There are numbers of them in the army—a few are actually there as soldiers, but the majority either teach the men or are responsible for their health and their living conditions. And they are reported to do this sort of work not only as well as, but on the whole better than, men, showing themselves in this particular range of activities more conscientious and sympathetic and less liable to corruption than male officials. And this in a country where the pre-war percentage of illiteracy among women was 65 per cent.

It is interesting to note that even here, where sex is actually no longer a bar to any occupation whatever, more women than men are studying administration and pedagogy, more men than women, technical subjects, such as engineering.

Yet it has to be noted, in spite of all this, that not one single outstanding figure in the direction of Russian affairs since the Revolution has been a woman. No women leaders have resisted the degenerative processes that have reduced the government of Russia from a group control to the harsh autocracy of Stalin. The opposition of Lenin's widow to Stalin was easily swept aside. No other women rallied to her. For all the releases and exposedness of women in Russia, the Soviet world remains a man-made, man-ruled world.

The change which is said to have taken place in the mentality of women in Russia may be exaggerated. Even if that is so, or even if, though real, it is a sort of adaptive coloration, it will still be interesting to consider the conditions which have produced it.

What are the operative factors?

In the first place, and as a key to the entire explanation, the women

of Soviet Russia have to do without comfort. And it is in their homes
that discomfort reaches its highest point. The overcrowding is appalling;
all attempts at private cosiness are doomed to failure. Everything hopeful, stimulating or interesting is part of corporate life, attaching to the
schools, the factories, the workmen's clubs, the communal farms. If
you do not come out and mix and share, you have nothing to do but
rot. Secondly, it is a time of intense intellectual excitement. Not only
is the air full of new ideas, but at any moment some or any of them
may be acted upon. In England we have come to rely upon a comfortable time-lag of fifty years or a century intervening between the perception that something ought to be done and a serious attempt to do
it. Even in America they have time to think things over if they want
to. Russia is obliged to think and act almost from day to day—it is
important for a woman to know something of what is being thought,
because at any moment it may be upon her, twisting the whole fabric
of her life. Lastly, in Russia women are legally equal, and they are really
free. They have as many opportunities as men, and as much money;
they are mistresses of their own bodies, and very great efforts are being
made by means of crèches, nursery-schools and so forth, to enable
them to shorten the periods during which economic dependence
through maternity is inevitable. Above all, they cannot sell their sex—
in Russia it simply is not possible to obtain a life of ease by physical
attraction plus a little lying and a great deal of flattery. Or even by
steadfast affection, personal loyalty and devotion to home duties. It is
not possible, indeed, to obtain a life of ease in any way whatever. What
is obtainable is a share in some of the most exciting work the world
can offer. There is a whole nation to be taught—9,000,000 women are
now taking the special classes for "the liquidation of illiteracy"—healed,
organized, inoculated with the new doctrines. Bodily life in Russia may
be sordid by Western standards, but the life of the mind seems to be
extraordinarily dramatic and stimulating. Moreover, all this woman's
work is manifestly wanted. That alone, for many women, must alter the
colour of life.

It would be wrong to draw any conclusion from the Russian experiment except that women are adaptable—that in certain circumstances
they can shake off that mental sloth and that intense concentration upon
their personal lives which obtain in most other countries. It may be
that in their hearts they are longing to slip back, that if, at length, the
Communist State achieves material prosperity, its women will return
with relief to reading fiction and following the fashions. Probably not.

For all over the world even though women may not be scaling the higher peaks of achievement, the steady and continuing release of their spirits and the steady and continuing rise in the general quality of their work are indisputable.

It may be that they have latent in them a coöperative steadiness denied to the normally less stable, less calculable, less tractable male. The rôle women have played in assistançe, reassurance and instigation has already been discussed in § 6. We return to the suggestions of that discussion here. The future unfolds a prospect of increasing teamwork in which women may have to play a steadying, harmonizing and sustaining rôle. In the past there have been countries and cultures where the support of women has defended religious observances and organizations against disintegration. Women have played the part of a social mortar. They seem able to accept more readily and with a greater simplicity, and they conserve more faithfully. In the more subtly moralized, highly educated and scientifically ruled world-society of the future, that world-society which is the sole alternative to human disaster, such a matrix function will be even more vitally necessary. That, rather than the star parts in the future, may be the general destiny of women. They will continue to mother, nurse, assist, protect, comfort, reward and hold mankind together.

Hitherto the rôle of woman has been decorative or ancillary. And to-day it seems to be still decorative or ancillary. Less frankly decorative, perhaps, and more honourably and willingly ancillary. Her recent gains in freedom have widened her choice of what she shall adorn or serve, but they have released no new initiatives in human affairs. This may not be pleasing to the enthusiastic feminist of the late *fin de siècle* school, but the facts are so. In a world in which the motive of service seems destined to become the dominant social motive, there is nothing in what we have brought forward here that any woman need deplore.

CHAPTER THE TWELFTH

THE GOVERNMENTS OF MANKIND AND THEIR ECONOMIC AND MILITARY WARFARE

§ 1. *Political Organizations*

HITHERTO, as far as possible, our survey of the human community has ignored political machinery. But we have now reached a point where we must take up the activities of governments and show how this world-wide plexus of work and acquisition and spending that we have spread before our readers is directed and controlled.

We shall still avoid politics so far as advocating measures, taking sides or discussing parties or policies go, but we must ask the reader to keep it clear in his mind that a description of political machinery is no more "politics" than a description of the stage is "drama" or a description of the human nervous system and its working, ethical exhortation. We are telling how things are. If at points they appear ridiculous, the fault is not in the description but in the facts.

And here we come to the broadest reality of the human situation to-day, which is this: that while the material forces man has evoked make, with an air of inevitability, for the unification of mankind into one world system of exchange and mutual service, the direction and control of his affairs is subdivided into a patchwork of over seventy* sovereign states, each theoretically independent of the others, free to go its own way and shape or misshape its destinies as though there existed no foreigners in the world. We have been brought already to recognize the profound evil of this divided control, in the matter of money and credit. Later in this chapter we shall trace the way in which the net of frontiers strangles economic life and keeps the world in constant imminent danger of a war catastrophe. But first, before we go on to this geographical fragmentation of human politics, let us examine some of these seventy-odd governments now in operation and, disregarding the

---

*Counting the United States as one but the British Empire and its Dominions, so far as they are separately represented at Geneva, apart.

question of frontiers and foreigners for a section or so altogether, consider the efficiency of these centres of management side by side, as it were, with the contemporary aëroplane, dynamo, biological laboratory or steel foundry.

By political organization we mean all the authorized activities that protect, direct, permit or prevent, in the name of the community. The State, in its various ramifications, is the political organ. Political life is the control, or the attempt to control, direct or influence State activities; it comprehends the minister in his bureau, the autocrat, the politician in opposition, the agitator at the street corner, and the conspirator in or out of jail. It is ostensibly if not actually the centralizing process of the community.

§ 2. *A Short Study of the British Government at Work**

Let us approach our first study of an existing government, that of Great Britain, by asking what it has to do, and what sort of arrangements would be made to house and organize it, if we entrusted the task to some intelligent specialist in the layout of industrial plants or the like. For the purposes of our present enquiry we may accept the existing ingredients: the monarch, an "upper" assembly of irremovable legislators, and a "lower" but more powerful body of elected representatives. (No one has ever yet attempted to run a business with an upper and a lower board of directors.) We will also assume the party system and cabinet government as they exist. We shall have a word or two to say about the number of these representatives and the method of their election, but beyond that we will merely consider the most expeditious and fruitful way of organizing the energies of all these factors.

The monarch we may, according to the best English precedents, leave out of our speculations. He is a constitutional monarch whose responsibility has been taken over entirely by his ministers. He is a ceremonial figure, the "golden link" of empire. He may not dispute about himself, and so, by an obvious courtesy, he is above criticism. He is tradition made inert like the Mace upon the table of the House of Commons. He —or rather "the crown"—is a time-honoured symbol of authority, and there is no reason whatever why a crown should not remain forever the emblem of authority in the commonweal. That, at any rate, is the

*For a more respectful account see Sir Erskine May's *Law, Privileges, Proceedings and Usage of Parliament.*

accepted theory and for many reasons we will refrain from any reflec-
tions upon that accepted theory. We will discuss the processes of
British government without the faintest flavour of lèse-majesté.

Now, first this government must be housed. Our expert would insist,
of course, upon a building of the very newest type. No great business
combine would dream to-day of carrying on its operations in a building
a hundred years old. It would have the soundest, best equipped structure conceivable, with every possible device and convenience to ensure
the well-being and facilitate the operations of its directors. Each of
these select and elected persons would have at least one private room,
well lit and fitted with telephone, special information and news tickers,
properly encased in soundproof covers, works of reference and so forth.
There would be stenographers and dactylographers swiftly available,
and there would be a big, efficiently organized library with a large and
competent staff present day and night to help and supply information.
Airy and pleasant dining rooms, newspaper rooms and conference
rooms go without saying, and the whole building would be linked by
lifts and passages planned elaborately to economize time and trouble.
The administrations of the various ministries of the State would no
doubt be housed in separate buildings of their own, but each would be
represented in the parliament house by a group of offices constituting
the bureau of the responsible minister. The prime minister would be
the chairman of the cabinet, the board of final decisions which would
meet in a convenient chamber near his bureau, whenever final decisions
were necessary.

The primary function of the elected members of the lower house is
to watch and question the proceedings of the ministries and the cabinet.
They mediate between the section of the community they represent
(and collectively for the community as a whole) and the administration of the ministries. They have also to function in legislation, that is
to say, in modifying the functions of the ministries. They would naturally be continually forming and reforming groups for those ends, for
the enforcement of protests and suggestions and the drafting of legislative extensions and amendments.

At intervals the upper and lower houses would meet to discuss and
decide upon these matters, and for this our government building would
have to have debating chambers. Every session in the debating chambers would be convoked for a specific end, *coram populo,* to repudiate
a minister or a line of action or to pass a law; it might adjourn, but it
would not disperse until it had got its business done. And the need

for such debates would determine the number of legislators in either house. There is a minimum below which the various interests of the realm would not be represented; there is a maximum beyond which an assembly begins to take on the lax, vaguely emotional quality, the fluctuations of excitement, and the boredom of a public meeting. These maxima and minima have never been worked out properly, but probably the best size for a businesslike deliberate assembly is somewhere between two hundred and fifty and three hundred and fifty persons. It is no good whatever to encumber government with more members than are needful. The elected house would represent the constituent element of the community, and in a world where distance has been abolished it is obvious that territorial constituencies, except upon a provincial scale, are out of date. . . .

But there is no reason why we should go on with this simple business statement of what is needed for the proper management and direction of Great Britain limited. The reader approaching this subject through museum avenues of business appliances, industrial layout, and rationalization expedients, will be in a position to imagine all the necessary efficiency. Let us, since our concern is not with what men might do but what they do now, turn rather to the actual working mechanism of British government in a period of dire stress and danger for all the world.

Our first intimation of incongruity comes when we contemplate the buildings, the Houses of Parliament, in which this great business is carried on. They do not look in the least businesslike. Nor do they make up in dignity or splendour of feeling what they lack in mechanical efficiency. They look as if a late Gothic cathedral had had an illegitimate child by a Flemish town hall. Even as an exhibition of the Victorian Gothic temperament, the building is less entertaining than (say) the London Law Courts or the Tower Bridge over the Thames.

A closer acquaintance suggests that the architects first designed the exterior and then rather inattentively fitted in an interior. There are the legislative chambers themselves with their lobbies, presidential throne, bilateral arrangement of seats for the "Ins" and the "Outs" in the struggle for office, galleries for admirers, and so forth, and beyond these there are a network of passages and staircases into which open various offices and chapel-like committee rooms devoid of any modern business convenience. The legislative chamber, in the case of the elected representatives, has seats for rather less than half the total number of members. But, of course, since forty-odd hours of oratory per week is

more than any but the hardiest can bear to listen to, most of its seats
are ordinarily empty. Scattered about the building are a few crypt-like
apartments, capable of accommodating perhaps five per cent of the
legislators, in which they can work individually with their secretaries.
There are, literally, miles of corridors, but only one lift to serve the four
floors used by members. Only ministers and under-ministers have rooms
of their own. A large proportion of these are of the kind which would
be set apart for the use of servants in Victorian dwelling-houses—ill-lit
and ill-ventilated. And as the building dates from Victorian times and
lends itself but poorly to modernization, many of them are still fitted
with a sacristy containing an ewer and basin for ablution. The ordinary
members have only small lockers of the kind allotted to schoolboys in
Victorian seminaries for their private books or papers. Every member
has a hook all to himself in the cloakroom, and to this hook a loop of
pink tape (renewed every session) is tied, in which he can hang his
sword! Interviews with visitors from outside must be carried on either
in corridors or in one or two underground tea or smoking rooms. There
is no modern system of communication between the various parts of the
building. As in primitive Africa, human porterage is relied upon as the
means of conveying messages, and an hour may easily elapse between a
visitor's arrival and the unearthing of the member he wishes to see.
What this method lacks in speed, however, it makes up in dignity, the
messengers being large and slow-moving men, wearing evening dress
even in daylight, and ornamented with large gilt chains and badges
after the manner of provincial mayors. Kitchens are interspersed among
committee rooms, and for a considerable period every evening favoured
regions of the building are pervaded by the sounds and the odours of
good, old-fashioned English cooking. These, however, are not the only
odours which are distributed by the ventilation. In some mysterious
manner the drainage in the Thames contributes an intermittent miasma
to a perennial stuffiness. Yet surely, for such important business as is
done here, it would be better to drench the workers in super-oxygenated
air of the utmost purity. Everywhere, even in the case of kitchens,
lockers, smoking rooms and lavatories, an elaborate imitation Gothic
scheme of decoration prevails. In his utmost privacy the member of
parliament still crouches in a niche.

The building is of a type of limestone exceptionally sensitive to the
acids of the London atmosphere, and a touch of eventfulness is given
to its façades by the occasional fall of lumps of the decaying stuff. This
is most felt upon the celebrated Terrace, a long narrow passage between

the building and the river. Here teas are served to members and their friends and constituents, heedless of the occasional avalanches. Here social influence is brought to bear up the legislator, as the student may learn from the still sufficiently contemporary novels of Mrs. Humphry Ward.

The enquiring stranger will naturally wish to be shown the library and the organization for prompt information. He will find three or four rooms lined chiefly with files of State papers and with collections of books on British birds and field sports—dating from the times when the majority of elected members were country gentlemen. True, a selection of the customary reference books to be found in clubs and hotels, and a few recently published political biographies, along with a small shelf of current books from a circulating library, indicate a faint recognition of modern requirements. But no effort is made, even from such pathetically inadequate material as this library comprises, to assemble for the use of members from time to time such books or papers as bear on subjects under discussion in the legislative chamber. There are no research workers, preparing synopses or abstracts of information: no effort, indeed, at all to relate the library, as such, to the specific needs of those who might use it.*

For obscure tactical reasons in the Party Game, the House of Commons consists of 615 members, a crowd too great for free deliberation and too small for mass meeting treatment. When most of them are present, a number must stand and cluster. There are about 760 peers in the House of Lords, about 28 are minors at the time of writing, and most of the others stay away, so that there is not the same congestion. At the risk of seeming farcical to the uninitiated it may be worth while to give some particulars of the way in which the business of a great empire is conducted in this ill-equipped, ill-ventilated and totally unsuitable building.

Every legislative measure must go through several stages of debate in the elected assembly—second reading,† committee, financial resolution (when money has to be found), report, third reading—before being sent to the hereditary chamber for further consideration and discussion there. It is the nominal aim of the Ins to keep the debates on each of these stages as short as possible, in order that the promises they have made to the electors may be redeemed at an early date. The ordinary

---

*No "wireless" is permitted anywhere in the Houses of Parliament.

†First reading has, surprisingly, been abbreviated to a mere formality occupying only a few seconds.

members on their side of the House are accordingly expected to remain silent, leaving it to their leaders to make explanatory statements and reply to the criticisms of the Outs. These latter, on the other hand, since the basic article of their creed is that everything proposed by the Ins is bad, and since furthermore they will, in the ordinary course of events, be outvoted anyhow, aim at lengthening out and delaying the debates as much as possible in order to hinder the Ins from carrying through their legislative programme. The business of talking is on their side, accordingly, not confined to the leaders, but is enthusiastically carried on by as many of their supporters as can contrive to speak for half-an-hour or more without too often repeating what has already been said several times, and without making too apparent their lack of knowledge of—and often indeed, lack of interest in—the subject under discussion. This kind of debating sometimes goes on into the small hours of the morning, sometimes right through the night, the Outs hoping that sheer physical fatigue may force the Ins upon "the rack," to make concessions. The Ins may retaliate by moving and carrying the closure of a debate, but they do this at the peril of being represented (by the Outs) to every elector in the country as enemies of freedom of debate, betrayers of democracy, etc. And although every elector knows that the voting which ultimately decides every question is carried out on strict party lines, and knows, too, that most members do not listen to the debates, he has been trained to the belief that this freedom of debate is a highly important thing, in the vein of Magna Carta and the Bill of Rights.

Recently a small group of members (including Sir Oswald Mosley and Mr. Maxton) became convinced that the economic situation demanded certain urgent remedies, and they did their best to work out how long these urgent measures would take. After the most careful enquiry and computation, they came to the conclusion that the measures immediately needed would take at least ten years of parliamentary time to put through.

This normal routine of parliamentary procedure may not strike the outside observer as an altogether dignified way of giving effect to the national will. But that is because he does not realize with what solemnity and formality it is carried on. There are certain honoured quaintnesses even in the discussion. All speeches must be addressed to "Mr. Speaker," the chairman of the assembly, and other members may only be alluded to by an elaborately circumlocutory form of address. For the convention of addressing the Speaker there is something to be said. It keeps debate impersonal; it prevents wrangling duels and direct insults "as man to man." But the other circumlocutions are a great strain. Ministers and ex-ministers are "right honourable gentlemen"; ordinary members "honourable gentlemen"; members with military or naval posts "honourable and gallant gentlemen"; and members who are also lawyers "honourable and learned gentlemen." Their surnames must never be used, but only the name of their constituencies. Plain Mr. X thus becomes "the honourable and learned gentleman, the member for ——." A similar rule forbids any direct mention of the hereditary chamber, the House of Lords, which can only be referred to as "another place." Furthermore, the proceedings are in costume. On his entry into the chamber Mr. Speaker, who is always attired in eighteenth-century court dress, plus a wig and gown, is attended by another functionary, the Sergeant-at-Arms (wearing a sword to justify his title), who carries the Mace, symbol of the Speaker's authority. This is deposited upon the table of the House, and it is removed as ceremoniously, and placed on two hooks under the table, when the assembly sits "in committee" and Mr. Speaker's place is taken by the Chairman of Ways and Means. There is no rule forbidding general conversation while someone is addressing the assembly; but there are strict rules against a member speaking with his hat on, though he may wear it while sitting.* And although members may walk in and out of the chamber as often as they please, whether anyone is speaking or not, they must always bow to Mr. Speaker or his deputy on entering or leaving. No member may stand in the chamber unless he is speaking, except on a certain marked-off area of the floor which is deemed to be outside the House. If a member's toe protrude across the line of tape (called "the Bar") marking the boundary of this area, he is guilty of a grave breach of decorum, and all those members in the chamber who have witnessed it are expected to chant, "Bar! Bar! Bar!" until the intruding toe is withdrawn. So too, if in the excitement of speech-making he chances to step away from his seat and set his foot in the gangway.

The debates are occasionally interrupted by a message from "another place" demanding Mr. Speaker's presence in the hereditary chamber to

*He must also put it on—or borrow someone else's to put on—if he wishes to rise to a point of order after a vote has been called. Otherwise, hatless, Mr. Speaker would not "see" him. There is much innocent fun when a large-headed member is thus forced to use a small-headed member's hat, or vice versa. The presence of women members has now brought in an added touch of humour when, for example, an eager hatless man finds nothing but a bonnet available to restore him to technical visibility.

hear some message from the King, or to witness the Royal Assent being given (in archaic French—*"le Roy le veult"*) to certain measures. The hereditary chamber thus asserts its superiority by compelling the attendance of representatives of the Lower House within its own precincts, while the latter saves its dignity by ceremoniously closing its door in the face of the peers' messenger and obliging him to knock and then knock again and then knock, three times altogether, before he is admitted. He then enters and delivers his invitation, and the Speaker, after repeating in full the invitation which everyone has just heard, heads a procession of members to the "other place." He and they cluster just outside the doorway and remain dutifully standing while the King's message is read. The procession then returns to the elected chamber, and the Speaker reads out the message in full once more.

The method of taking a vote of the members is as deliberate as the rest of the procedure. It is processional. (Edison invented a method of voting and counting all the votes in a minute or so without a member leaving his place, half a century ago. In Texas a mechanical voter is actually in use, and the result is recorded in twenty seconds.) Every member must leave his seat in the chamber and walk in queue through the fair way of one or other of two lobbies, the "Ayes" or the "Noes," passing through a sort of wicket, where he gives his name to a clerk, and then through a door where he is counted by two tellers. And so round the course home. When all have been counted, the tellers advance to the table of the House and, after bowing twice, read out their figures. This arrangement occupies from ten minutes to a quarter of an hour, and can even be made to last longer by the adoption of dilatory methods if either side is intent on hindering the course of the debates. Sometimes during the committee stage of a measure, votes on several amendments are taken in quick succession, members spend from two to three hours in a single evening filing through the lobbies.

This registering of his vote is, of course, the most important part of an ordinary member's duties. His efficiency, or otherwise, as a legislator is rated by his constituents according to the number of divisions in which he votes. Since he is seldom in the chamber when a vote is called, Whips appointed by his party are stationed at the door to tell him which lobby to enter and, if he is of the curious, troublesome type, what the voting is about. Apart from voting, his chief opportunity for individual participation in the business of legislation comes during question-time, when, during the first fifty minutes of each day's proceedings, he may put questions to Ministers on any matters of public importance. Questions in the main fall into three groups: those put down by the Outs with the aim of embarrassing the government by compelling them to make a definite statement on some issue about which the government prefers to be indefinite; those referring to matters of local constituency interest, put down by members to advertise to their constituents the fact of their presence in Parliament; and those which genuinely seek information on some point of policy or administration or aim at securing publicity for some genuine grievance.

But the student must not imagine that the private member may ask any questions he pleases. There are intricate rules and regulations about what he may or may not ask and about the form in which his question may be put. You would imagine that somewhere among the pillars and vaults and masonry a small bureau would have been established to which members would take their questions and have them put into acceptable form and passed, but that is not the Westminster way. The Member of Parliament must hand his questions, while debating is in progress around him, to the "Clerk at the Table" who sits immediately in front of the Speaker. He must then stand meekly by, like a schoolboy at the head master's desk, while the official ponders his question and discovers breaches of the rules in it. Having been instructed to alter it, but not daring to ask for any explanation lest he be called to order for brawling under the Speaker's very nose, he goes out and writes out another form of words. And so on, and so on—until the master is satisfied. A sufficiently lucid code of regulations as to the correct phrasing of questions could probably be drawn up in ten minutes and printed on a postcard. But apparently no one at Westminster has thought of this.

If he fails to obtain what he considers a satisfactory answer, our questioning member may announce his intention of raising the matter on the adjournment of the House, that is, after the business of the day is over, late at night, when both he and the Minister concerned are usually too tired to take more than a perfunctory interest in anything, and when, incidentally, it is too late to get any notice in the press of the matter. Or, if he feels acutely about the subject and desires some publicity for it, he may get himself suspended (i. e., expelled from the sittings of the chamber for a week or longer) by refusing to obey Mr. Speaker's order to him to sit down after his question has been dealt with. Then there is a "scene" in the House, which gets duly reported in the newspapers.

Often, when the question is inconvenient to the government, the member will get no open reply at all. He will be asked to wait while enquiries are made. Unless he is obstinately persistent he may hear no more about the subject. A special report from the department concerned may even be placed quietly in the library at some later date, but he will not necessarily be informed of this, and the information may lie safely hidden on a top shelf or in an obscure cupboard. This, of course, can happen very easily indeed to questions on foreign or colonial subjects, where some time must elapse before replies from the territory concerned can be obtained.

During certain parts of every session one day, sometimes two, in a week are set apart for the discussion of private members' motions or bills (which of them are thus discussed is decided by ballot). But as there is practically no likelihood of these debates influencing the course of legislation already decided upon by the government, they may be regarded as academic exercises, of use only to those members who desire practise in the art of speech-making.

We have noted the phases through which a bill must pass before it goes to "another place." That is only half its career. After the Commons it must go through similar stages in the House of Lords. But here business is expedited somewhat, and their lordships rarely sit longer than from tea-time to dinner-time.* (Voting is carried out in the same way as in the Commons, except that the lords, instead of being divided into "Ayes" and "Noes," declare themselves "Contents" or "Not Contents.") If a bill is passed by the lords it needs only the Royal Assent to become an Act of Parliament. In the event of the lords rejecting a bill, the commons may pass it again, this time with a minimum of formality and discussion; and if they repeat this procedure a year later, and again a year after that (which assumes that the Ins have not become Outs in the meantime), the bill becomes law without the consent of the lords.

The parliamentary session has a variable length, but is never less than a year (about eight months of actual sitting). It is opened by a King's Speech, written, of course, by ministers, which outlines in brief the programme of forthcoming legislation. This speech is read by the monarch himself to the assembled lords and commons, and the occasion is marked by a large amount of pageantry, with Gold-Sticks-in-Waiting and Gentlemen of the Household greatly in evidence.

At the end of the session all incomplete bills are dropped entirely. This is called the "Massacre of the Innocents" by "old parliamentary

*They have, of course, no budget or estimates to deal with, entire control of finance being vested in the Commons.

hands." Every scrap of work done upon these frustrated measures is absolutely wasted. Everything must begin again at the next session—the same stages, the same speeches, the same arguments, the same indignation—all over again.

For traditional reasons of a complex type, the government is regarded as a solid body of inseparables. If the members want to get rid of an incompetent minister of finance, they cannot do so without turning out the entire government and breaking off every other ministerial activity in progress. A prime minister, defeated or in a bad temper, may decide to advise the King to dissolve parliament, and then back go the affairs of the nation, in all their complexity and incompletenesses to the general population, under conditions we will consider a little more closely in our section on Assent.

Such are the machinery and working of the supreme government of what is still the greatest empire the world has ever seen. Our most effective comment is to turn our eyes for a mere instant back to Mr. Ford making motor cars, or to the mechanisms described at the end of Chapter IV.

The fact that the British Parliament is ceasing to be an efficient instrument for the government of a modern community has become so patent and painful to the more intelligent among politicians themselves that we find both Mr. Winston Churchill—who has sat in both Conservative and Liberal Cabinets—and Mrs. Sidney Webb—the wife of a Labour Cabinet Minister—putting forward schemes for its reform. Their plans have something in common: both start by pointing out that whereas the problems which confronted our ancestors were conceived in political terms, those that concern us to-day are mostly economic in character. And neither writer is able to regard our present House of Commons and House of Lords as suitable assemblies for the discovery or expression of economic truths. Mr. Churchill in his pamphlet "Parliamentary Government and the Economic Problem" states the position succinctly. What the peoples demand to-day, he says, is more prosperity. They ask to be delivered from "the new punishment—the Curse of Plenty"—a state in which they find themselves starving in the midst of world-wide "over-production." But the remedy he proposes for this is not particularly drastic. He wishes to set up an Economic Sub-Parliament, subordinate to Parliament, appointed by the party leaders in proportion to the number of their followers in the

House of Commons. These appointed members are to be possessed of "high technical qualifications"—that is, they are to consist of "40 members of the House of Commons experienced in economic subjects, and 80 business men, Trade Union representatives or economic authorities" among whom should be "not less than 20 members of the House of Lords." And the work he wishes them to do is to take over, with the consent of the House, bills which have passed their second reading, or any other bill or clause which they may be asked to consider, and debate them with fearless detachment from public opinion—and, one imagines, though he does not say so, equally fearless detachment from the opinion of the party leaders by whom they are appointed.

To this scheme one might put forward the objection that what is wanted is no mere discussion of bills after their principles have been settled, but a wider general knowledge of economics. The Macmillan Committee was a committee of experts of great brilliance and the highest standing. It was asked to advise on the financial policy of the country during the present crisis. In July, 1931, it reported that it is absolutely vital that a policy should be adopted which will tend to raise world-prices and increase consumption. In August, 1931, a National Government was formed in order to carry out a policy of checking consumption and forcing prices down still further. As we write efforts are being made to carry this out with the minimum of Parliamentary voting or discussion. In such a vortex what would happen to the straw of Mr. Churchill's economic parliamentary sub-committee?

But the main objection to his scheme, as our readers will have told themselves, is that economic problems are international. What is necessary is not that Trade Unionists and business men and members of the House of Lords shall have still another opportunity of stating their opinions, but that governments themselves shall consider their economic measures from a world point of view. The time to take expert advice is before the principles of bills are decided, the advice that is needed is that of real experts, and the danger to be overcome is that the present rules of the British democracy are too ignorant of finance and economics to be able to either understand or to criticize their pronouncements.

Mrs. Webb's scheme goes further towards meeting the first of these objections. She would have the range of questions which are generally called social removed from Parliament altogether and handed over to an elected National Assembly together with the government departments concerned with their administration. This would have great advantages.

It would relieve the pressure on Parliamentary time. It would mean that there was a far greater chance of bills being voted upon by people with some interest in their contents—the division into social questions on the one hand and foreign affairs, defense and imperial questions on the other does correspond to two different types of politician. It would revive cabinet government, which is made impossible at present by the sheer amount of work to be done. The weak link of the scheme is finance, which Mrs. Webb would leave in the main to the old Parliament after handing over certain sources of revenue to her National Assembly. Finance nowadays, as we are being sharply reminded, is more than the mere spending and raising of taxes. It is impossible to decide on wages or hours or unemployment insurance without reference to international money questions. And an assembly which had no responsibility for foreign affairs might tend to be even more insular than the existing Parliament. The parliaments of the future, if the world is not to relapse into chaos, must regard themselves as the local organs of the world state, and reforms which do not envisage this must fail at an essential point.*

§ 3. *The Permanent Official*

But does so clumsy, antiquated and slow an administrative machine really govern? The answer is that, except in a very broad and qualified sense, it does not. It has been partially superseded, just as the monarch has been almost entirely superseded, by other agencies. The King parades on public occasions as the head of the State. The members of the government parade as his responsible advisers. But what does not parade, and what is altogether less obvious to public observation, is the organization of departmental officials. A large and increasing share in government falls to this stratum of active workers, and it becomes necessary, therefore, that we should consider the rôle of administering and interpreting the law that falls to them.

Under all governments there has been this class, since civilized communities began. They were scribes, they were viziers, they were chamberlains and chancellors, they appear in endless variety, beside and behind the throne and spreading out over the administered country. A history of the Civil Service in Egypt throughout the dynasties has not yet been written. Probably Professor J. H. Breasted could tell us as

*For a fuller development of the matter in this section see the chapter on Political Institutions in Laski's *Grammar of Politics*.

much about it as anyone. There are studies still to be made of the Civil Service of the empires of Mesopotamia also, and we know far too little of what is to be known of the Civil Service of the Roman Empire. The thousands—generation after generation; I suppose it amounts altogether to millions—of men in these services, whose names are now for the most part forgotten, have held the machinery of civilization together and kept it going throughout the ages. Civilization could no more have existed without them than a human body without a nervous system. I would suggest that one of the chief contributing causes of the collapse of the great Mongol empire of the early thirteenth century and of the Arab empire of the eighth, so that they were blown out and burst like paper bags, was largely due to their inability to develop any effective civil service over the vast areas of their conquests in time to consolidate them. Some historians dwell upon the political incapacity of Mongol and Arab—perhaps unjustly. When the Mongol came upon an established machine of government in China, when the Arab found the same thing in Persia and Egypt, and the Turk in Byzantium, they founded enduring empires. Or rather, they took them over—and were taken over. A time may come when history, grown more penetrating, will have more to tell about clerks and less about conquerors.

In our analysis of the motivation of the human community in Chapter VIII, we gave some broad indications of the development and variation of the priestly persona. The departmental official, far more even than the teacher and the man of science, is in that tradition of honour and devotion. He has definitely put adventures in gain behind him. He is far more restricted in that respect than the official in any public utility or industrial enterprise run for profit. The latter type does for many reasons tend to assimilate to him as the scale of business enlarges, but the private official is generally more enterprising and bolder in accepting responsibility. The chief accusation against the public functionary throughout the ages has also been the chief grievance against priesthoods, conservatism; he is overdisposed, it is said, to follow precedents and refuse risks.

In the last two or three paragraphs suggestions have been thrown out for at least three enormous books. It is the privilege of a work like the present one to make such demands. Let us now ask for yet another great volume, with appendices and all complete, which shall be a full and careful study of the history, working and psychology of the British Civil Service for the last hundred years. It would be a most valuable and directive addition to the political science of the whole world. It would analyze problems at the very core of an organized world state.*

Great Britain, struggling with the unprecedented problems of an expanding industrialism at home and a spreading empire about the world, made its first break with patronage in 1856 and introduced a method of open competition for entrance to Haileybury College, leading on to the Indian Civil Service, which was further developed into a system of open competition for most home Civil Service appointments in 1870. There had been qualifying examinations for Haileybury since 1813, but not open competition. Open competition was really a primarily important innovation in administrative structure, and the outcome of a long and sustained discussion that had been going on for half a century. To Jeremy Bentham (1748–1832) we must ascribe the launching of this idea. His *Official Aptitude Maximised and Expense Minimised,* which was part of his great incomplete *Constitutional Code,* was a scheme for competitive examination for official appointments. The idea was supported vigorously by Sir Charles Trevelyan and Lord Macaulay. The speech of the latter upon the Indian Civil Service Charter Act in 1833 was a masterly statement of the case for the new method. The Indian Civil Service Charter Act in the days of Company rule in India was renewed every twenty years, and when it came up again in 1853 this great innovation was applied to India. A committee, Sir Charles Trevelyan's committee, sat from 1849 onward to bear fruit at last twenty-one years later. So the first modern civil service was born. The method of selection by open competition, hitherto unheard of in the Western world, has created a civil service, with a body of upper officials of a new and better type, singularly free from personal and party ties, exceptionally intelligent and intellectually enterprising. It lets in the "rank outsider" of ability and energy: that is its supreme merit.

No doubt the system of examination is open to very great improvement. The "subjects" to which marks were and are most heavily assigned in the competition are subjects remote from the realities with which the competitors will have to deal. It is possible for a Treasury clerk, for instance, to be blandly ignorant of economics, social and administrative science and psychology; he learns his business from the files of his department and is all too apt to absorb the shibboleths and habits of thought of the City financiers with whom his duties bring

---

*Dr. Finer, of the London School of Economics, has published various studies. An excellent, clear book, not too long, and full not only of fact but suggestion, is his *British Civil Service.*

him into contact. He has not the assurance and strength of scientific knowledge, and the City he should dominate, assimilates him. Good as the official by competitive examination is, an insistence on the social and political sciences as of dominant importance in his success would certainly make him better.

This new civil service presently revealed a spirit of enquiry into the objectives of government such as no other civil service had ever before displayed. It produced a novel ideology. Fabian Socialism is essentially a product of the British Civil Service. Both Sidney Webb (now Lord Passfield) and Sydney Olivier (now Lord Olivier) were among the chief creators of that school of nonrevolutionary administrative socialism, socialism by evolution. They were both civil servants, and it would be difficult to estimate how far the ideology of social reformers and public servants throughout the world at the present time has been affected by this remarkable initiative. Closely associated in its beginnings with the Fabian Society and with the activities of Webb and his brilliant wife, is the London School of Economics, still the most vigorous and efficient centre of modern social, political and economic thought in the world. These initiatives are, we say, in a large measure byproducts of the new British Civil Service; the expression of its bolder and more innovating spirits. They are cited here as evidence of what is possible and not of what is general as yet in the new type of civil servant. But each sweep of the competitive scythe brings in with the rest, a contingent of original minds. The majority of British permanent officials have proved less lucid and outspoken than these outstanding figures. They have done the tasks put before them without any overt excursions into general political suggestion, but their circumstances must dispose them to a very similar way of thinking.

Behind the antiquated and sometimes almost farcical forms and procedures of the British monarchy and parliament there now stands this stable organization of experienced and competent permanent officials, protected from the attacks of powerful and influential persons and legally excluded from party politics.

From top to bottom there are now almost 310,000 national civil servants in Great Britain; twenty times the number at the beginning of the nineteenth century. In addition there are 120,000 state industrial workers. Side by side with these there are the independently recruited local government officials (of the county councils, etc.) amounting to about the same total, to whom the principle of competitive examination has been as yet only partially applied. That 310,000, we must note, includes a multitude of postmen and suchlike subordinates with hardly any directive influence whatever. It is in the upper division chiefly that the vital and directive minds are to be found, a few hundreds (*circa* 1200) of them in all, but hundreds of extraordinary importance in the working of the governmental machine.* The politicians manœuvre against each other, fight their party battles in the country, repeat their catchwords, make their vast absurd promises and win their way to office. There they find themselves in the presence of complex administrative problems for which they have neither the necessary knowledge nor the aptitude. They find themselves nominally heads of departments but in reality intermediaries between departments they cannot handle and the enquiring private member. The newly appointed minister says unto this man go, and he goeth—but the minister never finds out how he manages to go; and to another come, and he cometh—with a dossier of documents sufficient to dismay the stoutest politician that ever shouted on a platform. The legislator cannot legislate without the help and instruction of his departmental staff. Between procedure on the one hand and the departmental official on the other the Member of Parliament and even the Minister is a sorely baffled man. He came to exercise power, and he finds himself not so much carrying on as being carried on.

It is impossible to overstress the significance of this modern type of civil service, which is neither elected from below nor appointed from above, but which emerges by a system of examination from the educational organization of the country. Elected, it would be, like the politician, merely a reflection and an exploitation of the self-pushing peasant type; appointed, it would be servile to the masterful predatory adventurer. It must be evident that in no section of the community is a modern ideology and a creative disposition of mind of greater importance and effectiveness than among these permanent officials. As the world of scientific workers emerges from the clerical traditions of the past, so also is the "trained" and "expert" official likely to emerge. They will be kindred types of similar origin.

We are still, so to speak, only in the first generation of the competitive civil service type, and already it is clear that it has a mind of its own. That distinctive mind is likely to develop to quite formidable proportions in the years ahead and to modify our conceptions of gov-

---

*There are four grades of British civil servant, responsible for taking decisions under a minister, with the following approximate membership: 1,150 administrative, 4,350 executive, 6,500 technical and scientific and an inspectorate of 2,150.

ernment and governmental possibility profoundly. And, though this is anticipating certain ideas we shall develop rather more fully later, it may be extraordinarily helpful to international coöperation in the future, if the meetings and interchanges of civil servants of different countries could be facilitated and multiplied. The meetings of the "great statesmen" of various nations at Geneva are apt to be rather like the casual meetings of Guys in the London streets on the fifth of November. The things flap about with their great eyes goggling at the photographers and reporters. The General Election bonfire will come sooner or later, and the next meeting may be of quite another pair of Guys. But the permanent official remains and returns and grows in significance.

§ 4. *A Collection of Governments**

It was rather amusing in § 2, even though it may have seemed a little irreverent to some of our readers, to survey the sacred procedures of the British Parliament in the light of modern rationalization. Manifestly we were dealing in this instance with a very old-established and intensely self-satisfied body. It has muddled along in the sunshine of British good luck for so long that it is still saturated with the idea that the sunshine is the outcome of its own peculiar virtues. It palavers, it plays its little slow game of processions and ceremonial, it rejoices in its leaders and "characters," it delays and obstructs human progress—with an unsullied conscience. Since the social machine does in a manner get along from day to day, and since the permanent official is relatively invisible, the public shares this delusion of the politician's essential importance. And there is no fundamental difference in quality, though there may be differences in degree, when we turn from the British government to other contemporary sovereign powers.

We find, for example, the government of the United States aloof from all the vital centres of American life in the District of Columbia. Washington has the better of Westminster at least in the possession of a comprehensive and admirably administered library. But the contact of the individual Congressman with the executive ministries is even more remote than that of the British Member of Parliament, because neither the President nor the Ministers he has selected sit in the House of

---

*A very readable, good little book on the subject of this section is *Parliament* (*History, Constitution and Practice*), by Sir Courtenay Ilbert. It is a pre-war book now brought up to date (1929). A more extensive study will be Dr. H. Finer's *Theory and Practice of Modern Government,* still in the press as this is being written.

Representatives. There is, therefore, no question time at Washington. The President may or may not assemble his Ministers after the fashion of the British Cabinet. There are 435 members of the House of Representatives; they sit for two years and legislate or serve on various standing committees which communicate with parallel committees of the Senate and with the ministries (departments). The individual Congressman may be even more ineffective and evanescent than the British Member of Parliament. He may feel even more like an uninvited stray dog in an unfamiliar house. Unless he is *in* with the party bosses, the rules of procedure paralyze him completely.

The Washington Senate is, however, a very different sort of body from the Assembly. There are ninety-six Senators at Washington, two for each state, who sit for six years, thirty-two are replaced or reëlected biennially, and the Senate is therefore, quite apart from its constitutional powers, a more permanent, homogeneous and effective body than the Lower House.

The framers of the Constitution contrived a complicated system of interlocking vetoes to prevent any possibility of convulsive political acts. The President may veto legislation, the Senate must endorse by a *two-thirds* majority every treaty with a foreign power. All save the minor processes and undertakings of American representatives abroad therefore are provisional and conditional upon the assent of the Senate. This has provided some stupendous surprises for the European mind, as, for example, the repudiation of the League of Nations by the Senate, after nearly every chief avenue in the European capitals had been rechristened Avenue Wilson. From first to last a European Foreign Office is never quite clear about what it is dealing with in America. Behind this formal government again move those great shadowy monsters, the Democratic and Republican party organizations. They become incarnate in Conventions; incarnate, they are seen to be creatures of frenzy and unreason. They produce "platforms" which straddle and evade every real issue, they menace, they make, and they break all the actors upon the Washington scene. They developed mainly between 1830 and 1840, they underwent great transformations through the Civil War, and they have ever since controlled the Washington government. They are in effect now as much the real government of the United States as Mussolini is at the time of writing the uncrowned King of Italy. The President is first and foremost a party man. He has been for a hundred years. He does not stand in the shoes of George Washington. He stands on one of his shoes. Moreover, this government at Washington is a government whose powers are strictly limited and defined. It has no concern over such (now) world-wide interests as labour legislation, marriage, divorce and general morals, public health, mineral resources, water power, company law, bankruptcy, insurance and education. These are affairs for the eight-and-forty sovereign governments constituent of the Union.

Senate, House and President are elected at different times for different periods. Hence a President, for a part or the whole of his term, may be confronted by a hostile Assembly.

At Washington and in each of the eight-and-forty state capitals, just as at Westminster, there centres a civil service organization. On the whole, the American Civil Service is not so stable and competent as the British equivalent. It varies in quality from state to state. The Federal Civil Service developed late in American history, and to its delayed and hampered development many weaknesses of the American government are to be ascribed. A hundred years ago the party machines, those two great party organizations behind the ostensible government, which actually dominate American politics, laid hold of Civil Service appointments and used them boldly as party bribes and rewards. No qualifications were exacted from the candidates for office, their salaries were taxed to contribute to the party funds, and, subject to the Four Years' Tenure of Office Act of 1820, they went in and out with their party.

This unfortunate arrangement has not only hampered the development of a great modern civil service in America, but it has introduced a perverted realism and a criminal bitterness into American party politics unknown in the British world. The gangster has stood close to the politician for a century. President Garfield, for example, was assassinated by a disappointed political gangster, and under one administration, a revenue service, appointed on this "spoils system," robbed the federal government of $75,000,000. After fifty years of ineffectual discontent, and following upon the shock of President Garfield's murder, the public rebelled, and the Federal Civil Service Act of 1883 (followed speedily by similar acts in the states of New York and Massachusetts), laid the foundations of a civil service in America adequate to the needs of a great modern community. Other states, however, still clung to gangster party officials, and only after 1905 did a new wave of purification sweep Wisconsin, Illinois, and several other states onward towards civilized civil services. And there at present things remain. The rest of the states have not been swept.

The Federal Civil Service Act itself was not altogether comprehensive; it excluded a number of appointments, higher grades of post-mastership, collectorship of customs and inland revenue and other administrative offices, which remain to this day party jobs subject to both appointment by the President and confirmation by the Senate. (If the President makes an appointment in defiance of party feelings, the Senate may not confirm. He must parley and choose again. Generally the President does not make these appointments at all, but leaves it to the interested Senator or party boss.) Because of this exclusion from the Acts there still remain in the United States about 17,000 federal officials of no particular competence, subordinating their proper duties to party intrigue. But the bulk of the Federal services (about 700,000 posts) is now carried on by permanent officials.

The struggle of the United States to establish and maintain scientific standards in these matters is by no means ended. The Senate clings obstinately to its patronage. The examination for even the higher grade appointments of the Federal service, says Graham Wallas, are not nearly so severe as the British, and for that and other reasons, they do not attract as good a type of man from the universities. It is a specialist's examination; it does not test general education and intelligence. In that respect the British conditions err on the other side. The pay in relation to the prevailing standard of life is low, and there is no effective superannuation. There is not the same career for an able man. The civil servant is not respected. He may be treated with great popular ingratitude. Citizens lack respect for the administration, and over great areas lawlessness prevails because the public services do not command respect.

And yet nowhere is this lawlessness absolute. In human affairs nothing is ever as good as it ought to be and nothing is ever as bad as it might be. Men may be crookedly appointed and still feel a sense of duty. There may be party politicians who may believe they are supporting the right thing—if a trifle subtly and indirectly—and at times they may even be roused to see that they get the right thing. Everywhere men value good report. In spite of every adverse force, the American nation is developing, slowly but surely, and in its own fashion, that essential organ for a modern state, a powerful and efficient civil service. Political entanglements notwithstanding, there are points upon which American public organization already compares favourably with any European parallels. The technicians, the economists, medical men, architects, chemists, draughtsmen and so forth, seem to be more severely chosen and chosen more definitely in relation to what they have to do. The prevalent hard thinking about efficiency methods permeates governmental work. There is not the same gap in sympathy between business procedure and public functionaries that we find in Great Britain. Professional organizations (of engineers, accountants, architects, e. g.) seem bolder and more vigorous and influential in America than in Europe, and make themselves better felt in the direction of public affairs.

When we turn to France we find a fine civil service (with which, in contrast to the British and American instances, the educational organization is combined), still rather disheartened and demoralized by an extensive reduction of salaries and prestige through the revaluation of the franc. The same thing has happened in Germany. Before the war the German bureaucracy was a very powerful body, appointed from above and responsible, says Finer, to no one but its conscience. It was appointed only after the most thorough education, selection, and probation—a system with two hundred years of history. It had public prestige of the highest degree, and a high tradition of efficiency, service, and liberal reform. It was sometimes overbearing, but just and clean. It was the state-conserving element in the Revolution of 1918 and the reaction of 1923. In spite of the temptations and tactics of political parties, it still preserves its professional dignity and capacity and becomes now more conscious than ever that it is the essential institution without which Germany must fail.

But we cannot embark here upon even the most elementary description of the working of the French or German governmental machinery. Or of any other governments. Treatise beyond treatise would arise. It was Aristotle, the Father of Systematic Knowledge, who made the first collection of governments (158 of them) as a supplement to his *Politics*. (Of this collection only the *Constitution of Athens* survives.) In that vast encyclopædic museum which overshadows our book there would be a complete display of the constitutions and methods of legislation and administration of mankind, it would be the list of Aristotle brought up to date. There the student would contemplate the housing and organization of the inkpot-throwing parliaments of eastern Europe (the members of the Mother of Parliaments have no inkpots handy), the highly disciplined Fascist legislature, to which Fascists only may be elected, the new parliamentary or pseudo-parliamentary organizations of China and Persia and Turkey, and those mass meetings which figure as parliaments in Soviet Russia.

I visited the Russian Duma in 1914; it conducted its deliberations in Potemkin's old riding school under a colossal portrait of the Tzar, enormously booted, and was otherwise a very good imitation of a modernized Western parliament, with priests and women among its members; and I visited and addressed the Soviet of the Commune of the North in Leningrad in 1920. That was a vast meeting of a couple of thousand people or more, a meeting completely dominated from the platform; and proceedings culminated in the showing of an anti-Imperialist film of Zinoviev and Zorin visiting the Caucasus; after which the assembly dispersed emotionally singing the "Internationale."

At Moscow I visited Lenin in the Kremlin, and I had a glimpse of the administration of one or two government departments. I got an impression everywhere of casual and amateurish administration. The post office was completely out of gear—I saw youthful stamp collectors, entrusted with letter sorting, picking foreign stamps off the envelopes of letters at the frontier bureau—and the new régime had practically taken over the personnel and methods of the Tzarist police. There never had been much of a civil service in Russia, and to a large extent its function (in 1920) was being performed by members of the Communist party, who sat in slovenly requisitioned rooms, and made up in zeal for what they lacked in efficiency. Possibly this improvised civil service has learnt much in the last ten years, but Stalin, who has succeeded the scientific-spirited Lenin, seems to possess all the vindictive romanticism of a typical Georgian, and his methodical removal of one after another of Lenin's trusted lieutenants cannot fail to injure and cripple the working of the huge new politico-economic machine he is trying to create. One symptom of inefficiency is the constant trials and frequent executions of officials and experts that still go on. The methods of terror, says H. R. Knickerbocker, still rule in Russia. The Terror in Russia has lasted thirteen years. It is a cruel and wasteful substitute for civil service morale.

But we cannot, we repeat, expand the catalogue of constitutions and administrations here. Those who are bent upon human unity and the great peace of the world must needs spend some pensive moments over this imagined gallery of contemporary governments at work, before they go on with our argument. This assemblage of creaky, clumsy, primary governing machines with their underpaid, corrupted or under-developed civil services, their encumbering traditions of procedure and their obstinate inefficiency, this miscellany of machines, all different, without "interchangeable parts" or any arrangements for interlocking, constitute at present the only available legal apparatus for regulating and reconstructing the common affairs of mankind. Our hope of a satisfactory substitute lies manifestly in the unobtrusive evolution of a series of scientifically organized civil services with ideas of world administration in common.

A very important and necessary linking system between the official civil services and the general activities of the developing modern community, Finer points out, is foreshadowed by what he calls vocational associations, such organizations as trade unions, federations of this or that industry, chambers of commerce and the like. On the one hand, such bodies can influence and instruct elected legislators directly; on the other, they are called in by the Civil Service before laws are drafted. They can coöperate in the work of special committees. More and more of the real administration work of modern governments is carried on by accessory committees. Such advisory committees before the departments as the German Economic Council, the French Economic Council, the English Economic Advisory Council, are all organized (if rudimentary) arrangements to supplement the work of Parliament by more effective consultative methods.*

§ 5. *Assent*

Let us for a section revert to the elementary psychology of human association with which we have already dealt in Chapter the Eighth. It has been difficult to consider the existing governments of mankind from the point of view of an efficient discharge of function, without a note of derision creeping into the account. That note will pass into dismay and monstrous foreboding as this chapter proceeds to the consideration of international relations and the clumsy dealings of these inept governments one with another. But when we consider them, not from that point of view, but as aspects in the slow, progressive adjustment of a very ego-centred and recalcitrant animal to social life, the calm of biology returns to us, we see how inevitable these evils were, and the flavour of exasperation and indignation fades out of our description.

Before we take up the activities of war and the mutual injuries of states, let us seek an explanation of this outstanding ineptitude which still pervades political life and which contrasts so vividly with man's present scientific and industrial achievement. Why are our ostensible

*Finer's book on *Representative Government* (1923) broke new ground in this matter. Since then Child's book on *Labour and Capital* in their relations with Parliament has analyzed the situation in the United States more closely and exhaustively. There is a compact and very suggestive discussion of these general administrative issues in Sir Arthur Salter's *A Scheme for an Economic Advisory Council in India*. 1931.

governments so manifestly inferior in their working and adjustments to railway engines or telephone exchanges?

The answer is latent in the account we have given of social origins. Man, we have to reiterate, is social in spite of himself. He is by nature self-centred, fierce and resentful, and to make up society it has been necessary that he should be educated, cajoled and subdued. Fear, superstitions and the gods, religions, histories, initiations and educations, example and precept have all played a part in the complex, always imperfect, process of breaking him in to collective life. Beating, promises, flattery and training have each contributed to win his assent to his rôle in the scheme of things, his willing participation in the give-and-take of the community.

In the smaller, simpler, stabler cities and states of the past, it was possible to browbeat and accustom ordinary people to the obediences and coöperations of collective life. The community carried on. If any chose to be recalcitrant, disapproval and compulsion of a practicable sort were close at hand. If in return the ruler proved too oppressive, a straightforward revolt and a change of ruler could occur and clean up the situation.

But with the growth and increasing complexity of modern communities, assent became a less simple matter. Government became distant, it became distant in space, and it receded from popular view behind a growing thicket of intermediaries. It ceased to feel the fluctuations of individual assent. Britain lost her American colonies because, weeks and weeks away across the Atlantic, men could get together and say freely what they thought of taxation by Westminster, while Westminster unaware could do nothing to suppress them or reconcile them. The French monarchy collapsed because France beyond Versailles would not assent to continually increasing taxation. Most of the social and political stresses of the past three centuries have been due to the dissentience of people out of touch with, and refusing assent to, governments. The nineteenth century, from first to last, was experimenting with representative democracy in the hope of sustaining the minimum of assent necessary for the working of a continually more extended, detailed (and more costly and taxing) governing machine.

On the one hand the traditional ruler was relinquishing more and more of the detailed application of power to the skilled or routine-guided official, while on the other he was still held responsible for all this increasing amount of government. So he found himself in continually greater need of the general assent of the community. The modern politician has arisen, in effect, to meet the needs of this situation. He is a dealer, a merchant or broker in assent. He lives by assent. He gathers it in, or makes believe to gather it in, from the vague and fluctuating masses of the great modern community, he consolidates it, or seems to consolidate it, always with a view to the approval of the assenting mass and a continuation of its favours, and so he transmits it to the officials, police, teachers, tax-gatherers, judiciary and so on. He interprets to the officials what the community approves and what they may do, and the officials inform him upon what issues the community needs to be instructed and directed. He has to pose as giving orders to the one and inspiration to the other. He is something quite different from a Roman Imperial statesman, an oriental vizier, or a statesman of the Middle Ages. One must go back to the city democracies of the Mediterranean to find anything like him. He is not indeed a statesman at all, or he is a statesman by the way. He is much more akin to the actor, the writer, and the popular journalist. He deals with audiences, as they do.

To realize the intervention of these assent-organizing activities and the conditions under which they must work is to begin to understand the otherwise inexplicable inefficiency of contemporary governing bodies. It was unfair to compare them to boards of directors or to any rationalized industrial organization. They neither embody definite plans nor pursue defined ends. Nobody is quite clear and precise about what they are for. They balance and sway in the balance. The will to rule which is supposed to exist in the electorate is not there. The will to rule has evaporated from the organization of the modern state. It is being concentrated afresh in the minds of political thinkers, business organizers, financial organizers and the modern civil service. But the politician has to pretend and sustain with all his power the pretense that the will to rule resides in the electorate. Directly it is proved that the ordinary man has no wish to rule at all, the reason for the politician's existence vanishes.

Our museum encyclopædia would detail all the multitudinous ways of looking at the state, still operative in the world. The religious royalist—in Britain, at least—would say that government is "for God and the King." It has to sustain the peace and order of the realm. Such Puritans as those who founded New England would have it that it is the embodiment of God's will on earth. Many minds with a Latin tradition would turn rather to the phrase of the Re-Public or the Common Weal. And then ask for an expert dictator—though dictators are never experts. But for the past century and a half theocracy and autocracy have been more or less thrust aside by the democratic idea, the idea that the state is the "embodied will" of the people, that all power comes from the people and all governmental service is ultimately the service of the people and of their common rights and liberties. In most other systems the people are supposed to assent passively; an element of natural or divine right in the ruler or rulers is assumed, and the people are understood to recognize that; in modern democratic systems popular assent is figured as active and continuous. The people are themselves supposed to watch and understand government and to signify their assent by their votes.

The next stage to representative democracy is Anarchism, in which theory no government whatever is required, since the people are supposed to be directly and immediately capable of solving whatever collective problems may arise.

Manifestly our contemporary populations neither watch nor understand government. That they do so is a legal fiction. But we have to get along with that fiction for the present, because no one has yet invented and worked out any better way of getting a general assent to administration and legislation. A much better way cannot be beyond human contriving, but it has not yet been contrived. Meanwhile the collective affairs of mankind have to be carried on through the mediation of a patchwork of seventy-odd governments, mostly of the elective democratic type. There is nothing else to be done but to work them as well as we can until a better way appears.

Again the reader must turn his imagination to vast shadowy galleries in our Museum of Human Activities. There would be exhibits to display the past and present of electioneering and the organization of democracies for political ends. All the machinery would be displayed from public meeting to polling station and vote counting; there should be a complete collection of election posters, cinema records of American processions and demonstrations, and a series of photographs of politicians in full harangue, with their faces distended and their uplifted and gesticulating hands and arms. In the special library there would be a collection to illustrate the relations of the press to political crises and studies of bribery under past and current conditions, intimidation, personation, the falsification of returns and the strategy of seat redistribution, freak candidatures and the like.

It is impossible, under modern conditions, for politicians to mould or direct opinion. They have to pick up and marshal such feelings and opinions as exist already in the community, to "crystallize" them in

catchwords, to use all the skill and science of the professional advertiser to impress their "personalities" and their panaceas on the popular
imagination. Even when they are standing for a real end, its statement
must be simplified down to the level of the average voter. Necessarily
they must seek and use the cheapest, widest appeals to prejudice that
the public intelligence will tolerate.

Cheapest and most effective of all such appeals is the appeal to
.patriotism. If patriotism had never existed before, modern politicians
would have invented it. And almost equally powerful are class jealousy
and class greed. Let the burthen of taxation fall on other people: that
has always been quite naturally a very popular cry. Fear of the unknown
is another great force for the politicians' purposes. All proposals for
reorganization must have their complexities, which may need half an
hour or so of explanation—and half an hour of explanation is nine-and-
twenty minutes too much for the average man. All, too, involve some
experimental reservations. A twist of misrepresentation, a misleading
nickname, a bold assertion of the certainty of disastrous consequences,
and the carefully elaborated scheme is doomed. The common voter,
unless he is in a panic or entirely desperate, will go down with the
ship, will stick to the ship, that is, so long as it is above water, rather
than risk the frightful jump into the lifeboat. Much more will he hold
back when there are politicians to tell him that the lifeboat is a life trap,
and as the ship always *has* floated he may trust it to float forever.

As corrective to this law, so to speak, of the maximum cheapness of
appeal in political life, there is nothing but a public understanding based
on a sound general education—education not of the formal school type,
but real education as we shall define it in Chapter XV. As the level of
sound education rises in a community, the quality of the politician's
appeal must rise. There will come a point at which the baser grades of
claptrap will discredit, and the politician will have to qualify this claptrap he uses with a certain consistency and sanity. An alert, intelligent
and honest press is a powerful restraint upon the worst impulses of
the politician. It can keep things in mind for and against him; it can be
a constant refresher to the public mind. Unhappily, economic developments have for a time cheapened the press mentality throughout the
world. But this we shall discuss later.

Posturing, intrigue and unscrupulous appeals to fear, class-jealousy,
and patriotism; favours, buttons, crystal and claptrap: these are the
forces that bring the politicians of the great powers of the world to
office. They come to government pledged to measures that must con-

A GOVERNMENT BUILDING
IN THE BEST HISTORICAL STYLE

THE Capitol Building at Washington, which recalls, by its name and architecture alike, the political traditions of Rome.

THE CROWD REJOICES

THE reception to Colonel Lindbergh in New York City. The air is white with rolls of ticker tape, torn up telephone books and infinite bits of torn paper. One of the principal ways in which New York shows its appreciation of a distinguished visitor is to shower tons of paper upon him.

fuse economic life, cripple trade and promote those international stresses that lead to war. As far as possible, the permanent official, the sane man in a position of responsibility, does his best to prevent or delay the realization of those pledges. And the necessary legislative and administrative incompetence of the democratic politician is also very helpful in assisting him to break his word. Moreover, as soon as his election to office is over, he has no longer any strong inducements to keep his word; it is much easier and pleasanter to let his pledges—he never, if he can help it, pledges anything tangible—slide. He promised to save the country, and is not his presence at the head of things a sufficient guarantee that the country has been saved?

In this manner it becomes clear how it is that the multitudinous governing machines that now divide human affairs so strangely between them are so inferior in efficiency to the aëroplane, the telephone exchange or the power station. When we scrutinize the psychology of human association the wonder is, not that it works badly, but that it works at all. We have seen how in a comparatively brief period of time human communities have passed from their ancient forced assent to the arbitrary will of Gods and masters, into this present state of alleged free assent—which is, to put it plainly, *humbugged* assent. Uncertainly and desperately the educationally minded toil to overtake the blundering developments of this new situation. The problem of government remains still the obscurest of all the vital problems that now challenge mankind.

We may, perhaps, glance for a moment at various proposals that have been advanced for the improvement of the modern democratic governing machine. They are all rather hopeless proposals because they are more or less plainly and openly projects for the abolition of the contemporary type of politician, and it is only with the consent of the contemporary type of politician that they can legally be brought into operation. The proposals fall into three groups: those which concern the method of election; those which concern the size and procedure of the legislative body, and those which turn upon the necessity of the checks and delays established by our forebears.

It is maintained by a very considerable number of intelligent people that the prevalent method of election by the division of the electorate into one-seat (or in a minority of cases two or more seat) constituencies, necessarily subordinates wide to local considerations, gives no representation whatever to the minority, though it may be only a few votes short of the majority, and leads inevitably to a two-party system which mocks at essential change. At times a party which really represents only a minority of the population, by winning a number of seats by narrow majority and losing a few by enormous minorites, may have an actual majority in the legislative chamber.

One remedy suggested by Thomas Hare (*The Election of Representatives*) in 1859 and supported by John Stuart Mill is Proportional Representation. In its original and most logical form it was a scheme for treating the whole country as one constituency and allowing a candidate to collect votes until he could obtain a quota qualifying him for election. "Practical" men have modified this project in 300 (!) different ways, but the most genuine form would have large constituencies returning up to 15 members (so Lord Courtney before the British Royal Commission in 1909) and long lists of candidates would be submitted to the electors who would mark their preferences 1, 2, 3, and so on. A candidate who secured more than sufficient 1's to achieve the quota, would have his surplus of 2's divided among candidates who had not yet received a quota, and so on, until a sufficient number of quotas would be accumulated and only a surplus of less than a quota would be left unrepresented. But this would tend to the election of outstanding representative men who are not simply party politicians. On that account it is that we have those three hundred variations of the method, all designed to keep government in the hands of party politicians by insisting upon the voters' second, third and later selection being not free but confined to tortuously fabricated party lists. These sophisticated forms of proportional representation, contrived as they are to restrict government to the professional politician, lead to a representative assembly with an inconvenient mosaic of small parties and make government a matter of tiresome bargaining and intrigue.

But the plain fact of the case is that proportional representation aims to get rid of the party politician altogether and to substitute for his interventions a real council of the nation. The world wants—just as far as it can—to get rid of the politician in managing its affairs, just as it wants to get rid of the middleman in trade. Both are interveners, making trouble rather than saving it. No true politician will ever concede silent working efficiency in administration if he can prevent it. He lives and dies by party. What has been overlooked in such experiments in so-called proportional representation as have been made thus far, is that the elected chamber must be much smaller than, for instance, the British House of Commons or the American House of Representatives, and that it should have no party structure. It must be a not too big committee of the nation rather than an unwieldy bilateral debating society. Its ministers must not be a block, going in and out of office together; they must be individually responsible to the entirely more intelligent and more representative assembly the proportional representative method would produce.

We cannot enter here into the detailed discussion of the proportional representative project. The best case against it is made by asserting that an election in a modern democracy has a double purpose. Its first end is the appointment of a legislator. But equally important, say these critics, is the education of the common citizen in public issues by the speeches and canvassing of the candidates. This is only possible in small, accessible constituencies. No candidate could cover the ground of a fifteen-member constituency; and so his instructive and exalting personality could not get into touch with the uninformed common man. Proportional representation would therefore throw more political power into the newspapers and (party) publicity machinery. But think of the average party candidate—as educating anybody! The fact is that to-day the guiding influences in modern elections are the newspaper, the party propaganda organization, priests (in many countries), and "movements" which canvass. A change over to proportional representation would not really alter this at all. Further it is argued that great numbers of voters would not vote at all. That might not prove a misfortune. To abstain is practically to assent.

But most criticism of genuine proportional representation is based on an uncritical and unimaginative belief in the necessity for party government because of its supposed stability. It is held to be an excellent preventive of any essential revolution, because the party out of office (though it consists of politicians differing in no essential respect from those in office) can pretend to take up and act for those who find the contemporary government intolerable. A change of personnel is thus foisted upon people who want a change of régime.

The whole apologetic for modern democratic government on the old party lines rests in fact upon this action in diverting and minimizing the forces of change in the interests of stability. It is not realized that there may be too much stability and not enough change. But the form of government suggested by the more thoroughgoing proportional representationists—a single small chamber of the size of a big committee of from 200 to 300 members, a circular chamber, that is, and not a bilateral one, a chamber elected by immense constituencies returning from 10 to 18 members each, would certainly give better scope for the broaching of dissentient views and for compromises with them, than the present system. It would accept or reject the ministers appointed by the premier individually, and it could go to the country triennially or quadrennially for new blood and the elimination of persons who had become unpopular. It would have far greater continuity of will and personnel than any existing government.

The professional politician has always clung as long as possible to the two-party system. When a community (as, for example, the British) has become so manifestly bored and thwarted with the Box and Cox alternation of governments, which, the more they changed, the more they remained the same thing, and has, in spite of every mechanical difficulty in its way, evoked a third or even a fourth party, then the politicians resort to the trick of the Second Ballot or Alternative Vote. These contrivances are designed to come into operation when there are three or more candidates, and none of them gets an absolute majority. The hindmost is eliminated, and the remaining two share his votes either in a second polling or by counting the second choice already marked on each voter's paper. These devices have recommended themselves to legislators because they admit a third professional politician to the chances of the election and nevertheless are entirely effective in excluding any publicist, however popular, who is not attached to a fully organized party machine. The trade in assent, with all its honours and profits, remains in professional hands and that, from the politician's point of view, is the most important consideration. It is hardly surprising that representative party government on such lines has been unable to prevent an anti-parliamentary revolution in the case of Poland and various other countries, when a bored and apathetic community has submitted to, and even found a certain relief in, a frank dictatorship. And already we have studied the desolating ineffectiveness and want of initiative of the Mother of Parliaments in the face of the dark urgencies of our time.

The fact that the prestige of the two-party system arose accidentally, because of a peculiar dynastic and religious stress in seventeenth-century England, is generally disregarded in the discussion of electoral methods. But it is a vitally important consideration. The fluctuations in English affairs which led to the successive replacement of the first Stuarts, the Commonweal, the late Stuarts, the House of Orange, the Tory reaction under Anne, the House of Hanover and the raids of the Old and Young Pretenders, within the brief space of a hundred years, established an exceptional duality in English political affairs. On the one hand was the Tory, Royalist, Anglo-Catholic or Roman Catholic, and presently agriculturalist and landlord; on the other the Whig, Middle-Class Republican, Aristocratic-Republican with a tame king as figurehead, Constitutionalist, Puritan, Dissenter or Low Church, often urban and interested in industrial development. When the British colonies in America developed beyond the scale of an exploited group of satellites, Tory and Whig fought for subjugation or independence—the City of London was for the colonists—and the two-party system was transferred without any question of its naturalness to American political life and fixed there permanently by the adoption of a method of voting that practically necessitates the restriction of an election to one of two candidates. Tory disappeared in America, and Whig split into Republican and Democrat—we omit the intermediate phases—but the dualism remained. The economic and political prosperity, first of Great Britain and then of the United States, gave everything Anglo-Saxon a flavour of success throughout the nineteenth century, and as other countries began to modernize their governments, this purely accidental bilateral arrangement of affairs, with its alleged efficacy in burking attempts at fundamental change by diverting them into the harmless channel of "opposition" politics, became a world-wide institution.

But there is no natural necessity for it; none whatever. It is a contemporary superstition.

Equally superstitious is the almost world-wide insistence upon two legislative chambers, devised to check and thwart each other. No one can give any satisfactory reasons, except what we may call "artful" reasons, for this double digestion of the community will. No sane business organizer would dream of an upper and lower board of directors with an "opposition" on each board and a cabinet of managers, who every one of them would have to throw up their jobs, if any single one of them failed to satisfy the boards. But that is the form of the British directorate, and that is more or less the spirit in which most of the seventy-odd, distinct and separate governments in the world have organized the conduct of their affairs.

Long ago Bentham remarked, "If a second chamber agrees with the first, it is superfluous; if it disagrees, it is obnoxious."

We have now to consider some of the broader consequences of this seventy-fold division of human control, among governments organized for conflict and specialized for the most tenacious and inveterate resistance to improvement or replacement.

§ 6. *Frontiers and the Official Intercommunication of Governments*

The division of human government into seventy-odd sovereign states does not merely impede the effective treatment of fundamentally important economic matters—that alone would be bad enough, but it goes much further towards evil and human frustration than that, because it keeps up the tradition of the militant state and turns men's faces towards war and war preparation, and towards destructive economic warfare in preparation for the military conflict. Enormous quantities of human energy are dissipated by this fragmentation of government, economic evolution is delayed by it, and the whole future of our species threatened.

We have to deal with these things here mainly as economic disturbances and diversions of creative power. We shall say very little of the cruelties and abominations of war. They are horrible indeed, but they are secondary. What concerns us with war in this general economic survey is not its soul-destroying cruelty, but it futility and the barrier it may set to man's attainment of any life ampler than the one he leads to-day.

Throughout this work stress has been laid on the profound change in human conditions brought about by increased facilities of transport and communication generally. That also is the main theme of the *Outline of History*. But since there exists as yet no real science of social structure, the connection of the vast change of scale in human operations, this enormous lengthening of the human reach, with the intensified economic and political tensions of our time, has not been understood. It was not realized that a drastic revision of our political institutions and economic conceptions to adapt them to this change of scale had become a logical and urgent necessity. It is only now that any considerable number of people are observing that the frontiers of the old political systems and the old areas of sympathetic association which fitted economic needs fairly well in the eighteenth century are becoming intolerably narrow, tight and dangerous. The *Outline of History* explains how in certain instances, in the preservation of the unity of the United States, for example, in the development of certain modern "empires," in the unification of Italy and Germany, the new forces operated, unthanked and almost unsuspected, and now the science of work and wealth must develop this conception of areas outgrown and set itself to a study of the "frontier" as a complication and an obstacle to the establishment of that world economic state which is so manifestly struggling to come into existence.

I had thought at first that we should begin here with the custom house as an ever present manifestation of this entanglement. But it opens up our discussion better to examine the nature of the obsolete traditional machinery which is fighting so obstinately to maintain the old patchwork of communities against the synthetic forces of the world, and then to treat the existence of tariff walls as one necessary concomitant of that machinery. The organization and work of foreign offices and of the diplomatic and consular services must first be brought into the picture. Here is the cue for the Foreign Minister in his becoming livery, the Foreign Office clerk, and even the King's messenger, with his impressively sealed bag, to pass across the stage.

All this is now established traditional stuff. But though its spirit is very ancient indeed, its present form was assumed in comparatively recent times. In its present form it is only about three centuries old— nine or ten generations of men. We must go back to the Peace of Westphalia (1648) for the inauguration of the system of international dealing we know to-day. Then it was, writes a friend from Geneva, that "the equal right of all states, whether great or small, Catholic or Protestant, to existence and independence was recognized, and also the virtual sovereignty of the princes and cities in the Holy Roman Empire. The practice of establishing permanent legations in each other's capitals was inaugurated at the Conference." And the board was set for that game between the powers, the Game of the Militant Powers, which has become now so monstrous a weight on social and industrial life and so stupendous a threat to the future of mankind.

Were we working on a truly encyclopædic scale, here would be the place for a study of the training and occupation of diplomatists, the relation of the diplomatic to the consular service, and the successful resistance offered by the diplomatic profession of the world, so far, to the natural consequences of the fact that it is now becoming materially possible for any Foreign Minister to talk to and see the face of any other Foreign Minister in any part of the world.

The diplomat of the eighteenth century, says Professor Alison Philips in his excellent article in the Encyclopædia Britannica, was frankly a national advocate, an "agent" for the proprietary rights of his sovereign. "Diplomacy thus resolved itself into a process of exalted haggling, conducted with an amazing disregard for the ordinary standards of morality, but with the most exquisite politeness, and in accordance with ever more and more elaborate rules." He cites Frederick de Marselaer (1626), however, as declaring that "it was the function of an ambassador not only to study the interests of his sovereign, but 'to work for the common peace and to study the convenience of foreign princes,'" and he also mentions François de Callières (1716) and Vattel (1756) as speaking "of Europe as a kind of republic which it was the function of diplomacy to preserve." In the nineteenth century Professor Philips traces a considerable relaxation of the original narrowness of the diplomatic idea and a certain diminution of the importance and responsibility of ambassadors with the advent of telegraph and railway. But at the same time there was a specialization and intensification of the mentality of the diplomatic services. Originally any intelligent competent person might be a diplomat (Louis XI sent his barber on diplomatic errands). But after the Treaty of Westphalia, the division of Europe among "sovereigns" and the centralization of power and authority about their courts, diplomacy became an "art" of the genteelest pretensions, reserved almost entirely for men of good family, skilled in etiquette and intrigue. They had to mingle with the "highest personages," to know the moods and feuds of influential people; to propitiate and hoodwink, to report and suggest. After Waterloo, Britain adopted the system of sending out to her various ambassadors one or two "attachés to be domesticated in his family."

"The attachés of the various embassies and legations in the European capitals," writes one bitter critic with an intimate knowledge of legation life, have been "a godsend to middle-aged women of position everywhere. They are State gigolos." This is perhaps a little harsh, but the advancement of these young men and their matrimonial successes are closely interwoven. An attaché who marries "beneath him" falls out of the service. Two "Labour" governments in Great Britain, approaching diplomacy in a state of conscious gentility, have done nothing to alter this state of affairs.

So the tradition of an elegant, manœuvering, "confidential," undemocratic service was built up, and it rules still, a little unsteadily, in the swaying and dangerous world of to-day. The British Foreign Office clerk has been mingled a little with the diplomatists proper, where knowledge and mental vigour were plainly more important than what is called breeding. And occasionally men of exceptional originality, such men as, for example, Lord d'Abernon in Berlin have achieved real creative statesmanship in spite of all tradition. There are also now always the military and naval attachés, who are there to observe and spy upon the military activities of the host country. And nowadays a commercial attaché creeps in. But of course there are no attachés whatever to study the scientific work, the philosophy, the art, and the social progress of the land. That sort of thing does not enter into Foreign Office mentality.

An ambassador has certain privileges; his embassy is treated as being part of his own country (extra-territoriality) in which he may maintain his native laws, and he is exempt from distraint for debt and may commit many of the lighter offenses, such as disregarding traffic regulations, indulging in prohibited drinks and the like, without prosecution. His more public duties are now largely formal; every contemporary ambassador is on the end of a telegraph wire from home; but there are obscurer activities for him to foster. The association of embassies with espionage, and during war time in neutral countries with the organization of incendiarism, the sinking of ships, raids and suchlike plotting, was natural and inevitable, and so, on the other side of the account, was the stealing of their code books and the furtive interception and examination of their correspondence.

For many reasons the diplomatic representatives of the United States of America have varied considerably from the normal European type, but there has been an increasing social assimilation in the present century. If the ordinary American ambassador is not now a nobleman, he is as much a nobleman as circumstances permit. Owing to many instabilities in their status and their greater novelty, the social assimilation of the representatives of Soviet Russia has hardly begun. They remain more than a little alien to the rest of the diplomatic world and are subjected to slights and insults no other diplomatists would endure.

§ 7. The Custom House

The obstinate resolve to treat the subjects of each of the sovereign states of the world as a community distinct from and in competition with the rest of humanity, which still dominates the political and educational organization of mankind is everywhere in the harshest conflict with the development of a world economic system. Of that we have a disagreeable reminder whenever we cross a frontier.

Nationalism is a vested interest and defends itself with all the disingenuousness of self-protection. The admission that a political world system is the natural expression of the continually more common material interests of mankind, means virtual social suicide for a vast complex of traditionally important people. It means the disappearance of diplomacy, of courts and royalties, and of every type professionally dependent upon assertive and aggressive patriotism. It means the obliteration of the nationalist politician and "statesman," who knows that in a world system he will sink to provincial or parochial importance. Or to no importance at all. There is consequently a world-wide and desperate resistance to the economic forces of our time at all the present headquarters of human organization. The parties of the right are patriotic and brutally for warfare; the patriotic parties of the left talk peace and will not ensue it, take care not to ensue it. The politician who really sought the peace of the world would need the courage and creative ability to make himself a world politician. He would do it at great personal risk. Whenever he displayed an interest in world problems or tried to acquire a wider point of view he would have to turn a defenceless back to his rivals at home. They would explain that he was growing too big for his boots, losing touch with his own people, neglecting the interests of his fatherland or motherland in his desire to strut upon a larger stage, and so on. World politicians will appear in time, no doubt; men working through such things as news agencies, books, and powerful international associations rather than through legislative assemblies, and so organizing a cosmopolitan assent to world-wide reconstruction; but such methods have still to be elaborated and made effective.

Meanwhile the sacred frontiers of the pre-railway era, and the ideals of the Foreign Offices of the eighteenth century, these strange geographical divisions for which we live and our sons may die, have under stresses of easier and easier transport to be fortified not simply against armed hosts but against marketable matter in motion; they have to be emphasized by a monstrous system of interferences with trade, to defend their obsolete romantic autonomy against the plain necessities of our time. The less the frontier is necessary the more it has to be exacerbated.

The story of the modern tariff system and its increase in importance after the eighteenth century is a complex and a curious one. Tariffs seem to have been first used extensively for quasi-belligerent purposes during the Napoleonic Wars. Originally a mere method of taxation for revenue—they have become a mitigated form of warfare, aiming at the relative advantage of the population interned behind the frontier and the relative damage and ruin of foreign industries. The nature of their interference, the way tariffs are imposed, their methods of administration, make a science in itself. A popular account of that science would have to be enlivened by pictures of custom-house officials at work; the searching of luggage upon a New York pier, for example, and the activities and methods of smugglers and revenue patrols. The profits and prospects of the professional smuggler, the salaries and opportunities for corruption of the revenue services would furnish interesting material.

How the normal hostilities of tariffs may be raised to the level of a blockade is shown by a study of the trade relations between Britain and Russia. Tariff obstruction at this higher level is, for all practical ends, *war at the frontier,* White War, the chronic as distinguished from that acute form in which invasion, bomb, bayonet and poison gas play leading parts, which more emphatic sort of warfare we may call Red War. It is not really a different thing; it is only a difference of tempo, instrument and colour.

Closely associated with the clogging and congestion of world trade by the custom house is the interference with the free movement of workers, business people, and the like, by the passport and permit system. The passport has other uses of a more strictly political sort, at which we shall glance later, but here it is, while we are still upon the subject of frontiers, that its origin and development can best be described. The passport grew out of a majestically feeble letter of recommendation addressed by one's foreign minister to all whom it might concern. That letter has shrunken to comparative insignificance in the contemporary booklet passport, which gathers impressions from the rubber stamps of all nations. Endless forms of trouble arise in various countries out of the passport mislaid, and there is a flourishing trade in stolen, transferred and forged passports wherever men and women go about their unlawful occasions.

§ 8. *War Preparation as an Industry*

From the passive and obstructive malignity of White War we must turn to the activities preparatory for the Red War phase in international dealings. In no other department of human affairs has tradition held its own so successfully against the creative forces of the new age and every reasonable disposition in mankind.

Our kings and presidents, in their military uniforms, our flags and sovereignties and the primary forms and conceptions of our states, all come down to us from the time of the localized community which was either predatory in a small local way upon its immediate neighbours or defensive against them. They remain with us, as dangerous as cancer starting points, because the development of the modern economic world system has so far been a planless process due to forces that are only now beginning to be apprehended as one whole.

At no time has the necessity of getting free from the outgrown rules and boundaries of the old régime been faced, and so the world's war equipment has followed blindly upon industrial advance until it has become a monstrous and immediate danger to the community. An encyclopædic review of modern war equipment might very well begin with an account of eighteenth-century war plant, its horse, its foot and its artillery of little field guns, and trace the accumulating consequences of big steel production and of inventions in gas and explosives, in transport, communication and the like. Finally that richly illustrated encyclopædia would become vivid with pictures of tanks, bombing planes, aëroplane carriers, battleships throwing out smoke-screens, and of munition works and casualty stations in full activity during the last great war. All that spectacle is part of the work of the world and a great misuse of wealth. It is essential to our review that it should come well into the picture.

The still unassembled galleries of this museum of the science of work and wealth we have dreamt of would display, therefore, the scale of the industry and the multitudes of men in training for it at the present time. And since the associated encyclopædia would be a full résumé of human occupations, it would have to give the abundant particulars of that training in its endless varieties. It would summarize the good and evil of barrack life.

At least military service uproots the peasant. That is a good thing. But this drilling of millions of young men, this incessant training of young Frenchmen mentally as well as physically to kill Italians and Germans, of Poles to kill Germans or Russians, of Russians and British and Americans to kill anybody who happens, is not a good thing. This morning ten thousand bugles and drums were noisy about the world, calling the boys out to the exercise yard, and hardly a moment passes without a machine gun rattling out its blank cartridges or a futile gun booming at a target for want of immediate flesh and blood to shatter.

There is a real breaking down of initiative in the well trained common soldier. The late Dr. Rivers in his brilliant report on "War Neurosis and Military Training," now reprinted in his *Instinct and the Unconscious,* tells how the army discipline exaggerates mental suggestibility until it may even induce that type of hysteria which is accompanied by partial paralysis and kindred crippling functional disorders. Numbers of men never recover from the drill-sergeant throughout their lives. They go out from the army and become citizens, to play a part in politics, to vote. But at the word of command they jump to attention.

Our encyclopædia would correlate these service disciplines with peace production on the one hand and the labour market on the other. On the one page it might give figures of so perfect a piece of mechanism as a modern submarine, and over against it photographs of the equipment of a one-roomed slum "home" in which heirs to our civilization have been born and are being reared. That home is what it is because neither labour nor material can be obtained to make it better. The home is subject to all the restrictions of private production for private property; the submarine is evoked by the collective buying of the community. Our schools wait; this ugly tribute starves our schools. The modern state "economizes" on schools; on submarines it dare not economize. We should have pictures of dockyard gates with the workers pouring in or out; the great workshops on which they toil and the streets in which they live. And there must also be an account of specialized technical training for warfare—specialized training as distinguished from the mere drilling of the rank and file. Every year in times of peace something between one and two thousand carefully chosen young men of exceptional physical quality are smashed, burnt alive, or otherwise destroyed in the training of the air forces of the world alone. There is also a steady destruction of choice young men in submarines.

Against this we must balance the braver shows of outright war. Our lavish encyclopædia would display kings, princes, and presidents and other militant heads of states arrayed in the brilliant uniforms that emphasize their fundamentally belligerent function, decorated with feathers, skins, manes of beasts, and so forth, reviewing and inspecting troops, presiding over military tattoos, parades, the trooping of the colors. It would give also a brief history of military and quasi-military costume in connection with belligerent psychology. A few score coloured plates might be devoted to the uniforms worn by the British royal family. Are soldiers particularly addicted to corsets and cosmetics? Some students allege they are. Little is known popularly of the motives and methods of those who design and vary the adornments of the military. It may be possible to discover some interesting symbolism from many objects that on the surface appear to be very aimless encumbrances and incrustations. Why, for instance, do the Grenadier Guards wear vast bearskins? Where are they made, and what do they cost? How many hands and eyes have been busied in decorating those unfortunate, bored and fatigued young men who stand for long hours heavily accoutred at the gates of Buckingham Palace? How long will it be before the last sentinel is relieved there and the whisper of the final password dies away into the eternal silences? These poor sentinels do nothing. The real guardians of the peace, the police, are there also, to save them from annoyance and preserve the dignity of the household within.

From these adornments an encyclopædic study of warfare would pass on to trace the progress in military methods, material, and machinery. The Science of Warfare is now a very active occupation. It is a sort of ugly and dwarfish little twin sister running at the side of scientific research. Her difference is that she tries to be secretive, and her ends are murderous. She is perpetually seeking to seize upon and pervert scientific advances.

But one must admit the fascinating vigour of many of her newer adaptations. There is something that stirs our unregenerate natures in the foaming advance of a great battleship and in the emphatic thud of gunfire, the flash, the swift ejection of a ball of dense smoke which slowly unfolds. Most of us could watch aërial warfare with undiluted pleasure if the promiscuous use of bombs were barred. We should follow with sympathetic delight the nimble dance of the conquering ace flying for position, tapping out the bullets from his exquisite gun with finished skill, sending, amidst our applause, his dead and wounded antagonists spinning down, poor rabbits, to their ultimate dramatic smash.

It would need another work as long as this one now, to tell fully of the post-war development of the tank and the mechanization of land warfare. Hitherto men have been stabbed, blown to pieces, buried alive, suffocated, scalded, burnt and smashed and eviscerated by projectiles in every conceivable way, but in the next war they will also have the prospect of being pulped into a sort of jam by glorified tanks. It will be a new experience. A really exhaustive treatise on war technique would include also the development of mine fields in the future and the next phase of warfare under the sea. A ship may hardly know it is hit before it goes under.

An inexpugnable nastiness and repulsiveness, however, invades the brightness of military science at the thought of "gas." The professional soldiers dislike it extremely. Nobody likes it. Yet no one in his senses believes that "gas" can be excluded from the next war. And no sane airman with a gas bomb will withhold it from the enemy's G. H. Q. if he gets a chance of delivering it there. But it is poor consolation for a civilization shattered, to know that a large proportion of military leaders will probably be choked to death in an extremely painful fashion if they get the war of their dreams. We also shall get the war of their dreams.

A comprehensive and impartial survey of what men do and how they gain their livings, if it were worked out in detail, would give ample attention to the Gas Warfare Department, describe the physical and moral effects of the latest and best gases, and weigh the prospects of an honest and capable young man or woman who selects that as a field for his or her life work. It would go into much detail about gas that we willingly spare our readers, telling of Lewisite, the gentle and insidious, so that you hardly know you are dead; of phosgene, which seems a small matter at the time and kills distressingly the next day; of the suffering caused by mustard gas, and of the fine gases that can get through any gas mask to the wearer within. These last do not kill, generally speaking; their purpose is to produce an intolerable discomfort so that the mask is torn off, and the heavier, deadlier gas given access to its victim. Gas treatment can now be extended to whole countrysides. It can constitute lines of defense that are for a time impenetrable. In the United States of America at least considerable advances have been made in the methods of disseminating disease germs from the air. It was found at first that the deadlier bacteria were in some cases too delicate and died during the process. Patient study has now made it possible to breed tougher strains of these organisms, and there is every prospect that in the next war all the more dreadful airborne infections will be released abundantly in the great cities of an enemy's country. Work has also been done upon the distribution of cattle and crop diseases over the countryside.

That better informed encyclopædia which hovers phantasmally at the back of our minds would also give certain figures I have not been able to ascertain, the number of grave, competent human beings who are now at work studying and experimenting upon these astounding refinements of human intercourse.

We cannot insist too emphatically here upon the fact that four countries alone are responsible for the continuation of armament at the present time, Great Britain, France, Germany and the United States of America. They and no others possess the complete industrial outfits needed to equip great modern armies. The iron and steel industry, the chemical industry, the electrical industry and the oil refineries are at the root of all armaments whatever. In concert they could suppress modernized warfare to-morrow. But they prefer to stimulate it. In 1925 exports of arms and munitions amounted to $48,438,000 of which the four great powers accounted for 90% (Great Britain 35 %, the U. S. A. 22.5%, Germany 16.9% and France 15.2%.) It is significant that imports recorded amounted to only $27,000,000, as follows:

British Dominions	$8,159,000
Japan	$7,561,000
China	$5,455,000
Mexico	$1,468,000
Rumania and Poland	$1,132,000

In other words twenty-one and a half million dollars worth of munitions *vanished;* their destinations were concealed or lied about.*

§ 9. The Rôle of the Armament Industry in Fostering Belligerence

Here is the place for an exhibit, an individual instance of the interplay of nationalist traditions and modern industrial progress, the life of Sir Basil Zaharoff. It is the story of an entirely honourable and honoured human being, exceptionally energetic and capable, reacting in a perfectly natural and legitimate way to the laws, traditions and institutions of our time. If this figure should seem to some imaginations to cast a very dark shadow upon the human spectacle, the fault lies rather with the pinnacle he stands upon and not with himself. His story is told by Richard Lewinsohn† with the endorsement of M. Skouloudis, the founder of Sir Basil's fortunes and a former Greek Foreign Minister.

SIR BASIL ZAHAROFF

Sir Basil, it seems, was born in an obscure village of Anatolia in 1849 of Greek parents who presently took him to Constantinople. There a kindly compatriot paid for his education at the English school, and in his teens he was able to earn his living as a guide and commissionaire attached to various hotels. Then he became the assistant of his uncle, Sevastopoulo, a draper, an infirm man whose affairs profited greatly by the energy and capacity the boy brought to them. The nephew was

---

*The report of an enquiry organized by the Inter-Parliamentary Union gives these figures from League of Nations sources, and contains much interesting material throughout.

†*Zaharoff l'Européen Mystérieux.*

promised a share in the proceeds of this business, but the uncle, either through meanness or the fear of losing the services of his useful relative if he became too independent, would not assent to the payment of the amount due to him. Accordingly young Zaharoff, having access to the money of the firm, paid himself off and, in the hope of avoiding any unpleasantness with his uncle, went to London to begin life anew. But the uncle, in a resentful mood, had him arrested there, accusing him of robbery. Things looked very bad indeed against the young man; he knew no one to bail him out, he was detained in prison until his uncle came to England to prosecute him. He was only saved from conviction and imprisonment by the dramatic discovery in the pocket of an old overcoat at the last moment before going into court, of a crumpled letter giving him full powers as a partner to buy, sell and pay out money as he thought fit. He had been hunting everywhere for that mislaid letter. The day when he had to go into court was cold, and he bethought himself of his overcoat, and in the pocket was something. . . . Sevastopoulo, confronted with it in court, could not deny his own handwriting. So by a fortunate accident young Basil Zaharoff was saved from prison to become, it is said, the richest man in the world.

How did this penniless adventurer clamber to that position, and what did he give the world in return for the enormous purchasing power he won from it?

Lewinsohn tells of a return to Athens, of struggles and difficulties, and then of the coming of opportunity. Zaharoff had gained the good-will and esteem of Skouloudis, and one day (in 1877) Skouloudis received a letter from the firm of Nordenfelt, makers of the earliest form of machine gun, asking him to recommend them an agent. Zaharoff was appointed to the vacant job with the warmest recommendation of Skouloudis at a salary of five pounds a week. Therewith, paying off various outstanding hotel bills, he commenced his march towards the inestimable millions of to-day.

He was to achieve wealth with honour, he was to become a British baronet and wear the magnificent plumes and robe of a G. C. B. in which he appears in his best known portrait. He is also, learn from Who's Who, a G. B. E. Oxford University has made him a D. C. L., and France has conferred upon him the Grand Cross of the Legion of Honour. And he has won not only honour but power. He exerted, says the Encyclopædia Britannica in an extremely insufficient and concise but extremely respectful biographical article, "a strong if indirect influence during the World War and at the Paris Conference, being a close friend and political admirer of Lloyd George, Venizelos, Clemenceau and Briand." To that we will return.

His first considerable step towards this influence and recognition was to sell a submarine to the Greek government. After years of trial, Nordenfelts had produced a submarine that not only went down under water but, generally speaking, came up again. It had been exhibited in the Sound between Sweden and Denmark, but the great naval powers had refused to take up this new engine of destruction. There seemed to be a conspiracy against it. The experts found it unnecessary and unpleasant. Zaharoff had the bright and patriotic idea of selling one on easy terms to Greece. He had friends in Greece. Then he went to Constantinople to tell them about it and ask what they thought of it. Turkey was indisposed to let Greece get ahead with a weapon that might prove effective in the Dardanelles. So Turkey ordered submarines also. The ball was set rolling. Russia could not let Turkey get ahead in this fashion. Soon the submarine was established as an item in armament competition.

But now the Nordenfelt gun was threatened by the invention of a certain Hiram Maxim. He had a machine gun one man could work; the Nordenfelt needed a crew of four. He exhibited it at Vienna. While he fired his gun at a target and demonstrated its powers, Zaharoff was busy explaining to expert observers that the whole thing was an exhibition of skill; that only Maxim could fire that gun, it would take years to train men to use it, and these new machines were delicate and difficult to make and could not be produced in quantities, and so forth. Maxim, after tracing the initials of the Emperor upon a target, prepared to receive orders. They were not forthcoming. He learnt that the Nordenfelt was simple and strong. This gun of his was a "scientific instrument" unfit for soldierly hands. His demonstration went for nothing. What had happened? He realized he was vis-à-vis with a salesman, a very formidable salesman. In the end he amalgamated with the salesman. Thereupon difficulties vanished, the Maxim gun ceased to be a scientific instrument and became a standard weapon. Nordenfelt and Maxim consolidated, and the fusion was financed with the eager support of the investing public. So Lewinsohn tells the story.

This was in 1888, and the instincts of the investing public marched with the spirit of the times. The age of armaments in which we still live had begun. The device of selling first to Greece was capable of infinite variation and repetition. Naval theory was developing and becoming more and more infected by mechanism—even though the military mind

still resisted what Lord Kitchener called "mechanical toys." The armament industry knew no boundaries. It was entirely modern in its
cosmopolitanism, and whenever it produced a model that met the taste
of Great Power A, Great Power B was invited to inspect the novelty
that might presently be used against it. Some powers increased their
state munition works, but the private armament industry, conceived on
a world-wide scale, was already growing larger and more inventive than
was possible for any single state. Presently (1897) Nordenfelt-Maxim
found themselves bought by the great British firm of Vickers for one
and a third million pounds, and Zaharoff carried his financial gifts and
his salesmanship on to a wider stage.

The Vickers firm was not merely an armament firm; it did a huge
business in iron and steel; it could carry through every stage in the
process from ore to battleship, a feat beyond the power of any state
arsenal. Vickers armed both sides in the Boer War, and the British who
were killed in that struggle had at least the satisfaction of being killed
by bullets "made in England." The profits of the Boer War enabled
Vickers to buy up the Wolseley Tool and Motor Co., and the Electric
and Ordnance Accessories Co., and so the process of amalgamation
went on. The prospect of any state undertakings rivalling the products
of the vast combination either in price, quantity, or quality became remoter and remoter.

It was less, perhaps, through ambition than through business necessity
that Zaharoff, the supreme salesman of this great system, entered upon
obscure but effective political and propagandist activities. He had never
paused in his brilliant career to indulge in philosophical speculations or
humanitarian dreams, and it was a natural and legitimate development
of his selling methods to avail himself of press support and, for example,
to secure an interest in such an enterprise as *Quotidiens illustrés,* which
published the well known journal *Excelsior* and to endow a chair of
aërodynamics in the University of Paris to hasten the day when aëroplanes (by Vickers) would be a necessary part of armaments all the
world over.

The Great War was harvest time for the trade in war munitions. It
would be unjust to historians, diplomatists, courts and patriots generally,
to say that the armament industry had sown the harvest, but certainly
for half a century it had done everything possible to stimulate the sowing. In Britain the industry was put under public control and a formal
limit was set to its profits, but its heads became very naturally the advisers and helpers of the belligerent governments. Greece was hesitating

about her rôle in the struggle, and Sir Basil found the money needed for a propaganda that would bring her into the war on the part of the Allies. Newspapers were bought and Greece came in, as Lewinsohn relates in detail.

The end of the war found the world extraordinarily weary of warfare, and there was a considerable possibility that the hugely distended world-armament industry would find itself facing a dispirited and declining market for its goods. Under these circumstances it was natural for those who were interested in its health and vigour to exert themselves to revive the romantic spirit of national assertion. And also Sir Basil loved Greece. He belonged to the Gladstonian age of national patriotism. A sentimental patriotism is probably the broadest, least ego-centred idea that ever entered his head; and we must not suppose too hastily that his motives in securing Western support for Greek aggressions upon Turkey, if complex, were necessarily disingenuous. But for Greece, in the harder, disillusioned, post-war world, the manœuvres that carried Greek armies to Angora and overwhelming defeat, that led to their disorderly retreat to the coast and the expulsion of the Greek population from Asia Minor, were altogether disastrous. The history of Greece and Turkey in the years following the war is too intricate, contentious and generally "shady" to deal with here; for us now its only importance is that it marks the culminating and conclusive effort of Sir Basil to exercise political power. Thereafter his activities have gone into channels that have little or nothing to do with this section of our work; operations with the deflated armament firms, metallurgical industries and petroleum, the exploitation of the Casino at Monte Carlo, and so forth. Our concern here is with the psychology of the armament maker as exemplified in his case.

Indisputably this man has spent a large part of his life in the equipment and promotion of human slaughter. And it is unjust and absurd to blame him for doing so. It is so cheap and easy for the sentimental pacifists to be indignant about him, but all of us are involved in the complex of processes that carried him to wealth and all of us have a share in his responsibility. Circumstances beyond his control built up his ideology. He has simply been modest enough not to question the standards of the world about him but to observe them faithfully and intelligently. It is plain that he has always accepted the making of money as a justification for his operations. Monetary success ought to be the indication of social service. If it is not, the fault is primarily with the political and business system and only secondarily with the individuals who make money. The organization of killing is inherent in our accepted ideology. The picture of an Anatolian Greek, overwhelmed by his riches, adorned with the highest honours France, Britain and Oxford can bestow, and amusing himself by running a gambling palace in his declining years, displayed against a background of innumerable millions of men maimed, tortured, scalded, mutilated and killed, may be an effective indictment of our political traditions, but in no sense is it a personal condemnation. Millions of his contemporaries would have played the same game had they thought of it and known how. There was nothing in their personas to prevent it. If anything is wrong it is in the educational influences and in the political, economic and financial opportunities that evoked those personas.

ALFRED KRUPP

We have taken the case of Sir Basil Zaharoff as the most picturesque illustration of the exploitation of our outgrown political suspicions and animosities by a particularly gifted salesman. An encyclopædia of the science of human industry would supplement his story with a constellation of biographies of kindred and associated spirits, all men no doubt amiable and pleasing in their private lives, and show how, acting strictly according to the business standards of the nineteenth century and on the lines of the education then provided, they were instrumental in imposing upon the civilized world first a colossal misapplication of its industrial machinery, then a vast load of taxation, and ultimately such an orgy of death, torment and destruction as the world has never seen before.

Victor Lefebure in his excellent book *Scientific Disarmament* tells how Lord Armstrong, the British armament vendor, when his new breech-loading rifled built-up gun was refused by the British government in 1863, went to Austria, Denmark, Spain and other countries and so put the British muzzle-loader out of fashion. It was the same forcing method that Zaharoff employed when he took the submarine to Greece. Lefebure gives also a brief résumé of the life of Alfred Krupp, another of these honest dealers in the destruction of mankind. Alfred Krupp was one of the earliest pioneers in the trade, and a pioneer also in that development of the steels which we have already described from the point of view of Substances, in Chapter II. Krupp's steel guns were little appreciated in Germany until, in 1856, the Khedive of Egypt quickened the business with an order for thirty-six of them. Prussia followed, and from that time onward for half a century the progress of the gun dominated European life. Krupp became the close friend of the first German Emperor William I and developed an unrivalled testing ground at Meppen with a range of fifteen miles, the world's showroom, as Lefebure calls it, for big artillery. Krupp reigned, the world's "Cannon King." No one could equal his guns; no one could equal his armour plate. For fifty years he toiled to achieve that immense superiority in heavy ordnance that Germany displayed at the outset of the war in 1914. The other countries laboured in a vain endeavour to keep pace with Krupp.

"How far," Lefebure asks, "would it help to remove war from reality if we could limit these unleashed forces of armament development under a definite policy of agreed control?"

Alfred Krupp, the Cannon King, died in 1887 at the age of sixty-five, and was succeeded by his son, Frederick Krupp, who died in 1902. His health was indifferent, and he died before he was fifty. This second Krupp had financial and organizing genius rather than the technical preoccupation of his father, and built up the vast industrial organization at Essen that flourishes to this day. He controlled an important section of the German press and did much to consolidate the aggressive patriotism of the German people. The third generation of the Krupp family was already passing the meridian when at last the final harvest, the second reaping after Alfred Krupp, arrived. Its members were already lapsing from the strenuous tradition of Alfred. One made an elegant withdrawal from the common life of mankind to the island of Capri, where his reputation mingles now with that of the Emperor Tiberius. In the excitement and resentment of the invasion of Belgium in 1914, many English writers, the present writer included, denounced the "Krupp-Kaiser combination" as the sole cause of the collapse of European peace. They forgot the Vickers-Armstrong side of the story and the aggressive British Imperialism of the Kipling period. The twin begetters of that war were the armament industry and aggressive patriotism wherever they appeared. Nevertheless, it was mainly the genius of Alfred Krupp, stimulating and being stimulated by the ambitions of the Hohenzollern dynasty, to which we must ascribe the full development of this strange, monstrous, morbid development of human industry, science, loyalty, greed, vanity and tradition, the armament trade. It has slaughtered twenty million people and still it towers menacingly over all human life.

§ 10. *Spying and Spy Hunting*

Our account of the war industry will not be complete without some description of espionage, counter espionage, newspaper corruption and secret service work generally. The prospective belligerent hides his plans, his inventions, his purpose, and he seeks incessantly to know what his neighbour is hiding. He wants to verify suspicions and sow the seeds of indecision and division in a camp that may at any time become hostile.

There are human types, and often they are by no means stupid types, which lend themselves very readily to the organization and performance of these obscure but logical developments of the patriotic spirit. There is an attractive element of mystery in the work, the possibility of intensely dramatic situations, revelations, the invocation of unsuspected power. There are also great opportunities of pay for nothing—except the taking of chances. A sound knowledge of languages is very helpful in the profession, a good memory, quiet observation, subtlety and histrionic ability.

Correlated with these activities of the spying sort and linking up by hidden strands with the overt diplomatic organization, every country maintains special bureaus, with classified dossiers, based largely on secret, unverified and often totally inaccurate informations made against a multitude of arbitrarily selected unfortunates, the "suspects." Being a "suspect" is an involuntary form of human activity of a particularly disagreeable sort. Nobody in the world knows what the secret service industry may not have filed against him in some police dossier of this or that country, or what threats, delays, inconveniences, arrests or physical injury may not descend upon him. He may merely have a name identical with or similar to that of someone else. The secret patriot is above reason or the law. Whether he is ever far above blackmailing is another question. And the curious reader who wants to know how much this branch of war work goes on in war-time, may read for himself in Somerset Maugham's grim *Ashenden* or in Compton Mackenzie's derisive *Extremes Meet* and *The Three Couriers*. Both these writers base their books on close personal experiences.

Our encyclopædia, when it comes to be compiled, may quote these writers, but it is to be hoped that much more exact details than they give will be available of the cost and range of this branch of work and reward, the nature of the duties to be performed and the emoluments of the practitioners. Few of us outside the profession realize the multitude of people now employed in watching the unwary, in sneaking about for information or pseudo-information, in steaming and stealing letters, playing tricks with the telegraph and telephone, provoking simpletons to indictable acts, filching documents, taking forbidden photographs, circulating rumours and so forth. It is a world screened and hidden. The census does not reckon with it, for all its practitioners mask themselves by professing some more reputable occupation. From secret service to the white slave trade, the drug trade and kindred criminality, seems but a step. All underhand callings tend to drift together, and the mentality of these activities is nearly identical, even if the relationship with the police is different. The arresting hand of the policeman is suddenly seized and lifted. "That man or woman is useful and not to be taken." The difficulty of suppressing this ugly development of the industrialization of vice is greatly enhanced and confused by the existence of this inevitable furtive fringe to modern war organization.

§ 11. *The Service Mentality*

But a complete survey of human motives and human interaction will have to go much more deeply into the belligerent process than the preceding sections have suggested. We have insisted and reiterated that this survey is essentially psychological. It seeks the roots of social motive. Its fundamental matter of study is "will systems." Shops, factories, railways, ports and shipping as we have passed them under review, are all realized will systems. They are to be explained completely as the product of desire and demand, experiment, suggestion, imitation and effort. Few people will believe that the continuing existence of organized White and Red War is completely explained by an association of traditional stupidity with self-protective blindness to manifest facts and mere short-sighted greediness. There is something better about army and navy than that. Let us now look on this better side of the military persona, the service will system.

Too much pacifist literature is devoted to the more manifest evils and absurdities of belligerence; too little to the hiatus that would be left in human life if, by a miracle, flags, frontiers, arms and disciplines were suddenly and completely abolished. The machine would not go on if they were merely abolished and nothing more. Something would have to replace them. It is comparatively rare to find any realization that when every allowance has been made for the inertia of tradition, for the blind vigour of threatened interests, and for the innate streak of fear-linked emotional cruelty in all men, there must still be other elements in the human make-up to keep this vast system of activities going. You cannot make a resistant system out of elements that are entirely rotten. Few people are prepared to declare that the professional soldier is simply a compound of idiocy, fierce cruelty, and dishonesty; and yet very little has been said here so far to admit any other interpretation of him. Yet most advocates of world peace and world unity have in their hearts a definite respect for the good soldier as a soldier, and for the spirit of military tradition.

It is when we turn upon the pacifist and confront him with that possibility of the concession of all his demands in the sudden obliteration of all the military systems in the world and ask him, "What then?" that we begin to realize the more fundamental and justifiable elements in the military and naval mentality.

And in the first place, it is well to be reminded, it is not our soldiers who are responsible for the horrors of modern warfare. To the best of their ability they have resisted the novelties forced upon them by civilian ingenuity. The British generals in the Great War refused to use and then failed to use the tank with a quite heroic obstinacy, and so they prolonged the indecisions of the war for two years. They completely defeated an attempt to mitigate the horrors and exhaustion of the journey to the front line by a system of telpherage. We have told of the British artillery authorities refusing Armstrong's guns and the Prussian War Office driving Krupp to sell a battery to Egypt before it could be brought to accept his improvements. Wellington opposed the adoption of the breech-loading rifle. Poison gas, mechanization, ironclads, torpedoes, submarines, aëroplanes, have all been forced upon unwilling service men by salesmen and financiers with the pitiless logic of material progress behind them. Such contrivances did not arise out of the intensely conservative service tradition. The civilian has been more reckless in his inventions and fiercer in their use.

In the next place it has to be remarked that the duty of preparing to kill and ultimately killing foreigners has never been recognized as more than half the work of the combatant services. Quite as important to the soldier was his rôle of guarding something central and precious, his rôle of protector. Only secondarily has he been a destroyer. Historically every specialized army system in the world had developed sooner or later a standing nucleus, a "Guard"—Pretorians, Mamelukes, Royal Guards or what not. Before that specialization, wars were wars of comparatively undisciplined levies, they were the wars of the natural man, and they were more cruel, predatory, indecisive, discursive, and destructive. The irruptions of Hun, Mongol, Northman and Moslim were far more frightful experiences than the conquests of Cæsar's legions.

We have already given the broad lines of a classification of the personas to which modern people shape their lives, and we have pointed out that the persona of the professional soldier is a blend of the nomadic with an increasing element of the educated persona; that he is not only a self-respecting fighting man but now also he is a specially disciplined and devoted, educated and educating man. To that idea we return. Let us compare the soldier with the scientific investigator, equally devoted and educated. Upon each there is impressed the same obligation to disregard mercenary considerations and all personal ends. Each has an acute and elaborate code of "honour," and each, it is assumed, would rather lose his life than save it at the price of betraying his essential purpose. But while there is this much resemblance, there is a wide divergence in the direction of the devotion. The man of science has to be devoted absolutely to the sense of truth within himself. He must doubt interminably rather than scamp his decisions to get to an end; he must not formulate half truths as truths. Until he passes from pure to applied science, he is rarely under the obligation to act. But the soldier lives alert for the call to a maximum of effective action. His, then, "not to reason why;" his "but to do or die." If his "orders" are to spy or cheat, he will obey.

His is therefore the type of persona most prone to uncritical loyalty. All his ideas march with the idea of saluting his superior officer and obeying "orders" implicitly. The navy is entirely with him in this respect. The "service" first and foremost, dominates such lives. Every established system, however decayed, has or has had its loyal, unquestioning "services." The King bolts to Varennes, but his Swiss Guard dies at its post. That is typical. Before everything else the good soldier fears attacks upon his own discipline and upon the discipline of the rank and file. He dreads the unsettling idea that creeps into his thoughts, and the leaflet at the barrack gates, with an equal unreasoning horror. To him these things mean not change but dissolution. He dreads that dissolution as much as the man of science welcomes the continual destruction and rebirth of generalizations. The "services" cannot be self-critical of their loyalties.

These loyalty systems radiating from the militant "services" devoted to the uncritical protection of the political institutions of the past, to King, however petty and absurd, and to Country, however restricted, are the living core about which the sweating employer, the munition profiteer, the financial adventurer, the beneficiary from old traditional privileges, the reckless journalist, the clinging adherent to bankrupt religions and every enemy of criticism, rationalization and open change, everyone who lives for to-day and not for to-morrow, rally and find their power of resistance. It is only by the capture of the imaginations that underlie every system of loyalty, by a gradual change in the direction of these loyalties as the error of their existing orientations is displayed beyond question, by the educational development of a new system of loyalties altogether and by the fusion and reconstruction of national services as world services, that the triumph of the new order can be attained. The new world state needs its own militant services, its own banded men of integrity and calculable action, even more than did the old order. If they are no longer needed to protect the State from the enemy without, they have to stand ready against brigandage, piracy and every form of disruption within. They have to keep safe the ways by sea and land and air from end to end of the earth. If they drop something of the decoration of the past, if they assimilate more and more to the realities of a land, sea and air police, they will, nevertheless, drop little of the sentiment and feeling that make the good service man what he is to-day.

Here, perhaps, we may recall the unsuccessful attempt of M. Léon Bourgeois to set up a cosmopolitan armed force at the disposal of the League of Nations and so provide the nucleus for a "world service" loyalty. M. Bourgeois has yet to be given his just meed of praise. He was, I fear, many decades in advance of his time. The need for such a nuclear beginning was also advocated very ably by the late Sir Mark Sykes.* It would be of extraordinary value now in allaying the irritation of minorities in such regions of mixed interest and mixed population as the Danzig corridor, Trieste and Macedonia. These obviously could be made into special neutral territories under direct League government, policed and administered by a more responsible international board of control. A League consular service is also an imaginative possibility, working to protect all foreigners in places where it is either inconvenient or undesirable to maintain separate consulates for each sovereign power.

---

*A book well worth reading in this connection is *The Problem of the Twentieth Century,* by David Davies (1930). The chapters in this book dealing with the plan for an international police force have been published as a separate book called "An International Police Force."

Would that we had space here to enter more fully into the policing of the wilder parts of the world. In the section devoted to housing and town planning we have already noted the regulative work of the police in big towns, and we have linked it to fire-fighting and other necessary services. But the world knows too little at present of the life and duties of the various types of armed service beyond its immediate ken. We have but the vaguest ideas of the life of the police who guard the sea and carry order into wild places, and scarcely more of the realities of our protection against every sort of malefactor. Roads, railways, grazing lands must be patrolled. False prophets and crazy insurrection may spring up like weeds after an unfavourable change in the economic weather or for no traceable reason at all.

The whales, the seals, the wild things of the waters, the deserts and wastes and forests call now for vigilant services on sea and land and air to save them from destruction. Seals, penguins, many sorts of fish have to be protected from cruel and wholesale massacre by semi-practical fishermen who will fight if need be. Kidnapping, forced labour and forced prostitution have to be prevented. Wherever there are crowds, again, there is danger of the collective lunatic breaking loose. Race conflicts and religious conflicts are not likely to die out for many generations. Even in the United States the vendetta and Judge Lynch still hold out against the powers of law and order. No civilization can save the world from earthquake, eruption, storm and physical disaster, and properly trained and disciplined services must be at hand to aid and shepherd the victims and clean up the débris. No longer loyal to local king and partisan flag, the services must be loyal to mankind and themselves.

Et quis custodiet ipsos custodes? Our imaginary encyclopædia, in its exhaustive study of these matters, must find place for a discussion of the most subtle of administrative problems, how to admit complaints, reverse decisions and sustain an adequate criticism of protective services without weakening them or hampering their just activities.

In a little book *The Moral Equivalent of War,* William James the psychologist made an interesting suggestion that is well worth noting here. He believed that there was a considerable moral benefit in a year or so of compulsory military service for all the young men of the community. He thought something of the kind might with advantage be extended to young women.

He was writing before the war in America, where nothing of the sort existed, and he had in mind a comparison of the younger generation of that country with their French and German coevals. It seemed to him that the young Americans were growing up with an irresponsible quality, that they took the order and security of life too much for granted, and that they needed to be reminded by some such universal imperative, of their obligations to the community which had produced them and protected them. This was in the restless but abundant times before the disillusionment of the Great War, and it seemed to him that definite military training was likely to become less and less necessary in the world. He thought therefore that, although the year or so of service ought still to be exacted because of its moral value, it ought now to be directed to non-belligerent ends, and particularly to such onerous tasks as can never be properly performed by people working merely in order to get wages. For example, for young women there are nursing and many kindred forms of social work, in prisons and asylums, there is the care and cheering of friendless, old and infirm people, and of young children who have no one to look after them, and for the young men all that multitude of police duties, from fire-fighting to fighting pestilence, and from traffic control to gang control, where the individual is necessarily on his honour to give his utmost, his life even, with entire self-forgetfulness. And there are many forms of arduous or dangerous toil, at which it does not become a civilization to keep a man or woman for a lifetime, which could also very well be made into special services.

A constant flow of young conscripts through all these and a multitude of other parallel activities would, it seemed to William James, give such organizations just that "ventilated" quality which would prevent them crystallizing into self-protective systems with a defensive attitude towards the general public—as they do tend to become if the whole personnel is making a life job of the employment. An ennobling quality would be given these services, and the associations of the conscript years would form the basis of later friendships and brotherhoods. Moreover, a large section of the general population would be brought, in this way, into touch with and watchful understanding of the official administrator.

Quite independently of William James, a parallel series of suggestions was made by his Austrian contemporary Joseph Popper (who died at Vienna in 1921 at the age of eighty-three), who is perhaps better known by his pen name of Lynkeus. His suggestion is of an economic conscription to produce all the prime necessities of mankind. He finds that from five to eight years of service will suffice. His chief work is *Die Allgemeine Nahrpflicht Als Losung Der Sozialen Frage* (Universal

Civil Service as the Solution of the Social Problem). His book has not the psychological quality of James's; he sees the problem as a material one. It is not available in an English translation, but an account of his proposals by Fritz Wittels has been translated into English by Eden and Cedar Paul under the title of *An End to Poverty*.

We shall recall these suggestions later when we are dealing with the educational state.

§ 12. *Passive Pacificism**

Our panegyric upon the police and the service type of persona has taken us away from the main issue of the danger of war to modern life, and to that we must now return. We had made a brief review of the existing machinery of government in the world—except only the League of Nations, to which we are soon coming—and we had shown the broad elements in the nature of these seventy-odd organizations, which make towards further war catastrophe. We will now consider the efforts that are being made to avert fresh warfare in the world. *Homo sapiens* is no longer carried mutely from disaster to disaster. He is protesting and using his wits with considerable vigour in the matter. How far has he got towards prevention?

We have insisted in § 3, and we here repeat, that economic war, the White War of peace time, and Red War, when all pretense even of peace is frankly set aside are merely the chronic and acute phases of the same disease—militant nationalism. They constitute one problem. The clue for the effective solution of this supreme riddle lies, we have argued, in the reorientation of loyalties through a realization of the essential unity of our species. In a phrase, loyalties have to be diverted from world subdivision to world union. That will give us a useful criterion by which to judge a great variety of anti-war activities in the world about us.

It would be a complex task to frame a list and classification of the anti-war movements of the present time. They fall into two main divisions. The first of them that will have to be considered may be termed roughly the non-participatory type of movement. The movements of this class base themselves on a resolve to have nothing whatever to do with war, to refuse military service, payment of taxes in wartime and so forth and so on. The more fundamental idea behind such a resolve is the complete renunciation of force in the dealings of

*The fullest and most recent statement of the case for Passive Pacificism is Devere Allen's *The Fight for Peace*.

man with man. But the renunciation of force means the renunciation of positive government. Fundamentally, therefore, in their absolute form, these passive pacificist movements are anarchist movements, and they merely apply the general non-resistance to evil professed by all Christians in their more exalted moments to the special case of war.

The second class of movement is more complex in its methods and less easy to examine and discuss. It looks to political arrangements, international courts, agreements between states, disarmament conventions, tariff unions and federations, to retard, mitigate, and ultimately abolish war. There are many intermediate shades of opinion and resolve between the definitive types of these main classes. Both are compatible with a vigorous agitation for that reform of history teaching, that change in the political basis of the normal persona, upon which so much stress is laid in this work. The new education, it goes without saying, is inherent in either type of proposal.

But before we can take up the positive proposals of our second class which aim at positive measures and laws to emasculate and end war, it will be necessary to make a very careful study of the mentality of the non-participating resister and to understand exactly why he or she takes up this curiously irresponsible attitude. They are very illuminating socially. There are wide differences in the conception of non-participation. There is first, in close approximation to the second group, what we may call conditional non-participation. Associations of various kinds exist whose members pledge themselves not to support their own government in war unless it has made the last possible effort to arbitrate the issue. Other associations go further. They will refuse service in any circumstances because they believe that it takes two governments to make a war, and that it is the business of all governments to avert a catastrophe at any cost. And quite logically they will refuse to receive or impart military training, because they declare war is now impossible without gross blundering on the part of their own government—whatever the enemy government may have done. Moreover, they hold, and perhaps soundly, that a government duly warned of the probable passive defection of considerable sections of its population will pursue a far less aggressive and confident policy than one assured of a unanimous people, ready to leap to arms at the roll of the drum, on no matter what occasion. And as a further step comes the public announcement, so to speak, of one's neutrality in *every* possible war. All these movements must weigh very usefully with governments in making them chary of belligerent gestures, but alone they may not only fail to pre-

vent war, but, it is alleged with some show of reason, they may even
provoke attack from without by weakening the potential resistance to
some more predatory state with a smaller proportion of peace idealists
in its community, or with ruder methods of restraining their propaganda.

After all, unless the whole story of human development told in this
work is wrong, it is by forcible assertion that the will for creative order
has thus far established its rule in the world. Let us not forget that
Education as we shall show later is to a large extent repression—
discipline. There is as much ape as angel in *Homo*. The policeman, not
the saint, is the guardian of freedom in the highways and byways. The
protective function of the militant "services" is not a sham. If it were
not for the potential force of orderly governments the whole world
would be given up to brigandage. Non-resistance has never been of the
slightest use in abolishing brigands. And a modern belligerent state,
waving its aggressive patriotism at its neighbours, boasting of its armaments and clamouring for expansion, differs only in the scale of its
offensiveness from some brigand chief in possession of a Chinese province, and he again from the gangster in a Chicago district. If the
resistance of the reasonable civilized elements in such a brigand state is
inadequate to control its government, it is not simply the right but the
duty of more civilized governments about it to restrain its aggressions.
And surely it is the duty of everyone within that state or without it, to
do whatever is possible to weaken its internal discipline, diminish its
credit and hamper its armament. It is childish to pretend, as so many
non-participatory pacificists do, that all governments are equally belligerent and equally pacificist. It is mere mental laziness to assert as
much. Values cannot be so easily ignored in international politics. The
power most closely associated with the armament industry was the
power most responsible for the war of 1914–18, and ten thousand able
writers cannot alter that. Preparation is aggression, and aggression is
brigandage. Brigandage will cease only when the last brigand is dead
or in the hands of the police. War will be at an end when the last
bellicose sovereign power lays down its arms before the united forces
of civilization. And not before.

These things the passive pacificists ignore with considerable perti-
nacity. And since they are often people of considerable culture and
ability, it is necessary to enquire into the ideology that enables them
to do this.

Their vision of the world seems to be defective in certain particulars.

Many of them seem to be the children of comfortable, secure homes and prosperous parents. There is a failure to realize that human affairs have to be kept going by the positive effort of a number of people. Before the Great War there was a curious feeling in the minds of many, that in spite of the visible armament competition in progress and the extraordinary swayings of European diplomacy, a big European war was unthinkable. There was an irrational persuasion that somewhere, somehow, it was being held off. I shared that baseless feeling. I was one of those pampered children of security. August 4, 1914, was an immense surprise to me, and I believe that a great number of comfortable, prosperous Europeans felt the same astonishment. The guns, of which we had watched the loading, were really going off! Although the forms of danger had been all about us, we had lived in such habitual security all our lives that our thoughts were bedded softly on that reasonless assurance.

It had certainly never occurred to us that we had to do anything in the matter—until the war was upon us. In America the war seemed still more archaic and incredible. Very few people really wanted war, and that had seemed to dispose of the matter. So America came into the war with more internal violence, more social persecution than any other belligerent. The war spirit had to be forced and fostered, or it would not have been adequate.

It is in the nature of all animals, and man is so far an animal, to live tranquilly until the ambushed eater rustles forward to his leap or the pursuer is visibly in sight. The anticipation and prevention of public catastrophe is a recent enterprise of the mind. Formerly the final direction of things public and general was left to Fate or the gods. The natural disposition of man is to keep happy as long as possible by denying the active evil in powerful, but not immediately hostile, things, to leave them alone unchallenged as long as they leave him alone and get what is to be got out of life meanwhile.

A great factor in this inactive pacificism is the disposition of fine and cultivated people to save their minds and lives from the complex distresses the positive prevention and forcible suppression of war adventurers would certainly cause them. There are so many fine, subtle, delicate, interesting and delightful things in life that it is intolerable that one should be forced to occupy good gray matter with these loutish, cruel, stupid, and abominable violences. But war is no more to be ended by saying, "No more war" and "I stand out," and declaring that every government that went into the Great War was just as bad as any other and indeed on the whole worse, than is burglary to be ended by speaking in tones of remonstrance to a policeman who uses his truncheon.

War is a necessary consequence of the political fragmentation of humanity. Until humanity constitutes a political unity, the mass of reasonable people will insist upon preparations for defensive war, and preparations for defensive war are indistinguishable in their nature and moral reactions from preparations for offensive war. There must be the same study and development of new and more dreadful war expedients. The only alternative to belligerent forces in the world is a common repressive and defensive force. Such a force has still with infinite toil and perplexity to be organized. But these passive pacificists seem to believe that in some remote and mystical form such a force exists already and can be invoked.

Let us admit that some of them, put to the test in the Great War, proved their faith in that unknown, unimplemented God of Peace in a very convincing manner. Many of the conscientious resisters were terribly broken in health, 71 died after arrest and 31 lost their reason in Great Britain. I would not because I criticize the efficacy of their methods, throw a doubt upon their courage and consistency.*

§ 13. *The League of Nations and Other Experiments in Internationalism*

We can now take the League of Nations into our account. Some readers will have wanted to consider it before. But for several reasons it has been preferable to glance down the diplomatic gallery, finish with our politicians and the Civil Service and see something of Scientific War before we came to this part of our Museum of Human Activities. We may figure the Peace Section now as a vast unfinished new wing to the collection. Much of that wing has still to be built; it is in the phase of mason's work and scaffolding in the open air, and even the galleries that are glazed and finished with cases and tables and open are far from full. It is through the League of Nations' display that we must pass to the greater possibilities beyond.

It is not really a very impressive display. One may figure it as a little clutter of beginnings amidst great spaces that are still eloquently vacant. It is only natural that it should be like that. The idea of a world League of Nations was unknown before the end of the first decade of

*See *Conscription and Conscience* by John W. Graham. 1922.

this century. The League itself was born in a sudden convulsion of human hope at the end of the Great War.

In the stirring up of men's ideas that resulted from the war catastrophe of 1914–18, there was a real disposition to break away from the competitive military and diplomatic methods that had contributed so greatly to bring about that disaster. There was much talk of "Open Diplomacy" and a phase when certain great political figures, and particularly President Wilson, had manifestly a world-wide appeal. The time seemed ripe for a bold break with the system of competitive independent sovereign states altogether and the establishment of a centralizing Pax Mundi, with the support and approval of the great majority of mankind. The thing seemed possible then. Whether it was really possible no man can say.

In the *Outline of History* we have told of the foundation of the League of Nations and shown how the nineteenth-century sentiment in favour of "little nations" which dominated the imagination of President Wilson, at a time when all the world was crying aloud for Federation, blocked the way to a reversal of the Westphalian tradition. The very name of League implies a binding association. But President Wilson did not pursue that implication. He was perhaps too much of an historian and not enough of a creator. He had surely a vision of what might be, but he was too punctiliously disposed to fit it into ancient and traditional formulæ. He thought not of mankind in chains to nationalism but of little nationalities struggling to be "free." The League of Nations from its birth onward, therefore, was dedicated to national sovereignty, and it was staffed largely by the diplomatic profession. It was to have made the world safe for democracy; it made it safe for more diplomacy. It has never yet recovered from this initial inoculation with the virus of nationalism. Perhaps it never will. It has displayed small power of growth or initiative in the past decade, and it has lost most or all of whatever hold it had taken upon the imaginations of common men. The world looks to it no longer as a beacon of hope.

Yet it was a very important initiative, and it would be premature to consider its possibilities as exhausted. Everyone interested in the present state of human affairs is bound to scrutinize its working and learn whatever it can teach or suggest to us, to be sceptical of its present pretensions and hopeful for its future usefulness.

A very good book on the organization and work of the League of Nations is Howard Ellis's *The Origin, Structure and Working of the League of Nations* (1928); another, *League of Nations; Ten Years of*

World Coöperation, written and published by the Secretariat (1930). A compacter work is Wilson Harris's *What the League of Nations Is.* To these works chiefly we are indebted for the facts we retail here. All these books set out the organization of Geneva in as hopeful a light as possible, and all make the reasons for looking on beyond it now to other unifying processes very clear. The claims and the apologetics of these writers are alike illuminating. A more critical study is H. R. G. Greaves' *The League Committees and World Order* (1931) and a useful treatment from the legal side is Norman L. Hill's *International Administration* (1931).

President Wilson seems to have had no very modern political philosophy. He had a legal rather than a psychological mind; his intelligence was of the nineteenth rather than the twentieth century; and the great opportunities of the time rushed upon him unheralded. And perhaps he was over self-reliant. His mind did not go out readily to others and he was apt to make or attempt to make men of his own calibre, his subordinates or his antagonists, rather than his helpers. The League, as he seems to have conceived it, was a sort of super-federal government, and he planned its constitution on lines that might have been drawn by one of the framers of the American Constitution. As he brought it into existence it was a quasi-parliamentary government of a type such as we have already criticized. It has an Upper and a Lower Chamber. The Assembly is a house of representative delegations from all the constituent countries of the League, each delegation casting one vote. The Council is a gathering with permanent representatives of the greater powers and a limited number of representatives of other states, who come in and go out of the Council at regular intervals.

We will not repeat here the story of Versailles and the subsequent refusal of the American Senate to allow the United States to enter the League. That is given with all the essential particulars in the *Outline of History.*

Once a year, usually in September, this Assembly, this partial parliament of mankind, meets, and the hotels of Geneva are packed with a polyglot multitude. There are not only the delegations from the constituent countries, but a great multitude of camp followers, journalists, publicists and interested people. Geneva becomes the most animated of towns; its quays are crowded, and everybody of consequence in international affairs seems to be hurrying in one direction or the other across the Pont du Mont Blanc. A delegation may consist of as many people as its country chooses to send, but it has only one vote. The

Assembly meets first in full session in an assembly room near the Grand Quai, the Salle de la Réformation, with a sternly Calvinistic gallery for strangers; it debates upon current international issues, resolves itself into a chamber of special committees which report to the concluding plenary session, and after that has been held and the reports have been considered, the tension upon the hotels relaxes again, and the delegations disperse north, east, west and south.

There can be no doubt that so far the Assembly has served a useful purpose for the public discussion of various issues of world importance. It is also commended as a meeting place for the politicians of remote countries, and as a medum for what Howard Ellis calls "hotel diplomacy," that is to say quiet friendly tentatives and undocumented understandings. It has been a convenient instrument for the formal discussion and settlement of various minor clashes in which the issues were not too strongly felt, the cases of frontier violence between Italy and Greece (1923) and Bolivia and Paraguay (1928), for example, and the Mosul frontier delimitation; but as regards War, either what we have described as the incessant White War of tariffs, or the Red War of military preparation and menace, it has proved a very ineffective body indeed. In September, 1931, while the Assembly was actually in session, warfare began between Japan and China. This was the beginning of a series of Japanese aggressions against which the League protested in vain. The reply of Japan to its belated remonstrances was to give notice of withdrawal from the League. In 1933 Germany also gave notice of withdrawal from the League so that only Britain, France and Italy remained as major powers in the Council. And Italy threatens to withdraw unless there is some drastic revision of the League's constitution. At present the League still carries on, with continually ebbing vitality. Even the idea of reconstituting it fails to stir human feeling. It exercises a number of directive functions, but the world's interest in its proceedings has become more and more flaccid with the spreading sense of its essential ineffectiveness. It meets and disperses without any conspicuous excitement in the European or American press. It meets without a splash and sends no thrill throughout the earth. Most people in the world are unaware of its gathering or dispersal.

But behind these parliamentary organs there is the Secretariat, the Civil Service of the League. After our examination of the modern needs and methods of government it is natural that we should turn to this with a very lively curiosity. It is appointed by a Secretary General (M. Joseph Avenol) and the whole staff numbers 680 persons (1933) drawn from nearly fifty different countries. There are a number of sections, Political, Economic and Financial, Transit, Mandated Territories, Disarmament, Health, Social Welfare, Intellectual Coöperation, Information and so on. There is a registry of treaties and various technical and advisory committees, some permanent and some gathered for special tasks, operated in correlation with the permanent sections. No part of this organization has any executive authority. It "studies," it "advises," it prepares material.

Except for leaves and vacations, the Secretariat is always to be found at Geneva. It has been housed in a number of converted hotels; the Hôtel National, which became the first Palais des Nations, being the chief; now special buildings are coming into existence to supplement these first emergency shelters. The personnel of the secretariat is drawn from among the available experts in political science and administration, and the original recommendation of the organizing committee in 1919 was that they should be men and women best qualified to perform the duties assigned to them without taking account of any supposed necessity for selecting persons from different nationalities. Qualifying this was a repudiation of any nation or group of nations monopolizing the staff appointments. Yet, clearly, if some one nation produces all the best experts, there is no sound reason why it should not "monopolize" all the service. "The members of the Secretariat, once appointed, are no longer in the service of their own country but become for the time being exclusively officials of the League. Their duties are not national but international."

It was hoped to develop in the Secretariat an "international" (i. e., a cosmopolitan) mind. But the spirit of national jealousy has never been exorcized from Geneva, and the personnel of the Secretariat is continually disturbed because this or that influential power objects that it is not getting a "fair share" in the official machine.

Now let us take one section of the League's activities and examine the spirit and vigour with which it does its work. Let us take as our sample that "Committee of Intellectual Coöperation" which was originally projected by M. Hymans at the Peace Conference of 1919 and organized in 1922. Unlike various other departments of the League's activities, it is a genuine post-war product; the League's very own.

Here we have a title, at least, which is full of promise. We think at once of a systematic enquiry into all the endless mental activities of mankind that are now calling for and feeling their way towards coöperative unification. The dream of a mightier Encyclopædism rises majestically before us. We think of men of science and influence coördinated to restrain the production of war inventions and to guide the spirit of our race towards unity.

Victor Lefebure, in his *Scientific Disarmament,* reproaches scientific men for the readiness with which they give their knowledge and inventive powers to the ends of national armament. He is particularly concerned by the possibilities of gas warfare. He wants a real pacificist organization of these at present irresponsible and mischievous experts. He wants a new scientific morale in regard to war, a cosmopolitan morale. This would be an obvious objective for a committee of intellectual coöperation throughout the world, but I find no evidence of any such attempt on the part of the existing organization.

The Introduction to this present work, and indeed all our present enterprise, is devoted to one of the main questions that such a committee should undertake, the question of a new education for a new age. The need to make over the schools of the world from the teaching of national to cosmopolitan history has been fairly evident since 1919. One man at least was alive to these great needs, that very original and creative thinker, that typical survivor of the old clear-headed French tradition, M. Léon Bourgeois. As he put it, it was to be a committee "to deal with questions of intellectual coöperation and *education.*" But the Second Assembly, which sanctioned the creation of this new organ, dropped the last two words and left the League with the Committee emasculated. Emasculated for such achievements as this—I quote a passage in the best prospectus style from the Secretariat's own *Ten Years of World Coöperation.*

"The Committee on Intellectual Coöperation consists entirely of persons chosen for their individual eminence in the world of thought. The object of the League in establishing it was to summon to its councils a carefully selected group of the best thinkers of the age drawn from the chief intellectual disciplines. Thus philosophy has been represented by the first chairman, M. Bergson, physics by Dr. Einstein, Mme Curie, Dr. Lorentz, M. Tanakadate, Dr. Hale and his successor Dr. Millikan, and, more recently, by M. Painlevé, Greek studies by Professor Gilbert Murray, literature by M. de Reynold, medicine by M. de Castro, biology by Mlle. Bonnevie and later by Sir Jagadis Bose, the arts by M. Destrée, history by M. Susta and law by Professor Ruffini (succeeded later by M. Rocco) and by M. Mariano H. Cornejo.

"To gather together such an array of talent, representing such a variety of specialisms, countries and intellectual traditions, was in itself no mean achievement, particularly at a moment when the contacts between scholars, which had been interrupted during the war, had not yet been renewed. The mere existence of the Committee has certainly been a considerable moral influence in favour of international understanding."

But did this astounding committee ever really exist—that is to say, as a conference with a purpose? What did it *do?* Nothing apparently for two years. In 1924 it suddenly remembered itself and its promise, and it found a material form as an institute lodged in the Palais Royal in Paris with an income provided by the French government and a staff and a secretary. But it chose to be limited by its terms of reference and displayed no power whatever, of conviction and will to break away from them. It has done nothing commensurate with our original hopes for the League. It has engaged in a few minor activities; the organization of a certain amount of relief for intellectual workers in countries impoverished by currency fluctuations, the exchange of publications between scientific societies, the formation of an "International Committee of Popular Arts"—whatever popular arts may be—and so on. These are very meritorious things to do in their way, but they have no more effect upon the broad intellectual processes of the world than the Council and Assembly have had upon the economic hostilities that impoverish mankind, or upon the gigantic preparations for another great war that are going on so vigorously everywhere. Perhaps the crowning achievement of this committee so far is the Resolution which, greatly daring, it passed in plenary session on July 25, 1931, on the initiative of Professor Murray and M. Painlevé.

"The International Committee on Intellectual Coöperation,
"Considering that the military burdens borne by the different nations render increasingly difficult the studies, the training and even the continued existence of an intellectual class, and thus hamper the intellectual progress of mankind;
"Considering further that the Committee has undertaken and is carrying out the duty of instructing youth in the principles of the League of Nations, of peace and of international coöperation;
"And that the whole development of the League of Nations is closely bound up with the progress of disarmament and of the international conventions ensuring Peace:
"Expresses the ardent hope that the General Conference which is to meet next February will achieve a substantial reduction in the land, sea and air armaments of the world under such conditions as will provide international guarantees for the security of each nation."

After which the banded Intellectuals appear to have slammed down the window very hard and dispersed in a threatening and portentous manner. No armament manufacturer could fail to realize the gravity of their disapproval.

It may be objected that it is not fair to judge the League by one of its feebler departments,* but that department has been taken because it was the League's own child. The International Labour Bureau, which has certainly done good work—and which carries a United States representative—is really only a continuation of the International Association for Labour Legislation founded in 1900, which held annual conferences and brought off such achievements as the Phosphorus Convention of 1906, in pre-war days. The League simply annexed and re-shaped it. It might have grown more vigorously outside the League. The International Court again is claimed as something new. It is, we are told, a "court of justice," and not merely a "tribunal for arbitration," like the Hague Court. That is what is new about it. But how a process in a court which has no power of enforcement whatever can differ from an arbitration is for the lawyers to decide. The pre-war court and the post-war League Court are linked closely together and share the same "Carnegie" Peace Palace at The Hague. The League's share in the business is chiefly an affiliation claim. Various other originally independent international organizations, such as the International Hydrographic Bureau of Monaco, have been brought under the auspices of the League without visible harm or benefit.

But it is not our purpose to indict the League of Nations for its very manifest superficiality and inadequacy. It puts up such claims as it can; the prospectus style of its account of itself was almost unavoidable. It does very little, and it puts a brave face on the matter. There is no touch of deep living pride, of high ambitions or creative imagination in its evasive and diplomatic direction, but in that way it escapes getting into difficulties with resentful governments. It might have been the rebellious heir of the old order, and it has become its clerk-valet. It does not lead the way to unity, but at times it makes a deferential and perhaps directive movement towards unifying courses. It has immobilized and killed that wide and dangerous desire, as it must have seemed to all diplomatists and most politicians, for a world super-government, that flamed out in men's minds in 1918. That desire may flame again as our

*For a criticism of the economic side of the League see H. R. G. Greaves, *The League Committees and World Order.* Another short and readable book criticizing the League is *Must the League Fail* by L. A. Zimmern.

troubles thicken, but one may doubt whether it will flame upon the Geneva altar.

Let us rather accept the League for what it is and for what it may be. It is a small achievement if we measure it by the scale upon which any real intellectual, economic and political consolidation of human affairs must be attempted, but it is an achievement. It is a ripple in the advancing tide of unifying realization. It is a useful, if modest, permanent addition to the governmental resources of mankind. If it is not the home of unity, it is for awhile a convenient postal address. It has been and is, and it may well continue to be, a point for assignations, for enquiries and meetings, and the preparation of more effective co-operations. It may play the rôle of a matrix for the casting of organizations wider in scope and more powerful than it can ever be. It will be serviceable in just the measure that it transmits, and it will be objectionable just so far as it attempts to arrest, control, annex and claim credit for, the unifying forces of the world.

THE RED CROSS

But now let us look at certain other experiments in internationalism, less pretentious than the League but possibly more illuminating in the way in which they have contrived to transcend nationalist limitations. Senior among these is the Red Cross. The Red Cross was founded by Henri Dunant in 1862, for the assistance of the wounded in war; it was begotten by his book, *Souvenirs de Solférino,* describing the horrible condition of things upon that battlefield. It has had Geneva for its headquarters since its inception and its International Committee treats with governments and with the League almost as if it were an independent sovereign power. It has sustained objections to various war cruelties. Its arrangements for the repatriation of prisoners after the Great War were ably executed, and it has recently developed a special "International Relief Union" for the prompter assistance of populations stricken by famine, earthquake or the like sudden disasters. Its work in sustaining a world standard of nursing and of medical material has been of inestimable value. It is a federation of national societies which among them all count somewhere about 17,000,000 members.

THE INTERNATIONAL INSTITUTE OF AGRICULTURE

Another very remarkable and important international experiment, which has the status of a sovereign power making actual treaties with governments, is the International Institute of Agriculture in Rome. This was the creation of an American, a man, as the world must some day admit, of a very wide economic and political vision, David Lubin. His object was to establish a continual survey of world production, a perennial census organization, first of food products and then of other staples, in relation to world consumption. Conventions were made in 1905 between Lubin and forty countries representing 90 per cent of the world's population, by which they agreed to furnish reports and subsidies to his institute. A special treaty was signed with the Italian government of Victor Emmanuel for the establishment of the Institute in a palace built for it by that monarch in the Villa Borghese. There it set to work. Its operations were shattered for a time by the Great War and Lubin never saw it restored to effective world influence. On the day that the main avenues of Rome were beflagged, crowded and lined with troops to receive President Wilson, fresh from the triumphs of Versailles, Lubin's obscure funeral was making its way by back streets to the cemetery.

It is only now that this potential economic world organ of his is struggling back to a functional existence. But the world agricultural census of 1930–31, which it has in hand at the time of writing, is evidence of its returning vitality. It has initiated congresses on meteorology, plant diseases and locust control, and collaborated on occasion both with the League of Nations and the International Labour Office. In the long run we may find that this institute, the International Red Cross and the modest bureau of the Postal Union at Berne—also sustained by contributions from all the countries of the world—are types of world coöperation more flexible and practicable than that rather old-fashioned pseudo-parliament at Geneva, with its upper and lower houses, its dreadful polyglot debates and its pervading diplomatic atmosphere. It is highly undesirable that these older tested experiments in internationalism should suffer incorporation with the League, or that the League should obstruct by any officious intervention the development of the many other similar federal organizations, the growing need for world action in such matters as disarmament and monetary and financial unifications, may evoke.

THE BANK OF INTERNATIONAL SETTLEMENTS AT BASLE

We have already noted in Chapter IX, § 10, the growing realization of the need to put finance (and possibly monetary affairs) upon a cosmopolitan footing. Very important in the development of this realization is the Bank of International Settlements set up in 1930 at Basle. Its ostensible objective was the handling and distribution of the payment of German reparations for the Great War of 1914–18. But from the beginning it was impossible to ignore the wider possibilities of any such institution, and it is already growing very remarkably beyond its original functions. It is empowered to assist in credit operations necessary for the development of countries arrested in their economic development. In other words, it is free, if it can, to weave together the highly industrialized countries of northwestern Europe into one economic system with the still mainly rural countries of the southeast. It has necessarily become a meeting place for the bankers of various countries and a centre of expert discussion. Its possibilities are enormous. Already there are attempts to evolve side by side with it a huge investment trust to lubricate the working of national industries throughout the world. A third possible member of this profoundly interesting embryo of a world business control is an international mortgage bank to irrigate the agricultural production of financially weak states by long term cosmopolitan lending.

Professor Gustav Cassel, the distinguished Swedish economist whose warnings against deflation before 1923–24 have been so amply justified by events, finds these international organizations insufficient in themselves. He supports a scheme, recently drawn up by representatives of the Bank of England, for a much bolder and larger international institute directing floating capital towards permanent investment, and organizing the central banks so as to coöperate in a radical and general reduction of interest upon those short-term loans which have played so large a part in the financial convulsions of the immediate past. (Chapter IX, § § 11 and 12.)

That is as much as we can say as yet of this new cosmopolitan banking. When, in a few years' time, this book is revised for a new edition, these paragraphs here may have to undergo a very considerable expansion. We may have to tell then of a world nucleus at least as important as the League itself.

OTHER INTERNATIONAL BODIES

Another international organ whose bureau is now seated at Geneva which has done very useful educational and organizing work, is the Inter-Parliamentary Union founded in 1888 by William Randal Cremer and Frédéric Passy. It holds annual conferences of cosmopolitan-minded members of parliament in various cities. At the Berlin Conference in 1928, 475 members representing 38 different countries assembled. And there is an International Bureau of Education with a constitution and an international status like the International Institute of Agriculture; it has been recently organized and as yet only a few countries have taken a share in it. So far it is no more than a poor timid, conferring body, afraid, it would seem, even of contemporary ideas. The blight of sentimental nationalism that cripples the Institute of International Co-operation manifestly lies upon it. Furthermore, there exist a multitude of purely propaganda organizations of a more or less thoroughly cosmopolitan trend, of which the British League of Nations Union and the Carnegie Endowment for International Peace under the presidency of Mr. Nicholas Murray Butler may be taken as samples. The latter organization distributes large funds, its publicity is wide and thorough, and the name of Nicholas Murray Butler has become a household word throughout the earth. With the International of Coöperatives we have already dealt in Chapter VII.

GENEVA AS A RENDEZVOUS OF SCHEMES

As an informal consequence of the establishment of the League of Nations at Geneva a multitude of voluntary organizations of every grade of scope and quality have concentrated upon the Lake. These too help to measure the scale of the League of Nations effort. Every question that has a world significance receives attention in this "Geneva outside the League," from the propaganda of Esperanto and the advocacy of suchlike artificial languages, to conferences on the bearing of sexual custom and hygiene upon population and international stresses. There are numerous organizations outside the pale which conduct enquiries and watch and seek to stimulate the League administration. Some act as centres for propaganda on behalf of the authority of the League. They have conferences; they sit in rooms talking, they constitute and reconstitute their societies, and no doubt they play a helpful part in maintaining international if not cosmopolitan ideals in a discouraged world. Many of the most active spirits in this outer circle at Geneva are wealthy Americans; many are less opulent students and enquirers seeking opportunity.

It is natural that a certain number of picturesque eccentrics should also be attracted to the lakeside to complete the picture. They walk on the quays, they cross the bridge to and fro, they wear rather distinctive costumes and carry important-looking portfolios.

Geneva is an interesting convergence of hopes and projects and pretensions, but if it is to be regarded as the sole centre and culmination of the organizing as opposed to the disintegrating forces in world politics, it is not a cheering resort for those who have any sense of the magnitude and urgency of the dangers which threaten our precarious civilization.

Happily Geneva is not all. Geneva is merely a rendezvous for a certain number of people who have been brought there or attracted thither by the expression it gives to creative forces that are at work everywhere. If Geneva and all that centres upon Geneva and the League were destroyed to-morrow, it would be a grave, but not an irreparable loss to mankind. These forces would find another rendezvous. The drive towards unification is in the logic of human association; it is the primary fact of history and social life.

§ 14. *Projects for Cosmopolitan Synthesis: Necessity Drives Us towards World Controls*

A distrust of the League's utility in the larger functions for which it was contrived is manifestly felt by most experienced politicians and statesmen. Ever since 1923 they have betrayed their dissatisfaction with the League by a search for supplementary devices to avert or mitigate war—whether White or Red.

It would need a long chapter of modern history to survey these supplementary efforts, from the Washington Disarmament Conference and Locarno, to the Kellogg Amphictyony and the proposals of M. Briand for a United States of Europe. It is necessary to distinguish clearly between such mere sentimental gestures as the Kellogg Pacts, however magnificent, and practical efforts to coöperate on super-national lines, however modest.

Perhaps the most hopeful element in all these post-war projects, conferences and the like, is their persistent resumption. There is a widespread uneasiness in the human mind that no fatuous renunciation of war "as a method of policy" will allay. Indefinable, various and universally dispersed urgencies are worrying the attention of our species towards some effectual unification, in spite of all the heavy thrust of tradition towards further conflicts.

Along one line of experiment we may note the various tentatives that have been made towards economic federations (with, of course, the correlative of military alliances) on a super-national scale. That may be as good a way as any of getting past the patriotic pickets. It may be true that Human Unity is too remote for a single imaginative stride. Pan-Europa seems, at the first glance at any rate, more practicable than Cosmopolis. Let us accept any proposal to go halfway there, in the sure conviction that once we are upon the road, we shall find our projected super-national combination no more than a wayside inn for the final political home-coming of mankind. M. Briand's scheme for the "United States of Europe,"* British projects for "Empire Free Trade,"† the reality of Pan-America,‡ the dream of an Anglo-Saxon alliance, and the like, may all serve a greater purpose. They may all help to break down the spirit of national and local egotism and to turn men's minds not simply to the possibility but the need of larger systems of co-operation. While such suggestions are materializing as negotiations and haggling their way to realization, the secular process of material liaison will continue its apparently inexorable advance and reinforce these suggestions by a multitude of practical confirmations.

None of these projects is very original. There have been schemes for the pacific unification of Europe since the days of Henri of Navarre. The Holy Alliance was an attempt to bring into European affairs the conception of a regal family, and Sir Charles Waldstein was advocating a United States of Europe project right up to the outbreak of 1914. No doubt a group of intelligent monarchs might have contrived a European merger at any time in the last two hundred years, but unhappily very few European monarchs in the last two hundred years have been even moderately intelligent, several have been stupidly and aggressively militarist, and most have clung like limpets to the romantic patriotic traditions on which their importance rests.

These practical proposals for political unifications we have considered, these unions, federations, empire free-trade systems and Zollvereins, are all attempts to achieve a partial unification of human interests geographically. But partial unification of human interests can also be arranged by function rather than region. World controls, it may be, are to be built up bit by bit. The world Postal Union, the International Institute of Agriculture, the International Labour Office, the Red Cross, are all examples of real cosmopolitan organs, working very efficiently for

*Based on R. N. Coudenhove Kalergis's *Pan Europa* (1923).

†See Lord Beaverbrook: *Case for Empire Free Trade*.

‡See C. E. Hughes: *Pan-American Peace Plans* (1930).

certain specific ends. Since the war the League of Nations may have obstructed rather than helped the development of further specific organizations of this type by its claim to be *the* international factotum. But, after all, such special conventions first for this end and then for that, may be the easier and better way to get past the Nationalist sentinels. The League was imposed upon the world by men whose imaginations were obsessed by the image of a legislative assembly in which politicians like themselves would play the leading rôles; they did not realize that world affairs may be handled and perhaps must be handled, by methods quite different from those of any modern sovereign government. Yet we may have a unified world securely at peace without either a president or a parliament of mankind. And even with most or all the old kings and presidents still robed and enthroned amidst their local gilding. There are possibilities of mediatizing the sovereign governments of the world bit by bit, with an extremely small amount of visible infringements of sovereignty.*

Consider first the problem of disarmament. The statesmen and diplomatists manœuvre and distinguish themselves, trust—I believe vainly—to the mercy of history for a favourable posthumous press, and achieve nothing of material importance. But manifestly no effectual disarmament is possible without, first, a world convention to take the armament industry out of the hands of profit-makers altogether,† and secondly, a permanent body, a commission, a convention, call it what you will, to watch, coördinate and restrain the armament of all the states party to the convention. Disarmament will remain the most ineffective of "gestures" until that International Armament Commission is in permanent authority. Sooner or later, if civilization is to go on, it *must* exist. The League of Nations is itself quite unsuitable for the function. The utmost the League can do is to facilitate and not hinder the establishment of that overriding body. And as soon as such a commission comes into being it will begin to develop its own personnel, and the world will begin the business of getting accustomed to and having confidence in its operations.

Next let us consider the growing realization throughout the world

---

*A good pre-war book on this subject, still well worth a student's attention, is L. S. Woolf's *International Government* (1916). A modern book (1931) which also sets out very plainly the large amount of international organization prior to and outside of the League machinery is Keith Clark's *International Communications: The American Attitude.*

†See *The Secret International. Armament Firms at Work,* published by the Union of Democratic Control, London.

that the economic distresses of our time are world stresses and that there is no hope of restoring and maintaining prosperity throughout the world except through cosmopolitan action. In this field, again, there may be a rapid acceleration of activities, as economic and social troubles increase. We have already noted in § 13 the extreme significance of the Bank for International Settlements at Basle and the buds it already bears. Its development into a real cosmopolitan organ is probable. Here, in another system of interests almost independent of the disarmament issues, we may presently find people adopting different agencies and different methods and working their way towards some sort of International Currency and Credit board. One can see that coming into existence by itself without any exacerbation of Nationalist feeling. It would need a considerable staff of its own even from the beginning. And from the beginning it could be in communication with the Disarmament Board.

The League of Nations Commission of Enquiry for European Union (1931), with its subcommittee on organization, with its examination of the world economic crisis, its projects for the international transmission of electric power and international coöperation in production, is an interesting preliminary exploration (within the limitations of the League) of the possibility of getting past political boundaries in economic matters.

Any such world boards or commissions would necessarily bring together into effective coöperation considerable contingents of the civil services of the various states. They would acquire ultra-national attitudes of mind. The foundations of a real world civil service, independent of national politics, would be assembled and laid. (Already, indeed, at Geneva, the League of Nations has a little rudimentary "world civil service" of five or six hundred employees.)

In § 12 we have already raised the possibility of international boards for the administration and control of *"macédoines"* of mixed populations and for a Geneva consular service. What we are suggesting here links very closely with the discussion in that section.

The Red Cross again could expand its work by degrees to become an effectual control of world health, no patriot objecting, and it could extend modern conceptions of sanitary regulation throughout the world. There are similar possibilities of development in the International Institute of Agriculture which might easily be associated with the Bank for International Settlements at Basle and the projected International Bank for Business Credits and the International Mortgage Bank in one great scheme of world statistics and world bookkeeping. Those who are acquainted with the writings of David Lubin will know that his ideas went far beyond the range of a mere bureau of statistics. He wanted not only a census of needs and production, but also a survey and control of methods of distribution. His own experiences as a merchant in America had impressed him with the primary significance of freights in trading, and one of his still undeveloped ideas was a progressive upward extension of the work of the world's post office, from letters and postcards to parcels of increasing bulk, until all the shipping and all the interstate transport of the world were brought into one tariffed scheme. Is a development of that foundation in Rome until it becomes a census and control—"control" because knowledge is power—not only of agricultural production but of all staple production *and distribution* also, an unthinkable thing? It would be something much less showy but infinitely more real than a world parliament.

An International Conservation Board, as the *Science of Life* shows, is already urgently needed for the protection of natural resources now being wasted, and particularly for the protection of many species of animals and plants threatened with speedy extinction. In less than a hundred years, while the statesmen and diplomatists wrangle, most of the forests of the world may be destroyed. Many smart men of business may make large fortunes out of the process, and that no doubt will reconcile them at least to living on a balder planet.

All these varied strands of world organization could be woven independently of one another, provided that we release our minds from the suggestion that now it is only through the straight and narrow way of the League of Nations that such things are to be attained. And another great power could be evoked if that Institute of Intellectual Coöperation could be rescued from the petty aims and the ridiculous nationalist ideology that affect it like a disease, and made an independent organization, open and accessible to all who are concerned in the intellectual processes of mankind. The original educational objectives of M. Léon Bourgeois could then be restored, and the vitally important task of examining, protesting against, controlling and ultimately suppressing patriotic and belligerent teaching throughout the world could be undertaken with some hope of success.

Later on (in Chapter XV) we shall return to the possibility that this Committee of Intellectual Coöperation might assist or direct the production of World Year Books and a World Encyclopædia.

Towards all these various ends people are working now. Every one of these desiderata carries with it vast possibilities of international con-fluence between public services and of international confluence between educational organizations. All such projects for world-wide special boards and services march side by side not only with each other but also with political projects for confederations and economic alliances, towards unity. The two types of coalescence, the geographical and the functional, are not in conflict. Together these two sorts of movement already constitute a very impressive array of devices, possibilities and hopes.

The greatest danger to such hopes seems to lie in the years immedi-ately ahead. All this experimenting and muddling towards world organization takes time. Meanwhile the old traditions remain very strongly established—in the legal forms of government, in social habit, in our schools. Particularly in our schools. The armament firms remain. They have not yet been brought to heel. The press, ignorant and short-sighted, is still very largely on the side of mischief.

This search for the methods of a world pax is essentially an intel-lectual matter, a psychological problem; it is an attempt to save mankind for the insane obsessions of patriotism; it is a race of educa-tion to avert another and greater catastrophe. The fundamental thing in human association is and always has been education; for what our education is, that also is our social organization and the quality of our lives.*

*The student who wishes to expand the matter of this and the preceding sections should read A. C. F. Beales' *History of Peace*.

CHAPTER THE THIRTEENTH

THE NUMBERS AND QUALITIES OF MANKIND

§ 1. *The Increase of the World's Population*

W E CAN now take up another important aspect of the lives of these nineteen hundred million inhabitants of the human anthill: their multiplication. That multiplication continues as I write. In the last minute the grand total has increased by twenty. It has been increasing for a long time, for several centuries. It is increasing now by about eleven million yearly. It may never have been nearly so great in any previous time.

Is this human population too great? Is it already consuming more of the available resources than nature renews? Or is it rapidly approaching that state of affairs? In a hundred years' time (A. D. 2031), at its present rate of increase it will number 4,000 millions. In two hundred years, 8,000 millions, in three hundred years 16,000 millions. These are overwhelming figures, the forecast of a stupendous breeding storm.

The answers to the questions we have asked here are discussed at greater length in the *Science of Life* and we have also approached these issues in Chapter IV, § 4 of this work. The earth is not fecund without limit, and in some of the needed alimentary substances it is even parsimonious. It seems, for example, to be grudging in its supply of phosphorus. The present great multitude of our own species is not now feeding upon the spontaneous gifts of our planet as other creatures are. Earth's gifts to us are in part already forced gifts. We depend on fertilizers for the fodder of our meat supply and for our vegetable food. And there is a limit to the supply of fertilizers. Every year the pressure on that supply increases. If the expansion of population continues, a time will come, whatever our efforts, when our species will return to the normal condition of most other species; that is to say, it will return to universal want and to a competition for bare subsistence.

In some parts of the world, in parts of Bengal, for example, humanity is now already at that level of bare subsistence. The peasants are so cheap that it does not pay to give them adequate protection against

594

wild beasts. It does not pay. Every year hundreds of them* are eaten by leopards, tigers and other carnivora. Man-eating beasts will come into their villages and carry off people in the night from their houses. Locks, bolts and bars cost money, and peasants cost nothing. They possess barely any clothing or furnishings, and though they breed abundantly, their rate of increase is kept down by their weakness and high mortality.

In a little while men of science may be in a position to estimate exactly what human population this earth can carry and go on carrying, at a tolerable level of existence, at a level of freedom, happiness, variety, direct relations to wild nature and full and complete living. At present such estimates are based upon insufficient assumptions; they are of no practical value. That estimated "optimum" of population, when we get it, may turn out to be above or below our present numbers, and it will certainly vary widely with what is taken as the standard of life. American authorities have put it as low as 350 million.† No doubt the earth could carry at a level of bare subsistence, for a few dismal decades, an enormously greater population of degraded human beings than 1,900 million. Some authorities go as high as 7,000 million. But who wants that? However high or low our standard may be, it will still leave us face to face with the facts that there is a limit to human increase and that it can be regulated and restrained or within certain limits encouraged and stimulated.

Since the time of Malthus it has generally been assumed that the human animal, like most other animals, has a reproductive urge sufficiently strong to keep its numbers pressing steadily upon the means of subsistence. But the readiness with which almost any human community to which the necessary knowledge was made available, has accepted and acted upon the suggestion of Birth Control, throws an increasing doubt upon that assumption. In various European countries, without any compulsion or any great pressure, merely through rising standards of life and the disinclination to bring children into the world at a disadvantage, the "natural" increase of the population has been checked and even converted into a decrease.

There are many interesting subtleties about the statistics of population into which we cannot enter very fully here, but, roughly stated, between 1876 and 1926 the birth rates of various European countries

---

*1794 in 1927.

†See *Nature*, February 7, 1931, p. 217. Account of discussion of American Society of Naturalists, New Year's Day, 1930; Professors W. F. Ogburn and E. M. East.

have fallen as follows: England and Wales 36.3 to 17.8 (16.3 in 1930); Germany 40.9 to 20.7; Italy 39.2 to 27.8; Sweden 30.8 to 16.9 and New Zealand 41.0 to 21.1. These are birth rates per thousand living at the time, and it is obvious that New Zealand, which was subjected to a steady immigration of people round about the age of marriage, was in a very different position from Great Britain, from which such young people were emigrating in considerable numbers during the last quarter of the nineteenth century. The New Zealand fall is really more striking than these figures at the first glance suggest. The British is less so. Yet, though such considerations mitigate or intensify the crude facts, they do not do so enough to alter their essential significance.

This fall in the birth rate has been accompanied by a fall in the death rate which has minimized its effect upon population totals. The figures for the countries just named are England and Wales 20.9 to 11.6 (11.5 in 1930); Germany 26.3 to about 11.9; Italy 28.8 to about 16.8; Sweden 19.9 to 11.8 and New Zealand 11.8 to 8.7. This gives an apparent fall in the rate of increase of population of all these countries of about 9 per thousand in the case of England and Wales, 7 in the case of New Zealand and similarly for the others. Had the death rate not fallen also, the "natural increase" would have been wiped out altogether and re-placed by an actual fall. During the period we are considering, the progress of hygiene saved so many infants that would otherwise have perished, and prolonged the life of so many people beyond middle age who would have died under earlier conditions, that the falling off at the source did not produce anything like its full effect upon the aggregate numbers. (The infant mortality for England and Wales sank to the record figure of 60 per 1,000 births in 1930.) It is only the saving of infant lives that has a real continuing effect on population. They will live and reproduce, but the increased proportion of people over the age of forty-five (from 18 to 25 per cent in twenty years in Great Britain) will add little or nothing to subsequent generations. The actual state of affairs is better displayed in another form. The number of children under fifteen in Great Britain in 1921 was no greater than in 1891; the number of scholars in Public Elementary schools in England and Wales reached its maximum in 1915 and has declined steadily ever since. In 1881, 883,600 children were born in England and Wales; in 1924 only 729,900.

So far as gross numbers are concerned, the problem of overpopulation is evidently not an insurmountable one. As modern civilization spreads a rising standard of life about the world, the fall of the birth rate goes with it. The full effects of a fall in the birth rate take some time to make themselves felt. If the birth rate in Great Britain remains at its present level, the population will cease to increase in about ten years' time and will then begin to diminish. No further cut in the birth rate is therefore needed in order to bring about a reduction of the population in the near future. The same holds good of all the countries of Northern and Western Europe.

Partly this falling off of births is due to a retardation of marriage, but nearly all authorities are agreed that it is due mainly to what is now known throughout the world by Margaret Sanger's term of Birth Control. This is the deliberate avoidance of offspring (by methods discussed more fully in the *Science of Life*), particularly during the earlier and formerly the most fertile years of married life (i. e., between twenty-five and thirty-five). This was first noticeable among the French peasants in the closing years of the eighteenth century and they adopted it to prevent the excessive division of their land. It has since become a general practice throughout the modernized Atlantic communities.

Its onset follows a practically uniform course as industrialism progresses, and as production and the standard of life rise. To begin with, in the ugly and "sweating" stage of industrial employment there is a phase of multiplication, and only after that does this brake come into action. The first result of modern industrialism in its cruder and crueller phases has always been to produce relative plenty at the price of onerous labour conditions. Anyone could "get a living" under the new régime, though it is a bare living of the most miserable sort. Previously there had been plain starvation. The new factory workers, ignorant, at a low level of subsistence, mostly young and thrown together with few restraining influences, were practically unable to avoid reproducing their kind. The first result of industrialization therefore was to foster a multiplication of the low grades of population. A rapid increase went on in Great Britain from the first appearance of factory manufacture in the eighteenth century up to the seventies of the nineteenth. Only then did a checking influence appear. Great Britain is the type instance in these matters. The story of the other industrialized countries upon the Atlantic, though it is not strictly parallel, is essentially similar, and the rest of the world's populations seem likely to follow these precedents one after another as industrialization reaches them; first will come proliferation through improved sanitation and increased production, then retardation.

The opening phase of proliferation has occurred in Japan and in the

modernized industrial centres of India and China. In Japan, population which had been practically stationary for a century (between 1723
and 1846) at about 29 million, leapt up with the extensive adoption of
European methods of production to its present congestion of 60 million. Japan is now, as Carr-Saunders has pointed out, in practically the
same phase as Great Britain in 1875, and there is no reason to suppose
she will not presently follow the other modernized countries towards
a reproductive arrest. This is the more probable since her people do not
emigrate readily to uncongenial climates, and most attractive emigration
areas are closed to them. They will feel the pressure the sooner for that
and resort to restriction sooner.*

We are still very ignorant of the state of affairs in China as a whole.
India, from the point of view of population, is a quite abnormal mass
of human beings. The heavy, protective paternalism of the British has
maintained a state of peace, prevented disease and famine, the natural
checks upon numbers in a barbaric community, and yet has done hardly
anything to educate or raise the standard of living of this multitude.
The Indian population in 1921 was 318,942,480. It had increased in spite
of an abnormal influenza mortality by 3,780,000 since 1911, and it continues to press upon the means of subsistence. Over the forty-nine years
from 1872, the date of the first (incomplete) Indian census, to 1921,
after making allowances for addition to area and improved methods of
enumeration, the real rate of increase has been about 20 per cent, or
an average of 4.1 per cent per decade, or .41 per cent per annum. The
increase from 1921–1931 however has been at the rate of 1.06 per cent
per annum, which approaches Italy with 1.1 per cent and New Zealand
with 1.24 per cent. The population of Russia, which probably declined
in the terrible early days of the Revolution is now (Chapter X, § 8) said
to be sweeping forward at the rate of three and three quarter millions
per annum, but these figures are subject to grave suspicion. It is doubtful whether there are at present any exact vital statistics for large regions
of Russia. Evidently we are dealing with very irregular movements
everywhere. An epidemic, a phase of economic or political disorder, a
change in social life, can reverse these increases very quickly. The proportion of Indians to the rest of the world's population is not increasing, or it is increasing only very slightly, and the uneasy multitudes of
China have probably an extremely low net increase at the present time.
India and China may be going forward in the population race, but the
European and American communities are still going forward also as

*See *The Japanese Population Problem,* by W. R. Crocker.

1931

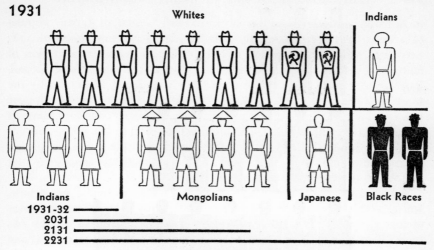

Whites Indians

Indians Mongolians Japanese Black Races

Indians
1931-32
2031
2131
2231

TOTAL POPULATION

2231

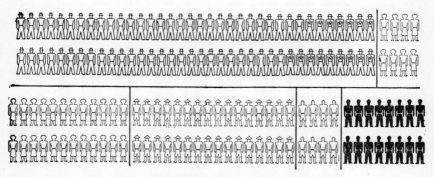

THE PROBLEM OF POPULATION

THE diagram at the top shows the present racial distribution of the people of the earth. The lower diagram, drawn within the same area, shows the crowding of populations three hundred years from now, provided that the present rate of increase is not checked. In both cases the figure of each man represents one hundred million people. The lower diagram indicates the tremendous overcrowding which increasing population will bring.

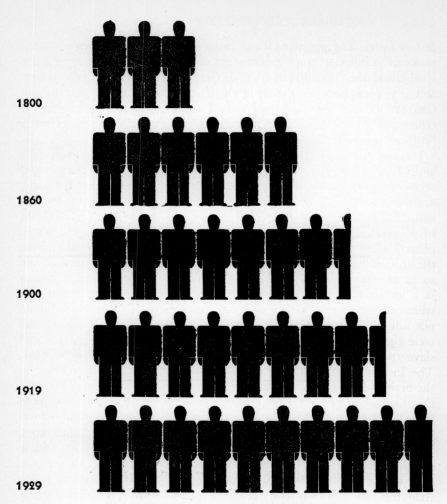

1800

1860

1900

1919

1929

THE GROWTH OF POPULATION

How the world's population has grown through the last century. Each figure of a man represents 200,000,000 persons.

fast or faster. The popular idea of India and China as great overflowing tanks of population ready to burst upon the rest of the world is quite a mistaken one. The "Rising Tide of Colour" is a scaremonger's fantasy. But it is constantly appearing in the discussion of these questions. In Chapter VII we have described a cruel and systematic depopulation of equatorial Africa during this current century which is all against a "colour" predominance.

It is not our affair here to speculate about the possible future of India and China. Both regions are manifestly in a phase of great change and reconstruction. But it is as reasonable as not to assume that the same economic and social forces that have brought, or are bringing, the advanced communities of the world nearer and nearer to a stabilization of population, will ultimately become operative throughout the whole planet. As the obsession of jealously competitive nationalism lifts from the still crazy mind of our race, there may even be a concerted return to an ascertained optimum lower than 1,900 millions. The lean Indian in a loincloth, living in a hut with a cow-dung floor, who tethers his worn-out cow on the jungle edge for the tiger to kill, because he must not kill her himself, is no more a permanent actor in the world spectacle than were the British savages in woad, or the Arab pirates and slave traders who raided the coasts of Provence in the Middle Ages. The Indian ryot is not there forever. The stuff that will be stirring in the brains of his grandchildren may be so different from that in his own, that his way of living may have become an almost incredible horror to them.

We are too chary with our imaginations about modern possibilities. The forces of modernization have still to play upon those Indian peasant swarms. The elementary school, the newspaper, the cinema, have not yet brought home to them that there are other ways of living than the routines they still accept as the inevitable formula for life. There has been a certain drift of a few millions altogether from the countryside to the dreadful factories of Calcutta, Bombay and Cawnpore, where conditions recalling Lancashire at its worst phase have been produced, but the greater part of that immense village population, so poor, so weak, so monotonous in its toil and debt and hunger, remains intact. A few decades of native administration may restore the vital balance to the stability of pre-British days.

So we put the vast sad sunlit plains of Bengal and its hundreds of millions toiling only to eat sparsely, into the background of our general survey of human activities. They are playing only a passive part in the drama. They are living, as it were, in a dream, and it is impossible to anticipate in what fashion the call of creative energy will presently awaken them to take up a positive rôle in our renascent world.

So far as present conditions go unless some outbreak of war upon a large scale dislocates the balance there does not seem any probability worth considering of very great change in the proportions of the human population in the years immediately before us. The total in hundreds of millions is rising towards 20; of these about 7 will be the children of the Europeans and Americans at present living under the modern capitalist system, of which seven, two will be English speaking; there will be 2 deriving from the present Soviet republics; 4 from the Indian mass and 5 Mongolian, of which something approaching 1 may be Japanese. There are thus 9 out of the 20, of what we may call the already Europeanized peoples, or 10 if we count in the Japanese. Two hundred million (or fewer) black people, chiefly in Africa, will complete the total. These are the great blocks which have to be built together into the coming world state. As their economic lives assimilate, their vital statistics are likely to move in unison, and the rate of increase or diminution become the same throughout the planet. There may be fluctuations in these proportions, but there does not seem to be the slightest probability that any section will be "swamped" by any other.

It is interesting to note how few are the people who may be considered answerable for the very great changes in the pressure of the more civilized populations we have just been considering. Until the last quarter of the nineteenth century birth control was a secret and shameful practice, known to occur but never discussed except to be disavowed or denounced. A few obscure societies, whose publications were in constant danger of prosecution, maintained what was then called the doctrines of Neo-Malthusianism in a world that feigned to ignore them. They had been active for three quarters of a century. Birth-control handbills were circulated in Manchester in 1823, it is believed at the instance of Francis Place, and books advocating birth control were published in America, the *Moral Physiology* of Dale Owen in 1830 and Dr. Knowlton's *Fruits of Philosophy* in 1833. *The Elements of Social Science* was published in London by Dr. George Drysdale in 1854.

The new views spread widely but quietly. They found their maximum application at first in France. They were talked over and applied more and more extensively, but it was left for quite a small number of resolute people to break the obscurantist convention and bring this fundamentally important issue in human affairs into the full light of open discussion. They did so under the provocation and threat of new prohibitive legislation, particularly of the laws passed by Congress and various state legislatures in America at the instance of Anthony Comstock's "Society for the Suppression of Vice." Anthony Comstock was not exactly the parent, but he was the stimulant of modern popular birth control. The pioneers for outspokenness in the English-speaking world were Charles Bradlaugh and Mrs. Besant, whose defiant republication of Dr. Knowlton's *Fruits of Philosophy* in 1877, and their subsequent prosecution, make indeed an epoch in human biology. A marked fall in the English birth rate followed this trial. The battle for the frank popularization of this kind of knowledge was fought and won in America by Mrs. Margaret Sanger, and in England by Dr. Marie Stopes. Margaret Sanger was a hospital nurse who had specialized in obstetric nursing. "During fourteen years of nursing in the homes of the New York poor," she writes, "I was brought face to face with such unbelievable misery that I reached the point where I could no longer face my own conscience without devoting myself to the relief of that misery at its source." Although she was happily married and the mother of three children, she embarked boldly and methodically upon a campaign first for the publicity of the issue, and then for its scientific development. Both she and her husband were imprisoned under the repressive Comstock Law—she twice—and she fought a stormy battle before she could win over public opinion to a rational attitude in the matter. Dr. Marie Stopes was a young doctor of science and a botanist of some distinction, who plunged into a parallel conflict in England, moved by the same pity for feminine wretchedness. England has had no Comstock, and it was not necessary for her to go to prison. Now in the English-speaking world at least, thanks mainly to these two valiant women, we may all talk, think and write without embarrassment of this quintessential of human biology.

But this freedom is not universal. In France and Italy, for example, the public discussion of birth control has been prohibited under penalties. In South Ireland also. Married women, in these countries, are in effect to be forced to bear children whether they want to do so or not. This does not prevent a fall in the birth rate in all three countries, but that fall is the result of forbidden knowledge, and it is associated with the utmost furtiveness, dirtiness, and shame. Indoor domestics, even when they are young married people, contrive to be as sterile in these lands of mystery as elsewhere, and the wife of the labourer and small shopkeeper no longer bears children until she dies exhausted in the good old fashion—whatever the authorities may forbid. But no one dare tell openly what is done. In France this obscurantism is by no means absolute. Those greater and better concepts of intellectual and personal freedom which are so inextricably interwoven in the French tradition, war against any such limitations of knowledge, and by way of medical and scientific conferences, more and more freely reported, and such courageous books as Victor Margeuritte's *Ton Corps est à Toi,* the possibilities of birth control are kept before the general mind.

The attempted suppression of birth control information in the Latin communities seems to be due mainly to a grotesque alliance between military feeling and the Roman Catholic organization. In Ireland, however, it is purely religious. The teaching of the Church as interpreted by the Papal Encyclical of January 8, 1931, denounces as sinful and unnatural any use of matrimony by which the production of offspring is evaded. (It is, indeed, as unnatural as stopping a tooth or wearing clothes.) No considerations of health or economics, says the Encyclical, are to justify this abstention. The good Roman Catholic must marry and breed or abstain, or he must not marry. Happily many Roman Catholics are not good Roman Catholics. Sterilization of the defective His Holiness declares is equally against the law of God. Sterilization, it is conceded, may be used by the civil power for the punishment of criminals but not as a social preventive measure. You may sterilize people to hurt and humiliate them, but not to do them and the world a benefit. The prospect of a world population of 16,000 million with an increasing population of imbeciles, in which no vow of poverty will be necessary, does not dismay the Church in the least.

This is "Providentialism" to the superlative degree; man is absolved from all practical responsibility in the matter, he is to observe the dogma and trust to the Church and Heaven. An age of famine and distress will afford great opportunities for holy living. The more sufferers, the more souls to be saved. There is a dreadful logic in this teaching.

This emphatic repudiation of any birth control whatever by the Roman Church is in marked opposition to the temporizing attitude of the Anglican Bishops expressed in the Lambeth Conference of 1930, and to the general disposition of enlightened people of all creeds; and from our present point of view at least it is regrettable that the mighty and venerable Roman Catholic organization should now have been put definitely and finally in a pose of antagonism to ordinary human welfare and happiness.

The opposition of the aggressive patriot springs from other than theological sources. It seems to be grafted upon a crude, brutish, and ignorant interpretation of what is called the "struggle for existence." President Roosevelt, for example, in his most "Bull Moose" style, reviled birth control as "race suicide." Why an attempt to husband the resources of mankind should be called race suicide, is difficult to imagine. A family that has restricted itself to three or four children has no more committed suicide than did Roosevelt when he took violent exercise in the presence of the reporters to keep his weight down. But the fear of being "outbred" by some imaginary, nasty but prolific "inferior race," though it has no support whatever in the figures we have just given, can be worked up into a very savage feeling indeed. To this terror of a pullulating flood of little brown, black and yellow babies which makes strenuous white men wake and cry out despairingly in the night, we will return when we discuss eugenics.

The Roman Catholic Church forbids birth control, but it makes no direct attempt to persecute hygienic propaganda. That it leaves to the secular arm. In France and Italy alike it is plainly not piety but the patriotic obsession, the insane entanglement of the mind with military delusions, which stands in the way of a frank and self-respecting practise of birth control. One must bear children for *la patrie*. "La France" wants soldiers, Italy's "destiny" is to recover the empire of the Cæsars. The Prince of Peace plays quite a secondary rôle in the active suppression of the Birth Control movement. He is merely an auxiliary argument. He stands for the crucifixion of the flesh rather than the glories of warfare. It is not souls to be saved but sons to be shot that the patriot is after—and particularly is he after other people's sons. It is to pacify the patriot rather than the priest that the poor tuberculous woman in the Parisian or Neapolitan slum is allowed, unwarned and unpitied, to bear her ninth or tenth diseased and hopeless child.

The general scheme of this work is to display human activities in one ensemble. But here we seem to be dealing for the most part with activities avoided rather than actual activities. We can add to our scene only a few figures here: a committee room with the mixed ingredients of every committee where "movements" are concerned, public halls and meeting rooms where an earnest speaker, often a woman, addresses a mixed crowd, or more intimately a special gathering of wives and mothers, or conferences of medical men. And we would evoke, too, a little room in a back street, which proclaims itself not too obtrusively a "Birth Control Clinic." Anxious furtive women with drawn faces and a persecuted expression come creeping in to tell a story in undertones.

If the reader wants to know the sort of stories they have to tell, he should read Margaret Sanger's *Motherhood* or Marie Stopes's *Mother England*.

Some of those who advocate a popular propaganda of birth control, like Professor MacBride, advocate it for others rather than for their own type and class, and they would supplement it with compulsory sterilization. Their minds are troubled by something called the "Rapid Multiplication of the Unfit," and by a gnawing vision of their own relative worthiness drowning in a sea of inferiors. This sort of birth control advocate is not really thinking of the population question at all, or, at any rate, he is making it a quite secondary consideration. What he has in mind is Eugenics, that is to say not Limited but Selective Breeding.

It is necessary to distinguish much more clearly than is usually done between these two different and separate ideas about reproduction, the idea of Birth Control and the idea of Eugenics. The former idea is an economic one based on the plain prospect of severe pressure upon the means and subsistence ahead of us, and it insists upon our attention here. The gross increase of population creates a problem immediately confronting mankind. This was the problem Malthus had in view in his celebrated *Essay on Population*. But there is also this other possibility, the possibility of improving the race by selective breeding, as races of dogs and horses have been improved, and as new and better Indian corn and wheat have been produced in recent years. This is a question for the biologist rather than the economist. In the *Science of Life* we tell of recent work in economic biology and we discuss and point out some of the difficulties in the way of human eugenics. We will recall these conclusions in a brief section following this one, to make it clear why Eugenics is not yet to be regarded as a practical proposition.

The question of Birth Control is a fairly straightforward one so soon as it is stripped of its eugenic entanglement. It has nothing to do with a "human stud farm," as some antagonists say it has. It is independent of quality. It is essentially a question of numbers and of quite practicable checks on their inordinate increase. The experience of the past few decades proves abundantly that where the standards of life are high, human beings, directly the conditions of parenthood become at all difficult and the necessary knowledge is available, are extremely ready and willing to lighten the burthen and anxieties of parentage. The possibility of overpopulation is formidable only in a darkened and ignorant community invaded in spite of itself by life-saving and food-increasing inventions from within or without, and even then it can be but a passing phase of distress.

§ 2. *Impact of Races and Cultures*

Our review of human lives as they are being lived at the present time takes us from high lights of spacious hopefulness to teeming wretchedness in the blackest of shadows. Our blackest, our most horrible section has been § 7 of Chapter VII, and frightful and disgusting as that section is, it has nevertheless been mitigated and toned down to make it endurable by the ordinary reader. It is really cannibalism that is occurring; not indeed the devouring of one man by another but the devouring of one human society by another. Whole populations have been and their remnants are still—now while the reader sits over this book—being tormented and crushed to produce saleable products, very much in the same fashion as the penguins of the Southern ocean are massacred and crushed for marketable oil. There is no Humanity, no *Homo sapiens,* embodied in a world government to protect them; there are only competing sovereign states, not concerned by their extirpation. How the "policies" of these competing states have barred enquiry in one case, we shall note later. It would be inhuman to leave this account we are giving of human populations at this; to give merely the account of these miseries without some discussion of what is being done and what is being promised and attempted to alleviate this frightful pressure of raw and undisciplined modernism upon backward and defenseless populations.

In the preceding section we have shown that in all probability the main pools of human population are likely to remain, for at least a very long period, with their general proportions to one another and their innate characters and qualities unchanged. But they are all under the influence of parallel cultural changes, and they are all being brought now into the same economic net. At a great number of points the chief "races" are either blending or becoming joint occupants of common territories without blending, or with various political and cultural complications they are in active conflict for the possession or control of disputed areas. The inequalities of social and economic progress during the past two centuries have given the "white" races and governments an inordinate destructive material advantage over the black, brown and yellow peoples, and the absence of any world government, and indeed of any operative world ideology for the common good, makes the regions of racial and cultural overlapping regions of disastrous dominance, brigandage, subjugation and revolt, while the world-wide exploitation of natural resources by white finance and economic enterprise is the cause everywhere of a hundred distresses for the disadvantaged millions of colour.

The broad reply to the question, "How is this present enslavement, torture and conflict of races and peoples to be ended?" is plainly to press on as fast as possible from our present division of the world's control among seventy-odd sovereign governments towards a world control and the scientific and comprehensive treatment of the matter as one whole. World controls and scientific planning are the broad remedies for most human ills. But that answer is so broad, so very broad, that it leaves us still without any clear ideas of what to advocate and what to do for the miseries of to-day and to-morrow, the immense miseries that actually oppress and threaten millions of our species who will never see and much less benefit by that world rule and world plan towards which things are moving. Nor does that broad reply give us any criterion for judgment upon the actual methods of dealing with these things at the present time.

Two preliminary questions, however, have to be asked before we can pass any judgments at all in this field. The first is the question whether, of the main races of mankind, some are "superior" and some "inferior," or whether there is a practical human equality throughout the earth. The second is whether there is anything formidable and undesirable about free mixture between the peoples of these broad divisions. Upon both questions there is a voluminous and unsatisfactory literature, only to be compared in quality and temper to the unlimited frothings of prejudice and rubbish, of which we have already complained in Chapter XI, evoked by the discussion of sexual relationships. As between white, yellow, brown and black, considered as wholes, it seems impossible to fix a scale of gradations that justifies any social subjection or servitude. The question is complicated by the existence of really primitive and undeveloped peoples in small numbers, like the white hairy Ainu or the pigmies or the Australian black-fellows, and by the fact that in populations of every colour inferior strains are perceptible. But these ethnological pockets and these bad streaks do nothing to justify broad colour generalizations. Professor J. W. Gregory* quotes ample

---

*The Menace of Colour (1925), Human Migrations and the Future (1928), Race as a Political Factor (1931).

authorities to sustain a virtual innate equality in the case most in dispute, the case of the American Negro. The Negro is different from the white or yellow man; that gives him advantages as well as disadvantages; he is better at this and worse at that; but it is only by marking all the points of difference in the white man's favour that the thesis of the white man's intrinsic superiority can be sustained. The "poor white" strain in Georgia compares badly with its coloured neighbours. In South Africa the black is so far from being inferior to the white that the Kaffir is debarred from education, skilled trades and various professions, to *protect* the white from his competition.

But while Professor Gregory admits the virtual equality of all men and would have no race subject to another, he displays a strong conviction against inter-marriage. He has collected various casual opinions about the inferiority of half-breeds to individuals who are what is called racially "pure," and he brings in his own widely travelled impression of the inferiority of the "mulatto." I note his impressions with respect but not his conclusions, and against them I put the much wider and more intimate experiences of such observers as Lord Olivier and Sir Harry Johnson.* Lord Olivier knows Jamaica as few other observers do. He was once Acting Governor, 1900–04, and once Governor, 1907–13, and he has revisited the island in 1930 and 1931. The population of Jamaica is about a million, of which 1,500 claim to be "pure white" and 150,000 mixed. The rest are definitely "black," but black drawn from very various African sources. "The administrative, professional, commercial and clerical classes are predominantly white or coloured, but include some who are pure black. The owners of the large estates are probably in most cases white, inheritors of the former white 'plantocracy,' but many are coloured, and there are great numbers of coloured and black proprietors of smaller farms and about 11,000 black and coloured landowners having from one to fifty acres. In this community there is no policy whatever in relation to contact between races. There is no colour bar and no discrimination of civil rights. There is a constant tendency to economic and social advance of the coloured and black people. The capable white people hold their own, and there is practically no poor white class in indigent circumstances. There is an aversion on the part of 'pure white' people to intermarriage with the coloured; but such marriages with near whites or reputed whites are not uncommon. The people of mixed race do not tend to disappear, nor do they constitute a separate class. Their proportion increases. Physically and intellectually

*Particularly his *Negro in the New World*.

they are vigorous. There is a very fine physical type of dark coloured men and women commonly called 'Sambos' which seems well established. They are energetic and independent in character."

Since he first knew the island Lord Olivier declares that the progress of coloured people has been conspicuously recognizable. There is still a certain amount of colour prejudice as between adjacent groups. But it is much less than it was forty years ago.

"Since I have been acquainted with Jamaica," writes Lord Olivier, "there has been a great increase in the facilities for the secondary education of coloured young persons of both sexes, and this has involved improvement in hygiene and athletic nurture. Coloured and black youths now hold their own in sports with those of any other race in the world. Note, for example, the recent performance of the West Indian Cricket team in Australia. . . ."

In "Jamaica, a Racial Mosaic" (in *Opportunity,* May, 1931) R. L. Buell insists that differences are more cultural than racial. "Black Jamaicans who are educated and well mannered are received upon a basis of complete equality."

The evidence of Lord Olivier is first-hand evidence of a very competent witness indeed, and it contradicts Professor Gregory flatly. It is Lord Olivier's opinion that the half-breed is so often a moral and social failure because he is a misfit; he falls between two stools; there is no established culture for him, and there is prejudice against him; given proper opportunity he might just as probably as not prove an interesting and successful blend of qualities; and there. is nothing in the uncontrolled verdicts Professor Gregory assembles to affect this explanation. Basing myself upon this evidence I do not share that fear of a free social and economic intercourse, even to the point of intermarriage betwen *all* racial types.

Another apparently successful mélange of races is to be found in Hawaii. There, says Professor Romanzo Adams, the Professor of Sociology in the University at Honolulu, practically all the main races of mankind mingle socially and genially.

Captain Leo L. Partlow, in an interestingly illustrated article in *Asia* for June, 1931, says:

"Former Governor Farrington once called the Territory of Hawaii 'the world's greatest adventure in friendship.' It may seem sentimental rather than scientific to suggest that there is such a thing as the 'Hawaiian atmosphere,' in which goodfellowship between races seems perfectly natural. Yet the various races in Hawaii do seem to accept one another as a part of the environment, without prejudice or favour. I should not quite say that they freely intermingle socially nor yet that they remain good-naturedly apart. They attend to their own affairs, and, if those affairs bring them together, they come together without antagonism or self-consciousness. If any but the whites have a feeling of racial superiority, I do not detect it. . . . Racial intermarriage is practised to some extent between all the various groups, but there is no indication that it is, or tends to become, general. Indeed, the Japanese never have intermarried to any great extent with any other race, and the inter-racial marriages of the Chinese—principally with the Hawaiians and Filipinos—are decreasing rather than increasing. Whatever may be the eventual outcome, nothing now indicates a homogenous physical blend."

To leave intermarriage free, one must remember, is not to make it universal or obligatory. It is a matter for individual preferences to settle. Mostly, I believe, like will marry like. I see nothing alarming, but much promise of varied interest, in a marginal mixed society—which is always likely to remain a marginal and intermediate society. The main pools of population will, I think, continue to absorb and assimilate what falls into them by virtue of the better adaptation of the regional type to regional conditions, and of its acquired resistances to local disease, and I see no necessity for emphasizing by bars and prohibitions racial conflicts and struggles in the areas overlapping. The setting up of racial barriers and segregations I regard as reactionary and mischievous and doomed to painful failure. These are, of course, merely personal opinions in a region of thought in which nothing better than opinions is yet possible.

So far as restrictions and prohibitions go, Lord Olivier is very insistent upon their bad imaginative results. "They will," he remarks, "produce very silly and very bloody romances." . . . They may produce such tragedies in great numbers. Plainly down that vista one can see race outrage and the moonlight pursuit, Judge Lynch and the Ku Klux Klan. And no end to that vista.

Obviously, with these primary issues still so much in dispute, our judgments upon actual methods of racial adjustment to modern stresses must remain to a large extent individual and provisional. Two systems of will and intention play against each other in this business. This has been very clearly expressed by Lord Lugard in his *Dual Mandate*. On the one hand there are the urgencies arising out of the idea of a modern world economy, using all the natural products of the earth, freely and thoroughly, for power and plenty. To that economy the distinctive products of every region of the earth must contribute, and it is necessary that, in unsettled or socially and politically backward lands where the local population is living under an ancient traditional savage or barbaric régime, some methods of exploitation should be adopted to bring these natural products into the new world system. Some invasion of the indigenous culture is inevitable, if the new system cannot work and cannot balance itself without these products in abundance.

How is that invasion to be made? The gravitation of these natural products to the modern centres of manufacture is so great that if the business is allowed to occur without control, tragedies of brigandage and cruelty, legal or quasi-legal, on the Congo and Putumayo pattern are inevitable. Free invasion and uncontrolled conflict is the way of nature, and the way of nature is not only cruel but disastrously wasteful. Like all exploitation for immediate private profit, like the present exploitation of forests everywhere, like the whale and sea fisheries and the penguin massacre, the modern private-profit system in these regions of coloured labour is getting natural resources too abundantly and too cheaply now while creating a shortage in the future. And in the cases we are now considering it is enslaving and destroying human beings to do so.

As this is apprehended there comes into action the second series of motives, the other command of the *Dual Mandate:* care not only for economic output but for the present and future welfare of the native. The economic invasion of these productive backward regions, we admit, must occur, but their human and other natural resources must be protected and conserved. This means a protective interference with the social life of the native in the place of a massacre. There is no other alternative. But that interference, it is held, can be and must be for the native's ultimate well-being. The economic annexation must needs be rapid, but the assimilation of the native into the world commonweal may need a lengthy education. The haste, therefore, must be canalized and restrained. The obvious dangers of hypocrisy and of a sham and enslaving "protection" are plain enough. Just how much interference there may be and what should be the quality of the interference is the question.

Now, there are four chief methods of interference possible. The first is to push the native aside from the coveted region of mines, forests, or cultivatable soil, into *reserves,* and to plant workers from some other region upon the district of exploitation. Usually under this method the native in the reserve dwindles away. The reserve is all too often a shrinking area of undesirable land. Imported white labour and imported Asiatic labour have proved failures in South and East Africa, but the Negro was established in this fashion in the days of frank slavery in the West Indies and America.

Or, secondly, the native can be pushed aside into a reserve, but from that reserve he is tempted to emerge as a wage-earner in the region of exploitation. The reserve is thus made a labour tank of supply. The trouble is that usually he will not be tempted in sufficient numbers to satisfy the impatient white planter or mine owner.

So we come to the third system of treatment, dear to the whites of British East Africa, for example, "pressure" on the reserves. The natives are, for example, taxed, a head tax or a hut tax, and the tax is payable solely in money, which can be got only by plantation work. Or in other ways up to actual conscription by the chiefs, the native is to be compelled to come in. And to keep him in the desired path he is to be restrained from occupations by which he may earn on his own account. Education which might "put him above" mine or plantation work, is to be denied him. So native labour, it is supposed, can be kept cheap, poor, inferior and submissive, and the white settler can have a reasonable prospect of an indolent competence while directing the exploitation of the invaded mines or lands. This is the Afrikander policy. In South Africa things are making clearly towards a dangerous two-caste society, in which a minority of whites will rule over an artificially restrained, uneducated, disenfranchised coloured labour majority. Olivier's *Anatomy of African Misery* (Chapter XI) deals faithfully with the frank economic purpose of Hertzog's Native Land and Labour Bills,* and he has been largely instrumental in the appointment of the Joint Select Committee which has arrested the development of a similar state of things in Kenya.

In his book, *Kenya,* Dr. Norman Leys indicts the white settlers of that colony very forcibly and effectively. General Smuts, in his *Africa and Some World Problems,* propounds a scheme for an Africa dominated throughout by a backbone of white settlers in the highlands, a scheme subjected to very destructive criticism by J. H. Oldham's *White and Black in Africa*. A network of restrictive legislation seems to be closing about the black peoples of the Dominion of South Africa. They are being deprived of educational opportunity and political expression. They are being driven towards the alternatives of mass insurrection or complete degradation.

A fourth line of treatment—which has a weaker appeal to the white

*See also Olivier's *White Capital and Coloured Labour,* chapters XIII and XIV.

settler in a hurry—is to treat the native fairly, to police his country, to teach and show him how to cultivate the desired product, to make it worth his while to produce it and gradually bring him into the position of a tenant farmer, with technical guidance and help and a sure market for his produce. This has been the British policy in the new cotton-growing areas of Nubia.* It marches with what we have developed in Chapter IV on the trend of agricultural reorganization throughout the world. In this way an intelligent native population might be brought step by step and freely and happily into line with modern conditions.

In Jamaica practically the same method has been followed, and a pros-perous and contented black and coloured peasantry has been raised from its original status of imported plantation labour to a level which compares favourably with many southeastern European cultivators. It is certainly as well prepared as they are to pass on towards that scien-tifically organized individual farming by state tenants under central control which we have given reasons (in Chapter IV) for regarding as the probable normal method of production in a completely modernized world.

The Gold Coast and the not very distant Portuguese islands of San Thomé and Principé are interesting exhibits for us here, since they offer a vivid contrast between the system of justly treated native production and what is practically slave labour. The cocoa-growing of the Gold Coast is due to native enterprise. The cacao tree is of South American origin; it has long been grown on the island of Fernando Po, and in 1879 a native blacksmith named Tette Kwesi had the energy and intel-ligence to bring a few pods to the Gold Coast. Other natives took up the cultivation, and in 1891 the colony exported eighty pounds of cocoa. The Gold Coast government follows the policy of encouragement to native farmers and prohibits the acquisition of land and the formation of plantations by white adventurers. Buying firms insist upon standards of quality and the Gold Coast Agricultural Department provides in-struction in planting, cultivating and preparing the cocoa. And behold the result! By 1929 that initial export of eighty pounds had grown to 233,000 tons, about 43 per cent of the whole world output, all grown by free native farmers, sanely governed and guided. In Ashanti and Nigeria the same methods have been adopted with a parallel success.

In San Thomé and Principé, a few hundred miles away, the planta-tion system rules in all its ugliness and misery. The attention of Cad-bury's, the British chocolate makers, was called to this fact in 1901 by

*See Odette Keun's *A Foreigner Looks at the British Sudan* (1930).

the offer for sale of a San Thomé plantation in which among other assets was an item of so many labourers at so much a head and an inferior grade of labourer at a lower price. The offer was declined, but that listing of labourers as chattels rankled in the mind of Mr. William Cadbury and led him to investigate further. He secured the coöperation of two other British firms, Fry and Rowntree, and the German firm of Stollwerck, and an investigator named Burtt was sent to prepare a report. It appeared in 1907 and was a thoroughly black one. It was a plain case of slave labour masquerading as contract labour. Most of the workers were caught in Angola, brought chained and under conditions of great hardship and cruelty to the coast, and shipped to the islands. There, with a view to outside criticism, they were made to go through the farce of signing a contract. But none was ever repatriated. When the contract expired they were forced to sign another.

We will not go on to tell the story of the efforts to end this state of affairs. They involved a libel action and other complications from which the cocoa firms concerned emerged very honourably. Foreign policy required that Great Britain should show great consideration for Portuguese feeling. But the cocoa firms named were able to secure the coöperation of their leading American competitors in a boycott of the tainted product, and by 1918 considerable reforms had been effected. How far these reforms were permanent is unhappily in doubt. San Thomé and Principé retain the plantation system, and in 1930 when the British Delegate at Geneva pressed for enquiry into the general question of slavery, the French, Italian, Portuguese and Abyssinian delegations opposed it successfully. France and Belgium have also refused a Forced Labour Convention with Britain. The better chocolate firms, the best known makes and names, still boycott plantation cocoa, but it finds a ready sale among their less scrupulous competitors. Thus, within an hour's flight of each other by aëroplane, you have the two contrasted systems of production in active competition. You have one black population being civilized and another being degraded and destroyed. And you have some intimation of the tangle of international politics which protects the evil method.

Let us return now to that other aspect of this problem of racial impact, which is raised by an exaggerated fear of miscegenation and by the prejudices of hates arising out of that fear. Here the writer's bias in favour of one human community is so strong that he finds it impossible to state the case against his own persuasion. He is convinced that in a properly educated world people can live in a state of racial

614 THE OUTLINE OF MAN'S WORK AND WEALTH

mingling without any tragedy at all, civilly and kindly. He disbelieves altogether in bars and permanent reserves. He accepts Jamaica and Hawaii as his justifying experiments. He believes that race hatreds and conflicts are due mainly to economic tension, bad traditions and diverse conceptions of pride and behaviour. They are stupidities, they are vulgarities that the schoolmaster should anticipate and destroy. There is indeed hardly any race conflict in the world that is not deeply rooted in economic motives. But since that is an abnormal point of view, let the writer stand aside here for Dr. Malinowski, Professor of Social Anthropology in London University, who has written as follows (*op. cit.*):

"What is the conclusion, then, to which we are forcibly driven by facts? Obviously, that the co-existence of two racial stocks side by side is inevitably a source of serious dangers and a starting-point of a long series of troubles. Once the process of mixture and conflict begins, the best we can hope is that one race should oust the other, or that a new preserve should be founded for the new mixed race. Why, then, not avoid the tragic process with all its evil implications and consequences? Why not frankly state that the only sound policy is that of racial and cultural preserves: the policy, that is, of indirect rule, of limited settlement for administrative purposes only, and the development of indigenous colonies on indigenous lines and, as far as possible, through indigenous enterprise? It would be untenable to object that this is not a practical policy. It is *de facto* the main principle of the policy of indirect rule which is, more or less, consistently carried out in the West African colonies. It has led to good results in Nigeria and in Uganda, in the Gold Coast and in the native protectorates of southern Africa.

"Moreover, the policy of racial exclusion is being carried out on a vast scale, consistently and efficiently. White Australia has resolutely closed its doors to superior Asiatic immigration, and it has deported in bulk inferior Kanaka labour. Similar racial preserves have been proclaimed in the Union of South Africa and in Canada, in Kenya and in many other white colonies. The United States of America have closed their frontiers completely on the West and very tightly on the East. Within Europe, Great Britain has excluded foreign immigrants.

"In all this we recognise a right policy, and we do not speak about violating the 'Dual Mandate,' though the 'world at large' would benefit appreciably if a score of million Asiatics were distributed over Queensland and the Pacific States, over the Northern Territory of Australia and the plains of Canada. Here is an immense wealth of fertile, unexploited regions wasted for the world, because the uplifting influence of effective Asiatic labour, of Chinese industry and Japanese organisation, is not being applied to it. This is the same moral argument as is used now to justify white settlement in East Africa. But both moral attitudes are wrong. Australia is not the yellow man's country, because, unless he could exterminate the few million whites there resident, he would create trouble for them and for himself. East Africa is not the white man's country because, again, he cannot exterminate the Negro; because he does not want to be blended racially, and because the only solution, a stratified community, is wrong all round."

Let there be a brief interpolation here. Dr. Malinowski was educated as a Pole, as a conscious aristocratic patriot (see Who's Who) in conflict with the central European synthesis. Most of us were brought up also on sound patriotic lines, and we cannot cast a stone at him on that account. But in what follows is it the Polish patriot or the emancipated London professor who is thinking?

"One more point must be made. The steam-roller of universal Western culture is undoubtedly levelling the cultures and societies of the world. . . . But, against this universal levelling, there is developing a strong reaction. The powerful assertion of political independence by the small nations in Europe was, perhaps, its initial symptom. National languages are revived, national religions set up, forms of national art and national literature cultivated, in opposition to the prevalent internationalism. Outside Europe, Egypt has claimed and received a considerable measure of independence; Turkey, while superficially adopting European ways and manners, has reasserted her national autonomy; Afghanistan has dealt even more drastically with spurious Westernisation; India is on the way to dominion status. In America, there is a strong resistance by the Latin-Indian nations against the cultural conquest of the North. Japan led the way in the fight for Eastern self-determination, and China may, in the future, completely reassert its cultural autonomy and achieve its national unity."

I repeat that I quote these views to disagree with them. This renewed fragmentation of mankind which Dr. Malinowski seems to welcome, this flickering back of his mind to nationalisms and autonomies, is a relapse from cosmopolitanism to Polish patriotism unworthy of the London School of Economics. The trend of material forces in the world is all towards unification of control however traditional sentiment and prejudice may resist that trend. Those more elemental directive influences will not tolerate these particularisms, these reversions to nationalism, these failures to tolerate or combine. Those post-war setbacks he cites, to the movement towards one great confluent human community having darker and fairer regions indeed but with no boundaries, castes or other fixed divisions, have occurred because that movement was, to begin with, so clumsy, planless and unforeseen. What

Dr. Malinowski calls "the steam-roller of universal Western culture" was in fact not a culture at all. It was a steam-roller of blind forces, that has yet to produce a conscious world culture. It was an economic rolling preparing the soil for a world culture. A halt and even a phase of reaction may be inevitable, but at best that is no more than an interlude, a resting pause, a phase for thinking things out better, before the conscious, measured and designed establishment of a world order and a world law in which all men will live at peace together is resumed.

§ 3. *Eugenics*

To make our review of human affairs comprehensive we have had to plan a considerable number of sections, bringing in this activity or that possibility. Here, for once, is a section about something that hardly comes in at all, Eugenics. We have to make clear as briefly as possible, why at present the practice of Eugenics does not come into a survey of contemporary mankind, and then we can dismiss the subject and proceed to other aspects of the human spectacle.

Eugenics dates from 1885. We owe the word to Sir Francis Galton, the founder of the science. He died in 1911, leaving money to found a Chair of Eugenics at University College, London. He worked in the days before the development of the science of genetics and before the dawn of any adequate classification of human quality. He was eager for immediate applications; he wanted to set about improving the race without any close critical examination of the assumptions on which his plans were to be based. He thought there were large, indisputably superior people in the world, moving about amidst the small inferior multitudes, and that it would be possible to pick out, mate, and breed these superiors. This he termed "positive eugenics." He thought also that there were people definably inferior whose breeding ought at all costs to be prevented. That was to be "negative eugenics."

But human relationships are complex and subtle, and the various attempts that have been made to measure "intelligence quotients" and the like, so as to show that there are social elements which have in their heredity a class superiority or a class inferiority to the average, are all open to very destructive critical objections. The only case that has been made out with any degree of conviction is the case for the segregation and sterilization of mental defectives.

There does seem to be a reasonable assumption that congenital defects of certain types are, so far as very many of them are concerned, hereditable, and at any rate, since restriction upon population is a world necessity, there is no reason why the slight unobtrusive and practically painless operation of sterilization should not be performed upon them. Nor is there any sound objection to the sterilization of criminals convicted of brutish violence. The balance of evidence tilts towards the conclusion that such qualities are transmissible and, even if that conclusion is unsound, nevertheless the suppression of offspring in these categories will eliminate the certainty of a number of children being born in unfavourable surroundings at a great social disadvantage. Again there is every reason for the temporary or permanent sterilization of those who have contracted hereditable diseases. For a fuller discussion of these points than is possible here the reader should consult Carr-Saunders' book on *Eugenics*. The sterilization of certain types of defectives is now (1930) the law in California, Connecticut, Delaware, Idaho, Iowa, Kansas, Maine, Michigan, Minnesota, Mississippi, Montana, Nebraska, New Hampshire, North and South Dakota, Oregon, Utah, Virginia, Washington and Wisconsin.

When we pass from such extreme and obvious application of negative eugenics towards positive eugenics, we find ourselves passing from a field of reasonable probabilities into a tangle of riddles.

In the early days of Galton it seemed reasonable to assume that a child was essentially a blend of all the qualities of its parents. Only a few acute observers, then, doubted that assumption. But the science of genetics has made it clear to us that the characteristics of an individual are not the expression of all his hereditable possibilities. In the *Science of Life,* with the help of diagram and full explanation, we have made clear how it is that this should be so, we have described the splitting of chromosomes, and we have shown how "recessive" qualities can be transmitted by parents in whose personal make-up they do not appear. Only the half of a human being's full equipment of hereditable qualities is handed on to any particular offspring, the other half comes from the other parent, and the combination of these two half sets may be quite a different selection from what appears in either the mother or the father. To take a simple instance, having blue eyes is, it seems, a "recessive" quality in heredity. Two brown-eyed people may each be carrying this recessive latent in their reproductive cells, and chance may pick this out from both of them to blend in making a blue-eyed child.

Manifestly, then, we are not going to produce miraculous beings with any certainty by mating people of outstanding beauty and intelligence. The delightful combination of these qualities in either case was an

accident not easily repeated. All sorts of recessives may pop out to
grimace at us from such a coupling. Who among us cannot recall the
half handsome children of the beautiful, the not very brilliant offspring
of the genius? Now and then, of course, there may be a run of luck,
but our best chance of getting any quality repeated, say the biologists, is
to inbreed closely, which at once brings us up against the restrictions of
current morality. We should turn back towards the primary social sin,
incest.

Even in negative eugenics there is no assurance that undesirable
qualities will be eliminated altogether. Certain types of mental deficiency are supposed to be "recessive." It is quite possible, therefore, that
two quite admirable people should have a defective child. Such
tragedies occur. The sterilization of defectives will not end, it will only
diminish, the supply of defectives. Recessives can hide from generation
to generation waiting to meet a kindred gene. When, therefore,
biological workers seek to evoke and fix a new variety of some plant or
animal, they resort to expedients quite outside our present liberties
with human material. The first thing is to discover the recessives by
the freest promiscuous breeding and interbreeding. Every undesirable
recessive thus brought to light is then thrown out of reproduction; every
individual known to carry a recessive is also cast out. When at last a
"pure" strain is achieved, all the rest are destroyed, sterilized, isolated,
or otherwise put beyond the possibility of reëntering the reproductive
stream.

And also, be it noted, in the case of plants and insects and so forth,
the breeder works for one simple quality. He wants a bigger ear of
wheat, he wants resisting power to some disease or to some degree of
cold. Nothing else concerns him. Everything else he can sweep away.
But we do not know with anything like that much narrowness what
we want in human beings. We do not want human beings to become
simply taller or swifter or web-footed or what not. We want a great
variety of human beings. And the qualities we want are complexes, not
simple hereditable elements. It sounds paradoxical, but it is probably
true that a large proportion of distinguished men and women are distinguished quite as much by a defect as by an outstanding gift. A man
who has a "gift" generally needs, in order to develop it, exceptional
freedom from secondary motives. He will specialize and concentrate all
the better if there is no other strong impulse in his composition to dis-
tract him from the call of his gift. So we hear that among distinguished
people so and so is sexless; so and so, strangely heartless with women;

so and so is incapable of managing his household or his business affairs; so and so, absent-minded and forgetful of engagements to the pitch of gross incivility. Yet one of these is, say, a great artist, another a great mathematician, a third a distinguished lawyer, the fourth a statesman. All of them might give the most disconcerting results with intelligence tests. A story is told of Einstein against himself that comes in amusingly here. He is a great mathematician, but he is not a ready reckoner, and during the crisis of the mark he thought that a tram conductor had given him back too much change—a hundred thousand marks or so—and had to be convinced of his error. "Everybody," said the kindly tram conductor, "hasn't the gift of calculation with these big figures. I mustn't take advantage of you. . . ." And Laplace, one of the greatest mathematicians the world has ever known, was dismissed from the Ministry of the Interior by Napoleon for the grossest incompetence. But our organizing world requires these exceptional individuals far more than it does an endless multitude of fairly-good-all-round people.

That is how things stand at present. Biology, like all sciences, may spring the unexpected upon us at any time, but unless some such surprise occurs, no deliberate improvement in human quality is likely to be attempted. We must tolerate much that is odd and weak lest we lose much that is glorious and divine. For man reproduction is so slow, and his conditions of survival so complex and individual at present, that no natural process of selection can now be in effective operation, whatever may have been the case with his shorter-lived ancestors. There is considerable finality about *Homo sapiens*. For many generations, and perhaps for long ages, we must reckon upon a population of human beings not very different from those we have to deal with to-day. We shall meet with the same mental and temperamental types and the same racial characteristics that we encounter in the cast of the human drama to-day. The deliberate improvement of man's inherent quality is at present unattainable. It is to a better education and to a better education alone, therefore, that we must look for any hope of ameliorating substantially the confusions and distresses of our present life.

CHAPTER THE FOURTEENTH

THE OVERFLOWING ENERGY OF MANKIND

§ 1. *A Short History of Leisure*

CHAPTERS XI and XII and XIII are the darkest chapters in our survey. They have dealt with waste and poverty, with the weaknesses of governments and the mischief of bad government, with war preparation and economic war, and with the black cloud of approaching over-population. They have also shown man apparently unable to save himself from grave disasters, caused by his own defective monetary arrangements. He is seen injuring and perhaps destroying himself—without waiting for external Nature to turn upon him. The note of confident progress that pervaded our recapitulation of human achievements grew weak and died out altogether in some of those sections.

But hope remained, waving a tattered flag above the panorama, if at times it was difficult not to wave it very much in the manner of a danger signal. We have now said about all there is to say in a work of this sort, about these vast instabilities. We shall glance at them once again in our chapter on Education, and weigh their gravity in our conclusion. But for the rest we will disregard them. If civilization crashes, the story ends, and this work is no more than the measure of a frustration which will matter in the end to no one. But civilization need not crash. If it does not crash, then it will go on, we may be sure, to the fullest realization of the hopes and liberties that scientific and mechanical progress have made possible.

One inevitable consequence of continuing human progress is a steady increase of human leisure and human resources. At present much of that leisure takes the form of unemployment and impoverishment, but that need not be so, and also, as needlessly, much of the wealth and vitality we have accumulated is guided by patriots and munition salesmen into the disagreeable and unprofitable expenditure of war preparation and the consequent war orgies. Nevertheless, for the present, at any rate, humanity enjoys much more surplus time and energy than the past ever knew. How that surplus time and energy is employed is a necessary part of the human spectacle. It is a developing aspect of that spectacle. It opens out a vista of very important and perhaps even very novel activities in the future.

No sociologist has yet attempted to measure the leisure of a community. No biologist indeed has yet devised a comparative scale for the surplus energy of a species. To the *Science of Life,* Julian Huxley contributed some very interesting and suggestive material on the play of animals. He wrote that living species for the most part stick closely to business; they do not play. Play appears only with the more intelligent vertebrates. It is of definite biological importance, and it is for the most part confined to the young. It is almost entirely an educational rehearsal of the serious activities ahead of the young. But among creatures at the level of dogs and cats, even the adults, in times of abundance, will lark about and exercise themselves. Generally, indeed, when they are grown up they sleep, digest and recuperate between exertions, but the play is there. When we come to the monkeys and apes, there is considerable restlessness and activity, even on the part of the mature, outside the food hunt and the sexual storm. They are not only sexually excessive but curious and experimental. Many birds also release exuberant energy in song beyond any biological need, and penguins, ravens and jackdaws will play in a very human manner.

Nomads and savages, in favourable seasons, have time on their hands and a surplus of energy to expend. They exercise and dance and play games, decorate themselves, make amusing objects. But the onset of the larger cultivating community, the onset of foresight, that is, and enforced toil, restricted the spontaneous activities of the multitude very greatly. Only a limited proportion of the people won to any notable share of free time and free activities. The mass was caught and remained entangled in the net of unavoidable work.

Throughout the ages of cultivation, the peasants, the great majority of mankind, have had little surplus energy. The life of the peasant is still a very continuous round of labour; in Christendom he goes to mass (itself the vestige of a fertility blood sacrifice) on Sunday morning, but often before and after that on Sunday he finds something to be done to his ground. His wife and womenfolk, and the wife and womenfolk of the smaller townspeople, seem unendingly busy. As the proverb goes, "A woman's work is never ended." For the peasant to be under-occupied is to be underfed. Over all the countries affected by the Hebrew tradition there is indeed the Sabbath, but that is not a day of leisure and the release of surplus energy; it is a day not of enjoyment but of ceremonial inactivity, a day of restraint. Chess may be played by the orthodox but not games for money, and the gad-about is restricted to the limits of a "Sabbath day's journey." The relationship of the Judæo-Christian Sabbath to other days when work is taboo, for workless days are found all over the world, is discussed in Hutton Webster's *Rest Days*.

The festivals of the cultivating communities, apart from seed time and harvest sacrifices, are few; they have lost the frequent dances, so stirring and hygienic, of the more savage people. Man, as we have insisted throughout this book, is not by nature a toiler: toil is a phase in his development; he has had to be subdued to toil, and whenever an excuse appears cheerfulness breaks through. Nevertheless, through the ages in which the main human community has been developing, through the last seven or eight thousand years, that is, the great industrious working majority has been almost devoid of surplus energy and spontaneous activities.

It was only at the centres where wealth accumulated or where a strong element of nomadism remained in the social mixture that holy days lost their severity and became holidays. The pastoral peoples have never given up their races, that exciting trying out of horses, and among them we find also the bull fight and suchlike sports. These mingle with foot races and combative exercises. The nomad trader brought his more eventful habits to meet the peasant spirit in the market and fair. The gipsy stirs up peasant life. The fair with its shows is a very ancient thing in social life. A few score times in his existence the peasant goes to the fair, partly to trade, but also to feast, dance, get drunk, fight, and, for a few precious hours, relax from his lifelong servitude to the soil.

Great towns, in which a large element of the population, like the Roman voters, for example, was exempted in some exceptional way from the need for continuous labour, display the maximum of leisure in the ancient world. In the classical period the architectural evidences of real holiday-keeping appear in amphitheatres and hippodromes. We find those clubs of the ancient world, the baths, becoming important features of the urban life. There and in groves and temple precincts we find also gentlemen of leisure meeting to walk and gossip, and presently to engage in philosophical discussion.

Except for the leisure of these favoured centres, a leisure which vanished again for long centuries with the collapse of the Roman system, the ordinary human life in the cultivating communities throughout history has had neither leisure nor recreation. It is only with the coming of power machinery and large industry, that the work of the common human being begins to be limited to regular hours leaving a daily margin of daylight and activity, and that a grudged but increasing amount of holiday appears. Nowadays there is leisure for all. The modern worker, under good conditions, gets his daily, weekly and annual leisure as he gets his daily bread. Never did the mediæval worker waste daylight as he does. It is quite a delusion to think that the past was a leisurely time and that this is a driving time. The past was a time of almost universal drudgery and insufficiency, and the ages of leisure and plenty lie ahead.

Some interesting books about leisure (C. E. M. Joad's *Diogenes or the Future of Leisure,* for example) have been written recently, but there is as yet no comprehensive survey of the ways in which this expanding element of surplus time and vigour is being used. That limitless encyclopædia of which we are always dreaming would trace in its ample pages how leisure has spread down from class to class in the last century or so, and how new occupations have been found for it. Man does not like prescribed toil, but man is an energetic creature and leisure has never meant idleness for him. Probably our encyclopædia would classify man's leisure activities roughly after this fashion: as (1) exercise and sports, (2) hygienically unprofitable games, (3) sexual dissipation, gluttony and drunkenness, (4) gossip, parading in costumes and loafing about, (5) seeing shows, (6) wandering and travelling to see and learn, (7) making things for pleasure or, as the Victorians called it, "hobbies," passing insensibly into (8) art, (9) philosophy, scientific enquiry and experiment.

The student of the general history of leisure will go very largely for his material to the contemporary novels, plays and accounts of lives and "characters" of the past. These begin to bear their witness about the period of the Reformation after a phase of pestilence and social warfare had strained the mediæval economy severely. There was little fun upon the toiling, needy countryside then except for the seasonal holidays, "May games, Whitsun ales, Morris dances, leaping and vaulting." The village seniors played skittles and quoits and drank beer, and the visit of a garrulous peddler was an event. A book of ancient "sports and pastimes" would not rouse the envy of a slum child to-day. Except perhaps the bull and bear baiting. The town worker had to practise his archery in any time he had to give it, and, to make sure that he did so, lapses into football and other games were legislated against and severely punished. Bowling was prohibited altogether in England "for the meane sort of people." After darkness stopped the work, before they went to sleep, there was taverning, "eaves dropping" in the villages and mischief in the dark streets. Only the fairly well-to-do had light enough for reading. The leisure of the common people, if one reads between the lines of the increasing literature of the times, shrinks rather than expands throughout the seventeenth and eighteenth centuries. People do not seem to be working vigorously, but they are incessantly drudging. They knew no better; they did not complain.

Meanwhile, in the accumulating mass of more prosperous people, the beginnings of all the nine categories of activity just enumerated were appearing. People who once rode about their business and hunted by necessity, now rode and hunted for health and pleasure. The deadly pastime of card games was elaborated, and a touch of reality given to its futility by gambling. It is less trying to the eyes to play cards than to read by candlelight. One got drunk in the dining room and made love discreetly in the drawing room, and the gentry periodically left their estates to their stewards and foregathered at Bath and Tunbridge and in London, observing and getting excitements out of the novel people they encountered. The theatre reappeared; not the informative miracle play of the Church, but the comedy and tragedy of the classical world adapted to modern needs. Much attention began to be paid to witticisms and sentiments. The reader may find the sort of witticisms in Swift's *Polite Conversation*. The novel developed.

There was, however, a steady resistance to "frivolity" in the puritanical household that played so large a part in the development of the capitalist system of business (see Weber's *Protestant Ethic*). This retarded the spread of leisure to the employee and directed the mind of the employer towards serious literary and scientific interest. Reading increased. The novel, at first merely tolerated on week days, presently, under a false claim of edification, invaded the Sabbath. The state of affairs for the employee in the early nineteenth century is shown in Samuel Warren's *Ten Thousand a Year*. His poor poverty-struck shopman works intolerable hours and has no form of leisure occupation at all, except dressing up "above his station" and going for a walk on Sunday, pretending to be a gentleman. "Going for a walk" was an important phase in the life of everyone who could afford the time in the serious nineteenth century. It was healthy; it was not frivolous. A hundred years ago it was the chief relaxation of the university student and the university don. All the country round Oxford and Cambridge was dotted daily with intent, wide-striding men. Sport, as an integral factor in university life, had still to come.

The onset of the annual "holidays" in civilized life would be matter for an interesting special monograph. In the Middle Ages the migratory urge, which has never been altogether eliminated from the human make-up, found a relief in pilgrimages. We do not know what proportion of the population went on pilgrimages or how often they went. Nor do we know the quantitative proportion of pilgrims in the world of Islam to-day. The German student and the German artisan have a mediæval knapsack tradition, but the latter wandered not so much for fun as to find work as a journeyman and settle down ultimately for good. For the bulk of people there was nothing like "the holidays" of the modern community, until the dawn of the railway era. Restless souls answered the call of the seas, of overseas adventure and of emigration. Lively lads enlisted or ran away to sea. For the most part, these restless souls went for good and never returned. Ordinary folks stayed where they were from start to finish. Samuel Warren's draper got no holidays, and had he got holidays he would have been hard put to it to find where to go. But people in prosperous strata above were already observing a seasonal migration to "town" and the "spa" in the seventeenth century. Directly the railways arrived, this fashion spread down into the middle classes. The railways assisted, by the introduction of excursion trains, which truly "supplied a long felt need." Now the whole working world takes holiday and our encyclopædia would have long histories of the seaside resort, of the battle against mixed bathing and against modern relaxations of costume, of the development of winter sport, of mountaineering and tourism. It would be a continuous unfolding of freedoms and refreshment, of new methods of catering and attraction, and on the whole it would be a very cheerful and encouraging history.

And, moreover, this great extension of leisure and this very considerable development of leisure occupations bear very importantly upon the economic and social difficulties we have discussed in Chapter XI, § § 5, 6 and 7. The primary needs of mankind, we have shown, are being satisfied by a smaller and smaller proportion of workers. Therefore, unless the standard of life rises, there must be a steadily growing proportion of the population unable to earn money, without spending power, and therefore without the ability, unless some form of "dole" steps in, to get and consume even their primary needs. By shortening hours, introducing more and more holidays, cutting down the working life at both ends, this surplus of unemployed workers may be reduced. But if also the standard of life for the primary productive workers rises by the development of leisure occupations, amusements, holidays and entertainments, there will not only be an increase of the numbers—or at any rate a check upon the shrinkage of the numbers employed in primary production, but also a new world of secondary employment will open up that may at last become as great a spectacle of activities as the old. This, indeed, without a revised currency credit system and a secure world pax, will not solve all the present perplexities of mankind, but it is a factor of very great importance indeed. Want more, live more fully, is the command of the new civilization; enjoy that others may also serve and enjoy.

§ 2. The Travel Bureau

There must be a section here, even if it has to be a very slight and allusive section, about the readiness with which human beings will at the slightest chance escape from fixed locality and everyday routines and set out to see the world. Hitherto there was not much chance for the generality of people; now every railway station appeals to the migrating impulse with gaily coloured posters of foreign scenery. Before the present age "over the hills and far away" was for most people an unrealizable reverie. There must have been a certain amount of coming and going in Greece at the season of the Olympiad. Tourists went up and down the Nile in the great times of Egyptian security and scratched their names on monuments and buildings already ancient and wonderful. And pilgrimages creep into history very early. There were pilgrimages in Egypt and Babylonia. I do not know of any good history of early travel, travel for piety or curiosity, or for the latter disguised as the former. The command of the prophet that all faithful Moslims should visit Mecca at least once in a lifetime made that form of wandering a great feature over all the East, and Christians began to resort to Jerusalem from the third century onward. All through the Middle Ages the pilgrim bands journeyed about Europe to this shrine or that, and for the sheer gad-about element in these wanderings see Chaucer's *Canterbury Tales*. In pre-revolutionary Russia the roads were pleasantly infested by tramps, each with his bundle and his kettle, seeing the world and living casually en route to pilgrimage centres. But there has never been anything before like the vast volume of journeys made frankly for pleasure that goes on to-day. Catering for pleasure travel is now an important industry.

There is no need to expand here what the reader can expand very amusingly for himself by applying to any travel agency. As this page is being read there must be hundreds of thousands of people in great liners upon the high seas, on pleasure journeys halfway round the world. There are scores of thousands of hotels full of transient visitors, trains of excursionists and trains de luxe rattling from country to country, and hardly a mountain pass or lovely highroad without its omnibus motor car of passengers agog. The "hiker" multiplies continually.

It is plain that, given prosperity and spare time, the great majority of human beings would go round the world two or three times and gratify an ample appetite for novel scenery and the different ways of men.

§ 3. *The World of Sport*

With the brief time at our disposal the writer and reader must now walk very quickly through another long, airy and attractive gallery in the vast museum of human activities this present work has evoked. This gallery is to represent all that efflorescence of athleticism and of looking-on at athleticism which goes on under the name of sport. It is an enormous and conspicuous aspect of modern life, and it may be capable of much further development.

Our gallery would pay its tribute to the athleticism of classical times. We have little record of sport in the older civilizations, except kingly hunting and the bullfights, gymnastics, and funeral games of the Cretan and other Mediterranean peoples. Those were palace affairs. The Aryan-speakers seem to have brought the chariot race with them when they flowed over and subjugated the ancient civilizations, and they seized upon and developed the sports of their predecessors. There were races on horseback so early as the third Olympiad, but the horse race never rivalled the chariot race in classical times.

We should trace the development of the Olympic games from a village festival to a great meeting which united all Hellas, and we should show how the gladiatorial fights of the Roman amphitheatre arose side by side with the Aryan chariot race in the hippodrome, out of a revival of the Etruscan sacrifices. Running, wrestling, boxing, weight throwing, were the main sports of the Greek meetings—and of all the ancient world. Roman gentlemen tossed balls to one another in the Baths, as Petronius tells us, but the widespread, regular playing of set ball games for exercise, from cricket and tennis to golf, seems to be a recent thing. There is scarcely a trace of it in the classical literature.

Games more or less like tennis and polo appear obscurely and intermittently in Persian, Arab and Egyptian records, but never as widespread practices. They were associated with mediæval courts and chivalry. To play tennis, the hard original tennis, you needed a castle moat.

The modern expansion of sport followed upon the industrial revolution and is closely associated with the revival of the universities. In the eighteenth century these institutions had shrunk very greatly, through the imposition of religious tests and the diversion of intelligent minds from scholarship to more interesting occupations. But the development of new types of well-off people, aware of a cultural inferiority, the general increase in wealth and the relaxation of sectarian jealousies, led to an influx of prosperous young men in the schools and colleges, anxious to become young gentlemen, but indisposed for any severe intellectual toil. The aristocratic conception of education through physical exercise appealed to them strongly.

The "sportsman" was already appearing in the first half of the eighteen hundreds. But "sport" was then a business of illicit boxing matches, dogfights, race meetings and the like, rather than real athleticism. It was frowned upon by the authorities. Cricket was discovering itself in England, indeed, and one or two English public schools had crude games of football with distinctive local rules. One found local sports of a traditional type in Scotland, a few Swiss villages and scattered unimportantly over the world. The big expansion of sport belongs to the latter half of the nineteenth century.

Then things went ahead very rapidly. The first athletic meeting in modern times, says Captain Webster in his British Encyclopædia article, was promoted by the Royal Military Academy, Woolwich, in 1849. Exeter College, Oxford, was next in 1850. Cambridge sports came in 1857. Oxford followed suit in '60, the Oxford and Cambridge meetings began in 1864, and English championships date from 1866. The American interuniversity meetings came soon after these British beginnings. International meetings appear in the record in the eighties. Thereafter there is a crescendo of sport. Our tale passes on to the revival of the Olympic games at Athens in 1896 and the appearance of great stadia for these gatherings, to remain as permanent additions to the athletic resources of the city of assembly. To such meetings Amsterdam owes its stadium; Paris, the Colombe stadium; London, the stadium at Shepherd's Bush (seating 50,000), Stockholm a stadium accommodating 15,000. These are far outdone in capacity by the Chicago (150,000), Yale

University (80,000), Illinois University (60,000) and Ohio State University (75,000) stadia, and London has since added to its resources the Wembley stadium of ten acres holding about 98,000. "The greatest capacities in the British Isles are now at Wembley Stadium, London, and Hampden Park, Glasgow; the highest recorded attendance, 129,810, occurred at the latter (in 1931), but at the opening of the former, in 1923, it is estimated that thousands more rushed the gates." In America, says the Encyclopædia Britannica (from which most of these figures are taken), there were only five stadia of importance in 1913, and now (1930) there are thirty. There is accommodation for two or three million spectators of athletic sport on any fine afternoon in the United States alone. The *English League* and *Scottish League* grounds (ignoring the hundreds of minor amateur and professional grounds) open every Saturday for football spectators are well over two and a half millions in capacity. There are four grounds holding over 60,000 in London alone (Wembley, Arsenal, Chelsea and the Crystal Palace Corinthians ground) and three others near 50,000 if not over (Tottenham, West Ham and Millwall). The original stadium at Athens which was reconstructed in marble upon its original ruins for the 1896 occasion held 60,000 people. The roman amphitheatres were never quite as vast as this; the very greatest, the Colosseum held, it is now estimated, about 50,000 (Talbot F. Hamlin).

These figures help one to understand the dimensions of the sporting world to-day. These gathering places are not like the Greek Olympic centre, used only once every one or two or four years. They are in frequent and habitual use. They add to our spectacle of factories, mines, plantations, transport, a vision of swarming myriads of usually sunlit folk in their places and in the arena, the shining bodies of beautifully fit and active racers, players and combatants, and the well drilled ranks of athletic associations in display.

And these stadia are not all. To them we must add the race courses with their grand stands, their coaches and parked automobiles, and the vast crowds of spectators and crowd-followers that assemble for such festivals as the English Derby or the Ascot week, and also we have to indicate such grounds as Lords and Kennington Oval, where they play cricket, and Wimbledon, with its tennis courts established for fifty years, must also come into the picture. And then from these culminating centres our eye must go outward, and all over the countryside of the modern communities are the football fields and baseball fields and cricket fields and tennis courts, where the balls fly and the healthy bodies flash to and fro. And then, in the less sunny weather, there are the running associations in vests and shorts, the "harriers" and paper chases, and so forth, and the resolute walking men, and the men in training loping cheerfully through the mud, fists clenched and lungs and heart at their steady busiest.

Add now to all this the paddled canoes, the single outriggers, the fours and eights and all the more leisurely rowing boats, that swarm upon every river near a great town. Add also the diving and swimming that go on in rivers, lakes, swimming pools and public baths. Add also the swarming beaches, the bathing places, and the basking lightly clad multitudes wherever there are sands by the sea. Bring in also the immense activities and pleasures of the snow sports that were almost unknown until the last decades of the nineteenth century, the luging, the ski jumping and the ski excursions. And the ice sports, the skating and curling. Mountain climbing is an older delight, but except for a few pioneers—De Saussure climbed Mont Blanc in 1787—it does not go back more than a century. And these pleasures are no longer monopolized by a small rich leisure class. There has been a great cheapening and distribution of athletic material—I do not know how far the development of rubber described in Chapter III has not made the balls so necessary for many games accessible to medium purses. Modern industrial methods have given the world cheap standardized balls. Without such balls the contemporary development of games could never have occurred. Football, one of the cheapest of games, has spread from the English industrial districts all over the Westernized world since the war. Any afternoon now one may see in the London parks a string of boys from some East End elementary school, who would already have been factory workers half a century ago, going out with a schoolmaster in charge of them to play their weekly game of football. Even in Egypt and the Sudan now the small boys play football.

All this in itself means human happiness on a world-wide scale. And never was there anything of the kind on earth before. Just like the swelling human population and the overwhelming production of staple goods, it is a consequence of the invention and discovery of the past century. There is no reason why we should not hope to see free, ample and lovely exercise in the open air brought within reach of every human being. There can be no limit to the beneficial extension of athletics.

But when we consider not the extension but the specialized intensification of athletic exercises and the domination of public attention and leisure by these activities, it becomes necessary to qualify our benedictions. It is good for a man to be fit and well developed; it is quite another matter when he gives, and is incited and driven to give, his whole being to the extreme exploitation of his neuro-muscular system. It is good for a community to have plenty of exercise; it is very bad for it to subordinate all other interests to sports and games. Athleticism in the present generation goes, it is admitted, too far. Reasonable sport accumulates energy, but excessive sport wastes it. From Euripides to Rudyard Kipling, with his "flannelled fool at the wicket" and his "muddied oaf in the goal," public-spirited men have had harsh words for the specialized athlete and game player.

The ascendency of sport is particularly remarkable in the United States of America. And from the United States universities come the boldest apologies for this tremendous concentration upon athleticism. Before the end of the nineteenth century university sports were mainly in undergraduate hands in America, as elsewhere. These were in part insurrectionary against the prevalent mental education. But the insurgent spirit of the richer and bolder students put the sporting side of the collective life into such prominence that the faculties of instruction had to accommodate themselves to the realities of the situation. The great "educational" value of sport was officially and formally discovered. An Intercollegiate Conference found sports could be used to "supplement and broaden modern education" and made the peak of a "physical education pyramid."

The "physical education pyramid" one can concede, but how careering about in fields in a semi-nude state can be supposed to "supplement and broaden" anything that an honest man would call education staggers the imagination.

However, on these assumptions and by much unsubstantial assertion of the moral benefits—"clean and healthful living" of athletes, for example, and "development of loyalty to the institution and to fellow members of the college community" (the gang spirit, in fact) the way was paved for the partial conversion of the American universities into athletic training centres. The athletic coach has now become the equal or superior in pay and dignity of the merely intellectual teachers, and the exhibition of sports an important source of funds for these institutions. Sport has indeed assisted in the financial revival of several state universities, whose merely intellectual teachers had failed to attract students in paying quantity. Conceivably some of them indeed might do even better financially by scrapping their intellectual faculties altogether, competing by scholarships for youngsters of athletic promise, and concentrating upon the stadium. The coach, the new "broadening" type of American professor, is sometimes a man educated on the older lines, sometimes a professor of modern hygiene, but often a promoted trainer or rubber or masseur.

In a list of "secondary objectives" in the statement of the Intercollegiate Conference, the realities of the situation peep out. Objectives 4 and 5 confess that these sports "provide opportunity to 'animal spirits' for legitimate physical expression" and "further the educational viewpoint and needs by securing and maintaining active interest of *alumni* and general public in the educational institutions through the field of greatest common interest and appeal." This concentration of sport in the universities is not in fact a development of education, but a distortion of the educational machine through an exuberant economic growth of the community which has swamped the country with endowments and with a multitude of people anxious to give their sons and daughters the social prestige of university graduation.

This inflation of sport is a natural and necessary result of the atmosphere of boredom created by crowding healthy adolescents who do not want to learn, into classrooms with teachers not particularly anxious to teach and not very clear about what should be taught, and its value as advertisement and its financial possibilities have been duly exploited by the college authorities. The influence of this development upon the general education of the community, and the desirability of withdrawing a large proportion of the better-class youth from general social and economic development to specialize as stadium performers and develop a gang feeling in intra- and inter-collegiate rivalries, lest worse befall, we will consider in the next chapter; our concern here is only with the physical aspect of the business and its radiation of health and excitement throughout the modern community. That radiation is undeniable. The health is for the moderate majority rather than the experts. The Encyclopædia Britannica states on the authority of the Carnegie Foundation for the Advancement of Teaching that twelve out of every hundred university football players receive "serious injuries." The figure given for all games is 3 per cent. These are the strenuous ones who are crippled, the vicarious offerings made for the well-being of the rank and file.

The same influences are at work in the promotion of athletics in the educational institutions of Europe as of America, but the European developments have not attained the same enormous scale nor devastated the intellectual life of the colleges to the same extent, because in their case there has not been the same steady advance in prosperity and spending power during the past two decades. The nearest approach to American conditions in Europe is to be found in the older English public schools. There an undernourished, underdeveloped slip of modern education travels, like an unwanted passenger in an overcrowded omnibus, between the captain of the cadet corps and the mighty cricketers and athletes whose attainments in the playing fields have determined their selection for the teaching staff.

One interesting aspect of athletic recreations is the organization of "records." In the past half century authoritative organizations have made the most precise and careful observations of human bodily achievements. We know now that man at his best can run 100 yards in 9 3/5 seconds. This has been done four times, by D. J. Kelly (1906), H. P. Drew (1914), C. W. Paddock (1921), and C. Coaffee (1922). Possibly it is a limiting record. C. W. Paddock also holds the 100 metre record (10 2/5 seconds). For longer distances the achievements of P. Nurmi, a Finn, remain unsurpassed. He ran a mile in 4 minutes 10 2/5 seconds (Stockholm, 1921), and he held all the records from a mile to 10,000 metres until Jules Ladoumègue did a mile 1/5 of a second quicker in October, 1931 (Paris). The highest jump so far recorded is 6 feet 8½ inches, by H. M. Osborne at Chicago in 1924, and the longest is D. H. Hubbards', of 25 feet 10 7/8 inches at the same meeting. J. Weissmuller swam 100 yards in 52 seconds and 100 metres in 57 2/5 seconds. But lists of records in a score of sports are to be found in every book of reference, and there is no need to give more of them here.

There seems to be no sensible objection to this exploration of human possibilities in every sort of bodily exertion. But in some directions a record hunt must necessarily take a murderous turn. For example, there is ski jumping. There is hardly any limit to the height a ski jumper, *with luck,* may not jump down and get away from. Up to a reasonable limit, men may compete and none be injured, unless for a broken ankle or so. Then as the dimensions increase, the adverse chances increase. The specially built hills from which the record jumps are made, increase in size and tend to increase still more. So that while people are willing to risk almost certain death or crippling injuries, there need be no limit to the record ski jump.

The same principle applies to many forms of mechanical record making, speed boats, aëroplane and motor-car races and the like. In these cases one is not dealing with a wholesome definite physical limit, nor is one really testing out a machine. More and more one is chancing the perfect smoothness or the perfect banking of a track or the limit of strength of a wing. Sir Henry Segrave was killed in his motor boat, *Miss England II,* on Lake Windermere, in an attack on the speed-boat record. The boat hit a scrap of flotsam at a speed of over 98¾ miles per hour, turned over in a cloud of spray, and sank stern downward. Mr. Hallwell, an engineer, went down with her. This *Miss England II* was recovered from the bottom of the lake, reconditioned, and on Lake Neagh, after a preliminary reconnaissance by aëroplane to make sure that the water was clear of driftage, Mr. Kaye Don got to an unofficial velocity of 107 miles per hour. But his official record made at Buenos Ayres was below this and he capsized but escaped uninjured in a later race. Then began a long struggle with Mr. Gar Wood, the record passing from one to the other and back. On Sep. 18th, 1932, Gar Wood in Miss America X attained an average of 124.91 miles per hour. Previously Sir Henry Segrave had made the record for automobile velocity on the Daytona beach 231 1/3 miles per hour, but his achievement was subsequently bettered by Captain Malcolm Campbell, who made an unofficial 260 miles per hour and an official record* of 246 miles per hour with the specially built car *Blue-Bird II.* A flight record of 357¾ miles per hour was made by squadron-leader Orlebar in September, 1929 and this was outdone by flight lieutenant G. H. Stainforth at Calshot on Sep. 29th, 1931, who reached a speed of 415.5 miles per hour and averaged 408.80 in four runs along the three kilometre course. Blériot, who was the first to fly across the Strait of Dover, is offering a prize for the first man who in any mechanical contrivance whatever achieves a horizontal speed at 1000 km.=621.37 miles, per hour. Quite possibly this is an attainable speed, but its attainment will exact a heavy toll of human lives.

It is possible that the development of record-breaking and display athleticism may be approaching its maximum now, or that in America it may even be passing its maximum. All the rational feats of bodily strength and skill may presently have been tried out to the limit. People will cease to beat records and only aspire to touch them. If the world's prosperity goes on increasing, the great majority of people may tire of the spectator's rôle in the stadium. They may find competing attractions. They may go to look on less frequently and less abundantly. There may be changes in the economic and industrial ordering of the world that will diminish the present supply of honourable amateurs for

Nature, February 14, 1931.

public games. Prosperous people may find some better method of launching their sons and daughters upon life than in offering them up to athletic uses. Public shows of games may become mainly professional displays of an exemplary sort. But this may not affect the wide diffusion of open-air recreation. That may be a permanent gain. If leisure increases, it seems likely to become more and more general, more and more a normal element in life.

THE SPORTING ELEMENT IN WAR, INSURRECTION AND MANY MURDERS

In a survey of human activities so essentially psychological as this that we are making, it is impossible to leave the question of sport and the sporting mentality without noting how closely allied are many of the impulses and motives that have been active in developing the world of modern sport, with those that are operative in maintaining war, and how closely allied complexes militate against order, tranquillity and security in everyday life. We have again to recall this fundamental fact in the human problems, that civilized man is a very imperfectly domesticated aggressive animal, that in each generation he has to be broken in again to social life, and that, whatever may be done to suppress, mitigate, or sublimate his fiercer, more combative impulses, there they are pressing against law, order and compromise. The American educationists find in athleticism a "legitimate" release for "animal spirits." Whether it is always adequate may be disputed, but there can be little dispute that the French Apache, the British Hooligan, the young American Tough on his way to become a gangster, are impelled very largely to their anti-social activities by impulses practically indistinguishable from the sporting spirit of their social betters.

So far we have said very little of hunting, shooting and other "blood" sports. We have still to note, for example, the almost pathetic spectacle of pink-clad huntsmen and hounds chasing rare and unpopular foxes, in spite of barbed wire, market gardeners, light railways, automobile-infested roads and chemical manure, across the suburban landscape of England, or rousing even the meek Egyptian fellahin to murderous protests. And here too we glance at the lined-up guns of a battue of pheasants, raised at great expense for the slaughter. These massacres are the last vestiges of the habitual amusement of monarch and noblemen throughout the whole course of history. The stir and effort, the triumph of slaughter, given by the hunt, have made it the dominant occupation of men of every race, who have found themselves free to follow it. And from the hunting of beasts to the man hunt was but a step. The two things mingle upon the painted walls of Egypt and the Assyrian sculptures. War and conquest was the sport of kings. And in all antiquity it is conquest and killing that is glorified. There is no trace in the record of any honest appreciation of an equal conflict fought out stoutly to an indecisive issue.

The American Indian was so great a sportsman that he subordinated all the rest of his life to the exaltation of the warpath. He inaugurated the season with mystical dances, and scalped and destroyed according to a precise and picturesque ritual. Throughout the ages, the historian can tell of communities, from the Huns to the Zulus, which have given over themselves (and their neighbours) altogether to the master sport of war. Clearly we have something in the human make-up here, very fundamental, fundamentally ineradicable, needing suppression and sublimation and likely to crop up again very obstinately whenever the suppression and sublimation relax. It is charged against the German Kaiser that he saw war as a sport and so precipitated the crash of 1914. It is at least equally true that Mr. Rudyard Kipling and his school, had presented imperial conquest as a sport to the minds of the British ruling classes. Only a few days before this was written some gallant British major-general—I made no note of his name—escaped from the control of his wife and wrote to the papers to say that war, the "man hunt," was the supreme sport of mankind.

How gladly would the unregenerate sportsman in ourselves chase that gallant gentleman into a gas cloud or drop him into a poisoned dugout and leave him there!

These "animal spirits," the American educationists recognize, crop up not only in the ragging and insubordination of students and the criminal violence of lower-class adolescents, but also, it is plain, in a certain proportion of adult crime. It is clear that certain uncontrolled human types, when they get the chance, will kill, as a cat or a tiger will kill, because it is in them to do so. We are not speaking here of lunatics; we are speaking only of a slight individual exaggeration of what is inherent and normal in man. Every man is a potential killer, warrior or murderer, and it is absurd to disregard that reality when we deal with the problems of economic organization and social and political control. Insurgent movements, insurrections, are a vast relief to the boredom of a countryside. Consider what a relief it must be to some poor devil, obsessed by a sense of social or racial inferiority, to make and throw a bomb, or waylay and murder a policeman, or riot and burn.

THURMAN ROTAN, FROM WORLD'S WORK.

MANKIND AT PLAY

A VIEW at Jones Beach, a new resort development on Long Island, owned and operated by the State of New York. It is one of the finest beaches in the United States, and almost the only one which has been designed with forethought and good taste.

THE CROWD RELAXES

THE beach at Coney Island, the greatest of all beach resorts in the United States. There is more than a mile of public beach, all of which is densely covered on a hot summer's day.

Many a revolution has been brought about by the want of sporting release, and as for war, the drums and trumpets, the martial music, the flags, the serried uniforms, the rhythmic jingle and tramping of marching men, and above all the sense of going off to a dramatic objective, call to all of us. It was necessary to spoil the sport of war by poison gas, air bombs, propaganda and the plain prospect of universal bankruptcy, before men would think seriously of giving it up. And when, if ever, we have "abolished war," we shall have to reckon much more thoroughly than we do now with the "blood" element in the sporting motive. Some forcible men will train and drill themselves and develop the service mentality, but not all; some bold spirits will hunt with a camera instead of a gun and be content with a picture instead of a skin, but not everyone will do that. Yet, if we can detach the adventurous element from cruelty, society will be the better able to keep cruelty under. With that first great pax in the world, the Roman Empire, the arena, the blood show, spread all over the civilized world. The civilized countries of to-day which are furthest removed from war display the greatest ruthlessness in sport. There is need for public watchfulness against the release of cruelty in sport. The world of sport, elaborately developed and firmly controlled, seems to be *inter alia* the most hopeful organ for excreting the more violent and adventurous ingredients in the surplus energy of mankind. *"Inter alia,"* we write, because sport leads also to greater fulness of life and beauty.

BETTING, GAMBLING, AND THE LOTTERY

Our survey of sport, to be complete, should include the betting world, gambling and playing for gain. One may raise the question whether these things are to be looked at under the heading of sport, or whether it would not have been advisable to treat them as an erratic branch of finance. And we may set aside either alternative with the suggestion that the reality beneath these things and beneath the lottery, which is prohibited in Great Britain, Belgium, Sweden, Switzerland and the United States, is something which is neither superfluous energy nor abnormal finance, but a craving to relieve a rather too dull everyday life by streaks of hope. To buy a lottery ticket is for most purchasers to buy something much more exciting than a novel or a cinema show. Until the drawing, the mind is pleasantly occupied by dreams of what will be done when the prize is paid. A bet (on reassuring information) at long odds, or a lottery ticket, is, at the worst, the key to many days of pleasant reverie. It is the imaginative stimulus for a dream that may come true.

That is from the point of view of the individual maker of bets. Energetic, fully and happily occupied people do not want these mitigations of an orderly life, and we may suppose that in a world growing more prosperous, various and interesting, betting will decline. The evil of betting comes in with the exploitation of this natural desire suddenly to get much for very little and so experience a bright, rare enhancement of life. The gambler soon comes to bet not with his odd superfluous coins but with his necessities. People will buy hope in such quantities that they deprive themselves of the necessities of life; too hopeful employees will borrow from the till on the strength of some tip or dream they have had; women will stake the housekeeping money, and men their wages. When the law intervenes with prohibitions, an illegal organization of betting arises in response to the attack. A full encyclopædia of human activities would include a small library upon anti-gaming and anti-gambling legislation and its evasions. It would be neither very entertaining nor very illuminating. Pictures of lottery drawing are very dull pictures. The only really agreeable thing about this complex dreary business is its multitude of gleams and states of hope. The actual prize winner, especially if the prize is big, is rather to be pitied than envied. Projected onto an unfamiliar plane of prosperity, socially transplanted, he or she in too many cases is destined to learn how little happiness can be bought in the world by an inexperienced buyer.

The habitual maker of bets and buyer of lottery tickets always loses in the long run. But specially attentive and industrious classes are able to make a living by ministering to the general gambler. Here we have no space for the ways and habits of tipsters, bookies and the like; for the journalistic side of gambling with its special sporting editions devoted to tips and starting prices, the organization of gambling clubs and houses, the corruption of games and the turf due to betting. From the prince's baccarat and Monte Carlo's roulette and *trente-et-quarante,* to the soldier's crown and anchor and the errand boy's pitch and toss, it is a history of stakes lost, relieved by incidents of irrational acquisition. It is a history of landslides in an account book. It is a pattern of slithering cards, dancing dice, spinning roulette wheels, coloured counters and scribbled computations on a background of green baize. It is a world parasitic on the general economic organization—fungoid and aimless, rather than cancerous and destructive, in its character. A stronger, happier organization would reabsorb it or slough it off altogether.

§ 4. *The World of Entertainment*

A field of human activities which seems certain to undergo great expansion and elaboration as human leisure and surplus energy increase, is the field of entertainment. Here the detail is enormously abundant and varied, and the alternative to a labyrinthine assembly of histories, panoramas and anecdotes of theatres and travelling companies, gipsy shows, bear-leaders, gymnasts and conjurors, street singers, menageries, circuses, clowns, fairs, hand, horse and steam roundabouts, minstrels and organ grinders, sing-songs, music halls, "variety" in all its forms, cabarets, revues, star actors and starry actresses, obscure actors and actresses, singers, musicians, music festivals, chamber music, concerts, Wagner, Reinhart, Crane, Barnum, Lord George Sanger, Mark Twain's immortal letter to Queen Victoria on the showman element in royalty, Maskelyne and Cooke, Mr. Charles Cochran, Mr. Ziegfeld, Mr. Frohman, the cinema, broadcasting, auditoria, admission, licensing, Sunday closing, censorship and prosecutions, books that profess to entertain, novels, novelists, playwrights, comic writers, comic papers, the newspapers as entertainment—is again to say "Museum" and evoke another ten miles or so of imaginary floor space, a cheerful deafening nightmare of glare, uproar, spangles and display. The record would go back into pre-history. The "funny man," the jester and the juggler, are probably as ancient as mankind. So are the singer, the story-teller, the acrobat, the dance and dressing up, the strange beast led about.

We may add, perhaps, a few general remarks about the entertainment world as a whole, about its atmosphere of thought and feeling, and then about what one may call its strangulation. For the strangling of entertainment is also serious business activity.

The psychology of the entertainer is peculiar. His persona lies outside any one of the three main types of persona described in Chapter VIII. Entertainers may be drawn from any class of mentality, but their peculiar circumstances lead very rapidly to the exaggeration of reactions that play only a secondary part in the lives of most human beings. The peasant's guiding principles are safety and profit, the nomad's, glory and swaggering advantage, the educated types, service and sound achievement. But the breath of the entertainer's nostrils is attention and applause. Only the modern politician approaches him in his sensitiveness to attention and applause. By them he lives, and for want of them he perishes—as an entertainer.

To a large extent entertainers are entertainers by heredity. This is truest of circus folk and performing folk generally, and least true of writers. Musicians are drawn very largely from professional musical families and music shops, if only on account of the advantage of early access to instruments and early stimulation. Nowadays, however, schools of dramatic art and music schools, and in America courses in story-writing and playwriting, introduce an unprecedented volume of new blood into the succession of those who would amuse.

Dependence upon applause produces characteristic traits. Applause is what the entertainer seeks, but what the normal human being desires in an entertainment is before anything else elation and laughter. Elation and laughter are the characteristic gifts of the best and most entertaining novels, plays, music and operas. These qualities compel applause. But since the great majority of professional entertainers have no very exceptional power of delighting, cheering and producing those happy surprises that stir the human heart to laughter, and since they have to live, they put it upon the common man in the audience that there are serious qualities in their work to which he must bring care and attention, that it behoves him to discriminate, to submit himself to instruction and learn to applaud not spontaneously but *properly*. He must be advised and shepherded by critics and reviewers, guided by a claque, and brought up to the applauding point in spite of his fundamental lack of response. Such are the essentials of the comedy of the entertaining world and so it is that that world is full of argument, assertion, detraction, plots and vile conspiracies, and infested by a great multitude of professional appraisers and praisers and suchlike critical journalists, clique organizers and advance agents; and why at the end of this chain of intermediaries the modern citizen sits before a long list of plays, shows, and entertainments of all kinds, by no means entertained, wondering distressfully where, if anywhere, he can go to find those rare, precious golden threads of self-forgetful happiness, those glittering, exalted moments which are the sole justification for any kind of entertainment whatever. And who among us has not stood before a row of books in a shop window, full of the same perplexity, gathering resentment against the authors without inspiration, the critics and publishers without discrimination, who live and flourish by seeming and failing to satisfy our universal frustrated desire?

Next only to prostitutes, no social class has been so needlessly pursued and vexed by administrators and magistrates as entertainers, and none has been so ruthlessly forestalled, hampered and crippled by commercial cunning. The entertainers, the artistes, preoccupied by their essential need for applause, and intent upon producing their effects, have little time or intelligence left over for the material arrangements of the publication or show. Here step in the impresario and the makers, owners, and conductors of exhibitions, theatres and other show places. They mediate between the public and the more or less gifted persons who would entertain the public, and they make their profits, and seek to make the utmost profits, according to the traditions of the ordinary entrepreneur.

There is consequently a disposition to restrict the output of popular displays with a view to higher prices, there are conspiracies to syndicate and monopolize theatres, music halls, and cinemas, to ration the most attractive stuff and serve it out diluted with less amusing or exciting matter, to buy up and monopolize and restrain the performance of star performers, and to cut the market of outstandingly original star performers by advertising and pushing inferior rivals and mere imitators into prominence. These traders in entertainment corner joy; they ration joy; they adulterate joy. All these activities intervene between us and our moments of real happiness in entertainment. They thwart and irritate us.

No need for museum exhibits here, for nearly everyone can fill in these general statements from what we have all known and felt. Not only do we not get nearly all the good entertainers and delightful entertainment or anything like the amount of their work that we might have, but we have a quite excessive amount of weak, plausible, sham entertainment foisted upon us. It is well to have a rationalized oil or coal industry, because here we deal with a standard commodity, but entertainment can never be standardized, and these ingenious people who quasi-standardize it and flatten and deaden it are real destroyers of human initiatives and of human happiness and well-being. This is one side, the commercial side, of this very real problem of contemporary life, the restriction and strangulation of entertainment.

It is a complex and difficult problem, and here we can offer no suggestion of how free trade in entertainment can be established and maintained. The municipalization of theatres and show places and their separate local management may alleviate this unofficial commercial strangulation of the entertainer. A municipal free-house working in competition with just as many private entrepreneurs as appear would check monopoly, but combined with a municipal regulation of privately owned show places it may easily develop into the second form of strangulation—strangulation by authority. A public authority may very well require that a show place for the public should be safe, sound, healthy and with a reasonable standard of comfort and elbow room. Further than that it is doubtful whether the public authority should interfere. But it does interfere most persistently. In all ages rulers, religious organizations and governments have regarded uncontrolled entertainment and particularly uncontrolled mirth, with suspicion. Mirth is a powerful solvent: the *aqua regia* of thought. All human authority is more or less haunted by the fear of ridicule. No doubt the Old Man in the primitive squatting place became restive at any unexplained laughter. Few people, even the most potent and flattered, are free from some element of self-distrust, and laughter is the natural enemy of all authoritative conventions. Even the court of Louis XIV must have had moments when it realized that it was just a little preposterous, and the Church of his time, that it was more than a little pretentious. The laws against sceptical or disrespectful jesting in the eighteenth century were severe. Actors and minstrels were vagabonds. No writer who wrote against authority could call his ears his own or hope to keep out of the pillory. And for the better protection of the realm, all who would act must be licensed as the King's Servants. Academies were founded in France to elevate the aims and ambitions of writers and keep the intellectual life of the community in due subjection to the great apex of the pyramid, and every English poet who did not delight outrageously might hope to become Poet Laureate. There was a real sustained effort during the eighteenth century, in Catholic quite as much as in Puritanical countries, to stand between the industrious masses of the realm and levity. Reading "light books," such as novels or poetry, was discouraged in the respectable home. "Fun," said the ruler, "by all means," and begged the whole question by adding, "innocent fun."

Is there ever any fun without its streak of naughtiness?

There has been much emancipation since the phase of high control in the eighteenth century, but not by any means complete emancipation. A cat may look at a king in all his majesty, but it will certainly be indicted for the worst possible taste and probably turned out of doors if it laugh aloud at him. The utmost absurdities of theology are still taboo. Only very little, remote, pearl-eyed, shark-toothed Polynesian gods may be laughed at freely. People may now protest "seriously" against current sexual institutions and sentiment, but good honest laughter in these matters is decried. You may leer and snigger a little, but Peeping Tom's giggle is the very opposite to the healthy "ha-ha" of a mind released. The absurdest military or naval proceedings, again, command and get attitudes of respectful homage. A marshal, spurred and feathered like a Bantam cock and claiming credit for a victory that happened to him, overwhelms us with awe. Who dare mock him on the stage? At the loyal and patriotic anthem we stand up and look as stiff and meekly dangerous as possible. People dare not laugh at these preposterous things, cannot laugh at them, because they have never been shown how to laugh at them. Yet the world is full of vast, solemn, disastrous old conventions and institutions that only a gale of laughter or the despairing fury of revolution can ever sweep away.

And so we go out from our entertainments into the streets again smug and subdued, like a genteel congregation leaving church; elation and laughter well drained out of us.

§ 5. *Art as a Product of Leisure*

Between Entertainment and Art there is no boundary. All entertainers claim to be artistes, even if there is much Art that does not condescend to entertain. Art is the larger term, and we are bound to attempt some generalizations about the immense variety of forms in which it expresses itself, before this chapter can be considered complete.

What is Art? That question was asked and answered with endless variations in ten thousand nineteenth-century debating societies. But from the biological approach it is seen as a special form of play which takes a constructive form. There are no precise boundaries between other forms of play at which one can say: Here play ceases and Art begins. Play is the happy overflow of energy of a more or less secure and satisfied creature under no immediate practical urgency. With dogs and cats and young human beings it takes the form of wild caperings and mock battles. Such caperings become rhythmic, pass insensibly into dancing, just as shouts and noises pass into song.

Human life is full of overflow and by-products. Nature, we may say, supplies the urge and conditions of life; the creature she evokes must have impulses to drive it, senses, feelings, preferences, discriminations. Then it will survive and multiply itself, and that is as much as concerns her. It is no affair of hers if the impulses are in excess and if these senses, feelings, discriminations and preferences open up beyond the world of mere existing propagation and survival, realms of effect beyond utility, and delights and emotions that serve no manifest biological end. You may say that all this world of feelings and responses that art explores is a mere superfluity upon the material scheme, like the colours of a bubble or the delight and beauty of a flower. Or you may say that it is an escape from the material scheme, that Nature, the careless old sloven, has quite heedlessly put a key into our hands that opens the portals of a universe of super-reality, more important than material being, a sublimated universe of emancipated and intense effectiveness.

This last attitude is that generally adopted by the artist and the art critic. They have to choose the alternatives we have stated, and the latter is the one they are practically obliged to choose. The former alternative would be intolerable for an artist with a normal persona, an admission of triviality that would take all the spirit out of life for him. Hence the artistic persona is almost always a mystical and arbitrary one, and the attentive critic toils, vaguely expressive, in pursuit. The real artist, with his music, his paint, his chisel, his pencil or his pen, explores his kingdom beyond space and time, explores his magical overworld, and endeavours to convey his not always very certain impression of his discoveries to appreciative minds. He shows. You must take it or leave it—if you do not get it then it is not for you—and therein he differs from the man of science who explores as boldly as the artist, but within material limits and with repeated experiment and reasoned demonstration so that he can prove and compel your acquiescence.

For this part of our survey of the human ant-hill we need invoke no imaginary collections, for all over the world there exist art museums and galleries; it is impossible to guess how many hundred miles of Art have been segregated from the general life and come to rest in these places. And we can point, too, to countless myriads of books about art, and still there will be the poets and the romancers and the fine writers to consider. But let us turn from these accumulations of achievement to the activities of painters, composers, poets, designers, contemporary playwrights and novelists. It is in many ways a distressful life. No artist is an artist all the time; he has his moments of serene divinity when he is absolutely sure of himself and his vision; the great artist has long periods of such assurance; but for the rest, the artist is an unsure, straining creature, miserably in need of reassurance and failing in courage. He has glimpses of his kingdom, and then it is hidden from him. And since in our present state of affairs much prestige and some profit come to the successful artist, he is jostled by a great number of pretenders, without vision, who imitate and put out the results of a pretended and fabricated inspiration. Many of these pretenders do indeed have gleams of artistic insight mingling with their dross, no great artist has been altogether free from dull moments of forced and routine performance, and there is every gradation between the almost perfect genius and the absolute impostor. The world of art is made feverish and miserable by its evident need for continual criticism, appraisal and condemnation. Critics are mostly very human in the worst sense of the word, so that no artist gets his perfect praise. Not for him is the full-bodied applause that greets the successful entertainer, nor the sure and certain "record" of the athlete. He may have done his utmost and be driven frantic by some stupidity of interpretation.

It exacerbates the sensitiveness of the genuine artist that he has generally to make a living by his art. He must sell his picture or his novel, he must get his composition performed. He cannot keep his mind indifferent to those banalities of criticism and publicity, on which his reputation and his income depend. And in this world of shareholders he finds himself working amidst a half competitive swarm of people who have larger or smaller independent incomes, who are attracted by the charm and picturesqueness of a literary or artistic atmosphere, who feel they "want to do something."

But we have said enough to account for the expression of tormented defiance that looks out upon us from under the extravagantly slouched hat and disordered hair and over the wild large tie of the artist. He is a tragic hybrid. He is divine; he is pitifully human. We can hurt him even without malice, stupidly and enormously. He puts up his distinctive fight against us in his own fashion.

Here we will but name the rest of the world of art and artistic literature, the picture dealers, the exhibitions, the publishers, the musical recitals and concerts, the new multiplication of music by radio and gramophone, a world which passes without any boundary into the world of entertainment. We can but glance and pass on.

Steadily through art, life explores the realms of human possibility beyond the limits of material necessity, as athleticism explores to the utmost the physical possibilities of human life, and entertainment sustains its continual protest against a purely rational interpretation of existence. "Eat and drink," says the hard rationalist, "and be merry" adds the entertainer, and opens one door at least upon the wonderland of art. It seems inevitable that as man conquers the three major problems that at present confront him, as he escapes from the suicidal obsession of warfare, the plain danger of overpopulation and the perplexities of economic strangulation, his released energy, his ever increasing free energy, will find its satisfactions very largely in immense artistic undertakings. No doubt it will also flow into the service of science, but though science illuminates, its main product is power—and it is art alone which can find uses for power.

Therefore, if we are not on the verge of a phase of disaster, it seems plain that we must be on the verge of an age of mighty art, and particularly of mighty architecture and musical spectacle. Architecture and music may be regarded as the primary arts. Painting, sculpture, all furnishing and decoration, are the escaped subsidiaries of architecture, and may return very largely to their old dependence. Spectacle is architecture animated, and music also, through the dance and the sound drama, leads the way to spectacle. There may be a very great rehabitation of poetry and fine prose composition under the influence of radio. For two or three generations we have read our poetry in books; we may return again to hearing it.

But it is not for us to attempt a prophecy of the coming forms of art. It is absurd to suppose that all that we now call art, the masterpieces, the supreme attainments, is anything more than an intimation of what the surplus energy of mankind may presently achieve.

CHAPTER THE FIFTEENTH

How Mankind Is Taught and Disciplined

§ 1. *What Is Education?*

SO WE come to the culminating chapter of our review of human activities. We have shown the factories at work, the houses being built, the armies drilled, the trains running, the food distributed, the population clothed, and the human race maintained and reproduced and increased from day to day, by the interplay of need and desire, guided by idea systems, by conceptions of how and why one ought to behave, and what is due to self and to others in this vast coöperation. We have introduced Jung's convenient new term, the persona in that exposition, and it has proved very useful indeed in handling this discussion. We have attempted a rough, obvious classification of the various types of persona by which human conduct is guided, and we have indicated how the social economic life of our communities is shaped by the multitudinous interplay of these various kinds of persona. But so far we have been vague upon the way in which these guiding personas are built up in human brains. Yet obviously, unless the entire psychological analysis on which we have based ourselves is wrong, the building of these personas and their associated ideology in the one thousand nine hundred-odd million brains of mankind is the central reality of human association.

Every human being is to some extent an educable creature. If it were not so, the loosely knit world community which already exists would be impossible.

And here we use educable and education in the widest sense. We are using it in the biological sense of the modification and elaboration of instinct, of innate dispositions that is, to behave in this way or that, through experience. Experiences enhance or restrain the original mechanical responses; the creature learns. As the *Science of Life* explains very carefully, this educability is vastly greater in mammals than in any other creatures, greater in the primates than any other mammals and immensely greater in man. In all these "higher animals" there is a

647

distinctive organ, the cerebral cortex, which is specially associated with this learning through experience. But in many animals, and particularly among the primates, there appear the rudiments of deliberate instruction. In man educability is carried to unprecedented levels by the use of symbols and particularly by the use of words. And now almost universally he draws and writes and so supplements his gestures and talking in their task of conveying and receiving suggestions. The education and instruction of even the highest anthropoid ape is quite immeasurably below the education of the most primitive savage.

The education of the savage, and also the education of a great proportion of simple and primitive people, is limited to the precept, examples and warnings of the small social group in which the individual is reared. He is shown and told what is needed for conduct in that restricted group in which he is to play his part. If he is a savage, he is shown the use of weapons, the simpler tactics of war and hunting, the use and manufacture of a few implements. It is suggested to him that certain things are things to be proud of and certain things are things to be ashamed of. And there are the imperatives of primitive law, the tabus, sexual limitations, respect for the property of others, minor specific restrictions, which must be observed under penalty. Everyone drums them into him. Everyone will see that he observes them. That suffices for his elemental needs. In the more restricted and specialized sense of the word, the normal sense of the word "educated," he is not educated at all. He is in ordinary language an uneducated person.

In that narrower sense he only begins to be educated when he is given definite and deliberate instruction in the exacter use of words, almost always with instruction in the elements of writing and counting, and when he is made to learn and remember histories which seem to explain the group and the world to him and assist him to play his part not only in the intimate domestic life, but in wider relationships. Even that much education is not yet administered to the whole of mankind. Up to a very recent date it was the privilege of comparatively limited classes even in the most advanced societies. Universal elementary education in a community is a thing of yesterday, and it is still imperfectly established. The extension of education to the whole of adult life in every class has hardly begun. Education is only dawning upon the world.

But education is being forced upon everyone by that rapid increase in the range, complexity and instability of social coöperation that is the fundamental characteristic of contemporary experience. Men have to read and write if only to understand messages, render accounts and adapt themselves to incessantly changing processes. You cannot train them and leave them. The traditional equipment of the peasant and the wandering herdsman and hunter has now to be enlarged and supplemented at a hundred points, if he is to maintain himself among the constantly multiplying exigencies of the present world. Everywhere, now, the teaching of reading and writing spreads: into the peasant life of Russia and Turkey, into the wilds of America and Siberia, into the dense peasant masses of India and China. That is to say, thin threads of understanding relationship are spreading into the minds of populations whose towns and villages were formerly as incoherent one with another, politically and economically, as grains of desert sand. The need for an extension of education created by the new economic life has been perceived, and perceived so plainly, in all the Western communities that, in spite of the jealous opposition of the baser sort of employer and of privileged people with limited ideas, it has already been carried through to the extent of creating an almost completely literate population. Nearly everybody in America and western Europe has learnt to read and write nowadays. Illiteracy recedes everywhere.

That an extension of the educational elements was bound to bring great changes in the ideology and the personas of the newly instructed was not at first evident. But reading and writing involved the penetration of general ideas into a majority of minds that had hitherto been untouched by them.

Instead of certain instructed and privileged classes the whole community is now accessible to wide general ideas and capable of incalculable interventions in the economic and political organization. The broadest ideology may appear now in action at any level in the social body. The educated persona which dominates the public services more and more, which has permeated even into the militant services, is now infecting and changing both the entrepreneur and the worker. The sense of service is spreading; it is becoming an ingredient in a growing proportion of personas. We are visibly moving towards an entirely literate and disciplined world, more and more clearly informed about its origins and its destinies.

The civilized world-state of the future will develop and can only develop in correlation with that spread of the educated persona. In the end that, with its variations, must become the universal human persona. The motive of service must replace the motives of profit and privilege altogether.

§ 2. *The Nature of Primitive Education*

When that encyclopædia of work and wealth we have projected is completed, or when our industrial museums have been extended to cover the whole field of human activities, there will be great sections devoted to education in its more specialized sense. They will show a continually broadening scope and a steady invasion of the everyday persona by large ideas.

The earliest formal education must have been instruction in the meaning of hieroglyphic signs and symbols, the teaching, that is, of reading and writing and the art of counting. There are learners' cuneiform writing tablets still in existence, four thousand years old and more, Sumerian pot-hooks and hangers. This was the substantial basis of all education for vast ages. To that was added a certain amount of explanatory lore. In our sufficiently spacious museum we should have models or paintings as well as specimens to illustrate types of primordial primary education; pictures of hedge-schools and dame schools, samples of horn books and alphabets, the abacus in use, slates and slate pencils, copy books and the like. That great educational museum of ours, which has yet to find its Oskar von Miller, will show scores of charming groups of the world's children at work upon their "elements." Rabindranath Tagore described to me how, in the schools he endowed upon his family estates, little Indians sat under trees in the open air learning after the fashion of the past to make their letters with styles upon big leaves. I remember learning my A B C from my mother with the help of a sheet of letters which she had stuck up in the kitchen, and the first word I wrote was "butter" on a scrap of paper put against the window to trace over the copy she had made. From such primitive methods our museum will ascend to that more systematic and scientific training, not only in letters and figures, but in shapes, colours and outline that has been developed from Froebel's initiatives in the kindergarten.

Many of my contemporaries got their "elements" in the same old-fashioned way as I. They learnt the numbers as shapes and their "tables" of multiplication, and so forth, long before they realized what it was all about. Such propositions as "five and two are seven" or "twice five are ten" were learnt as dogmas. A single unsoundness in the set of dogmas thus acquired was enough to send all their summing wrong and give them a lifelong dread of the uncertainties of calculation and the perplexities of mathematics. Their "sums" came out wrong, and there was no way of checking and discovering the faulty tendency. A little boy who had slipped into the heresy that $5+7=11$ or that $7\times8=48$ might have his life embittered and suffer punishments and impositions for years through the operation of that one undetected defect.

Interesting modern developments will be displayed in these collections showing how the accidental misconceptions and physical idiosyncrasies of children can now be observed and detected and corrected. Hitherto astigmatism and other optical defects have made adding and suchlike processes in column, and the swift recognition of figures, difficult for multitudes in every generation, and have stamped this swarm of unfortunates with an unjustifiable sense of their lack of "gift" in these matters. Defects of hearing and obscure mental resistances have led to a similar imputation of stupidity in the use of words. The old elementary teaching was a wasteful process because it was unobservant. At every stage it left crippled and uncompleted minds by the wayside.

Superposed on the necessary first-grade instruction in the codes of intercommunication comes the teaching of social explanations, the teaching of the common ideas that hold the community together, its history and its usages. This lore and the way in which it is imparted vary enormously throughout the educational spectacle. Here again we contemplate a vast region of fact that still awaits the labours of an army of investigators. The persona of the adult is made in the mould of this elucidatory and initiatory teaching, and through the aggregate of the personas of the community flow all its activities. At this most important part of our enquiry into the motive forces of the human ant-hill we find ourselves again in uncharted and unsettled territory.

That anthropological part of our coming encyclopædia, that still uncrystallized Museum of Human Education, when it has been brought into being, will display, arranged in order, an intricate, strange variety of methods adopted by savage and barbaric peoples throughout the earth. Just as there was a stage in the development of agricultural processes when the sowing of seed and the beginning of a new year seem to have been inseparably associated with human sacrifices, so almost everywhere we find traces of cruel, dark and grotesque ceremonies at the dawn of sexual maturity. Fasts, vigils, torture, mutilations, the knocking out of teeth, the tattooing of the body were inflicted. And after various dire tests and strains, there generally appeared a pretense of imparting profound secrets. The incidence of these initiations varied widely. Some were the lot of everyone in the tribe, or they fell most heavily on the men, or they were restricted to particular ranks in the social body or made exceptionally onerous for those ranks. They were the crown of the popular education of all the folk concerned, or they were the culmination of the special education of the priests and medicine men.

The teaching of the young savage about himself and the conditions of his life, what he was, what the tribe was, what he might do, what he might not do, what powers he should respect and why, was manifestly threaded into this testing, straining, and breaking-in process. But at present our knowledge of the psychological forces concerned, what were the motives and ideas of the elders who imposed these ceremonies, and how they reacted upon the persona of the neophyte, is very obscure. Even our accounts of the actual rituals in many cases are extremely imperfect and unsatisfactory. More often than not the idea which led to the adoption of this or that ceremony is lost completely in the remote past. Each generation has gone on repeating what was done before, with occasional elaborations and mutations of the things done, reverence increasing and deepening as the last rays of rationality vanish. When the ceremony has become a mystery and a sacrament, then its establishment is secure.

There is a streak of original cruelty in the human make-up, a disposition to experiment upon our fellows, a taste for strange, impressive, and terrifying behaviour. All peoples seem to like grotesque masks, monstrous images and antics, throbbing and menacing music and ceremonious dances for their own sake; but the normal human disposition is all against admitting that these things are mere play and purposeless excess; they are justified therefore in inventing deep reasons and grave imperatives. In an earlier chapter of this work (Chapter I, § 5) we have shown how the human community grew against resistances and particularly against the dispersive influence of the jealousy of senior for junior. There may be an appeasing element mixed up in initiation; there may be a vindictive and dominating factor in the primitive educational process. The jealousy of the seniors works itself off. We do not merely teach the young, we "larn 'em."

The disposition to inflict suffering and impose submission is still plainly perceptible in our records of the education of the growing civilizations of ancient and modern times. The teacher approached his pupil in the mood of a snarling dog, hardly concealing the implements of discipline, the rod, the cane, the birch, the leather strap. It is all too plain that he did not mean to use them only in the last resort; he meant to use them at the first opportunity. Our Educational Museum will have cases and diagrams of these once necessary instruments, and all literature will be ransacked for our encyclopædia to find illuminating quotations about this flagellatory phase in the teaching of mankind.

Even the "elements" were taught harshly and clumsily in primitive education, and the comparison of savage initiations with one another and with classical and mediæval educational methods will, I think, reveal more and more that the second stage of education has aimed partly indeed to impart a history and an explanation, but mainly to cow, abase, break in, and so socialize the presumably recalcitrant and insubordinate newcomer. Even to this day it is charged against the English public schoolboy that he has been given a morbidly exaggerated sense of "good form," that he is a moral coward, afraid to think for himself or look hostile public opinion in the face. He is subjugated not only by the teaching staff, but by the conservative influence of the senior forms entrusted with the "traditions of the school"; he has all the individual "nonsense" knocked out of him. So the prize boy becomes the orthodox second-rate man. That particular indictment we will not discuss here. But it is plain in any realistic and circumstantial account of schools throughout the ages that the pedagogue has had a very aggressive way of leaping upon his human material and driving it before him. And much of the amelioration of upper-class schools in the last hundred years or so has been rather a relaxation of pedagogic energy, fierceness and clumsiness, under the protests of parents and public, than any very definite revolution in the teachers' conception of educational method.

The extensive disappearance of violence and dogmatic compulsion from education in recent times is apparently only one aspect of a general mitigation of the relations of human beings one to another. It has gone on parallel with the decline in the beating and ill-treatment of servants and workers, and the diminished arrogance of employers, and it is due to deeper causes than any specific educational reform. We have already indicated how far the greater prosperity of our species and the civilizing influence of the machine have contributed to this amelioration of life. "Democracy" is one of the terms we use to express this changed spirit in the world. We are not so sure who are inferiors and who are superiors as we used to be. Projects are explained to people instead of being imposed upon them, and the imperative mood gives place to persuasion.

The world has discovered that the common man is neither so stupid nor so obstinate as was once supposed; a large part of industrial progress has consisted in taking the worker into the confidence of the entrepreneur, and a quite parallel change in spirit has gone on throughout the educational organization. The declared object of education is no longer to make a suitable instrument for the carrying out of a subjugating and restraining tradition; it has become the stimulation and release of a willing collaborator in an adventurous enterprise.

This implies not only an extensive change in the spirit and method of teaching, but also a revolutionary change in the content of education. The persona evoked has not only to be of a different quality, but it has to look in a different direction.

To the development of that change of direction this entire work is devoted, and we now approach its concluding definition.*

§ 3. *Religions and Education*

Here it is we must bring in the church spires, the towers, the minarets, the modest chapels, the cathedrals, cloisters and episcopal palaces, the church house, the monastery, the nunnery, the lamasery, the religious retreats, pilgrimage centres and wayside shrines, scattered about our world. Or rather we must bring in the activities of all the men, women and children which centre upon these, who perform ceremonies, celebrate occasions, chant, fast, pray, and watch in and protect these picturesque and often very beautiful aspects of the human landscape. What do they signify to us in our review of the human ensemble? What in fact is the social significance of religion?

Let us recall the limitations we have set ourselves in this work. As we defined our scope in Chapter II, § 4, we are dealing with "man's gradual and at last methodical extension of mastery over the forces and substances about him—in space and time as he experiences them, in existence as he knows it." We have refused to follow the new-fashioned mathematician or the old-fashioned theologian beyond this everyday life, and we are concerned with religion therefore only in so far as it now influences the activities of people and affords occupations for them. It is not for us to discuss here whether this universe has in fact existed forever or (what is for all practical purposes the same thing) that it was flung into being in the year 4004 B. C. as a going concern so

*A good general account of modern educational experiments is to be found in *Towards a New Education*, edited by William Boyd and published by the New Education Fellowship. See also *Training for Citizenship* by E. M. Hubback and E. D. Simon.

contrived that it implied an infinite past. It does not concern us whether (in some profoundly symbolic fashion, of course) the cosmos rests on a tortoise which rests on an elephant whose legs reach "all the way down," or that it is all a thought in the mind of a Jeans-like Deity whose symbol is the square root of minus one, who started his vast meditation with the simple proposition, "Let there be light" and gradually worked things out—a game of Patience played by a Being of Infinite Leisure—to produce a recognizable reflection of Himself in the mind of a popular savant. These and every other form of cosmic poetry, logomachy and "mystical" interpretation of Being are outside our scope altogether. We refuse all theological controversy. We do not interpret Being here. We accept Being. However Being may be interpreted, it remains for man mainly an affair of economic coöperation in which his to-day is filled with the cares of to-morrow. That employs him, and that is what concerns us here. We deal with Being here only as it presents itself in the everyday life, and with religion only as a social fact in a spectacle of facts.

In fact, religion appears at first in the human story as something as practical as a flint arrowhead. Its gods were once as actual and material as men. Its chief festivals turned on seedtime and harvest, and its sacrifices and the benefits it promised were, so far as we are able to tell, entirely mundane. Even when the idea of immortality came in, it was to begin with a quite materialist immortality, a resurrection of the actual body, or a life in happy hunting grounds as real as earth.

We are profoundly ignorant of the religion of palæolithic man. There are guesses that he had a sort of fetishism, and that he imagined minds and wills in everything. They are just guesses. It is doubtful if the present beliefs and customs of still savage people furnish very sound indications of the working of those archaic minds. A savage is as many generations away from primitive man as we are.

Still less do we understand the mental operations of the generations transitional to the early agricultural peoples. Advancing psychology may presently find acceptable explanations of the steps which led to the specialized priest and the altar. Through stage after stage we may build up again in our imaginations that mighty growth of fears and personifications, of symbols that were living realities to the worshipper, of vast overhanging imperatives and assurances. Now it is only in rare flashes of intuition that we glimpse the gods and spirits and powers that our ancestors knew for real. The early civilizations, as archæology reveals them, show a threefold society of peasant, of nomad conqueror and trader and of initiated priest, already established, believing in the gods and in the guidance of those gods. The religion as prehistory displays it is intensely practical, and the priest monopolizes the thought and knowledge of the community. He is astronomer, man of science, doctor, lawyer, banker, architect and art director. He is subjugated to his god and to his order, and he is saturated with the idea of service. The whole mental life of the community is in fact at that early stage religious.

So, still very largely unexplained, Neolithic society breaks upon our knowledge.

The collective mental life has long since lapsed from its homogeneity in the early communities, by the distinction and disentanglement of the learned and technical callings from the religious priesthood, pure and simple; by the escape through specialization of this great service and of that, from immediate association with the temple. The professions specialized away from the religious body, but the religious body to the best of its ability remained generalized and directive. It did not accept any specialization, though a sort of specialization was thrust upon it. By the later Middle Ages, the lawyer and the study of law, the medical profession, philosophy, science, finance, banking were all practically secularized, and the formal religious organization, though still the directive power of society, no longer permeated the whole net of intellectual activities.

Finance had indeed been secularized since classical times. When the great Semitic civilizations of Mesopotamia and the Mediterranean had collapsed before Aryan conquerors, the cruder religious organization of these latter never took over the banking, loaning and insurance of the ancient Temples. That remained in Semitic hands.

From the time of the Greek republics onward, whenever a class of independent gentlemen arose there was also an escape of philosophy and science from the priests. But though they escaped they were still subordinated. If men thought and experimented with a certain freedom they did so under God or under the gods. Plato, Socrates, Euripides pursued the most penetrating and subversive enquiries, but they saluted the gods with respect. They could think and say what they liked within limits and to their own special circle, but they had to respect the divine control of the general community. The earliest scientific society dedicated itself to the Muses.

Education has been the last field of intellectual activity to pass out of religious control, and it is still imperfectly and doubtfully released.

General education was still almost entirely in consecrated hands in the sixteenth century, and most of the great statesmen were still clerics. There is a manifest reason why there should be this sustained association of school and altar. The lawyer could begin as a special sort of priest and presently cease to be a priest at all, because explaining the moral order of the universe and keeping contact with the gods had manifestly ceased to be any part of his business. But the teacher who began as a special sort of priest has remained priest because he has, even more than most priests, to explain the moral order of the universe and keep up the contact between the learner and the gods.

In our own times in England and France we have seen a great movement to "secularize" education and a powerful resistance to that movement. The conflict has played a large part in the political life of both these countries for half a century, and the disentanglement of school and Church is still very incomplete. It is, in fact, an impossible disentanglement. The moral order of the community must be expounded in some fashion; if the gods and creeds are to go, there must be another story told and a fresh creed explained.

Secularism cannot do without the religious function; it cannot banish a rationalized devotion. Quite as much as religion it has to present life in an ordered series of values in which self takes a subordinate place.

If the reader will recall the chief religious revolutions, revivals and new beginnings throughout the world, he will, I think, agree that in all cases they were animated by the desire to restore the original comprehensiveness of religious direction. They are educational resumptions or attempted resumptions, a bracing up of education. They all arose in times of change and mental confusion, and either they sought to recall the old gods or formulæ in an invigorated state, or they attempted to substitute new ones. Buddhism, Christianity, Islam, Communism arose, all of them, not as new and interesting discoveries (or denials) in the field of theology, but as complete new ways of life, to which law, hygienic régime and medicine, social custom, thought and enquiry had to be reoriented. In each the convert had to be "born again." He had to come out from the City of Destruction. He had to learn a new way of life. They were all "teachings"; they were all in essence educational, a new sort of training for a new sort of living.

Throughout the ages religion in its various forms has always been providing or attempting to provide *the common explanation of the community;* to state, so to speak, the community's "articles of association." It has held communities together even if it has never, in historical times and so far as we know, completely and entirely bound them into perfect organized unities.

If we consider the histories of the main religious beginnings and reform movements of the historical period we shall find a sort of parallel development among them all. They arise with a sort of glory in men's souls. The common things of life are transfigured. To begin with, the new faith is always intensely practical, always. It demands a change of the whole life. Things have got into a dreadful state, and they have to start afresh. Whatever the revelations, theories and mysteries on which the new teaching professes to be based, a new sort of behaviour is its substantial aspect. The normal everyday life, the "world," has to be renounced altogether. It is the new religious life or nothing. The rich young man has to sell all that he has and follow in the footsteps of the Teacher. All men are to be converted and brought under the yoke of the faith. Manifestly all education has to be renewed from the ground upward.

But soon the teaching is taken up by disciples who hand it on to other disciples. They go out from the inspiration of the Master to obdurate and inattentive people already set in established ways of living but who, they feel, ought to be attracted and persuaded. And presently the Master is no longer with his disciples to revive their flagging zeal and criticize their interpretations. Compromise creeps in. The new faith reduces its terms. Things are made easy for those who will come part of the way but not all the way. A distinction is made between those who lead a full religious life and the lay adherent. Times and seasons are prescribed for religious duties, and the rest of the daily life is tacitly released from the grip of the advancing religion.

A process of "spiritualization" begins. The Master taught, perhaps, that the spirit was more important than the letter, but now this is interpreted to justify a mitigation of practical applications. A distinction is drawn between *deadly sins,* like denial, blasphemy, failure to respect the prescribed sacraments and the like, which break up the organization and so remain of vital importance, and *venial sins* which merely disregard the rules of personal conduct. Sins of the flesh, usury, dishonesties, these the religious specialist will forgive on reasonable terms so long as you will not attack the fundamentals of his organization and creed. Make the sign of the cross, or repeat the formula that Allah alone is God, admit that your sins are sins, and you may sin in comparative peace.

And not only is the practical influence of the spreading faith thus attenuated and detached, but also it becomes "tolerant." It is tacitly admitted that it is, after all, not supremely important. Islam, which began with the alternative of conversion or the sword, presently arrived at the more practicable alternative of conversion or tax-paying. The believer and the damned meet with increasing amiability as this attenuation of religion proceeds.

It becomes less and less possible to distinguish the converted by any external tests. Even their spiritualized religious exercises begin to be neglected. The formulæ remain devitalized and dying. Yet the organizations fight for existence, and the sincere believers fight against this broadening decadence. Many are diverted into partisanship and into a preservative persecution of the scoffer and the open unbeliever. There is a struggle against mixed marriages, against unsympathetic talk and books, against novel practices. Instead of the "glad tidings" of the opening phase appears orthodoxy indignant in an inattentive world. What was once an inspiration has become an obstruction; from conquest the creed has passed into opposition. Religions begin as the dawn of God and end with their backs to the wall.

Such is the common history of religions as the world has known them since history began. It is as true of sectarian departures, of Quakerism and Calvinism for example, as of Christianity as a whole. Religious impulses are always "fading out" and always being renewed. They do not disappear, but they lose emphasis. They lose fire and quality. They are great impulses in life, and they spread and spend themselves in conquest. The flash ends in ashes.

Yet the need of religion for a comprehensive statement of life and right conduct is perennial. Religion after religion is evoked by that need; each tries to recapture that completeness of control over life which was originally exercised by belief and fear in the early communities, and each in its turn fails.

At present great multitudes of us are living in a state of faded religiosity. The formal religious organizations of the Atlantic world are little more than the spiritualized husks and trappings of long abandoned efforts to begin a new way of living for mankind. About each there has clustered an accumulation of buildings, endowments and methods of feeling and behaviour. These things go on by a certain inertia and by the imponderable elements in the human make-up. The new way of living, the new rule of life has largely or entirely disappeared or become the "rule" of some professing order, but the "spiritualized" functions and ceremonies still exert an emotional and habitual appeal. So far from revolutionizing life and taking people out of worldly routines, religions in their last phase serve rather to allay restlessness, silence uneasy questionings and reassure by their atmosphere of conviction and ultimate knowledge.

Least faded of all the variations of Christianity is the Roman Catholic Church. This does maintain not merely a struggle for its own existence and an obstinate grip upon its schools, but a stout and definite attempt to control the lives of its adherents. Not in economic life. In economic life the control of the church is and always has been very weak, it repudiates Socialism without any clear definition of the sin involved, but in things biological and intimate its determination to direct is real and living. We have noted this already in Chapter XIII, § 1. Upon the fundamental issue of birth control there was a phase of hesitation on the part of the Church. Bishop Bovier of Le Mans, for instance, in 1842 warned the Pope that to prohibit the practise of contraception would weaken the power of the Church in France. It was only in December, 1930, that the Pope finally slammed the door upon "toleration" in this matter and restored the sacrament of marriage to an unambiguous material significance.

The Roman Catholic Church thus remains as a body the most practical, the least "spiritualized," of all the main sects of Christianity. It confronts its adherents with a definite way of living which in this respect at least is in plain antagonism to modern ideas. It has launched upon a deliberate struggle to deflect education from modern ends. Roman Catholics have now no choice but to obey, or to disobey and lie about it (which the confessional makes difficult) or to leave the Church.

In Moscow I have been told there is a Museum of Religion of a bitterly polemical type. But it is possible to imagine a Museum of Comparative Religion void of all polemical suggestion that would bring together in a very illuminating way the altars, rituals, symbols, costumes and prescribed types of building of all the world's creeds from Rome to Hayti and from Tibet to Yucatan. We should trace how Persia, ancient Etruria, Hellenic Alexandria, have contributed to the temples of to-day. There could be gramophone records of music, of revivalist preaching and chants, working models of genuflexions and prostrations, and all the instruments and methods of purification, mortification, and penance. All these things a museum could show, but no museum can recapture the hopes, the ecstasies and despairs, the passions of devotion, the abasement and the ennoblement of minds, of which these things are the sounds and hulls and instruments. Throughout the ages ten thousand million souls have been lit and have flamed upward, consoled and exalted by religion.

A myriad religious activities are in progress as this page is read, and our panorama of all that occupies mankind would not be complete without them. At Benares fakirs and saints are doing the strangest things, sitting cross-legged, their arms limp, their palms upward, squinting at the tips of their own noses in a meditative ecstasy, lying on beds of spikes, maintaining incredible attitudes; yellow-robed, shaven-headed men are tending the wind-driven praying wheels of Tibet; there are pilgrimages afoot in every quarter of the globe, chantings, kneeling, sacrifices. At Altotting, in Bavaria, on nearly every day in the year there are men and women on their knees dragging heavy wooden crucifixes round the Chapel of the Black Virgin. Wherever you are, there are probably men and women fasting and praying within a few miles of you. There is exhortation going on at this moment in cathedrals, in great public halls, in little plain chapels, at the street corners, in forest clearings.

All this religious doing is as much a part of the world of work and wealth as the beating of foundry hammers and the clatter of looms. It may be withdrawn a little from the main stream of production and distribution and consumption, but it draws its impetus from the same sources, and it moves forward together with the rest of the living flood. It reacts upon production, consumption, buying and selling, population and practically all the material concerns of life.

Statistics, such as they are, suggest that the current of these ceremonies and devotions has dwindled relatively to the main stream of life in the past century or so. It is difficult to ascertain what proportion of the world's population is now under vows, consecrated to a religious life. There do not seem to be any statistics to show the increase or decrease of the monastic and conventual life. The maximum, so far as Christendom goes, is believed to have occurred in the thirteenth century. Nor are there figures to show the waxing or waning of Buddhist monasticism. The Christian churches complain of diminished attendances of the laity. The churches open their doors for service, the church bells peal, but the swelling torrent of modern life seems to heed these invitations less and less.

Perhaps the most vital contemporary religion—as we have defined religion—is embodied in the disciplines of the Communist party. It is vital in the fact that it is still in continuous contact with conduct. It is elaborately protected against "spiritualization" by an insistent dogmatic materialism. It admits no significance for life whatever except here and now. The Communist prides himself upon this implacable materialism. He, at least, he is resolved, will not fall away from the intense practicality which all other religions have so conspicuously lost.

If he does fall away in the future, it will be in the name not of spirituality but of strategy and tactics. He may *reculer pour mieux sauter,* and then never return for the leap. Christianity started with a community of goods which it presently became convenient to disregard. The sense of this danger of "weakening off" haunts the Communist world and produces, just as it has produced in other religions, a heavy stressing of orthodoxy. The religion is fighting hard for great ends, and there is a heavy strategical disadvantage in any modifications of doctrine in the face of the "enemy." It fears criticism for exactly the same reason that the military type fears criticism, because it weakens discipline and breaks the fighting front.

Communism clings to orthodoxy, the true and only faith, and already there have been heresy hunts in the Communist body. There is a sort of Inquisition into the sincerity of professed believers and servants, and there has been a panic lest the faith be betrayed. Eminent officials are accused; they are subjected to rigorous enquiries, they confess and submit gratefully to discipline. If the Five Year Plan falls short, it will be through conspiracies and sabotage, for it is contrary to the creed that the Five Year Plan should fail through any inherent defect. For the edification of the weaker brethren there are now prophets and saints, Marx and Lenin to begin with, whose intelligence and character must no longer be questioned, whose every utterance was divine. And there is even a mystical communism, affecting the art and literature of Moscow profoundly, whose aim is self-identification with "the Proletarian." "The Proletarian" is a superhuman entity with whom the devout Marxist seeks and attains spiritual communion. The individuality of the worshipper is merged therein. From the Proletarian springs "Prolet-art," for example, among the first fruits of the new spirit. It is art without individuality. Proletarian thought, proletarian science, proletarian conduct have, it is believed by the devout Communist, strange and novel superiorities of their own.

Already Fülop-Miller in the *Spirit and Face of Bolshevism* has initiated the study of these developments. The comparative theologian will find close and interesting analogies between these aspects of Communism and Christian and Moslem mysticism.

From our present point of view Communism is only the latest and not the last of the world religions. We may foretell, but it is difficult to anticipate, others. One guess may be permitted here. Communism may be the last wave of dogmatic religion. It seems probable to the writer that the development of religion in the future may differ in one important respect from the way in which all religions, up to and including Communism, have arisen in the past. In the future there may be a religious organization without a Founder or an initial inalterable Teaching.

All religions hitherto have begun with extreme definition; with the assumption that the final truth was now revealed. That was on all fours with the mental dispositions of the ages of tradition. But just as nowadays all sciences are consciously progressive, working towards more truth but never attaining absolute truth, so modern religion may become also a continually progressive thing. Do not modern conditions indeed necessitate such a new type of religious approach? Our world is now launched upon a perpetual investigation and innovation, and its ideal of education is no longer the establishment of a static ideology, but the creation of a receptive and coöperative alertness. For that no fixed inalterable teaching will suffice.

All those forms of mental service we have considered in our study of the priestly persona, that have escaped one by one, as we have said, from the original comprehensiveness of religion, need now to be brought back into a common understanding. They left organized and formulated religion behind very largely because of its inflexibility. They left it high and dry and flowed out into the world. So that the world has become more and more scattered in its ideals and aims. Education, law, finance, research, literature, all begotten by the priestly tradition, have ceased now to have even ceremonial relations with organized religion. Liberal minds conceive education nowadays as divested of any existing religious form. Nevertheless, we realize the necessity of some more comprehensive teaching that shall restore the declining unity of human motives. If we cannot teach imperatives we have to teach aims. We have to restore unifying power to education. We seek a new education to achieve the synthesis of the new world community.

But if we are seeking to frame out a new education in view of the new ways of living that open before us, we are thereby and at the same time starting religion anew.

§ 4. *Universities*

Just as the forms and methods of the new economic organization of mankind spring from the social order of the Atlantic civilizations, so the types of educational method that now prevail and spread over the earth are mainly the fruits of Western Christendom. The two things have gone together. In the educational museum of the future, the young Moslim shrilly learning the Koran by rote, the Chinese student toiling to recognize and shape one complex character after another and acquiring a miscellany of phrase and information in the process, will be found in side galleries leading nowhere. The main aisle will carry us from the schools of Rome through the schools of mediæval and modern Europe to the world education of to-day.

Latin education under the Empire had separated itself very widely from religion. Religion had passed into one of its most attenuated phases, and the recognized worship of the gods was being supplemented by that variety of cults, Neoplatonism, Isis worship, Mithraism, primitive Christianity, and so forth, out of which orthodox Catholicism arose at last triumphant. The school and the pedagogue had practically nothing to do with these religious developments. Formal education concerned itself with the teaching of Greek and Latin and with rhetoric, and it was restricted to a limited class. What ideology the young received came to them from the world about them. There was no religious doctrine in formal education. There was not, therefore, as Cloudesley Brereton points out very clearly in his excellent article in the current Encyclopædia Britannica, any violent conflict between ascendent Christianity and the pagan schools. They were taken over by the Christian synthesis.

The dark ages of barbaric disorder and social confusion in Europe attenuated but did not break the Latin educational tradition. The curriculum of the schools that emerge in the ninth and tenth centuries is recognizably the same as that of the schools of the second century B. C. plus an ideology—to wit doctrinal Christianity—and minus any Greek learning. The Latin language, some Latin literature, logical reasoning, an astrological astronomy, rudimentary (and quite bookish) science, counting and a little computation and vocal music, constituted the substantial equipment of an educated man. And even this much education did not extend far beyond the organized clergy.

From such schools, with the restoration of social order in the eleventh and twelfth centuries, there presently arose those distinctive centralizing organs of the European educational systems, the universities. They were developed in close relation to the Church and monasticism; their organization was essentially monastic. Salerno stands out as an exception. It arose in the tolerant atmosphere of tenth century Sicily, where Moslim Christian and Jew could meet and exchange ideas, and it was primarily a school of medicine. Its growth was fostered by that pioneer rebel against the Papacy, the Emperor Frederick II. The others were aggregates of scholars, aggregates growing out of local schools, as learning spread and the increasing social stability made law more important and a knowledge of law desirable.

The teachers and scholars in these expanding schools organized for mutual assistance in guilds under an elected rector. The typical university was, to begin with, a teachers' and students' association. It was not created by a ruling authority. At first the students lodged haphazard, but later came residential colleges. The method of teaching was chiefly by lecture and notebook. At these concentrations, law, bookish medicine and theology were studied, and at a lower level was the preparatory "arts" course for those insufficiently prepared for the major studies. The "arts" were Latin, logic, rhetoric, stale book-science, music, descriptive astronomy and a little summing. The arts student graduated B. A. and, if he meant to teach, M. A. The teaching in all faculties was the teaching of tradition.

"The methods of instruction," says Mr. Cloudesley Brereton, in the article already cited, "—by lecture, or commentary on received texts; and by disputation, in which the scholars acquired dexterity in the use of the knowledge they had absorbed—were in harmony with this conception, and were undoubtedly thoroughly well suited to the requirements of an age in which the ideal of human thought was not discovery, but order, and in which knowledge was regarded as a set of established propositions, the work of reason being to harmonize these propositions in subordination to the authoritative doctrines of the Church."

The growth of the universities of this pattern throughout Europe was accompanied by a development of local schools preparing for the "arts" course. These, represented in England by the public schools and grammar schools, made no attempt to educate the general population. They simply prepared aspirants for the three great professions and supplied instruction in the "elements" and a smattering of learning for the sons of prosperous people. By the thirteenth century the formal education of Europe was firmly established upon these lines, and the essentially traditional universities had secured a controlling grip upon educational organization that endures to this day. Some reading and summing leaked out beyond the established schools, men and women learnt to write their names and so on, and an outline of Christian ideology was imparted to nearly everybody in the community by the priest, who used the painted walls of his church and its carved decorations as a picture book for the illiterate.

But this organization leading up to the clerical universities was not the only medium for the transmission of knowledge and ideas in the Middle Ages. By its side there were other educational processes going on, sometimes waxing and sometimes waning in relative importance. The rich and powerful employed private tutors for their children. There was an education of the castle as well as an education of the schools. The young gentleman began as page and learnt equestrian and military science; he learnt estate management; he was trained in instrumental music, versification and good manners. In the presence of the dingy erudite he carried himself with pride. He rarely went near a university to learn. His crowning graduation was foreign travel.

In the fifteenth century, the increase in the number of intelligent gentlemen was making this other line of education more and more important. They were reading and thinking. The education of the universities was fading, just as in the preceding section we have described religion as fading. It was failing to cover the realities of life. It was like a small cloak shrinking to the dimensions of a handkerchief on a growing body. The drive towards trade expansion and exploration in the fifteenth century and most of the intellectual stir of the time were not coming through the universities at all.

The acceptance of Greek and of a study of the Greek and Latin literatures for their own sakes, were forced upon the universities through the influence of the merchant princes of Italy, the princes of Germany and the sumptuous ecclesiastics of Rome. Tradition fought against these innovations. The convulsion of the Reformation saw a great decline in the entire university-school organization, and more especially in the Protestant countries. Education retreated for a time to the gentleman's library and study. It was the counter reformation under the Jesuits that salvaged the schools and universities of the Catholic countries and set a pattern for the Anglican public school.

The attempt to reorganize education in the seventeenth century would make a long history. Oxford and Cambridge counted their students by hundreds then, where once they had counted thousands.

Severe religious tests excluded the Catholic and the Nonconformist from these centres. The intellectual thrust of the new times was embodied in such new institutions as the Scientific Academies whose development we have already discussed in Chapter II, § 5. The most rigorous and energetic of the Protestant sects evolved their own teaching institutions. Max Weber in his *Protestant Ethic and the Spirit of Capitalism* shows how closely the religious revivalism of the time, the "new life" of the Calvinists in particular, was associated in spirit with the business methods that are now grouped together under the name of Capitalism. It was not simply a religious break-away that occurred. It was an educational break-away. It was equally a break-away from the faded clerical tradition of the time embodied in the universities. In our analysis of social motives we have pointed out some of the results of this detachment of the entrepreneur from the clerical tradition. The "uneducated" man really had an advantage at that time over the "educated" in his boldness of initiative and in his closer grip upon reality. He had no use for "book learning" emasculated by generations of "scholars." That he had certain moral deficiencies was not so apparent and interfered not at all with his crude success in that industrial revolution which preceded the mechanical.

It would be too long and subtle an undertaking to tell here how the European university-school system after its ebb towards the middle of the seventeenth century came back again to its present formal predominance in educational organization. This recovery has been made by a series of adaptive abandonments. Conspicuous among these has been the extensive abandonment of religious restrictions, bringing the Nonconformist and the Jew, as well as in Protestant countries the exiled Roman Catholic, back to the depopulated lecture rooms.

This was only one aspect of a still profounder abandonment: the abandonment of the idea that the chief function of a university is to preserve traditional learning. Reluctantly but steadily during the last two centuries the idea of intellectual progress has been accepted. "Scholarship" has ceased to rule the teacher's world. Side by side with the older disciplines the gymnastics of mathematics arose. The astronomy of the telescope followed mathematics into these centres. Then, as the nineteenth century ripened, the experimental sciences won their way to academic protection and encouragement. We have noted the fashion in which this came about in Chapter II, § 5. Now the universities of the world are conscientiously progressive. No man or woman of powerful intellectual initiative need despair nowadays of at least posthumous recognition by these chastened and reinvigorated institutions.

And as an aspect of this renascence the universities have taken up exterior teaching also—before it was too late. They have just prevented the development of a school system independent of them, planned on novel lines to meet new needs.

One may doubt whether this has been altogether a fortunate thing for the community. By great but measured concessions to the more formidable forces of our time they have brought the whole system of secondary education under their sway. The popular State schools that have spread about the world since the need of at least an elementary universal education has been recognized, came into existence largely beyond their purview, but they are gradually bringing these also into relationship by means of a scholarship ladder and the infiltration of the ranks of teachers and inspectors with their graduates. If they have really begotten very little of modern education they have at least now enormously adopted it. New educational institutions have been shaped to their pattern. The new great University of London and scores of other modern educational centres throughout the civilized world, recall the more venerable institutions in a hundred particulars. They even ape their antiquated costumes and ceremonies; they imitate their "degrees" and courses.

With a difference. Imagine the encounter of a bright young modern-spirited girl in traditional doctor's cap and scarlet robes, dedicated by a scholarship at the London School of Economics to, let us say, "sociological research," with a learned doctor, robe, hood, and cap essentially the same, a monster of erudition, a great bag of quotations, a mighty "scholar" resuscitated from the dignified mental repletion of seventeenth-century Oxford. On the one hand we should have an effect of masquerading impertinence, on the other, I fear, apoplexy.

The universities of Christendom have survived because of the enormous concessions they have made, because of their sedulous propitiation of the strong and successful; they have spread all over the world with the general Europeanization of the world; but it is permissible to question whether they and the conceptions of education they embody are destined to any very prolonged predominance over the intellectual processes of mankind.

In spite of all their apparent modernization the universities have never yet discovered how to lead a community. They have a timidity in their hearts; they would rather propitiate than dominate. They have

THE LINKING OF SCIENCE AND INDUSTRY

THE cold testing of motors in a refrigerating chamber in the Physical
Laboratory of a great automobile plant in Detroit.

SCIENCE AND INDUSTRY

CHEMICAL research laboratory in a great industrial plant. It is research of this sort, carried on at great expense by various manufacturers, which has almost done away with the old-time inventor and has made many of the greatest strides in recent scientific development possible.

simply substituted the tradition of yesterday for inalterable tradition to save themselves. They have almost come up to date, and they have been carried on prosperously by a hurrying and not too critical world. But they will always be by their very nature, by their instinct for following power instead of exercising it, not quite up to date. It is difficult to imagine how they can ever get beyond yesterday. With their fundamental hieratic prepossessions, their degrees and examinations, their curricula and direction of study, they must always remain organizations for the confirmation and transmission of what has already been accepted in the unorganized world of free intelligence. They cannot handle knowledge in this fashion until it is more or less traditionalized. They may be of service in stereotyping ideas for general distribution, but they can neither monopolize nor control the spontaneous directive processes of human thought. These last, in a world where there are no longer any educational limitations to class or type, must play freely through the general intellectual community.

The university in its origin and essence is the culmination of a great system of classrooms in which teachers talk and exercises are done. But is it necessary now that the classroom should extend up to the adult level? For the more or less systematized teaching of the elements and for the establishment of a common ideology the gathering of very young people into classrooms may still be desirable. This we will examine in a later section. But the present fashion of sending young men and women of from seventeen to twenty-two or three to universities for a modernized "arts" degree may give way very rapidly before a clearer conception of education.

The recovery of the universities from their decadence in the eighteenth century was due very largely to the growth of new social types, keenly aware of their educational deficiencies, but by no means clear about the education they needed. The primitive entrepreneur despised book learning, literature, science. His successor demanded education as he demanded a standing among the gentry.

The old universities were distended and reanimated by the requirements of these people. Rich men, stirred by creative impulses, founded new ones in the naïve persuasion that any learning was good knowledge. We have devoted a brief section already to the civilization of the entrepreneur (Chapter VIII, § 5). The wealth won by innovation bowed down in the halls of tradition and founded new halls. But as its intelligence grew it became critical, and then it was that the old universities began to affect that air and complexion of youth and achieved that

remarkable rejuvenation we are dealing with now. The more fashionable became in effect concerns for the flattering of the prosperous old
and the entertainment of the prosperous young. The classroom is at
last only the venerable nucleus for institutions essentially modern, a
formal centre for the playing fields, the boating, the picnicking, the
making of helpful friendships, the amateur music, the amateur dramatic
societies, the gay, fantastic ragging. Learning indeed is still pursued in
real earnest, but only by a despised minority. These are like those persistent mystics attached to various religions who are understood to save
all the sinners of the world by their unseen and unheeded exercises and
mortifications.

The newer and less wealthy foundations to the best of their ability
have imitated the pattern set them by the older ones. If they cannot be
as meretricious as their great exemplars, they are at any rate as gay and
sporting as their means and circumstances permit. The idea of training
and breaking in people to disinterested service which was the sustaining
idea of the mediæval university has evaporated altogether from the universities of to-day. They are an unstable rebirth, clad in the garments
and buildings of ancient institutions. They impart no intelligible ideology because that would "arouse controversy." Modern universities are
the last places in the world for controversy. They are imposingly frivolous. They flourish and are indicted.

Nowadays the intelligent rich are becoming more circumspect in their
endowments and more careful with their sons. They endow special
research institutions, and they begin to think out special courses of training for their own boys and girls. In many matters the fashion set by the
rich to-day is taken up by the ordinarily prosperous classes to-morrow
and becomes the general usage of the day after. This may be the case
in education. The break-up of the universities may be at hand in their
very phase of maximum expansion. The undergraduate body may melt
away quite suddenly, dispersing to forms of work and training of a
more specialized and continuous sort, and with that the university
properly speaking, that immense obsolescent educational gesture, that
miscellaneous great gathering of students and teachers, will achieve a
culminating gala of sport and splendour—and cease.

For "research universities" and "post-graduate universities" are clearly
a contradiction in terms; they are something new. We are not writing
of them here. We are not writing of the working, thinking and innovating minority which is found in nearly every university in the world.
The original university knew no more of research than it did of

athleticism. It taught, and you learnt, and when you had learnt everything you were a "doctor," and its task was done.

An encyclopædia of work and wealth might supply us here with a
mass of statistics about university and college funds and attendances
throughout the world. They would be impressive, but useless for the
ends we have in view, and so would be lists of various types of continuation schools, technical schools and the like. Classification and
nomenclature have still to be brought into line with reality in the field
of education. What is called a college here may be classed as a school
there; the schools in one country may be doing the "arts" work of the
universities in another. All comparisons between the educational level
of one country and that of another are unsound, and most of them very
irritating to the country which appears at a disadvantage.

More interesting would be that part of the Museum of Education
containing pictures and plans of university layout and a display of the
architecture and sanitation of existing universities, from Oxford's dreaming spires to the single great skyscraper of forty stories designed to
hold the entire University of Pittsburgh. The Museum of Education
would have to assemble great masses of detail and range widely, to
make its presentation complete. There might be gramophone records
of the discourses of typical university lectures and studies of actual
laboratory instruction, and there would certainly be a display of the
use of the talking film as a substitute for anatomical and other scientific
demonstrations. A picturesque side section would display the peculiar
costumes that students wear, the spatterdashes of Lisbon, the corps caps
of Germany and the red gowns of Glasgow, and a complete collection
of academic robes, hoods and decorations.

A large and striking range of the museum galleries would be devoted
to university sports and the rôle of scholarly athleticism in relation to
the sporting world. All the present abundance of university sport
surged up out of the unpretending relaxations of the mediæval student
at a quite recent date. It became conspicuous about the middle of the
nineteenth century, and it has since played a large part in advertising
and popularizing the modernized university. The training of athletes
is now a recognized function of universities, a function that would
have shocked Roger Ascham beyond measure. For to the tutor of Queen
Elizabeth all sports but archery were "vile."

The Oxford and Cambridge boat race rowed every spring at Putney
must not be forgotten in the story of university athleticism. It marked
the first public display and popularization of the university as a sport-

ing centre. The first inter-university boat race was as early as 1828, though it did not become a regular public function until later. Since then, as we have told in Chapter XIV, § 3, the expansion of the play side of the universities has been—magnificent. In America the faculties have frankly adopted sport as a main business of a university; the sports coach is as important as any other professor, and the sporting side is supposed to develop the distinctive qualities of American public life in their highest manifestation. Great stadia are a feature of all the wealthier American universities—that of Stanford University is capable of holding 88,000 people. But we have already described these developments and noted the claims made on their behalf.

The whole effect of this mélange of bright activities, youthful exuberance and picturesque tradition, this exhibition of schools and universities, would, I think, be indeed one of rapid and spontaneous development but also one of imperfect adjustment, of much energy misdirected, aiming awry or aiming not at all at the realization through mental training of the vast possibilities of man's present attainment.

§ 5. *Education Outside the Classroom*

In the preceding short history of formal education it has been made clear that never at any time since reading and writing began has formal education been the whole of education. This is a very important distinction on which we would lay the utmost stress. People nowadays have a habit of associating education with the classroom, the professor and the schoolmaster. But the professor and schoolmaster are no more inseparable from education than the galley slave or the mule are inseparable from transport. They are just the operators of one way of education. They are connected with education, but it is not an essential connection. Great intelligent communities have carried on without them. Hellas knew of no schools, as we understand schools to-day, and we have noted how the universities seemed to be fading out in the sixteenth and seventeenth centuries.

Not only has the intellectual process of mankind gone on steadily far beyond the boundaries of professional intellectual activities, whenever there were security and leisure, but also there has always been more or less informal transmission and communication of the results of this free, extra-mural thinking to the general body of mentally active people. The advent of the printed book and the diffusion of reading, the newspaper and the popular press have progressively increased this external educational work, and now such new devices as the cinema and broadcasting are carrying the informal diffusion of fact and ideas still further.

The proportion of stuff in the mind of the "educated" man and woman of to-day, which is of school or college origin, to the stuff that has come to them from extra scholastic sources, is enormously less to-day than it would have been in the case of their social equivalents a century ago. Turn out the mind of a bachelor of arts to-day and see how much his school and university have given him. A little store of Latin, rusting through disuse, a scrap or so of Greek, a very imperfect knowledge of one or two foreign languages and literatures, the views of various learned gentlemen on his own language and literature, scraps of, ten-year-old science, the incomplete foundations of mathematical computation, and some "period" history.

But a word here about that "period" history. At its worst, it can be amazingly bad. It is partly like heavy stale gossip about incredible individuals, partly like trying to get interested in the litigation of unknown people in a remote country, and partly like watching a university don playing soldiers on his study floor. (How he loves his "Decisive Battles of the World"!) The murder or execution of one or another of the more tiresome characters in the story comes as an all too rare relief. A certain feverish liveliness is sought by grossly patriotic appeals. In the growing citizen's childhood, home, governesses, playfellows, friends and a world beflagged, have conspired to distend to the utmost his natural disposition towards tribal partisanship. The "period" historian of the pre-war tradition, who is still all too far from extinction, plays upon this predisposition, because by giving a certain pseudo-personal flavour to his narrative he hopes to redeem its essential dreariness. He incites his students to say "we." "We," it seems, were the Royalists or the Puritans or the Balts or the Medici or the Knights of Malta. "We" conquered India; "we" defeated the French; "we" crossed the plains to the Pacific and bested the Spanish. In this mouldering paste of corrupting facts dates are set like pebbles on an unappetizing cake. They are for production under examination in evidence that the stuff has been swallowed. Such is still the historical equipment of too many a contemporary. It fades and lies forgotten after his last "exam." Beyond that, and with no vital connection with it, he has a score of skills he has acquired, and a whole universe of ideas, in which this poor little old "education" of his lies like a worm-eaten nut that has been dropped by chance into a salad.

Things are altering however in the field of history. The current syllabus of the Joint Board for the Higher and Schools Certificates in England shows a very marked departure from the older type of teaching. There is a real breadth of reference in the reading prescribed, and an effective direction of the mind to economic and social forces at work in the shaping of events.

Beyond the school subjects in the after-school and out-of-school acquisitions, lies a large and still uncharted region for the sociological observer. We have no orderly account, no working classification of the actual educational influences that play over the minds of girls and boys and adolescents in the world to-day. They are various, unequal, good and evil, unpremeditated as educational influences, and mostly quite accidental. They are controlled in the feeblest way. There are certain censorships, the contracted vestiges of far more extensive restrictions in the past. Everywhere there still exists a standard of sexual decency maintained by the law, that is justified wholly and solely by educational considerations. Youth must not be stimulated prematurely: that is the generally accepted idea; it is good for social growth to delay and minimize sexual adolescence. Conceptions of stimulation vary widely, but that we cannot discuss here; the general agreement against deliberate and even careless stimulation is undeniable. Apart from these legal restraints there is scarcely any screen now between the young and the relatively immense conflict of suggestions, the information, the appeals that rain upon them from the world beyond the schoolmaster's collection of exhibits. The illustrated newspapers, books, magazines, the cinema and a multitude of shows, an immense clangour of advertisement, build up a vision of the round world in their minds infinitely more vivid than the instruction of the schoolroom. Discussion of a hundred urgent questions, from birth control to tariff reform and from military service to immortality, is forbidden nowhere except in the academic preparation for life. Within the schoolhouse, at least, the orthodox religious formulas are treated with infinite solicitude, and only examiners may ask questions about them. School is no longer an enlargement but a withdrawal. It is like an embanked canal running far out into the lake of adult life and keeping the current needlessly apart from the waters with which it must ultimately mix.

Moreover, it has to be noted that the "educated" man whose mental content we are considering is still actively learning. There again we have a remarkable change that has happened to us by swift yet almost imperceptible degrees. The old order was permeated with the idea that for every rank of life there was a definite, sufficient, once-for-all education. You graduated, and the task was over. You learnt, and you stopped learning and worked out the consequences. But now we never stop learning. We add to our ideas, we modify and replace them daily. The process of informal education that begins directly a child opens its eyes upon the world proceeds crescendo throughout its entire life. Schools and universities are losing their importance because, so far as ideas and information go, the whole community is now in fact its own school. It is an undisciplined, ill-planned school, if you will, but it is vocal, explanatory and directive as no community has ever been before.

Let us attempt a brief survey of what this ultra-scholastic education consists of and of the nature and quality of its principal media. Three main things it gives the citizen. In the first place he gets News, that is to say a constant development, correction and elaboration of his view of the world about him. History is written and revised under his nose. The things he knew before are recalled to him, brightened, emphasized, added to. He gets fresh intimations of human character and conduct; he learns of discoveries and inventions; daily, geography unfolds itself anew before him, and particularly the human side of geography. Map, diagram and picture, in newspaper and in the increasing multitude of ephemeral books about contemporary things, informed him and inform him, and now the cinema and the radio increase the service. He makes the tour of the world in an armchair.

On the whole, it is sound stuff he gets. We have traced the sordid origins of the newspaper, we have noted how the spirit of propaganda and the influence of the advertiser can deflect and censor particular streaks of news; nevertheless, the bulk of trustworthy statement that gets through is very great. A newspaper cannot lie comprehensively; its lies are no good to it unless it is generally credible, and every propaganda from its very nature goes on in the teeth of counter propaganda. Concealment is special and occasional. Newspaper history is far more veracious than the dogmas of some biassed pedagogue unchecked in his classroom. So far as libel goes there is law, even in the United States, faint but pursuing.

No doubt the modern newspaper has found retailing the unimportant and exciting, more to its advantage than studiously balanced statement. But how far newspapers, even if they are conducted on absolutely mercenary lines, can venture to be trivial depends upon the general moral and intellectual atmosphere. Even our most tawdry and sensational prints retain the affectation of a certain dignity. The common man may be a fool in a hurry, readier to laugh or marvel than learn, but he is not an absolute fool, he takes thought occasionally, and his apologists can point to a fairly steady improvement in the quality of the world's news service in the last hundred years. More and better news gets now to more people than it ever did before.

It would need a specialist who was a very subtle psychologist to expound all the mysteries and complications of a journalist's honour. But the most base, overbearing, energetic and subtle of newspaper proprietors will still find himself with intractable material between himself and the public he would hoodwink and control. And for the other side of the medal, the honest realization of his duties as well as his opportunities, is his sure and certain way to wealth, influence and the conspicuous and splendid service of mankind.

The second educational thing that the ordinary man gets from the ultra-scholastic educational influences of the time is a constant revision and extension of his general ideas. He need not go, as the Greek had to do, to the Agora to hear of some new thing; all about him is the Agora, the Forum. The increase of public discussion in the last decade or so is one of the most remarkable of contemporary phenomena. The character of the newspaper has changed completely with regard to opinion. There was a time when there was about as much free thinking in the column of a newspaper as there is in Little Bethel. The editor did the thinking, with his staff well under control; he told his readers what they thought about things, and if the strain became too great they changed their paper. If anyone objected to the pronouncements of the paper they could write a letter on the chance of its being printed, without pay, in the "Correspondence." But within the past quarter century, it dawned upon various newspaper directors that it would attract quite a number of the curious and arouse very little resentment among the faithful if they opened their columns to heterodox views, provided these were properly disavowed in an editorial note. This ventilation of opinion has developed very rapidly. It was a draw; it made the paper exciting in a new direction. The philosophers, religious teachers, radicals, and scientific men were very reasonable about fees, and these debates cost far less than, for example, sending special correspondents and commissioners to investigate the latest murder. The usage was established very rapidly, and now it would be difficult to abandon it. For the ordinary man wants to have his views discussed and reanimated just as he wants to know and to vivify his knowledge. The note of interroga-

tion which is born in the nature of every human being has been released.

The newspaper changes continually. In the early nineteenth century,
when printing was a comparatively primitive business, newspapers were
largely the creation of "great journalists," and their influence was relatively much greater than their capital value. Their mentality was of
more importance than their machinery. But they reached only to the
middle class. The masses had no newspaper at all. Like every other
social concern, the newspaper has experienced the "change of scale" of
our period. The change reached it late because it was first necessary
that the elementary education of the working masses should prepare a
public to justify large-scale production. That wider public only became
effective in the eighties and nineties of last century. Then came, first
the mechanization, and then the popularization, of the "new" newspaper. The mechanical advances that made the printing house of a
modern newspaper a great factory of costly and beautiful machines, not
simply printing but folding and counting and packing, made newspapers huge business enterprises demanding an immense initial outlay
of capital. The traditions of the old type of journalist proprietor were
all against a ready adaptation to the new requirements. Because of this
the newspaper passed very largely into the hands and is still in the
hands of highly individualized entrepreneurs, much more akin in their
character to the ordinary financial adventurer than the older type of
newspaper owner.

The contemporary press is a new thing and not a real continuation
of the nineteenth-century press—even when old periodicals have been
made over to the new methods. It is still very largely dominated by the
commercialized development of the peasant persona. It is in the first
phase of industrialization. Its conscientiousness about the quality of its
goods and the use of flavour, colour, diluents, and substitutes is at about
the same level as that of the jam trade noted in our chapter on Food.
There the new press follows behind other great industrial organizations,
such as the steel or chemical industry, which are for the most part passing from individual to group ownership and control, coming under the
"service" mentality of the official and paying a close regard to the
quality and purity of their products.

Some great periodicals indeed are now owned and directed by special
organizations; the *Christian Science Monitor,* the property of a sect, is a
very attractive and trustworthy daily, and the London *Times* has be-

come a quasi-public institution whose ownership is controlled by a body of trustees designed to save it from falling under merely profiteering influences. But these periodicals are exceptions to current conditions.

It is possible that a movement towards responsibility in the newspaper world may be developing behind the scenes similar to that which has made banking and insurance semi-official and public-minded. Much will certainly happen to change the newspaper in the days before us. If it becomes semi-official and responsible-minded, its trustworthiness may increase at the expense of its liveliness, and it may cease either to discuss boldly or to entertain. There may be a definite split and distinction between the responsible papers we shall buy and trust and the irresponsible papers we shall buy to entertain, excite or irritate us. Or Opinion, after its present rush into the newspaper columns, may presently find the editors growing restrictive, interfering or stingy, and resort to the intermittent instead of the periodical press, to pamphlets and special periodicals. We want the news every morning, but it may be to the taste of many of us to have our arguments by the week or occasionally, for us to take up when we are so disposed. What concerns us here is whether the common man is likely to get as good news or better in the future than he does now and whether there is likely to be any diminution of his present free access to every sort of opinion about every possible subject. There is little or no indication of any reversal of the general advance in these matters.

In imaginative works about the future, the writers are apt to abolish the newspaper altogether and represent the news and so forth as being distributed entirely by wireless, cinemas and the like ultra-modern devices. But it may be doubted whether such contrivances will ever do more than act as supplements and stimulants to the reading of books and newspapers. For all these other things you must go to an appointed place or listen at an appointed time. You cannot choose your programme or consider your own convenience. But the book and newspaper, with an almost canine fidelity, follow you meekly everywhere and brighten up when you turn to them, at any hour.

Within their limitations and on account of certain advantages of presentation the newer media are extraordinarily helpful accessories in the general task of informing and quickening men's minds. In Great Britain the distribution of sound by radio is the monopoly of the British Broadcasting Corporation, and there have been some very lively contests at the headquarters of the organization between the educationists and the entertainers. These struggles are very illuminating when the educational value of these new media is under discussion. The B. B. C. has made a great feature of talks by the most stimulating thinkers in the world. Keenly appreciated by many hearers, these talks are bitterly denounced by others, who want light music and facetiæ all the time, and who do not wish to have their guiding ideas loosened or modified insidiously. The Roman Catholic hierarchy wishes to confine the discussion of theology and the deeper things of life to qualified specialists, which it naturally identifies with the Roman Catholic hierarchy. The war rages with varying fortunes, and the educational light of the B. B. C. flares and wanes. Possibly it may be blown out altogether.

The educational film is equally a part of a programme and equally subject to suppression, if a majority, or even a truculent minority, objects. And always there are the limitations of a set time and place for each item.

Listening-in and the cinema, so far as they are educational at all, seem likely to supply only high lights in education, and tend less to sate curiosity than to send men and women back with quickened appetites to the printed word. In the immediate future, as in the recent past, the press seems likely to be the main medium of news and the principal forum for popular discussion, and the editorial journalist, whether he likes it or not, one of the most important agents in the education of the world.

News and the forum; these are the first and second things that the shows, noises and newspapers of our contemporary world bring to the normal man. But, as we have already suggested in the Introduction of this work, his mind has been rather stimulated than satisfied by the incoherent masses of news that come to it, and the battles of thought, propaganda and persuasion that go on round and about himself. He wants to know in a more orderly fashion. He asks for education—adult education—long before education goes out to find him. In response to this demand, a considerable and increasing mass of published matter has developed which is neither trivial nor original, which summarizes what is known in this or that wide field of reality and puts it forth in a plain, assimilable, trustworthy fashion. This present work with its associates, the *Outline of History* and the *Science of Life,* and various collateral works, is a sample of this new literature of information. Other works of the same character will occur to the reader. So far such enterprises have had to be produced upon strictly commercial lines, and they have many of the characteristic defects of a production for profit. But the need for such comprehensive digests for ordinary intelligent people is so manifest that in due time these pioneer attempts to state a complete modern ideology are bound to be replaced by sounder and more authoritative successors.

Besides these "outlines" and "summaries," which give a mental framework and stand-by, there is and there has been now for half a century a steady production of informative books in series, by various firms of publishers. There seems to be an insatiable market for little books that will give, or appear to give, the latest results of modern research and discussion in this department or that, in an assimilable form. More often than not they are written by eminent specialists and are generally years in advance of the textbooks used in our schools.

This literature of information is only one aspect of the way in which the demand for after-school education has outrun the supply. We have to put beside it also the spectacle of the classroom, abandoning school and university, so to speak, and starting off across country, in pursuit of adults still eager to learn but unable to afford the time and money needed for residence at an educational centre. At the proper time, school and university missed these people, and now they are learning in a pseudo-academic manner from extension teachers. So we get also in a loose coöperation with those educational Ishmaelites we have noted, "Adult Education," a sincere attempt of the university to recover this lost clientele. We find, for example, a British Institute of Adult Education, and a World Association for Adult Education, active in developing the organization of the ordinary man's after-school thought and reading.

By Adult Education here is meant, of course, real post-school education and not merely the belated teaching of the "elements" to totally uneducated grown-up people such as is going on now in Russia and Anatolia. Adult Education is a rapidly expanding movement. It is not a substitute for general reading, but its value in directing, steadying, confirming and disciplining such reading must be very great.

The English universities (since Oxford initiated the movement in 1907), working in association with the Board of Education, developed Tutorial Classes, of which in 1925 there were 500 with 12,000 students. All these students were volunteers, with no immediate mercenary reward in view. The classes have usually a weekly hour's lecture throughout the winter followed by an hour's discussion, and the student undertakes to follow the course for three years, and to read and to do written work for it. Similar activities are to be found in most intellectually living countries. *An Adventure in Working Class Education,* by Albert Mansbridge, who is the chairman of the World Association for Adult Education, gives the spirit and intention of, and fuller particulars about, this type of educational enterprise, which is after all, considerable as it is in itself, merely one intimation of the wide hunger for real knowledge and mental disciplines in the contemporary world.

It is interesting to contrast the Workers' Educational Association, which is a frank attempt to shepherd back this widespread appetite for self-education into the university fold, with what is called the Labour College movement. The Workers' Educational Association was a development of the University Extension movement, and although, in response to the demand of many of its working-class students in the industrial centres, the classes carried on under its auspices often deal with economics, history and the social sciences, it has always tried to stress the importance of bringing general culture—in the quite orthodox sense—into working-class life. It would teach about Italian art or Gothic architecture with extreme readiness. The Labour College movement (formerly the Plebs League) is on the contrary frankly and aggressively independent of both academic organization and inspiration. It claims to be a spontaneous expression of the need felt by manual workers themselves—miners, railwaymen, engineers, building workers—for an education based on an attitude critical of the existing social order, and it concentrates primarily on such subjects as will fit its students to think and act politically. To which my friend Professor Carr-Saunders adds, on reading these proofs, that the Labour Colleges claim freedom in one form in order to abandon it in another. They teach the religion of Marx. They are theological colleges.

§ 6. Mental Training

So far our account of the world's formal education amounts very largely to a summary of insufficiencies and to a compensatory display of the very extensive and growing system of activities outside it and independent of it, which now supply the bulk of the material of a contemporary ideology. We have shown how, concurrently with this shrinkage of the primary rôles of school and college, these bodies have taken on a secondary function in the organization of athleticism. We have shown them, indeed, as diverting rather than directing energy. But is this a condemnation of formal education? Is it a glorification of press and show as the only education needed? By no means. It is indeed a

very grave criticism of the existing organs of general education throughout the world, as a stocktaking encyclopædia would have to display
them. But the criticism is that they fail to supply the formal education
they should supply: not that a formal education is unwanted. To-day
still there is everywhere a clear distinction in people's minds between
an "educated" and an "uneducated" man, and to the nature of that
difference we will now give our attention.

In our analysis of the personas operative in our world we have
stressed the rôle played in the progressive development of society by
what we have called the "educated" or priestly type. The essential fact
about that type, as we have defined it for the purposes of this book, is
that its dominating motive is service as distinguished from the peasant's
motive of gain by toil and the nomad's motive of gain by gallant
violence. The gist indeed of our study of the working of the human
ant-hill has been to accentuate the primary importance of this educated
element as priest, administrator, lawyer, in keeping the coöperations
going, and to show how the conception of conscientious service has
ruled professional medicine and law, saturated the official classes, and
passed over to the professional scientific and technical worker and even
to the man of letters and the artist of to-day. We have pointed out
again and again how the grade of social organization possible at any
time or in any country is dependent upon the educational level of a
community and we have maintained throughout that our hope of our
racial future—our sole reason for hope—lies in the extension of this
"educated" quality to the whole of mankind.

Our gravamen therefore is not against formal education, but against
the existing organs of formal education, because they are insufficient
and beside the mark. Our study of the present "faded" state of religion
is manifestly associated with this exposure of the inadequacy of deliberate education. Formal education to-day is also in a faded phase. We
have shown how immensely exterior forces now supplement the schools
so far as knowledge and suggestion go, but that substitution of newspaper, book and cinema for the classroom lesson does not in any way
abolish the need for a drilling, ordering and invigoration of the minds
subjected to this tumultuous invasion. Rather it intensifies that need.
The establishment, confirmation and diffusion of the spirit of service
are more than ever necessary in the presence of this stupendous froth
of knowledge and ideas.

A certain moral disinterestedness is not the only characteristic we
evoke when we speak of an "educated" man. We also imply a certain

mental power and fastidiousness. Through the ages, a proper use of language has been a main objective in education. This world-wide contemporary education, deriving from the European schools, has, even in its weariest, most decadent phases, set itself to that end. The attempt to make language an instrument of precision and to keep thinking lucid and exact, has never been altogether relaxed. For all the informative-suggestive uproar of our time there is very little training to be got outside school and university in the exactitudes of mathematics. Our complaint is that there is not enough within those institutions. It is our gravest accusation against present-day universities that they will now graduate men and women who speak and write inexactly, have no framework of general ideas, and think no better than labourers who have left school at twelve or thirteen. It is the most damning charge that can be brought against them.

So that for our complete encyclopædia of Work and Wealth, in addition to that broad review of the visible apparatus of education we have made in the preceding sections, there must be a more difficult and profounder study. We have to go into the precise details of the mental processes involved. How is language taught, its grammatical and its logical use? Language is far less important as a means of talking about things than as a means of thinking about things, but we use it now almost entirely as a means of talking about things. What might be done with human minds in sharpening and tempering this instrument, and what is done? Do any real exercises in thought survive at all in an ordinary education? How are they supplied? How can they be supplied? Mathematical studies can be a fine exercise in precision. How far are they used in that way? But they do not cover the whole field of thought; they do not quicken the observation nor strengthen the judgment. We have roundly asserted (in Chapter II, § 2) that the world to-day suffers greatly from the shelving of the discussion between Realism and Nominalism at the Renascence. To that we return. The issue between the one and the many is an issue of perennial importance —and our alleged education does not even raise it. There can be no fine thought or fine understanding widespread throughout the community until that has been understood and remedied.

Everyone has heard that Plato and Aristotle were exceedingly wise men and that our world is infinitely in their debt. And everybody knows that Plato wrote divers dialogues that are understood to have a beauty no modern writing can rival. (Everyone should try a dialogue or so in translation.) And these two were associated with a certain

Socrates who so irritated the public of his time by insisting upon clear thinking so far as he understood it, that he was obliged to drink an infusion of hemlock and die. But how many people in a cinema theatre know *why* or want to know why we are so profoundly in debt to Plato and Aristotle and what these unparalleled people were talking about so continuously in their academy? If it was unimportant, the Academy ought to be forgotten by this time, and if it was important, the gist of its teaching ought to have got by now to the ears of all the men and women in the cinema theatre.

These Greek philosophers were, in fact, opening out that same debate between the one and the many, the species and the individual, which also exercised the schoolmen. It has never been altogether dropped, but it goes on now in other forms. Modern biology has had to rediscover and revive these fundamental exercises in its examination of the nature of individuality, and modern physics in its rediscovery of the uniqueness of "events." There is no lack of material nor of means of approach to these mind-sharpening issues, but the truth about our present education is that they are not even approached. Even the university honours-man with pretensions to philosophy is not put through these disciplines at all effectively. Directly the old issues appear in modern dress, he seems unprepared for them. Nothing is more amazing to the enquiring and intelligent humble in the pursuit of understanding than the realization of the intellectual sloppiness and defensiveness of the academic dignitary.

I believe that an exhaustive enquiry into the intellectual training that is going on in our world to-day would reveal an amazing deficiency of sound, thorough instruction in the processes and dangers of thinking. There is a certain amount of logical training in Catholic seminaries, but to judge from contemporary controversies it is of the thirteenth-century Realist type. Contemporary thinking, alas! outside those circles "comes by nature." One may go through school and college to-day and never once be reproached for a foolish generalization, an unjustifiable inference, an unsound conclusion. We ought to have experts everywhere, like food and drink inspectors, exposing the torrent of invalidity in the newspapers and public utterances of the day. But few people are sufficiently keen on lucidity to follow such exposures. The public would be restive. It would say these experts were splitting hairs, that they were highbrows; they would be bawled down by loud journalists. We pick up good or bad habits of thinking as luck and our natural brightness may determine. In thought and statement we are all untrained amateurs. A very large part of contemporary discussion is spent in misunderstand-ings due to our universal intellectual slovenliness.

And it is not simply that we are untrained amateurs; we are also con-ceited amateurs. We resent correction. We *like* the rich confused stuff in our minds. When we hear a thing repeated twenty times with emphasis we believe it. It would trouble us not to believe it. It does not trouble us in the least that it should be entirely incompatible with some other equally emphatic belief we have adopted. We have not had that sort of training. We need it badly. At present a few adult classes in logic and methods of reasoning are all we have in the world to set against the undisciplined confusions of modern thought.

§ 7. *Education for the Modern Progressive Community*

After this résumé of the world's education to-day we can turn to its objectives and consider the actual needs of the nineteen hundred-odd million human beings who are being drawn together, dangerously and with infinite complication and difficulty, by the forces of mechanical invention into one great economic community.

Suppose we allow ourselves a brief respite from the crowded as-semblage of fact and imagine we have a free hand to plan an education for all the world. We have studied education in the preceding sections, faint but pursuing, toiling along behind the disappearance of distance, the acceleration of communications, the mechanical revolution of the world, to preserve understanding and a proper spirit in our human coöperations. Let us now imagine the schoolmaster not kicked along by powers beyond his control, but coming to meet and assist them. What would that new, helpful education give, and what would be the machinery it would use?

First let us plan out what it would give and what it would impose upon the normal human persona.

The foundations of education are laid in early infancy. The psy-chological work of the past thirty years has brought out the immense importance to the adult of his infantile impressions. It is by them that the foundations of his character are laid, and his dispositions estab-lished. By the time the young human being goes to school, he has already gone far either along the road of adapting himself happily to the requirements of civilization or towards failure, towards the estab-lishment of those instabilities whose consequences we consider in the last section of this chapter. Pre-school education in a civilized world will be based upon a scientific knowledge of children's minds. That is not a thing of to-morrow. For it presupposes parents not only educated in a general sense but equipped for their task with a certain definite body of training and information—information which can hardly be considered accessible at present. To attain it one must still wade through a mass of highly technical psychological literature, fiercely polemical in character and made particularly repugnant to the ordinary mind by its lack of grace and literary dexterity. And even when that literature is read the enquirer will find that what he is studying is the treatment of abnormality rather than the needs of the normal child. The normal child, however, is also being studied—a few courageous schoolmasters here and there are actively experimenting in the treatment of more normal types. It becomes manifest that a great proportion of later recalcitrance, inadequacy, dullness, irresponsibility and actual physical illness is due to the mishandling, with the best intentions, of children's minds. For the pre-school education of the days ahead we may reasonably hope for a body of principles simple and clear enough to be understood and applied by men and women who are not specialists. Modern methods of dissemination will make that body of principles part of the mental equipment of the entire population. And through the application of these principles the mass of the children of the future will arrive at their formal education with free and balanced minds. To that formal education, to the schooling of the modern state, as it should be, we will now proceed.

To begin this we require universal elementary teaching. That use of language which is picked up from the circle of folks immediately around a child must be made finer and fuller and extended to reading, writing and calculation. How that can best be taught is a highly technical question. It can be done, educationists assure us, much more swiftly and efficiently than it is usually done. And they tell us too that every normal child can learn to draw. An educational world net, by the bye, would also be very convenient in noting and doing what is possible to correct various physical defects (of eyes, ears, teeth and so forth) and hereditary taints. That is not education, but a good thing that can be very conveniently saddled upon an educational institution. Moreover, there is a phase somewhere between five and sixteen when children are most apt to learn foreign languages and, with modern methods and means (gramophones, the radio lesson, etc.), it would not be any very great additional burthen on the educational machine to give every child a sound and practical knowledge of at least one of the great world languages, English, French, German, Spanish, Russian, in addition to its mother tongue. The possibility of one of these languages becoming so widely understood as to serve as a world lingua franca is not very remote.

And speaking of a *lingua franca* we may perhaps note here the ingenious project of Mr. C. K. Ogden of what he calls Basic English. By a most elaborate study of the science of meaning he has been able to produce a vocabulary of something under a thousand English words and a small group of grammatical constructions by which practically any meaning can be expressed, with only a very slight loss of vividness and compactness. An English speaker can learn in a very little time to confine himself within the limits of this simplified speech; a foreigner can learn it in a few weeks. They can then converse and correspond with the utmost ease, and the foreigner can make himself understood by any English-speaking person. It is possible that "Basic" forms of other languages may also be worked out, and that in many cases these Basic idioms may be used as a first stage to a closer familiarity. But the peculiar simplicity of Basic English is due to the absence of inflexions, and no other tongue lends itself so easily to simplification.

Need children go to school continuously for a number of years for these elements? This is a question for the expert. But there is a widespread persuasion now that classroom work should be intensive and restricted to brief periods. Children should go into a bright, well lit and well ventilated classroom only when they are fresh and alert; they should meet keen, active and highly competent teachers, and the teaching and learning alike should be vigorous and direct. One should go into a classroom as one goes onto a tennis court, for brisk, continuous action. In a classroom one should work *hard*. Learning is a special exertion. The future world citizen cannot acquire too early the idea that effort is required in learning. If schools are to be used as places where the young are to spend whole days and long periods of time, they must have rooms other than classrooms; they must have rest rooms and playrooms and playgrounds where the activities are not intense. Here the less specific factors of the educational process come into play. Here is where the youngster acquires a regard for others, civility, sociability and a habit of reciprocal and coöperative action. Here is where the impulse to make, to draw, to write and invent is given scope and satisfaction. The rôle of the teacher here is to be supervisor and helper; encouraging tactfully, restraining bad conduct, but compelling not at all.

For this primary stage of education, large, beautiful, healthy schools are required throughout the world with a proper equipment, toys, books, apparatus, the gramophone, the demonstration cinema. Music and singing will play a large part in this schooling phase. The productive energy of the world is now fully able to provide all this for every child on earth. If you would know why this is not done now, go back to Chapter IX again and read what has been told about Hetty Green, Lowenstein, and the Great Slump of 1930–31. Read too of Sir Basil Zaharoff in Chapter XII and of the paradox of overproduction in Chapter XI. We cannot afford this manifestly necessary education, although all the material is ready and the workers stand idle. That is the absurd truth, the idiotic truth, of our situation. When the world has found its way to collective buying, the weaving of this planetary net of schools will be its first concern.

Next, using perhaps those same school buildings, the children of the new age will be learning to think. Logic should not be separated from grammatical teaching, and both should be associated with an acute attention to precise meaning. The boy or girl should be accustomed to use language like a rapier, should despise a clumsiness in inference as if it were a foul in a game. The classes should collect blunders, disingenuous statements and false conclusions from public discussion. They should botanize for errors and bring the precious finds to the classroom for dissection. They will also go as far as their willingness and aptitudes will take them in the exact and rigid reasoning processes of mathematics. And they will learn of the growth of knowledge and the methods of the scientific investigator with his measurements, his experiments, and his controls. They will do some exemplary scientific work at this stage, not for the sake of knowledge but as mental exercise. The discussion of theories and generalizations will be more important here than the accumulation of facts. Far more important than scientific knowledge is scientific method. This much, and watchfully directed bodily exercise, is surely all that there need to be in the universal primary education of mankind.

But this is merely equipment and the sharpening of the human instrument. Next follows the socially more important part of the task of education, the establishment of a persona which will lead to the service of the race and protect the individual from social mischief, economic offenses, political delusions, frustrations, disappointments and evil conduct towards others. A picture of the world and of the ways of the world in relation to the self, and what is honourable and right for the self, has to be imposed upon the growing mind. The foundations of its ideology have to be laid.

Now, as we have made perfectly clear in § 6, the school alone can contribute only a small part of a contemporary ideology. That grows and changes day by day under the thousandfold impacts of reality. But we are speaking here of certain foundation ideas upon which this living and developing fabric can be poised. First there is the idea of man's history as one whole. A child has to be guarded against early infection by picturesque false, and short-sighted national traditions. The effectual exorcism for that sort of thing is the plain, straightforward teaching of human history as one progressive adventure in which all races have helped and all have sinned. Picture and book, story and lecture, cinema and school museum must converge upon that rational presentation of man's collective life. And secondly the citizen of the world must have a sound conception of the evolution of life and its nature, that is, he must have learnt elementary biology thoroughly. Thirdly he must learn geography and the economic layout of the world as one coöperative field of enterprise. These are the three pillars of a modern ideology, the three branches of knowledge which constitute that "New Education," of which I have already written something in my Introduction. This is the essential instructional material for a modern world vision. All the rest is training and equipment.

Here we will not expand the suggestions already made in the chapter on Housing, that the primitive "home" in which a swarm of children, servants and poor relations centre upon father and mother has already broken up for a great majority of the European peoples and given way to new social units. All prosperous people in the advanced communities entrust their children to nurses, tutors and governesses, whenever they can, and send them away to preparatory schools; the continuous contact of parent and child does not seem to be either desirable or desired. In the case of the small family there is also a considerable educational advantage in associating children with their equals in strength and age. All this points to the ordinary general school as having a third function as the modern form of "home." In many cases it may be a boarding school; or in a town or village it may be a day home. In the happier world-state to which we look forward, the struggle of various "faded" religious organizations to capture and control as many schools as possible in order to preserve the distinctive "atmosphere," the graceful legends and misleading assurances of this or that cult, will, we presume, have died away.

The "elements," a foreign language or so, directed opportunities for artistic "play," mental training and the elementary knowledge of history, biology and social relations necessary as a basis for a modern ideology: this is really as much as the general school need give a human being.

I do not know how far it may be possible or desirable to control some of this general education by examinations. That is a question for the sociological educationist. Maybe the common citizen of the future will have to pass a leaving examination before he sets about his special adventure in life. Maybe he will have to pass a matriculation test before he embarks upon various definite callings. Or it may be found that the compulsion of these tests is not required.

But from the end of the school stage onward—which ought to be completed at latest in the middle teens—I can see no use for any further general education in school. Everything necessary for a common mental foundation will be there. The ordinary "arts" course in our older universities to-day is merely a wasteful prolongation of puerility.

In Chapter XII, at the end of § 6, we have noted a suggestion made long ago by Professor William James that everyone should do a year or so of compulsory service for the State. We may refer to that suggestion again here. Such a term of service might do very much to strengthen the sense of citizenship in the individual. We shall return to that idea when we deal with certain difficultes in the staffing of public institutions in § 10.

After, or concurrently with, the closing years of the general school course in the middle teens, specialization will begin. But special and technical instruction is not a task for the upper forms of general schools where the stabilizing, standardizing, unstimulating scholastic mentality is bound to prevail, but for schools carefully planned to achieve the particular end in view and in close contact with real activities. The adolescent citizen will take up his or her technical (or professional) education, and that may or may not be combined with actual productive work. In Chapter VII, § 6, we pointed out how the organizations of great industrial enterprises are becoming interlocked with technical schools, and how continuation schools supplying scientific instruction can carry on through the whole career of a worker and keep his knowledge up-to-date and effective. For the worker ceases now to be a *hand;* he is chemist in a thousand forms, he is electrician, he is engineer, he is artist. The various sorts of scientific investigator for which the coming order will have an insatiable demand, the medical man, the cultivator of plants and animals, the sociologist, policeman and lawyer, the archi-tect and local administrator, the industrial organizer, the statistician and banker, and all the multitudinous variations of the active citizen, will follow their special trainings from the general school onward and the nature of those trainings, the methods of qualification and gradua-tion, will vary as endlessly as the occupation. Training will be given where it is most conveniently given. Educational vacations, when workers from one region of the world may visit the museums and hold conferences with those of another, interprofessional gatherings when, for example, the student-practitioners of medicine may meet lawyers and sociologists, may play a very important part in this lifelong educa-tional process.

But though the common citizen will have done with the general school and turned to specialized work and study by the time he is adolescent, he will not have done with general education. He will now be carrying it on—or the world about him will be carrying it on—through all those multifarious agencies of suggestion and information to which we have referred in § 6. He will go on being educated until he dies.

We have touched upon those agencies outside the classrooms and their development at various points in this work. We have glanced at current developments of book and newspaper and their new educa-tional auxiliaries. We are describing the present and not imagining the future in this survey, and so we will refrain from any Utopian specula-tions about the educational community of the years to come, the com-munity that will be in itself educational. How can one mind foretell where thousands of minds of the liveliest sort are inventing, contriving, trying, and judging new methods of presentation, distribution and stimulus? But we may at least go so far as to anticipate that the in-formation and suggestions that will beat upon the minds of our grand-children will be far less confused and confusing, unequal and casual, than those amidst which our own generation lives. In this chapter, thus far, we have noted an immense amount of incoherent learning in progress; a clamour of statement, misstatement and counterstatement; summaries of knowledge read by perhaps one man in a hundred and counted great successes, and innumerable series of little books and radio talks, flying, hit or miss, through the mental atmosphere. It is possible that the presentation of reality to the mind of the ordinary man may presently become much less haphazard, much more orderly and deliberate. There may be a systematic ordering and drawing together of human thought and knowledge. To that possibility we will now address ourselves. It is a possibility all too little apprehended at the present time.

§ 8. *The Rôle of an Encyclopædia in a Progressive Civilization*

The importance of the encyclopædia as a necessary educational organ and the possibilities and probabilities of considerable developments of the encyclopædic idea are still very imperfectly understood. For some centuries a limited number of men have been aware of the importance of a general summary of thought and knowledge which will serve as the basis for common understandings between specialists and for the ideology of education, and so become a guiding centre for the intellectual activities of mankind. But the mass of the public is still quite heedless of this need. It takes its knowledge as it takes its milk, without enquiring how it came to the door.

Attempts to get ideas and knowledge together for general use were made in the classical world, and the peculiarities of the Chinese writing made encyclopædic lexicons a natural development of Chinese learning. The great Chinese encyclopædias, however, are something different from our current idea of an encyclopædia; they are collections of extracts from the classics rather than summaries of knowledge, and most of them were overwhelmingly vast. Condensation and simplification are Western tendencies. I do not know why it should be so, but the Chinese seem to have a real preference for elaboration, in their games, in their art, in their life; they have nothing like the Western aptitude for short cuts. A failure to simplify writing is probably, as the *Outline of History* explains, the main reason for the Western advantage over China to-day. Even to-day the Chinese find themselves unable to send telegrams in their own language because it has no alphabet adapted to the purpose. The various Chinese literary and scientific collections, for that is really what they should be called—the Yung Lo assemblage ran to 22,937 volumes—date from the tenth to the seventeenth century and they are not really equivalent to our modern European encyclopædias at all. We mention them because the reader is sure to have heard of them, simply to note that they are beside our present discussion.

The first important movement towards encyclopædism—which, however, did not actually produce an encyclopædia—was due largely to the initiatives of Aristotle. Perhaps he was one of the first of men to be altogether possessed and directed by the passion for assembling and ordering knowledge. To him we must ascribe Alexander's foundation of the Museum at Alexandria with its great library and its book-copying organization. It was plainly modelled on the pattern of the Lyceum at Athens, which also was dedicated to the Muses, and had a library, maps and possibly other assembled material. (And, says Mr. Ernest Barker, it had its college dinners and even its own plate.) This home of the Muses at Alexandria was much more like the encyclopædic world-organization we shall presently foreshadow than any mediæval university. The *Outline of History* tells of its achievements and its decline. Latin culture produced nothing to compare with the Hellenic initiative at Alexandria, but it can claim at least to have produced the first encyclopædic book, Pliny's *Natural History*.

Manifestly while hand-copying was the only means of multiplying a work, an encyclopædia was a thing of very limited effect. The bigger, more comprehensive it was, the more impossible it was to distribute it to many people. It was a rarity for the erudite, and not an educational instrument. It was easier for the student to go to the knowledge at the museum or the university than for the knowledge to place itself at the disposal of the student in book form. It was only with the onset of printing on paper from movable type that the thing we call an encyclopædia to-day became a practical possibility.

First came "dictionaries" with long explicit articles. John Harris, the first secretary of the Royal Society, produced a Universal Dictionary of Arts and Sciences in 1704 and Zedler's Universal Lexicon in 64 volumes (Leipzig, 1732–50) was a great and comprehensive work. The Encyclopædia Britannica lists a number of parallel undertakings. It was the genius of Diderot (1713–84) which first revealed the power and importance latent in these great gatherings of fact and theory. Comenius, the Bohemian educationist, had, however, anticipated his idea of a synthesis of current knowledge in a pamphlet published at Oxford in 1637 (*Conatum Comenianorum Praeludia*), but he was unable to carry out his scheme. Diderot was invoked to revise and rearrange the translation of an English work, Chambers' Cyclopædia (of the Arts and Sciences), and it is clear that the light of a great opportunity dawned upon him as he struggled with this task. He proposed to the bookseller who had brought it to him to scrap the English original entirely and embark upon an altogether bolder, more comprehensive undertaking. He had definite ideas and much enthusiasm, and he won a considerable amount of support among the liberal spirits of his time.

His scheme was plainly to make his encyclopædia the substantial basis of a modernized ideology, gather together the accumulating criticism of tradition and established usage, and organize the new and growing knowledge of the age into an effective instrument for social, political and religious reconstruction. His Encyclopédie was something new; the Encyclopédistes constituted a definite movement towards a new education and a new social life. The first volume was issued in 1751. It was only as the subsequent volumes appeared that the full force of his design became apparent. The story of its production is a complicated and stormy one. The work was held up after the second volume appeared in 1752, as a danger to religion and the King's authority, but after a delay of a year its resumption was permitted. In 1759 the still incomplete Encyclopédie was formally suppressed and its sale forbidden. It was continued furtively and in fear of the police. The last volume of letter-press was published in 1765, and the final volume of plates only reached the subscribers in 1772. The work was distributed secretly in Paris and Versailles. Altogether 4,250 people subscribed to it: a formidable body of opinion for that time. The later volumes were emasculated by the cowardice and treachery of the printer Lebreton. He had the articles set up in type exactly as the authors sent them in, and when the final proofs had been corrected by Diderot, "he and his foreman, hastily, secretly and by night . . . cut out whatever seemed to them daring, or likely to give offence, mutilated most of the best articles without any regard to the consecutiveness of what was left, and burnt the manuscript. . . ."* Diderot knew nothing of what was going on until he saw the printed book. What an amazing, embittering, heartbreaking experience it must have been for him to turn from page to page and find clear statement and crucial argument, blunted, weakened, made absurd!

So, crippled, damaged, uneven, the first encyclopædia of power came into the world. Defective as it was, it was of cardinal importance in the great intellectual movements of the time. There was enough left to get through to men's imaginations. Its influence in giving an ideological content to the first French Revolution was immense. It radiated far beyond France; it released minds and steadied progressive thought everywhere where men read books; it set a pattern for all kindred enterprises—in this respect at least, that henceforth they treated ideas historically and recognized diversity of opinion.

The first edition of the Encyclopædia Britannica appeared in 1768 onward, and its very title shows its indebtedness to and its competition

*Encyclopædia Britannica: Article, *Encyclopædia*.

with its French predecessor. The ideology was conservative and patriotic, and the dedication to a supplement to the third edition, in 1800, refers to the Encyclopédie as a "pestiferous work." But the likeness to the parent increased with each edition and compensated for this ungracious repudiation. It is against nature that a comprehensive survey of reality should be reactionary. In 1812 we hear a very different note; we find general introductions being planned to show the progress of science since Bacon, similar to "the excellent discourse prefixed by D'Alembert to the French Encyclopédie." The breadth and power of each new edition increased. It is a question whether the ninth (with supplements, the tenth) or the eleventh (with successive supplements, the twelfth and the thirteenth) edition is to be counted the better and more influential. Both were widely distributed by modern methods of marketing and still constitute a sort of intellectual backbone for the body of English speaking and writing, for teachers, preachers, journalists, authors and intelligent people generally.

The article in the fourteenth edition to which we are indebted for these present facts gives a résumé of the other leading encyclopædias that have served the Atlantic world since our age of organized knowledge commenced. The Conversations Lexicon of Brockhaus is the chief among these, but there is scarcely a European language now without a reasonably good encyclopædia. The contemporary French mind has been moulded to a very remarkable extent by the dictionaries and encyclopædias initiated by Pierre Larousse. There is a pre-revolutionary Russian encyclopædia based on Brockhaus and a Communist Bolshaya Sovietskaya Entsiklopediya is now said to be in hand. That should prove an exceptionally interesting production. There is an excellent Jewish Encyclopædia and the Jesuits have produced a Catholic Encyclopædia of their own which is also very characteristic in its spirit and quality.

But if Diderot could return to this world, learn the vast potentialities of our age, and sense our present intellectual atmosphere, I doubt if he would be content with the current phase of "encyclopædization," widespread though it is. Encyclopædias have multiplied and spread considerably, but the mechanical structure of our world and our economic and social organization have developed out of all proportion to their increase. The modern encyclopædia should bear the same relation to the Encyclopédie or the early Encyclopædia Britannica that a transcontinental railway engine bears to Cugnot's steam road car. But does it do so? Let us take, for example, the current edition (the fourteenth) of the Encyclopædia Britannica as the last achievement in this great movement towards a guiding synthesis of human knowledge and ask whether it is not capable of further very great invigoration and development.

We are criticizing a fairly good thing here to which indeed we are manifestly indebted, and when we criticize, it is not to say that the work is bad but to suggest that it has not fully realized the measure of contemporary necessity. You will find in it some magnificent articles to stir the creative imagination, the article upon architecture, for example. It is full of the stimulating statement of concrete achievements and possibilities. I repeat it is impossible for any encyclopædia to be truly reactionary. Such articles as the one on pottery and porcelain are marvels of illustration and copious information. But they are out of proportion. Full justice is done to the actual wealth and vigour of our times. But when it comes to a question of directive general ideas such as the idea of property, or the creative possibilities of financial or political reorganization, it is mute or unstimulating; it speaks with an uncertain mind. For the most part, and in its preface and general scheme, it seems to assume political institutions and financial methods that even the man in the street is questioning. And one discovers odd gaps. I wanted some particulars about the enquiry into the labour atrocities of Putumayo and its outcome, and I could find nothing. Nor is there a word about Sanderson of Oundle, most original and stimulating of British schoolmasters. This latest compilation is to say the least of it lacking in just that stirring sense of a better ordering of things at hand, ours for the effort of realization, which was the heroic quality, the essential and power-giving quality, of Diderot's great endeavour. And indeed, in his Preface, Mr. J. L. Garvin, the editor, frankly abandons the *Encyclopédiste* ambition. The world, he says, has become so multitudinous, so overwhelming that a directive synthesis is impossible. It is as if a general had failed to conceive a plan of campaign and ordered his army very eloquently to advance in all directions. It is a diffusion, not a synthesis. He had great difficulties in his task, one can understand. Perhaps his hands were not altogether free. But his encyclopædia, in its abandonment of synthesis, is a reversion to the "cyclopædias" and universal dictionaries that existed before the days of Diderot, rather than an advance beyond its predecessors. It is an all too characteristic product of our time. It is multitudinous, defective and discursive in just this present phase of the world's history when the need for directive general concepts, gripped firmly and held steadfastly, is the supreme need of our race.

But impermanence is the lot of all encyclopædias, and though the

Britannica, after some decades of virtuous excitement, shows now these marks of advanced maturity, of "middle-aged spread," that is no reason for supposing that the spirit of Diderot is dead, or that this impulse towards comprehensive intellectual coördination, which has been going on through the past two centuries as if it were a natural necessity for the human mind, will not continue. Perhaps the days when the making and issuing of encyclopædias could be regarded as legitimate business enterprises are drawing to an end, and our world is near realizing that the assembling and presentation of knowledge and ideas, of ideological material, that is, should become a primary function of the educational community.

The encyclopædia of the future may conceivably be prepared and kept by an endowed organization employing thousands of workers permanently, spending and recovering millions of pounds yearly, mediating between the original thinker, the scientific investigator, the statistician, the creative worker and the reporter of realities on the one hand and the general intelligence of the public on the other. But such an organization would outgrow in scale and influence alike any single university that exists, and it would inevitably tend to take the place of the loose-knit university system of the world in the concentration of research and thought and the direction of the general education of mankind.

The World Encyclopædia organization as we are here conceiving it would reach down to direct the ideological side of human education. But it could scarcely come into existence without on the other hand creating organic relations with the main statistical activities of the world. It would almost inevitably develop a centralized system of world statistics in direct relation to its needs. It would have its Year Book volumes. So it would be a natural collaborator with Lubin's pioneer Institute in Rome for an annual world census of cultivation and staple production generally. Moreover, it would be a natural nucleus about which specific researches could cluster very conveniently, and it could undertake with advantage that systematic indexing, abstracting and exchange of research publications, to which Madame Curie has directed the attention of the International Institute of Intellectual Coöperation. At present the old universities, in spite of their encumbrance with tradition, sport, entertainment and the belated unspecialized education of backward young men and women, are the natural recipients of endowments for research, because they still seem to be the only possible agents in the matter. An encyclopædia organization, reviving on a modern scale the high ambitions of the Alexandria Museum, would change all that. It would become the logical nucleus of the world's research universities and post-graduate studies. It would be the central Museum of a world, Hellenized anew after the long twilight of Latin predominance.

In another direction one sees this convenient centre annexing or duplicating the League of Nations' registry of treaties and organizing a world digest of laws.

How far this establishment of an encyclopædia as a recognized central organ in the mental life of mankind may be attainable by a transformation of university activities, by the formation of special societies and groups of learned, wealthy and influential people, by inspired feats of publication, and by state action, I will not venture to speculate; nor how closely it may be associated with a world system of informative and demonstrative museums. Nor do I know how closely it will be linked with the research laboratories, experimental farms and reserves and statistical bureaus of the advancing world. But the need for it and the existence of forces making for it are undeniable. And whatever other functions it had, its main function would be to irradiate the ideological teaching of every common school in the world.

If no great catastrophe arrests or delays the present prosperous advance of our race, the coming of a world encyclopædia is a matter—it may be—only of decades. It is an enterprise that the League of Nations' Institute of Intellectual Coöperation might very well consider. That body, given the necessary organizing ability, is in a position of exceptional advantage to bring together large groups of publishers, writers and universities for such an associated production. And we can prophesy with considerable assurance that so soon as it comes into existence this culminating Encyclopædia will be made available in all the chief languages (the Conversations Lexicon of Brockhaus, with wide variations of title and considerable local adaptation, has gone into most of them already), and that it will be undergoing constant revision and reprinting. This suggests the desirability of considerable detachability and interchangeability between its parts. A faint prevision of the rows of volumes of this coming encyclopædia is evoked by these considerations. We can even foretell some probable details of arrangement. Many of the earlier encyclopædias did not have numbered pages—perhaps in view of possible insertions—and it may be desirable at any rate not to have numbered volumes. There seems little reason for retaining the alphabetical arrangement of the whole book. It might be divided into main sections which could be lettered and there could be one or more numbered volumes under each letter. Then any section could be revised independently and its one or two volumes replaced by three or four without disturbing the general arrangement. Within a section there might be a retention of the convenient system of major articles and alphabetically arranged minor articles characteristic of the Britannica.

To speculate in this fashion about the form in which a world encyclopædia may presently appear falls very properly into our present design. We may even make an anticipatory summary of the arrangement and contents of the work. Such a summary is not in the least irrelevant to our enterprise, for it enables us to make a survey of all contemporary knowledge and all contemporary ideas, and so evoke another set of figures to add to our grand ensemble of human activities, which would be otherwise difficult to introduce. There are the men and women, more men as yet than women, who are engaged in original thought. They are the men and women who know best, the men and women who think and express best, the sources. What sort of people are they?

For the most part they will have to be presented sitting at well-lit writing tables and desks in conveniently appointed apartments lined with books. They read, they make notes, the pen scratches over the paper, some perhaps dictate to stenographers or use dictaphones, and within easy reach of many of them are typists with their typewriters, the first step towards print, towards stereo plates and the roaring presses that will bring the new idea, the novel suggestion, the illuminating comment into the common mental life. One sheet of manuscript follows another, and presently the day's work or the night's work is done and pinned together.

The rooms of these individuals are sometimes in the dignified colleges of universities, sometimes in carefully sought country retreats, sometimes in the quieter streets of great towns. An increasing number work in laboratories now, and in the reserved rooms of the ever extending museums of our time. The laboratories may be of the largest or smallest type, elaborate with the most extraordinary apparatus, or simple with some little object rendering its secret under examination. Others of these intellectual workers watch in observatories or scrutinize the stellar photographs observatories have made under their directions. Many of these men and women who are "sources" explore now and excavate with teams of trained workers, amidst Arctic severities or under a tropical sun. Then back they come with their finds, to explain, write up what they have done, compare and discuss.

These fundamental people are not very gregarious as a rule; they have not much time to spare for small talk; but they have their sociable moments and may even ventilate their preoccupations by two's and three's or in little groups, or you may find them assembled in attentive roomfuls while one of them reads a paper and ideas are interchanged. Some are negligently dressed and distraught in their bearing, but for the most part they look fairly well cared for and have little or nothing to mark them off from the ordinary bourgeoisie. You may pass Mr. Einstein, who upset all our ideas of space and movement, carrying his violin in the streets of Berlin and take him for nothing but a smiling fiddler on his way to a recital; you may dine with the Royal Society, and it looks remarkably like the company at an ordinary city dinner. In the more inaccessible parts of the sunny East we are given to understand that beautiful sages of manifest and immediately recognizable sagacity, meditate profoundly in propitious attitudes amidst their adoring disciples. Little that is worth while comes through to us from them, and until it does, it is to those other scattered, busy, unposed, unpretentious and often quite obscure-looking Westerners, that we must ascribe the essential living thought of the world. Altogether their actual thinking is physically a very unobtrusive series of activities. A single shipyard at work makes more noise than all the original thought of the world put together.

But generally these individuals we have termed the "sources" are not in direct communication with the general mind. They will contribute to the World Encyclopædia, no doubt, and they will in their own sphere of interest exercise powers of revision and criticism of its contents, but much even of that work of explanation and correlation can be done by their student associates as well or even better than they can do it themselves. But such a vigorous and original thinker as Professor T. H. Huxley (Darwin's Huxley) found the delivery of a course of elementary lectures or the occasional production of a textbook a very illuminating and beneficial exercise for himself because it obliged him to put his abbreviated technical thoughts into plain and simple language. There are endless pitfalls in technicality, and many temptations to retire from the general intelligence into a cloud where one's proceedings can no longer be checked.

Between the original "sources" and the common thought of the world there intervenes a much more abundant and almost as various a multitude of busy individuals. There are interpreters, would-be interpreters and mis-interpreters. There are also the sham sages, the presumptious, conceited and ambitious among the intellectual workers. Some serve a useful purpose, some sting and stimulate and some obstruct and corrupt. In all the big centres of population are great libraries, as, for example, the British Museum library, and thither converge daily a swarm of preoccupied individuals, with portfolios and notebooks. Some of these may be original workers of importance, "sources" themselves. Most of them are the transmitting, intervening, checking categories. Manifestly this present work you are reading falls into this mediatory grade of transmission. And from these we pass on to such types as the specially qualified interviewer consulting the savant for the press. He brings us to scientific and technical journalism, a little world in itself, still very underdeveloped, and so to all these popular means of diffusion we have already discussed. One of the most useful and unpretending of transmission organs is that weekly paper *Nature,* which serves for intellectual exchanges, as far as science goes, throughout the whole English-speaking, English-reading world. A World Encyclopædia kept sedulously in direct contact with as many as possible of these fundamental minds we have considered would be of enormous value in steadying, controlling and informing this secondary network of transmission, correlation and interpretation.

And if we think of all these primary intellectual activities on which the progress of the world depends, gathered together and summarized into a World Encyclopædia, what are the main sections of that work likely to be? Let us sketch a provisional answer to that question.

Manifestly the opening section would have to be an account of the philosophies of the world, compared critically and searchingly in an Introduction. Then, in separate articles, there would be accounts of the main systems of philosophy with their variants and the lives of the chief philosophers. There would have to be a history of philosophies and of the development of general ideas. There would be an account of logic, of what used to be called "significs," the values of language. Philosophical and comparative philology would be dealt with, for we are approaching a time when a real history of languages becomes possible, and a study of grammar and idiom in relation to turns and habits of thought. Then would come the origins and development of writing. Number and the mathematical exploitation of form and conceptions of space and time would follow, and an account of mathematical signs and symbols and their relation to realities. A history, classification and analysis of fallacies and of superstitions and prevalent errors arising out of the incautious use of symbols would seem to be indicated. This would constitute the opening section.

From it there would probably branch off a section devoted to specific languages and the literary cultures associated with them, and a third section would deal with the detailed development of pure mathematics.

The fourth section would be a compendium of pure physics, chemistry and astronomy, the whole of what is still best called "material science." Biographies of the men who have built up this body of science would be given, and a history of its development.

Next would come a fifth section—the general science of life and a great series of articles devoted to the forms of life. Biographies of biologists and a history of biological science would be added.

From this fifth section there might branch off a sixth. Health and medicine would be dealt with in this, mental health as well as bodily health, and with that might come an account of sport, exercise and pastimes.

Then in a seventh section there would be a fuller treatment of human biology and the general history of mankind. The history of exploration would form a subsection of this.

The histories of various peoples and political systems, e. g. Greek and Roman history, would make an eighth section, and here would come a political Atlas and general biography, the stories of outstanding men and women, except the artists and men of science whose lives will be treated elsewhere.

The ninth section would deal with education, religion and ethics treated objectively and historically, the science and art of education, the laws of conduct and the treatment of crime.

Then two huge parallel sections would give a double-barrelled treatment of economic life, one from the point of view of production and industrial organization, and the other from the points of view of distribution and finance. Here the principles and laws of property would be dealt with and here would come an economic geography and Atlas of the world. These really constitute that as yet imaginary *Science of Work and Wealth* which has served so useful a purpose in easing the burthen of detail in this work.

The twelfth section of our World Encyclopædia would stand somewhat apart in spirit from the rest of the enterprise, and it would deal with beauty. It would be devoted to the æsthetic concepts and accomplishments of our race, with music, with every form of art, with poetry and all that can be called creative literature. In it æsthetic criticism would pursue its wild, incalculable, unstandardized career, mystically distributing praise and blame. Here would come the lives and critical studies of the work of poets and artists of every kind; the history of the drama; of opera; architecture considered as cultural expression; the high mystery of the Novel, as it was understood by Henry James. And here the multiplying new resources of artistry, the cinema, radio, gramophone and the like, of which the mechanical and financial sides would have been considered elsewhere, would be treated from the point of view of their æsthetic possibilities. The artist in his studio, the composer in his music room and all the multitude who invent and write down their inventions, have hardly figured as yet in our world panorama, and even now we can give them but a passing sentence or so. They are an efflorescence, a lovely and purifying efflorescence on life. And still more of an efflorescence is that vastly greater multitude of painters who cannot paint, of sculptors who leave us colder than their marble, of musicians who have but to approach a piano to put us to insincerely apologetic flight, and of an endlessly brawling, posturing, insulting, lusciously appreciating swarm of people—for the most part of small independent means—who write, talk, fight and bore about art. All this clamorous obscurity we glance at under the lower edge of this twelfth section of our World Encyclopædia, contemplate ambiguously for a moment and dismiss.

With that twelfth volume the great survey of human wisdom and initiatives would be complete. Then would come a dictionary index, with brief definitions for use as a dictionary, and the fullest index references to the encyclopædia. Good indexing is absolutely essential to an efficient encyclopædia. Every section should be indexed, every main article should have an index and a full bibliography, and in addition there should be this comprehensive general dictionary index, a section in itself.

Manifestly this is a much completer enterprise than any encyclopædia hitherto attempted. But then the resources of our world are vastly greater than they were in the days of Diderot and the first Encyclopædia Britannica. It would indeed do little more than bring those gallant pioneer essays properly up to date and scale. It would need as much money to bring it into existence as would launch a modern battleship. Are there no anti-Zaharoffs to bring back money to these better uses? And when it was launched it would need half a million pounds a year at least to keep it under constant revision. It would maintain as large a permanent staff as all the faculties of three or four great universities and unless it sold by the million sets it would not possibly *pay*. It would probably have to be a stupendously endowed enterprise. Yet in relation to Diderot's achievement it would be in no greater proportion than a modern liner is to the little sailing ships that lay in the Downs waiting for a change in the wind a century and a half ago.

And consider its certain effects. It would become the central ganglion, as it were, of the collective human brain. It would keep the thought of the world in a perpetual lively interchange. It would be the living source of a true *Outline of History,* instead of the poor sketch the world buys to-day, of a lucid *Science of Life,* of an understandable summary of the business of the world. It would sustain the common ideology of mankind. It would be the world organ of our correlated activities. And after all, at its most magnificent, if it used some thousands of men continually, it would not cost a tithe of the money spent upon such aimless, excessively dangerous extravagances as the French army which may never fight, or the American fleet, or the British fleet, or the militant forces the Germans are now endeavouring to restore.

§ 9. *Open Conspiracy*

And now that this great spectacle of human toil and effort rises to its culmination a crowning question becomes manifest. Wherein does true sovereignty reside? What is ruling and directing this millionfold diversity of activity towards its objective of synthesis order and power?

It is clear that existing governments do not really govern. We have shown how provisional and sometimes how obstructive and dangerous are these formal governments of our time. Their origin was combative. They drift by an inherited necessity towards war. They are not really governing any more than our formal educational organizations are really educating, or our religious bodies really inspiring and shaping human lives.

The world needs a world government to supplement, control or supersede these traditional governments, a recasting of its schools to meet the needs of a new education, and a formulation of modern religious feeling that will free us from the entangling rags of ancient superstitions. And the strange thing is that in spite of the conscious and unconscious resistance of governments, schools and religious bodies, and the whole machinery of mental and material direction, in spite of the absence of any real progressive organization of the world, mankind does move forwards towards that new world, has moved indeed with increasing rapidity for the past two centuries, and still struggles with gathering vigour and effect against the restraints of the past. What is the power that sustains this forward urge? What is it that inspires so many of us with the hope of presently making an end to war and of so marshalling our present confusions as to achieve a world of justice, health, achievement and happiness such as life has never known before?

In our analysis of the social motives of humanity, we have already found some intimations of an answer. We have drawn attention to the peculiar effect, the almost paradoxical effect, of the priestly training in turning minds to the scrutiny and revision of tradition. Men can be broken in to all sorts of submissions but the last thing you can break in is thinking. Every system of shams, every system once living that has become unreal, carries with it that ferment of skepticism. In spite of profit and advantage, in spite of the universal longing for peace and comfort, there is a disposition—it is as deep almost as an instinct—for truth, at work in us all. But that is not the only strain that is making for the revision of our world. The nomad, the autocrat, has never come into civilization submissively. He may not be a noble creature—*Homo sapiens* is not as yet a noble animal—but he has pride. His tradition is all against suppressions and smothered whispers. Tell the truth though the heavens fall, is the heroic phrasing of it.

And further, man has brought down from his arboreal ancestry, an unsleeping curiosity, an incessant disposition to experiment and invent.

Now these various sources of unrest have worked together, altogether unconsciously, to frame out this new world civilization that dawns upon us amidst the institutions and traditions of the old. The critical man, the inventive man, the adventurous and outspoken man, have worked together for consequences greater than they knew. When Stephenson watched his "Active" pull out the first passenger train upon the Stockton & Darlington Railway, it did not dawn upon him that this puffing and hissing contraption was destined to ensure the unity of the United States and make every frontier in Europe too tight. When Franklin flew his kite on a thundery day and drew sparks from the key at the end of his string, he had no idea that he was one small link in the huge chain of thought and realizations that was to throw a mantle of instant intelligence about the whole world. One step of curious enquiry, one act of simple mental integrity, multiplied a millionfold, has made the possibilities and opportunities of to-day. Behind these more recent and more successful innovators are others, more tragic and heroic. These are the men who told the truth as they conceived it about the heavens, though the churchmen of the time and all the established powers thundered together against them; there is Socrates drinking his hemlock because his genius had forced him to quicken the minds of the young.

Before that unpremeditated convergence of criticism, enquiry, suggestions, experiment and outspoken denial, the traditional order has become unreal in our minds to-day, and a new way of living opens before us. All that innovating, subversive activity was an unconscious conspiracy to evoke a new world.

But latterly that once unconscious conspiracy has been developing an awareness of itself, at first dimly but now more clearly. For a century and a half, at least, the idea of a conscious handling of the future of humanity has been establishing itself in our minds. Man finding knowledge and power growing in his hands and his range of possibilities increasing continually, has gone on to the obvious next step of putting his knowledge in order and making his attainment of yet more knowledge and yet more power, purposive and systematic. For that new apprehension we have made Diderot, with his poor burked and mangled and persecuted Encyclopédie, our symbol. We would put him against his monarch, making the latter, with his preposterous robes and ceremonies, his pretentious magnificence, his infinite self-complacency, his "foreign policy," his diplomatists, his mistresses and his piety, the very crown and embodiment of vulgar tradition. Who at that time would have imagined that Diderot would be alive to-day, a power and an inspiration, and his gorgeous sovereign as gone and happily gone out of human admiration and imitation as Nero or Cambyses before him.

With Diderot at last, that hitherto unconscious conspiracy for progress began to know itself for what it was. The nineteenth century was the century of liberalism, of the undermining of privilege and restriction. Progress came to be regarded as a necessary, rather than a merely possible, good. Lord Tennyson was the laureate not only of progress but of that limited reactionary little lady, Queen Victoria; and he reconciled the two without a qualm by presenting her as a veritable queen of light and guidance. Since he felt the world must surely "broaden down from precedent to precedent," how could she be anything but that? It was only a limited number of people who realized the finer truth that the secular development of a world civilization is not inevitable, but the outcome of constant effort and critical vigilance. Progress went on in that age of good fortune as though it went on by itself. It was the catastrophe of the Great War which has recalled us to the fact that the malignant possibilities of tradition had also been enhanced amidst the accumulated opportunities of that prolific awakening century which revealed to man all that he might hope and dare. After the Great

War the impulse towards planned effort, towards the timely repudiation of obsolete institutions and towards educational reorganization has grown exceedingly. And it still grows. The word "plan" grows upon us. The Five Year Plan is only the first of many such plans to come.

To-day it is impossible to estimate how far human affairs are still drifting by hazard and material forces, and how far conscious scientific construction is making head against the adverse elements, within us and without, that would turn us back to outworn methods and racial recession. Our review of human affairs has been a display of almost unqualified growth under the influence of what we have just styled the "unconscious conspiracy" of original thought and innovation and experiment. But throughout we have had to note defects and waste in the working of this developing ant-hill for which no inevitable compensations appear, and dangers that have grown at least as vigorously as the rest of men's concerns. We have had at every step to qualify the confident effortless progressivism of the nineteenth century. The nineteenth century was a run of luck for mankind, a gust of good fortune, that may never recur. We see now plainly that we live in a world advancing still—but advancing dangerously and stumbling as it advances. We have shown political and financial science and method, lagging behind mechanical invention, and education faltering at its task. It seems that we can no longer rely upon the successful working of that "unconscious conspiracy" alone, to carry our intricate politico-economic system through the great dangers and stresses, so manifestly ahead, so rapidly drawing near. There is a quickening sense of this need for more concerted action, that is to say, for a new way of living, if the promise of humanity is to be fulfilled.

What are the activities to which men and women should now address and adjust their lives? They are, we shall find, activities that cannot be done by isolated men in out-of-the-way places or by energetic groups working for partial ends and heedless of the general drift of things. Railways could be spread by such groups—the governments of the time and the bulk of men scarcely heeding the network that grew about them and their planet—telegraphs, automobile and aëroplane could arrive without asking for any general consent. But the organization of a world peace can come into existence only through the previous acquiescence of at least all the chief governments in the world. That change must come about in a different fashion from the preceding changes. Men must be brought to a common mind in the matter, and that can be done only by the concerted efforts of a great number of influential and devoted people organizing propaganda and action. They must know themselves and each other, for that action to be effectual. There must be a Five Year Plan or a Ten Year Plan for all the world to understand if world pacification and disarmament are to be achieved. And similarly the readjustment of our cash-credit arrangements whose entanglements promise to strangle our growing prosperity, must be a world-wide, conscious undertaking to which governments must assent. You cannot introduce a new economic method in New Jersey or Denmark while the rest of the world abstains. The failure of a score of hopeful Utopian experiments in the nineteenth century demonstrated that. Concerted action by numbers of energetic men in all the great communities can alone meet this occasion. The world must have a plan like a banner that all men may follow, if the tariff walls are to crumble out of sight and a new money serve all the planet. Both these great tasks, the political and the economic, which mankind must perform or perish, are associated with and dependent on a concurrent world-wide renewal of education, which must equally be planned and carried out in the light of day. Restraint of population too must be world-wide.

We are forced therefore towards the conclusion that the phase of the "unconscious conspiracy" is drawing to its end, and that the further stages in the development of the new order of human life have to be achieved only through a world-wide movement conscious of itself.

Elsewhere I have used the term "open conspiracy" to express such a movement of men of ability and understanding towards world-wide concerted effort. As I conceive it, "open conspiracy" is not in itself the name of a defined project, but a term to accentuate and to help people to the realization of this present need for conscious and stated creative coöperations. It is something already going on; the unconscious conspiracy of effort and circumstance in the past becomes open conspiracy by imperceptible degrees, as the necessity for combined effort becomes plain and its recognition outspoken. All political, economic, and social service that is free and unhampered by patriotic limitations is open conspiracy. All biological work is that, all physical science and all straightforward industrial innovation, in so far as it sets no limits to its inferences and makes an unrestrained communication of its results and suggestions to the whole world. All these forces will gain enormously in effectiveness by common protection and support, one for the other, and by a clear formulation of their common end.

As I conceive it this open conspiracy of the educated is dawning now. Unless I misread the signs of the time it should grow articulate and spread very rapidly through the world's educational organizations. It should find a response and expression in literature and art. It should quicken the imaginations of financial and industrial directors and organizers, and it should bring them into understanding relation with the civil services of the world's governments. It should become the dominating idea of an increasing multitude of active personalities. In our Chapter XII, § 13, the problem of world unity was discussed, and it was shown how pressing and probable great world commissions for world planning in such fields as disarmament and international trade have become. These must bring to a head, into a common constellation of activities, just such elements as I have indicated here as the formative threads of this open conspiracy. The open conspiracy is not a remote utopian project; it is something very probable, almost actual, close at hand.

In this idea of a concerted world-wide effort to sustain and continue the progress of the past two centuries, we have surely just that criterion of the value of conduct, that indication of an end for our activities, that the decay of the old faiths and explanations has deprived us of. We have the call for a new type of devotion and the indications for a new system of disciplines. We have indeed, at the practical level at which all this book is written—for life in space and time—the working elements of a new religion. But it is a religion that emerges, without founder or dogma or any finality, from the factors of social effort and desire that have been fostered and elaborated in the mind of man, by and throughout his developing social life. If man is to continue and still progress, it can only be by such a direct and simple apprehension of his world of work and achievement.

If the line of thought pursued in this book is sound, then what is here called open conspiracy is the practical form modern religion must assume, and the aim of modern education, as we have unfolded it here, must be to make every possible man and woman in the world an open conspirator.

To bring about this reconstruction of education and economic affairs, the mere general diffusion of liberal ideas may prove insufficient, and many people are thinking to-day of the need of a more organized movement of modernization in social, political and educational life. The practical successes of such bodies as the Communist Party and the Fascist organization has stimulated the imaginations of many of the younger generation and there are some so bold as to dream of a movement, so wide in aim and so far-reaching that it will become in the long run the directive and educational power of the world. They point out that in effect now the Communist Party *is* Russia and the Fascisti *are* Italy, and they do not quail from the proposition that a similar but more greatly conceived initiative of devoted and disciplined adherents might in itself become the living modern World State.

In Chapter VIII § § 6 and 8, we have introduced an idea to which we attach very great importance, namely the idea of the *Competent Receiver* as a primary necessity to any large-scale handling of human affairs. The Communist Party attempts to be the competent receiver for the property and responsibility of the dispossessed landlord and profiteering entrepreneur of Russia. The World Society of this greater dream would set itself to become the competent receiver of the whole world's business. It would be the militant form of the Open Conspiracy. And it is certainly very difficult to imagine how mankind can escape from the conflicting tangle of its present governments without some such overt and definite world organization of will and aim.

§ 10. *The Recalcitrant*

In the preceding section we have ventured in criticism and forecast far beyond our enterprise of presentation. Let us return now to some very hard and serious realities in the shadow of the human community with which our enumeration of human life schemes must conclude.

The community breaks in the individual by education, and sometimes that education involves disciplines of some severity. Education passes by insensible degrees into adult government, into the public control of conduct, into the infliction of restraints, pains, and penalties. There is no gap, no real dividing line between education proper and the prevention and punishment of crime; they are two aspects of one thing.*

Let us consider what crime is, in the light of contemporary knowledge. Man at the level of *Sinanthropus* probably had no more conception of crime and sin than any other animal. He had still to begin to be broken in to organized social life. He was like a dog which will commit incest, murder another dog, steal a bone—without feeling a stain upon its character. He may have had a certain awe of his master or his assembled fellows, as a dog has. We can only guess about that.

*A good recent work on the repression or cure of the recalcitrant is Dr. Pailthorpe's *What We Put in Prison,* published by the London Association for the Scientific Treatment of Criminals.

We have stated the broad facts of the prehistoric process of breaking-in of *Homo* in our Chapter I telling how Man became an economic animal. Restraint was imposed upon him by taboos. He was brought to restrain his sexual impulses by the incest taboo, and to respect property by the tabooing of this object or that to all but its owner. He had to restrict his impulse to violence. There is no instinct, psychologists tell us, against murder, robbery, theft or incest. There is no natural inherent virtue. Virtue is an artificial thing, an achievement, which is why we praise it to one another. A system of inhibitions is built up in our minds from our earliest days against these society-destroying impulses. For most of us, this system of inhibitions is sufficiently strong, under normal conditions, to keep us out of mischief. But it helps almost all of us to know that behind these acquired dispositions of ours is the law, with its pains and penalties.

So long as our moral education holds, and reasonable social circumstances and our good fortune keep us out of temptation, we do not release the potential murderer or robber within us, but there he is, nevertheless. Our ideologies, our conception of ourselves and our world, keep him out of sight even of our introspection. But whenever a murderer goes to be hanged, "there but for the grace of God" go the reader and the writer.

There was a fashion some years ago for denying this fairly evident truth. An Italian psychologist, Cesare Lombroso, produced a book, *L'Uomo Delinquente,* in which he declared that for the most part criminals had distinctive physical traits, "criminal" ears, thumbs and so forth. This idea carried out to its proper conclusion would enable us to hang our murderers on anthropometric grounds before they killed anyone. He modified his views later, but that qualification was less exciting "news" and did not get the same publicity. After his book on criminals Lombroso published a book in which he attempted to show that men of genius are defectives and akin to the insane. As everybody who writes believes himself or herself to be a genius, this gave Lombroso what literary circles call a "bad press," and his reputation collapsed. But his views have been more convincingly disposed of by Dr. Goring (*The English Convict,* 1913) who has shown that there is no distinctive physical or mental criminal type. Dr. Kischway (Encyclopædia Britannica, under Criminology) questions the latter half of Dr. Goring's conclusion, namely that there is no mental difference. The truth of the matter may lie in the fact that though there is no innate criminal quality there are probably certain distinctive qualities in the ideology established in the mind which resorts to crime. There may be unstable types in which a criminal ideology is established with facility. Professor Burt lays stress on this in his *Young Delinquent*. In America they talk glibly of "morons" as if they were a specially defined class of human being. In effect "moron" is simply a term of prejudice and abuse. There is no such class. The practical distinction of innate and acquired qualities is a difficult one. There are certainly criminal types of persona.

We return to our assumption that crimes and offenses are artificial, they are restrictions imposed upon the normal "natural man" in order that the community may exist and work. There is no real difference in anything but degree between the man who outrages and robs his aunt, the man who deliberately drives an automobile round a corner on the wrong side of the road in order to get a thrill, the man who pulls a railway communication cord without proper excuse, and the man who uses a cleaned-up postage stamp over again. Each is giving way to his own impulses regardless of conventions established for the general good. The right or wrong of what they do is relative to society; there is no absolute right or wrong. A certain sanctity has been imposed upon the lives of aunts and the defacement of postage stamps, and the offender has refused to respect it. The social organization cannot afford to ignore this disregard. The artificial nature of crime becomes very plain when we consider such an offense as forgery. The precise imitation of a bank note or of a private signature on a cheque is made a serious offence in order to keep our cash and credit systems in working order. Otherwise it would be merely an elegant accomplishment. As a magistrate I have committed forgers for trial without feeling the slightest moral disapproval of them. There was a case came before the Folkestone bench: A prosperous gipsy woman bought a horse and almost immediately went mad; her nephew, who worked with her, took her cheque book and signed her name to pay for the horse. In perfect good faith. He did not even try to imitate her signature. What could have been more straightforward? How many women suddenly left penniless by a husband's insanity must have been disposed to do likewise? But the law has never been able to devise special arrangements for such hard cases, and so "forger" is established in our minds side by side with "robber" and "murderer" as a specially tainted being.

Crime, then, is that much of recalcitrance to the established processes and regulations, laws and by-laws of the social organization, which is punishable by law, and our best way of approaching it is by some preliminary considerations about recalcitrance in general. Why do people suddenly or of set habit and disposition refuse to "play the game" and disorganize the social operations about them?

This is a question that can be addressed in precisely the same terms to a school disciplinarian. The problem of order in society is one with the problem of order in the school. The latter is only the former in an earlier and simpler phase. The educationist's discipline is merely the prelude to the policeman and the criminal law. His science, which has advanced immensely in the last century, tells him to get just as much of right conduct as possible into the persona, to build up continually by example and precept, encouragement and disapproval, the suggestion that this is "done" and that is "not done." As far as possible he avoids reasoning about things; there is less friction if a type of act is established as being in itself "right" or "wrong." Telling the truth, avoiding and objecting to cruelty, playing fair, can all be put into a mind as handsome and creditable things by a competent teacher without any discussion at all. One of his most important disciplinary forces, is "the tone of the school." Individual ideas float on ideas generally prevalent. The preservation of the tone of the school is his constant solicitude. He resorts nowadays to compulsion and punishment only when the equipment of the persona is inadequate. But the youngsters over whom he rules are not passive wax for his moulding. His example and precept must be a consistent system in itself and consistent also with the general conception of the world that is developing in the developing mind. Suggest that one must be brave and independent, and some of the subordinations you are imposing may take on a timid look; suggest that one must be loyal and you raise perplexing issues between the chum in trouble and the law. The schoolmaster has to discriminate between individuals. Some are more vigorously egotistical than others, some are reserved and secretive. The former sort are apt to clamour for justice and consideration, exclusively directed to themselves. They are excitable; they flare up and rebel easily. They are dramatic. They clamour for popular approval or defy it. The subtle ones make their private reservations about right and wrong.

The school is already dealing in miniature with the two chief types of recalcitrant. The former is the open recalcitrant, the rebel, the violent breaker of rules, the type which needs open suppression, and the latter is the incredulous sneak, who accepts outwardly all the conventions of the community for the advantage of contravening them while others do not do so. But these two main classes by no means exhaust the disciplinary problems of the schoolmaster. There are exceptional types which seem to have an inherent mental twist against the restraints of social life, they are extravagantly egoistic and fail to "adjust," or they are dull and brutish and cannot establish or cannot sustain the necessary nervous connections. These are the mentally unstable and defective. The schoolmaster rejects the more marked individuals of this group; they must go to special institutions for such special compensatory or curative treatment as may be possible. Already across the crowd of normal educable youth in a school fall the shadows of rebellion, crime, defectiveness and lunacy. These shadows darken but do not change in their essential forms as we pass up to adult life.

The schoolmaster has got a certain proportion of the new generation morally educated. In no case, however, will he have suppressed the primordial human being altogether. The adolescent he turns out as one of his successes, is still an egotist, but now with his anti-social impulses sufficiently minimized to remain ineffective or altogether latent throughout life. He wants sincerely to be a good citizen. He would be a good citizen because of his education, were there no law, no policeman, no jail. But that is the more perfect product in the educationist's output. Of such is the Kingdom of Heaven—and the Utopia of the anarchist. A number, probably a larger number, are sufficiently tamed and well disposed to refrain from anti-social behaviour while there is a reasonable prospect of detection, unpopularity and punishment. Finally there are those who will give trouble anyhow, the recalcitrants and the "mental cases."

The proportion of the recalcitrants to the rest of the population will vary enormously with the social atmosphere, which is the adult equivalent of the schoolmaster's "tone of the school." Where the community is saturated with common understandings, where the law and social usage are but little questioned and in harmony with the prevailing temperament, recalcitrants may fall to a very low percentage of the community. We get what is called a law-abiding community. A generally accepted law is what is called a "just" law, and the administration in a justly organized community can carry on its work with an air of righteousness and justice. Everyone helps and nobody hinders.

Where, on the other hand, the law is widely vexatious in any respect, as, for instance, Prohibition is vexatious in the United States of America; where there is a mixed population or an alien government with a consequent conflict of ideals and the suspicion of partiality; or where economic stresses fall unequally, the essential artificiality of right and wrong becomes apparent, the administration loses moral prestige and the proportion of recalcitrants rises. As recalcitrance rises the administration necessarily becomes more and more repressive. A community with a large proportion of recalcitrants is parallel to a school of which the tone has degenerated through mismanagement or has still to be raised to a high level, and which is consequently "out of hand." Punishment has to be vivid and unsparing, the forces of law and order vigorously aggressive.

We have shown that in the past education was a much more violent breaking-in than it is to-day. The modern teacher has a subtlety, gentleness and success of which no previous age ever dreamt. The treatment of social recalcitrance has undergone and is still undergoing a parallel amelioration.

The methods adopted in the past to maintain the health of the social body, to educate the community to seemly coöperation, make a terrible chapter in the history of mankind. The main purpose of all punishment is exemplary. The plain logical thing to do therefore, it seemed, was to exhibit the punishment to the crowd and make it as impressive as possible. "Do likewise and so it shall be with you," said the lawgiver. A kind of moral rage was excited in the struggling ruler by the breach of social rules, he lost his beneficence, and so the idea of teaching and reforming the malefactor himself played only a secondary rôle in the affair. The welfare of the wretch had passed out of consideration. What the ruler had to do was to demonstrate that he had got the better of the wretch and not the wretch of him.

In the old-fashioned education, birchings and floggings, the wearing of the foolscap and standing in painful attitudes, were inflicted if possible in the presence of the whole school for the benefit of all. The same publicity characterized the penal code. The stocks were still a common discipline a century and a half ago; the cangue was used in China within the lifetime of most of us—I am not sure that it is entirely disused even now; the seventeenth-century pillory, where exposure in discomfort was often combined with the mutilation of ears or nose, carried an inscription defining the offense committed. Executions were public festivals. Our projected Educational Museum must needs have its chamber of horrors, accessible only to those of a stout stomach, in which we shall pass from the more familiar instruments of school discipline to apparatus for the most terrifying executions. All these things played their part in the social education of man, the heavy-handed breaking-in of the past.

It is with a note of apology nowadays that one even mentions torture, but the world-wide use of torture before the days of Voltaire and the French Revolution, had a certain illuminating justification. There was a remarkable objection to putting a malefactor to death until he confessed his crime. He was tortured to produce a confession. Nothing could bring out more plainly the fundamentally pedagogic attitude of criminal law. It was not simply avenging an outrage upon society. The victim was being *taught* in spite of himself. If he died contumacious, he had not learnt his lesson, and, so far as he was concerned, the ruler had suffered defeat.

For obvious reasons the punishment of crime in primitive communities has always been summary, killing or beating or hurting in some way. Before the Middle Ages imprisonment was not widely used as a punishment, and prisons were simply mews for persons awaiting trial or execution. Sir Basil Thomson (whose *Story of Dartmoor* is well worth reading) ascribes our modern use of imprisonment to the influence of monastic Christianity, which regards solitude as a great help to penitence. Monks were among the first to be punished by imprisonment, and the aim in their cases was quite definitely educational. The oubliettes, dungeons and so forth of the mediæval castle were rather guest chambers for people the lord of the castle disliked and wished to treat as disagreeably as possible, than places of punitive restraint; they may have been persuasive in some cases, but they were not penal. They were revengeful. Such prisons as the Bastille in Paris or the Tower of London were essentially places of detention, and it was only after the First French Revolution that the legal sentence of imprisonment came into effect in France to replace a variety of brutal summary penalties. Under the vanished monarchy, French law had been almost as bloody as the English, which still in the first two decades of the nineteenth century hung men, women and children for thefts of a greater value than forty shillings. (But before the Revolution there were prisons for women and minor offenders in Holland and in 1703 Pope Clement XI built a special prison for youthful offenders.)

Throughout the ages the practise of selling recalcitrants into slavery and using them for mines, galleys and other excessive forms of labour has appealed very strongly to economical governments. It was a favourite expedient of the British in the provision of cheap labour for their earlier colonies. In Defoe's *Moll Flanders* transportation to the West Indies is highly commended as a way of starting life anew. In Soviet Russia, it is said, engineers and other skilled workers are charged with sabotage, sentenced to death, and then have their sentences commuted to so many years of unpaid work. But through a large part of the modern world now, except for capital sentences and the brutalities of army training, the only physical punishment inflicted is imprisonment.*

The use of prisons for convicted criminals was a distinct step forward from the public cruelties inflicted upon the recalcitrant in earlier times. Partly it may have been due, as Sir Basil seems to suggest, to the Christian idea of reforming the sinner, but mainly it was a product of the increasing decency and civilization of the world, which so quickened sympathy for those who might be condemned that witnesses would not come forward to give evidence nor juries, with the dire penalties of the time in view, convict. Severity defeated itself, and the offender went scot free. The public sufferings of the condemned advertised the atrociousness of the law. In the eighteenth century in Britain, though the yearly massacre of criminals was counted by the thousand, the annual depredations upon property lying in the Thames, says Sir Basil, amounted to half a million sterling, and no mail coach out of London was safe without an armed escort.

The prisons of the new régime of comparative mercy that followed the French Revolution were not indeed very wholesome places for repentance. They had to be improvised by authorities with not too much money to spend, and often with little sympathy for the new ideas. The intention of the law, no doubt, has always been something in the way of a rigorously clean little cell, a hard bed, simple, barely adequate food, cheerless exercise and meditation. Or labour upon quarries or public buildings conducted austerely in an edifying spirit. But these things are easier to launch than to keep in order. The trouble in all prisons throughout the world is at bottom the same double-headed trouble— expense and the staff. It is a trouble that also affects mental homes and lunatic asylums, which we may therefore bring into the picture very conveniently here. It is almost impossible to say where responsible recalcitrance ends and irresponsible recalcitrance begins. The taxpayer, the press, protest at the "pampering" of offenders, and there is a widespread feeling that their treatment should be below the lowest standard of life outside. There is a similar jealous objection that a mental asylum should not be a "palace."

It is the greatest tragedy of lunacy that the afflicted speedily become unendurably tiresome even to their intimate friends and close relations; so that they have few champions except a few philanthropic specialists.

*In 1920 flogging for certain types of robbery with violence was restored to the British penal code.

Both classes of establishment therefore are very subject to the economizing "axe." During the war the lunatics of Europe had a very bad
time; in nearly every belligerent country they were half starved. Prisons
and mental homes alike are by their very nature secret places, secluded
from casual inspection. And the difficulty in getting an adequate staff
of a suitable quality is very great. The ordinary warder or asylum attendant is not highly paid, and few people would undertake the work,
unless for religious reasons, who could find equally well paid employment outside. A prison governorship is not regarded as a great prize.
Economy understaffs and makes the work more exacting. The demands
for patience and self-control in dealing with recalcitrants under restraint
are enormous, and the normal lunatic, not simply from lack of understanding, but often because of an inherent maliciousness, can be in-
credibly vexatious.

All this leads, not indeed to tragic and horrifying events, but to a
régime of petty tyrannies, illegal beatings, spiteful deprivations and
misery. Most warders and attendants, when one meets them, are manifestly honest and worthy people; the community certainly gets its
money's worth from this class; but they are bothered from morning to
night, teased and overstrained. The monotony of a prison must be
dreadful for all who have to keep it in a going state. The prisons of the
world, rest assured, are cold, hard and needy places; the mental homes
and asylums are full of wretchedness. In neither category are they, as
yet, the organizations for cure, reform and adaptation they might well
become.

One very dreadful result of the understaffing of mental homes is the
reluctance these establishments frequently display in releasing the almost sane, once they are brought into the institution. Because, you see,
the almost sane are so manageable comparatively and they can "help
with the others." This is a clear and natural outcome of the instinctive
abandonment and essential parsimony with which these unfortunates
are treated.

As far as possible the insane and feeble-minded are given work to
do that will keep their minds moving in tolerable paths. They follow
various industries in the institutions provided for them; they work in
the open air inside the high walls of the asylum grounds. There is no
absolute difference between ordinary sane and law-abiding people,
criminals, lunatics and the feeble-minded; there are only differences of
degree. They feel as we do; if they do not act as we do, they act after

the same fashion, with the same sort of mental sequences—at least, until their disease has gone on for some time. The criminal guides himself by a persona that permits him to do forbidden things more readily than the normal citizen. The lunatic's moods and interpretations fluctuate as ours do, but more widely and convulsively. He has impulse systems that get the better of him more completely than our impulse systems; his attempts to rationalize his world into harmony with the demands of his egotism are more extravagant than ours. We all comfort ourselves by delusions about our charm, our value, our ability, but he becomes God, or the King of the World, or the "mysterious European," or the Napoleon of the press. As far as he can he acts accordingly. The bulk of asylum patients may all have been curable at an early stage; there is no insane *type* any more than there is any criminal type; at most there is an excessive excitability which may soon, with advancing medical science, be quite controllable by glandular treatment; and in every asylum there are certainly men and women who were originally quite balanced but whose minds have been overwhelmed by some adverse chance too great to square with their general view of existence. Whether it is inherent or the result of misfortune, a defective or a misshapen and untrustworthy persona is what the alienist has to deal with. The picture within is wrong. The ideology is at issue with society. It is an incurable discordance rather than a deliberate recalcitrance that takes these afflicted individuals out of the world. It is not that they will not, but that they can no longer will.

The visitor to a modern mental home feels the distress of it only by degrees. His first impression is one of space, light and cheerfulness. He sees tennis courts and cricket fields; men working in gardens, people promenading and talking. He scarcely heeds the high wall that closes it all in from the world. He enters the building and finds people sitting about reading newspapers, talking, smoking. Then he notes as he goes from floor to floor the sound of keys being turned. And he begins to remark a certain listlessness here or a smouldering excitement there. He finds patients sitting inert, or muttering to themselves, or repeating some phrase or some movement mechanically and endlessly. They are doing very much as we do when we are greatly strained and troubled. They have been forced into uncongenial associations; they bore one another frightfully and increase each other's malady.

By comparison the appearance of a jail is dark and gloomy. The inmates are under a closer discipline and more obviously subjugated. They sit in separate cells doing some daily task, or they sit still. The peeping visitor speculates about what is going on in that cropped averted head. Does that particular criminal think he was justified? Was he treated fairly? The law has got him now, but next time will he get away with it? There is little or nothing in cell or exercising yard to cause a rebirth to a braver, more generous system of ideas. There is little to restore confidence in one's fellow men.

Since the days of Jeremy Bentham there has been a steady movement towards the development of the reformatory type of prison for at least young offenders, in spite of many financial and administrative obstacles. Borstal in Kent was the germ of the new methods so far as Britain is concerned. The Borstal idea is essentially adolescent reëducation, on the principle of better late than never. It deals with young criminals be- tween the ages of sixteen and twenty-three. They have grown up, it is assumed, in a bad environment; they have got false ideas, a bad ide- ology, a warped persona, and that has to be set right before it is fixed forever. So they are treated with an austere kindliness, set to learn useful trades, encouraged to play social games that evoke the concepts of team-play and fair-play, and released under supervision to start the world anew. The method is so far successful that of 6,000 cases ob- served, two thirds have never troubled the law again.

But it has to be noted that the Borstal prisons, of which there are now four in England, are not *cheap* prisons to run, and that they de- mand a certain very special enthusiasm on the part of governor, house master and staff. That one can get for one pioneer prison, for four prisons even, amidst the stir and hope of a new movement. But how far can the methods be extended before the strain on the supply of devoted officials becomes excessive? People like Mr. Alec Patterson, the Prisons Commissioner for the Borstal Institutions, Sir Wemyss Grant Wilson who founded the After Care work, and Miss Lillian Barker of the girls' Borstal, do not grow on every family tree.

The name of Thomas Mott Osborne is closely associated with the parallel movement in America to make the prison educational. He trained himself in the matter by undergoing a term of voluntary im- prisonment at Auburn, New York. Under him, the New York State Prison at Sing Sing was the scene of some very remarkable and success- ful experiments in social rehabilitation. The punitive factor was reduced to a minimum. He even introduced a form of convict self-government known as the "mutual welfare league." But note that I write with caution; I write "under him." Lately (1930) there has been grave trouble in Sing Sing. The celebrated Juvenile Court of Judge Lindsay in Denver also was a one-man court, a self-embodiment rather than an autonomous machine.

In these cases, as in all such cases, the directive personality in a prison seems to be the supremely important thing. Good educational prisons are still exceptional prisons. They have not been made into machines with replaceable parts, and perhaps that will never be possible. It needs only a little relaxation of guidance for them to lose their educational quality and lapse into irritation and unhappiness. The same is true of the lunatic asylum and the mental hospital. The relation of warder and prisoner, or attendant and defective, is normally one of restraint and resistance, and so it is always close to the keen edge of exasperation. The history of reform in both these types of human institution from the days of John Howard and Beccaria onward, is a history of indignant and devoted personalities. Such reformers capture the imaginations of authorities and helpers and force up the tone of the business—for a time. But the normal, healthy human mind, with an instinctive economy of effort and feeling, turns itself away from the fate of the recalcitrant and ill-adjusted. It is a special job for a special type, which responds to what religious people speak of as a "call."

What hope have we then that this painful substratum of social life may be mitigated or reduced to nothing in the future? Will the world solve this problem of personal management and staffing? To what may we look for a steady and if necessary an increased supply of service?

Our first hope lies in the schools of the future and in the general educational atmosphere of the community. These will fail to establish the law-sustaining persona with a smaller and smaller percentage of the young. They will be cutting off the criminal supply at the source.

And there may be a further interception of possible criminals with defective personas at the leaving school stage. The juvenile prison at Wandsworth is interesting in this respect. Young persons under remand are put through the same sort of examination as we have mentioned in Chapter VII, § 6, our account of the London Institute of Industrial Psychology. A very material proportion of young criminals commit offenses because they are misfits and unhappy in the calling chosen for them. The juvenile prison affords every facility for a change over to congenial and satisfying jobs. Here again is another preventive force to diminish the load upon the prison at least, if not upon the mental retreat.*

*A good summary of Children's Courts throughout the world is given in W. Clarke Hall's book with that title. This has ample references to the general literature of the

Next, to keep down the criminal load there is the deterrent force of efficient policing. It is a proved and tested maxim of the criminologist that the surer the conviction of the offender, the less likely he is to offend. Light but inevitable punishments are far more effective than uncertain heavy ones. Sentences can be reduced therefore with every improvement in policing, and there will be fewer people in prison, and they will be there for shorter terms.

Turn now to the mental home, and here again there is a reasonable hope of a great reduction in the number of cases. Actual lunacy, as we have remarked already, may soon become much more curable if taken in time than it is at present; it is to begin with a disorder of the thoughts associated with the misbehaviour of the endocrinal glands, both controllable things. The psychoanalyst may come to the help of the family doctor, and the standard of medical education may be raised very greatly in this field. The load upon asylums may also be lightened presently by the sterilization of mental defectives (discussed in Chapter X, § 6).

While the load is thus being reduced, it may be possible to supplement and improve the staffing of both series of institutions very considerably. There is the possibility of a reinvigorated moral education and a revival of the religious spirit among the young. I have already noted in two places (Chapter XII, § 7, and in this chapter, § 7) William James's suggestion of a year or so of universal public service for all the young people in the community. A certain proportion of these, carefully selected by a scientific testing of character and intelligence, would find an ennobling use in the responsibilities of prison and asylum work.

There is also another and perhaps even more valuable element in the population that could be brought to bear upon both prison and asylum. That is the student who proposes to specialize as a doctor and in particular as a mental doctor, or as a lawyer, educationist or practising teacher. We have already commented (Chapter VIII, § 7) on the remarkable general ignorance of solicitors. In no class of men is an acute sense of the defects and dangers of human impulse more necessary than in these modern successors of the father confessor of the past. The lawyer in training also might well supplement his law studies with a year or so of practical work among the extremer cases of impulse, defect

subject. Professor Cyril Burt's *Young Delinquent* is a fuller treatment of this most interesting borderland between normal education and police restraint. Apart from the interest of the subject itself, these books introduce the reader to a very cheering and inspiring group of inspectors and court officials, sterling good people that one is the better for knowing about.

and recalcitrance. There is a strong case for impressing the law student for this work. When we take into consideration all these possibilities of improved and scientific staffing on the one hand and of restricted supply on the other, the ultimate complete civilization of both prison and mental seclusion ceases to appear an impossible dream and takes on the character of a finite and solvable problem. But their ultimate abolition is a remoter issue altogether.

And now, with a sigh of relief, let us turn our backs upon those museum galleries of past and present restraint and repression we have had to conjure up, with their models of prisons and cells, their effigies in convict clothing, their handcuffs, stretchers and straitjackets, their frightful disciplines and intimidations, and all that depressing but unavoidable display of human frustration, and let us turn our subject about and ask, "What is recalcitrance?" What, that is, are the things society considers it desirable and justifiable to insist upon in its individuals, and what are the tendencies it must restrain or suppress if individuals will not or cannot do so?

In the past, through the clumsiness of the current conceptions of social relationships, a great number of acts and attitudes were regarded as inimical to social well-being which we, with our broader outlook, know to be matters of indifference. Ceremonial negligences, the questioning of received opinions, disregard of various obsolete taboos, alchemy, magic practises, witchcraft, heresy, the eating of forbidden things, unorthodox fashions of life and behaviour, were supposed to offend the Higher Powers so gravely as to bring misfortune on the community. Accordingly, such acts were prosecuted and punished, often very cruelly. We speak of these things as "persecutions," but from the point of view of the persecutor they were as much crimes as murder or theft or forgery. They awakened the same horror and the same vindictive passion in the well disposed. To this day, in those darker corners of the earth where savage life still lingers, there are sacrifices to avert disaster, but in most of our world there are now no involuntary offences and no propitiatory sacrifices, and there has been an immense release of thought and act from the narrower, fear-haunted ideology of the past.

Every new phase in social development must create new offenses and supersede old ones. The progressive organization of world unity will, for example, abolish the offenses of smuggling and espionage. You will be able to take anything anywhere, look at anything, and tell anybody what you have seen. On the other hand, a modern state may suddenly bring new spheres of activity within the criminal code. Before the war the brewing, sale and delivery of beer was as honourable an occupation in New York as it is still in London. By a constitutional amendment this has been changed in the United States against the will and conscience of great numbers of hitherto decent people, and as a consequence of this and of a pedantic deliberation, and possibly a certain venality, in the machinery of the law, a new and formidable criminal organization has been evoked in that country. The attempt to control a particular detail of conduct in a community accustomed to great freedom of personal initiative was manifestly entirely unscientific. The voters in that democratic country should have been educated to a clearer idea of what a law can and cannot do. The ante-war saloon was no doubt a very great social and political nuisance, but its impatient, crude suppression has replaced it by far greater evils and done a very deep injury to the American morale.

The Soviet Republic, in its attempt to replace a mediæval autocracy by a scientifically organized collectivist state, has had to revise its code of right and wrong in the most drastic fashion. It had for instance to make an offense of "speculation," punishable in the case of members of the Communist party by death. Speculation was simply buying to sell again at a profit instead of buying for use. Every shopkeeper and every pedlar became a criminal. A more vaguely defined offense, "economic sabotage," has also been pursued with implacable fury. "Economic sabotage" seems to be failing, "with intent," to get the very best result out of every machine or organization of which one is in control. Indeed, a whole series of offenses has been created in defense of the Soviet régime. What the rest of the world would call political opposition has become stark treason in Russia. To point out defects in the Five Year Plan or suggest coöperation with capitalist Europe is a crime.

Never have the definitions of right and wrong fluctuated so wildly as they do to-day. They change and are bound to change with every attempt to adjust our overstrained and dislocated economic, political and social ideologies to the vast new needs of the time. In this comprehensive statement and analysis of human coöperations we have attempted, it is made plain that in all existing political and commercial systems there are the gravest defects and dangers. They are undergoing adjustment amidst great stresses. It has been impossible to describe them without condemning their past and foreshadowing the future. The so-called Capitalist System is not in being, it is continually becoming. But to forecast developments is to forecast new methods of dealing and new rules of conduct, and that is to open up a new list of offenses.

We advance into no anarchist paradise. Progress is only possible through repression. For example, we have traced lightly but sufficiently the growth of the armament industry in the last half century. We have seen how the conduct of a small number of energetic individuals pursuing profits on entirely legal and permissible lines, has already contributed to a monstrous destruction of human life, happiness and material. Largely that was possible because incitement to war, whether secret or public, in school or press, is not a criminal offense. But now at least it ought to be a criminal offense, if the Kellogg Pact means anything at all. Incitement to general murder ought to be brought into line with incitement to murder specific individuals. And the speculative manufacture of arms by private individuals so that their purchase can be forced upon reluctant governments, and the public sale of lethal weapons, are manifestly much more socially injurious and should be made at least as criminal as brewing or the sale of cocaine has been made in the United States of America. Both indeed would be extremely easy to suppress were there the will for it.

Moreover, we have shown how badly, and at present how ominously, the system of production for profit with its current methods of credit, works. It is clear it has to be changed and made to work in a new spirit if we are to avoid a catastrophe. By successive replacements at this point and that, production for use and large measures of collective buying have to supercede profit production and the incoherent direction of the unorganized purchaser. And in personal conduct the spirit of service, and service as a criterion of moral quality, have to be brought in to modify the deliberate and admitted self-seeking that rules our economic life to-day. These developments involve a correlated adjustment of instruction and the law. The persona has to be set in certain new directions by education, and the criminal law has to confirm that bias.

There is need of a sustained, continuing scrutiny of the methods of banking, the manipulation of money and credit, the permissible devices of trading, the financing of enterprises. There is need of a progressive modification of the law in association with this scrutiny. Our economic life has to be brought more and more into harmony with the concept of collective effort for the common welfare to avert the disaster the tradition of chaotic competition, the legacy of the peasant, and the predatory nomad will otherwise bring upon us all. The fierce and drastic suppressions of economic recalcitrance in Russia are violent beyond any necessity of the Atlantic communities, but it is plain that since, under the compulsion of new dangers and stresses, all the world, and not Russia alone, struggles towards more highly organized mutual service, a more deliberate, parallel restraint upon anti-social individual enterprise becomes inevitable in the non-Communist communities also.

The aim of this work throughout is to translate the abstract ideas of economics and sociology into terms of concrete human beings, and there need be no apology offered for an attempt to present "anti-social individual enterprise" in the form of living types. What manner of man and woman, what sort of persona, does that phrase "anti-social individual enterprise" convey?

I would suggest that the type of crime this age will find most difficult to deal with is not the rough, overt recalcitrance of former times. So much of that as still gets past preventive education can be dealt with by competent police methods. The comparative abundance of violent crimes in the United States is a temporary phase, due to short-sighted repressive legislation and an ill-organized police system; both of which disadvantages one may count upon the American people to overcome. In the rest of the world, as school, reformatory, police integrity, and efficiency advance, the open recalcitrants diminish. But on the other hand, in certain types of crime, in the possibility of undetected hidden crimes and in acts, plainly antisocial but not yet definitely made criminal, it is not so easy to congratulate ourselves. The police organization plays a long and difficult game against, for example, the intelligent poisoner. The law finds itself in constant perplexity about the intricate cheat. Sir Basil Thomson found most of his "old lags" at the convict prison of Dartmoor men of poor education and inferior mental quality. The proportion of educated cheats and middle class criminals who come into jail seemed to him unaccountably small, in view of all the cheating and overreaching that was going on in the world outside.

From America comes a sobriquet I find attractive, "Smart Alec." I propose to use it here. It raises in my mind a figure of just the qualities I have in view. Smart Alec is a sharp lad, who retains the peasant persona, polished to an extreme brightness, in spite of all the modern educational forces that may have been brought to bear upon him. For some reason of innate quality or faulty suggestion, the ideas of honour, service, frankness, and truth do not "take" with him. He professes to accept them, but within they have no hold on him. His persona is pervaded by the persuasion that he is "not a fool." Fools take these things as fundamental, but not he. He has ends of his own, private standards of what is desirable. These ends may be the gratifications of sense or vanity or the secret triumphs of advantage and avarice. An immense vanity and a profound secret self-reliance are in his make-up. He does not trust. Even with those he values and cares for, he does not give himself away, or he does so by some lapse into boasting. From this angle it is that Smart Alec comes into the game of life.

(I write of Smart Alec to economize my third personal pronouns. There are Smart Alexandras—with certain differences of aim and method; it may be, as abundant.)

He comes into the game of life with the idea not of serving, but of beating the community, and the community, so far as it is wisely guarded, sets itself to defeat and if possible "save the soul" of Smart Alec. All up and down the scale of misdemeanour and punishment we find Smart Alec being found out, and how many Smart Alecs are never found out we cannot estimate. Some are caught cheating in school, and some are caught cheating at games. They get a check, and perhaps they mend their ways. But the abler or more fortunate Smart Alec has a finer discretion and does not cheat too crudely. He studies the weaknesses of his masters and wins good marks with a minimum of exertion. He plays his games according to the rules. His companions say that he plays for his own hand, but playing for one's own hand is not yet scheduled as an offense. He watches his averages and gets through his examinations. He pushes out into the world alert for opportunity.

Where is there most opportunity? That may vary with the circumstances in which he is launched, with his special aptitudes, with his general intelligence. He may choose a trade or a profession. Law has had some brilliant, unscrupulous successes to fire the imagination of an ambitious youngster. A political career, particularly for a smart and smartly bold lawyer, offers a way to prominence and many glittering prizes. A lawyer may do many things a layman dare not do. He knows the law better and within limits, if men denounce him, he can trust to the instinct of professional solidarity. There are some good prizes in the Church, too, and less competition than there was in former days. But industry, commerce and especially financial organization, beckon to Smart Alec with both hands.

There at present he finds his richest field. There is an amazing tolerance in finance for the man who plays for himself alone. Boldness with property ceases to be heroic in the business man's imagination only when it comes into the dock. Some of the older banks may distrust youthful brilliance and lay snares for its feet, but the prevailing standards of the financial world still blend the traditions of peasant and raider. In Chapter X we have exposed all this region of human activities to the light of a careful analysis and shown what a danger its unplanned looseness of play is to the whole human organization. The task of its adjustment would still be enormously difficult if everyone concerned in it were giving himself unreservedly to assist. But nothing of the sort is going on. Smart Alec meets one at every twist and turn, ready to oppose everything that will embarrass him, alert to snatch and take advantage. He stretches the poor old law to the utmost and cheats a little when it is likely to inconvenience him. He has his confederates in the legislature; his friends who own and direct newspapers; Smart Alecs likewise.

The man of good-will, as we call him, himself by no means perfect, thinks and plans to save and serve the civilization that in his mind has come to be something more significant than himself. He is part of that once unconscious conspiracy that now becomes conscious, the conspiracy of constructive service to sustain and continue civilization. He has no ambition to flare across the heavens as the richest man in the world. He has his own conception of satisfaction and his less obvious and deeper standards of success and failure. He is an official, or a man of science, or a lawyer with an enlightened sense of honour, a teacher, or he may be many other serviceable things. His wealth, his power, so far as that depends on wealth, and his knack of getting, may be, man for man, almost incalculably inferior to that of any of the more flagrantly successful Smart Alecs, but there is this on his side and on the side of civilization, that he is capable of wider and wider coöperations, while Smart Alec is by his very nature an individualist, playing for his own skin. Smart Alec does this and that and one Smart Alec skins another Smart Alec, Smart Alecs are cannibals among themselves, the gross, limited and ignorant crowd thrusts stupidly this way or that or lapses into collective inertia, but the open conspiracy will go on more and more steadfastly doing the same system of things, working toward a more and more clearly defined objective.

Between Smart Alec and the conscientious, devoted, all too pedagogic makers of order and progress, the limited, instinctive traditional life of the multitude blunders along, at once protected and entangled, in a fabric of laws and methods that is still manifestly casual, unstable and incalculable. The multitude is ignorant, and Smart Alec can lie to it convincingly and brilliantly; he can fool its dim impulses to do right and turn them against his toiling pursuers. Its loyalties are dull and strong, attached to decaying idols and superseded necessities, but

Smart Alec will champion and defend and utilize the honoured tradition, the ancient institution, and reward and advance himself with all the picturesque honours it can confer. Or some devitalized religion spreads its attractive endowments about the world for Smart Alec to seize upon and sustain. He is to be found playing the rôle of the enthusiastic Nationalist, the acute Protectionist, for of all systems of opportunity for the alert, war and war preparation are the greatest. A staff uniform becomes him well. In the trenches and tortures of warfare men may come to see Smart Alec plainly, in a blaze of revelation, but there is no going back for them then; he is well out of range. And now that Smart Alec has been so busy with our currencies and prices that this swarming world of work and wealth hangs dangerously on the verge of panic and despair, the Smart Alecs continue their reckless manœuvres, sell to keep the depression going and buy at bedrock prices, traverse every effort to unify the incoherence of a divided economic front, and bid fair to accomplish the ruin of our civilization. Then, amidst the discomforts of a brigand world, Smart Alec, with his gains mysteriously gone and his comforts and indulgences shattered beyond recovery, will adjust himself knowingly and briskly to new occasions.

Unless we of the open conspiracy who hunt him incessantly can net him tightly enough to save our world from his exploits.

These are the fundamental sides of the internal conflict of the human community as we see them to-day. Education, law, an advancing psychology, and social science have the brute, the dull and the defective well in hand. That much may be counted as done. The broad task now is a vast and difficult political and economic reconstruction of the world's affairs, with Smart Alec as the main recalcitrant. Law, like a living, self-repairing net, seeks for him. The mind of the race in literature and social psychology sustains a perpetually closer criticism of motive and conduct and so exposes and pursues him. Continually the modern community, thoughtfully, steadfastly, powerfully, must be anticipating, circumventing, defeating, and, as may be necessary, punishing Smart Alec. For Smart Alec is now the chief enemy of mankind. He is the antagonist and betrayer of open conspiracy; his rôle is to prevent the salvaging of civilization. We have to fight him in the whole world about us. We have to fight him by school, by art and literature and law. We have to meet and fight him in our daily transactions. We have to fight him in ourselves.

And conversely, Smart Alec is rarely if ever found—how shall I put it?—in a state of chemical purity, a hundred per cent Smart Alec.

Nearly always, if not always, his private self, his persona, will have been infected with some qualities of a wider, less personal scope. He has a conscience. There are moments when the Smartest Alec sees himself for what he is.

If, in space and time, but outside of and above our world of work and wealth altogether, some commanding intelligence could survey and appraise it in its simplest form, the whole spectacle of our activities, our desires, our efforts, and our defeats would appear as one continuing struggle between the creative synthetic will and thought of the human mind on one hand, and the subtle, endlessly various self-centred recalcitrance of the individual man on the other.

CHAPTER THE SIXTEENTH

THE OUTLOOK OF MANKIND

§ 1. *The Next Phase Latent in the Present Situation*

WE HAVE now completed our general account of this little world of men, our survey of the activities and interaction of the one thousand nine hundred million souls who make up the human garment of our globe. We have shown how things are with that film of life to-day. We have shown how it stirs and carries on. We have ranged from the financial adventurer in his aëroplane to the miner hacking at the seam, and from the work girl in the atelier, and the peasant bent down to his soil, to the film star and the military commander; clerks and machine minders, stokers and cabmen, the parson in the pulpit, and the fur trapper in the snow have all figured in the reckoning. We have noted, if only by mere indicative gestures, a hundred culs-de-sac and out-of-the-way corners, the prisoner in his cell, the burglar "at work," the lunatic under treatment, the religious ascetic wrung with prayer, the noiseless jungle savage. It is the main masses that have chiefly held our attention; it is the broad realities we have examined. So human beings live, so they work, so hating and loving and bickering and bargaining they serve and depend upon one another and pass away.

What has evolved this multitude? What has woven this magic network of aid and service between them? That has been asked and in a manner answered here. Example, imitation, teaching, intricate educational processes. It is a psychological net. Why has this world of ours so many corrupting kinks and morbid developments, so many parasites, rebels and betrayers? Because of the imperfections of its educational adaptations. The web is not perfectly woven. To crown our work we turned to the teachers, preachers, writers, innovators, propagandists and all that miscellany of people who keep ideas alive and operative and weave new conceptions of action and new threads of relationship into the dispersed millions of our kind. We showed their retardations and

731

their difficulties. They are always a little behind the mechanical drift of things, as the upthrust of a wave is behind its crest.

This planetary ant-hill of interrelated living creatures is changing as the reader turns these pages. It never pauses in its changes. In the past three seconds, six human beings have been born upon this globe as it spins steadily through space, from day to night and from night to day, born each with a blank new brain, upon which the first writing has already begun: those first impressions, those foundations of dim experience which will be built at length into a unique, unprecedented persona with all the intricate reactions of self-conscious, self-directive individual life. And in the last three seconds—unless there has been some exceptional catastrophe—five human beings have died, taking with them, each one of them, a world.

Many of those so recently dead, dying while the last few paragraphs were read, were quite young creatures, some just born; but most of them carried with them out of the impulses of mankind, unforgettable memories, obstinate prepossessions, life-worn traditions, obsolete skills and responses, unteachable determinations. Over the teeming minds of the young play the suggestions, traditions, examples, preachments and reasonings of our newer time. These minds in their turn are going on to hope and desire, struggle and consume, suppress disagreeable facts and exaggerate pleasant ones, embrace self-protective delusions, conduct themselves according to their lights and so act their parts. They too will be shaped and set and hardened, but not exactly as their predecessors were. The pattern is always changing. Work goes on day by day about the planet, and wealth is gathered and spent. The threads interweave, and the pattern passes into new shapes and new promises. In the end these others also will pass away. Man is forever dying and forever being born, and it is impossible to tell of what is, without passing on forthwith to the only aspect that gives the present significance and reality, the things that now arise out of the things that are.

§ 2. *Uncertainties in the Human Outlook*

Let us before we conclude devote a section to the possibility that this human adventure will fail. We have no guarantee whatever against many sorts of cosmic disaster. There is the risk, an infinitesimal but real risk, of meteoric bodies hurtling through our system, bodies so large and coming so near to us as to destroy our planet as a home for life. So remote is such a mischance that Sir James Jeans can dismiss it as negligible. If the lot falls against us in spite of the odds, there is nothing more to be said or done. Fate will end the story.

But other sinister possibilities, less catastrophic but in the end as decisive, are not so easily dismissed. We still know very little of the secular changes of climate, and it is conceivable that in quite a few years, in a hundred thousand or a thousand thousand, that is to say, this planet may be returning to a phase of wide-spread glaciation, or temperature may be rising to universal tropical and ultra-tropical conditions. Within the sun, for all we know, explosive forces are brewing—or on our earth itself—to heat or chill or shatter. Or again, if steady urgencies of upheaval and disturbance are not still astir under the feet of our race, the rains and rivers and waves will presently wear down our mountains and hills and flatten out our lands until one monotonous landscape of plains of exhausted soil and swamps and lagoons of tepid water has replaced the familiar scenery of our time. Or if these terrestrial tensions increase, our race will pass into a period of volcanic violence and earthquakes, forces from within breaking loose to thrust up new mountain chains and giving fresh directions to wind and sea current, and the conditions of life may become extreme and diversified beyond adjustment.

Here plainly we are still under the sway of the Fates. Presently we may be able to foretell; later we may even control such fluctuations, but certainly the sun and planets and our little globe have their own motions and changes regardless of our needs and desires. The cards as they are played are being swept up for a fresh deal. The hand our race must play to-morrow may be very different from the hand we play to-day. There are no fixed conditions to human life, and if this newborn world community of ours is to go on through vast periods of time, man will have to be forever guessing new riddles. Will he be able to get so far with his science as to map out at length in their due order all the coming throws of the planetary roulette? Or get a mastery of the wheel? There will have to be an encyclopædia of knowledge for such feats as that, vaster than anything we can dream of to-day. There will have to be a mightier sort of man, very marvellously educated, and perhaps by virtue of an advancing science of eugenics innately better, to do things on that scale.

Such are the difficulties and problems for our descendants, that must slowly develop themselves age by age, even if they solve the riddles of our present civilization. But will mankind ever solve these immediate problems? There was recently published a very suggestive and amusing book by Olaf Stapledon, *Last and First Men*. It is an imaginary history upon an astronomical scale of the future of humanity, a grimly cheerful mixture of biology, burlesque, and satire. He sees our present species blundering through some further great wars and unified at last under American rule into one world state, a world state of a harshly plutocratic type which undergoes an entirely incredible moral and intellectual degeneration and ends in a new Dark Age. *Homo sapiens* is then practically exterminated by a catastrophe he has himself provoked, and only a few individuals survive obscurely to become the progenitors of two species of *Homo* who presently increase and come into conflict. The remoter speculations of Mr. Stapledon about the succession of the latter Hominidae and their final extinction, vivid and amusing though they are, and stimulating as they will prove to those unversed in biological and cosmological possibilities, need not be discussed here. But the nearer issues he broaches, do pose very disturbingly the considerable probability of a failure in our contemporary civilization to anticipate and prevent fresh world warfare and an economic crash. I see that possible economic crash nearer and larger and more important than he does, as a greater menace, indeed, than the militant nationalism from which it arises. But I believe in human sanity more than he does, I believe that that widely diffused will and understanding which I have termed "open conspiracy" may be strong enough to carry the race through the economic stresses ahead of us, and to delay, minimize and finally repulse the onset of war.

There has been a great quickening of the general intelligence about political and economic life in recent years, and the man of action and the man of thought have been drawn nearer together. There may be some dark chapters in human history still to be written, and provisional governments and a mightier Judge Lynch may figure in the drama. The forces that will carry on, develop and realize the abounding promise of our present civilization are by no means sure of victory; they may experience huge and tragic setbacks; but the balance of probability seems to be largely in their favour. If they win out, it will be men of our own kind, better, according to our present values, but men still—not beings specifically different and beyond our sympathy—who with a whole planet organized for the conflict, will face those greater problems, the long-period problems of terrestrial and cosmic changes which advance upon us behind the skirmishing dangers of to-day.

But nothing is certain. Men may breed and bicker too long, be overtaken by some swift universal epidemic they have had no time to arrest, perish of a phosphorous famine, or be destroyed by some war machine they have had the ability to invent but not the intelligence to control. In the Mesozoic Age great reptiles multiplied and dominated the earth, and suddenly they passed away. In the Miocene flourished countless varieties of huge mammals, now altogether extinguished. Why should we suppose that we are specially favoured items in the spectacle of existence? Millions of us are wearied, chased about, heartbroken, wounded and killed, for no evident good, in war; millions are destroyed by accidents without apparent reason or justice; beasts of prey in India and Africa slay and eat their thousands of "man the master" every year; millions die in unalleviated pain through a multitude of cruel diseases. Is there any difference in quality between one single case of a dear human being killed by cancer and the murder of a world? It is simply a difference of numbers and scale. If the universe can kill a child unjustly, so it can kill a race or a planet unjustly. If so many individual lives end tragically, why should not the whole species end tragically?

We may say, "It shall not," but what weight have such words?

§ 3. *Hope and Courage Are Inevitable*

What have we to put into the scale against this presentation of the whole human adventure, as nothing better than a freak of chance, flung up in the incomprehensible play of forces forever outside our understanding, and destined to be reversed as casually and wiped out of being altogether?

So far as our powers and knowledge go, we have nothing. We are forced back upon something more fundamental in us than knowledge or reason; the innate inevitable faith in itself that every healthy conscious being must necessarily possess. "Where there is life," says the old proverb, "there is hope." A creature with no faith in itself will die and pass out of the reckoning, leaving the world to those whose faith remains. We are unable to believe that the universe that has evoked the will to live in us can be without will. We can no more believe the universe insane by our measure of sanity and altogether indifferent to our urgencies than we can prove it sane.

But the pessimist also can prove nothing. He argues that the antagonists are very strong; he does not show they are invincible. He reminds us that we are not insured against this or that gloomy mischance. But there is no inevitability about any of these gloomy mischances. The unknown is full of possible surprises for mankind. There is no more probability of these surprises being dreadful than there is of their being delightful. The chances are strictly even. When everything has gone into either scale, there still remains this fact to tilt the balance in our favour; that here we are with courage in us.

What is the culminating effect of a survey of history, of the science of life, and of existing conditions? It is an effect of steadily accelerated growth in power, range, and understanding. All these things lead up to us—and how could they seem to do otherwise? Progress continues in spite of every human fear and folly. Men are borne along through space and time regardless of themselves, as if to the awakening greatness of Man.

Why should we not believe that amidst the stars ahead of us the world-state will be won, and that long ages of progressive civilization, ages of accumulating life and power open out before our kind? And though that is the present frame of our vision, why should we suppose that any end has been set to the growth and advancement of our race while the time garment still wraps about it and veils its eyes? For our history is just a story in space and time, and to its very last moment it must remain adventure. We have no ultimate measure of life's potentialities, no reason for supposing that what seems to us to be insurmountable obstacles will not dissolve to nothing before an ever increasing knowledge and resourcefulness. Our vision is limited indeed, but not by any fated and assured end. Even these ingenious paradoxes by which space and time merge into one another and all our absolutes and infinities dissolve away have no quality of finality about them. One feels there is more to be said; much still to be thought out. They challenge; they do not capture and convince. Our most fundamental ideas are provisional ideas, no doubt, but as yet there is nothing to replace them. Ten thousand or ten million years from now will still be ten thousand or ten million years from now. So far and beyond, this adventure may continue and our race survive. The impenetrable clouds that bound our life at last in every direction may hide innumerable trials and dangers, but there are no conclusive limitations even in their deepest shadows, and there are times and seasons, there are moods of exaltation—moments, as it were, of revelation—when the whole universe about us seems bright with the presence of as yet unimaginable things.

THE END

INDEX

A